ANNUAL EDITIONS

Anthropology

Thirty-first Edition

08/09

Editor

Elvio Angeloni
Pasadena City College

Elvio Angeloni received his B.A. from UCLA in 1963, his M.A. in anthropology from UCLA in 1965, and his M.A. in communication arts from Loyola Marymount University in 1976. He has produced several films, including *Little Warrior,* winner of the Cinemedia VI Best Bicentennial Theme, and *Broken Bottles,* shown on PBS. He served as an academic adviser on the instructional television series *Faces of Culture.* He received the Pasadena City College Outstanding Teacher Award in 2006. He is also the academic editor of *Annual Editions: Physical Anthropology, Classic Edition Sources: Anthropology* and co-editor of *Annual Editions: Archeology.* His primary area of interest has been indigenous peoples of the American Southwest.

Mc Graw Hill **Higher Education**

Boston   Burr Ridge, IL   Dubuque, IA   New York   San Francisco   St. Louis
Bangkok   Bogotá   Caracas   Kuala Lumpur   Lisbon   London   Madrid   Mexico City
Milan   Montreal   New Delhi   Santiago   Seoul   Singapore   Sydney   Taipei   Toronto

ANNUAL EDITIONS: ANTHROPOLOGY, THIRTY-FIRST EDITION

This book is printed on recycled, acid-free paper containing 10% postconsumer waste.

1 2 3 4 5 6 7 8 9 0 QPD/QPD 0 9 8

ISBN 978–0–07–339754–2
MHID 0–07–339754–7
ISSN 1091–613X

Managing Editor: *Larry Loeppke*
Production Manager: *Faye Schilling*
Developmental Editor: *Jade Bennedict*
Editorial Assistant: *Nancy Meissner*
Production Service Assistant: *Rita Hingtgen*
Permissions Coordinator: *Lenny Behnke*
Senior Marketing Manager: *Julie Keck*
Marketing Communications Specialist: *Mary Klein*
Marketing Coordinator: *Alice Link*
Project Manager: *Jean Smith*
Design Specialist: *Tara McDermott*
Senior Administrative Assistant: *DeAnna Dausener*
Senior Operations Manager: *Pat Koch Krieger*
Cover Graphics: *Maggie Lytle*

Compositor: Laserwords Private Limited
Cover Image: © Erin Koran and Glen Allison/Getty Images

Library in Congress Cataloging-in-Publication Data
Main entry under title: Annual Editions: Anthropology. 2008/2009.
  1. Anthropology—Periodicals. I. Angeloni, Elvio, *comp.* II. Title: Anthropology.
658'.05

www.mhhe.com

Editors/Advisory Board

Members of the Advisory Board are instrumental in the final selection of articles for each edition of ANNUAL EDITIONS. Their review of articles for content, level, currentness, and appropriateness provides critical direction to the editor and staff. We think that you will find their careful consideration well reflected in this volume.

Preface

In publishing ANNUAL EDITIONS we recognize the enormous role played by the magazines, newspapers, and journals of the public press in providing current, first-rate educational information in a broad spectrum of interest areas. Many of these articles are appropriate for students, researchers, and professionals seeking accurate, current material to help bridge the gap between principles and theories and the real world. These articles, however, become more useful for study when those of lasting value are carefully collected, organized, indexed, and reproduced in a low-cost format, which provides easy and permanent access when the material is needed. That is the role played by ANNUAL EDITIONS.

This thirty-first edition of *Annual Editions: Anthropology* contains a variety of articles on contemporary issues in social and cultural anthropology. In contrast to the broad range of topics and minimum depth typical of standard textbooks, this anthology provides an opportunity to read firsthand accounts by anthropologists of their own research. In allowing scholars to speak for themselves about the issues on which they are expert, we are better able to understand the kind of questions anthropologists ask, the ways in which they ask them, and how they go about searching for answers. Indeed, where there is disagreement among anthropologists, this format allows the readers to draw their own conclusions.

Given the very broad scope of anthropology—in time, space, and subject matter—the present collection of highly readable articles has been selected according to certain criteria. The articles have been chosen from both professional and nonprofessional publications for the purpose of supplementing the standard textbook in cultural anthropology that is used in introductory courses. Some of the articles are considered classics in the field, while others have been selected for their timely relevance.

Included in this volume are a number of features designed to make it useful for students, researchers, and professionals in the field of anthropology. While the articles are arranged along the lines of broadly unifying themes, the *Topic Guide* can be used to establish specific reading assignments tailored to the needs of a particular course of study. Other useful features include the *Table of Contents* abstracts, which summarize each article and present key concepts in italics. In addition, each unit is preceded by an overview, which provides a background for informed reading of the articles, emphasizes critical issues, and presents *key points to consider*.

Finally, there are *Internet References* that can be used to further explore the topics.

Annual Editions: Anthropology 08/09 will continue to be updated annually. Those involved in producing the volume wish to make the next one as useful and effective as possible. Your criticism and advice always are welcome. Please fill out the postage-paid article rating form on the last page of the book and let us know your opinions. Any anthology can be improved. This continues to be—annually.

Elvio Angeloni

Elvio Angeloni
Editor

Contents

UNIT 1
Anthropological Perspectives

The concepts in bold italics are developed in the article. For further expansion, please refer to the Topic Guide.

UNIT 2
Culture and Communication

UNIT 3
The Organization of Society and Culture

The concepts in bold italics are developed in the article. For further expansion, please refer to the Topic Guide.

UNIT 4
Other Families, Other Ways

The concepts in bold italics are developed in the article. For further expansion, please refer to the Topic Guide.

UNIT 5
Gender and Status

UNIT 6
Religion, Belief, and Ritual

The concepts in bold italics are developed in the article. For further expansion, please refer to the Topic Guide.

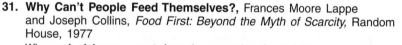

UNIT 7
Sociocultural Change: The Impact of the West

The concepts in bold italics are developed in the article. For further expansion, please refer to the Topic Guide.

The concepts in bold italics are developed in the article. For further expansion, please refer to the Topic Guide.

Topic Guide

This topic guide suggests how the selections in this book relate to the subjects covered in your course. You may want to use the topics listed on these pages to search the Web more easily.

On the following pages a number of Web sites have been gathered specifically for this book. They are arranged to reflect the units of this *Annual Edition*. You can link to these sites by going to the student online support site at *http://www.mhcls.com/online/*.

ALL THE ARTICLES THAT RELATE TO EACH TOPIC ARE LISTED BELOW THE BOLD-FACED TERM.

Acculturation
1. Before: The Sixties
5. One Hundred Percent American
20. Who Needs Love! In Japan, Many Couples Don't
24. Eyes of the Ngangas: Ethnomedicine and Power in Central Africa
32. The Arrow of Disease
34. The Price of Progress
35. The Battle for Cattle
36. Rangers by Birth
37. Digging Into the Roots of Research Ethics
38. Can Minority Languages Be Saved?
39. What Native Peoples Deserve

Aggression
32. The Arrow of Disease
33. Burying the White Gods: New Perspectives on the Conquest of Mexico
39. What Native Peoples Deserve

Altruism
2. Eating Christmas in the Kalahari
13. Meeting the Maasai: Messages for Management
14. Too Many Bananas, Not Enough Pineapples, and No Watermelon at All
15. Ties That Bind

Child care
17. Death Without Weeping
23. Where Fat Is a Mark of Beauty

Children
17. Death Without Weeping
23. Where Fat Is a Mark of Beauty
27. Remapping the World of Autism

Communication
6. Who's Speech Is Better?
7. Do You Speak American?
8. Fighting for Our Lives
9. "I Can't Even Open My Mouth"
10. Shakespeare in the Bush
15. Ties That Bind
38. Can Minority Languages Be Saved?

Cooperation
1. Before: The Sixties
13. Meeting the Maasai: Messages for Management
14. Too Many Bananas, Not Enough Pineapples, and No Watermelon at All

Cross-cultural experience
2. Eating Christmas in the Kalahari
5. One Hundred Percent American
6. Who's Speech Is Better?
10. Shakespeare in the Bush
11. Understanding Eskimo Science
12. The Inuit Paradox
13. Meeting the Maasai: Messages for Management

---

14. Too Many Bananas, Not Enough Pineapples, and No Watermelon at All
15. Ties That Bind
17. Death Without Weeping
19. Arranging a Marriage in India
24. Eyes of the Ngangas: Ethnomedicine and Power in Central Africa
27. Remapping the World of Autism
37. Digging Into the Roots of Research Ethics
38. Can Minority Languages Be Saved?

Cultural change
5. One Hundred Percent American
7. Do You Speak American?
12. The Inuit Paradox
18. What's Love Got to Do with It
20. Who Needs Love! In Japan, Many Couples Don't
31. Why Can't People Feed Themselves?
32. The Arrow of Disease
33. Burying the White Gods: New Perspectives on the Conquest of Mexico
34. The Price of Progress
35. The Battle for Cattle
36. Rangers by Birth
37. Digging Into the Roots of Research Ethics
38. Can Minority Languages Be Saved?

Cultural diversity
5. One Hundred Percent American
6. Who's Speech Is Better?
7. Do You Speak American?
13. Meeting the Maasai: Messages for Management
15. Ties That Bind
18. What's Love Got to Do with It
19. Arranging a Marriage in India
21. The Berdache Tradition
24. Eyes of the Ngangas: Ethnomedicine and Power in Central Africa
27. Remapping the World of Autism
37. Digging Into the Roots of Research Ethics
38. Can Minority Languages Be Saved?

Cultural identity
5. One Hundred Percent American
6. Who's Speech Is Better?
12. The Inuit Paradox
13. Meeting the Maasai: Messages for Management
15. Ties That Bind
23. Where Fat Is a Mark of Beauty
26. The Adaptive Value of Religious Ritual
37. Digging Into the Roots of Research Ethics
38. Can Minority Languages Be Saved?
39. What Native Peoples Deserve

Cultural relativity
2. Eating Christmas in the Kalahari
6. Who's Speech Is Better?
7. Do You Speak American?
12. The Inuit Paradox
13. Meeting the Maasai: Messages for Management
15. Ties That Bind

Internet References

The following Internet sites have been carefully researched and selected to support the articles found in this reader. The easiest way to access these selected sites is to go to our student online support site at *http://www.mhcls.com/online/*.

AE: Anthropology 08/09

The following sites were available at the time of publication. Visit our Web site—we update our student online support site regularly to reflect any changes.

General Sources

American Anthropologist Association
http://www.aaanet.org

Check out this site—the home page of the American Anthropology Association—for general information about the field of anthropology as well as access to a wide variety of articles.

Anthropology Links
http://anthropology.gmu.edu/

George Mason University's Department of Anthropology Web site provides a number of interesting links.

Latin American Studies
http://www.library.arizona.edu/search/subjects/

Click on Latin American Studies to access an extensive list of resources—links to encyclopedias, journals, indexes, almanacs, and handbooks, and to the Latin American Network Information Center and Internet Resources for Latin American Studies.

Web Resources for Visual Anthropology
http://www.usc.edu/dept/elab/urlist/index.html

This UR-List offers a mouse-click selection of Web resources by cross-indexing 375 anthropological sites according to 22 subject categories.

UNIT 1: Anthropological Perspectives

Archaeology and Anthropology Computing and Study Skills
http://www.isca.ox.ac.uk/index.html

Consult this site of the Institute of Social and Cultural Anthropology to learn about ways to use the computer as an aid in conducting fieldwork, methodology, and analysis.

Introduction to Anthropological Fieldwork and Ethnography
http://web.mit.edu/dumit/www/syl-anth.html

This class outline can serve as an invaluable resource for conducting anthropological fieldwork. Addressing such topics as The Interview and Power Relations in the Field, the site identifies many important books and articles for further reading.

Theory in Anthropology
http://www.indiana.edu/~wanthro/theory.htm

These Web pages cover subdisciplines within anthropology, changes in perspectives over time, and prominent theorists, reflecting 30 years of dramatic changes in the field.

UNIT 2: Culture and Communication

Exploratorium Magazine: "The Evolution of Languages"
http://www.exploratorium.edu/exploring/language

Where did languages come from and how did they evolve? This educational site explains the history and origin of language. You can also investigate words, word stems, and the similarities between different languages.

Hypertext and Ethnography
http://www.umanitoba.ca/anthropology

Presented by Brian Schwimmer of the University of Manitoba, this site will be of great value to people who are interested in culture and communication. Schwimmer addresses such topics as multivocality and complex symbolization.

Language Extinction
http://www.colorado.edu/iec

"An often overlooked fact in the ecological race against environmental extinction is that many of the world's languages are disappearing at an alarming rate." This article investigates language extinction and its possible consequences.

Showcase Anthropology
http://www.anthropology.wisc.edu

Examples of documents that make innovative use of the Web as a tool for "an anthropology of the future"—one consisting of multimedia representations in a nonlinear and interactive form—are provided on this Web site.

UNIT 3: The Organization of Society and Culture

Smithsonian Institution Web Site
http://www.si.edu

Looking through this site, which provides access to many of the enormous resources of the Smithsonian, will give a sense of the scope of anthropological inquiry today.

Sociology Guy's Anthropology Links
http://www.trinity.edu/~mkearl/anthro.html

This list of anthropology resources on the Web is suggested by a sociology professor at Trinity University and includes cultures of Asia, Africa, the Middle East; Aztecan, Mayan, and aboriginal cultures; sections on Mythology, Folklore, Legends, and Archaeology; plus much more.

UNIT 4: Other Families, Other Ways

Kinship and Social Organization
http://www.umanitoba.ca/anthropology

Kinship, marriage systems, residence rules, incest taboos, and cousin marriages are explored in this kinship tutorial.

www.mhcls.com/online/

UNIT 5: Gender and Status

Arranged Marriages
http://women3rdworld.miningco.com/cs/arrangedmarriage/

This site, provided by ABOUT, contains a number of papers on arranged marriages. It also has links to other related women's issues, subjects, and forums.

Bonobo Sex and Society
http://songweaver.com/info/bonobos.html

This site includes a Scientific American article discussing a primate's behavior that challenges traditional assumptions about male supremacy in human evolution.

FGM Research
http://www.amnesty.org/ailib/intcam/femgen/fgm1.htm

Dedicated to research pertaining to Female Genital Mutilation (FGM), this site presents a variety of perspectives: psychological, cultural, sexual, human rights, and so on.

OMIM Home Page-Online Mendelian Inheritance in Man
http://www3.ncbi.nlm.nih.gov/omim/

This National Center for Biotechnology Information database is a catalog of human genes and genetic disorders. It contains text, pictures, and reference information.

Reflections on Sinai Bedouin Women
http://www.sherryart.com/women/bedouin.html

Social anthropologist Ann Gardner tells something of her culture shock while first living with a Sinai Bedouin family as a teenager. She provides links to sites about organization of society and culture, particularly with regard to women.

UNIT 6: Religion, Belief, and Ritual

Anthropology Resources Page
http://www.usd.edu/anth/

Many topics can be accessed from this University of South Dakota Web site. Repatriation and reburial are just two.

Yahoo: Society and Culture: Death
http://dir.yahoo.com/Society_and_Culture/Death_and_Dying/

This Yahoo site has an extensive index to diverse issues related to how different people approach death, such as beliefs about euthanasia, reincarnation, and burial.

UNIT 7: Sociocultural Change: The Impact of the West

Human Rights and Humanitarian Assistance
http://www.etown.edu/vl/humrts.html

Through this site you can conduct research into a number of human rights topics and issues affecting indigenous peoples in the modern era.

The Indigenous Rights Movement in the Pacific
http://www.inmotionmagazine.com/pacific.html

This article addresses issues that pertain to the problems of the Pacific Island peoples as a result of U.S. colonial expansion in the Pacific and Caribbean 100 years ago.

RomNews Network—Online
http://www.romnews.com/community/index.php

This is a Web site dedicated to news and information for and about the Roma (European Gypsies). Visit here to learn more about their culture and the discrimination they constantly face.

WWW Virtual Library: Indigenous Studies
http://www.cwis.org/wwwvl/indig-vl.html

This site presents resources collected by the Center for World Indigenous Studies (CWIS) in Africa, Asia and the Middle East, Central and South America, Europe, and the Pacific.

We highly recommend that you review our Web site for expanded information and our other product lines. We are continually updating and adding links to our Web site in order to offer you the most usable and useful information that will support and expand the value of your Annual Editions. You can reach us at: http://www.mhcls.com/annualeditions/.

World Map

Scale: 1 to 125,000,000

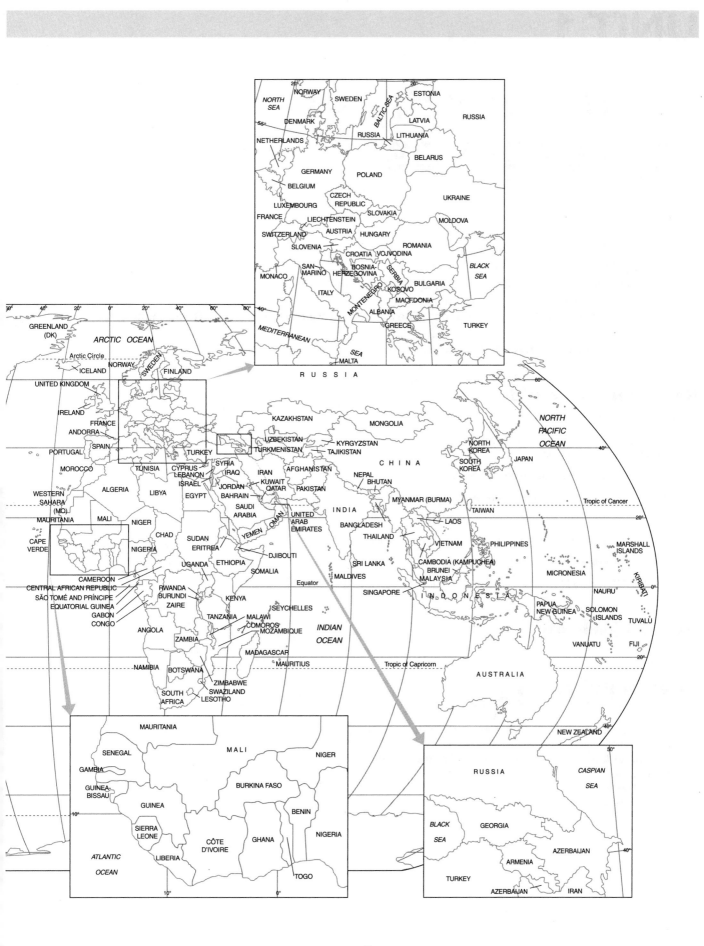

UNIT 1

Anthropological Perspectives

Unit Selections

Key Points to Consider

- What is "culture shock?"

- How can anthropologists who become personally involved with a community through participant observation maintain their objectivity as scientists?

- What kinds of ethical obligations do fieldworkers have toward their informants?

- In what ways do the results of fieldwork depend on the kinds of questions asked?

- In what sense is sharing intrinsic to egalitarianism?

- What lessons can be learned about one's own culture by going into the field?

- Should anthropologists participate in counterinsurgency programs?

- Why is it meaningless to claim that one is "one hundred percent American?"

Student Web Site

www.mhcls.com/online

Internet References

Further information regarding these Web sites may be found in this book's preface or online.

Archaeology and Anthropology Computing and Study Skills
http://www.isca.ox.ac.uk/index.html

Introduction to Anthropological Fieldwork and Ethnography
http://web.mit.edu/dumit/www/syl-anth.html

Theory in Anthropology
http://www.indiana.edu/~wanthro/theory.htm

For at least a century, the goals of anthropology have been to describe societies and cultures throughout the world and to compare the differences and similarities among them. Anthropologists study in a variety of settings and situations, ranging from small hamlets and villages to neighborhoods and corporate offices of major urban centers throughout the world. They study hunters and gatherers, peasants, farmers, labor leaders, politicians, and bureaucrats. They examine religious life in Latin America as well as revolutionary movements.

Wherever practicable, anthropologists take on the role of "participant observer." Through active involvement in the lifeways of people, they hope to gain an insider's perspective without sacrificing the objectivity of the trained scientist. Sometimes the conditions for achieving such a goal seem to form an almost insurmountable barrier, but anthropologists call on persistence, adaptability, and imagination to overcome the odds against them.

The diversity of focus in anthropology means that it is earmarked less by its particular subject matter than by its perspective. Although the discipline relates to both the biological and social sciences, anthropologists know that the boundaries drawn between disciplines are highly artificial. For example, while in theory it is possible to examine only the social organization of a family unit or the organization of political power in a nation-state, in reality it is impossible to separate the biological from the social, from the economic, from the political. The explanatory perspective of anthropology, as the articles in this unit demonstrate, is to seek out interrelationships among all these factors.

The first three articles in this section illustrate varying degrees of difficulty that an anthropologist may encounter in taking on the role of the participant observer. Conrad Phillip Kottak's essay,

"Assault on Paradise," shows the hardships imposed by certain physical conditions as well as the "culture shock" experienced as a result of "being away," that is, cut off from the world-at-large.

Richard Lee, in "Eating Christmas in the Kalahari," apparently had few problems with the physical conditions and the personalities of the people he was studying. He did, however, come to realize that his behavior conveyed a certain attitude incompatible with the values of his hosts. In the process, he learned a important lesson about how these hunter-gatherers have been able to survive for so long under conditions which we would consider marginal at best.

Then, of course, there is "Tricking and Tripping: Fieldwork on Prostitution in the Era of AIDS," in which Claire E. Sterk describes the problems, both professional and personal, involved in trying to understand the precarious lives of prostitutes on the urban streets of America.

The final two articles in this unit deal with larger issues. In "Anthropology and Counterinsurgency," Montgomery McFate combines her experience in anthropology and the law to argue for increased involvement on the part of anthropologists in United States counterinsurgency programs. In the classic essay, "One Hundred Percent American," Ralph Linton shows that even modern America, as technologically innovative as is, will forever owe a great debt to all those inventive cultures that came before.

Much is at stake in these discussions as we attempt to achieve a more objective understanding of the diversity of peoples' ways. After all, the purpose of anthropology is not only to describe and explain, but also to develop a special vision of the world in which cultural alternatives (past, present, and future) can be measured against one another and used as guides for human action.

Before: The Sixties

CONRAD PHILLIP KOTTAK

It Began by Accident

This is a story of change, but it didn't start out to be that. It began by accident. I first lived in Arembepe during the (North American) summer of 1962. That was between my junior and senior years at New York City's Columbia College (of Columbia University), where I was majoring in anthropology. I went to Arembepe as a participant in a now defunct program designed to give undergraduates an experience in ethnography—the firsthand study of local culture and social life. The program's cumbersome title, the Columbia-Cornell-Harvard-Illinois Summer Field Studies Program in Anthropology, reflected participation by four universities, each with a different field station. The other field sites were in Peru, Mexico, and Ecuador. The area around Salvador, Brazil, had just been chosen for the Columbia field station.

The field team leader was Professor Marvin Harris, who was later to become my adviser and doctoral dissertation committee chair during my graduate work in anthropology at Columbia University, which began in 1963. Also in Salvador that year was Professor Charles Wagley, another Columbia anthropologist, who had worked with Harris and others to establish the program. Through their links with Bahian social scientists, Harris and Wagley chose two villages that were anthropologically interesting but close enough to Salvador to maintain contact with the undergraduates. The two communities lay along the same road. Abrantes, the agricultural village, nearer to Salvador, was the district seat for Arembepe, the more remote fishing village. Liking the coast, I preferred Arembepe, where I was assigned, with fellow team member David Epstein. Harris arranged for us to rent the dilapidated summer house of a city man who sometimes vacationed in Arembepe.

Meanwhile, Professor Wagley's daughter, Betty, a Barnard College student also majoring in anthropology, arrived to spend the summer with her parents in Salvador. She went with us to visit Abrantes and Arembepe and decided she also wanted to do fieldwork in the latter. Betty arranged lodging with a local woman, but since David and I had hired a cook, she ate with us and shared the cost of food and supplies. Betty's mother was Brazilian, and Betty, herself born in Brazil, is bilingual in Portuguese (her first language). This made her more adept at fieldwork than either David or I was. She was also kind enough to translate for us many times.

Having taught anthropology now for more than 30 years, I realize how unusual my first field experience was. Most anthropologists begin fieldwork, which is required for the doctorate, after a few years of graduate study and not as undergraduates. They usually choose the part of the world they want to work in and the topic they will investigate there. For example, my own longest ethnographic project came just after graduate school. Having taken courses about several world areas, I became particularly interested in Madagascar, a large island off the southeast coast of Africa. I read as much as I could about the cultures of Madagascar. I focused on a problem—the social implications of an economic change, the expansion of irrigated agriculture—that I could investigate there.

With Arembepe, by contrast, someone else—the directors of the field program—selected the area, even the village, for me. I didn't have time to do the extensive background reading that normally precedes fieldwork. Nor did I have much time to study the language I would be using in the field.

Although I didn't control the initial choice of Arembepe, I *did* decide to keep on studying it, particularly when, by 1973, it was evident that Arembepe had changed more rapidly in less than two decades than some places change in centuries. Longitudinal (long-term, ongoing) fieldwork during that transformation is the basis of this book.

Most of my preparation for my 1962 fieldwork was in a prefield seminar that Harris offered at Columbia and another seminar about ethnographic field methods

(Conrad P. Kottak)

"We always got stuck at least once." The road to Arembepe, passing through the district seat, Abrantes, in 1964.

on Brazilian racial classification, which I discuss later in this chapter.

Although I prepared myself to investigate Brazilian race relations, my preparation in Brazilian Portuguese was insufficient. Language was my biggest barrier in the field. I had never been abroad and had no experience speaking a foreign language: high school (Latin) and college (German) had barely taught me how to read one. As a result, I spent most of the summer of 1962 asking Brazilians to repeat everything they said to me. This led Arembepeiros to call me a *papagaio* (parrot)—because I could only echo words that someone else had originated. I discovered that it's difficult to gain much insight into native social life when you can't converse as well as a five-year-old can.

The Sixties

In June 1962, when I first set eyes on Arembepe, the 55-kilometer trip from Salvador was neither simple nor sure. It took three hours in a vehicle with four-wheel drive. Located about 13 degrees south of the equator and at sea level, Arembepe is never cold, but June and July are rainy, making travel difficult. The clay-surfaced road was usually muddy, and we always got stuck at least once in any round trip. The task of getting our heavy jeep station wagon unstuck usually required a work group of field team members and a dozen helpful onlookers.

Sand, lagoons, and more sand came after the mud. After heavy rains, crossing the freshwater lagoons that bordered Arembepe on the west made the jeep seem like a motorboat. High water washed onto the cabin floor and sometimes stalled the engine. After the lagoons came the dunes, with closely planted coconut trees— posing another traffic hazard. Making it into the village required finding another vehicle's tracks and flooring the accelerator. Once, as a frustrating drive out seemed over, I pulled up in front of the house I was renting to find that the brakes had failed. Frantic pumping kept me from crashing through the kitchen wall.

But Arembepe was worth the trip. I can't imagine a more beautiful field setting. The village was strung along a narrow strip of land (less than a kilometer) between ocean and lagoons. It was more spectacular than any South Sea island I later visited. Arembepe's houses— brightly painted in tones of blue, pink, purple, and orange—stood under lofty coconut palms. To the east, stretches of smooth white sand and protected swimming areas alternated with jagged rocks and churning Atlantic waves. On a sunny day in August, Arembepe was alive

taught by Professor Lambros Comitas. In Harris's class, students talked about the kinds of research we planned to do when we got to Brazil. Harris urged us to do micro-projects, focusing on limited aspects of community life that we could investigate easily in three months. The program's founders didn't intend our work to be traditional holistic ethnography—intensive study of all aspects of local life through long-term residence and participant observation. Comitas's seminar, on the other hand, had introduced me to techniques used in long-term, in-depth ethnography. One of my problems in doing fieldwork in Arembepe in 1962 was the conflict between my wish to do a holistic study and the program's preference for a microproject.

The program's goals were modest. I now realize that this was realistic, because we were novices. Harris and the other leaders wanted us to get our feet wet—to see if we liked fieldwork enough to pursue a career in cultural anthropology. Our experience would also prepare us for later, longer fieldwork. As training for our microprojects, our prefield seminar assignment was to write a library research paper on the topic we planned to investigate in Brazil.

Harris suggested I study race relations, which already had a large literature. Comparisons of race relations in Brazil and the United States are appropriate because both countries have a heritage of slavery. In both there has been considerable mixture of Europeans, Africans, and Native Americans. For the seminar, I read extensively. I learned the main differences between the role of race in Brazil and the United States and wrote a research paper on my findings. Harris and I later worked out a specific microproject

(Conrad P. Kottak)

During the 1960s, as we approached Arembepe, the clay road yielded to sand.

with color: the green-blue hues of ocean and lagoons, orange-red of brick and roof tiles, pinks and blues of houses, greens of palms, and white of sand. Colorful fishing boats anchored evenings and Sundays in the port, just east of the central square and the small, white Roman Catholic chapel. The harbor is formed by a rugged, partially submerged reef. Each morning the boats rowed through its narrow channels, then raised their sun-bleached sails to travel to their destinations for the day.

The conjunction of natural beauty with the middle-class appeal of a quaint fishing village had already drawn a handful of tourists and summer residents to Arembepe in 1962. Still, the poor quality of the road made it a hard trip even in summer, the dry season (December to February). Only a few residents of the capital—mainly middle-class and lower-middle-class people—had summer homes in Arembepe. Limited bus service began in 1965, but it brought few visitors until the road was improved in 1970.

Poverty and poor public health were blights that made Arembepe—despite the title of this book—something less than paradise. In theory, Arembepeiros got their drinking water from Big Well, a tiny settlement 2 kilometers away. An entrepreneur who lived there made money selling barrels of water in Arembepe. When well water wasn't readily available, villagers sometimes drank water from the freshwater lagoon. Some mothers even used lagoon water in the powdered milk they mixed for their children. Considering these traditional uses of water—and that the bushes where villagers relieved themselves were on the edge of the lagoon, which rose in the rainy season—it's easy to understand why children suffered from intestinal disorders and extreme malnutrition (the latter partly caused by parasites in their bodies).

Malinowski and Microprojects

I entered this romantic yet imperfect setting as a fledgling ethnographer with ambitious goals and a huge linguistic impediment. Two dimensions of my work in Arembepe bear discussion here. One involves my scientific and professional aims. The second has to do with my personal reactions to an alien setting. First the scientific goals.

As a conscientious anthropology major, I wanted to put the lessons from my classes into practice. I wanted to do the things that Bronislaw Malinowski describes as the ethnographer's work in the first chapter of his classic *Argonauts of the Western Pacific,* a field study of fishers and traders in Melanesia.

I often compared my experiences with Malinowski's. Even our field settings struck me as similar. He had also worked in a tropical South Sea setting (the Trobriand Islands). Though Arembepe is on the mainland, the phrase "South Sea island" kept running through my head. Reading Malinowski's description of the moment when the ethnographer set foot upon a beach reminded me of my own situation. I imagined myself in his sandals. Like me, Malinowski initially had trouble communicating with local people. "I was quite unable to enter any more detailed or explicit conversation with them at first. I knew well that the best remedy for this was to collect concrete data, and accordingly I took a village census, wrote down genealogies, drew up plans and collected the terms of kinship" (Malinowski 1961, p. 5).

I was eager to do those things that Malinowski had done, especially to census the village. But field leader Harris discouraged me, offering another lesson: Before I could gather the detailed and accurate data that ethnography demands, I needed to build rapport; people would have to get to know and trust me. I would have to convince them I wasn't dangerous and that it wouldn't be to their disadvantage to answer my questions. Furthermore, I didn't yet know enough about village life to devise pertinent questions to ask during a census. Accordingly, but regretfully, I put the census on hold and set about building rapport. David Epstein and Betty Wagley, my companions in the field, were doing the same thing.

How does one build rapport? "Get to know the men," Marvin told me. To do this I started joining the fishermen for their evening bath in the lagoon. I had my first doubts about the wisdom of this participant observation when I accidentally swatted a floating piece of donkey dung (I like to think I identified the correct mammal) during my third bath. I gave up lagoon bathing when I learned of the lagoon system's infestation by schistosomes—liver flukes. After that, I was careful to avoid the lagoon. I followed the advice of public health officials to rub exposed body parts

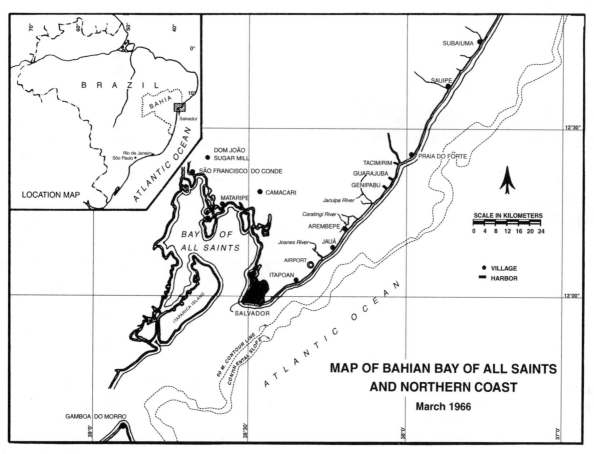

**MAP OF BAHIAN BAY OF ALL SAINTS
AND NORTHERN COAST**

March 1966

with alcohol whenever I came into contact with lagoon water. Arembepeiros found these precautions laughable: Not to worry, they said—small fish in the lagoon ate the liver flukes (and germs in general).

If the lagoon was now off-limits, there was still the chapel stoop, where each evening, after the fleet had returned, baths had been taken, and the day's main meal consumed, men would gather to talk. This was male territory. Among females, only small girls and old women dared approach. David and I would sit and try to talk. My Portuguese was rudimentary. Still, villagers tossed questions my way. They were curious about the United States, but their questions were hardly scintillating: "Were there camels in the United States?" "Elephants?" "Monkeys?" They went through a litany of animals they had seen on the lottery tickets people brought back from Salvador. "Look! Up in the sky. It's a jet from the United States heading for Rio," they observed every other night, reflecting the airline's schedule. Whenever, after arduous mental rehearsal, I found the words to ask a question about Arembepe, I'd get an incomprehensible reply, followed by some such query as "Have you ever seen a bear, Conrado?"

"Bear, bear," I parroted.

"Parrot, parrot," they guffawed.

"Yes, I have seen a bear. I have seen a bear in a zoo."

Rapport building was fascinating indeed.

Visions of Malinowski danced in my head as I came to resent this kind of activity as a waste of time. I was eager to do something "more scientific." The microproject that Harris and I had planned involved testing a difference between race relations in Brazil and the United States. In the United States a rule of descent determines racial identity. If an American has one black (African-American) parent and one white one, he or she is assigned, automatically at birth and without regard for physical appearance, to the black race. In Brazil, it seemed that several factors determine racial identity and that no descent rule operates. Since, however, no one had systematically demonstrated that Brazil lacks such a rule, we decided that a genetically and phenotypically (physically) mixed community like Arembepe would be a good place to test it.

When an automatic descent rule operates, full siblings belong to the same group. Thus in the United States, full siblings can't belong to different races. In Arembepe, we

(Courtesy Jerald T. Milanich)

The beautiful, microbe-infested, freshwater lagoon that borders Arembepe to the west, at sundown.

set out to find full siblings who were physically very different, to see if they were assigned to different races. We found three sisters with widely varying skin shades, hair types, and facial features. After we photographed them, I finally got to do something more challenging than reporting on North American animals. I chose a sample of 100 villagers and showed the photo of the sisters to all, asking them to tell me each girl's race. Sure enough, I found that many different terms were used, that in Brazil full siblings could belong to different races.

New questions about race emerged from that first survey. We devised another set of questions, based on drawings of individuals who contrasted phenotypically. By questioning another sample of villagers, I found that Arembepeiros used many more racial terms (over 40) than had previously been reported for a Brazilian community. They also used them inconsistently, so that the racial term used for another person might vary from day to day, as might even self-identification. By the time my three months in Arembepe were up, I was fluent in Brazilian racial terminology, and Harris and I had the basis for a couple of journal articles. Although I still felt guilty that I hadn't managed to do a Malinowskian census, I did think I'd accomplished something in my first field experience.

To work again in Brazil, I knew I'd have to improve my Portuguese. I could get only so far talking about race relations. I spent the next summer (1963) taking an intensive course in Brazilian Portuguese at Columbia University while another field team lived in Arembepe. Also in the summer of 1963, Betty Wagley and I, whose romance had begun under Arembepe's full moon, got married; and I began graduate school in the fall.

I was delighted, the following spring, to be offered the job of assistant leader of the 1964 field team. I returned to Arembepe in June 1964 determined to do my census. And not just a census. By then I had studied more anthropology, and my Portuguese had improved dramatically. I felt I was ready to do a full-fledged interview schedule (a kind of questionnaire). Peter Gorlin, who now holds a Ph.D. in anthropology and an M.D. degree, was an undergraduate field team member stationed in Jauá, the next village south of Arembepe. Peter had read Malinowski, too; he was also eager to use Malinowski's "method of concrete, statistical documentation" (1961, p. 24), to satisfy the ethnographer's "fundamental obligation of giving a complete survey of the phenomena, and not of picking out the sensational [and] the singular" (1961, p. 11).

I was ready to do a survey of all the households in Arembepe, and Peter wanted to do the same thing in Jauá. But we needed an instrument. Our team leader, the renowned Bahian physician and anthropologist Thales de Azevedo, supplied us with one—an interview schedule that had been used in southern Bahia. We revised the schedule for the fishing villages and had it printed.

An *interview schedule* differs from a standard questionnaire in that the ethnographer talks directly, face to face, with informants, asks the questions, and writes down the answers. Questionnaire procedures, which sociologists routinely use, tend to be more indirect and impersonal; often the respondent fills in the form. Sociologists normally work with literate people, who can fill out the answer sheets or questionnaire forms themselves. Anthropologists, by contrast, haven't usually worked in places where most people are literate, so we have to record the answers ourselves.

Because we are in charge of pacing, we can choose to digress temporarily from the scheduled questions to follow up intriguing bits of information that emerge in the interview. Thus the ethnographer can keep interviews open-ended and exploratory while asking a basic set of questions, to gather comparable, quantifiable information. I learned as much about Arembepe from the open-ended questioning as I did from the formal queries.

Our interviews in Arembepe illustrate still another difference between the research techniques of anthropologists and sociologists. Because sociologists normally deal with large populations, such as the United States, they must use *sampling techniques,* which enable them to make inferences about a larger group from a detailed study of a smaller one. We didn't need to do sampling in Arembepe, because it was small enough for us to do a

(Conrad P. Kottak)

1964 field team members Peter Gorlin (second from left) and Erica Bressler with their host family in Jauá, the fishing village just south of Arembepe. Note the range of physical variation among the local people.

total sample—that is, to complete the schedule with all the households there—159 of them.

A final contrast between cultural anthropology and sociology is worth mentioning. Sociologists often distribute their questionnaires by mail or hire research assistants to administer, code, and analyze them. Ethnographers, by contrast, work right in the community, where they encounter a series of real-world obstacles. My main problem as I interviewed in Arembepe wasn't the few villagers who slammed doors in my face or even the droopy-nosed kids who used my pants as a handkerchief. My problem was fleas. I recall my third or fourth interview, in a sand-floored hut. Asking my questions to a dozen smiling members of an extended family, I began to itch in places I was embarrassed to scratch. I made it to the end of the form, but I didn't tarry for open-ended inquiry. Instead I ran home, through the house, out the back door, right into the harbor at high tide. I let the salt water burn into my flea wounds. Fleas bothered most of us, especially Betty, that summer. The remedy for the men was to wear pants and sprinkle our cuffs with flea powder. We managed to interview in almost all Arembepe's households, despite the predatory sand fleas.

Our interview schedule was eight pages long. We asked questions (for each household member) about age, gender, racial identity, diet, job, religious beliefs and practices, education, political preferences, possessions, consumption patterns, and ownership of livestock, boats, coconut trees, land, and farms. I encouraged Peter not to do a microproject but to follow the Malinowskian path I'd wanted to tread. He did it with gusto; in two months he'd

finished the schedule with all the households in Jauá. He hiked up the beach to spend August helping Betty and me finish the interviewing in Arembepe.

There are advantages, I now realize, in both models for brief fieldwork. A microproject is easily manageable and holds out the promise of a modest research paper. The holistic Malinowskian approach is also valuable. I'm convinced my Portuguese would have improved much more if I'd done the interview schedule the first summer, rather than limiting my talk to rapport building and race relations. Peter Gorlin's work with the schedule in Jauá and Arembepe in 1964 helped him improve his Portuguese much more quickly than I had done in 1962.

Doing the schedule had an added benefit I didn't fully realize in 1964: It got at least one member of the field team into every home in Arembepe. Years later I was to hear from many villagers that they remembered those visits warmly. Our questions, asked in their homes, had communicated our personal interest and showed we didn't look down on Arembepeiros.

I found the people of Arembepe to be open, warm, and hospitable, much less wary of outsiders than the Betsileo of Madagascar, whom I studied for 14 months in 1966–1967. Most Arembepeiros welcomed us to their homes and gladly answered our questions. Only a handful played hard to get, slamming windows and doors as we approached, telling neighbors they wouldn't answer our questions. I had to settle for sketchier information about them and could only make estimates of their incomes and consumption patterns, using public information and behavior. Fortunately (since the 1964 data are the basis for much of the detailed comparison between Arembepe in the 1960s and later), fewer than a dozen households, scattered throughout the village, refused to let us do the schedule.

The interview schedule wasn't the only thing I did in Arembepe in 1964. Soon after my arrival, I met an excellent informant, Alberto, whose name figures prominently in the story that follows. Then a 40-year-old fisherman, Alberto was the eldest brother of our cook. He felt free to visit our house almost every night, and he was eager to teach me about the fishing industry. I also got information about fishing by talking to fishermen and fish marketers on the beach and by going out in several boats, including that of Tomé, Arembepe's most successful boat captain and owner. Tomé's name, too, is a prominent one in Arembepe's recent history.

In 1965 I had my third chance to study Arembepe. The results of analyzing the interview schedules and my information on fishing had been so promising that both Marvin

Harris and I felt that I might, with another summer of field-work, amass sufficient data to write my doctoral dissertation about Arembepe, which I did. This time Betty and I weren't part of a field team but on our own. A graduate fellowship and grant supported my work, and living was still cheap in cash-poor Arembepe. In summer 1965 I again followed the Malinowskian plan, but I already had much of the statistical and observational data needed for the "firm, clear outline" of my community's organization and the "anatomy of its culture" (Malinowski 1961, p. 24).

What I needed now was flesh for the skeleton. So I spent the summer of 1965 gathering data on the "imponderabilia of actual life . . . collected through minute, detailed observations . . . made possible by close contact with native life" (Malinowski 1961, p. 24). By this time, I didn't really have to harken back to Malinowski to know that although I had the bare bones, I still needed to find out more about local opinions, values, and feelings; to listen to stories, examine cases, and gather intimate, basic details about everyday life. Like Napoleon Chagnon, the principal ethnographer of the Yanomamo Indians of Venezuela, I knew "how much I enjoyed reading monographs that were sprinkled with real people, that described real events, and that had some sweat and tears, some smells and sentiments mingled with the words" (Chagnon 1977, p. xi). I wanted to add such dimensions—feeling tones—to my ethnography of Arembepe.

It Was an Alien Place

Those were some of my professional goals and research methods. Another part of ethnography is more personal. No matter how objective and scientific they fancy themselves, anthropologists are not mechanical measuring instruments. We are inevitably *participant* observers, taking part in—and by so doing modifying, no matter how slightly—the phenomena we are investigating and trying to understand. Not recording machines but people, anthropologists grow up in particular cultural traditions, possess idiosyncratic personality traits and experiences, have their own motivations, impressions, values, and reactions. Nor are our informants alike; we come to appreciate them differently. Some we never appreciate; an occasional one we detest.

Raised in one culture, curious about others, anthropologists still experience culture shock, especially on the first field trip. *Culture shock* refers to the whole set of feelings about being in an alien setting and the resulting reactions. It is a chilly, creepy feeling of alienation, of being without some of the most ordinary, trivial—and therefore basic—cues of one's culture of origin.

As I planned to set off for Brazil in 1962, I couldn't know how naked I would feel without the cloak of my language and culture. My sojourn in Arembepe would be my first trip outside the United States. I was an urban boy who had grown up in Atlanta, Georgia, and New York City. I had little experience with rural life in my country, none with Latin America, and I had received only minimal training in the Portuguese language.

New York City direct to Salvador, Bahia, Brazil. Just a brief stopover in Rio de Janeiro; a longer visit would be a reward at the end of fieldwork. As our plane approached tropical Salvador, I couldn't believe the whiteness of the sand. "That's not snow, is it?" I remarked to a fellow field team member. Marvin Harris had arranged our food and lodging at the Paradise Hotel, overlooking Bahia's magnificent, endlessly blue, All Saints' Bay. My first impressions of Bahia were of smells—alien odors of ripe and decaying mangoes, bananas, and passion fruit—and of swatting ubiquitous flies. There were strange concoctions of rice, black beans, and gobs of unidentified meats and floating pieces of skin. Coffee was strong and sugar crude. Every table top had containers for toothpicks and manioc (cassava) flour, to sprinkle, like parmesan cheese, on anything one might eat. I remember oatmeal soup and a slimy stew of beef tongue in tomatoes. At one meal a disintegrating fish head, eyes still attached, but barely, stared up at me as its body floated in a bowl of bright orange palm oil. Bearing my culture's don't-drink-the-water complex, it took me a few days to discover that plain mineral water quenched thirst better than the gaseous variety. Downstairs from the hotel was the Boite Clock, a nightclub whose rhythmic bossa nova music often kept us from sleeping.

I only vaguely remember my first day in Arembepe. Unlike ethnographers who have studied remote tribes in the tropical forests of South America or the highlands of New Guinea, I didn't hike or ride a canoe for days to arrive at my field site. Arembepe wasn't isolated compared with those places—only compared with every place *I*'d ever been. My first contact with Arembepe was just a visit, to arrange lodging. We found the crumbling summer house of a man who lived in Salvador and arranged to rent it and have it cleaned. We hired Dora, a 25-year-old unmarried mother of two, to cook for us, and another woman to clean house and do our laundry. My first visit to Arembepe didn't leave much of an impression. I knew I'd still have a few more days at the Paradise Hotel, with a real toilet and shower, before having to rough it in the field.

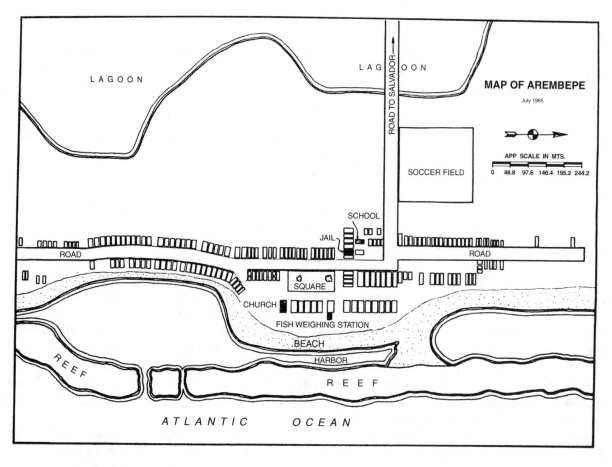

Back in the city, using her fluency in Brazilian language and culture, Betty Wagley bargained for our cots, pots, pans, flashlights, and other supplies. I don't remember our actual move to Arembepe or who accompanied us. Harris had employed a chauffeur; we stopped to deposit some field team members in Abrantes. I do recall what happened when we got to Arembepe. A crowd of children pursued our car through the sand and streets until we parked in front of our house, near the central square. We spent our first few days with children following us everywhere. For weeks we had little daytime privacy. Kids watched our every move through our living room window. Sometimes one made an incomprehensible remark. Usually they just stood there. Occasionally they would groom one another's hair, chewing on the lice they found.

Outcasts from an urban culture, David and I locked our doors. Once he went into Salvador while I stayed the night alone.

"Conrado's scared," said Dora, our cook. "He's afraid of the *bichos* [beasts, real and imaginary] outside." There was really nothing to be afraid of, she assured me. A dan-

gerous *bicho* had never bothered anyone in Arembepe; most people didn't even have locks on their doors.

The sounds, sensations, sights, smells, and tastes of life in Arembepe slowly grew familiar. I grew accustomed to this world without Kleenex, where globs of mucus drooped from the noses of village children whenever a cold passed through. A world where, seemingly without effort, women with gracefully swaying hips carried 18-liter kerosene cans of water on their heads, where boys sailed kites and sported at catching houseflies in their bare hands, where old women smoked pipes, storekeepers offered *cachaça* (common rum) at nine in the morning, and men played dominoes on lazy afternoons when there was no fishing. I was in a world where life was oriented toward water—the sea, where men fished, and the lagoon, where women communally washed clothing, dishes, and their bodies.

Arembepe was a compact village, where the walls of most houses touched those of their neighbors. Privacy was a scarce commodity. No wonder villagers didn't lock their doors—who could steal anything and have it stay a secret? Young lovers found what privacy they could at night.

Even more dramatically than in other places without electricity, Arembepe's night life was transformed when the moon was full. Reflected everywhere by the sand and water, moonlight turned the village by night into almost day. Young people strolled in the streets and courted on the beach. Fishermen sought octopus and "lobster" (Atlantic crayfish) on the reef. Accustomed to the electrified, artificial pace of city life, I was enchanted by the moonlight and its effect on this remote village. Moonless nights impressed me, too. For the first time I could understand how the Milky Way got its name. Only in a planetarium had I seen a sky so crammed with stars. Looking south, distant Salvador's electric lights just barely dimmed the white stars against the coal-black sky, and for the first time I could view the Southern Cross in its magnificence.

Even a devout astrologer would have been impressed with the extent to which activities were governed by the phases of the moon. This was a slower and more natural epoch in Arembepe's history than the years that were to follow. People awakened near sunrise and went to bed early. Moonlight and a calm sea permitted occasional nighttime fishing, but the pattern was for the fleet to leave in the early morning and return in the late afternoon. Boats usually went out five or six days a week; as Christians, Arembepeiros took Sunday as a day of rest. But generally, life in Arembepe followed the availability of natural light and the passing of day and night.

Another force of nature, the weather, influenced the rhythm of life. My visits to Arembepe were during the season of rain and rough seas. Sailboats were vulnerable to high winds and stormy weather, and it was dangerous to negotiate the narrow channels in the rocky reef when racing home to escape a sudden squall. Storms usually lasted no more than a week, but I remember one three-week lull, in 1964. People speculated incessantly about when the weather would improve; they had no access to weather reports. Villagers lamented that they couldn't work. Eventually they began to complain of hunger. Cattle were brought in from farms to be butchered and sold, but many households were too poor to buy beef. Villagers said they were hungry for fish, for something with flesh to complement a diet of coffee, sugar, and manioc flour. The weather even forced us to let up on our interviewing. Our schedule had a whole section on diet—the quantities of various foods that people bought or ate per day, week, or month. We felt embarrassed asking people what they ate in normal or good times when they were starving for

protein and, indeed, for all items whose purchase required cash.

The tropical rainy season meant constant high humidity, a perfect climate for molds. My black leather dress shoes turned white with mildew. Peter Gorlin had bought a navy blue drip-dry suit before his trip to Bahia in 1964. Since we attended few formal affairs in Salvador, Peter let his suit hang in a wardrobe in Jauá until he finally needed it. Discovering, a few hours before a party, that it was covered with mildew, Peter checked into a Salvador hotel, took a shower with his suit on, lathered and rinsed it, wore it to the party, and dripped dry for the next few hours.

The tile roofs of the houses we rented in Arembepe were never very effective in keeping the moisture (and bats) out. Whenever it rained, we had to avoid the large leaks, but there was no place we could be completely dry. One rainy day during the three-week fishing lull, Dora told us that lately, smelling the moist walls of her wattle-and-daub (stick-and-mud) hut, she had remembered her craving as a child to lick, even eat, dirt from the mud walls. Arembepeiros sometimes did eat earth, she told us. This geophagy may have been a symptom of iron deficiency in lean times.

I can summarize my feelings about living in Arembepe in the 1960s by saying that I had a profound sense of being away. In those days, almost no one except a fish buyer from Salvador ever drove a car into Arembepe. I felt cut off from the world. Only a few villagers owned radios, which rarely brought news of the rest of the world anyway. I pored over every word of *Time*'s Latin American edition on each visit to Salvador. We sometimes planned our trips into Salvador to coincide with the day the new *Time* came out.

Even for Betty Wagley Kottak, a Brazilian (of dual nationality), Arembepe was unfamiliar. It was far removed from the sophistication, social stratification, and style consciousness of Rio de Janeiro and São Paulo, which she knew well. Betty had been exposed to much of Brazil's "Great Tradition" (to use Robert Redfield's term for the culture of literate, mainly urban, elites) but not the "little traditions" of its peasants and rural poor. For both of us, then, as for the other field team members, Arembepe provided a strong contrast with all previous settings in our lives.

I think that our work in Arembepe also gave us a better understanding of rural America as recently as the 1930s and 1940s. Then, in many isolated pockets, especially among the poor, night life still went on by candle and lantern. This was before business, government, and media had fully introduced rural folk to the industrial world's vast inventory of benefits and costs.

We learned firsthand about the habits and values of Arembepeiros, how they tried to make ends meet, how they dealt with fortune and adversity. We got to know many people as individuals and as friends. Characters like Alberto, Dora, and Tomé, whose words, stories, and experiences are laced through this chronicle of a changing Arembepe, are much more to me than informants. They are people I value as I do my friends and special colleagues in the United States. Yet they are the kind of people that few outsiders will ever have a chance to meet. The anthropologist's special obligation is to tell their story for them.

Eating Christmas in the Kalahari

RICHARD BORSHAY LEE

The !Kung Bushmen's knowledge of Christmas is third-hand. The London Missionary Society brought the holiday to the southern Tswana tribes in the early nineteenth century. Later, native catechists spread the idea far and wide among the Bantu-speaking pastoralists, even in the remotest corners of the Kalahari Desert. The Bushmen's idea of the Christmas story, stripped to its essentials, is "praise the birth of white man's god-chief"; what keeps their interest in the holiday high is the Tswana-Herero custom of slaughtering an ox for his Bushmen neighbors as an annual goodwill gesture. Since the 1930's, part of the Bushmen's annual round of activities has included a December congregation at the cattle posts for trading, marriage brokering, and several days of trance-dance feasting at which the local Tswana headman is host.

As a social anthropologist working with !Kung Bushmen, I found that the Christmas ox custom suited my purposes. I had come to the Kalahari to study the hunting and gathering subsistence economy of the !Kung, and to accomplish this it was essential not to provide them with food, share my own food, or interfere in any way with their food-gathering activities. While liberal handouts of tobacco and medical supplies were appreciated, they were scarcely adequate to erase the glaring disparity in wealth between the anthropologist, who maintained a two-month inventory of canned goods, and the Bushmen, who rarely had a day's supply of food on hand. My approach, while paying off in terms of data, left me open to frequent accusations of stinginess and hard-heartedness. By their lights, I was a miser.

The Christmas ox was to be my way of saying thank you for the cooperation of the past year; and since it was to be our last Christmas in the field, I determined to slaughter the largest, meatiest ox that money could buy, insuring that the feast and trance-dance would be a success.

Through December I kept my eyes open at the wells as the cattle were brought down for watering. Several animals were offered, but none had quite the grossness that I had in mind. Then, ten days before the holiday, a Herero friend led an ox of astonishing size and mass up to our camp. It was solid black, stood five feet high at the shoulder, had a five-foot span of horns, and must have weighed 1,200 pounds on the hoof. Food consumption calculations are my specialty, and I quickly figured that bones and viscera aside, there was enough meat—at least four pounds—for every man, woman, and child of the 150 Bushmen in the vicinity of /ai/ai who were expected at the feast.

Having found the right animal at last, I paid the Herero £20 ($56) and asked him to keep the beast with his herd until Christmas day. The next morning word spread among the people that the big solid black one was the ox chosen by /ontah (my Bushman name; it means, roughly, "whitey") for the Christmas feast. That afternoon I received the first delegation. Ben!a, an outspoken sixty-year-old mother of five, came to the point slowly.

"Where were you planning to eat Christmas?"

"Right here at /ai/ai," I replied.

"Alone or with others?"

"I expect to invite all the people to eat Christmas with me."

"Eat what?"

"I have purchased Yehave's black ox, and I am going to slaughter and cook it."

"That's what we were told at the well but refused to believe it until we heard it from yourself."

"Well, it's the black one," I replied expansively, although wondering what she was driving at.

"Oh, no!" Ben!a groaned, turning to her group. "They were right." Turning back to me she asked, "Do you expect us to eat that bag of bones?"

"Bag of bones! It's the biggest ox at /ai/ai."

"Big, yes, but old. And thin. Everybody knows there's no meat on that old ox. What did you expect us to eat off it, the horns?"

Everybody chuckled at Ben!a's one-liner as they walked away, but all I could manage was a weak grin.

That evening it was the turn of the young men. They came to sit at our evening fire. /gaugo, about my age, spoke to me man-to-man.

"/ontah, you have always been square with us," he lied. "What has happened to change your heart? That sack of guts and bones of Yehave's will hardly feed one camp, let alone all the Bushmen around ai/ai." And he proceeded to enumerate the seven camps in the /ai/ai vicinity, family by family. "Perhaps you have forgotten that we are not few, but many. Or are you too blind to tell the difference between a proper cow and an old wreck? That ox is thin to the point of death."

"Look, you guys," I retorted, "that is a beautiful animal, and I'm sure you will eat it with pleasure at Christmas."

"Of course we will eat it; it's food. But it won't fill us up to the point where we will have enough strength to dance. We will eat and go home to bed with stomachs rumbling."

That night as we turned in, I asked my wife, Nancy: "What did you think of the black ox?"

"It looked enormous to me. Why?"

"Well, about eight different people have told me I got gypped; that the ox is nothing but bones."

"What's the angle?" Nancy asked. "Did they have a better one to sell?"

"No, they just said that it was going to be a grim Christmas because there won't be enough meat to go around. Maybe I'll get an independent judge to look at the beast in the morning."

Bright and early, Halingisi, a Tswana cattle owner, appeared at our camp. But before I could ask him to give me his opinion on Yehave's black ox, he gave me the eye signal that indicated a confidential chat. We left the camp and sat down.

"/ontah, I'm surprised at you: you've lived here for three years and still haven't learned anything about cattle."

"But what else can a person do but choose the biggest, strongest animal one can find?" I retorted.

"Look, just because an animal is big doesn't mean that it has plenty of meat on it. The black one was a beauty when it was younger, but now it is thin to the point of death."

"Well I've already bought it. What can I do at this stage?"

"Bought it already? I thought you were just considering it. Well, you'll have to kill it and serve it, I suppose. But don't expect much of a dance to follow."

My spirits dropped rapidly. I could believe that Ben!a and /gaugo just might be putting me on about the black ox, but Halingisi seemed to be an impartial critic. I went around that day feeling as though I had bought a lemon of a used car.

In the afternoon it was Tomazo's turn. Tomazo is a fine hunter, a top trance performer . . . and one of my most reliable informants. He approached the subject of the Christmas cow as part of my continuing Bushman education.

"My friend, the way it is with us Bushmen," he began, "is that we love meat. And even more than that, we love fat. When we hunt we always search for the fat ones, the ones dripping with layers of white fat: fat that turns into a clear, thick oil in the cooking pot, fat that slides down your gullet, fills your stomach and gives you a roaring diarrhea," he rhapsodized.

"So, feeling as we do," he continued, "it gives us pain to be served such a scrawny thing as Yehave's black ox. It is big, yes, and no doubt its giant bones are good for soup, but fat is what we really crave and so we will eat Christmas this year with a heavy heart."

The prospect of a gloomy Christmas now had me worried, so I asked Tomazo what I could do about it.

"Look for a fat one, a young one . . . smaller, but fat. Fat enough to make us //gom ('evacuate the bowels'), then we will be happy."

My suspicions were aroused when Tomazo said that he happened to know of a young, fat, barren cow that the owner was willing to part with. Was Tomazo working on commission, I wondered? But I dispelled this unworthy thought when we approached the Herero owner of the cow in question and found that he had decided not to sell.

The scrawny wreck of a Christmas ox now became the talk of the /ai/ai water hole and was the first news told to the outlying groups as they began to come in from the bush for the feast. What finally convinced me that real trouble might be brewing was the visit from u!au, an old conservative with a reputation for fierceness. His nickname meant spear and referred to an incident thirty years ago in which he had speared a man to death. He had an intense manner; fixing me with his eyes, he said in clipped tones:

"I have only just heard about the black ox today, or else I would have come here earlier. /ontah, do you honestly think you can serve meat like that to people and avoid a fight?" He paused, letting the implications sink in. "I don't mean fight you, /ontah; you are a white man. I mean a fight between Bushmen. There are many fierce ones here, and with such a small quantity of meat to distribute, how can you give everybody a fair share? Someone is sure to accuse another of taking too much or hogging all the choice pieces. Then you will see what happens when some go hungry while others eat."

The possibility of at least a serious argument struck me as all too real. I had witnessed the tension that surrounds the distribution of meat from a kudu or gemsbok kill, and had documented many arguments that sprang up from a real or imagined slight in meat distribution. The owners of a kill may spend up to two hours arranging and rearranging the piles of meat under the gaze of a circle of recipients before handing them out. And I also knew that the Christmas feast at /ai/ai would be bringing together groups that had feuded in the past.

Convinced now of the gravity of the situation, I went in earnest to search for a second cow; but all my inquiries failed to turn one up.

The Christmas feast was evidently going to be a disaster, and the incessant complaints about the meagerness of the ox had already taken the fun out of it for me. Moreover, I was getting bored with the wisecracks, and after losing my temper a few times, I resolved to serve the beast anyway. If the meat fell short, the hell with it. In the Bushmen idiom, I announced to all who would listen:

"I am a poor man and blind. If I have chosen one that is too old and too thin, we will eat it anyway and see if there is enough meat there to quiet the rumbling of our stomachs."

On hearing this speech, Ben!a offered me a rare word of comfort. "It's thin," she said philosophically, "but the bones will make a good soup."

At dawn Christmas morning, instinct told me to turn over the butchering and cooking to a friend and take off with Nancy to spend Christmas alone in the bush. But curiosity kept me from retreating. I wanted to see what such a scrawny ox looked like on butchering and if there *was* going to be a fight, I wanted to catch every word of it. Anthropologists are incurable that way.

The great beast was driven up to our dancing ground, and a shot in the forehead dropped it in its tracks. Then, freshly cut branches were heaped around the fallen carcass to receive the meat. Ten men volunteered to help with the cutting. I asked /gaugo to make the breast bone cut. This cut, which begins the butchering process for most large game, offers easy access for removal of the viscera. But it also allows the hunter to spot-check the amount of fat on the animal. A fat game animal carries a white layer up to an inch thick on the chest, while in a thin one, the knife will quickly cut to bone. All eyes fixed on his hand as /gaugo, dwarfed by the great carcass, knelt to the breast. The first cut opened a pool of solid white in the black skin. The second and third cut widened and deepened the creamy white. Still no bone. It was pure fat; it must have been two inches thick.

"Hey /gau," I burst out, "that ox is loaded with fat. What's this about the ox being too thin to bother eating? Are you out of your mind?"

"Fat?" /gau shot back, "You call that fat? This wreck is thin, sick, dead!" And he broke out laughing. So did everyone else. They rolled on the ground, paralyzed with laughter. Everybody laughed except me; I was thinking.

I ran back to the tent and burst in just as Nancy was getting up. "Hey, the black ox. It's fat as hell! They were kidding about it being too thin to eat. It was a joke or something. A put-on. Everyone is really delighted with it!"

"Some joke," my wife replied. "It was so funny that you were ready to pack up and leave /ai/ai."

If it had indeed been a joke, it had been an extraordinarily convincing one, and tinged, I thought, with more than a touch of malice as many jokes are. Nevertheless, that it was a joke lifted my spirits considerably, and I returned to the butchering site where the shape of the ox was rapidly disappearing under the axes and knives of the butchers. The atmosphere had become festive. Grinning broadly, their arms covered with blood well past the elbow, men packed chunks of meat into the big cast-iron cooking pots, fifty pounds to the load, and muttered and chuckled all the while about the thinness and worthlessness of the animal and /ontah's poor judgment.

We danced and ate that ox two days and two nights; we cooked and distributed fourteen potfuls of meat and no one went home hungry and no fights broke out.

But the "joke" stayed in my mind. I had a growing feeling that something important had happened in my relationship with the Bushmen and that the clue lay in the meaning of the joke. Several days later, when most of the people had dispersed back to the bush camps, I raised the question with Hakekgose, a Tswana man who had grown up among the !Kung, married a !Kung girl, and who probably knew their culture better than any other non-Bushman.

"With us whites," I began, "Christmas is supposed to be the day of friendship and brotherly love. What I can't figure out is why the Bushmen went to such lengths to criticize and belittle the ox I had bought for the feast. The animal was perfectly good and their jokes and wisecracks practically ruined the holiday for me."

"So it really did bother you," said Hakekgose. "Well, that's the way they always talk. When I take my rifle and go hunting with them, if I miss, they laugh at me for the rest of the day. But even if I hit and bring one down, it's no better. To them, the kill is always too small or too old or too thin; and as we sit down on

the kill site to cook and eat the liver, they keep grumbling, even with their mouths full of meat. They say things like, 'Oh this is awful! What a worthless animal! Whatever made me think that this Tswana rascal could hunt!'"

"Is this the way outsiders are treated?" I asked.

"No, it is their custom; they talk that way to each other too. Go and ask them."

/gaugo had been one of the most enthusiastic in making me feel bad about the merit of the Christmas ox. I sought him out first.

"Why did you tell me the black ox was worthless, when you could see that it was loaded with fat and meat?"

"It is our way," he said smiling. "We always like to fool people about that. Say there is a Bushman who has been hunting. He must not come home and announce like a braggard, 'I have killed a big one in the bush!' He must first sit down in silence until I or someone else comes up to his fire and asks, 'What did you see today?' He replies quietly, 'Ah, I'm no good for hunting. I saw nothing at all [pause] just a little tiny one.' Then I smile to myself," /gaugo continued, "because I know he has killed something big."

"In the morning we make up a party of four or five people to cut up and carry the meat back to the camp. When we arrive at the kill we examine it and cry out, 'You mean to say you have dragged us all the way out here in order to make us cart home your pile of bones? Oh, if I had known it was this thin I wouldn't have come.' Another one pipes up, 'People, to think I gave up a nice day in the shade for this. At home we may be hungry but at least we have nice cool water to drink.' If the horns are big, someone says, 'Did you think that somehow you were going to boil down the horns for soup?'"

"To all this you must respond in kind. 'I agree,' you say, 'this one is not worth the effort; let's just cook the liver for strength and leave the rest for the hyenas. It is not too late to hunt today and even a duiker or a steenbok would be better than this mess.'"

"Then you set to work nevertheless; butcher the animal, carry the meat back to the camp and everyone eats," /gaugo concluded.

Things were beginning to make sense. Next, I went to Tomazo. He corroborated /gaugo's story of the obligatory insults over a kill and added a few details of his own.

"But," I asked, "why insult a man after he has gone to all that trouble to track and kill an animal and when he is going to share the meat with you so that your children will have something to eat?"

"Arrogance," was his cryptic answer.

"Arrogance?"

"Yes, when a young man kills much meat he comes to think of himself as a chief or a big man, and he thinks of the rest of us as his servants or inferiors. We can't accept this. We refuse one who boasts, for someday his pride will make him kill somebody. So we always speak of his meat as worthless. This way we cool his heart and make him gentle."

"But why didn't you tell me this before?" I asked Tomazo with some heat.

"Because you never asked me," said Tomazo, echoing the refrain that has come to haunt every field ethnographer.

The pieces now fell into place. I had known for a long time that in situations of social conflict with Bushmen I held all the cards. I was the only source of tobacco in a thousand square miles, and I was not incapable of cutting an individual off for non-cooperation. Though my boycott never lasted longer than a few days, it was an indication of my strength. People resented my presence at the water hole, yet simultaneously dreaded my leaving. In short I was a perfect target for the charge of arrogance and for the Bushmen tactic of enforcing humility.

I had been taught an object lesson by the Bushmen; it had come from an unexpected corner and had hurt me in a vulnerable area. For the big black ox was to be the one totally generous, unstinting act of my year at /ai/ai, and I was quite unprepared for the reaction I received.

As I read it, their message was this: There are no totally generous acts. All "acts" have an element of calculation. One black ox slaughtered at Christmas does not wipe out a year of careful manipulation of gifts given to serve your own ends. After all,

to kill an animal and share the meat with people is really no more than Bushmen do for each other every day and with far less fanfare.

In the end, I had to admire how the Bushmen had played out the farce—collectively straight-faced to the end. Curiously, the episode reminded me of the *Good Soldier Schweik* and his marvelous encounters with authority. Like Schweik, the Bushmen had retained a thorough-going skepticism of good intentions. Was it this independence of spirit, I wondered, that had kept them culturally viable in the face of generations of contact with more powerful societies, both black and white? The thought that the Bushmen were alive and well in the Kalahari was strangely comforting. Perhaps, armed with that independence and with their superb knowledge of their environment, they might yet survive the future.

Richard Borshay Lee is a full professor of anthropology at the University of Toronto. He has done extensive fieldwork in southern Africa, is coeditor of *Man the Hunter* (1968) and *Kalahari Hunter-Gatherers* (1976), and author of *The !Kung San: Men, Women, and Work in a Foraging Society.*

From *Natural History,* December 1969, pp. 14–22, 60–64. Copyright © 1969 by Natural History Magazine. Reprinted by permission.

Tricking and Tripping
Fieldwork on Prostitution in the Era of AIDS

CLAIRE E. STERK

S tudents often think of anthropological fieldwork as requiring travel to exotic tropical locations, but that is not necessarily the case. This reading is based on fieldwork in the United States—on the streets in New York City as well as Atlanta. Claire Sterk is an anthropologist who works in a school of public health and is primarily interested in issues of women's health, particularly as it relates to sexual behavior. In this selection, an introduction to a recent book by the same title, she describes the basic fieldwork methods she used to study these women and their communities. Like most cultural anthropologists, Sterk's primary goal was to describe "the life" of prostitution from the women's own point of view. To do this, she had to be patient, brave, sympathetic, trustworthy, curious, and nonjudgmental. You will notice these characteristics in this selection; for example, Sterk begins her book with a poem written by one of her informants. Fieldwork is a slow process, because it takes time to win people's confidence and to learn their language and way of seeing the world. In this regard, there are probably few differences between the work of a qualitative sociologist and that of a cultural anthropologist (although anthropologists would not use the term "deviant" to describe another society or a segment of their own society).

Throughout the world, HIV/AIDS is fast becoming a disease found particularly in poor women. Sex workers or prostitutes have often been blamed for AIDS, and they have been further stigmatized because of their profession. In reality, however, entry into prostitution is not a career choice; rather, these women and girls are themselves most often victims of circumstances such as violence and poverty. Public health officials want to know why sex workers do not always protect their health by making men wear condoms. To answer such questions, we must know more about the daily life of these women. The way to do that, the cultural anthropologist would say, is to ask and to listen.

As you read this selection, ask yourself the following questions:

- What happens when Sterk says, "I'm sorry for you" to one of her informants? Why?
- Why do you think fieldwork might be a difficult job?
- Do you think that the fact that Sterk grew up in Amsterdam, where prostitution is legal, affected her research?

- Which of the six themes of this work, described at the end of the article, do you think is most important?

The following terms discussed in this selection are included in the Glossary at the back of the book:

demography	*sample*
fieldwork	*stroll*
key respondent	

O ne night in March of 1987 business was slow. I was hanging out on a stroll with a group of street prostitutes. After a few hours in a nearby diner/coffee shop, we were kicked out. The waitress felt bad, but she needed our table for some new customers. Four of us decided to sit in my car until the rain stopped. While three of us chatted about life, Piper wrote this poem. As soon as she read it to us, the conversation shifted to more serious topics—pimps, customers, cops, the many hassles of being a prostitute, to name a few. We decided that if I ever finished a book about prostitution, the book would start with her poem.

This book is about the women who work in the lower echelons of the prostitution world. They worked in the streets and other public settings as well as crack houses. Some of these women viewed themselves primarily as prostitutes, and a number of them used drugs to cope with the pressures of the life. Others identified themselves more as drug users, and their main reason for having sex for money or other goods was to support their own drug use and often the habit of their male partner. A small group of women interviewed for this book had left prostitution, and most of them were still struggling to integrate their past experiences as prostitutes in their current lives.

The stories told by the women who participated in this project revealed how pimps, customers, and others such as police officers and social and health service providers treated them as "fallen" women. However, their accounts also showed their strengths and the many strategies they developed to challenge these others. Circumstances, including their drug use, often forced them to sell sex, but they all resisted the notion that they might be selling themselves. Because they engaged in an illegal profession, these women had little status: their working conditions were poor, and their work was physically and mentally exhausting. Nevertheless, many women described the ways in which they gained a sense of control over their lives. For instance, they learned how to manipulate pimps, how to control the types of services and length of time bought by their customers, and how to select customers. While none of these schemes explicitly enhanced their working conditions, they did make the women feel stronger and better about themselves.

In this book, I present prostitution from the point of view of the women themselves. To understand their current lives, it was necessary to learn how they got started in the life, the various processes involved in their continued prostitution careers, the link between prostitution and drug use, the women's interactions with their pimps and customers, and the impact of the AIDS epidemic and increasing violence on their experiences. I also examined the implications for women. Although my goal was to present the women's thoughts, feelings, and actions in their own words, the final text is a sociological monograph compiled by me as the researcher. Some women are quoted more than others because I developed a closer relationship with them, because they were more able to verbalize and capture their circumstances, or simply because they were more outspoken.

The Sample

The data for this book are qualitative. The research was conducted during the last ten years in the New York City and Atlanta metropolitan areas. One main data source was participant observation on streets, in hotels and other settings known for prostitution activity, and in drug-use settings, especially those that allowed sex-for-drug exchanges. Another data source was in-depth, life-history interviews with 180 women ranging in age from 18 to 59 years, with an average age of 34. One in two women was African-American and one in three white; the remaining women were Latina. Three in four had completed high school, and among them almost two-thirds had one or more years of additional educational training. Thirty women had graduated from college.

Forty women worked as street prostitutes and did not use drugs. On average, they had been prostitutes for 11 years. Forty women began using drugs an average of three years after they began working as prostitutes, and the average time they had worked as prostitutes was nine years. Forty women used drugs an average of five years before they became prostitutes, and on the average they had worked as prostitutes for eight years. Another forty women began smoking crack and exchanging sex for crack almost simultaneously, with an average of four years in the life. Twenty women who were interviewed were ex-prostitutes.

Comments on Methodology

When I tell people about my research, the most frequent question I am asked is how I gained access to the women rather than what I learned from the research. For many, prostitution is an unusual topic of conversation, and many people have expressed

surprise that I, as a woman, conducted the research. During my research some customers indeed thought I was a working woman, a fact that almost always amuses those who hear about my work. However, few people want to hear stories about the women's struggles and sadness. Sometimes they ask questions about the reasons why women become prostitutes. Most of the time, they are surprised when I tell them that the prostitutes as well as their customers represent all layers of society. Before presenting the findings, it seems important to discuss the research process, including gaining access to the women, developing relationships, interviewing, and then leaving the field.[1]

Locating Prostitutes and Gaining Entree

One of the first challenges I faced was to identify locations where street prostitution took place. Many of these women worked on strolls, streets where prostitution activity is concentrated, or in hotels known for prostitution activity. Others, such as the crack prostitutes, worked in less public settings such as a crack house that might be someone's apartment.

I often learned of well-known public places from professional experts, such as law enforcement officials and health care providers at emergency rooms and sexually transmitted disease clinics. I gained other insights from lay experts, including taxi drivers, bartenders, and community representatives such as members of neighborhood associations. The contacts universally mentioned some strolls as the places where many women worked, where the local police focused attention, or where residents had organized protests against prostitution in their neighborhoods.

As I began visiting various locales, I continued to learn about new settings. In one sense, I was developing ethnographic maps of street prostitution. After several visits to a specific area, I also was able to expand these maps by adding information about the general atmosphere on the stroll, general characteristics of the various people present, the ways in which the women and customers connected, and the overall flow of action. In addition, my visits allowed the regular actors to notice me.

I soon learned that being an unknown woman in an area known for prostitution may cause many people to notice you, even stare at you, but it fails to yield many verbal interactions. Most of the time when I tried to make eye contact with one of the women, she quickly averted her eyes. Pimps, on the other hand, would stare at me straight on and I ended up being the one to look away. Customers would stop, blow their horn, or wave me over, frequently yelling obscenities when I ignored them. I realized that gaining entree into the prostitution world was not going to be as easy as I imagined it. Although I lacked such training in any of my qualitative methods classes, I decided to move slowly and not force any interaction. The most I said during the initial weeks in a new area was limited to "how are you" or "hi." This strategy paid off during my first visits to one of the strolls in Brooklyn, New York. After several appearances, one of the women walked up to me and sarcastically asked if I was looking for something. She caught me off guard, and all the answers I had practiced did not seem to make sense. I mumbled something about just wanting to walk around. She did not like my answer, but she did like my accent. We ended up talking about the latter and she was especially excited when I told her I came from Amsterdam. One of her friends had gone to Europe with her boyfriend, who was in the military. She understood from her that prostitution and drugs were legal in the Netherlands. While explaining to her that some of her friend's impressions were incorrect, I was able to show off some of my knowledge about prostitution. I mentioned that I was interested in prostitution and wanted to write a book about it.

Despite the fascination with my background and intentions, the prostitute immediately put me through a Streetwalker 101 test, and apparently I passed. She told me to make sure to come back. By the time I left, I not only had my first conversation but also my first connection to the scene. Variations of this entry process occurred on the other strolls. The main lesson I learned in these early efforts was the importance of having some knowledge of the lives of the people I wanted to study, while at the same time refraining from presenting myself as an expert.

Qualitative researchers often refer to their initial connections as gatekeepers and key respondents. Throughout my fieldwork I learned that some key respondents are important in providing initial access, but they become less central as the research evolves. For example, one of the women who introduced me to her lover, who was also her pimp, was arrested and disappeared for months. Another entered drug treatment soon after she facilitated my access. Other key respondents provided access to only a segment of the players on a scene. For example, if a woman worked for a pimp, [she] was unlikely . . . to introduce me to women working for another pimp. On one stroll my initial contact was with a pimp whom nobody liked. By associating with him, I almost lost the opportunity to meet other pimps. Some key respondents were less connected than promised—for example, some of the women who worked the street to support their drug habit. Often their connections were more frequently with drug users and less so with prostitutes.

Key respondents tend to be individuals central to the local scene, such as, in this case, pimps and the more senior prostitutes. Their function as gatekeepers often is to protect the scene and to screen outsiders. Many times I had to prove that I was not an undercover police officer or a woman with ambitions to become a streetwalker. While I thought I had gained entree, I quickly learned that many insiders subsequently wondered about my motives and approached me with suspicion and distrust.

Another lesson involved the need to proceed cautiously with self-nominated key respondents. For example, one of the women presented herself as knowing everyone on the stroll. While she did know everyone, she was not a central figure. On the contrary, the other prostitutes viewed her as a failed streetwalker whose drug use caused her to act unprofessionally. By associating with me, she hoped to regain some of her status. For me, however, it meant limited access to the other women because I affiliated myself with a woman who was marginal to the scene. On another occasion, my main key respondent was a man who claimed to own three crack houses in the neighborhood. However, he had a negative reputation, and people accused him of cheating on others. My initial alliance with him delayed, and almost blocked, my access to others in the neighborhood. He intentionally tried to keep me from others on the scene, not because he would gain something from that transaction but because it made him feel powerful. When I told him I was going to hang out with some of the other people, he threatened me until one of the other dealers stepped in and told him to stay away. The two of them argued back and forth, and finally I was free to go. Fortunately, the dealer who had spoken up for me was much more central and positively associated with the local scene. Finally, I am unsure if I would have had success in gaining entrance to the scene had I not been a woman.

Developing Relationships and Trust

The processes involved in developing relationships in research situations amplify those involved in developing relationships in general. Both parties need to get to know each other, become aware and accepting of each other's roles, and engage in a reciprocal relationship. Being supportive and providing practical assistance were the most visible and direct ways for me as the researcher to develop a relationship. Throughout the years, I have given countless rides, provided child care on numerous occasions, bought groceries, and listened for hours to stories that were unrelated to my initial research questions. Gradually, my role allowed me to become part of these women's lives and to build rapport with many of them.

Over time, many women also realized that I was uninterested in being a prostitute and that I genuinely was interested in learning as much as possible about their lives. Many felt flattered that someone wanted to learn from them and that they had knowledge to offer. Allowing women to tell their stories and engaging in a dialogue with them probably were the single most important techniques that allowed me to develop relationships with them. Had I only wanted to focus on the questions I had in mind, developing such relationships might have been more difficult.

At times, I was able to get to know a woman only after her pimp endorsed our contact. One of my scariest experiences occurred before I knew to work through the pimps, and one such man had some of his friends follow me on my way home one night. I will never know what plans they had in mind for me because I fortunately was able to escape with only a few bruises. Over a year later, the woman acknowledged that her pimp had gotten upset and told her he was going to teach me a lesson.

On other occasions, I first needed to be screened by owners and managers of crack houses before the research could continue. Interestingly, screenings always were done by a man even if the person who vouched for me was a man himself. While the women also were cautious, the ways in which they checked me out tended to be much more subtle. For example, one of them would tell me a story, indicating that it was a secret about another person on the stroll. Although I failed to realize this at the time, my field notes revealed that frequently after such a conversation, others would ask me questions about related topics. One woman later acknowledged that putting out such stories was a test to see if I would keep information confidential.

Learning more about the women and gaining a better understanding of their lives also raised many ethical questions. No textbook told me how to handle situations in which a pimp abused a woman, a customer forced a woman to engage in unwanted sex acts, a customer requested unprotected sex from a woman who knew she was HIV infected, or a boyfriend had realistic expectations regarding a woman's earnings to support his drug habit. I failed to know the proper response when asked to engage in illegal activities such as holding drugs or money a woman had stolen from a customer. In general, my response was to explain that I was there as a researcher. During those occasions when pressures became too severe, I decided to leave a scene. For example, I never returned to certain crack houses because pimps there continued to ask me to consider working for them.

Over time, I was fortunate to develop relationships with people who "watched my back." One pimp in particular intervened if he perceived other pimps, customers, or passersby harassing me. He also was the one who gave me my street name: Whitie (indicating my racial background) or Ms. Whitie for those who disrespected me. While this was my first street name, I subsequently had others. Being given a street name was a symbolic gesture of acceptance. Gradually, I developed an identity that allowed me to be both an insider and an outsider. While hanging out on the strolls and other gathering places, including crack houses, I had to deal with some of the same uncomfortable conditions as the prostitutes, such as cold or warm weather, lack of access to a rest room, refusals from owners for me to patronize a restaurant, and of course, harassment by customers and the police.

I participated in many informal conversations. Unless pushed to do so, I seldom divulged my opinions. I was more open with my feelings about situations and showed empathy. I learned quickly that providing an opinion can backfire. I agreed that one of the women was struggling a lot and stated that I felt sorry for her. While I meant to indicate my "genuine concern for her, she heard that I felt sorry for her because she was a failure. When she finally, after several weeks, talked with me again, I was able to explain to "her that I was not judging her, but rather felt concerned for her. She remained cynical and many times asked me for favors to make up for my mistake. It took me months before I felt comfortable telling her that I felt I had done enough and that it was time to let go. However, if she was not ready, she needed to know that I would no longer go along. This was one of many occasions when I learned that although I wanted to facilitate my work as a researcher, that I wanted people to like and trust me, I also needed to set boundaries.

Rainy and slow nights often provided good opportunities for me to participate in conversations with groups of women. Popular topics included how to work safely, what to do about condom use, how to make more money. I often served as a health educator and a supplier of condoms, gels, vaginal douches, and other feminine products. Many women were very worried about the AIDS epidemic. However, they also were worried about how to use a condom when a customer refused to do so.

They worried particularly about condom use when they needed money badly and, consequently, did not want to propose that the customer use one for fear of rejection. While some women became experts at "making" their customers use a condom—for example, "by hiding it in their mouth prior to beginning oral sex—others would carry condoms to please me but never pull one out. If a woman was HIV positive and I knew she failed to use a condom, I faced the ethical dilemma of challenging her or staying out of it.

Developing trusting relationships with crack prostitutes was more difficult. Crack houses were not the right environment for informal conversations. Typically, the atmosphere was tense and everyone was suspicious of each other. The best times to talk with these women were when we bought groceries together, when I helped them clean their homes, or when we shared a meal. Often the women were very different when they were not high than they were when they were high or craving crack. In my conversations with them, I learned that while I might have observed their actions the night before, they themselves might not remember them. Once I realized this, I would be very careful to omit any detail unless I knew that the woman herself did remember the event.

In-Depth Interviews

All interviews were conducted in a private setting, including women's residences, my car or my office, a restaurant of the women's choice, or any other setting the women selected. I did not begin conducting official interviews until I developed relationships with the women. Acquiring written informed consent prior to the interview was problematic. It made me feel awkward. Here I was asking the women to sign a form after they had begun to trust me. However, often I felt more upset about this technicality than the women themselves. As soon as they realized that the form was something the university required, they seemed to understand. Often they laughed about the official statements, and some asked if I was sure the form was to protect them and not the school.[2] None of the women refused to sign the consent form, although some refused to sign it right away and asked to be interviewed later.

In some instances the consent procedures caused the women to expect a formal interview. Some of them were disappointed when they saw I only had a few structured questions about demographic characteristics, followed by a long list of open-ended questions. When this disappointment occurred, I reminded the women that I wanted to learn from them and that the best way to do so was by engaging in a dialogue rather than interrogating them. Only by letting the women identify their salient issues and the topics they wanted to address was I able to gain an insider's perspective. By being a careful listener and probing for additional information and explanation, I as the interviewer, together with the women, was able to uncover the complexities of their lives. In addition, the nature of the interview allowed me to ask questions about contradictions in a woman's story. For example, sometimes a woman would say that she always used a condom. However, later on in the conversation she would indicate that if she needed drugs she would never use one. By asking her to elaborate on this, I was able to begin developing insights into condom use by type of partner, type of sex acts, and social context.

The interviewer becomes much more a part of the interview when the conversations are in-depth than when a structured questionnaire is used. Because I was so integral to the process, the way the women viewed me may have biased their answers. On the one hand, this bias might be reduced because of the extent to which both parties already knew each other; on the other, a woman might fail to give her true opinion and reveal her actions if she knew that these went against the interviewer's opinion. I suspected that some women played down the ways in which their pimps manipulated them once they knew that I was not too fond of these men. However, some might have taken more time to explain the relationship with their pimp in order to "correct" my image.

My background, so different from that of these women, most likely affected the nature of the interviews. I occupied a higher socioeconomic status. I had a place to live and a job. In contrast to the nonwhite women, I came from a different racial background. While I don't know to what extent these differences played a role, I acknowledge that they must have had some effect on this research.

Leaving the Field

Leaving the field was not something that occurred after completion of the fieldwork, but an event that took place daily. Although I sometimes stayed on the strolls all night or hung out for several days, I always had a home to return to. I had a house with electricity, a warm shower, a comfortable bed, and a kitchen. My house sat on a street where I had no fear of being shot on my way there and where I did not find condoms or syringes on my doorstep.

During several stages of the study, I had access to a car, which I used to give the women rides or to run errands together. However, I will never forget the cold night when everyone on the street was freezing, and I left to go home. I turned up the heat in my car, and tears streamed down my cheeks. I appreciated the heat, but I felt more guilty about that luxury than ever before. I truly felt like an outsider, or maybe even more appropriate, a betrayer.

Throughout the years of fieldwork, there were a number of times when I left the scene temporarily. For example, when so many people were dying from AIDS, I was unable to ignore the devastating impact of this disease. I needed an emotional break.

Physically removing myself from the scene was common when I experienced difficulty remaining objective. Once I became too involved in a woman's life and almost adopted her and her family. Another time I felt a true hatred for a crack house owner and was unable to adhere to the rules of courteous interactions. Still another time, I got angry with a woman whose steady partner was HIV positive when she failed to ask him to use a condom when they had sex.

I also took temporary breaks from a particular scene by shifting settings and neighborhoods. For example, I would invest most of my time in women from a particular crack house for several weeks. Then I would shift to spending more time on one of the strolls, while making shorter and less frequent visits to the crack house. By shifting scenes, I was able to tell people why I was leaving and to remind all of us of my researcher role.

While I focused on leaving the field, I became interested in women who had left the life. It seemed important to have an understanding of their past and current circumstances. I knew some of them from the days when they were working, but identifying others was a challenge. There was no gathering place for ex-prostitutes. Informal networking, advertisements in local newspapers; and local clinics and community settings allowed me to reach twenty of these women. Conducting interviews with them later in the data collection process prepared me to ask specific questions. I realized that I had learned enough about the life to know what to ask. Interviewing ex-prostitutes also prepared me for moving from the fieldwork to writing.

It is hard to determine exactly when I left the field. It seems like a process that never ends. Although I was more physically removed from the scene, I continued to be involved while analyzing the data and writing this book. I also created opportunities to go back, for example, by asking women to give me feedback on parts of the manuscript or at times when I experienced writer's block and my car seemed to automatically steer itself to one of the strolls. I also have developed other research projects in some of the same communities. For example, both a project on intergenerational drug use and a gender-specific intervention project to help women remain HIV negative have brought me back to the same population. Some of the women have become key respondents in these new projects, while others now are members of a research team. For example, Beth, one of the women who has left prostitution, works as an outreach worker on another project.

Six Themes in the Ethnography of Prostitution

The main intention of my work is to provide the reader with a perspective on street prostitution from the point of view of the women themselves. There are six fundamental aspects of the women's lives as prostitutes that must be considered. The first concerns the women's own explanations for their involvement in prostitution and their descriptions of the various circumstances that led them to become prostitutes. Their stories include justifications such as traumatic past experiences, especially sexual abuse, the lack of love they experienced as children, pressures by friends and pimps, the need for drugs, and most prominently, the economic forces that pushed them into the life. A number of women describe these justifications as excuses, as reflective explanations they have developed after becoming a prostitute.

The women describe the nature of their initial experiences, which often involved alienation from those outside the life. They also show the differences in the processes between women who work as prostitutes and use drugs and women who do not use drugs.

Although all these women work either on the street or in drug-use settings, their lives do differ. My second theme is a typology that captures these differences, looking at the women's prostitution versus drug-use identities. The typology distinguishes among (a) streetwalkers, women who work strolls and who do not use drugs; (b) hooked prostitutes, women who identify themselves mainly as prostitutes but who upon their entrance into the life also began using drugs; (c) prostituting addicts, women who view themselves mainly as drug users and who became prostitutes to support their drug habit; and (d) crack prostitutes, women who trade sex for crack.

This typology explains the differences in the women's strategies for soliciting customers, their screening of customers, pricing of sex acts, and bargaining for services. For example, the streetwalkers have the most bargaining power, while such power appears to be lacking among the crack prostitutes.

Few prostitutes work in a vacuum. The third theme is the role of pimps, a label that most women dislike and for which they prefer to substitute "old man" or "boyfriend." Among the pimps, one finds entrepreneur lovers, men who mainly employ streetwalkers and hooked prostitutes and sometimes prostituting addicts. Entrepreneur lovers engage in the life for business reasons. They treat the women as their employees or their property and view them primarily as an economic commodity. The more successful a woman is in earning them money, the more difficult it is for that woman to leave her entrepreneur pimp.

Most prostituting addicts and some hooked prostitutes work for a lover pimp, a man who is their steady partner but who also lives off their earnings. Typically, such pimps employ only one woman. The dynamics in the relationship between a prostitute and her lover pimp become more complex when both partners use drugs. Drugs often become the glue of the relationship.

For many crack prostitutes, their crack addiction serves as a pimp. Few plan to exchange sex for crack when they first begin using; often several weeks or months pass before a woman who barters sex for crack realizes that she is a prostitute.

Historically, society has blamed prostitutes for introducing sexually transmitted diseases into the general population. Similarly, it makes them scapegoats for the spread of HIV/AIDS. Yet their pimps and customers are not held accountable. The fourth theme in the anthropological study of prostitution is the impact of the AIDS epidemic on the women's lives. Although most are knowledgeable about HIV risk behaviors and the ways to reduce their risk, many misconceptions exist. The women describe the complexities of condom use, especially with steady partners but also with paying customers. Many women have mixed feelings about HIV testing, wondering how to cope with a positive test result while no cure is available. A few of the women already knew their HIV-infected status, and the discussion touches on their dilemmas as well.

The fifth theme is the violence and abuse that make common appearances in the women's lives. An ethnography of prostitution must allow the women to describe violence in their neighborhoods as well as violence in prostitution and drug-use settings. The most common violence they encounter is from customers. These men often assume that because they pay for sex they buy a woman. Apparently, casual customers pose more of a danger than those who are regulars. The types of abuse the women encounter are emotional, physical, and sexual. In addition to customers, pimps and boyfriends abuse the women. Finally, the women discuss harassment by law enforcement officers.

When I talked with the women, it often seemed that there were no opportunities to escape from the life. Yet the sixth and final theme must be the escape from prostitution. Women who have left prostitution can describe the process of their exit from prostitution. As ex-prostitutes they struggle with the stigma of their past, the challenges of developing a new identity, and the impact of their past on current intimate relationships. Those who were also drug users often view themselves as ex-prostitutes and recovering addicts, a perspective that seems to create a role conflict. Overall, most ex-prostitutes find that their past follows them like a bad hangover.

Notes

1. For more information about qualitative research methods, see, for example, Patricia Adler and Peter Adler, *Membership Roles in Field Research* (Newbury Park: Sage, 1987); Michael Agar, *The Professional Stranger* (New York: Academic Press, 1980) and *Speaking of Ethnography* (Beverly Hills: Sage, 1986); Howard Becker and Blanche Geer, "Participant Observation and Interviewing: A Comparison," *Human Organization* 16 (1957): 28–32; Norman Denzin, *Sociological Methods: A Sourcebook* (Chicago: Aldine, 1970); Barney Glaser and Anselm Strauss, *The Discovery of Grounded Theory: Strategies for Qualitative Research* (Chicago: Aldine, 1967); Y. Lincoln and E. Guba, *Naturalistic Inquiry* (Beverly Hills: Sage, 1985); John Lofland, "Analytic Ethnography: Features, Failings, and Futures," *Journal of Contemporary Ethnography* 24 (1996): 30–67; and James Spradley, *The Ethnographic Interview* (New York: Holt, Rinehart and Winston, 1979) and *Participant Observation* (New York: Holt, Rinehart and Winston, 1980).

2. For a more extensive discussion of informed consent procedures and related ethical issues, see Bruce L. Berg, *Qualitative Research Methods for the Social Sciences,* 3rd edition, Chapter 3: "Ethical Issues" (Boston: Allyn and Bacon, 1998).

Anthropology and Counterinsurgency: The Strange Story of Their Curious Relationship

MONTGOMERY MCFATE

Something mysterious is going on inside the U.S. Department of Defense (DOD). Over the past 2 years, senior leaders have been calling for something unusual and unexpected—cultural knowledge of the adversary. In July 2004, retired Major General Robert H. Scales, Jr., wrote an article for the Naval War College's Proceedings magazine that opposed the commonly held view within the U.S. military that success in war is best achieved by overwhelming technological advantage. Scales argues that the type of conflict we are now witnessing in Iraq requires "an exceptional ability to understand people, their culture, and their motivation."[1] In October 2004, Arthur Cebrowski, Director of the Office of Force Transformation, concluded that "knowledge of one's enemy and his culture and society may be more important than knowledge of his order of battle."[2] In November 2004, the Office of Naval Research and the Defense Advanced Research Projects Agency (DARPA) sponsored the Adversary Cultural Knowledge and National Security Conference, the first major DOD conference on the social sciences since 1962.

Why has cultural knowledge suddenly become such an imperative? Primarily because traditional methods of warfighting have proven inadequate in Iraq and Afghanistan. U.S. technology, training, and doctrine designed to counter the Soviet threat are not designed for low-intensity counterinsurgency operations where civilians mingle freely with combatants in complex urban terrain.

The major combat operations that toppled Saddam Hussein's regime were relatively simple because they required the U.S. military to do what it does best—conduct maneuver warfare in flat terrain using overwhelming firepower with air support. However, since the end of the "hot" phase of the war, coalition forces have been fighting a complex war against an enemy they do not understand. The insurgents' organizational structure is not military, but tribal. Their tactics are not conventional, but asymmetrical. Their weapons are not tanks and fighter planes, but improvised explosive devices (IEDs). They do not abide by the Geneva Conventions, nor do they appear to have any informal rules of engagement.

Countering the insurgency in Iraq requires cultural and social knowledge of the adversary. Yet, none of the elements of U.S. national power—diplomatic, military, intelligence, or economic—explicitly take adversary culture into account in the formation or execution of policy. This cultural knowledge gap has a simple cause—the almost total absence of anthropology within the national-security establishment.

Once called "the handmaiden of colonialism," anthropology has had a long, fruitful relationship with various elements of national power, which ended suddenly following the Vietnam War. The strange story of anthropology's birth as a warfighting discipline, and its sudden plunge into the abyss of postmodernism, is intertwined with the U.S. failure in Vietnam. The curious and conspicuous lack of anthropology in the national-security arena since the Vietnam War has had grave consequences for countering the insurgency in Iraq, particularly because political policy and military operations based on partial and incomplete cultural knowledge are often worse than none at all.

A Lack of Cultural Awareness

In a conflict between symmetric adversaries, where both are evenly matched and using similar technology, understanding the adversary's culture is largely irrelevant. The Cold War, for all its complexity, pitted two powers of European heritage against each other. In a counterinsurgency operation against a non-Western adversary, however, culture matters. U.S. Department of the Army Field Manual (FM) (interim) 3-07.22, Counterinsurgency Operations, defines insurgency as an "organized movement aimed at the overthrow of a constituted government through use of subversion and armed conflict. It is a protracted politico-military struggle designed to weaken government control and legitimacy while increasing insurgent control. Political power is the central issue in an insurgency [emphasis added]." Political considerations must therefore circumscribe military action as a fundamental matter of strategy. As British Field Marshall Gerald Templar explained in 1953, "The answer lies not in pouring more troops into the jungle, but rests in the hearts and minds of the . . . people." Winning hearts and minds requires understanding the local culture.[3]

Aside from Special Forces, most U.S. soldiers are not trained to understand or operate in foreign cultures and societies. One U.S.

Army captain in Iraq said, "I was never given classes on how to sit down with a sheik. . . . He is giving me the traditional dishdasha and the entire outfit of a sheik because he claims that I am a new sheik in town so I must be dressed as one. I don't know if he is trying to gain favor with me because he wants something [or if it is] something good or something bad." In fact, as soon as coalition forces toppled Saddam Hussein, they became de facto players in the Iraqi social system. The young captain had indeed become the new sheik in town and was being properly honored by his Iraqi host.[4]

As this example indicates, U.S. forces frequently do not know who their friends are, and just as often they do not know who their enemies are. A returning commander from the 3d Infantry Division observed: "I had perfect situational awareness. What I lacked was cultural awareness. I knew where every enemy tank was dug in on the outskirts of Tallil. Only problem was, my soldiers had to fight fanatics charging on foot or in pickups and firing AK-47s and RPGs [rocket-propelled grenades]. Great technical intelligence. Wrong enemy."[5]

While the consequences of a lack of cultural knowledge might be most apparent (or perhaps most deadly) in a counterinsurgency, a failure to understand foreign cultures has been a major contributing factor in multiple national-security and intelligence failures. In her 1962 study, Pearl Harbor: Warning and Decision, Roberta Wohlstetter demonstrated that although the U.S. Government picked up Japanese signals (including conversations, decoded cables, and ship movements), it failed to distinguish signals from noise—to understand which signals were meaningful—because it was unimaginable that the Japanese might do something as "irrational" as attacking the headquarters of the U.S. Pacific fleet.[6]

Such ethnocentrism (the inability to put aside one's own cultural attitudes and imagine the world from the perspective of a different group) is especially dangerous in a national-security context because it can distort strategic thinking and result in assumptions that the adversary will behave exactly as one might behave. India's nuclear tests on 11 and 13 May 1998 came as a complete surprise because of this type of "mirror-imaging" among CIA analysts. According to the internal investigation conducted by former Vice Chairman of the Joint Chiefs of Staff David Jeremiah, the real problem was an assumption by intelligence analysts and policymakers that the Indians would not test their nuclear weapons because Americans would not test nuclear weapons in similar circumstances. According to Jeremiah, "The intelligence and the policy communities had an underlying mind-set going into these tests that the B.J.P [Bharatiya Janata Party] would behave as we [would] behave."[7]

The United States suffers from a lack of cultural knowledge in its national-security establishment for two primary, interrelated reasons. First, anthropology is largely and conspicuously absent as a discipline within our national-security enterprise, especially within the intelligence community and DOD. Anthropology is a social science discipline whose primary object of study has traditionally been non-Western, tribal societies. The methodologies of anthropology include participant observation, fieldwork, and historical research. One of the central epistemological tenets of anthropology is cultural relativism—understanding other societies from within their own framework.

The primary task of anthropology has historically been translating knowledge gained in the "field" back to the West. While it might seem self-evident that such a perspective would be benefi-

cial to the national-security establishment, only one of the national defense universities (which provide master's degree-level education to military personnel) currently has an anthropologist on its faculty. At West Point, which traditionally places a heavy emphasis on engineering, anthropology is disparagingly referred to by cadets as "nuts and huts." And, although political science is well represented as a discipline in senior policymaking circles, there has never been an anthropologist on the National Security Council.

The second and related reason for the current lack of cultural knowledge is the failure of the U.S. military to achieve anything resembling victory in Vietnam. Following the Vietnam War, the Joint Chiefs of Staff collectively put their heads in the sand and determined they would never fight an unconventional war again. From a purely military perspective, it was easier for them to focus on the threat of Soviet tanks rolling through the Fulda Gap, prompting a major European land war—a war they could easily fight using existing doctrine and technology and that would have a clear, unequivocal winner.[8]

The preference for the use of overwhelming force and clear campaign objectives was formalized in what has become known as the Weinberger doctrine. In a 1984 speech, Secretary of Defense Caspar Weinberger articulated six principles designed to ensure the Nation would never become involved in another Vietnam. By the mid-1980s, there was cause for concern: deployment of troops to El Salvador seemed likely and the involvement in Lebanon had proved disastrous following the bombing of the U.S. Marine barracks in Beirut. Responding to these events, Weinberger believed troops should be committed only if U.S. national interests were at stake; only in support of clearly defined political and military objectives; and only "with the clear intention of winning."[9]

In 1994, Chairman of the Joint Chiefs of Staff Colin Powell (formerly a military assistant to Weinberger) rearticulated the Weinberger doctrine's fundamental elements, placing a strong emphasis on the idea that force, when used, should be overwhelming and disproportionate to the force used by the enemy. The Powell-Weinberger doctrine institutionalized a preference for "major combat operations"—big wars—as a matter of national preference. Although the Powell-Weinberger doctrine was eroded during the Clinton years; during operations other than war in Haiti, Somali, and Bosnia; and during the second Bush Administration's pre-emptive strikes in Afghanistan and Iraq, no alternative doctrine has emerged to take its place.[10]

We have no doctrine for "nationbuilding," which the military eschews as a responsibility because it is not covered by Title 10 of the U.S. Code, which outlines the responsibilities of the military as an element of national power. Field Manual 3-07, Stability Operations and Support Operations, was not finalized until February 2003, despite the fact the U.S. military was already deeply engaged in such operations in Iraq. Field Manual 3-07.22—meant to be a temporary document—is still primarily geared toward fighting an enemy engaged in Maoist revolutionary warfare, a type of insurgency that has little application to the situation in Iraq where multiple organizations are competing for multiple, confusing objectives.[11]

Since 1923, the core tenet of U.S. warfighting strategy has been that overwhelming force deployed against an equally powerful state will result in military victory. Yet in a counterinsurgency situation such as the one the United States currently faces in Iraq, "winning" through overwhelming force is often inapplicable as a concept, if not problematic as a goal. While negotiating in Hanoi a few days before Saigon fell, U.S. Army Colonel Harry Summers, Jr., said to a North Vietnamese colonel, "You know, you never defeated us on the battlefield." The Vietnamese colonel replied, "That may be so, but it is also irrelevant."[12] The same could be said of the conflict in Iraq.

Winning on the battlefield is irrelevant against an insurgent adversary because the struggle for power and legitimacy among competing factions has no purely military solution. Often, the application of overwhelming force has the negative, unintended effect of strengthening the insurgency by creating martyrs, increasing recruitment, and demonstrating the "brutality" of state forces.

The alternative approach to fighting insurgency, such as the British eventually adopted through trial and error in Northern Ireland, involves the following: A comprehensive plan to alleviate the political conditions behind the insurgency; civil-military cooperation; the application of minimum force; deep intelligence; and an acceptance of the protracted nature of the conflict. Deep cultural knowledge of the adversary is inherent to the British approach.[13]

Although cultural knowledge of the adversary matters in counterinsurgency, it has little importance in major combat operations. Because the Powell-Weinberger doctrine meant conventional, large-scale war was the only acceptable type of conflict, no discernable present or future need existed to develop doctrine and expertise in unconventional war, including counterinsurgency. Thus, there was no need to incorporate cultural knowledge into doctrine, training, or warfighting. Until now, that is.

On 21 October 2003, the House Armed Services Committee held a hearing to examine lessons learned from Operation Iraqi Freedom. Scales' testimony at the hearing prompted U.S. Representative "Ike" Skelton to write a letter to Secretary of Defense Donald Rumsfeld in which he said: "In simple terms, if we had better understood the Iraqi culture and mindset, our war plans would have been even better than they were, the plan for the postwar period and all of its challenges would have been far better, and we [would have been] better prepared for the 'long slog' . . . to win the peace in Iraq."[14]

Even such DOD luminaries as Andrew Marshall, the mysterious director of the Pentagon's Office of Net Assessment, are now calling for "anthropology-level knowledge of a wide range of cultures" because such knowledge will prove essential to conducting future operations. Although senior U.S. Government officials such as Skelton are calling for "personnel in our civilian ranks who have cultural knowledge and understanding to inform the policy process," there are few anthropologists either available or willing to play in the same sandbox with the military.[15]

. . . The Perils of Incomplete Knowledge

DOD yearns for cultural knowledge, but anthropologists en masse, bound by their own ethical code and sunk in a mire of postmodernism, are unlikely to contribute much of value to reshaping national-security policy or practice. Yet, if anthropologists remain disengaged, who will provide the relevant subject matter expertise? As Anna Simons, an anthropologist who teaches at the Naval Postgraduate School, points out: "If anthropologists want to put their heads in the sand and not assist, then who will the military, the CIA, and other agencies turn to for information? They'll turn to people who will give them the kind of information that should make anthropologists want to rip their hair out because the information won't be nearly as directly connected to what's going on on the local landscape."[16]

Regardless of whether anthropologists decide to enter the national-security arena, cultural information will inevitably be used as the basis of military operations and public policy. And, if anthropologists refuse to contribute, how reliable will that information be? The result of using incomplete "bad" anthropology is, invariably, failed operations and failed policy. In a May 2004 New Yorker article, "The Gray Zone: How a Secret Pentagon Program Came to Abu Ghraib," Seymour Hersh notes that Raphael Patai's 1973 study of Arab culture and psychology, The Arab Mind, was the basis of the military's understanding of the psychological vulnerabilities of Arabs, particularly to sexual shame and humiliation.[17]

Patai says: "The segregation of the sexes, the veiling of the women . . . , and all the other minute rules that govern and restrict contact between men and women, have the effect of making sex a prime mental preoccupation in the Arab world." Apparently, the goal of photographing the sexual humiliation was to blackmail Iraqi victims into becoming informants against the insurgency. To prevent the dissemination of photos to family and friends, it was believed Iraqi men would do almost anything.[18]

As Bernard Brodie said of the French Army in 1914, "This was neither the first nor the last time that bad anthropology contributed to bad strategy." Using sexual humiliation to blackmail Iraqi men into becoming informants could never have worked as a strategy since it only destroys honor, and for Iraqis, lost honor requires its restoration through the appeasement of blood. This concept is well developed in Iraqi culture, and there is even a specific Arabic word for it: al-sharaf, upholding one's manly honor. The alleged use of Patai's book as the basis of the psychological torment at Abu Ghraib, devoid of any understanding of the broader context of Iraqi culture, demonstrates the folly of using decontextualized culture as the basis of policy.[19]

Successful counterinsurgency depends on attaining a holistic, total understanding of local culture. This cultural understanding must be thorough and deep if it is to have any practical benefit at all. This fact is not lost on the Army. In the language of interim FM 3-07.22: "The center of gravity in counterinsurgency operations is the population. Therefore, understanding the local society and gaining its support is critical to success. For U.S. forces to operate effectively among a local population and gain and maintain their support, it is important to develop a thorough understanding of the society and its culture, including its history, tribal/family/social structure, values, religions, customs, and needs."[20]

To defeat the insurgency in Iraq, U.S. and coalition forces must recognize and exploit the underlying tribal structure of the country; the power wielded by traditional authority figures; the use of Islam as a political ideology; the competing interests of the Shia, the Sunni, and the Kurds; the psychological effects of totalitarianism; and the divide between urban and rural, among other things.

Interim FM 3-07.22 continues: "Understanding and working within the social fabric of a local area is initially the most influential factor in the conduct of counterinsurgency operations. Unfortunately, this is often the factor most neglected by U.S. forces."[21]

And, unfortunately, anthropologists, whose assistance is urgently needed in time of war, entirely neglect U.S. forces. Despite the fact that military applications of cultural knowledge might be distasteful to ethically inclined anthropologists, their assistance is necessary.

Notes

1. MG Robert H. Scales, Jr., "Culture-Centric Warfare," Proceedings (October 2004).

2. Megan Scully, "'Social Intel' New Tool For U.S. Military," Defense News, 26 April 2004, 21.

3. U.S. Department of the Army Field Manual (FM) (Interim) 3-07.22, Counterinsurgency Operations (Washington, DC: U.S. Government Printing Office [GPO], 1 October 2004), sec. 1-1; David Charters, "From Palestine to Northern Ireland: British Adaptation to Low-Intensity Operations," in Armies in Low-Intensity Conflict." A Comparative Analysis, eds., D. Charters and M. Tugwell (London: Brassey's Defence Publishers, 1989), 195.

4. Leonard Wong, "Developing Adaptive Leaders: The Crucible Experience of Operation Iraqi Freedom," Strategic Studies Institute, U.S. Army War College, Carlisle Barracks, Pennsylvania, July 2004, 14.

5. Scales, "Army Transformation: Implications for the Future," testimony before the House Armed Services Committee, Washington, D.C., 15 July 2004.

6. Roberta Wohlstetter, Pearl Harbor: Warning and Decision (California: Stanford University Press, 1962).

7. Jeffrey Goldberg, "The Unknown: The C.I.A. and the Pentagon take another look at Al Qaeda and Iraq," The New Yorker, 10 February 2003.

8. See Max Boot, The Savage Wars of Peace: Small Wars and the Rise of American Power (New York: Basic Books, 2003).

9. Casper W. Weinberger, "The Uses of Military Power," speech at the National Press Club, Washington, D.C., 28 November 1984.

10. Jeffrey Record, "Weinberger-Powell Doctrine Doesn't Cut It," Proceedings (October 2000) The Powell doctrine also "translates into a powerful reluctance to engage in decisive combat, or to even risk combat, and an inordinate emphasis at every level of command on force protection." Stan Goff, "Full-Spectrum Entropy: Special Operations in a Special Period," Freedom Road Magazine, on-line at www.freedom.read.org/fr/03/english/07_entropy.html, accessed 18 February 2005.

11. U.S. Code, Title 10, "Armed Forces," on-line at www.access.gpo.gov/uscode/ title10/title10.html, accessed 18 February 2005; FM 3-07, Stability Operations and Support Operations (Washington, DC: GPO, February, 2003); FM 3-07.22, Interim.

12. The 1923 Field Service Regulations postulate that the ultimate objective of all military operations is the destruction of the enemy's armed forces and that decisive results are obtained only by the offensive. The Regulations state that the Army must prepare to tight against an "opponent organized for war on modern principles and equipped with all the means of modern warfare. . . ." The preference for use of offensive force is found continuously in U.S. military thought, most recently in FM 3-0, Operations (Washington, DC: GPO, 2001), which says: "The doctrine holds warfighting as the Army's primary focus and recognizes that the ability of Army forces to dominate land warfare also provide the ability to dominate any situation in military operations other than war"; Richard Darilek and David Johnson, "Occupation of Hostile Territory: History, Theory, Doctrine; Past and Future Practice, "conference presentation, Future Warfare Seminar V. Carlisle, Pennsylvania, 18 January 2005; Peter Grier, "Should US Fight War in Bosnia? Question Opens an Old Debate," Christian Science Monitor, 14 September 1992, 9.

13. For a full discussion of British principles of counterinsurgency, see Thomas Mockaitis, British Counterinsurgency, 1919–1960 (New York: St. Martin's Press, 1990); Ian Beckett and John Pimlott, eds., Armed Forces and modern Counter-Insurgency (London: Croom Helm, 1985)

14. Office of Congressman Ike Skelton, "Skelton Urges Rumsfeld To Improve Cultural Awareness Training," press release, 23 October 2003, on-line at www.house.gov/skelton/pr031023.html, accessed 18 February 2005.

15. Jeremy Feller, "Marshall US. Needs To Sustain Long-Distance Power Projection," Inside The Pentagon, 4 March 2004, 15.

16. Renee Montagne, "Interview: Anna Simons and Catherine Lutz on the involvement of anthropologists in war," National Public Radio's Morning Edition, 14 August 2002.

17. Raphael Patai in Seymour M. Hersh, "The Gray Zone How a secret Pentagon program came to Abu Ghraib," The New Yorker, 24 May 2004; Patai, The Arab Mind (Now York: Scribner's 1973).

18. Patai.

19. Bernard Brodie, Strategy in the Missile Age (New Jersey: Princeton University Press, 1959), 52.

20. Amatzia Baram, "Victory in Iraq, One Tribe at a Time," New York Times, 28 October 2003; FM (Interim) 3-07.22, sec 4–11.

21. FM (Interim) 3-07.22, sec. 4–13.

MONTGOMERY MCFATE, J.D., PhD, is an American Association for the Advancement of Science Defense Policy Fellow at the Office of Naval Research, Arlington, Virginia. She received a B.A. from the University of California at Berkeley, an M.A., M. Phil., and a Ph.D. from Yale University, and a J.D. from Harvard Law School. She was formerly at RAND's Intelligence Policy Center.

From *Military Review*, March/April 2005. Published in 2005 by Military Review, a publication of the U.S. Army.

One Hundred Percent American[1]

Ralph Linton[2]

There can be no question about the average American's Americanism or his desire to preserve this precious heritage at all costs. Nevertheless, some insidious foreign ideas have already wormed their way into his civilization without his realizing what was going on. Thus dawn finds the unsuspecting patriot garbed in pajamas, a garment of East Indian origin; and lying in a bed built on a pattern which originated in either Persia or Asia Minor.[3] He is muffled to the ears in un-American materials: cotton, first domesticated in India; linen, domesticated in the Near East; wool from an animal native to Asia Minor; or silk whose uses were first discovered by the Chinese. All these substances have been transformed into cloth by methods invented in Southwestern Asia. If the weather is cold enough he may even be sleeping under an eiderdown quilt invented in Scandinavia.

On awakening he glances at the clock, a medieval European invention, uses one potent Latin word in abbreviated form, rises in haste, and goes to the bathroom. Here, if he stops to think about it, he must feel himself in the presence of a great American institution; he will have heard stories of both the quality and frequency of foreign plumbing and will know that in no other country does the average man perform his ablutions in the midst of such splendor. But the insidious foreign influence pursues him even here. Glass was invented by the ancient Egyptians, the use of glazed tiles for floors and walls in the Near East, porcelain in China, and the art of enameling on metal by Mediterranean artisans of the Bronze Age. Even his bathtub and toilet are but slightly modified copies of Roman originals. The only purely American contribution to the ensemble is the steam radiator, against which our patriot very briefly and unintentionally places his posterior.

In this bathroom the American washes with soap invented by the ancient Gauls. Next he cleans his teeth, a subversive European practice which did not invade America until the latter part of the eighteenth century. He then shaves, a masochistic rite first developed by the heathen priests of ancient Egypt and Sumer. The process is made less of a penance by the fact that his razor is of steel, an iron-carbon alloy discovered in either India or Turkestan. Lastly, he dries himself on a Turkish towel.

Returning to the bedroom, the unconscious victim of un-American practices removes his clothes from a chair, invented in the Near East, and proceeds to dress. He puts on close-fitting tailored garments whose form derives from the skin clothing of the ancient nomads of the Asiatic steppes and fastens them with buttons whose prototypes appeared in Europe at the close of the Stone Age. This costume is appropriate enough for outdoor exercise in a cold climate, but is quite unsuited to American summers, steam-heated houses, and Pullmans.[4] Nevertheless, foreign ideas and habits hold the unfortunate man in thrall even when common sense tells him that the authentically American costume of gee string and moccasins would be far more comfortable. He puts on his feet stiff coverings made from hide prepared by a process invented in ancient Egypt and cut to a pattern which can be traced back to ancient Greece, and makes sure that they are properly polished, also a Greek idea. Lastly, he ties about his neck a strip of bright-colored cloth which is a vestigial survival of the shoulder shawls worn by seventeenth century Greeks. He gives himself a final appraisal in the mirror, an old Mediterranean invention, and goes downstairs to breakfast.

Here a whole new series of foreign things confronts him. His food and drink are placed before him in pottery vessels, the proper name of which—china—is sufficient evidence of their origin. His fork is a medieval Italian invention and his spoon a copy of a Roman original. He will usually begin the meal with coffee, an Abyssinian[5] plant first discovered by the Arabs. The American is quite likely to need it to dispel the morning-after effects of overindulgence in fermented drinks, invented in the Near East; or distilled ones, invented by the alchemists of medieval Europe.[6] Whereas the Arabs took their coffee straight, he will probably sweeten it with sugar, discovered in India; and dilute it with cream, both the domestication of cattle and the technique of milking having originated in Asia Minor.

If our patriot is old-fashioned enough to adhere to the so-called American breakfast, his coffee will be accompanied by an orange, domesticated in the Mediterranean region, a cantaloupe domesticated in Persia, or grapes domesticated in Asia Minor. He will follow this with a bowl of cereal made from grain domesticated in the Near East and prepared by methods also invented there. From this he will go on to waffles, a Scandinavian invention with plenty of butter, originally a Near Eastern cosmetic. As a side dish he may have the egg of a bird domesticated in Southeastern Asia or strips of the flesh of an animal domesticated in the same region, which has been salted and smoked by a process invented in Northern Europe.

Breakfast over, he places upon his head a molded piece of felt, invented by the nomads of Eastern Asia, and, if it looks like rain, puts on outer shoes of rubber, discovered by the ancient Mexicans, and takes an umbrella, invented in India. He then sprints for his train—the train, not sprinting, being an English invention. At the station he pauses for a moment to buy a newspaper, paying for it with coins invented in ancient Lydia.[7] Once on board he settles back to inhale the fumes of a cigarette invented in Mexico, or a cigar invented in Brazil.[8] Meanwhile, he reads the news of the day, imprinted in characters invented by the ancient Semites by a process invented in Germany upon a material invented in China. As he scans the latest editorial pointing out the dire results to our institutions of accepting foreign ideas, he will not fail to thank a Hebrew God in an Indo-European language that he is a one hundred percent (decimal system invented by the Greeks) American (from Americus Vespucci, Italian geographer).

Notes

1. With additional comments added by Parman.

2. American anthropologist. The article was published in *The American Mercury* in 1937 (40:427–429), a time of unrest just before WWII.

3. A peninsula in West Asia between the Black and Mediterranean seas, including most of Asiatic Turkey. (Part of Turkey is in Europe.)

4. Railroad sleeping car or parlor invented by the 19th-century American inventor and railroad car designer, George Mortimer.

5. Ethiopian.

6. According to the *Oxford English Dictionary,* the word "alcohol" derives from a process of sublimation (a Latin word that means to purify, as through distillation) invented by the Arabs by which powders were produced (Arab *al-koh'l,* collyrium, the fine powder used to stain the eyelids). The word "alcohol" itself appears in English in the 16th century, from medieval Latin, referring to the process of distillation of fluids (an extension of the concept of distillation or purification of powder).

7. An ancient kingdom in West Asia Minor; under Croesus, a wealthy empire including most of Asia Minor. See footnote 3.

8. Tobacco is indigenous to the New World, just as the "Irish potato" is indigenous to the New World.

From *The Study of Man* by Ralph Linton (Appleton–Century Company, 1936).

UNIT 2
Culture and Communication

Unit Selections

Key Points to Consider

- In what sense are all languages "equal?"

- How can language restrict our thought processes?

- Should the monitors of the English language, such as teachers and dictionaries, be prescriptive or descriptive?

- In what ways is communication difficult in a cross-cultural situation?

- How has the "argument culture" affected the way we conduct ourselves vis-à-vis others?

- How has this section enhanced your ability to communicate more effectively?

Student Web Site
www.mhcls.com/online

Internet References
Further information regarding these Web sites may be found in this book's preface or online.

Exploratorium Magazine: "The Evolution of Languages"
    http://www.exploratorium.edu/exploring/language
Hypertext and Ethnography
    http://www.umanitoba.ca/anthropology
Language Extinction
    http://www.colorado.edu/iec
Showcase Anthropology
    http://www.anthropology.wisc.edu

Anthropologists are interested in all aspects of human behavior and how they interrelate with each other. Language is a form of such behavior (albeit primarily verbal behavior) and, therefore, worthy of study. Although it changes over time, language is patterned and passed down from one generation to the next through learning, not instinct. In keeping with the idea that language is integral to human social interaction, it has long been recognized that human communication through language is by its nature different from the kind of communication found among other animals. Central to this difference is the fact that humans communicate abstractly, with symbols that have meaning independent of the immediate sensory experiences of either the sender or the receiver of messages. Thus, for instance, humans are able to refer to the future and the past instead of just the here-and-now.

Recent experiments have shown that anthropoid apes can be taught a small portion of Ameslan or American Sign Language. It must be remembered, however, that their very rudimentary ability has to be tapped by painstaking human effort, and that the degree of difference between apes and humans serves only to emphasize the peculiarly human need for, and development of, language.

Just as the abstract quality of symbols lifts our thoughts beyond immediate sense perception, it also inhibits our ability to think about and convey the full meaning of our personal experience. No categorical term can do justice to its referents—the variety of forms to which the term refers. The degree to which this is an obstacle to clarity of thought and communication relates to the degree of abstraction in the symbols involved. The word "chair," for instance, would not present much difficulty, since it has objective referents. However, consider the trouble we have in thinking and communicating with words whose referents are not tied to immediate sense perception—words such as "freedom," "democracy," and "justice." Deborah Tannen's discussion of the "argument culture" (in "Fighting for our Lives") is a prime example of this. At best, the likely result is symbolic confusion: an inability to think or communicate in objectively definable symbols. At worst, language may be used to purposefully obfuscate.

A related issue has to do with the fact that languages differ as to what is relatively easy to express within the restrictions of their particular vocabularies. Thus, although a given language may not have enough words to cope with a new situation or a new field of activity, the typical solution is to invent words or to borrow them. In this way, it may be said that any language can be used

Rob Melnychuk/Getty Images

to teach anything. This point is illustrated by Laura Bohannan's attempt to convey the "true" meaning of Shakespeare's *Hamlet* to the West African Tiv (see "Shakespeare in the Bush"). Much of her task was devoted to finding the most appropriate words in the Tiv language to convey her Western thoughts. At least part of her failure was due to the fact that some of the words are just not there, and her inventions were unacceptable to the Tiv.

In a somewhat different manner, both Donna Jo Napoli in "Whose Language Is Better?" and Deborah Tannen in "I Can't Even Open My Mouth," point out that there are subtleties to language that cannot be found in a dictionary and whose meaning can only be interpreted in the context of the social situation. In fact, Robert MacNeil shows in "Do You Speak American?" that linguistic diversity within the United States is alive and well and, in spite of the homogenizing effects of the mass media, is actually on the increase.

Taken collectively, the articles in this unit show how symbolic confusion may occur between individuals or groups. In addition, they demonstrate the tremendous potential of recent research to enhance effective communication among all of us.

Whose Speech Is Better?

DONNA JO NAPOLI

Not all speakers of a given language speak the same way. You've noticed speech variations on television. Maybe you've seen the movie *My Fair Lady,* in which Henry Higgins believes that the Queen's English is the superior language of England (and, perhaps, of the world). So the question arises, whose speech is better? And this question is subsumed under the larger question of whether any language is intrinsically superior to another.

Before facing this issue, though, we need to face another matter. Consider these utterances:

Would you mind if I borrowed that cushion for a few moments?

Could I have that pillow for a sec?

Give me that, would you?

All of these utterances could be used to request a pillow.

Which one(s) would you use in addressing a stranger? If you use the first one, perhaps you sense that the stranger is quite different from you (such as a much older person or a person with more stature or authority). Perhaps you're trying to show that you're polite or refined or not a threat. Pay attention to the use of the word "cushion" instead of "pillow." Pillows often belong behind our heads, typically in bed. If you wanted to avoid any hint of intimacy, you might choose to use the word "cushion" for what is clearly a pillow.

Consider the third sentence. It's harder for some people to imagine using this one with a stranger. When I help to renovate urban housing for the poor with a group called Chester Community Improvement Project and I am pounding in nails next to some guy and sweat is dripping off both our brows, I have no hesitation in using this style sentence. With the informality of such a sentence, I'm implying, or perhaps trying to bring about, a sense of comradery.

Of course, it's easy to imagine a scene in which you could use the second sentence with a stranger.

Which one(s) would you use in addressing someone you know well? Again, it could be all three. But now if you use the first one, you might be insulting the addressee. It's not hard to think of a scenario in which this sentence carries a nasty tone rather than a polite one. And you can describe scenarios for the second and third sentences easily.

The point is that we command different registers of language. We can use talk that is fancy or ordinary or extremely informal, and we can choose which register to use in which situations to get the desired effect. So we have lots of variation in our own speech in the ways we phrase things (syntax) and the words we use (lexicon vocabulary).

Other variation in an individual's speech involves sound rules (phonology). Say the third sentence aloud several times, playing with different ways of saying it. Contrast "give me" to "gimme" and "would you" to "wudja." When we say words in a sequence, sometimes we contract them, but even a single word can be said in multiple ways. Say the word "interesting" in several sentences, imagining scenarios that differ in formality. Probably your normal (or least marked) pronunciation has three syllables: "in-tres-ting." But maybe it has four, and if it does, they are probably "in-er-es-ting."

The pronunciation that is closest to the spelling ("in-ter-es-ting") is more formal and, as a result, is sometimes used for humor (as in "very in-ter-es-ting," with a noticeably foreign flair to the pronunciation of "very" or with a drawn-out "e" in "very").

So you have plenty of variation in your own speech, no matter who you are, and the more different speech communities you belong to, the more variation you will have. With my mother's relatives, I will say, for example, "I hate lobsters anymore," whereas with other people I'm more likely to say, "I hate lobsters these days." This particular use of "anymore" is common to people from certain geographical areas (the North and South Midland, meaning the area from Philadelphia westward through southern Pennsylvania, northern West Virginia, Ohio, Indiana, and Illinois to the Mississippi River) but not to people from other places, who may not even understand what I mean. With my sister, I used to say, "Ain't nobody gonna tell me what to do," but I'd never say that to my mother or to other people unless I was trying to make a sociolinguistic point. This kind of talk signaled for us a comradery outside of the socioeconomic group my mother aspired to. In a speech to a convention of librarians recently, I said, "That had to change, for I, like you, do not lead a charmed life," but I'd probably never say that in conversation to anyone—it's speech talk. Also, think about the language you use in e-mail and contrast it to your job-related writings, for example.

Although we cannot explicitly state the rules of our language, we do choose to use different rules in different contexts. We happily exploit variation, which we encounter in a wide range, from simple differences in pronunciation and vocabulary to more marked differences that involve phrasing and sentence structure. When the differences are greater and more numerous, we tend to talk of dialects rather than just variations. Thus the languages of upper class and lower class Bostonians would probably be called variations of American English, whereas the languages of upper class and lower class Londoners (Queen's English versus Cockney) would probably be called dialects of British English. When the dialects are so different as to be mutually incomprehensible and/or when they gain a cultural or political status, we tend to talk of separate languages (such as French versus Spanish).

There's one more point I want to make before we return to our original question. I often ask classes to play the game of telephone in the following way. We line up twenty-one chairs, and volunteers sit on them. Then I whisper in the middle person's ear, perhaps something very simple, such as "Come with me to the store." The middle person then whispers the phrase into the ears of people on both sides, and the whisper chain goes on to each end of the line. Finally, the first and twenty-first persons say aloud what they heard.

Next we do the same experiment but this time with a sentence that's a little more tricky, perhaps something such as "Why choose white shoes for winter sports?" Then we do the experiment with a sentence in a language that the first whisperer (who is often not me at this point) speaks reasonably well and might be familiar to some of the twenty-one people in the chairs—perhaps something such as *La lune, c'est magnifique* (which in French means "the moon is wonderful"). Finally, we do the experiment with a sentence whispered initially by a native speaker of a language that none of the twenty-one people speak.

Typically, the first and twenty-first persons do not come up with the same results. Furthermore, the distance between them seems greater with each successive experiment.

Part of the problem is in the listening. We don't all hear things the same way. When we haven't heard something clearly, we ask people to repeat what they said. But sometimes we don't realize we haven't heard something clearly, until our inappropriate response is corrected. At times the other person doesn't correct us and the miscommunication remains, leading to various other difficulties.

Part of the problem in the experiment is in the repeating. You may say, "My economics class is a bore," and you begin the second word with the syllable "eek." I might repeat the sentence but use my pronunciation of the second word, which would begin with "ek." If you speak French well, you might say "magnifique" quite differently from me. In high school or college language classes, the teacher drilled the pronunciation of certain words over and over—but some people never mimicked to her satisfaction. A linguist told me a story about a little girl who introduced herself as "Litha." The man she was introducing herself to said, "Litha?" The child said, "No, Litha." The man said, "Litha?" The child said, "No, no. Litha. Li-tha." The man said, "Lisa?" The child smiled and said, "Right." Repetitions are not exact and lead to change.

Imperfections in hearing and repeating are two of the reasons that language must change over time. When the Romans marched into Gaul and into the Iberian peninsula and northeastward into what is now Romania, they brought large populations who stayed and spoke a form of street Latin. But over time, the street Latin in Gaul developed into French; that in the Iberian Peninsula developed into Portuguese along the west and Spanish along the east and central portions; that in Romania developed into Romanian. Moreover, the street Latin spoken in the original community on the Italian peninsula changed as well, developing into Italian.

Other factors (besides our imperfections in hearing and in repeating sounds) can influence the speed with which language changes and the ways in which it changes—but the fact is that living languages necessarily change. They always have and they always will.

Many political groups have tried to control language change. During the French Revolution, a controlling faction decided that a standard language would pave the way for unity. Parish priests, who were ordered to survey spoken language, found that many dialects were spoken in different geographic areas, and many of them were quite distinct from the dialect of Paris. Primary schools in every region of France were established with teachers proficient in the Parisian dialect. The effect of this educational reform was not significant until 1881, when state education became free and mandatory, and the standard dialect (that is, Parisian) took hold more firmly. Still, the geographic dialects continued, though weakened, and most important, the standard kept changing. Standard French today is different from the Parisian dialect of 1790. In addition, new varieties of French have formed, as new subcultures have appeared. Social dialects persist and/or arise even when geographic dialects are squelched. Change is the rule in language, so variation will always be with us.

Now we can ask whose speech is better. This is a serious question because our attitudes about language affect how we treat speakers in personal, as well as in business and professional, situations. In what follows I will use the term "standard American English" (a term riddled with problems, which will become more and more apparent as you read)—the variety that we hear in news reports on television and radio. It doesn't seem to be strongly associated with any particular area of the country, although those who aren't from the Midwest often call it midwestern. This variety is also more frequently associated with the middle class than with the lower class, and it is more frequently associated with whites than with other races.

A few years ago a white student from Atlanta, Georgia, recorded herself reading a passage of James Joyce both in standard American English pronunciation and in her Atlanta pronunciation. She then asked strangers (adults of varying ages who lived in the town of Swarthmore, Pennsylvania) to listen to the two readings and answer a set of questions she had prepared. She did not tell the strangers that the recordings were made by a single person (nor that they were made by her). Without exception, the strangers judged the person who read the passage with standard English pronunciation as smarter and better educated, and most of them judged the person who read the passage with Atlanta pronunciation as nicer and more laid-back. This was just a small, informal study, but its findings are consistent with those of larger studies.

Studies have shown that prejudice against certain varieties of speech can lead to discriminatory practices. For example, Professor John Baugh of Stanford University directed a study of housing in which he used different English pronunciations when telephoning people who had advertised apartments for rent. In one call he would use standard American pronunciation; in another, African-American; in another, Latino. (He is African American, but he grew up in the middle class in Los Angeles with many Latino friends. He can sound white, African American, or Latino, at will.) He said exactly the same words in every call, and he controlled for the order in which he made the calls (i.e., sometimes the Latino pronunciation would be used first, sometimes the African-American, and sometimes the standard). He asked if the apartments were still available. More were available when he used the standard pronunciation. Thus it is essential that we examine carefully the question of "better" with regard to language variety.

When I knock on a door and my friend inside says, "Who's there?" I'm likely to answer, "It's me," but I don't say, "It's I" (or, even more unlikely for me, "It is I"). Do you? If you do, do you say that naturally, that is, not self-consciously? Or do you say it because you've been taught that that's the correct thing to say? If you do it naturally, your speech contains an archaism—a little fossil from the past. We all have little fossils. I say, "I'm different from you." Most people today would say, "I'm different than you." My use of "from" after "different" was typical in earlier generations, but it's not typical today. Some of us hold onto archaisms longer than others, and even the most linguistically innovative of us probably have some. So don't be embarrassed by your fossils: They're a fact of language.

But if you say "It's I" self-consciously because you've been taught that that's correct, what does "correct" mean in this situation? If that's what most people used to say but is not what most people say today, you're saying it's correct either because you revere the past (which many of us do) or because you believe that there's a rule of language that's being obeyed by "It's I" and being broken by "It's me."

I'm going to push the analysis of just this one contrast—"It's I" versus "It's me"—quite a distance because I believe that many relevant issues about how people view language will come out of the discussion. Consider the former reason for preferring "It's I," that of revering the past. Many people have this reason for using archaic speech patterns and for preferring that others use them. For some reason, language is treated in a unique way here. We certainly don't hold up the past as superior in other areas, for example, mathematics or physics. So why do some of us feel that changes in language are evidence of decay?

If it were true that the older way of saying something were better simply because it's older, your grandparents spoke better than your parents and your great-grandparents spoke better than your grandparents and so on. Did Chaucer speak a form of English superior to that spoken by Shakespeare? Shall we go further back than Chaucer for our model? There is no natural stopping point. We can go all the way to prehistoric times if we use "older" as the only standard for "better."

The latter reason—believing that "It's I" obeys a rule that "It's me" breaks—is more defensible, if it is indeed true. Defenders of the "It's I" school of speech point out that with the verb "be" the elements on both sides of it are grammatically equivalent—so they should naturally have the same case.

I've used a linguistic term here: "case." To understand it (or review it), look at these Hungarian sentences:

Megnézhetem a szobát?

Van rádió a szobában?

Hol a szoba?

May I see the room?

Is there a radio in the room?

Where's the room?

I have translated the sentences in a natural way rather than word by word. Can you pick out the word in each sentence that means "room"? I hope you chose *szobát, szobában,* and *szoba.* These three forms can be thought of as variants of the same word. The difference in form is called case marking. Textbooks on Hungarian typically claim that a form like *szoba* is used when the word is the subject of the sentence, a form like *szobát* when the word is the direct object, and a form like *szobában* when the word conveys a certain kind of location (comparable to the object of the preposition "in" in English). So a word can have various forms—various cases—based on how it is used in the sentence.

English does not have different case forms for nouns (with the exception of genitive nouns, such as "boy's" in "the boy's book"). So in the English translations of the Hungarian sentences above, the word "room" was invariable. However, English does have different case forms for pronouns:

I like tennis.

That tennis racket is mine.

Everyone likes me.

These three forms indicate the first-person singular: "I," "mine," and "me." They distinguish subjects ("I") from genitives ("mine") from everything else ("me").

Now let's return to "It's I." Must elements on either side of "be" be equivalent? In the following three sentences, different syntactic categories are on either side of "be" (here "NP" stands for "noun phrase"):

Bill is tall

Bill is off his rocker.

Bill is to die for.

NP "be" AP

NP "be" PP

NP "be" VP

"Tall" is an adjective (here, an adjective phrase, AP). "Off" is a preposition, and it's part of the prepositional phrase (PP) "off his rocker." "To die for" is a verb phrase (VP). Thus the two elements that flank "be" do not have to be equivalent in category.

Still, in the sentence "It's I," the elements that flank "be" are both pronouns ("It" and "I"), so maybe these elements are equivalent in this sentence. Let's test that claim by looking at agreement. Verbs agree with their subject in English, whether that subject precedes or follows them:

John's nice.

Is John nice?

But "be" in our focus sentence agrees with the NP to its left, not to its right:

It's I.

*It am I.

No one would say "It am I." Therefore, the NP to the right of "be" is not the subject of the sentence, which means that the NPs flanking "be" are not equivalent—"It" is the subject, but "I" is not.

Perhaps you think that the equivalency that matters here has to do with meaning, not with syntax. Let's pursue that: Do "It" and "I" have equivalent meaning in "It's I"? Notice that you can also say:

"It's you."

In fact, the slot after "It's" can be filled by several different pronouns. "It" in these sentences is not meaningful; it is simply a place holder, just as in sentences about time and weather:

It's four o'clock.

It's hailing.

But "I" is meaningful because it refers to a person (the speaker). Therefore, "It" and "I" are not equivalent in meaning in the sentence "It's I."

In sum, it's not clear that the elements on either side of "be" in the sentence "It's I" are equivalent in any linguistic way. We can conclude something even stronger. We noted that "It" in these sentences is the subject and that the pronoun following a form of "be" is not the subject. But the pronoun following "be" is also not a genitive. Given the pronoun case system of English discussed above, we expect the pronoun to take the third form (the "elsewhere" form), which is "me," not "I." In other words, our case system would lead us to claim that "It's me" is the grammatical sentence.

I am not saying "It's I" is ungrammatical. I want to show that the issue may not be as clean-cut as you might have thought. Indeed, the conclusion I come to is that more than one case system is at play here. Those who say "It's me" are employing regular case rules. But those who say "It's I" have a special case rule for certain sentences that contain "be." The important point is that both sets of speakers have rules that determine what they say. Their speech is systematic; they are not speaking randomly.

That is the key issue of this whole chapter. When we consider variation in language, we must give up the idea of errors and accept the idea of patterns. Some people produce one pattern because they are following one set of rules; other people produce a different pattern because they are following a different

set of rules. (For several different types of language variations in English, visit the websites of the West Virginia Dialect Project: http://www.as.wvu.edu/dialect.) From a linguistic perspective, asking whose speech is better would amount to asking whose system is better. But what standards do we have for evaluating systems? What standards do you, as a speaker of the language, employ when you judge between varieties of speech? To answer that question, consider variation in your own speech. Do you consider some varieties better than others? And which ones? If you're like most people, you consider formal or polite speech to be better. But that standard concerns behavior in society—behavior that may reveal or perhaps even determine one's position. We tend to think that the speech of those who hold cultural, economic, or other social power is better, but this has little to do with linguistic structure. Now ask yourself what standards you are using to judge the speech of others.

Such questions often boil down to your politics (who do you esteem?) or to your experience (what are you familiar with?) but not to your grammatical rules. Consider the common claim that some varieties of speech are lazy. Try to find a recording of English speech that you consider lazy. Now mimic it. Some people are good at mimicking the speech of others, but accurately mimicking the speech of anyone else (anyone at all) takes a good ear, good control over the parts of your body that produce speech, and mostly a grasp of the sound rules that are being used. So the speech you thought was lazy wasn't lazy at all. Rather, different rules are being employed in different varieties of speech. What makes each variety distinct from others is its inventory of rules.

Consider learning a foreign language. People who feel confident about their ability to speak and to understand a foreign language in a classroom often visit a place where that language is spoken, only to find that no one is speaking the classroom variety. One of the big differences is usually speed: Ordinary speech can be quite rapid. Again, some claim that fast speech is sloppy, but fast speech is notoriously hard to mimic. It is typically packed with sound rules, so it takes more experience with the language to master all the rules and to be able to produce fast speech.

Among American speakers a common misconception is that British speech is superior to American speech. Part of this belief follows from reverence of the past, already discussed. Part of it follows from the misperception that American upper class speech is closer to British speech—so British speech is associated with high society and with politeness. In fact, the speech of the British changed over time, just as the speech of the American colonialists changed over time. Therefore, modern British speech is not, in general, closer to older forms of English than American speech is. Pockets of conservative varieties of English occur both in the British Isles and in the United States, but most varieties on either side of the Atlantic Ocean have changed considerably. Also, British society is stratified, just as American society is, and not all British speech is either upper class or polite.

Linguists claim that all varieties of a language—all dialects and all languages, for that matter—are equal linguistic citizens. Linguists have recognized that all languages are systematic, obeying certain universal principles regarding the organization and interaction of sounds, the ways we build words and phrases and sentences, and how we code meaning. However, this doesn't mean that all language is esthetically equal. I can recognize a beautiful line in a poem or a story, as I'm sure you can (though we might not agree). But that beautiful line might be in archaic English, formal contemporary English, ordinary contemporary English, very informal contemporary English, African-American Atlanta English, Italian-American Yonkers English, Philadelphia gay English, Chinese-American Seattle English, or so many others. Within our different varieties of speech, we can speak in ways that affect people's hearts or resonate in their minds, or we can speak in ways that are unremarkable. These are personal (esthetic or political) choices.

Some possible effects of the goal of the English only movement (EOM) of minimizing certain language variations in the United States [exist]. But even if English were declared the official language of the United States, variation would not be wiped out. What would be threatened is the richness of the range of variation most speakers are exposed to. Once that exposure is lost, Americans might start thinking that English is a superior language simply because they would no longer hear other languages being spoken by people they know personally and respect. They might become severely provincial in their linguistic attitudes, and given the necessity of global respect these days, such provincialism could be dangerous.

The fact that variation in language is both unavoidable and sometimes the result of esthetic and political choices does not mean that educational institutions should not insist that children master whatever variety of language has been deemed the standard—just for purely practical reasons. There's little doubt that linguistic prejudice is a reality. The adult who cannot speak and write the standard variety may encounter a range of difficulties, from finding suitable employment to achieving social advancement.

At the same time, all of us—and educational institutions, in particular—should respect all varieties of language and show that respect in relevant ways. Look at one notorious controversy: In 1996 the school board in Oakland, California, declared Ebonics to be the official language of the district's African-American students. Given funding regulations for bilingual education in that time and place, this decision had the effect of allowing the school district to use funds set aside for bilingual education to teach their African-American children in Ebonics, as well as in the standard language.

The debate was particularly hot, I believe, because of the sociological issues involved. Many people thought that Ebonics should be kept out of the classroom purely because the dialect was associated with race. Some of these people were African Americans who did not want their children to be disadvantaged by linguistic prejudice; they were afraid that teaching in Ebonics would exaggerate racial linguistic prejudice rather than redress it. Many good books written about the Ebonics controversy for the general public look at the issue from a variety of perspectives (see the suggested readings). But from a linguistic perspective, the issue is more a question of bilingual (or bi-dialectal) education than anything else.

In sum, variation in language is something we all participate in, and, as a linguist and a writer, I believe it's something we should revel in. Language is not a monolith, nor can it be, nor should it be, given the complexity of culture and the fact that language is the fabric of culture. Some of us are more eloquent than others, and all of us have moments of greater or lesser eloquence. But that range in eloquence is found in every language, every dialect, and every variety of speech.

Further Reading on Variation

Andersson, L. G., and P. Trudgill. 1990. *Bad language.* Cambridge: Blackwell.

Baron, D. 1994. *Guide to home language repair.* Champaign, Ill.: National Council of Teachers of English.

Baugh, J. 1999. *Out of the mouths of slaves.* Austin: University of Texas Press.

Biber, D., and E. Finegan. 1997. *Sociolinguistic perspectives on register.* Oxford: Oxford University Press.

Cameron, D. 1995. *Verbal hygiene.* London: Routledge.

Carver, C. 1989. *American regional dialects: A word geography.* Ann Arbor: University of Michigan Press.

Coulmas, F. 1998. *Handbook of sociolinguistics.* Cambridge: Blackwell.

Fasold, R. 1984. *The sociolinguistics of society.* New York: Blackwell.

Finegan, E. 1980. *Attitudes toward language usage.* New York: Teachers College Press.

Fishman, J. 1968. *Readings in the sociology of language.* Paris: Mouton.

Herman, L. H., and M. S. Herman. 1947. *Manual of American dialects for radio, stage, screen, and television.* New York: Ziff Davis.

Hock, H., and B. Joseph. 1996. *An introduction to historical and comparative linguistics.* Berlin: Mouton de Gruyter.

Labov, W. 1972. *The logic of nonstandard English in language and social context: Selected readings.* Compiled by Pier Paolo Giglioli. Baltimore Md.: Penguin.

Labov, W. 1972. *Sociolinguistic patterns.* Philadelphia: University of Pennsylvania Press.

LeClerc, F., Schmitt, B. H., and Dube, L. 1994, May. Foreign branding and its effects on product perceptions and attitudes. *Journal of Marketing Research,* 31: 263–270.

Lippi-Green, R. 1997. *English with an accent.* New York: Routledge.

McCrum, R., W. Cran, and R. MacNeil. 1986. *The story of English.* New York: Viking Penguin.

Millward, C. M. 1989. *A biography of the English language.* Orlando, Fla.: Holt, Rinehart and Winston.

Milroy, J., and L. Milroy. 1991. *Authority in language,* 2nd ed. London: Routledge.

Moss, B., and K. Walters. 1993. Rethinking diversity: Axes of difference in the writing classroom. In L. Odell, ed., *Theory and practice in the teaching of writing: Rethinking the discipline.* Carbondale: Southern Illinois University Press.

Peyton, J., S. McGinnis, and D. Ranard, eds. 2001. *Heritage languages in America: Preserving a national resource* (from Delta Systems, phone 800–323–8270), Arlington, Va.

Romaine, S. 1994. *Language in society: An introduction to sociolinguistics.* Oxford: Oxford University Press.

Scherer, K., and H. Giles, eds. 1979. *Social markers in speech.* New York: Cambridge University Press.

Seligman, C. R., G. R. Tucker, and W. Lambert. 1972. The effects of speech style and other attributes on teachers' attitudes toward pupils. *Language and Society,* 1: 131–42.

Trask, R. L. 1994. *Language change.* London: Routledge.

Weinreich, U. [1953] 1968. *Languages in contact.* The Hague: Mouton.

Wolfram, W. 1991. *Dialects and American English.* Englewood Cliffs, N.J.: Prentice Hall.

Wolfram, W., and N. Schilling-Estes. 1998. *American English— dialects and variation.* Oxford: Blackwell.

Further Reading on Ebonics

Adger, C. 1994. Enhancing the delivery of services to black special education students from non-standard English backgrounds. Final Report. University of Maryland, Institute for the Study of Exceptional Children and Youth. (Available through ERIC Document Reproduction Service. Document No. ED 370 377.)

Adger, C., D. Christian, and O. Taylor. 1999. *Making the connection: Language and academic achievement among African American students.* Washington, D.C. and McHenry, Ill.: Center for Applied Linguistics and Delta Systems.

Adger, C., W. Wolfram, and J. Detwyler. 1993. Language differences: A new approach for special educators. *Teaching Exceptional Children,* 26, no. (1): 44–47.

Adger, C., W. Wolfram, J. Detwyler, and B. Harry. 1993. Confronting dialect minority issues in special education: Reactive and proactive perspectives. In *Proceedings of the Third National Research Symposium on Limited English Proficient Student Issues: Focus on Middle and High School Issues,* 2: 737–62. U.S. Department of Education, Office of Bilingual Education and Minority Languages Affairs. (Available through ERIC Document Reproduction Service. Document No. ED 356 673.)

Baratz, J. C., and R. W. Shuy, eds. 1969. Teaching black children to read. Available as reprints from the University of Michigan, Ann Arbor (313-761-4700).

Baugh, J. 2000. *Beyond Ebonics.* New York: Oxford University Press.

Christian, D. 1997. Vernacular dialects and standard American English in the classroom. ERIC Minibib. Washington, D.C.: ERIC Clearinghouse on Languages and Linguistics. (This minibibliography cites seven journal articles and eight documents related to dialect usage in the classroom. The documents can be accessed on microfiche at any institution with the ERIC collection, or they can be ordered directly from EDRS.)

Dillard, J. L. 1972. *Black English: Its history and use in the U.S.* New York: Random House.

Fasold, R. W. 1972. Tense marking in black English: A linguistic and social analysis. Available as reprints from the University of Michigan, Ann Arbor (313-761-4700).

Fasold, R. W., and R. W. Shuy, eds. 1970. *Teaching standard English in the inner city.* Washington, D.C.: Center for Applied Linguistics.

Wiley, T. G. 1996. The case of African American language. In *Literacy and language diversity in the United States,* pp. 125–32. Washington, D. C.: Center for Applied Linguistics and Delta Systems.

Wolfram, W. 1969. A sociolinguistic description of Detroit Negro speech. Available as reprints from the University of Michigan, Ann Arbor (313-761-4700).

Wolfram, W. 1990, February. Incorporating dialect study into the language arts class. *ERIC Digest.* Available from the ERIC Clearinghouse on Languages and Linguistics, Center for Applied Linguistics, 4646 40th Street NW, Washington, D.C. 20016-1859, (202-362-0700).

Wolfram, W. 1994. Bidialectal literacy in the United States. In D. Spencer, ed., *Adult biliteracy in the United States,* pp. 71–88. Washington, D.C.: Center for Applied Linguistics and Delta Systems.

Wolfram, W., and C. Adger. 1993. *Handbook on language differences and speech and language pathology: Baltimore City public schools.* Washington, D.C.: Center for Applied Linguistics.

Wolfram, W., C. Adger, and D. Christian. 1999. Dialects in schools and communities. Mahwah, N.J.: Erlbaum.

Wolfram, W., and N. Clarke, eds. 1971. *Black-white speech relationships.* Washington, D.C.: Center for Applied Linguistics.

Do You Speak American?

**"Well, butter my butt and call me a biscuit"; a documentary
on the English language, as spoken in the U.S., is airing on PBS.**

Robert MacNeil

On Columbus Avenue in New York, a young wait-ress approaches our table and asks, "How are you guys doin'?" My wife and I are old enough to be her grandparents, but we are "you guys" to her. Today, in Ameri-can English, guys can be guys, girls, or grandmothers. Girls call themselves guys, even dudes. For a while, young women scorned the word girls, but that is cool again, probably because African-American women use it and it can be real cool—even empowering—to whites to borrow black talk, like the word cool. It is empowering to gay men to call themselves queer, once a hated homophobic term, but now used to satirize the whole shifting scene of gender attitudes in the TV reality show, "Queer Eye for the Straight Guy." As society changes, so does language, and American society has changed enormously in recent decades. Moreover, when new norms are resented or feared, language often is the target of that fear or resentment.

How we use the English language became a hot topic dur-ing the 1960s, and it remains so today—a charged ingredient in the culture wars, as intensely studied and disputed as any other part of our society. That is appropriate because nothing is more central to our identity and sense of who we are and where we belong. "Aside from a person's physical appearance, the first thing someone will be judged by is how he or she talks," main-tains linguist Dennis Baron.

Many feel that the growing informality of American life, the retreat from fixed standards, ("the march of casualization," *The New York Times* recently called it)—in clothing, manners, sexual mores—is reflected in our language and is corrupting it. They see schools lax about teaching grammar and hear nonstan-dard forms accepted in broadcasting, newspapers, politics, and advertising. They believe the slogan "Winston tastes good like a cigarette should" is so embedded in the national psyche that few Americans would now balk at the use of "like" (instead of "as") because that usage is fast becoming the new standard. They hate such changes in the language and they despair for our culture.

Others, however, believe language is thriving—as inventive and vigorous as English was in the time of the Elizabethans—and they see American English as the engine driving what is now a global language.

This deep disagreement is one of the issues explored in a survey producer William Cran and I recently completed and a three-hour documentary, "Do You Speak American?"

We address the controversies, issues, anxieties, and assump-tions swirling around language today—some highly emotional and political. Why are black and white Americans speaking less and less like each other? We explain. Does Hispanic immigra-tion threaten the English language? We do not think so. Is our exposure to national media wiping out regional differences and causing us all to speak the same? We think not. Is the language really in serious decline? Well, we have quite a debate about that.

The people who believe so are known as prescriptivists: those who want us to obey prescribed rules of grammar. They do not mind being called curmudgeons and they alternate between pleasure and despair—pleasure in correcting their fel-low citizens: despair that they cannot stop the language from going to hell in our generation.

The Prince of Prescriptivists

One of the leading curmudgeons of our time—he has been called the Prince of Prescriptivists—is John Simon, theater critic for *New York Magazine,* and he comes to do battle in "Do You Speak American?" Simon sees the language today as "unhealthy, poor, sad, depressing, and probably fairly hopeless." In the foreword to a new book, *The Dictionary of Disagreeable English,* he writes: "No damsel was ever in such distress, no drayhorse more flogged, no defenseless child more drunkenly abused than the English language today."

The enemies for Simon are the descriptivists, those content to describe language as it actually is used. They include the editors of great dictionaries who, Simon charges, have grown dangerously permissive, abandoning advice on what is correct and what is not. He calls descriptivist linguists "a curse on their race."

One such individual is Jesse Sheidlower. American editor of the august *Oxford English Dictionary.* Does he believe the language is being ruined by the great informality of American life? "No, it is not being ruined at all," he replies. Sheidlower believes that Simon and other language conservatives actually are complaining that linguists and dictionary writers no longer are focused on the language of the elite. They look at the old days and say, "Well, everything used to be very proper, and now we have all these bad words and people are being careless, and so forth." In fact, he insists people always have spoken that way. "It's just that you didn't hear them because the media would only report on the language of the educated upper middle class," Sheidlower points out. "Nowadays . . . we see the language of other groups, of other social groups, of other income levels, in a way that we never used to.

"Language change happens and there's nothing you can do about it." To which Simon replies, "Maybe change is inevitable—maybe. Maybe dying from cancer is also inevitable, but I don't think we should help it along."

Helping it along, to Simon, would mean surrendering to the word "hopefully," one of his pet peeves. "To say, 'Hopefully it won't rain tomorrow'—who, or what, is filled with hope? Nothing. So you have to say, 'I hope it won't rain tomorrow.' But you can say, 'I enter a room hopefully,' because you are the vessel for that hopefulness."

Sheidlower replies that modern computer databases make it possible to check texts back over the centuries: "We see that 'hopefully' is not in fact very new. . . . It goes back hundreds of years, and it has been very common even in highly educated speech for much of the time."

This battle—the stuff of angry skirmishes in books, magazines, and seminars—is only one part of what makes our language news today. Other findings may surprise many people because they challenge widely held popular conceptions, or misconceptions, about the language.

Our study took the form of a journey starting in the Northeast, down to the mid-Atlantic states, west to the Great Lakes, Midwest, Appalachia, then toward the South, through Louisiana, Texas, and California into the Pacific Northwest. In linguistic terms, we traveled through the main dialect areas of the nation. Professional linguists, students of the science of language, were the key to our understanding of the forces changing the language as rapidly as the society has changed in the past 50 years.

While computers, information technology, globalization, digital communications, and satellites have revolutionized how we work, equally potent revolutions have occurred concerning the home, family structure and marriage, sexual mores, the role of women, race relations, and the rise of teenagers as a major consumer and marketing force. With this has come alterations in our public manners, eating habits, clothing, and tolerance of different lifestyles—all of which have been swept by a tide of informality.

Linguists Spring into Action

Observing how these rapid social changes have altered our language have been the linguists, whose new branch of the social sciences really came into its own in the 1960s, followed more recently by sociolinguistics, the study of how language and society interact. They have produced a body of fascinating

research that usually is couched in technical language difficult for non-linguists to understand. Dozens of linguists have lent their skills to help us translate their findings, and marry their scholarship to our sampling of the actual speech of ordinary Americans in all its variety, vitality, and humor, drawn from the widest social spectrum. They include waitresses, cowboys, hip-hop artists, Marine drill sergeants, Border Patrol agents, Mexican immigrants, Cajun musicians, African-American and Hispanic broadcasters, and Silicon Valley techies (who try to make computers talk like real people), as well as writers and editors, teachers and teenagers, surfers and snowboarders, actors and screenwriters, and presidents and politicians.

Did they all sound the same? One of the most common assumptions is that our total immersion in the same mass media is making us all speak in a similar manner. Not true, claim the linguists. We are not talking more alike, but less.

One of the enduring themes in American life is the pull of national against regional interests and regret for local distinctiveness erased in the relentless march of uniformity. It surfaced in the song "Little Boxes" by Pete Seeger, about people put into little boxes of identical houses made of "ticky tacky" and who all come out the same. Today, with more and more national franchising of basic elements—food, mobile homes, clothing, hotels, recreation—the U.S. can seem like one giant theme park endlessly reduplicated, the triumph of the cookie cutter culture and its distinctive art form, the national TV commercial.

Paradoxically, however, language is one fundamental aspect of our cultural identity in which growing homogenization is a myth. While some national trends are apparent, regional speech differences not only thrive, in some places they are becoming more distinctive. Local differences, pride, and identity with place are asserting themselves strongly, perhaps as instinctive resistance to the homogenizing forces of globalization. One remarkable example is the speech of urban African-Americans, which is diverging from standard mainstream English. After decades of progress in civil rights, and the growth of a large and successful black middle class, African-American speech in our big cities dramatically is going its own way.

Two linguists, Guy Bailey, provost of the University of Texas at San Antonio, and Patricia Cukor-Avila of the University of North Texas at Denton have documented this. For 18 years, they have studied a small community in East Central Texas they named "Springville," which appears to live in a time warp from a century ago, when it was the center for local cotton sharecroppers, black and white. Little remains now but the original general store. During the late 1930s, the Works Progress Administration recorded the voices of elderly blacks, some former slaves, some the children of slaves.

One of them, Laura Smalley, was born to a slave mother. She was nine at the time of Emancipation in 1863. She told how the slave owner kept them ignorant of Lincoln's Proclamation for six months. "An' I thought ol' master was dead, but he wasn'. . . . He'd been off to the war an' come back. All the niggers gathered aroun' to see ol' master again. You know, an' ol' master didn' tell, you know, they was free. . . . They worked there, I think now they say they worked them six months after that, six months. And turn them loose on the 19th of June.

That's why, you know, they celebrate that day. Colored folks celebrates that day."

Black and White Dialects

Reviewing the speech of Smalley and others, the linguists were taken by how similar it was to the speech of rural whites of that time and place, but now dissimilar to the speech of blacks today. Features characteristic of modern black speech, what linguists call African-American vernacular English—such as the invariant "be," as in "they 'be' working," or the deleted copular, leaving out the auxiliary verb in "they working"—were absent.

Here are samples of modern speech of African-Americans in large cities:

> "When the baby be sleep, and the othe' kids be at school, and my husband be at work, then . . . I might can finally sit down."

> "She told David they Mama had went to Chicago to see her sister and her sister's new baby."

These examples show the invariant "be," and the construction "had went." Bailey and Cukor-Avila say that these features did not exist in black speech before World War II. They conclude that, after the great migration to the North from World War I to the 1970s, blacks were segregated in urban ghettoes, had less contact with whites than they had in places like Springville, and their speech began to develop new features, as all human speech does when people are separated culturally and have little communication.

This has serious consequences in efforts to reduce the school dropout rate among blacks. Not only white teachers, but many African-American instructors, despise the "street talk" or "slang" as they call it, and often treat the children as if they were stupid or uneducable. In 1979, a Federal judge in Detroit ruled that an Ann Arbor, Mich., school, ironically named after Martin Luther King, Jr., was discriminating against black kids because of their language and ordered the school to remedy it. Yet, the prejudice lives on elsewhere. In 1997, Oakland schools tried to get black speech recognized not as a dialect of English but a separate language, Ebonics, to qualify for Federal money to teach English as a second language. That backfired amid furious protests nationally from black and white educators.

What is shocking to linguists is the manner in which many newspaper columnists excoriate black English, using terms such as "gibberish." In the linguistic community, black English is recognized as having its own internal consistency and grammatical forms. It certainly is not gibberish (which means something unintelligible) because it works effectively for communication within the urban community.

One of the first to give black English this measure of respect was William Labov of the University of Pennsylvania, who testified at a Senate hearing during the Ebonics furor in 1997: "This African-American vernacular English . . . is not a set of slang words, or a random set of grammatical mistakes, but a well-formed set of rules of grammar and pronunciation that is capable of conveying complex logic and reasoning."

To linguists, the fault lies not in a particular dialect, but in what attitudes others bring to it. Steve Harvey, an African-American who hosts the most popular morning radio show in Los Angeles, told us: "I speak good enough American. You know, I think there's variations of speaking American. I don't think there's any one set way, because America's so diverse." He added, "You do have to be bilingual in this country, which means you can be very adept at slang, but you also have to be adept at getting through the job interview."

Now, without fanfare, some Los Angeles schools have been trying a more sympathetic approach to help minority students become bilingual—by teaching them the differences between African-American Language, as they call it, and Mainstream American English. We visited PS 100 in Watts to watch fifth-graders play a "Jeopardy"-like game in which they won points for "translating" such sentences as "Last night we bake cookies."

Teacher: "What language is it in?"

Student: "AAL."

Teacher: "It is in African-American Language. What linguistic feature is in AAL?"

Student: "Past-tense marker-ed."

Teacher: "Past-tense marker-ed. That's cool! And how do you code-switch it to Mainstream American English?"

Student: "Last night we baked cookies."

Teacher: "You got five hundred more points." Big cheers from the kids.

So, four decades after the passage of landmark legislation outlawing racial discrimination, the news is that it blatantly survives in language. Columnists would not dream of describing other attributes of being African-American with epithets like "gibberish." They could, however, get away with it in writing about black language, which remains a significant barrier to success in school and ultimately in the job market and housing—pathways to the American dream.

Ironically, as much as it is despised, black English is embraced and borrowed by whites, especially young whites in thrall to the appeal of hip hop music. There are divergences just as dramatic within the English of white Americans. Around the Great Lakes, people are making what Labov believes are "revolutionary changes in the pronunciation of short vowels that have remained relatively stable in the language for a thousand years."

Labov is director of an effort to determine the boundaries of different dialects within American speech. Traditionally, that was achieved by comparing distinctive local or regional words people used for every day things. One surviving example is the different terms for the long sandwich that contains cold cuts, cheese, and lettuce—a grinder in some parts of New England; a wedge in Rhode Island: a spuky in Boston; a hero in New York; a hoagie in Philadelphia; a submarine in Ohio and farther west. By drawing lines around places where each term is used, linguists can form maps of dialect areas. Many such regional terms are dying out because old craft skills are replaced by products marketed nationally. Labov leads a new method in which the different ways people pronounce words are recorded with colored dots on a map of the U.S. Connecting the dots produces the Atlas of North American English.

Labov and his colleagues found startling pronunciation changes in cities such as Chicago, Cleveland, and Detroit and New York State's Rochester and Syracuse. On a computer in his office in Philadelphia, we heard a woman say the word "black," then the complete phrase: "Old senior citizens living on one 'black,' and it was apparent that she was pronouncing "block" like "black." Similarly, another woman mentions what sounds like "bosses." The full sentence reveals she means "buses:" "I can vaguely remember when we had 'bosses' with the antennas on top."

When one vowel changes, so do the neighboring ones: "caught" shifts toward "cot," "cot" toward "cat," "cat" toward "kit" or "keeyat." Labov thinks these changes are quite important. "From our point of view as linguists, we want to understand why people should become more different from each other. We're all watching the same radio and television; we live side by side. And it's important to recognize that people don't always want to behave in the same way."

Labov has a theory that, behind changes like these, are women, the primary transmitters of language. Traditionally enjoying less economic power than men, women rely on the symbolic power offered by words. Labov believes women are more apt than men to adopt "prestige forms" of language and symbols of nonconformism—new or "stigmatized forms" that can acquire a kind of "covert prestige." Labov writes that women are quicker and more forceful in employing the new social symbolism, whatever it may be. Working on his landmark study, "The Principles of Linguistic Change," he identifies a particular type of woman—working class, well-established in her community—who takes pleasure in being nonconformist and is strong enough to influence others. He sees parallels between leadership in fashion and language change. Most young women are alert to novelty in fashion; some have the confidence to embrace it and the natural authority to induce others to follow.

These are mysterious forces working on our language from underneath, as it were, and producing startling changes that, far from homogenizing our speech, actually create more diversity. Despite all the forces of global and national uniformity in products and trends, Americans clearly still want to do their own thing linguistically. An example is Pittsburgh, where the local dialect, or Pittsburghese, is celebrated, constantly talked about, and made a commodity. They know themselves as "Yinzers," from "yinz," the plural of "you," or "you ones." They use "slippy" for "slippery"; "red up" means to "tidy up"; and "anymore" as in "'Anymore,' there's so many new buildings you can't tell which is which." In downtown Pittsburgh—pronounced "dahntahn"— the question, "Did you eat yet?" sounds like "Jeet jet?" If you haven't, the response is, "No, 'jew?"

Barbara Johnstone, a linguist from Pittsburgh, thinks the pride in their local speech is a way for Pittsburghers to talk about who they are and what it means to live there. People treasure their local accents, because where they come from, or

where they feel they belong, still does matter. In the words of California linguist, Carmen Fought, "People want to talk like the people they want to be like." This contradicts the common assumption that media exposure is making everyone sound the same.

Local Accents Prevail

Yet, amusingly, people often are quite unaware of how their own speech sounds to others. Linguists we met were full of stories about people in Texas or coastal North Carolina with strong local accents who were convinced they sounded like Walter Cronkite. It happened to me. I grew up in the Canadian province of Nova Scotia, so fascinated with words that I called a memoir of my childhood *Wordstruck*. Even in my own family, I often heard the same words said differently. My grandfather, from Nova Scotia's south shore, said "garridge" while his daughter, my mother, said "gar-aghe."

Until I first came to the U.S. in 1952, I was unaware how different my speech was even from that of neighboring New England. I was 21 and (briefly, thank God!) an aspiring actor, thrilled to be working in a summer theater in Massachusetts. The first time I stepped on to the stage and opened my mouth, the director said, "You can't talk like that." I was stunned, not knowing until that moment that I was pronouncing "out" to rhyme with "oat," and "about" with "aboat"—still the common Nova Scotian pronunciation. Anxious not to close any career doors, I immediately began trying to modify the "oat" sound, but 50 years later, when I am tired or back with my brothers in Canada, I still slip into the pronunciations I grew up with.

What appears to be the determining force in whether regional dialects survive or disappear is not media influence, but rather the movements of people. We talked to John Coffin, a lobsterman in South Freeport, Me. Once a quiet fishing and ship-building harbor but now a bustling outlet shopping center, the town has attracted so many new visitors and residents that Coffin fears the Maine way of speaking—with its characteristic "ayeh" for "yes"—is disappearing: "I think in this area it's going to be a lost thing," and that makes him sad. "I'd like to think my children and grandchildren talk that way, whether people laugh at you, wherever we go—whatever." Do people laugh at his Maine accent? "Oh, yes, lots of times. When I was in the military, they made fun of me wicked."

"Wicked" is a typical Maine word, meaning "very," as in" "wicked' good."

This homogenizing trend is obvious on some of the islands, like Ocrakoke, off the coast of North Carolina, home of the Hoi Toiders, people who pronounce "high tide" as "hoi toid." These islands have become meccas for individuals from elsewhere building vacation homes, displacing locals and their dialect.

Still, the national media are having some effect: Labov notes two sound changes that have spread nationally, probably from California. One is the vowel in "do," which increasingly sounds like "dew." Labov calls it "oo-fronting"; the sound is produced more to the front of the mouth. You also hear it in the word "so," which sounds like "so-ew." Another trend, more noticeable among young women, but also some men, is a rising inflection at the ends of sentences, making statements such as "The bus station is around *the corner*" sound like a query. One of the regions where "oo-fronting" is common is the South, where there are changes just as dramatic as those in the North. Southern ghosts do not say "boo," but "bew."

The most prevalent shift is that Southerners increasingly are pronouncing the "r" at the ends of words such as father. In part, this is due to the large migration of Northerners to Southern cities. Partly it is the historic decline in influence of the coastal Southern areas that once boasted the great slave-holding plantation culture, and the kind of r-less pronunciation we associated with languid belles posing in hoop skirts on the porches of ante-bellum houses. This advancing "r" marks the growing prestige of what linguists call Inland Southern, the speech deriving from Appalachia. That pattern goes back to the earliest days of British settlement, when people from parts of England who did not pronounce "r" settled the coastal areas, while the Scots-Irish, settlers from Northern Ireland who spoke with a strong "r," moved into the hills of Appalachia because the easily-cultivated coastal land already was taken.

Their speech has been given a huge boost by the rise of country music, no longer a regional craze, but a national phenomenon. Those who "sing country," wherever they come from, "talk country" and "talkin' country" has become a kind of default way of speaking informal American. It is considered easygoing and friendly. Pres. George W. Bush has made it his trademark, with no disadvantage politically because, like him, a great many Americans say, "Howya doin'? Doin' fine!" and they are not more particular than he is about making subject agree with verb in sentences such as, "There's no negotiations with North Korea."

The economic rise of the South has had another startling result. So many Americans have moved into the South and Southwest and happily adopted Southernisms—such as "y'all" and "fixin' to" and pronouncing "I" as "all," not the Northern "eye-ee"—that more Americans now speak some variety of Southern than any other dialect. That is the conclusion of linguist John Fought, who believes that, as the population shift to the Sun Belt continues, "In time, we should expect 'r-full' southern to become accepted as standard American speech."

That news will come as a shock to Northerners conditioned over generations to despise Southern talk, considering it evidence of stupidity and backwardness. In the film "Sweet Home Alabama," the good ol' boy played by Josh Lucas says to his Northernized wife, Reese Witherspoon, "Just because I talk slow, doesn't mean I'm stupid." The context leads the audience to believe him.

The comedian Jeff Foxworthy still fills huge theaters North and South with his hilarious routine ridiculing Southern speech and Northern attitudes towards it. He kills them with his list of Southern "words:'"

"May-o-naise. Man, a's a lotta people here tonight,"

"Urinal. I told my brother, 'You're in a lotta trouble when Daddy gets home."

"Wichadidja. Hey, you didn't bring your track with you, did you?"

Northern attitudes to Southerners may be ameliorating slightly, possibly because it no longer is uncool in Northern cities to like country music and the culture that goes with it. Yet, an ingrained sense of the prestige of some dialects and scorn for others is very much alive. Linguist Dennis Preston of Michigan State University has spent years studying the prejudices Americans have concerning speech different from their own. He joined us on a train west from Philadelphia, demonstrating his regular technique. Establishing quick rapport with other passengers, he got them to mark on a map of the U.S. where they thought people spoke differently. Almost without exception, they circled the South and New York to locate the worst English. Referring to New York, a Pennsylvania woman told Preston contemptuously, "They say waader!" Preston asked, "What do you say?" "Water!" she declared proudly.

A Distinct New York Voice

Preston, though, detects another emotion creeping in beneath the scorn, and that is pleasure. People may think Southern or New York speech is not good, but they find them charming, and that must be partly an effect of media exposure, for instance, to the sympathetic New York characters in the TV series "Law and Order." Linguists believe that broadcasting and the movies help all Americans understand different dialects, perhaps appreciating the diversity in our culture. Moreover, no matter how they themselves speak, Americans learn to understand the language of network broadcasters, which is the closest thing to an overall American standard. That standard coincides with the speech that Preston's subjects inevitably identify as the best American speech—that of the Midwest—because it has the fewest regional features.

That Midwest standard is relevant to the cutting edge of computer research in Silicon Valley. There is heavy investment in efforts to make computers speak like us and understand us. The researchers believe they will achieve that in 10 to 15 years but it is an incredible challenge.

What these efforts demonstrate is how infinitely complex our language and understanding of it is, how meaning turns on the subtlest changes in intonation, how vast any computer data base must be to catch all the nuances we take for granted. How do you program a computer to avoid those charming errors in context which foreigners make in perfectly grammatical sentences? For instance, a sign in an Egyptian hotel states: "Patrons need have no anxiety about the water. It has all been passed by the management." Or, this in a Swiss hotel: "Due to the impropriety of entertaining guests of the opposite sex in the bedrooms, it is suggested that the lobby be used for this purpose."

The effort to make computers understand speech raises other questions about the future of language. Will the technology, and the business imperatives behind it, create an irresistible drive toward more standard speech? If so, which accents or varieties of American speech will that leave out? Whom will it disenfranchise because of their dialect—African-Americans, Hispanics, Cajuns in Louisiana'? A couple of years ago, the police chief of Shreveport, La., complained that the computer voice-recognition system used to route nonemergency calls did not understand the local accent. Researchers point out, however, that if you speak like someone from the Midwest, computers will understand you.

The emerging technology is irresistible for business. When United Airlines introduced a computerized voice-recognition system for flight information–replacing live bodies—it saved a reported $25,000,000. As these systems become more sophisticated, a lot of companies will want them to replace expensive warm bodies. Inevitably, more and more of our lives will involve talking to and being understood by computers. Being understood will be increasingly important. Will the technology work to reinforce existing linguistic stereotypes—about your race, ethnicity, gender, or where you live—or help to break them down? Will we have to talk as computers would like us to in order for them to obey us?

During the California portion of filming "Do You Speak American?" I drove a car equipped with an elaborate voice-recognition system. I speak a version of standard broadcast American English, and I tried to enunciate clearly. Occasionally, it worked, but often it did not and the car kept saying, "Pardon me? Pardon me?" and I gave it up.

Everything in the American experience, each new frontier encountered—geographical, spiritual, technological—has altered our language. What kind of a frontier are we crossing by teaching computers our most fundamental human skill, that of the spoken word?

ROBERT MACNEIL, former co-anchor of PBS's Emmy Award-winning "MacNeil/Lehrer NewsHour," is a member of the Television Academy Hall of Fame and the author of several books.

Fighting for Our Lives

Deborah Tannen, PhD

This is not another book about civility. "Civility" suggests a superficial, pinky-in-the-air veneer of politeness spread thin over human relations like a layer of marmalade over toast. This book is about a pervasive warlike atmosphere that makes us approach public dialogue, and just about anything we need to accomplish, as if it were a fight. It is a tendency in Western culture in general, and in the United States in particular, that has a long history and a deep, thick, and far-ranging root system. It has served us well in many ways but in recent years has become so exaggerated that it is getting in the way of solving our problems. Our spirits are corroded by living in an atmosphere of unrelenting contention—an argument culture.

The argument culture urges us to approach the world—and the people in it—in an adversarial frame of mind. It rests on the assumption that opposition is the best way to get anything done: The best way to discuss an idea is to set up a debate; the best way to cover news is to find spokespeople who express the most extreme, polarized views and present them as "both sides"; the best way to settle disputes is litigation that pits one party against the other; the best way to begin an essay is to attack someone; and the best way to show you're really thinking is to criticize.

Our public interactions have become more and more like having an argument with a spouse. Conflict can't be avoided in our public lives any more than we can avoid conflict with people we love. One of the great strengths of our society is that we can express these conflicts openly. But just as spouses have to learn ways of settling their differences without inflicting real damage on each other, so we, as a society, have to find constructive ways of resolving disputes and differences. Public discourse requires *making* an argument for a point of view, not *having* an argument—as in having a fight.

The war on drugs, the war on cancer, the battle of the sexes, politicians' turf battles—in the argument culture, war metaphors pervade our talk and shape our thinking. Nearly everything is framed as a battle or game in which winning or losing is the main concern. These all have their uses and their place, but they are not the only way—and often not the best way—to understand and approach our world. Conflict and opposition are as necessary as cooperation and agreement, but the scale is off balance, with conflict and opposition overweighted. In this book, I show how deeply entrenched the argument culture is, the forms it takes, and how it affects us every day—sometimes in useful ways, but often creating more problems than it solves, causing

rather than avoiding damage. As a sociolinguist, a social scientist, I am trained to observe and explain language and its role in human relations, and that is my biggest job here. But I will also point toward other ways for us to talk to each other and get things done in our public lives.

The Battle of the Sexes

My interest in the topic of opposition in public discourse intensified in the years following the publication of *You Just Don't Understand,* my book about communication between women and men. In the first year I appeared on many television and radio shows and was interviewed for many print articles in newspapers and magazines. For the most part, that coverage was extremely fair, and I was—and remain—indebted to the many journalists who found my ideas interesting enough to make them known to viewers, listeners, and readers. But from time to time—more often than I expected—I encountered producers who insisted on setting up a television show as a fight (either between the host and me or between another guest and me) and print journalists who made multiple phone calls to my colleagues, trying to find someone who would criticize my work. This got me thinking about what kind of information comes across on shows and in articles that take this approach, compared to those that approach topics in other ways.

At the same time, my experience of the academic world that had long been my intellectual home began to change. For the most part, other scholars, like most journalists, were welcoming and respectful in their responses to my work, even if they disagreed on specific points or had alternative views to suggest. But about a year after *You Just Don't Understand* became a best-seller—the wheels of academia grind more slowly than those of the popular press—I began reading attacks on my work that completely misrepresented it. I had been in academia for over fifteen years by then, and had valued my interaction with other researchers as one of the greatest rewards of academic life. Why, I wondered, would someone represent me as having said things I had never said or as having failed to say things I had said?

The answer crystallized when I put the question to a writer who I felt had misrepresented my work: "Why do you need to make others wrong for you to be right?" Her response: "It's an argument!" Aha, I thought, that explains it. When you're having an argument with someone, your goal is not to listen and understand. Instead, you use every tactic you can think of—including distorting what your opponent just said—in order to win the argument.

Not only the level of attention *You Just Don't Understand* received but, even more, the subject of women and men, triggered the tendency to polarize. This tendency to stage a fight on television or in print was posited on the conviction that opposition leads to truth. Sometimes it does. But the trouble is, sometimes it doesn't. I was asked at the start of more than one talk show or print interview, "What is the most controversial thing about your book?" Opposition does not lead to truth when the most controversial thing is not the most important.

The conviction that opposition leads to truth can tempt not only members of the press but just about anyone seeking to attract an audience to frame discussions as a fight between irreconcilable opposites. Even the Smithsonian Institution, to celebrate its 150th anniversary, sponsored a series of talks billed as debates. They invited me to take part in one titled "The Battle of the Sexes." The organizer preempted my objection: "I know you won't be happy with this title, but we want to get people interested." This is one of many assumptions I question in this book: Is it necessary to frame an interchange as a battle to get people interested? And even if doing so succeeds in capturing attention, does it risk dampening interest in the long run, as audiences weary of the din and begin to hunger for more substance?

Thought-Provoking or Just Provocative?

In the spring of 1995, Horizons Theatre in Arlington, Virginia, produced two one-act plays I had written about family relationships. The director, wanting to contribute to the reconciliation between Blacks and Jews, mounted my plays in repertory with two one-act plays by an African American playwright, Caleen Sinnette Jennings. We had both written plays about three sisters that explored the ethnic identities of our families (Jewish for me, African-American for her) and the relationship between those identities and the American context in which we grew up. To stir interest in the plays and to explore the parallels between her work and mine, the theater planned a public dialogue between Jennings and me, to be held before the plays opened.

As production got under way, I attended the audition of actors for my plays. After the auditions ended, just before everyone headed home, the theater's public relations volunteer distributed copies of the flyer announcing the public dialogue that she had readied for distribution. I was horrified. The flyer announced that Caleen and I would discuss "how past traumas create understanding and conflict between Blacks and Jews today." The flyer was trying to grab by the throat the issue that we wished to address indirectly. Yes, we were concerned with conflicts between Blacks and Jews, but neither of us is an authority on that conflict, and we had no intention of expounding on it. We hoped to do our part to ameliorate the conflict by focusing on commonalities. Our plays had many resonances between them. We wanted to talk about our work and let the resonances speak for themselves.

Fortunately, we were able to stop the flyers before they were distributed and devise new ones that promised something we could deliver: "a discussion of heritage, identity, and complex family relationships in African-American and Jewish-American culture as represented in their plays." Jennings noticed that the original flyer said the evening would be "provocative" and changed it to "thought-provoking." What a world of difference is implied in that small change: how much better to make people think, rather than simply to "provoke" them—as often as not, to anger.

It is easy to understand why conflict is so often highlighted: Writers of headlines or promotional copy want to catch attention and attract an audience. They are usually under time pressure, which lures them to established, conventionalized ways of expressing ideas in the absence of leisure to think up entirely new ones. The promise of controversy seems an easy and natural way to rouse interest. But serious consequences are often unintended: Stirring up animosities to get a rise out of people, though easy and "provocative," can open old wounds or create new ones that are hard to heal. This is one of many dangers inherent in the argument culture.

For the Sake of Argument

In the argument culture, criticism, attack, or opposition are the predominant if not the the only ways of responding to people or ideas. I use the phrase "culture of critique" to capture this aspect. "Critique" in this sense is not a general term for analysis or interpretation but rather a synonym for criticism.

It is the *automatic* nature of this response that I am calling attention to—and calling into question. Sometimes passionate opposition, strong verbal attack, are appropriate and called for. No one knows this better than those who have lived under repressive regimes that forbid public opposition. The Yugoslavian-born poet Charles Simic is one. "There are moments in life," he writes, "when true invective is called for, when it becomes an absolute necessity, out of a deep sense of justice, to denounce, mock, vituperate, lash out, in the strongest possible language." I applaud and endorse this view. There are times when it is necessary and right to fight—to defend your country or yourself, to argue for right against wrong or against offensive or dangerous ideas or actions.

What I question is the ubiquity, the knee-jerk nature, of approaching almost any issue, problem, or public person in an adversarial way. One of the dangers of the habitual use of adversarial rhetoric is a kind of verbal inflation—a rhetorical boy who cried wolf: The legitimate, necessary denunciation is muted, even lost, in the general cacophony of oppositional shouting. What I question is using opposition to accomplish *every* goal, even those that do not require fighting but might also (or better) be accomplished by other means, such as exploring, expanding, discussing, investigating, and the exchanging of ideas suggested by the word "dialogue." I am questioning the assumption that *everything* is a matter of polarized opposites, the proverbial "two sides to every question" that we think embodies open-mindedness and expansive thinking.

In a word, the type of opposition I am questioning is what I call "agonism." I use this term, which derives from the Greek word for "contest," *agonia,* to mean an automatic warlike stance— not the literal opposition of fighting against an attacker or the unavoidable opposition that arises organically in response to conflicting ideas or actions. An agonistic response, to me, is a kind of programmed contentiousness—a prepatterned, unthinking use of fighting to accomplish goals that do not necessarily require it.

How Useful Are Fights?

Noticing that public discourse so often takes the form of heated arguments—of having a fight—made me ask how useful it is in our personal lives to settle differences by arguing. Given what I know about having arguments in private life, I had to conclude that it is, in many cases, not very useful.

In close relationships it is possible to find ways of arguing that result in better understanding and solving problems. But with most arguments, little is resolved, worked out, or achieved when two people get angrier and less rational by the minute. When you're having an argument with someone, you're usually not trying to understand what the other person is saying, or what in their experience leads them to say it. Instead, you're readying your response: listening for weaknesses in logic to leap on, points you can distort to make the other person look bad and yourself look good. Sometimes you know, on some back burner of your mind, that you're doing this—that there's a kernel of truth in what your adversary is saying and a bit of unfair twisting in what you're saying. Sometimes you do this because you're angry, but sometimes it's just the temptation to take aim at a point made along the way because it's an easy target.

Here's an example of how this happened in an argument between a couple who had been married for over fifty years. The husband wanted to join an HMO by signing over their Medicare benefits to save money. The wife objected because it would mean she could no longer see the doctor she knew and trusted. In arguing her point of view, she said, "I like Dr. B. He knows me, he's interested in me. He calls me by my first name." The husband parried the last point: "I don't like that. He's much younger than we are. He shouldn't be calling us by first name." But the form of address Dr. B. uses was irrelevant. The wife was trying to communicate that she felt comfortable with the doctor she knew, that she had a relationship with him. His calling her by first name was just one of a list of details she was marshaling to explain her comfort with him. Picking on this one detail did not change her view—and did not address her concern. It was just a way to win the argument.

We all are guilty, at times, of seizing on irrelevant details, distorting someone else's position the better to oppose it, when we're arguing with those we're closest to. But we are rarely dependent on these fights as sources of information. The same tactics are common when public discourse is carried out on the model of personal fights. And the results are dangerous when listeners are looking to these interchanges to get needed information or practical results.

Fights have winners and losers. If you're fighting to win, the temptation is great to deny facts that support your opponent's views and to filter what you know, saying only what supports your side. In the extreme form, it encourages people to misrepresent or even to lie. We accept this risk because we believe we can tell when someone is lying. The problem is, we can't.

Paul Ekman, a psychologist at the University of California, San Francisco, studies lying. He set up experiments in which individuals were videotaped talking about their emotions, actions, or beliefs—some truthfully, some not. He has shown these videotapes to thousands of people, asking them to identify the liars and also to say how sure they were about their judgments. His findings are chilling: Most people performed not much better than chance, and those who did the worst had just as much confidence in their judgments as the few who were really able to detect lies. Intrigued by the implications of this research in various walks of life, Dr. Ekman repeated this experiment with groups of people whose jobs require them to sniff out lies: judges, lawyers, police, psychotherapists, and employees of the CIA, FBI, and ATF (Bureau of Alcohol, Tobacco, and Firearms). They were no better at detecting who was telling the truth than the rest of us. The only group that did significantly better were members of the U.S. Secret Service. This finding gives some comfort when it comes to the Secret Service but not much when it comes to every other facet of public life.

Two Sides to Every Question

Our determination to pursue truth by setting up a fight between two sides leads us to believe that every issue has two sides—no more, no less: If both sides are given a forum to confront each other, all the relevant information will emerge, and the best case will be made for each side. But opposition does not lead to truth when an issue is not composed of two opposing sides but is a crystal of many sides. Often the truth is in the complex middle, not the oversimplified extremes.

We love using the word "debate" as a way of representing issues: the abortion debate, the health care debate, the affirmative action debate—even "the great backpacking vs. car camping debate." The ubiquity of this word in itself shows our tendency to conceptualize issues in a way that predisposes public discussion to be polarized, framed as two opposing sides that give each other no ground. There are many problems with this approach. If you begin with the assumption that there *must* be an "other side," you may end up scouring the margins of science or the fringes of lunacy to find it. As a result, proven facts, such as what we know about how the earth and its inhabitants evolved, are set on a par with claims that are known to have no basis in fact, such as creationism.

The conviction that there are two sides to every story can prompt writers or producers to dig up an "other side," so kooks who state outright falsehoods are given a platform in public discourse. This accounts, in part, for the bizarre phenomenon of Holocaust denial. Deniers, as Emory University professor Deborah Lipstadt shows, have been successful in gaining television airtime and campus newspaper coverage by masquerading as "the other side" in a "debate."

Appearance in print or on television has a way of lending legitimacy, so baseless claims take on a mantle of possibility. Lipstadt shows how Holocaust deniers dispute established facts of history, and then reasonable spokespersons use their having been disputed as a basis for questioning known facts. The actor Robert Mitchum, for example, interviewed in *Esquire,* expressed doubt about the Holocaust. When the interviewer asked about the slaughter of six million Jews, Mitchum replied, "I don't know. People dispute that." Continual reference to "the other side" results in a pervasive conviction that everything has another side—with the result that people begin to doubt the existence of any facts at all.

The Expense of Time and Spirit

Lipstadt's book meticulously exposes the methods used by deniers to falsify the overwhelming historic evidence that the Holocaust occurred. That a scholar had to invest years of her professional life writing a book unraveling efforts to deny something that was about as well known and well documented as any historical fact has ever been—while those who personally experienced and witnessed it are still alive—is testament to another way that the argument culture limits our knowledge rather than expanding it. Talent and effort was wasted when individuals who have been unfairly attacked must spend years of their creative lives defending themselves rather than advancing their work. The entire society loses their creative efforts. This is what happened with scientist Robert Gallo.

Dr. Gallo is the American virologist who codiscovered the AIDS virus. He is also the one who developed the technique for studying T-cells, which made that discovery possible. And Gallo's work was seminal in developing the test to detect the AIDS virus in blood, the first and for a long time the only means known of stemming the tide of death from AIDS. But in 1989, Gallo became the object of a four-year investigation into allegations that he had stolen the AIDS virus from Luc Montagnier of the Pasteur Institute in Paris, who had independently identified the AIDS virus. Simultaneous investigations by the National Institutes of Health, the office of Michigan Congressman John Dingell, and the National Academy of Sciences barreled ahead long after Gallo and Montagnier settled the dispute to their mutual satisfaction. In 1993 the investigations concluded that Gallo had done nothing wrong. Nothing. But this exoneration cannot be considered a happy ending. Never mind the personal suffering of Gallo, who was reviled when he should have been heralded as a hero. Never mind that, in his words, "These were the most painful years and horrible years of my life." The dreadful, unconscionable result of the fruitless investigations is that Gallo had to spend four years fighting the accusations instead of fighting AIDS.

The investigations, according to journalist Nicholas Wade, were sparked by an article about Gallo written in the currently popular spirit of demonography: not to praise the person it features but to bury him—to show his weaknesses, his villainous side. The implication that Gallo has stolen the AIDS virus was created to fill a requirement of the discourse: In demonography, writers must find negative sides of their subjects to display for readers who enjoy seeing heroes transformed into villains. The suspicion led to investigations, and the investigations became a juggernaut that acquired a life of its own, fed by the enthusiasm for attack on public figures that is the culture of critique.

Metaphors: We Are What We Speak

Perhaps one reason suspicions of Robert Gallo were so zealously investigated is that the scenario of an ambitious scientist ready to do anything to defeat a rival appeals to our sense of story; it is the kind of narrative we are ready to believe. Culture, in a sense, is an environment of narratives that we hear repeatedly until they seem to make self-evident sense in explaining human behavior. Thinking of human interactions as battles is a metaphorical frame through which we learn to regard the world and the people in it.

All language uses metaphors to express ideas; some metaphoric words and expressions are novel, made up for the occasion, but more are calcified in the language. They are simply the way we think it is natural to express ideas. We don't think of them as metaphors. Someone who says, "Be careful: You aren't a cat, you don't have nine lives," is explicitly comparing you to a cat, because the cat is named in words. But what if someone says, "Don't pussyfoot around; get to the point"? There is no explicit comparison to a cat, but the comparison is there nonetheless, implied in the word "pussyfoot." This expression probably developed as a reference to the movement of a cat cautiously circling a suspicious object. I doubt that individuals using the word "pussyfoot" think consciously of cats. More often than not, we use expressions without thinking about their metaphoric implications. But that doesn't mean those implications are not influencing us.

At a meeting, a general discussion became so animated that a participant who wanted to comment prefaced his remark by saying, "I'd like to leap into the fray." Another participant called out, "Or share your thoughts." Everyone laughed. By suggesting a different phrasing, she called attention to what would probably have otherwise gone unnoticed: "Leap into the fray" characterized the lively discussion as a metaphorical battle.

Americans talk about almost everything as if it were a war. A book about the history of linguistics is called *The Linguistics Wars.* A magazine article about claims that science is not completely objective is titled "The Science Wars." One about breast cancer detection is "The Mammogram War"; about competition among caterers, "Party Wars"—and on and on in a potentially endless list. Politics, of course, is a prime candidate. One of innumerable possible examples, the headline of a story reporting that the Democratic National Convention nominated Bill Clinton to run for a second term declares, "DEMOCRATS SEND CLINTON INTO BATTLE FOR A 2D TERM." But medicine is as frequent a candidate, as we talk about battling and conquering disease.

Headlines are intentionally devised to attract attention, but we all use military or attack imagery in everyday expressions without thinking about it: "Take a shot at it," "I don't want to be shot down," "He went off half cocked," "That's half the battle." Why does it matter that our public discourse is filled with military metaphors? Aren't they just words? Why not talk about something that matters—like actions?

Because words matter. When we think we are using language, language is using us. As linguist Dwight Bolinger put it (employing a military metaphor), language is like a loaded gun: It can be fired intentionally, but it can wound or kill just as surely when fired accidentally. The terms in which we talk about something shape the way we think about it—and even what we see.

The power of words to shape perception has been proven by researchers in controlled experiments. Psychologist Elizabeth Loftus and John Palmer, for example, found that the terms in which people are asked to recall something affect what they recall. The researchers showed subjects a film of two cars colliding, then asked how fast the cars were going; one week later, they asked whether there had been any broken glass. Some subjects were asked, "About how fast were the cars going when they smashed into each other?" Those who read the question with the verb "smashed" estimated that the cars were going faster. They were also more likely to "remember" having seen broken glass. (There wasn't any.)

This is how language works. It invisibly molds our way of thinking about people, actions, and the world around us. Military metaphors train us to think about—and see—everything in terms of fighting, conflict, and war. This perspective then limits our imaginations when we consider what we can do about situations we would like to understand or change.

Even in science, common metaphors that are taken for granted influence how researchers think about natural phenomena. Evelyn Fox Keller describes a case in which acceptance of a metaphor led scientists to see something that was not there. A mathematical biologist, Keller outlines the fascinating behavior of cellular slime mold. This unique mold can take two completely different forms: It can exist as single-cell organisms, or the separate cells can come together to form multicellular aggregates. The puzzle facing scientists was: What triggers aggregation? In other words, what makes the single cells join together? Scientist focused their investigations by asking what entity issued the order to start aggregating. They first called this bosslike entity a "founder cell," and later a "pacemaker cell," even though no one had seen any evidence for the existence of such a cell. Proceeding nonetheless from the assumption that such a cell must exist, they ignored evidence to the contrary: For example, when the center of the aggregate is removed, other centers form.

Scientists studying slime mold did not examine the interrelationship between the cells and their environment, nor the interrelationship between the functional systems within each cell, because they were busy looking for the pacemaker cell, which, as eventually became evident, did not exist. Instead, under conditions of nutritional deprivation, each individual cell begins to feel the urge to merge with others to form the conglomerate. It is a reaction of the cells to their environment, not to the orders of a boss. Keller recounts this tale to illustrate her insight that we tend to view nature through our understanding of human relations as hierarchical. In her words, "We risk imposing on nature the very stories we like to hear." In other words, the conceptual metaphor of hierarchical governance made scientists "see" something—a pacemaker cell—that wasn't there.

Among the stories many Americans most like to hear are war stories. According to historian Michael Sherry, the American war movie developed during World War II and has been with us ever since. He shows that movies not explicitly about war were also war movies at heart, such as westerns with their good guy–bad guy battles settled with guns. *High Noon,* for example, which became a model for later westerns, was an allegory of the Second World War: The happy ending hinges on the pacifist taking up arms. We can also see this story line in contemporary adventure films: Think of *Star Wars,* with its stirring finale in which Han Solo, having professed no interest in or taste for battle, returns at the last moment to destroy the enemy and save the day. And precisely the same theme is found in a contemporary low-budget independent film, *Sling Blade,* in which a peace-loving retarded man becomes a hero at the end by murdering the man who has been tormenting the family he has come to love.

Put Up Your Dukes

If war provides the metaphors through which we view the world and each other, we come to view others—and ourselves—as warriors in battle. Almost any human encounter can be framed as a fight between two opponents. Looking at it this way brings particular aspects of the event into focus and obscures others.

Framing interactions as fights affects not only the participants but also the viewers. At a performance, the audience, as well as the performers, can be transformed. This effect was noted by a reviewer in *The New York Times,* commenting on a musical event:

> **Showdown at Lincoln Center.** Jazz's ideological war of the last several years led to a pitched battle in August between John Lincoln Collier, the writer, and Wynton Marsalis, the trumpeter, in a debate at Lincoln Center. Mr. Marsalis demolished Mr. Collier, point after point after point, but what made the debate unpleasant was the crowd's blood lust; humiliation, not elucidation, was the desired end.

Military imagery pervades this account: the difference of opinions between Collier and Marsalis was an "ideological war," and the "debate" was a "pitched battle" in which Marsalis "demolished" Collier (not his arguments, but him). What the commentator regrets, however, is that the audience got swept up in the mood instigated by the way the debate was carried out: "the crowd's blood lust" for Collier's defeat.

This is one of the most dangerous aspects of regarding intellectual interchange as a fight. It contributes to an atmosphere of animosity that spreads like a fever. In a society that includes people who express their anger by shooting, the result of demonizing those with whom we disagree can be truly tragic.

But do audiences necessarily harbor within themselves a "blood lust," or is it stirred in them by the performances they are offered? Another arts event was set up as a debate between a playwright and a theater director. In this case, the metaphor through which the debate was viewed was not war but boxing—a sport that is in itself, like a debate, a metaphorical battle that pitches one side against the other in an all-out effort to win. A headline describing the event set the frame: "AND IN THIS CORNER . . . ," followed by the subhead "A Black Playwright and White Critic Duke It Out." The story then reports:

the face-off between August Wilson, the most successful black playwright in the American theater, and Robert Brustein, longtime drama critic for The New Republic and artistic director of the American Repertory Theatre in Cambridge, Mass. These two heavyweights had been battling in print since last June. . . .

Entering from opposite sides of the stage, the two men shook hands and came out fighting—or at least sparring.

Wilson, the article explains, had given a speech in which he opposed Black performers taking "white" roles in color-blind casting; Brustein had written a column disagreeing; and both followed up with further responses to each other.

According to the article, "The drama of the Wilson-Brustein confrontation lies in their mutual intransigence." No one would question that audiences crave drama. But is intransigence the most appealing source of drama? I happened to hear this debate broadcast on the radio. The line that triggered the loudest cheers from the audience was the final question put to the two men by the moderator, Anna Deavere Smith: "What did you each learn from the other in this debate?" The loud applause was evidence that the audience did not crave intransigence. They wanted to see another kind of drama: the drama of change—change that comes from genuinely listening to someone with a different point of view, not the transitory drama of two intransigent positions in stalemate.

To encourage the staging of more dramas of change and fewer of intransigence, we need new metaphors to supplement and complement the pervasive war and boxing match metaphors through which we take it for granted issues and events are best talked about and viewed.

Mud Splatters

Our fondness for the fight scenario leads us to frame many complex human interactions as a battle between two sides. This then shapes the way we understand what happened and how we regard the participants. One unfortunate result is that fights make a mess in which everyone is muddied. The person attacked is often deemed just as guilty as the attacker.

The injustice of this is clear if you think back to childhood. Many of us still harbor anger as we recall a time (or many times) a sibling or playmate started a fight—but both of us got blamed. Actions occur in a stream, each a response to what came before. Where you punctuate them can change their meaning just as you can change the meaning of a sentence by punctuating it in one place or another.

Like a parent despairing of trying to sort out which child started a fight, people often respond to those involved in a public dispute as if both were equally guilty. When champion figure skater Nancy Kerrigan was struck on the knee shortly before the 1994 Olympics in Norway and the then-husband of another champion skater, Tonya Harding, implicated his wife in planning the attack, the event was characterized as a fight between two skaters that obscured their differing roles. As both skaters headed for the Olympic competition, their potential meeting

was described as a "long-anticipated figure-skating shootout." Two years later, the event was referred to not as "the attack on Nancy Kerrigan" but as "the rivalry surrounding Tonya Harding and Nancy Kerrigan."

By a similar process, the Senate Judiciary Committee hearings to consider the nomination of Clarence Thomas for Supreme Court justice at which Anita Hill was called to testify are regularly referred to as the "Hill-Thomas hearings," obscuring the very different roles played by Hill and Thomas. Although testimony by Anita Hill was the occasion for reopening the hearings, they were still the Clarence Thomas confirmation hearings: Their purpose was to evaluate Thomas's candidacy. Framing these hearings as a two-sides dispute between Hill and Thomas allowed the senators to focus their investigation on cross-examining Hill rather than seeking other sorts of evidence, for example by consulting experts on sexual harassment to ascertain whether Hill's account seemed plausible.

Slash-and-Burn Thinking

Approaching situations like warriors in battle leads to the assumption that intellectual inquiry, too, is a game of attack, counterattack, and self-defense. In this spirit, critical thinking is synonymous with criticizing. In many classrooms, students are encouraged to read someone's life work, then rip it to shreds. Though criticism is one form of critical thinking—and an essential one—so are integrating ideas from disparate fields and examining the context out of which ideas grew. Opposition does not lead to the whole truth when we ask only "What's wrong with this?" and never "What can we use from this in building a new theory, a new understanding?"

There are many ways that unrelenting criticism is destructive in itself. In innumerable small dramas mirroring what happened to Robert Gallo (but on a much more modest scale), our most creative thinkers can waste time and effort responding to critics motivated less by a genuine concern about weaknesses in their work than by a desire to find something to attack. All of society loses when creative people are discouraged from their pursuits by unfair criticism. (This is particularly likely to happen since, as Kay Redfield Jamison shows in her book Touched with Fire, many of those who are unusually creative are also unusually sensitive; their sensitivity often drives their creativity.)

If the criticism is unwarranted, many will say, you are free to argue against it, to defend yourself. But there are problems with this, too. Not only does self-defense take time and draw off energy that would better be spent on new creative work, but any move to defend yourself makes you appear, well, defensive. For example, when an author wrote a letter to the editor protesting a review he considered unfair, the reviewer (who is typically given the last word) turned the very fact that the author defended himself into a weapon with which to attack again. The reviewer's response began, "I haven't much time to waste on the kind of writer who squanders his talent drafting angry letters to reviewers."

The argument culture limits the information we get rather than broadening it in another way. When a certain kind of interaction is the norm, those who feel comfortable with that type of interaction are drawn to participate, and those who do not feel comfortable with it recoil and go elsewhere. If public discourse included a broad range of types, we would be making room for individuals with different temperaments to take part and contribute their perspectives and insights. But when debate, opposition, and fights overwhelmingly predominate, those who enjoy verbal sparring are likely to take part—by calling in to talk shows, writing letters to the editor or articles, becoming journalists—and those who cannot comfortably take part in oppositional discourse, or do not wish to, are likely to opt out.

This winnowing process is easy to see in apprenticeship programs such as acting school, law school, and graduate school. A woman who was identified in her university drama program as showing exceptional promise was encouraged to go to New York to study acting. Full of enthusiasm, she was accepted by a famous acting school where the teaching method entailed the teacher screaming at students, goading and insulting them as a way to bring out the best in them. This worked well with many of the students but not with her. Rather than rising to the occasion when attacked, she cringed, becoming less able to draw on her talent, not more. After a year, she dropped out. It could be that she simply didn't have what it took—but this will never be known, because the adversarial style of teaching did not allow her to show what talent she had.

Polarizing Complexity: Nature or Nurture?

Few issues come with two neat, and neatly opposed, sides. Again, I have seen this in the domain of gender. One common polarization is an opposition between two sources of differences between women and men: "culture," or "nurture," on one hand and "biology," or "nature," on the other.

Shortly after the publication of *You Just Don't Understand,* I was asked by a journalist what question I most often encountered about women's and men's conversational styles. I told her, "Whether the differences I describe are biological or cultural." The journalist laughed. Puzzled, I asked why this made her laugh. She explained that she had always been so certain that any significant differences are cultural rather than biological in origin that the question struck her as absurd. So I should not have been surprised when I read, in the article she wrote, that the two questions I am most frequently asked are "Why do women nag?" and "Why won't men ask for directions?" Her ideological certainty that the question I am most frequently asked was absurd led her to ignore my answer and get a fact wrong in her report of my experience.

Some people are convinced that any significant differences between men and women are entirely or overwhelmingly due to cultural influences—the way we treat girls and boys, and men's dominance of women in society. Others are convinced that any significant differences are entirely or overwhelmingly due to biology: the physical facts of female and male bodies, hormones, and reproductive functions. Many problems are caused by framing the question as a dichotomy: Are behaviors that pattern by sex biological or cultural? This polarization encourages those on

one side to demonize those who take the other view, which leads in turn to misrepresenting the work of those who are assigned to the opposing camp. Finally, and most devastatingly, it prevents us from exploring the interaction of biological and cultural factors—factors that must, and can only, be understood together. By posing the question as either/or, we reinforce a false assumption that biological and cultural factors are separable and preclude the investigations that would help us understand their interrelationship. When a problem is posed in a way that polarizes, the solution is often obscured before the search is under way.

Who's Up? Who's Down?

Related to polarization is another aspect of the argument culture: our obsession with ratings and rankings. Magazines offer the 10, 50, or 100 best of everything: restaurants, mutual funds, hospitals, even judges. Newsmagazines tell us Who's up, Who's down, as in *Newsweek*'s "Conventional Wisdom Watch" and *Time*'s "Winners and Losers." Rankings and ratings pit restaurants, products, schools, and people against each other on a single scale, obscuring the myriad differences among them. Maybe a small Thai restaurant in one neighborhood can't really be compared to a pricey French one in another, any more than judges with a vast range of abilities and beliefs can be compared on a single scale. And timing can skew results: Ohio State University protested to *Time* magazine when its football team was ranked at the bottom of a scale because only 29 percent of the team graduated. The year before it would have ranked among the top six with 72 percent.

After a political debate, analysts comment not on what the candidates said but on the question "Who won?" After the president delivers an important speech, such as the State of the Union Address, expert commentators are asked to give it a grade. Like ranking, grading establishes a competition. The biggest problem with asking what grade the president's speech deserves, or who won and who lost a campaign debate, is what is not asked and is therefore not answered: What was said, and what is the significance of this for the country?

An Ethic of Aggression

In an argument culture aggressive tactics are valued for their own sake. For example, a woman called in to a talk show on which I was a guest to say, "When I'm in a place where a man is smoking, and there's a no-smoking sign, instead of saying to him 'You aren't allowed to smoke in here. Put that out,' I say, 'I'm awfully sorry, but I have asthma, so your smoking makes it hard for me to breathe. Would you mind terribly not smoking?' Whenever I say this, the man is extremely polite and solicitous, and he puts his cigarette out, and I say, 'Oh, thank you, thank you!' as if he's done a wonderful thing for me. Why do I do that?"

I think this woman expected me to say that she needs assertiveness training to learn to confront smokers in a more aggressive manner. Instead, I told her that there was nothing wrong with her style of getting the man to stop smoking. She gave him a face-saving way of doing what she asked, one that allowed him to feel chivalrous rather than chastised. This is kind to him, but it is also kind to herself, since it is more likely to lead to the result she desires. If she tried to alter his behavior by reminding him of the rules, he might well rebel: "Who made you the enforcer? Mind your own business!" Indeed, who gives any of us the authority to set others straight when we think they're breaking rules?

Another caller disagreed with me, saying the first caller's style was "self-abasing" and there was no reason for her to use it. But I persisted: There is nothing necessarily destructive about conventional self-effacement. Human relations depend on the agreement to use such verbal conventions. I believe the mistake this caller was making—a mistake many of us make—was to confuse *ritual* self-effacement with the literal kind. All human relations require us to find ways to get what we want from others without seeming to dominate them. Allowing others to feel they are doing what you want for a reason less humiliating to them fulfills this need.

Thinking of yourself as the wronged party who is victimized by a lawbreaking boor makes it harder to see the value of this method. But suppose you are the person addicted to smoking who lights up (knowingly or not) in a no-smoking zone. Would you like strangers to yell at you to stop smoking, or would you rather be allowed to save face by being asked politely to stop in order to help them out? Or imagine yourself having broken a rule inadvertently (which is not to imply rules are broken only by mistake; it is only to say that sometimes they are). Would you like some stranger to swoop down on you and begin berating you, or would you rather be asked politely to comply?

As this example shows, conflicts can sometimes be resolved without confrontational tactics, but current conventional wisdom often devalues less confrontational tactics even if they work well, favoring more aggressive strategies even if they get less favorable results. It's as if we value a fight for its own sake, not for its effectiveness in resolving disputes.

This ethic shows up in many contexts. In a review of a contentious book, for example, a reviewer wrote, "Always provocative, sometimes infuriating, this collection reminds us that the purpose of art is not to confirm and coddle but to provoke and confront." This false dichotomy encapsulates the belief that if you are not provoking and confronting, then you are conforming and coddling—as if there weren't myriad other ways to question and learn. What about exploring, exposing, delving, analyzing, understanding, moving, connecting, integrating, illuminating . . . or any of innumerable verbs that capture other aspects of what art can do?

The Broader Picture

The increasingly adversarial spirit of our contemporary lives is fundamentally related to a phenomenon that has been much remarked upon in recent years: the breakdown of a sense of community. In this spirit, distinguished journalist and author Orville Schell points out that in his day journalists routinely based their writing on a sense of connection to their subjects—and that this sense of connection is missing from much that is written by journalists today. Quite the contrary, a spirit of demonography

often prevails that has just the opposite effect: Far from encouraging us to feel connected to the subjects, it encourages us to feel critical, superior—and, as a result, distanced. The cumulative effect is that citizens feel more and more cut off from the people in public life they read about.

The argument culture dovetails with a general disconnection and breakdown of community in another way as well. Community norms and pressures exercise a restraint on the expression of hostility and destruction. Many cultures have rituals to channel and contain aggressive impulses, especially those of adolescent males. In just this spirit, at the 1996 Republican National Convention, both Colin Powell and Bob Dole talked about growing up in small communities where everyone knew who they were. This meant that many people would look out for them, but also that if they did something wrong, it would get back to their parents. Many Americans grew up in ethnic neighborhoods that worked the same way. If a young man stole something, committed vandalism, or broke a rule or law, it would be reported to his relatives, who would punish him or tell him how his actions were shaming the family. American culture today often lacks these brakes.

Community is a blend of connections and authority, and we are losing both. As Robert Bly shows in his book by that title, we now have a *Sibling Society:* Citizens are like squabbling siblings with no authority figures who can command enough respect to contain and channel their aggressive impulses. It is as if every day is a day with a substitute teacher who cannot control the class and maintain order.

The argument culture is both a product of and a contributor to this alienation, separating people, disconnecting them from each other and from those who are or might have been their leaders.

What Other Way Is There?

Philosopher John Dewey said, on his ninetieth birthday, "Democracy begins in conversation." I fear that it gets derailed in polarized debate.

In conversation we form the interpersonal ties that bind individuals together in personal relationships; in public discourse, we form similar ties on a larger scale, binding individuals into a community. In conversation, we exchange the many types of information we need to live our lives as members of a community. In public discourse, we exchange the information that citizens in a democracy need in order to decide how to vote. If public discourse provides entertainment first and foremost—and if entertainment is first and foremost watching fights—then citizens do not get the information they need to make meaningful use of their right to vote.

Of course it is the responsibility of intellectuals to explore potential weaknesses in others' arguments, and of journalists to represent serious opposition when it exists. But when opposition becomes the overwhelming avenue of inquiry—a formula that *requires* another side to be found or a criticism to be voiced; when the lust for opposition privileges extreme views and obscures complexity; when our eagerness to find weaknesses blinds us to strengths; when the atmosphere of animosity precludes respect and poisons our relations with one another; then the argument culture is doing more damage than good.

I offer this book not as a formal assault in the argument culture. That would be in the spirit of attack that I am questioning. It is an attempt to examine the argument culture—our use of attack, opposition, and debate in public discourse—to ask, What are its limits as well as its strengths? How has it served us well, but also how has it failed us? How is it related to culture and gender? What other options do we have?

I do not believe we should put aside the argument model of public discourse entirely, but we need to rethink whether this is the *only* way, or *always* the best way, to carry out our affairs. A step toward broadening our repertoires would be to pioneer reform by experimenting with metaphors other than sports and war, and with formats other than debate for framing the exchange of ideas. The change might be as simple as introducing a plural form. Instead of asking "What's the other side?" we might ask instead, "What are the other sides?" Instead of insisting on hearing "both sides," we might insist on hearing "all sides."

Another option is to expand our notion of "debate" to include more dialogue. This does not mean there can be no negativity, criticism, or disagreement. It simply means we can be more creative in our ways of managing all of these, which are inevitable and useful. In dialogue, each statement that one person makes is qualified by a statement made by someone else, until the series of statements and qualifications moves everyone closer to a fuller truth. Dialogue does not preclude negativity. Even saying "I agree" makes sense only against the background assumption that you might disagree. In dialogue, there is opposition, yes, but no head-on collision. Smashing heads does not open minds.

There are times when we need to disagree, criticize, oppose, and attack—to hold debates and view issues as polarized battles. Even cooperation, after all, is not the absence of conflict but a means of managing conflict. My goal is not a make-nice false veneer of agreement or a dangerous ignoring of true opposition. I'm questioning the *automatic* use of adversarial formats—the assumption that it's *always* best to address problems and issues by fighting over them. I'm hoping for a broader repertoire of ways to talk to each other and address issues vital to us.

Notes

Note: Sources referred to by short form are cited in full in the References.

[Numbers indicate page numbers of original document. Ed]

7. *"culture of critique"*: I first introduced this term in an op-ed essay, "The Triumph of the Yell," *The New York Times,* Jan. 14, 1994, p. A29.

7. *"There are moments"*: Charles Simic, "In Praise of Invective," *Harper's,* Aug. 1997, pp. 24, 26–27; the quote is from p. 26. The article is excerpted from *Orphan Factory* (Ann Arbor: University of Michigan Press, 1997). I am grateful to Amitai Etizioni for calling this article to my attention.

8. Both the term "agonism" and the phrase "programmed contentiousness" come from Walter Ong, *Fighting for Life.*

10. *"the great backpacking vs. car camping debate"*: Steven Hendrix, "Hatchback vs. Backpack," *The Washington Post Weekend,* Mar. 1, 1996, p. 6.

11. *creationism:* See, for example, Jessica Mathews, "Creationism Makes a Comeback," *The Washington Post,* Apr. 8, 1996, p. A21.

11. *"People dispute that"*: Lipstadt, *Denying the Holocaust,* p. 15. Lipstadt cites *Esquire,* Feb. 1983, for the interview with Mitchum.

12. *Gallo had to spend:* See Nicholas Wade, "Method and Madness: The Vindication of Robert Gallo," *The New York Times Magazine,* Dec. 26, 1993, p. 12, and Elaine Richman, "The Once and Future King," *The Sciences,* Nov.–Dec. 1996, pp. 12–15. The investigations of Gallo were among a series of overly zealous investigations of suspected scientific misconduct—all of which ended in the exoneration of the accused, but not before they had caused immense personal anguish and professional setbacks. Others similarly victimized were Gallo's colleague Mike Popovic, immunologist Thereza Imanishi-Kari, and her coauthor (not accused of wrongdoing but harmed as a result of his defense of her), Nobel Prize winner David Baltimore. On Popovic, see Malcolm Gladwell, "Science Friction," *The Washington Post Magazine,* Dec. 6, 1992, pp. 18–21, 49–51. On Imanishi-Kari and Baltimore, see *The New Yorker,* May 27, 1996, pp. 94–98ff.

14. *potentially endless list:* Randy Allen Harris, *The Linguistics Wars* (New York: Oxford University Press, 1993); "The Science Wars," *Newsweek,* Apr. 21, 1997, p. 54; "The Mammogram War," *Newsweek,* Feb. 24, 1997, p. 54; "Party Wars," *New York,* June 2, 1997, cover. The subhead of the latter reads, "In the battle to feed New York's elite, the top caterers are taking off their white gloves and sharpening their knives."

14. *"DEMOCRATS SEND CLINTON"*: *The New York Times,* Aug. 29, 1996, p. A1.

15. *"We risk imposing"*: Keller, *Reflections on Gender and Science,* p. 157. Another such case is explained by paleontologist Stephen Jay Gould in his book *Wonderful Life* about the Burgess shale—a spectacular deposit of 530-million-year-old fossils. In 1909, the first scientist to study these fossils missed the significance of the find, because he "shoehorned every last Burgess animal into a modern group, viewing the fauna collectively as a set of primitive or ancestral versions of later, improved forms" (p. 24). Years later, observers looked at the Burgess shale fossils with a fresh eye and saw a very different reality: a panoply of life forms, far more diverse and numerous than what exists today. The early scientists missed what was right before their eyes because, Gould shows, they proceeded from a metaphoric understanding of evolution as a linear march of progress from the ancient and primitive to the modern and complex, with humans the inevitable, most complex apex. Accepting the metaphor of "the cone of increasing diversity" prevented the early scientists from seeing what was really there.

16. *"Showdown at Lincoln Center"*: Peter Watrous, "The Year in the Arts: Pop & Jazz/1994," *The New York Times,* Dec. 25, 1994, sec. 2, p. 36.

17. *"the face-off between"*: Jack Kroll, "And in This Corner . . . ," *Newsweek,* Feb. 10, 1997, p. 65.

18. *a fight between two skaters:* Though Harding was demonized somewhat more as an unfeminine, boorish "Wicked Witch of the West" (George Vecsey, "Let's Begin the Legal Olympics," *The New York Times,* Feb. 13, 1994, sec. 8, p. 1.), Kerrigan was also demonized as cold and aloof, an "ice princess."

18. *"long-anticipated figure-skating shootout"*: Jere Longman, "Kerrigan Glides Through Compulsory Interviews," *The New York Times,* Feb. 13, 1994, sec. 8, p. 9.

18. *"the rivalry surrounding"*: Paul Farhi, "For NBC, Games Not Just for Guys; Network Tailors Its Coverage to Entice Women to Watch," *The Washington Post,* July 26, 1996, p. A1.

20. *"I haven't time"*: *The Washington Post Book World,* June 16, 1996, p. 14.

21. *even judges: Washingtonian,* June 1996, ranked judges.

22. *Ohio State University protested:* Letter to the editor by Malcolm S. Baroway, Executive Director, University Communications, *Time,* Oct. 3, 1994, p. 14.

22. Overlaid on the talk show example is the gender issue: The woman who called wished she had the courage to stand up to a man and saw her habitual way of speaking as evidence of her insecurity. This interpretation is suggested by our assumptions about women and men. Many people, researchers included, start from the assumption that women are insecure, so ways they speak are scrutinized for evidence of insecurity. The result is often a failure to understand or appreciate women's styles on their own terms, so women are misinterpreted as defective men.

23. *"Always provocative, sometimes infuriating"*: Jill Nelson, "Fighting Words," review of Ishmael Reed, *Airing Dirty Laundry, The New York Times Book Review,* Feb. 13, 1994, p. 28.

24. *In this spirit:* John Krich, "To Teach Is Glorious: A Conversation with the New Dean of Cal's Journalism School," Orville Schell, *Express,* Aug. 23, 1996, pp. 1, 14–16, 18, 20–22. The remark is from p. 15.

24. *Many cultures have rituals:* See Schlegel and Barry, *Adolescence.*

25. *"Democracy begins in conversation"*: *Dialogue on John Dewey,* Corliss Lamont, ed. (New York: Horizon Press, 1959), p. 88. Thanks to Pete Becker for this reference.

26. *In dialogue, there is:* This insight comes from Walter Ong, who writes, "There is opposition here but no head-on collision, which stops dialogue. (Of course, sometimes dialogue has to be stopped, but that is another story.)" (*Fighting for Life,* p. 32).

References

Gould, Stephen Jay. *Wonderful Life: The Burgess Shale and the Nature of History* (New York: W. W. Norton, 1989).

Keller, Evelyn Fox. *Reflections on Gender and Science* (New Haven: Yale University Press, 1985).

Krich, John. "To Teach Is Glorious: A Conversation with the New Dean of Cal's Journalism School, Orville Schell." *Express,* Aug. 23, 1996, pp. 1, 14–16, 18, 20–22.

Lipstadt, Deborah. *Denying the Holocaust: The Growing Assault on Truth and Memory* (New York: Free Press, 1993).

Ong, Walter J. *Fighting for Life: Contest, Sexuality, and Consciousness* (Ithaca, N.Y.: Cornell University Press, 1981).

Schlegel, Alice, and Herbert Barry III. *Adolescence: An Anthropological Inquiry* (New York: Free Press, 1991).

DEBORAH TANNEN is best known as the author of *You Just Don't Understand: Women and Men in Conversation,* which was on *The New York Times* bestseller list for nearly four years, including eight months as number one, and has been translated into twenty-four languages. Her book, *Talking from 9 to 5: Women and Men in the Workplace: Language, Sex, and Power,* was a *New York Times* Business bestseller. She has written for and been featured in *The New York Times, Newsweek, Time, USA Today, People,* and *The Washington Post.* Her many national television and radio appearances include *20/20, 48 Hours,* CBS *News,* ABC *World News Tonight,* and *Good Morning America.* She is one of only three University Professors at Georgetown University in Washington, D.C., where she is on the Linguistics Department faculty. *The Argument Culture* is her sixteenth book.

Deborah Tannen has also published short stories, essays, and poems. Her first play, *An Act of Devotion,* is included in *Best Short Plays 1993–1994.* It was produced, together with her play *Sisters,* by Horizons Theatre in Arlington, VA.

"I Can't Even Open My Mouth"
Separating Messages from Metamessages in Family Talk

DEBORAH TANNEN

"Do you really need another piece of cake?" Donna asks George.

"You bet I do," he replies, with that edge to his voice that implies, "If I wasn't sure I needed it before, I am darned sure now."

Donna feels hamstrung. She knows that George is going to say later that he wished he hadn't had that second piece of cake.

"Why are you always watching what I eat?" George asks.

"I was just watching out for you," Donna replies. "I only say it because I love you."

Elizabeth, in her late twenties, is happy to be making Thanksgiving dinner for her extended family in her own home. Her mother, who is visiting, is helping out in the kitchen. As Elizabeth prepares the stuffing for the turkey, her mother remarks, "Oh, you put onions in the stuffing?"

Feeling suddenly as if she were sixteen years old again, Elizabeth turns on her mother and says, "*I'm* making the stuffing, Mom. Why do you have to criticize everything I do?"

"I didn't criticize," her mother replies. "I just asked a question. What's got into you? I can't even open my mouth."

The allure of family—which is, at heart, the allure of love—is to have someone who knows you so well that you don't have to explain yourself. It is the promise of someone who cares enough about you to protect you against the world of strangers who do not wish you well. Yet, by an odd and cruel twist, it is the family itself that often causes pain. Those we love are looking at us so close-up that they see all our blemishes—see them as if through a magnifying glass. Family members have innumerable opportunities to witness our faults and feel they have a right to point them out. Often their intention is to help us improve. They feel, as Donna did, "I only say it because I love you."

Family members also have a long shared history, so everything we say in a conversation today echoes with meanings from the past. If you have a tendency to be late, your parent, sibling, or spouse may say, "We have to leave at eight"—and then add, "It's really important. Don't be late. Please start your shower at seven, not seven-thirty!" These extra injunctions are demeaning and interfering, but they are based on experience. At the same time, having experienced negative judgments in the past, we develop a sixth sense to sniff out criticism in almost anything a loved one says—even an innocent question about ingredients in the stuffing. That's why Elizabeth's mother ends up feeling as if she can't even open her mouth—and Elizabeth ends up feeling criticized.

When we are children our family constitutes the world. When we grow up, family members—not only our spouses but also our grown-up children and adult sisters and brothers—keep this larger-than-life aura. We overreact to their judgments because it feels as if they were handed down by the Supreme Court and are unassailable assessments of our value as human beings. We bristle because these judgments seem unjust; or because we sense a kernel of truth we would rather not face; or because we fear that if someone who knows us so well judges us harshly we must really be guilty, so we risk losing not only that person's love but everyone else's, too. Along with this heavy load of implications comes a dark resentment that a loved one is judging us at all—and has such power to wound.

"I still fight with my father," a man who had reached a high position in journalism said to me. "He's been dead twenty-one years." I asked for an example. "He'd tell me that I had to comb my hair and dress better, that I'd learn when I grew up that appearance is important." When he said this I noticed that his hair was uncombed, and the tails of his faded shirt were creeping out from the waist of his pants. He went on, "I told him I'd ignore that. And now sometimes when I'm going somewhere important, I'll look in the mirror and think—I'll say to him in my mind, 'See? I *am* a success and it didn't matter.'"

This man's "fights" with his father are about approval. No matter what age we've reached, no matter whether our parents are alive or dead, whether we were close to them or not, there are times when theirs are the eyes through which we view ourselves, theirs the standards against which we measure ourselves when we wonder whether we have measured up. The criticism of parents carries extra weight, even when children are adults.

I Care, Therefore I Criticize

Some family members feel they have not only a right but an obligation to tell you when they think you're doing something wrong. A woman from Thailand recalls that when she was in her late teens and early twenties, her mother frequently had talks with her in which she tried to set her daughter straight. "At the end of each lecture," the woman says, "my mother would always tell me, 'I have to complain about you because I am your mother and I love you. Nobody else will talk to you the way I do because they don't care.'"

It sometimes seems that family members operate under the tenet "I care, therefore I criticize." To the one who is being told to do things differently, what comes through loudest and clearest is the criticism. But the one offering suggestions and judgments is usually focused on the caring. A mother, for example, was expressing concern about her daughter's boyfriend: He didn't have a serious job, he didn't seem to want one, and she didn't think he was a good prospect for marriage. The daughter protested that her mother disapproved of everyone she dated. Her mother responded indignantly, "Would you rather I didn't care?"

As family members we wonder why our parents, children, siblings, and spouses are so critical of us. But as family members we also feel frustrated because comments we make in the spirit of caring are taken as criticizing.

Both sentiments are explained by the double meaning of giving advice: a loving sign of caring, a hurtful sign of criticizing. It's impossible to say which is right; both meanings are there. Sorting out the ambiguous meanings of caring and criticizing is difficult because language works on two levels: the message and the metamessage. Separating these levels—and being aware of both—is crucial to improving communication in the family.

The Intimate Critic: When Metamessages Hurt

Because those closest to us have front-row seats to view our faults, we quickly react—sometimes overreact—to any hint of criticism. The result can be downright comic, as in Phyllis Richman's novel *Who's Afraid of Virginia Ham?* One scene, a conversation between the narrator and her adult daughter, Lily, shows how criticism can be the metronome providing the beat for the family theme song. The dialogue goes like this:

LILY: Am I too critical of people?

MOTHER: What people? Me?

LILY: Mamma, don't be so self-centered.

MOTHER: Lily, don't be so critical.

LILY: I knew it. You do think I'm critical. Mamma, why do you always have to find something wrong with me?

The mother then protests that it was Lily who asked if she was too critical, and now she's criticizing her mother for answering. Lily responds, "I can't follow this. Sometimes you're impossibly hard to talk to."

It turns out that Lily is upset because her boyfriend, Brian, told her she is too critical of him. She made a great effort to stop criticizing, but now she's having a hard time keeping her resolve. He gave her a sexy outfit for her birthday—it's expensive and beautiful—but the generous gift made her angry because she took it as criticism of the way she usually dresses.

In this brief exchange Richman captures the layers of meaning that can make the most well-intentioned comment or action a source of conflict and hurt among family members. Key to understanding why Lily finds the conversation so hard to follow—and her mother so hard to talk to—is separating messages from metamessages. The *message* is the meaning of the words and sentences spoken, what anyone with a dictionary and a grammar book could figure out. Two people in a conversation usually agree on what the message is. The *metamessage* is meaning that is not said—at least not in so many words—but that we glean from every aspect of context: the way something is said, who is saying it, or the fact that it is said at all.

Because they do not reside in the words themselves, metamessages are hard to deal with. Yet they are often the source of both comfort and hurt. The message (as I've said) is the word meaning while the metamessage is the heart meaning—the meaning that we react to most strongly, that triggers emotion.

When Lily asked her mother if she was too critical of people, the message was a question about Lily's own personality. But her mother responded to what she perceived as the metamessage: that Lily was feeling critical of *her*. This was probably based on experience: Her daughter had been critical of her in the past. If Lily had responded to the message alone, she would have answered, "No, not you. I was thinking of Brian." But she, too, is reacting to a metamessage—that her mother had made herself the point of a comment that was not about her mother at all. Perhaps Lily's resentment was also triggered because her mother still looms so large in her life.

The mixing up of message and metamessage also explains Lily's confused response to the gift of sexy clothing from her boyfriend. The message is the gift. But what made Lily angry was what she thought the gift implied: that Brian finds the way she usually dresses not sexy enough—and unattractive. This implication is the metamessage, and it is what made Lily critical of the gift, of Brian, and of herself. Metamessages speak louder than messages, so this is what Lily reacted to most strongly.

It's impossible to know whether Brian intended this metamessage. It's possible that he wishes Lily would dress differently; it's also possible that he likes the way she dresses just fine but simply thought this particular outfit would look good on her. That's what makes metamessages so difficult to pinpoint and talk about: They're implicit, not explicit.

When we talk about messages, we are talking about the meanings of words. But when we talk about metamessages, we are talking about relationships. And when family members react to each other's comments, it's metamessages they are usually responding to. Richman's dialogue is funny because it shows how we all get confused between messages and metamessages when we talk to those we are close to. But when it happens in the context of a relationship we care about, our reactions often lead to hurt rather than to humor.

In all the conversations that follow, both in this chapter and throughout the book, a key to improving relationships within the family is distinguishing the message from the metamessage, and being clear about which one you are reacting to. One way you can do this is *metacommunicating*—talking about communication.

"What's Wrong with French Bread?" Try Metacommunicating

The movie *Divorce American Style* begins with Debbie Reynolds and Dick Van Dyke preparing for dinner guests—and arguing. She lodges a complaint: that all he does is criticize. He protests that he doesn't. She says she can't discuss it right then because she has to take the French bread out of the oven. He asks, "French bread?"

A simple question, right? Not even a question, just an observation. But on hearing it Debbie Reynolds turns on him, hands on hips, ready for battle: "What's wrong with French bread?" she asks, her voice full of challenge.

"Nothing," he says, all innocence. "It's just that I really like those little dinner rolls you usually make." This is like the bell that sets in motion a boxing match, which is stopped by another bell—the one at the front door announcing their guests have arrived.

Did he criticize or didn't he? On the message level, no. He simply asked a question to confirm what type of bread she was preparing. But on the metamessage level, yes. If he were satisfied with her choice of bread, he would not comment, except perhaps to compliment. Still, you might ask, So what? So what if he prefers the dinner rolls she usually makes to French bread? Why is it such a big deal? The big deal is explained by her original complaint: She feels that he is *always* criticizing—always telling her to do things differently than she chose to do them.

The big deal, in a larger sense, is a paradox of family: We depend on those closest to us to see our best side, and often they do. But because they are so close, they also see our worst side. You want the one you love to be an intimate ally who reassures you that you're doing things right, but sometimes you find instead an intimate critic who implies, time and again, that you're doing things wrong. It's the cumulative effect of minor, innocent suggestions that creates major problems. You will never work things out if you continue to talk about the message—about French bread versus dinner rolls—rather than the metamessage—the implication that your partner is dissatisfied with everything you do. (*Divorce American Style* was made in 1967; that it still rings true today is evidence of how common—and how recalcitrant—such conversational quagmires are.)

One way to approach a dilemma like this is to *metacommunicate*—to talk about ways of talking. He might *say* that he feels he can't open his mouth to make a suggestion or comment because she takes everything as criticism. She might *say* that she feels he's always dissatisfied with what she does, rather than turn on him in a challenging way. Once they both understand this dynamic, they will come up with their own ideas about how to address it. For example, he might decide to preface his question with a disclaimer: "I'm not criticizing the French bread." Or maybe he *does* want to make a request—a direct one—that she please make dinner rolls because he likes

them. They might also set a limit on how many actions of hers he can question in a day. The important thing is to talk about the metamessage she is reacting to: that having too many of her actions questioned makes her feel that her partner in life has changed into an in-house inspection agent, on the lookout for wrong moves.

Living with the Recycling Police

"This is recyclable," Helen exclaims, brandishing a small gray cylinder that was once at the center of a roll of toilet paper. There she stops, as if the damning evidence is sufficient to rest her case.

"I know it's recyclable," says Samuel. "You don't have to tell me." He approves of recycling and generally practices it, if not quite as enthusiastically (he would say obsessively) as Helen. But this time he slipped: In a moment of haste he tossed the cardboard toilet paper tube into the wastebasket. Now Helen has found it and wants to know why it was there. "You can't go through the garbage looking for things I threw away," Samuel protests. "Our relationship is more important than a toilet paper carcass."

"I'm not talking about our relationship," Helen protests. "I'm talking about recycling."

Helen was right: She *was* talking about recycling. But Samuel was right, too. If you feel like you're living with the recycling police—or the diet police, or the neatness police—someone who assumes the role of judge of your actions and repeatedly finds you guilty—it takes the joy out of living together. Sometimes it even makes you wish, for a fleeting moment, that you lived alone, in peace. In that sense, Samuel was talking about the relationship.

Helen was focusing on the message: the benefits of recycling. Samuel was focusing on the metamessage: the implication he perceives that Helen is enforcing rules and telling him he broke one. Perhaps, too, he is reacting to the metamessage of moral superiority in Helen's being the more fervent recycler. Because messages lie in words, Helen's position is more obviously defensible. But it's metamessages that have clout, because they stir emotions, and emotions are the currency of relationships.

In understanding Samuel's reaction, it's also crucial to bear in mind that the meaning of Helen's remark resides not just in the conversation of the moment but in the resonance of all the conversations on the subject they've had in their years together—as well as the conversations Samuel had before that, especially while growing up in his own family. Furthermore, it's her *repeatedly* remarking on what he does or does not recycle that gives Samuel the impression that living with Helen is like living with the recycling police.

Give Me Connection, Give Me Control

There is another dimension to this argument—another aspect of communication that complicates everything we say to each other but that is especially powerful in families. That is our simultaneous but conflicting desires for connection and for control.

In her view Helen is simply calling her husband's attention to a small oversight in their mutual pursuit of a moral good—an expression of their connection. Their shared policy on recycling reflects their shared life: his trash is her trash. But Samuel feels that by installing herself as the judge of his actions, she is placing herself one-up. In protest he accuses, "You're trying to control me."

Both connection and control are at the heart of family. There is no relationship as close—and none as deeply hierarchical—as the relationship between parent and child, or between older and younger sibling. To understand what goes on when family members talk to each other, you have to understand how the forces of connection and control reflect both closeness and hierarchy in a family.

"He's like family," my mother says of someone she likes. Underlying this remark is the assumption that *family* connotes closeness, being connected to each other. We all seek connection: It makes us feel safe; it makes us feel loved. But being close means you care about what those you are close to think. Whatever you do has an impact on them, so you have to take their needs and preferences into account. This gives them power to control your actions, limiting your independence and making you feel hemmed in.

Parents and older siblings have power over children and younger siblings as a result of their age and their roles in the family. At the same time, *ways of talking create power.* Younger siblings or children can make life wonderful or miserable for older siblings or parents by what they say—or refuse to say. Some family members increase their chances of getting their way by frequently speaking up, or by speaking more loudly and more forcefully. Some increase their influence by holding their tongues, so others become more and more concerned about winning them over.

"Don't tell me what to do. Don't try to control me" are frequent protests within families. It is automatic for many of us to think in terms of power relations and to see others' incursions on our freedom as control maneuvers. We are less likely to think of them as connection maneuvers, but they often are that, too. At every moment we're struggling not only for control but also for love, approval, and involvement. What's tough is that the *same* actions and comments can be either control maneuvers or connection maneuvers—or, as in most cases, both at once.

Control Maneuver or Connection Maneuver?

"Don't start eating yet," Louis says to Claudia as he walks out of the kitchen. "I'll be right there."

Famished, Claudia eyes the pizza before her. The aroma of tomato sauce and melted cheese is so sweet, her mouth thinks she has taken a bite. But Louis, always slow-moving, does not return, and the pizza is cooling. Claudia feels a bit like their dog Muffin when she was being trained: "Wait!" the instructor told Muffin, as the hungry dog poised pitifully beside her bowl of food. After pausing long enough to be convinced Muffin would wait forever, the trainer would say, "Okay!" Only then would Muffin fall into the food.

Was Louis intentionally taking his time in order to prove he could make Claudia wait no matter how hungry she was? Or was he just eager for them to sit down to dinner together? In other words, when he said, "Don't start eating yet," was it a control maneuver, to make her adjust to his pace and timing, or a connection maneuver, to preserve their evening ritual of sharing food? The answer is, it was both. Eating together is one of the most evocative rituals that bond individuals as a family. At the same time, the requirement that they sit down to dinner together gave Louis the power to make Claudia wait. So the need for connection entailed control, and controlling each other is in itself a kind of connection.

Control and connection are intertwined, often conflicting forces that thread through everything said in a family. These dual forces explain the double meaning of caring and criticizing. Giving advice, suggesting changes, and making observations are signs of caring when looked at through the lens of connection. But looked at through the lens of control, they are put-downs, interfering with our desire to manage our own lives and actions, telling us to do things differently than we choose to do them. That's why caring and criticizing are tied up like a knot.

The drives toward connection and toward control are the forces that underlie our reactions to metamessages. So the second step in improving communication in the family—after distinguishing between message and metamessage—is understanding the double meaning of control and connection. Once these multiple layers are sorted out and brought into focus, talking about ways of talking—metacommunicating—can help solve family problems rather than making them worse.

Small Spark, Big Explosion

Given the intricacies of messages and metamessages, and of connection and control, the tiniest suggestion or correction can spark an explosion fueled by the stored energy of a history of criticism. One day, for example, Vivian was washing dishes. She tried to fix the drain cup in an open position so it would catch debris and still allow water to drain, but it kept falling into the closed position. With a mental shrug of her shoulders, she decided to leave it, since she didn't have many dishes to wash and the amount of water that would fill the sink wouldn't be that great. But a moment later her husband, Mel, happened by and glanced at the sink. "You should keep the drain open," he said, "so the water can drain."

This sounds innocent enough in the telling. Vivian could have said, "I tried, but it kept slipping in, so I figured it didn't matter that much." Or she could have said, "It's irritating to feel that you're looking over my shoulder all the time, telling me to do things differently from the way I'm doing them." This was, in fact, what she was feeling—and why she experienced, in reaction to Mel's suggestion, a small eruption of anger that she had to expend effort to suppress.

Vivian was surprised at what she did say. She made up a reason and implied she had acted on purpose: "I figured it would be easier to clean the strainer if I let it drain all at once." This thought *had* occurred to her when she decided not to struggle any longer to balance the drain cup in an open position, though it wasn't true that she did it on purpose for that reason. But by justifying her actions, Vivian gave Mel the opening to argue for his method, which he did.

"The whole sink gets dirty if you let it fill up with water," Mel said. Vivian decided to let it drop and remained silent. Had she spoken up, the result would probably have been an argument.

Throughout this interchange Vivian and Mel focused on the message: When you wash the dishes, should the drain cup be open or closed? Just laying out the dilemma in these terms shows how ridiculous it is to argue about. Wars are being fought; people are dying; accident or illness could throw this family into turmoil at any moment. The position of the drain cup in the sink is not a major factor in their lives. But the conversation wasn't really about the message—the drain cup—at least not for Vivian.

Mel probably thought he was just making a suggestion about the drain cup, and in the immediate context he was. But messages always bring metamessages in tow: In the context of the history of their relationship, Mel's comment was not so much about a drain cup as it was about Vivian's ability to do things right and Mel's role as judge of her actions.

This was clear to Vivian, which is why she bristled at his comment, but it was less clear to Mel. Our field of vision is different depending on whether we're criticizing or being criticized. The critic tends to focus on the message: "I just made a suggestion. Why are you so touchy?" The one who feels criticized, however, is responding to the metamessage, which is harder to explain. If Vivian had complained, "You're always telling me how to do things," Mel would surely have felt, and might well have said, "I can't even open my mouth."

At the same time, connection and control are in play. Mel's assumption that he and Vivian are on the same team makes him feel comfortable giving her pointers. Furthermore, if a problem develops with the sink's drainage, he's the one who will have to fix it. Their lives are intertwined; that's where the connection lies. But if Vivian feels she can't even wash dishes without Mel telling her to do it differently, then it seems to her that he is trying to control her. It's as if she has a boss to answer to in her own kitchen.

Vivian might explain her reaction in terms of metamessages. Understanding and respecting her perspective, Mel might decide to limit his suggestions and corrections. Or Vivian might decide that she is overinterpreting the metamessage and make an effort to focus more on the message, taking some of Mel's suggestions and ignoring others. Once they both understand the metamessages as well as the messages they are communicating and reacting to, they can metacommunicate: talk about each other's ways of talking and how they might talk differently to avoid hurt and recriminations.

"Wouldn't You Rather Have Salmon?"

Irene and David are looking over their menus in a restaurant. David says he will order a steak. Irene says, "Did you notice they also have salmon?"

This question exasperates David; he protests, "Will you please stop criticizing what I eat?"

Irene feels unfairly accused: "I didn't criticize. I just pointed out something on the menu I thought you might like."

The question "Did you notice they also have salmon?" is not, on the message level, a criticism. It could easily be friendly and helpful, calling attention to a menu item her husband might have missed. But, again, conversations between spouses—or between any two people who have a history—are always part of an ongoing relationship. David knows that Irene thinks he eats too much red meat, too much dessert, and, generally speaking, too much.

Against the background of this aspect of their relationship, any indication that Irene is noticing what he is eating is a reminder to David that she disapproves of his eating habits. That's why the question "Do you really want to have dessert?" will be heard as "You shouldn't have dessert," and the observation "That's a big piece of cake" will communicate "That piece of cake is too big," regardless of how they're intended. The impression of disapproval comes not from the message—the words spoken—but from the metamessage, which grows out of their shared history.

It's possible that Irene really was not feeling disapproval when she pointed out the salmon on the menu, but it's also possible that she was and preferred not to admit it. Asking a question is a handy way of expressing disapproval without seeming to. But to the extent that the disapproval comes through, such indirect means of communicating can make for more arguments, and more hurt feelings on both sides. Irene sees David overreacting to an innocent, even helpful, remark, and he sees her hounding him about what he eats and then denying having done so. Suppose he had announced he was going to order salmon. Would she have said, "Did you notice they also have steak?" Not likely. It is reasonable, in this context, to interpret any alternative suggestion to an announced decision as dissatisfaction with that decision.

Though Irene and David's argument has much in common with the previous examples, the salmon versus steak decision is weightier than French bread versus dinner rolls, recycling, or drain cups. Irene feels that David's health—maybe even his life—is at stake. He has high cholesterol, and his father died young of a heart attack. Irene has good reason to want David to eat less red meat. She loves him, and his health and life are irrevocably intertwined with hers. Here is another paradox of family: A blessing of being close is knowing that someone cares about you: cares what you do and what happens to you. But caring also means interference and disapproval.

In other words, here again is the paradox of connection and control. From the perspective of control, Irene is judging and interfering; from the perspective of connection, she is simply recognizing that her life and David's are intertwined. This potent brew is family: Just knowing that someone has the closeness to care and the right to pass judgment—and that you care so much about that judgment—creates resentment that can turn into anger.

Crying Literal Meaning: How Not to Resolve Arguments

When Irene protested, "I didn't criticize," she was crying literal meaning: taking refuge in the message level of talk, ducking the metamessage. All of us do that when we want to avoid a fight but still get our point across. In many cases this defense is sincere, though it does not justify ignoring or denying the metamessage someone else may have perceived. If the person we're talking to believes it wasn't "just a suggestion," keeping the conversation focused on the message can result in interchanges that sound like a tape loop playing over and over. Let's look more closely at an actual conversation in which this happened—one that was taped by the people who had it.

Sitting at the dining room table, Evelyn is filling out an application. Because Joel is the one who has access to a copy machine at work, the last step of the process will rest on his shoulders. Evelyn explains, "Okay, so you'll have to attach the voided check here, after you make the Xerox copy. Okay?" Joel takes the papers, but Evelyn goes on: "Okay just—Please get that out tomorrow. I'm counting on you, hon. I'm counting on you, love."

Joel reacts with annoyance: "Oh, for Pete's sake."

Evelyn is miffed in turn: "What do you mean by that?"

Joel turns her words back on her: "What do *you* mean by that?"

The question "What do you mean by that?" is a challenge. When communication runs smoothly, the meanings of words are self-evident, or at least we assume they are. (We may discover later that we misinterpreted them.) Although "What do you mean?" might be an innocent request for clarification, adding "by that" usually signals not so much that you didn't understand what the other person meant but that you understood—all too well—the *implication* of the words, and you didn't like it.

Evelyn cries literal meaning. She sticks to the message: "Oh, honey, I just mean I'm *counting* on you."

Joel calls attention to the metamessage: "Yes, but you say it in a way that suggests I can't be counted on."

Evelyn protests, accurately, "I never said that."

But Joel points to evidence of the metamessage: "I'm talking about your *tone*."

I suspect Joel was using *tone* as a catchall way of describing the metamessage level of talk. Moreover, it probably wasn't only the way Evelyn spoke—her tone—that he was reacting to but the fact that Evelyn said it at all. If she really felt she could count on him, she would just hand over the task. "I'm counting on you" is what people say to reinforce the importance of doing something when they believe extra reinforcement is needed. Here, the shared history of the relationship adds meaning to the metamessage as well. Joel has reason to believe that Evelyn feels she can't count on him.

Later in the same conversation, Joel takes a turn crying literal meaning. He unplugs the radio from the wall in the kitchen and brings it into the dining room so they can listen to the news. He sets it on the table and turns it on.

"Why aren't you using the plug?" Evelyn asks. "Why waste the batteries?" This sparks a heated discussion about the relative importance of saving batteries. Evelyn then suggests, "Well, we could plug it in right here," and offers Joel the wire.

Joel shoots her a look.

Evelyn protests, "Why are you giving me a dirty look?"

And Joel cries literal meaning: "I'm not!" After all, you can't prove a facial expression; it's not in the message.

"You are!" Evelyn insists, reacting to the metamessage: "Just because I'm handing this to you to plug in."

I have no doubt that Joel did look at Evelyn with annoyance or worse, but not because she handed him a plug—that would be literal meaning, too. He was surely reacting to the metamessage of being corrected, of her judging his actions. For her part, Evelyn probably felt Joel was irrationally refusing to plug in the radio when an electrical outlet was staring them in the face.

How to sort through this jumble of messages and metamessages? The message level is a draw. Some people prefer the convenience of letting the radio run on batteries when it's moved from its normal perch to a temporary one. Others find it obviously reasonable to plug the radio in when there's an outlet handy, to save batteries. Convenience or frugality, take your pick. We all do. But when you live with someone else—caution! It may seem natural to suggest that others do things the way you would do them, but that is taking account only of the message. Giving the metamessage its due, the expense in spirit and goodwill is more costly than batteries. Being corrected all the time is wearying. And it's even more frustrating when you try to talk about what you believe they implied and they cry literal meaning—denying having "said" what you know they communicated.

Consider, too, the role of connection and control. Telling someone what to do is a control maneuver. But it is also a connection maneuver: Your lives are intertwined, and anything one person does has an impact on the other. In the earlier example, when Evelyn said, "I'm counting on you," I suspect some readers sympathized with Joel and others with Evelyn, depending on their own experience with people they've lived with. Does it affect your reaction to learn that Joel forgot to mail the application? Evelyn had good reason, based on years of living with Joel, to have doubts about whether he would remember to do what he said he would do.

Given this shared history, it might have been more constructive for Evelyn to admit that she did not feel she could completely count on Joel, rather than cry literal meaning and deny the metamessage of her words. Taking into account Joel's forgetfulness—or maybe his being overburdened at work—they could devise a plan: Joel might write himself a reminder and place it strategically in his briefcase. Or Evelyn might consider mailing the form herself, even though that would mean a trip to make copies. Whatever they decide, they stand a better chance of avoiding arguments—and getting the application mailed on time—if they acknowledge their metamessages and the reasons motivating them.

Who Burned the Popcorn?

Living together means coordinating so many tasks, it's inevitable that family members will have different ideas of how to perform those tasks. In addition, everyone makes mistakes; sometimes the dish breaks, you forget to mail the application, the drain cup falls into the closed position. At work, lines of responsibility and authority are clear (at least in principle). But in a family—especially when adults are trying to share responsibilities and authority—there are fewer and fewer domains that belong solely to one person. As couples share responsibility for more and more tasks, they also develop unique and firm opinions about how those tasks should be done—and a belief in their right to express their opinions.

Even the most mundane activity, such as making popcorn (unless you buy the microwave type or an electric popper), can spark conflict. First, it takes a little going, and people have their own ideas of how to do it best. Second, popcorn is often made in the evening, when everyone's tired. Add to that the paradox of connection and control—wanting the person you love to approve of what you do, yet having someone right there to witness and judge mistakes—and you have a potful of kernels sizzling in oil, ready to pop right out of the pot.

More than one couple have told me of arguments about how to make popcorn. One such argument broke out between another couple who were taping their conversations. Since their words were recorded, we have a rare opportunity to listen in on a conversation very much like innumerable ones that vanish into air in homes all around the country. And we have the chance to think about how it could have been handled differently.

The seed of trouble is planted when Molly is in the kitchen and Kevin is watching their four-year-old son, Benny. Kevin calls out, "Molly! Mol! Let's switch. You take care of him. I'll do whatever you're doing."

"I'm making popcorn," Molly calls back. "You always burn it."

Molly's reply is, first and foremost, a sign of resistance. She doesn't want to switch jobs with Kevin. Maybe she's had enough of a four-year-old's company and is looking forward to being on her own in the kitchen. Maybe she is enjoying making popcorn. And maybe her reason is truly the one she gives: She doesn't want Kevin to make the popcorn because he always burns it. Whatever her motivation, Molly resists the switch Kevin proposes by impugning his ability to make popcorn. And this comes across as a call to arms.

Kevin protests, "No I don't! I never burn it. I make it perfect." He joins Molly in the kitchen and peers over her shoulder. "You making popcorn? In the big pot?" (Remember this line; it will become important later.)

"Yes," Molly says, "but you're going to ruin it."

"No I won't," Kevin says. "I'll get it just right." With that they make the switch. Kevin becomes the popcorn chef, Molly the caretaker. But she is not a happy caretaker.

Seeing a way she can be both caretaker and popcorn chef, Molly asks Benny, "You want to help Mommy make popcorn? Let's not let Daddy do it. Come on."

Hearing this, Kevin insists, "I know how to make popcorn!" Then he ups the ante: "I can make popcorn better than you can!" After that the argument heats up faster than the popcorn. "I cook every kernel!" Kevin says.

"No you won't," says Molly.

"I will too! It's never burned!" Kevin defends himself. And he adds, "It always burns when you do it!"

"Don't make excuses!"

"There's a trick to it," he says.

And she says, "I know the trick!"

"No you don't," he retorts, "'cause you always burn it."

I do not!" she says. "What are you, crazy?"

It is possible that Kevin is right—that Molly, not he, is the one who always burns the popcorn. It is also possible that Molly is right—that he always burns the popcorn, that she doesn't, and that he has turned the accusation back onto her as a self-defense strategy. Move 1: I am not guilty. Move 2: You are guilty.

In any case, Kevin continues as popcorn chef. After a while Molly returns to the kitchen. "Just heat it!" she tells Kevin. "Heat it! No, I don't want you—"

"It's going, it's going," Kevin assures her. "Hear it?"

Molly is not reassured, because she does not like what she hears. "It's too slow," she says. "It's all soaking in. You hear that little—"

"It's not soaking in," Kevin insists. "It's fine."

"It's just a few kernels," Molly disagrees.

But Kevin is adamant: "All the popcorn is being popped!"

Acting on her mounting unease about the sounds coming from the popping corn, Molly makes another suggestion. She reminds Kevin, "You gotta take the trash outside."

But Kevin isn't buying. "I can't," he says. "I'm doing the popcorn." And he declines Molly's offer to watch it while he takes out the trash.

In the end Molly gets to say, "See, what'd I tell you?" But Kevin doesn't see the burned popcorn as a reason to admit fault. Remember his earlier question, "In the big pot?" Now he protests, "Well, I never *use* this pot, I use the other pot."

Molly comes back, "It's not the pot! It's you!"

"It's the pot," Kevin persists. "It doesn't heat up properly. If it did, then it would get hot." But pots can't really be at fault; those who choose pots can. So Kevin accuses, "You should have let me do it from the start."

"You *did* it from the start!" Molly says.

"No, I didn't," says Kevin. "You chose this pan. I would've chosen a different pan." So it's the pot's fault, and Molly's fault for choosing the pot.

This interchange is almost funny, especially for those of us—most of us, I'd bet—who have found ourselves in similar clashes.

How could Kevin and Molly have avoided this argument? Things might have turned out better if they had talked about their motivations: Is either one of them eager to get a brief respite from caring for Benny? If so, is there another way they can accomplish that goal? (Perhaps they could set Benny up with a task he enjoys on his own.) With this motivation out in the open, Molly might have declined to switch places when Kevin proposed it, saying something like, "I'm making popcorn. I'm enjoying making it. I'd rather not switch." The justification Molly used, "You always burn it," may have seemed to her a better tactic because it claims her right to keep making popcorn on the basis of the family good rather than her own preference. But the metamessage of incompetence can come across as provocative, in addition to being hurtful.

It's understandable that Kevin would be offended to have his popcorn-making skills impugned, but he would have done better to avoid the temptation to counterattack by insisting he does it better, that it's Molly who burns it. He could have prevented the argument rather than escalate it if he had metacommunicated: "You can make the popcorn if you want," he might have said, "but you don't have to say I can't do it." For both Molly and Kevin—as for any two people negotiating who's going to do what—metacommunicating is a way to avoid the flying metamessages of incompetence.

"I Know a Thing or Two"

One of the most hurtful metamessages, and one of the most frequent, that family talk entails is the implication of incompetence—even (if not especially) when children grow up. Now that we're adults we feel we should be entitled to make our own decisions, lead our own lives, imperfect though they may be. But we still want to feel that our parents are proud of us, that they believe in our competence. That's the metamessage we yearn for. Indeed, it's because we want their approval so much that we find the opposite metamessage—that they don't trust our competence—so distressing.

Martin and Gail knew that Gail's mother tended to be critical of whatever they did, so they put off letting her see their new home until the purchase was final. Once the deal was sealed they showed her, with pride, the home they had chosen while the previous owner's furniture was still in it. They were sure she would be impressed by the house they were now able to afford, as well as its spotless condition. But she managed to find something to criticize—even if it was invisible: "They may've told you it's in move-in condition," she said with authority, "but I know a thing or two, and when they take those pictures off the wall, there will be holes!" Even though they were familiar with her tendency to find fault, Gail and Martin were flummoxed.

The aspect of the house Gail's mother found to criticize was profoundly insignificant: Every home has pictures on the wall, every picture taken down leaves holes, and holes are easily spackled in and painted over. It seems that Gail's mother was really reaching to find *something* about their new home to criticize. From the perspective of control, it would be easy to conclude that Gail's mother was trying to take the role of expert in order to put them down, or even to spoil the joy of their momentous purchase. But consider the perspective of connection. Pointing out a problem that her children might not have noticed shows that she can still be of use, even though they are grown and have found this wonderful house without her help.

She was being protective, watching out for them, making sure no one pulled the wool over their eyes.

Because control and connection are inextricably intertwined, protection implies incompetence. If Gail and Martin need her mother's guidance, they are incapable of taking care of themselves. Though Gail's mother may well have been reacting to—and trying to overcome—the metamessage that they don't need her anymore, the metamessage they heard is that she can't approve wholeheartedly of anything they do.

"She Knew What Was Right"

In addition to concern about their children's choice of home, parents often have strong opinions about adult children's partners, jobs, and—especially—how they treat their own children. Raising children is something at which parents self-evidently have more experience, but metamessages of criticism in this area, though particularly common, are also particularly hurtful, because young parents want so much to be good parents.

A woman of seventy still recalls the pain she felt when her children were small and her mother-in-law regarded her as an incompetent parent. It started in the first week of her first child's life. Her mother-in-law had come to help—and didn't want to go home. Finally, her father-in-law told his wife it was time to leave the young couple on their own. Unconvinced, she said outright—in front of her son and his wife—"I can't trust them with the baby."

Usually signs of distrust are more subtle. For example, during a dinner conversation among three sisters and their mother, the sisters were discussing what the toddlers like to eat. When one said that her two-year-old liked fish, their mother cautioned, "Watch the bones." How easy it would be to take offense (though there was no indication this woman did): "You think I'm such an incompetent mother that I'm going to let my child swallow fish bones?" Yet the grandmother's comment was her way of making a contribution to the conversation—one that exercises her lifelong responsibility of protecting children.

It is easy to scoff at the mother-in-law who did not want to leave her son and his wife alone with their own baby. But consider the predicament of parents who become grandparents and see (or believe they see) their beloved grandchildren treated in ways they feel are hurtful. One woman told me that she loves being a grandmother—but the hardest part is having to bite her tongue when her daughter-in-law treats her child in a way the grandmother feels is misguided, unfair, or even harmful. "You see your children doing things you think aren't right," she commented, "but at least they're adults; they'll suffer the consequences. But a child is so defenseless."

In some cases grandparents really do know best. My parents recall with lingering guilt a time they refused to take a grandparent's advice—and later wished they had. When their first child, my sister Naomi, was born, my parents, like many of their generation, relied on expert advice for guidance in what was best for their child. At the time, the experts counseled that, once bedtime comes, a child who cries should not be picked up. After all, the reasoning went, that would simply encourage the baby to cry rather than go to sleep.

One night when she was about a year old, Naomi was crying after being put to sleep in her crib. My mother's mother, who lived with my parents, wanted to go in and pick her up, but my parents wouldn't let her. "It tore us apart to hear her cry," my father recalls, "but we wanted to do what was best for her." It later turned out that Naomi was crying because she was sick. My parents cringe when they tell this story. "My mother pleaded with us to pick her up," my mother says. "She knew what was right."

I'm Grown Up Now

Often a parent's criticism is hurtful—or makes us angry—even when we know it is right, maybe especially if we sense it is right. That comes clear in the following example.

Two couples were having dinner together. One husband, Barry, was telling about how he had finally—at the age of forty-five—learned to ignore his mother's criticism. His mother, he said, had commented that he is too invested in wanting the latest computer gizmo, the most up-to-date laptop, regardless of whether he needs it. At that point his wife interrupted. "It's true, you are," she said—and laughed. He laughed, too: "I know it's true." Then he went back to his story and continued, unfazed, about how in the past he would have been hurt by his mother's comment and would have tried to justify himself to her, but this time he just let it pass. How easily Barry acknowledged the validity of his mother's criticism—when it was his wife making it. Yet acknowledging that the criticism was valid didn't change his view of his mother's comment one whit: He still thought she was wrong to criticize him.

When we grow up we feel we should be free from our parents' judgment (even though we still want their approval). Ironically, there is often extra urgency in parents' tendency to judge children's behavior when children are adults, because parents have a lot riding on how their children turn out. If the results are good, everything they did as parents gets a seal of approval. My father, for example, recalls that as a young married man he visited an older cousin, a woman he did not know well. After a short time the cousin remarked, "Your mother did a good job." Apparently, my father had favorably impressed her, but instead of complimenting him, she credited his mother.

By the same token, if their adult children have problems—if they seem irresponsible or make wrong decisions—parents feel their life's work of child rearing has been a failure, and those around them feel that way, too. This gives extra intensity to parents' desire to set their children straight. But it also can blind them to the impact of their corrections and suggestions, just as those in power often underestimate the power they wield.

When adult children move into their own homes, the lid is lifted off the pressure cooker of family interaction, though the pot may still be simmering on the range. If they move far away—as more and more do—visits turn into intense interactions during which the pressure cooker lid is clicked back in place and the steam builds up once again. Many adult children feel like they're kids again when they stay with their parents. And parents often feel the same way: that their adult children are acting like kids. Visits become immersion courses in return-to-family.

Parents with children living at home have the ultimate power—asking their children to move out. But visiting adult children have a new power of their own: They can threaten not to return, or to stay somewhere else. Margaret was thrilled that her daughter Amanda, who lives in Oregon, would be coming home for a visit to the family farm in Minnesota. It had been nearly a year since Margaret had seen her grandchildren, and she was eager to get reacquainted with them. But near the end of the visit, there was a flare-up. Margaret questioned whether Amanda's children should be allowed to run outside barefoot. Margaret thought it was dangerous; Amanda thought it was harmless. And Amanda unsheathed her sword: "This isn't working," she said. "Next time I won't stay at the farm. I'll find somewhere else to stay." Because Margaret wants connection—time with her daughter and grandchildren—the ability to dole out that connection gives her daughter power that used to be in Margaret's hands.

The Paradox of Family

When I was a child I walked to elementary school along Coney Island Avenue in Brooklyn, praying that if a war came I'd be home with my family when it happened. During my childhood in the 1950s my teachers periodically surprised the class by calling out, "Take cover!" At that cry we all ducked under our desks and curled up in the way we had been taught: elbows and knees tucked in, heads down, hands clasped over our necks. With the possibility of a nuclear attack made vivid by these exercises, I walked to school in dread—not of war but of the possibility that it might strike when I was away from my family.

But there is another side to family, the one I have been exploring in this chapter. My nephew Joshua Marx, at thirteen, pointed out this paradox: "If you live with someone for too long, you notice things about them," he said. "That's the reason you don't like your parents, your brother. There's a kid I know who said about his friend, 'Wouldn't it be cool if we were brothers?' and I said, 'Then you'd hate him.'"

We look to communication as a way through the minefield of this paradox. And often talking helps. But communication itself is a minefield because of the complex workings of message and metamessage. Distinguishing messages from metamessages, and taking into account the underlying needs for connection and control, provides a basis for metacommunicating. With these insights as foundation, we can delve further into the intricacies of family talk. Given our shared and individual histories of talk in relationships, and the enormous promise of love, understanding, and listening that family holds out, it's worth the struggle to continue juggling—and talking.

Shakespeare in the Bush

LAURA BOHANNAN

Just before I left Oxford for the Tiv in West Africa, conversation turned to the season at Stratford. "You Americans," said a friend, "often have difficulty with Shakespeare. He was, after all, a very English poet, and one can easily misinterpret the universal by misunderstanding the particular."

I protested that human nature is pretty much the same the whole world over; at least the general plot and motivation of the greater tragedies would always be clear—everywhere—although some details of custom might have to be explained and difficulties of translation might produce other slight changes. To end an argument we could not conclude, my friend gave me a copy of *Hamlet* to study in the African bush: it would, he hoped, lift my mind above its primitive surroundings, and possibly I might, by prolonged meditation, achieve the grace of correct interpretation.

It was my second field trip to that African tribe, and I thought myself ready to live in one of its remote sections—an area difficult to cross even on foot. I eventually settled on the hillock of a very knowledgeable old man, the head of a homestead of some hundred and forty people, all of whom were either his close relatives or their wives and children. Like the other elders of the vicinity, the old man spent most of his time performing ceremonies seldom seen these days in the more accessible parts of the tribe. I was delighted. Soon there would be three months of enforced isolation and leisure, between the harvest that takes place just before the rising of the swamps and the clearing of new farms when the water goes down. Then, I thought, they would have even more time to perform ceremonies and explain them to me.

I was quite mistaken. Most of the ceremonies demanded the presence of elders from several homesteads. As the swamps rose, the old men found it too difficult to walk from one homestead to the next, and the ceremonies gradually ceased. As the swamps rose even higher, all activities but one came to an end. The women brewed beer from maize and millet. Men, women, and children sat on their hillocks and drank it.

People began to drink at dawn. By midmorning the whole homestead was singing, dancing, and drumming. When it rained, people had to sit inside their huts: there they drank and sang or they drank and told stories. In any case, by noon or before, I either had to join the party or retire to my own hut and my books. "One does not discuss serious matters when there is beer. Come, drink with us." Since I lacked their capacity for the thick native beer, I spent more and more time with *Hamlet*. Before the end of the second month, grace descended on me. I was quite sure that *Hamlet* had only one possible interpretation, and that one universally obvious.

Early every morning, in the hope of having some serious talk before the beer party, I used to call on the old man at his reception hut—a circle of posts supporting a thatched roof above a low mud wall to keep out wind and rain. One day I crawled through the low doorway and found most of the men of the homestead sitting huddled in their ragged cloths on stools, low plank beds, and reclining chairs, warming themselves against the chill of the rain around a smoky fire. In the center were three pots of beer. The party had started.

The old man greeted me cordially. "Sit down and drink." I accepted a large calabash full of beer, poured some into a small drinking gourd, and tossed it down. Then I poured some more into the same gourd for the man second in seniority to my host before I handed my calabash over to a young man for further distribution. Important people shouldn't ladle beer themselves.

"It is better like this," the old man said, looking at me approvingly and plucking at the thatch that had caught in my hair. "You should sit and drink with us more often. Your servants tell me that when you are not with us, you sit inside your hut looking at a paper."

The old man was acquainted with four kinds of "papers": tax receipts, bride price receipts, court fee receipts, and letters. The messenger who brought him letters from the chief used them mainly as a badge of office, for he always knew what was in them and told the old man. Personal letters for the few who had relatives in the government or mission stations were kept until someone went to a large market where there was a letter writer and reader. Since my arrival, letters were brought to me to be read. A few men also brought me bride price receipts, privately, with requests to change the figures to a higher sum. I found moral arguments were of no avail, since in-laws are fair game, and the technical hazards of forgery difficult to explain to an illiterate people. I did not wish them to think me silly enough to look at any such papers for days on end, and I hastily explained that my "paper" was one of the "things of long ago" of my country.

"Ah," said the old man. "Tell us."

I protested that I was not a storyteller. Story telling is a skilled art among them; their standards are high, and the audiences critical—and vocal in their criticism. I protested in vain. This morning they wanted to hear a story while they drank. They threatened to tell me no more stories until I told them one of mine. Finally, the old man promised that no one would criticize my style "for we know you are struggling with our language." "But," put in one of the elders, "you must explain what we do not understand, as we do when we tell you our stories." Realizing that here was my chance to prove *Hamlet* universally intelligible, I agreed.

The old man handed me some more beer to help me on with my storytelling. Men filled their long wooden pipes and knocked coals from the fire to place in the pipe bowls; then, puffing contentedly, they sat back to listen. I began in the proper style, "Not yesterday, not yesterday, but long ago, a thing occurred. One night three men were keeping watch outside the homestead of the great chief, when suddenly they saw the former chief approach them."

"Why was he no longer their chief?"

"He was dead," I explained. "That is why they were troubled and afraid when they saw him."

"Impossible," began one of the elders, handing his pipe on to his neighbor, who interrupted, "Of course it wasn't the dead chief. It was an omen sent by a witch. Go on."

Slightly shaken, I continued. "One of these three was a man who knew things"—the closest translation for scholar, but unfortunately it also meant witch. The second elder looked triumphantly at the first. "So he spoke to the dead chief saying, 'Tell us what we must do so you may rest in your grave,' but the dead chief did not answer. He vanished, and they could see him no more. Then the man who knew things—his name was Horatio—said this event was the affair of the dead chief's son, Hamlet."

There was a general shaking of heads round the circle. "Had the dead chief no living brothers? Or was this son the chief?"

"No," I replied. "That is, he had one living brother who became the chief when the elder brother died."

The old men muttered: such omens were matters for chiefs and elders, not for youngsters; no good could come of going behind a chief's back; clearly Horatio was not a man who knew things.

"Yes, he was," I insisted, shooing a chicken away from my beer. "In our country the son is next to the father. The dead chief's younger brother had become the great chief. He had also married his elder brother's widow only about a month after the funeral."

"He did well," the old man beamed and announced to the others, "I told you that if we knew more about Europeans, we would find they really were very like us. In our country also," he added to me, "the younger brother marries the elder brother's widow and becomes the father of his children. Now, if your uncle, who married your widowed mother, is your father's full brother, then he will be a real father to you. Did Hamlet's father and uncle have one mother?"

His question barely penetrated my mind; I was too upset and thrown too far off balance by having one of the most important elements of *Hamlet* knocked straight out of the picture. Rather uncertainly I said that I thought they had the same mother, but I wasn't sure—the story didn't say. The old man told me severely that these genealogical details made all the difference and that when I got home I must ask the elders about it. He shouted out the door to one of his younger wives to bring his goatskin bag.

Determined to save what I could of the mother motif, I took a deep breath and began again. "The son Hamlet was very sad because his mother had married again so quickly. There was no need for her to do so, and it is our custom for a widow not to go to her next husband until she has mourned for two years."

"Two years is too long," objected the wife, who had appeared with the old man's battered goatskin bag. "Who will hoe your farms for you while you have no husband?"

"Hamlet," I retorted without thinking, "was old enough to hoe his mother's farms himself. There was no need for her to remarry." No one looked convinced. I gave up. "His mother and the great chief told Hamlet not to be sad, for the great chief himself would be a father to Hamlet. Furthermore, Hamlet would be the next chief: therefore he must stay to learn the things of a chief. Hamlet agreed to remain, and all the rest went off to drink beer."

While I paused, perplexed at how to render Hamlet's disgusted soliloquy to an audience convinced that Claudius and Gertrude had behaved in the best possible manner, one of the younger men asked me who had married the other wives of the dead chief.

"He had no other wives," I told him.

"But a chief must have many wives! How else can he brew beer and prepare food for all his guests?"

I said firmly that in our country even chiefs had only one wife, that they had servants to do their work, and that they paid them from tax money.

It was better, they returned, for a chief to have many wives and sons who would help him hoe his farms and feed his people; then everyone loved the chief who gave much and took nothing—taxes were a bad thing.

I agreed with the last comment, but for the rest fell back on their favorite way of fobbing off my questions: "That is the way it is done, so that is how we do it."

I decided to skip the soliloquy. Even if Claudius was here thought quite right to marry his brother's widow, there remained the poison motif, and I knew they would disapprove of fratricide. More hopefully I resumed, "That night Hamlet kept watch with the three who had seen his dead father. The dead chief again appeared, and although the others were afraid, Hamlet followed his dead father off to one side. When they were alone, Hamlet's dead father spoke."

"Omens can't talk!" The old man was emphatic.

"Hamlet's dead father wasn't an omen. Seeing him might have been an omen, but he was not." My audience looked as confused as I sounded. "It *was* Hamlet's dead father. It was a thing we call a 'ghost.'" I had to use the English word, for unlike many of the neighboring tribes, these people didn't believe in the survival after death of any individuating part of the personality.

"What is a 'ghost?' An omen?"

"No, a 'ghost' is someone who is dead but who walks around and can talk, and people can hear him and see him but not touch him."

They objected. "One can touch zombis."

"No, no! It was not a dead body the witches had animated to sacrifice and eat. No one else made Hamlet's dead father walk. He did it himself."

"Dead men can't walk," protested my audience as one man.

I was quite willing to compromise. "A 'ghost' is the dead man's shadow."

But again they objected. "Dead men cast no shadows."

"They do in my country," I snapped.

The old man quelled the babble of disbelief that arose immediately and told me with that insincere, but courteous, agreement one extends to the fancies of the young, ignorant, and superstitious, "No doubt in your country the dead can also walk without being zombis." From the depths of his bag he produced a withered fragment of kola nut, bit off one end to show it wasn't poisoned, and handed me the rest as a peace offering.

"Anyhow," I resumed, "Hamlet's dead father said that his own brother, the one who became chief, had poisoned him. He wanted Hamlet to avenge him. Hamlet believed this in his heart, for he did not like his father's brother." I took another swallow of beer. "In the country of the great chief, living in the same homestead, for it was a very large one, was an important elder who was often with the chief to advise and help him. His name was Polonius. Hamlet was courting his daughter, but her father and her brother . . . [I cast hastily about for some tribal analogy] warned her not to let Hamlet visit her when she was alone on her farm, for he would be a great chief and so could not marry her."

"Why not?" asked the wife, who had settled down on the edge of the old man's chair. He frowned at her for asking stupid questions and growled, "They lived in the same homestead."

"That was not the reason," I informed them. "Polonius was a stranger who lived in the homestead because he helped the chief, not because he was a relative."

"Then why couldn't Hamlet marry her?"

"He could have," I explained, "but Polonius didn't think he would. After all, Hamlet was a man of great importance who ought to marry a chief's daughter, for in his country a man could have only one wife. Polonius was afraid that if Hamlet made love to his daughter, then no one else would give a high price for her."

"That might be true," remarked one of the shrewder elders, "but a chief's son would give his mistress's father enough presents and patronage to more than make up the difference. Polonius sounds like a fool to me."

"Many people think he was," I agreed. "Meanwhile Polonius sent his son Laertes off to Paris to learn the things of that country, for it was the homestead of a very great chief indeed. Because he was afraid that Laertes might waste a lot of money on beer and women and gambling, or get into trouble by fighting, he sent one of his servants to Paris secretly, to spy out what Laertes was doing. One day Hamlet came upon Polonius's daughter Ophelia. He behaved so oddly he frightened her. Indeed"—I was fumbling for words to express the dubious quality of Hamlet's madness—"the chief and many others had also noticed that when Hamlet talked one could understand the words but not what they meant. Many people thought that he had become mad." My audience suddenly became much more

attentive. "The great chief wanted to know what was wrong with Hamlet, so he sent for two of Hamlet's age mates [school friends would have taken long explanation] to talk to Hamlet and find out what troubled his heart. Hamlet, seeing that they had been bribed by the chief to betray him, told them nothing. Polonius, however, insisted that Hamlet was mad because he had been forbidden to see Ophelia, whom he loved."

"Why," inquired a bewildered voice, "should anyone bewitch Hamlet on that account?"

"Bewitch him?"

"Yes, only witchcraft can make anyone mad, unless, of course, one sees the beings that lurk in the forest."

I stopped being a storyteller, took out my notebook and demanded to be told more about these two causes of madness. Even while they spoke and I jotted notes, I tried to calculate the effect of this new factor on the plot. Hamlet had not been exposed to the beings that lurk in the forests. Only his relatives in the male line could bewitch him. Barring relatives not mentioned by Shakespeare, it had to be Claudius who was attempting to harm him. And, of course, it was.

For the moment I staved off questions by saying that the great chief also refused to believe that Hamlet was mad for the love of Ophelia and nothing else. "He was sure that something much more important was troubling Hamlet's heart."

"Now Hamlet's age mates," I continued, "had brought with them a famous storyteller. Hamlet decided to have this man tell the chief and all his homestead a story about a man who had poisoned his brother because he desired his brother's wife and wished to be chief himself. Hamlet was sure the great chief could not hear the story without making a sign if he was indeed guilty, and then he would discover whether his dead father had told him the truth."

The old man interrupted, with deep cunning, "Why should a father lie to his son?" he asked.

I hedged: "Hamlet wasn't sure that it really was his dead father." It was impossible to say anything, in that language, about devil-inspired visions.

"You mean," he said, "it actually was an omen, and he knew witches sometimes send false ones. Hamlet was a fool not to go to one skilled in reading omens and divining the truth in the first place. A man-who-sees-the-truth could have told him how his father died, if he really had been poisoned, and if there was witchcraft in it; then Hamlet could have called the elders to settle the matter."

The shrewd elder ventured to disagree. "Because his father's brother was a great chief, one-who-sees-the-truth might therefore have been afraid to tell it. I think it was for that reason that a friend of Hamlet's father—a witch and an elder—sent an omen so his friend's son would know. Was the omen true?"

"Yes," I said, abandoning ghosts and the devil; a witch-sent omen it would have to be. "It was true, for when the storyteller was telling his tale before all the homestead, the great chief rose in fear. Afraid that Hamlet knew his secret he planned to have him killed."

The stage set of the next bit presented some difficulties of translation. I began cautiously. "The great chief told Hamlet's mother to find out from her son what he knew. But because a woman's children are always first in her heart, he had the important elder Polonius hide behind a cloth that hung against the wall of Hamlet's mother's sleeping hut. Hamlet started to scold his mother for what she had done."

There was a shocked murmur from everyone. A man should never scold his mother.

"She called out in fear, and Polonius moved behind the cloth. Shouting, 'A rat!' Hamlet took his machete and slashed through the cloth." I paused for dramatic effect. "He had killed Polonius!"

The old men looked at each other in supreme disgust. "That Polonius truly was a fool and a man who knew nothing! What child would not know enough to shout, 'It's me!'" With a pang, I remembered that these people are ardent hunters, always armed with bow, arrow, and machete; at the first rustle in the grass an arrow is aimed and ready, and the hunter shouts "Game!" If no human voice answers immediately, the arrow speeds on its way. Like a good hunter Hamlet had shouted, "A rat!"

I rushed in to save Polonius's reputation. "Polonius did speak. Hamlet heard him. But he thought it was the chief and wished to kill him earlier that evening. . . ." I broke down, unable to describe to these pagans, who had no belief in individual after-life, the difference between dying at one's prayers and dying "unhousell'd, disappointed, unaneled."

This time I had shocked my audience seriously. "For a man to raise his hand against his father's brother and the one who has become his father—that is a terrible thing. The elders ought to let such a man be bewitched."

I nibbled at my kola nut in some perplexity, then pointed out that after all the man had killed Hamlet's father.

"No," pronounced the old man, speaking less to me than to the young men sitting behind the elders. "If your father's brother has killed your father, you must appeal to your father's age mates; *they* may avenge him. No man may use violence against his senior relatives." Another thought struck him. "But if his father's brother had indeed been wicked enough to bewitch Hamlet and make him mad that would be a good story indeed, for it would be his fault that Hamlet, being mad, no longer had any sense and thus was ready to kill his father's brother."

There was a murmur of applause. *Hamlet* was again a good story to them, but it no longer seemed quite the same story to me. As I thought over the coming complications of plot and motive, I lost courage and decided to skim over dangerous ground quickly.

"The great chief," I went on, "was not sorry that Hamlet had killed Polonius. It gave him a reason to send Hamlet away, with his two treacherous mates, with letters to a chief of a far country, saying that Hamlet should be killed. But Hamlet changed the writing on their papers, so that the chief killed his age mates instead." I encountered a reproachful glare from one of the men whom I had told undetectable forgery was not merely immoral but beyond human skill. I looked the other way.

"Before Hamlet could return, Laertes came back for his father's funeral. The great chief told him Hamlet had killed Polonius. Laertes swore to kill Hamlet because of this, and because his sister Ophelia, hearing her father had been killed by the man she loved, went mad and drowned in the river."

"Have you already forgotten what we told you?" The old man was reproachful. "One cannot take vengeance on a madman;

Hamlet killed Polonius in his madness. As for the girl, she not only went mad, she was drowned. Only witches can make people drown. Water itself can't hurt anything. It is merely something one drinks and bathes in."

I began to get cross. "If you don't like the story, I'll stop."

The old man made soothing noises and himself poured me some more beer. "You tell the story well, and we are listening. But it is clear that the elders of your country have never told you what the story really means. No, don't interrupt! We believe you when you say your marriage customs are different, or your clothes and weapons. But people are the same everywhere; therefore, there are always witches and it is we, the elders, who know how witches work. We told you it was the great chief who wished to kill Hamlet, and now your own words have proved us right. Who were Ophelia's male relatives?"

"There were only her father and her brother." *Hamlet* was clearly out of my hands.

"There must have been many more; this also you must ask of your elders when you get back to your country. From what you tell us, since Polonius was dead, it must have been Laertes who killed Ophelia, although I do not see the reason for it."

We had emptied one pot of beer, and the old men argued the point with slightly tipsy interest. Finally one of them demanded of me, "What did the servant of Polonius say on his return?"

With difficulty I recollected Reynaldo and his mission. "I don't think he did return before Polonius was killed."

"Listen," said the elder, "and I will tell you how it was and how your story will go, then you may tell me if I am right. Polonius knew his son would get into trouble, and so he did. He had many fines to pay for fighting, and debts from gambling. But he had only two ways of getting money quickly. One was to marry off his sister at once, but it is difficult to find a man who will marry a woman desired by the son of a chief. For if the chief's heir commits adultery with your wife, what can you do? Only a fool calls a case against a man who will someday be his judge. Therefore Laertes had to take the second way: he killed his sister by witchcraft, drowning her so he could secretly sell her body to the witches."

I raised an objection. "They found her body and buried it. Indeed Laertes jumped into the grave to see his sister once more—so, you see, the body was truly there. Hamlet, who had just come back, jumped in after him."

"What did I tell you?" The elder appealed to the others. "Laertes was up to no good with his sister's body. Hamlet prevented him, because the chief's heir, like a chief, does not wish any other man to grow rich and powerful. Laertes would be angry, because he would have killed his sister without benefit to himself. In our country he would try to kill Hamlet for that reason. Is this not what happened?"

"More or less," I admitted. "When the great chief found Hamlet was still alive, he encouraged Laertes to try to kill Hamlet and arranged a fight with machetes between them. In the fight both the young men were wounded to death. Hamlet's mother drank the poisoned beer that the chief meant for Hamlet in case he won the fight. When he saw his mother die of poison, Hamlet, dying, managed to kill his father's brother with his machete."

"You see, I was right!" exclaimed the elder.

"That was a very good story," added the old man, "and you told it with very few mistakes. There was just one more error, at the very end. The poison Hamlet's mother drank was obviously meant for the survivor of the fight, whichever it was. If Laertes had won, the great chief would have poisoned him, for no one would know that he arranged Hamlet's death. Then, too, he need not fear Laertes' witchcraft; it takes a strong heart to kill one's only sister by witchcraft.

"Sometime," concluded the old man, gathering his ragged toga about him, "you must tell us some more stories of your country. We, who are elders, will instruct you in their true meaning, so that when you return to your own land your elders will see that you have not been sitting in the bush, but among those who know things and who have taught you wisdom."

LAURA BOHANNAN is a former professor of anthropology at the University of Illinois, at Chicago.

From *Natural History*, August/September 1966. Copyright © 1966 by Laura Bohannan. Reprinted by permission of the author.

UNIT 3

The Organization of Society and Culture

Unit Selections

Key Points to Consider

- What traditional Inuit (Eskimo) practices do you find contrary to values professed in your society but important to Eskimo survival under certain circumstances?

- What can contemporary hunter-collector societies tell us about the quality of life in the prehistoric past?

- What is the "Inuit paradox" and what can we learn from it regarding modern-day eating practices?

- How do the Maasai achieve social harmony through a "collectivist" culture? Can a modern business model be based upon the lessons learned?

- What is the significance of "the gift" in traditional Hopi society?

Student Web Site

www.mhcls.com/online

Internet References

Further information regarding these Web sites may be found in this book's preface or online.

Smithsonian Institution Web Site
http://www.si.edu
Sociology Guy's Anthropology Links
http://www.trinity.edu/~mkearl/anthro.html

U.S. Air Force photo by Master Sgt. Efran Gonzalez

Human beings do not interact with one another or think about their world in random fashion. Instead, they engage in both structured and recurrent physical and mental activities. In this section, such patterns of behavior and thought—referred to here as the organization of society and culture—may be seen in a number of different contexts, from the hunting tactics of the Inupiaq Eskimos of the Arctic (see "Understanding Eskimo Science") to the value the Hopi place on the gift as a symbol of social relations built on kinship and altruism (as discussed in "Ties That Bind").

Of special importance are the ways in which people make a living—in other words, the production, distribution, and consumption of goods and services. It is only by knowing the basic subsistence systems that we can hope to gain insight into the other levels of social and cultural phenomena, for, as Nigel Nicholson shows in "Meeting the Maasai: Messages for Management," they are all inextricably bound together.

Noting the various aspects of a socio-cultural system in harmonious balance, however, does not imply an anthropological seal of approval. To understand infanticide (killing of the newborn) in the manner that it is practiced among some peoples is

neither to condone nor condemn it. The adaptive patterns that have been in existence for a great length of time, such as many of the patterns of hunters and gatherers, probably owe their existence to their contributions to long-term human survival (see "The Inuit Paradox"). Anthropologists, however, are not content with the data derived from individual experience. On the contrary, personal descriptions must become the basis for sound anthropological theory. Otherwise, they remain meaningless, isolated relics of culture in the manner of museum pieces. Thus, in "Too Many Bananas, Not Enough Pineapples, and No Watermelon at All: Three Object Lessons in Living with Reciprocity," David Counts provides us with ground rules for reciprocity that were derived from his own particular field of experience and yet are cross-culturally applicable.

In other words, while the articles in this unit are to some extent descriptive, they also serve to challenge both academic and commonsense notions about why people behave and think as they do. They remind us that assumptions are never really safe. Anytime anthropologists can be kept on their toes, their field as a whole is the better for it.

Understanding Eskimo Science

Traditional hunters' insights into the natural world are worth rediscovering.

RICHARD NELSON

Just below the Arctic Circle in the boreal forest of interior Alaska; an amber afternoon in mid-November; the temperature −20°; the air adrift with frost crystals, presaging the onset of deeper cold.

Five men—Koyukon Indians—lean over the carcass of an exceptionally large black bear. For two days they've traversed the Koyukuk River valley, searching for bears that have recently entered hibernation dens. The animals are in prime condition at this season but extremely hard to find. Den entrances, hidden beneath 18 inches of powdery snow, are betrayed only by the subtlest of clues—patches where no grass protrudes from the surface because it's been clawed away for insulation, faint concavities hinting of footprint depressions in the moss below.

Earlier this morning the hunters took a yearling bear. In accordance with Koyukon tradition, they followed elaborate rules for the proper treatment of killed animals. For example, the bear's feet were removed first, to keep its spirit from wandering. Also, certain parts were to be eaten away from the village, at a kind of funeral feast. All the rest would be eaten either at home or at community events, as people here have done for countless generations.

Koyukon hunters know that an animal's life ebbs slowly, that it remains aware and sensitive to how people treat its body. This is especially true for the potent and demanding spirit of the bear.

The leader of the hunting group is Moses Sam, a man in his 60s who has trapped in this territory since childhood. He is known for his detailed knowledge of the land and for his extraordinary success as a bear hunter. "No one else has that kind of luck with bears," I've been told. "Some people are born with it. He always takes good care of his animals—respects them. That's how he keeps his luck."

Moses pulls a small knife from his pocket, kneels beside the bear's head, and carefully slits the clear domes of its eyes. "Now," he explains softly, "the bear won't see if one of us makes a mistake or does something wrong."

Contemporary Americans are likely to find this story exotic, but over the course of time episodes like this have been utterly commonplace, the essence of people's relationship to the natural world. After all, for 99 percent of human history we lived exclusively as hunter-gatherers; by comparison, agriculture has existed only for a moment and urban societies scarcely more than a blink.

From this perspective, much of human experience over the past several million years lies beyond our grasp. Probably no society has been so deeply alienated as ours from the community of nature, has viewed the natural world from a greater distance of mind, has lapsed into a murkier comprehension of its connections with the sustaining environment. Because of this, we have great difficulty understanding our rootedness to earth, our affinities with nonhuman life.

I believe it's essential that we learn from traditional societies, especially those whose livelihood depends on the harvest of a wild environment—hunters, fishers, trappers, and gatherers. These people have accumulated bodies of knowledge much like our own sciences. And they can give us vital insights about responsible membership in the community of life, insights founded on a wisdom we'd long forgotten and now are beginning to rediscover.

Since the mid-1960s I have worked as an ethnographer in Alaska, living intermittently in remote northern communities and recording native traditions centered around the natural world. I spent about two years in Koyukon Indian villages and just over a year with Inupiaq Eskimos on the Arctic coast—traveling by dog team and snowmobile, recording traditional knowledge, and learning the hunter's way.

Eskimos have long inhabited some of the harshest environments on earth, and they are among the most exquisitely adapted of all human groups. Because plant life is so scarce in their northern terrain, Eskimos depend more than any other people on hunting.

Eskimos are famous for the cleverness of their technology—kayaks, harpoons, skin clothing, snow houses, dog teams. But I believe their greatest genius, and the basis of their success, lies in the less tangible realm of the intellect—the nexus of mind and nature. For what repeatedly struck me above all else was their profound knowledge of the environment.

Several times, when my Inupiaq hunting companion did something especially clever, he'd point to his head and declare: "You see—Eskimo scientist!" At first I took it as hyperbole, but as time went by I realized he was speaking the truth. Scientists had often come to his village, and he saw in them a familiar commitment to the empirical method.

Traditional Inupiaq hunters spend a lifetime acquiring knowledge—from others in the community and from their own observations. If they are to survive, they must have absolutely reliable information. When I first went to live with Inupiaq people, I doubted many things they told me. But the longer I stayed, the more I trusted their teachings.

For example, hunters say that ringed seals surfacing in open leads—wide cracks in the sea ice—can reliably forecast the weather. Because an unexpected gale might set people adrift on the pack ice, accurate prediction is a matter of life and death. When seals rise chest-high in the water, snout pointed skyward, not going anywhere in particular, it indicates stable weather, the Inupiaq say. But if they surface briefly, head low, snout parallel to the water, and show themselves only once or twice, watch for a sudden storm. And take special heed if you've also noticed the sled dogs howling incessantly, stars twinkling erratically, or the current running strong from the south. As time passed, my own experiences with seals and winter storms affirmed what the Eskimos said.

Like a young Inupiaq in training, I gradually grew less skeptical and started to apply what I was told. For example, had I ever been rushed by a polar bear, I would have jumped away to the animal's *right* side. Inupiaq elders say polar bears are left-handed, so you have a slightly better chance to avoid their right paw, which is slower and less accurate. I'm pleased to say I never had the chance for a field test. But in judging assertions like this, remember that Eskimos have had close contact with polar bears for several thousand years.

The Inupiaq hunter possesses as much knowledge as a highly trained scientist in our own society

During winter, ringed and bearded seals maintain tunnel-like breathing holes in ice that is many feet thick. These holes are often capped with an igloo-shaped dome created by water sloshing onto the surface when the animal enters from below. Inupiaq elders told me that polar bears are clever enough to excavate around the base of this dome, leaving it perfectly intact but weak enough that a hard swat will shatter the ice and smash the seal's skull. I couldn't help wondering if this were really true; but then a younger man told me he'd recently followed the tracks of a bear that had excavated one seal hole after another, exactly as the elders had described.

In the village where I lived, the most respected hunter was Igruk, a man in his 70s. He had an extraordinary sense of animals—a gift for understanding and predicting their behavior. Although he was no longer quick and strong, he joined a crew hunting bowhead whales during the spring migration, his main role being that of adviser. Each time Igruk spotted a whale coming from the south, he counted the number of blows, timed how

long it stayed down, and noted the distance it traveled along the open lead, until it vanished toward the north. This way he learned to predict, with uncanny accuracy, where hunters could expect the whale to resurface.

I believe the expert Inupiaq hunter possesses as much knowledge as a highly trained scientist in our own society, although the information may be of a different sort. Volumes could be written on the behavior, ecology, and utilization of Arctic animals—polar bear, walrus, bowhead whale, beluga, bearded seal, ringed seal, caribou, musk ox, and others—based entirely on Eskimo knowledge.

Comparable bodies of knowledge existed in every Native American culture before the time of Columbus. Since then, even in the far north, Western education and cultural change have steadily eroded these traditions. Reflecting on a time before Europeans arrived, we can imagine the whole array of North American animal species—deer, elk, black bear, wolf, mountain lion, beaver, coyote, Canada goose, ruffed grouse, passenger pigeon, northern pike—each known in hundreds of different ways by tribal communities; the entire continent, sheathed in intricate webs of knowledge. Taken as a whole, this composed a vast intellectual legacy, born of intimacy with the natural world. Sadly, not more than a hint of it has ever been recorded.

Like other Native Americans, the Inupiaq acquired their knowledge through gradual accretion of naturalistic observations—year after year, lifetime after lifetime, generation after generation, century after century. Modern science often relies on other techniques—specialized full-time observation, controlled experiments, captive-animal studies, technological devices like radio collars—which can provide similar information much more quickly.

Yet Eskimo people have learned not only *about* animals but also *from* them. Polar bears hunt seals not only by waiting at their winter breathing holes, but also by stalking seals that crawl up on the ice to bask in the spring warmth. Both methods depend on being silent, staying downwind, keeping out of sight, and moving only when the seal is asleep or distracted. According to the elders, a stalking bear will even use one paw to cover its conspicuous black nose.

Inupiaq methods for hunting seals, both at breathing holes and atop the spring ice, are nearly identical to those of the polar bear. Is this a case of independent invention? Or did ancestral Eskimos learn the techniques by watching polar bears, who had perfected an adaptation to the sea-ice-environment long before humans arrived in the Arctic?

The hunter's genius centers on knowing an animal's behavior so well he can turn it to his advantage. For instance, Igruk once saw a polar bear far off across flat ice, where he couldn't stalk it without being seen. But he knew an old technique of mimicking a seal. He lay down in plain sight, conspicuous in his dark parka and pants, then lifted and dropped his head like a seal, scratched the ice, and imitated flippers with his hands. The bear mistook his pursuer for prey. Each time Igruk lifted his head the animal kept still; whenever Igruk "slept" the bear crept closer. When it came near enough, a gunshot pierced the snowy silence. That night, polar bear meat was shared among the villagers.

A traditional hunter like Igruk plumbs the depths of his intellect—his capacity to manipulate complex knowledge. But he also delves into his animal nature, drawing from intuitions of sense and body and heart: feeling the wind's touch, listening for the tick of moving ice, peering from crannies, hiding as if he himself were the hunted. He moves in a world of eyes, where everything watches—the bear, the seal, the wind, the moon and stars, the drifting ice, the silent waters below. He is beholden to powers we have long forgotten or ignored.

In Western society we rest comfortably on our own accepted truths about the nature of nature. We treat the environment as if it were numb to our presence and blind to our behavior. Yet despite our certainty on this matter, accounts of traditional people throughout the world reveal that most of humankind has concluded otherwise. Perhaps our scientific method really does follow the path to a single, absolute truth. But there may be wisdom in accepting other possibilities and opening ourselves to different views of the world.

I remember asking a Koyukon man about the behavior and temperament of the Canada goose. He described it as a gentle and good-natured animal, then added: "Even if [a goose] had the power to knock you over, I don't think it would do it."

For me, his words carried a deep metaphorical wisdom. They exemplified the Koyukon people's own restraint toward the world around them. And they offered a contrast to our culture, in which possessing the power to overwhelm the environment has long been sufficient justification for its use.

"Each animal knows way more than you do," a Koyukon Indian elder was fond of telling me.

We often think of this continent as having been a pristine wilderness when the first Europeans arrived. Yet for at least 12,000 years, and possibly twice that long, Native American people had inhabited and intensively utilized the land; had gathered, hunted, fished, settled, and cultivated; had learned the terrain in all its details, infusing it with meaning and memory; and had shaped every aspect of their life around it. That humans could sustain membership in a natural community for such an enormous span of time without profoundly degrading it fairly staggers the imagination. And it gives strong testimony to the adaptation of mind—the braiding together of knowledge and ideology—that linked North America's indigenous people with their environment.

A Koyukon elder, who took it upon himself to be my teacher, was fond of telling me: "Each animal knows way more than you do." He spoke as if it summarized all that he understood and believed.

This statement epitomizes relationships to the natural world among many Native American people. And it goes far in explaining the diversity and fecundity of life on our continent when the first sailing ship approached these shores.

There's been much discussion in recent years about what biologist E. O. Wilson has termed "biophilia"—a deep, pervasive, ubiquitous, all-embracing affinity for nonhuman life. Evidence for this "instinct" may be elusive in Western cultures, but not among traditional societies. People like the Koyukon manifest biophilia in virtually all dimensions of their existence. Connectedness with nonhuman life infuses the whole spectrum of their thought, behavior, and belief.

It's often said that a fish might have no concept of water, never having left it. In the same way, traditional peoples might never stand far enough outside themselves to imagine a generalized concept of biophilia. Perhaps it would be impossible for people to intimately bound with the natural world, people who recognize that all nature is our own embracing community. Perhaps, to bring a word like *biophilia* into their language, they would first need to separate themselves from nature.

In April 1971 I was in a whaling camp several miles off the Arctic coast with a group of Inupiaq hunters, including Igruk, who understood animals so well he almost seemed to enter their minds.

Onshore winds had closed the lead that migrating whales usually follow, but one large opening remained, and here the Inupiaq men placed their camp. For a couple of days there had been no whales, so everyone stayed inside the warm tent, talking and relaxing. The old man rested on a soft bed of caribou skins with his eyes closed. Then, suddenly, he interrupted the conversation: "I think a whale is coming, and perhaps it will surface very close. . . ."

To my amazement everyone jumped into action, although none had seen or heard anything except Igruk's words. Only he stayed behind, while the others rushed for the water's edge. I was last to leave the tent. Seconds after I stepped outside, a broad, shining back cleaved the still water near the opposite side of the opening, accompanied by the burst of a whale's blow.

Later, when I asked how he'd known, Igruk said, "There was a ringing inside my ears." I have no explanation other than his; I can only report what I saw. None of the Inupiaq crew members even commented afterward, as if nothing out of the ordinary had happened.

The Inuit Paradox

How can people who gorge on fat and rarely see a vegetable be healthier than we are?

PATRICIA GADSBY

P atricia Cochran, an Inupiat from Northwestern Alaska, is talking about the native foods of her childhood: "We pretty much had a subsistence way of life. Our food supply was right outside our front door. We did our hunting and foraging on the Seward Peninsula and along the Bering Sea."

"Our meat was seal and walrus, marine mammals that live in cold water and have lots of fat. We used seal oil for our cooking and as a dipping sauce for food. We had moose, caribou, and reindeer. We hunted ducks, geese, and little land birds like quail, called ptarmigan. We caught crab and lots of fish—salmon, whitefish, tomcod, pike, and char. Our fish were cooked, dried, smoked, or frozen. We ate frozen raw whitefish, sliced thin. The elders liked stinkfish, fish buried in seal bags or cans in the tundra and left to ferment. And fermented seal flipper, they liked that too."

Cochran's family also received shipments of whale meat from kin living farther north, near Barrow. Beluga was one she liked; raw muktuk, which is whale skin with its underlying blubber, she definitely did not. "To me it has a chew-on-a-tire consistency," she says, "but to many people it's a mainstay." In the short subarctic summers, the family searched for roots and greens and, best of all from a child's point of view, wild blueberries, crowberries, or salmonberries, which her aunts would mix with whipped fat to make a special treat called *akutuq*—in colloquial English, Eskimo ice cream.

Now Cochran directs the Alaska Native Science Commission, which promotes research on native cultures and the health and environmental issues that affect them. She sits at her keyboard in Anchorage, a bustling city offering fare from Taco Bell to French cuisine. But at home Cochran keeps a freezer filled with fish, seal, walrus, reindeer, and whale meat, sent by her family up north, and she and her husband fish and go berry picking—"sometimes a challenge in Anchorage," she adds, laughing. "I eat fifty-fifty," she explains, half traditional, half regular American.

No one, not even residents of the northernmost villages on Earth, eats an entirely traditional northern diet anymore. Even the groups we came to know as Eskimo—which include the Inupiat and the Yupiks of Alaska, the Canadian Inuit and

Inuvialuit, Inuit Greenlanders, and the Siberian Yupiks—have probably seen more changes in their diet in a lifetime than their ancestors did over thousands of years. The closer people live to towns and the more access they have to stores and cash-paying jobs, the more likely they are to have westernized their eating. And with westernization, at least on the North American continent, comes processed foods and cheap carbohydrates—Crisco, Tang, soda, cookies, chips, pizza, fries. "The young and urbanized," says Harriet Kuhnlein, director of the Centre for Indigenous Peoples' Nutrition and Environment at McGill University in Montreal, "are increasingly into fast food." So much so that type 2 diabetes, obesity, and other diseases of Western civilization are becoming causes for concern there too.

Today, when diet books top the best-seller list and nobody seems sure of what to eat to stay healthy, it's surprising to learn how well the Eskimo did on a high-protein, high-fat diet. Shaped by glacial temperatures, stark landscapes, and protracted winters, the traditional Eskimo diet had little in the way of plant food, no agricultural or dairy products, and was unusually low in carbohydrates. Mostly people subsisted on what they hunted and fished. Inland dwellers took advantage of caribou feeding on tundra mosses, lichens, and plants too tough for humans to stomach (though predigested vegetation in the animals' paunches became dinner as well). Coastal people exploited the sea. The main nutritional challenge was avoiding starvation in late winter if primary meat sources became too scarce or lean.

These foods hardly make up the "balanced" diet most of us grew up with, and they look nothing like the mix of grains, fruits, vegetables, meat, eggs, and dairy we're accustomed to seeing in conventional food pyramid diagrams. How could such a diet possibly be adequate? How did people get along on little else but fat and animal protein?

'The diet of the Far North shows that there are no essential foods—only essential nutrients'

What the diet of the Far North illustrates, says Harold Draper, a biochemist and expert in Eskimo nutrition, is that there are no essential foods—only essential nutrients. And humans can get those nutrients from diverse and eye-opening sources.

One might, for instance, imagine gross vitamin deficiencies arising from a diet with scarcely any fruits and vegetables. What furnishes vitamin A, vital for eyes and bones? We derive much of ours from colorful plant foods, constructing it from pigmented plant precursors called carotenoids (as in carrots). But vitamin A, which is oil soluble, is also plentiful in the oils of cold-water fishes and sea mammals, as well as in the animals' livers, where fat is processed. These dietary staples also provide vitamin D, another oil-soluble vitamin needed for bones. Those of us living in temperate and tropical climates, on the other hand, usually make vitamin D indirectly by exposing skin to strong sun—hardly an option in the Arctic winter—and by consuming fortified cow's milk, to which the indigenous northern groups had little access until recent decades and often don't tolerate all that well.

As for vitamin C, the source in the Eskimo diet was long a mystery. Most animals can synthesize their own vitamin C, or ascorbic acid, in their livers, but humans are among the exceptions, along with other primates and oddballs like guinea pigs and bats. If we don't ingest enough of it, we fall apart from scurvy, a gruesome connective-tissue disease. In the United States today we can get ample supplies from orange juice, citrus fruits, and fresh vegetables. But vitamin C oxidizes with time; getting enough from a ship's provisions was tricky for early 18th- and 19th-century voyagers to the polar regions. Scurvy—joint pain, rotting gums, leaky blood vessels, physical and mental degeneration—plagued European and U.S. expeditions even in the 20th century. However, Arctic peoples living on fresh fish and meat were free of the disease.

Impressed, the explorer Vilhjalmur Stefansson adopted an Eskimo-style diet for five years during the two Arctic expeditions he led between 1908 and 1918. "The thing to do is to find your antiscorbutics where you are," he wrote. "Pick them up as you go." In 1928, to convince skeptics, he and a young colleague spent a year on an Americanized version of the diet under medical supervision at Bellevue Hospital in New York City. The pair ate steaks, chops, organ meats like brain and liver, poultry, fish, and fat with gusto. "If you have some fresh meat in your diet every day and don't overcook it," Stefansson declared triumphantly, "there will be enough C from that source alone to prevent scurvy."

In fact, all it takes to ward off scurvy is a daily dose of 10 milligrams, says Karen Fediuk, a consulting dietitian and former graduate student of Harriet Kuhnlein's who did her master's thesis on vitamin C. (That's far less than the U.S. recommended daily allowance of 75 to 90 milligrams—75 for women, 90 for men.) Native foods easily supply those 10 milligrams of scurvy prevention, especially when organ meats—preferably raw—are on the menu. For a study published with Kuhnlein in 2002, Fediuk compared the vitamin C content of 100-gram (3.55-ounce) samples of foods eaten by Inuit women living in the Canadian Arctic: Raw caribou liver supplied almost 24 milligrams, seal brain close to 15 milligrams, and raw kelp more

than 28 milligrams. Still higher levels were found in whale skin and muktuk.

As you might guess from its antiscorbutic role, vitamin C is crucial for the synthesis of connective tissue, including the matrix of skin. "Wherever collagen's made, you can expect vitamin C," says Kuhnlein. Thick skinned, chewy, and collagen rich, raw muktuk can serve up an impressive 36 milligrams in a 100-gram piece, according to Fediuk's analyses. "Weight for weight, it's as good as orange juice," she says. Traditional Inuit practices like freezing meat and fish and frequently eating them raw, she notes, conserve vitamin C, which is easily cooked off and lost in food processing.

Hunter-gatherer diets like those eaten by these northern groups and other traditional diets based on nomadic herding or subsistence farming are among the older approaches to human eating. Some of these eating plans might seem strange to us— diets centered around milk, meat, and blood among the East African pastoralists, enthusiastic tuber eating by the Quechua living in the High Andes, the staple use of the mongongo nut in the southern African !Kung—but all proved resourceful adaptations to particular eco-niches. No people, though, may have been forced to push the nutritional envelope further than those living at Earth's frozen extremes. The unusual makeup of the far-northern diet led Loren Cordain, a professor of evolutionary nutrition at Colorado State University at Fort Collins, to make an intriguing observation.

Four years ago, Cordain reviewed the macronutrient content (protein, carbohydrates, fat) in the diets of 229 hunter-gatherer groups listed in a series of journal articles collectively known as the Ethnographic Atlas. These are some of the oldest surviving human diets. In general, hunter-gatherers tend to eat more animal protein than we do in our standard Western diet, with its reliance on agriculture and carbohydrates derived from grains and starchy plants. Lowest of all in carbohydrate, and highest in combined fat and protein, are the diets of peoples living in the Far North, where they make up for fewer plant foods with extra fish. What's equally striking, though, says Cordain, is that these meat-and-fish diets also exhibit a natural "protein ceiling." Protein accounts for no more than 35 to 40 percent of their total calories, which suggests to him that that's all the protein humans can comfortably handle.

'Wild-animal fats are different from other fats. Farm animals typically have lots of highly saturated fat'

This ceiling, Cordain thinks, could be imposed by the way we process protein for energy. The simplest, fastest way to make energy is to convert carbohydrates into glucose, our body's primary fuel. But if the body is out of carbs, it can burn fat, or if necessary, break down protein. The name given to the convoluted business of making glucose from protein is gluconeogenesis. It takes place in the liver, uses a dizzying slew of enzymes, and creates nitrogen waste that has to be converted into urea and disposed of through the kidneys. On a truly traditional diet, says Draper, recalling his studies in the 1970s, Arctic people had plenty of protein but little carbohydrate, so they often relied on gluconeogenesis. Not only did they have bigger livers to handle the additional work but their urine volumes were also typically larger to get rid of the extra urea. Nonetheless, there appears to be a limit on how much protein the human liver can safely cope with: Too much overwhelms the liver's waste-disposal system, leading to protein poisoning—nausea, diarrhea, wasting, and death.

Whatever the metabolic reason for this syndrome, says John Speth, an archaeologist at the University of Michigan's Museum of Anthropology, plenty of evidence shows that hunters through the ages avoided protein excesses, discarding fat-depleted animals even when food was scarce. Early pioneers and trappers in North America encountered what looks like a similar affliction, sometimes referred to as rabbit starvation because rabbit meat is notoriously lean. Forced to subsist on fat-deficient meat, the men would gorge themselves, yet wither away. Protein can't be the sole source of energy for humans, concludes Cordain. Anyone eating a meaty diet that is low in carbohydrates must have fat as well.

Stefansson had arrived at this conclusion, too, while living among the Copper Eskimo. He recalled how he and his Eskimo companions had become quite ill after weeks of eating "caribou so skinny that there was no appreciable fat behind the eyes or in the marrow." Later he agreed to repeat the miserable experience at Bellevue Hospital, for science's sake, and for a while ate nothing but defatted meat. "The symptoms brought on at Bellevue by an incomplete meat diet [lean without fat] were exactly the same as in the Arctic . . . diarrhea and a feeling of general baffling discomfort," he wrote. He was restored with a fat fix but "had lost considerable weight." For the remainder of his year on meat, Stefansson tucked into his rations of chops and steaks with fat intact. "A normal meat diet is not a high-protein diet," he pronounced. "We were really getting three-quarters of our calories from fat." (Fat is more than twice as calorie dense as protein or carbohydrate, but even so, that's a lot of lard. A typical U.S diet provides about 35 percent of its calories from fat.)

Stefansson dropped 10 pounds on his meat-and-fat regimen and remarked on its "slenderizing" aspect, so perhaps it's no surprise he's been co-opted as a posthumous poster boy for Atkins-type diets. No discussion about diet these days can avoid Atkins. Even some researchers interviewed for this article couldn't resist referring to the Inuit way of eating as the "original Atkins." "Superficially, at a macronutrient level, the two diets certainly look similar," allows Samuel Klein, a nutrition researcher at Washington University in St. Louis, who's attempting to study how Atkins stacks up against conventional weight-loss diets. Like the Inuit diet, Atkins is low in carbohydrates and very high in fat. But numerous researchers, including Klein, point out that there are profound differences between the two diets, beginning with the type of meat and fat eaten.

Fats have been demonized in the United States, says Eric Dewailly, a professor of preventive medicine at Laval University in Quebec. But all fats are not created equal. This lies at the heart of a paradox—the Inuit paradox, if you will. In the Nunavik villages in northern Quebec, adults over 40 get almost half their calories from native foods, says Dewailly, and they don't die of heart attacks at nearly the same rates as other Canadians or Americans. Their cardiac death rate is about half of ours, he says. As someone who looks for links between diet and cardiovascular health, he's intrigued by that reduced risk. Because the traditional Inuit diet is "so restricted," he says, it's easier to study than the famously heart-healthy Mediterranean diet, with its cornucopia of vegetables, fruits, grains, herbs, spices, olive oil, and red wine.

A key difference in the typical Nunavik Inuit's diet is that more than 50 percent of the calories in Inuit native foods come from fats. Much more important, the fats come from wild animals.

Wild-animal fats are different from both farm-animal fats and processed fats, says Dewailly. Farm animals, cooped up and stuffed with agricultural grains (carbohydrates) typically have lots of solid, highly saturated fat. Much of our processed food is also riddled with solid fats, or so-called trans fats, such as the reengineered vegetable oils and shortenings cached in baked goods and snacks. "A lot of the packaged food on supermarket shelves contains them. So do commercial french fries," Dewailly adds.

Trans fats are polyunsaturated vegetable oils tricked up to make them more solid at room temperature. Manufacturers do this by hydrogenating the oils—adding extra hydrogen atoms to their molecular structures—which "twists" their shapes. Dewailly makes twisting sound less like a chemical transformation than a perversion, an act of public-health sabotage: "These man-made fats are dangerous, even worse for the heart than saturated fats." They not only lower high-density lipoprotein cholesterol (HDL, the "good" cholesterol) but they also raise low-density lipoprotein cholesterol (LDL, the "bad" cholesterol) and triglycerides, he says. In the process, trans fats set the stage for heart attacks because they lead to the increase of fatty buildup in artery walls.

Wild animals that range freely and eat what nature intended, says Dewailly, have fat that is far more healthful. Less of their fat is saturated, and more of it is in the monounsaturated form (like olive oil). What's more, cold-water fishes and sea mammals are particularly rich in polyunsaturated fats called n-3 fatty acids or omega-3 fatty acids. These fats appear to benefit the heart and vascular system. But the polyunsaturated fats in most Americans' diets are the omega-6 fatty acids supplied by vegetable oils. By contrast, whale blubber consists of 70 percent monounsaturated fat and close to 30 percent omega-3s, says Dewailly.

'Dieting is the price we pay for too little exercise and too much mass-produced food'

Omega-3s evidently help raise HDL cholesterol, lower triglycerides, and are known for anticlotting effects. (Ethnographers have remarked on an Eskimo propensity for nosebleeds.) These fatty acids are believed to protect the heart from life-threatening arrhythmias that can lead to sudden cardiac death. And like a "natural aspirin," adds Dewailly, omega-3 polyunsaturated fats help put a damper on runaway inflammatory processes, which play a part in atherosclerosis, arthritis, diabetes, and other so-called diseases of civilization.

You can be sure, however, that Atkins devotees aren't routinely eating seal and whale blubber. Besides the acquired taste problem, their commerce is extremely restricted in the United States by the Marine Mammal Protection Act, says Bruce Holub, a nutritional biochemist in the department of human biology and nutritional sciences at the University of Guelph in Ontario.

"In heartland America it's probable they're not eating in an Eskimo-like way," says Gary Foster, clinical director of the Weight and Eating Disorders Program at the Pennsylvania School of Medicine. Foster, who describes himself as open-minded about Atkins, says he'd nonetheless worry if people saw the diet as a green light to eat all the butter and bacon—saturated fats—they want. Just before rumors surfaced that Robert Atkins had heart and weight problems when he died, Atkins officials themselves were stressing saturated fat should account for no more than 20 percent of dieters' calories. This seems to be a clear retreat from the diet's original don't-count-the-calories approach to bacon and butter and its happy exhortations to "plow into those prime ribs." Furthermore, 20 percent of calories from saturated fats is *double* what most nutritionists advise. Before plowing into those prime ribs, readers of a recent edition of the *Dr. Atkins' New Diet Revolution* are urged to take omega-3 pills to help protect their hearts. "If you watch carefully," says Holub wryly, "you'll see many popular U.S. diets have quietly added omega-3 pills, in the form of fish oil or flaxseed capsules, as supplements."

Needless to say, the subsistence diets of the Far North are not "dieting." Dieting is the price we pay for too little exercise and too much mass-produced food. Northern diets were a way of life in places too cold for agriculture, where food, whether hunted, fished, or foraged, could not be taken for granted. They were about keeping weight on.

This is not to say that people in the Far North were fat: Subsistence living requires exercise—hard physical work. Indeed, among the good reasons for native people to maintain their old way of eating, as far as it's possible today, is that it provides a hedge against obesity, type 2 diabetes, and heart disease. Unfortunately, no place on Earth is immune to the spreading taint of growth and development. The very well-being of the northern food chain is coming under threat from global warming, land development, and industrial pollutants in the marine environment. "I'm a pragmatist," says Cochran, whose organization is involved in pollution monitoring and disseminating food-safety information to native villages. "Global warming we don't have control over. But we can, for example, do cleanups of military sites in Alaska or of communication cables leaching lead into fish-spawning areas. We can help communities make informed food choices. A young woman of childbearing age may choose not to eat certain organ meats that concentrate contaminants. As individuals, we do have options. And eating our salmon and our seal is still a heck of a better option than pulling something processed that's full of additives off a store shelf."

Not often in our industrial society do we hear someone speak so familiarly about "our" food animals. We don't talk of "our pig" and "our beef." We've lost that creature feeling, that sense of kinship with food sources. "You're taught to think in boxes," says Cochran. "In our culture the connectivity between humans, animals, plants, the land they live on, and the air they share is ingrained in us from birth.

"You truthfully can't separate the way we get our food from the way we live," she says. "How we get our food is intrinsic to our culture. It's how we pass on our values and knowledge to the young. When you go out with your aunts and uncles to hunt or to gather, you learn to smell the air, watch the wind, understand the way the ice moves, know the land. You get to know where to pick which plant and what animal to take."

"It's part, too, of your development as a person. You share food with your community. You show respect to your elders by offering them the first catch. You give thanks to the animal that gave up its life for your sustenance. So you get all the physical activity of harvesting your own food, all the social activity of sharing and preparing it, and all the spiritual aspects as well," says Cochran. "You certainly don't get all that, do you, when you buy prepackaged food from a store."

"That's why some of us here in Anchorage are working to protect what's ours, so that others can continue to live back home in the villages," she adds. "Because if we don't take care of our food, it won't be there for us in the future. And if we lose our foods, we lose who we are." The word Inupiat means "the real people." "That's who we are," says Cochran.

Meeting the Maasai: Messages for Management

Nigel Nicholson

Is it possible to learn anything of value from the study of cultures far removed from contemporary business experience? A positive answer would rest on two ideas. One is the idea that our social systems are the result of implicit choices we make about work and organization, which contrasts can help to highlight. The other is the idea that similarities forms and functioning of organizations and societies.

It was with these principles in mind that I embarked early in 2004 on a week-long ethnographic field trip to a remote part of Northern Kenya, off the tourist track, to stay with a remote Maasai tribe. My interest was stimulated partly from my work on the new Darwinism—what is called evolutionary psychology—and its application to contemporary business (Nicholson, 1997, 2000). I wanted to see how the same ideas might be relevant to a radically different context. This was also linked with my primary research interest: the study of family firms. The underlying proposition of my work in this area is that family businesses have special qualities arising from the infusion of kinship into organizations and their operations (Nicholson & Björnberg, 2004). Accordingly, my method of inquiry was to study them, the Maasai, as if they were a family business, which in one sense they are, as a kinship and affiliate community centered around a common economic objective: the raising of livestock. The underlying intent was to see by what stretch one could find parallels with family and other businesses or what one might learn from failing to find any.

In this article, I set out a number of general principles and themes that emerged from this inquiry.

Who Are the Maasai?

One can divide the primal social systems of world peoples into three broad historical groupings: hunter gatherers, whose way of life has predominated for 99% of human history; pastoralists (often nomadic); and agrarians (farmers). In modern times (i.e., the last 3,000 years), we can add such categories as slave and feudal states, command economies or dictatorships, and latterly, liberal democracies; but it is the first three that have been the way of life for most people for the past 10,000 years (Diamond, 1997; Runciman, 1998). The Maasai fall into the second group: pastoralists who have subsisted on breeding livestock, periodically shifting their grazing across their geographically bounded range—a way of life that has remained pretty much unchanged for 3,000 years. There have been interruptions and incursions in this period, from the spread of farming and later the advent of colonial rule. But now the Maasai are protected in a large conservation area of upland bush veldt and scrub desert, mainly in Northern Kenya and Tanzania.

Their social system revolves around a simple system of production and exchange involving the breeding and herding of cattle and goats.

Where they have little contact with the outside world, they are for the most part non-literate and non-monetary. Their units of production—animals—are their currency along with other materials and services through barter. Their way of life is intensely communal, consisting of tribes aggregating from regionally networked clans. A key theme in their culture is the cult of the warrior. Warriors form a pivotal segment of their social structure, which forms around the divisions of the age set: 14-year periods that govern the lives, responsibilities, and rights of cohorts of males. The rules governing men and women make a very sharp differentiation between the sexes.

In my interviews, my companions and I spoke to four groups: children, women, warriors, and elders. I was one of a party of four Europeans supported by two local men with tents and four-wheel drives to enable us to live among the people in their home area. We were also accompanied by a Turkana,[1] a native of the northern desert area of the Maasai range, who was a freelance journalist fluent in local dialects and who acted as translator and cultural interpreter for us. At the end of our trip, in Nairobi, we also interviewed a prominent Maasai scholar and writer, currently publishing an authoritative series of monographs on Maasai life and customs, to check key facts and impressions.[2] Interviews were semi-structured and, in most cases, recorded on videotape. Various sources were consulted for background intelligence to ensure that we did not waste time uncovering what is already known about the Maasai. Our desire was to understand their experience of life and work and how it might relate to the challenges, tasks, and roles we see in working organizations in the West.

This article is based on field notes from our interviews and observations. Each day for 6 days, we conducted intensive interviews throughout the day and some evenings with individuals and groups of Laikipiak tribespeople in a region to the north of Nairobi, in the foothills of Mount Kenya.[3] In each location, we camped just outside the boma, the thorn enclosure that surrounds a manyatta. The manyatta—literally, "warrior village"—is usually a small collection of mud and wattle huts, usually no more than a dozen per enclosure. Each of these villages houses kinship groups of women, children, and elders (men in age sets superior to the warriors, i.e., from around 30 upwards). The boma acts as a nighttime enclosure protecting livestock from predators (lions and hyenas, principally).

Our interviews took place within the manyattas as well as in the field—wherever we came across warriors, children, women, and elders willing to talk. They almost always were very happy to stop and answer our inquiries. They were almost as interested in us as we in them, and we gave them small gifts of pens, pocketknives, and Polaroid prints of themselves as tokens of appreciation. In content, the schedule of interview questions covered issues of kinship, family life, work, leadership, decision making, and community, including the following topics:

- the roles and responsibilities of specific demographic groups
- leadership role expectations
- governance and decision-making structures
- cultural mores, norms, and taboos
- leadership succession practices
- ownership and wealth management
- critical incidents and everyday problem solving
- conflict management and difficult relationships
- crime and punishment
- health and well-being
- change, especially the incursion of education, money, and other forms of modernity into their way of life

Overall Impressions

My first impression was of a society as far removed from my own as it is possible to imagine. The absence of electricity, running water, consumer goods, written material, and any kind of mechanization, including transport, provides an immediate and visible contrast with any developed economy. You know you are in another world. The physical appearance of the Maasai sends the same message. Most are attired traditionally, wearing the bright red shawl, or shuka, that is emblematic of their identity. Unwed girls and warriors are intensely decorated with elaborate beaded necklaces, circlets, jewelry, and headgear. Many have dyed and braided hair. Male warriors typically carry spears and clubs—ceremonial emblems of their status. In the locality of our inquiry, there was an evident passion for headgear incorporating plastic flowers, a small sign of how materials from other cultures can be imported and absorbed without disturbance to the culture. Elders and married women are more plainly attired, with the only swathes of color being that of their shawls and shukas, especially featuring the famous Maasai crimson. Children, especially boys, are more conventionally ragged urchins in appearance.

The demeanor of people is gentle, self-confident, and positive. Around the boma, one encounters women, infants, and elders during the day. The women are mainly engaged in tending the very young livestock, keeping the fires going, maintaining the enclosure, and doing other local domestic labors. The elders sit around in groups, mainly gossiping and story telling. The women do much the same when not otherwise engaged, for in times of plenty, as we found them after they had experienced the unexpected bonus of un-seasonal rain, this is an undemanding lifestyle. At times of drought or other extremity, life is harder in the struggle to preserve dwindling stock, but during our sojourn, we observed a pace of life that was leisurely and decidedly un-pressured. Around the village, warriors tend to come and go in twos and threes; hang out for a while, talking to the women and elders; and then wander off. When we went walking in the bush, it was these proud and gaudy young men we would mostly encounter out on their patrol duties.

The cycle of the day follows the rhythm of herding. Early repast is followed by the animals being led out of the boma for grazing (keeping young livestock separate from their mothers to preserve their milk supply). They are brought back in at dusk, at which time the women and children do the milking. Evenings are a quiet time for these groups, though warrior groups are given to communal chanting and dancing. In their dance, warriors and unmarried girls set up a hypnotic rhythm of vocalizing and dancing. The men display their agility and athleticism in the famous vertical springing action[4] often featured on travelogue films of the region, whereas the girls rock their bodies in rhythm—a motion visually amplified by the exaggerated sway of their broad flat

neckbands. No such evening celebration takes place if the pattern of normalcy has been disturbed, such as when an animal has gone astray during the day's grazing. Then, searching replaces partying. The Maasai have much larger periodic gatherings and ceremonials to mark the major life events and transitions of the tribe—the most important being age-set succession: the passing of the warrior age-set into elder-hood and the initiation of an entering cohort.

These and other practices are extensively documented elsewhere (D. M. Anderson, 1995; Spear & Waller, 1993) and will not detain us here, for the aim here is rather to extract lessons of wider relevance from observations of how the Maasai see themselves, the world around them, and the prospect of change.

These can be distilled around themes and points of contrast between their world and ours, which I shall summarize here as eight messages for management.

Eight Messages for Management
Clarity and Uniformity Define a Strong Culture

In interviewing the Maasai, one encounters a confidence that is born of clarity. No one seems in any doubt about his or her role, purpose, and responsibilities. The parameters of their world are secure. Within our party, Anthony Willoughby and Jo Owen[5] are practitioners in a territory-mapping technique that engages people from all kinds of societies in the figurative portrayal of their worlds and the tensions within them and in the ways forward to solving problems. In societies such as the Maasai there is not just absolute clarity but uniformity of view. What they draw on their maps repeatedly depicts a focus on the constant priorities of their existence: their livestock, water supply, and grazing and their community and the potential threat to its boundaries by raiders.

Transpose to the Western corporation, and you have as many world-views as you do people. The maps that business people draw show a yearning for strong cultures but an experience that consists of coalitions of fragmented (often quasi-tribal) subcultures. How can one hope to build community under such circumstances? The inconsistent perceptions that the mapping technique exposes in our businesses show how far we are from a communitarian ideal, by virtue of an absence of shared experience and common perspectives. When family firms draw their territory maps, it appears that the sense of true community is less of a problem than in other types of business, partly as a function of reduced size and complexity, strong cultural values, and secure identity. How much does the Maasai clarity depend on small size and short lines of communication? Probably not much. The Maasai people are populous, but their people are dispersed in small groups, linked by almost no modern communication technologies—bush telegraph is literally practiced here—yet our experience of the Maasai was not idiosyncratic. What we observed corresponds to what can be read in the scholarly works on the people.

Does clarity for our business communities depend on size? It does to the extent that evolutionary psychology tells us (Dunbar, 1996) that above the size 150, it is hard to maintain what the 19th-century sociologist Tonnies (1887/1957) called gemeinschaft—the feeling of true community. Large firms do it by maintaining viable subgroups of these dimensions, linking them by weak ties (Burt, 1992; Nicholson, 2000). Additionally, the experience of large family firms seems to suggest that you can spread a "family feeling" through a community by consistency and clarity of vision and values.

The lesson we can derive from Maasai experience here is that clarity matters, and we would do well to ruthlessly expose incongruence and confusion in people's views of the organization and its environment to understand what it would take to move toward greater consistency. But perhaps consistency is not what we want. We love our diversity and revel in our individuality. If we are not prepared to forgo these qualities, then we need to realize that they may impose substantial costs on our capacity to work together. Family firms may supply examples of where some of these costs can be circumvented by cultural integration, for within them, the natural diversity of human types in the firm are, at their best, brought together in a powerful and rich weave of themes around a clear business focus (Tagiuri & Davis, 1996). At their worst, the family mix is explosive and destroys the business—a risk that seems absent among the Maasai.

Minimalism Yields Harmony

One theme of our interrogations was a search for the dynamics driving adaptation and development in the Maasai, as one might seek it in a business, through the sources of creative tension, difference, and conflict resolution. This proved to be difficult. We uncovered accounts of small disputes and everyday jealousies, but we found few signs of significant conflicts, even through indirect inquiries we made to assess whether our hosts were concealing a more turbulent reality from us. By every account we received, this was plainly not the case. We had entered a society where, despite evident privations, there was uniformity, contentment, and harmony among people. The men, women, and children we spoke with expressed in word and manner an unaffected happiness and contentment with life. "We all love each other," we were told. "We are all one family." When we asked them about threats to their existence, they were strongly resistant to the idea, expressing great confidence in their values and continuity. Anthropologists are wise to be cautious of the gloss that is given to accounts of everyday life given by people flattered by the unusual attention of ethnographic inquiry. We prefer to accept our impressions as genuine for three reasons. First, we were not so exotic to them as they were to us; they had mostly seen White people before,[6] though they had not been questioned in this manner. Second, our impressions were corroborated across more than one group, independently. Third, we tested all our impressions with our Turkana interpreter and subsequently in discussions after the trip with a Maasai scholar. As the former, our translator affirmed, "No, they are not romancing. People here don't carry baggage. They have no word for 'sorry.'" However, in other respects, we did find quite a lot of romancing about their existence, as we shall see. Some of the facts of people's reports were quite far removed from their lived reality.

The chief point here, however, is that it would appear that the real peace and amity we observed was delivered partly by virtue of the extreme un-demand and simplicity of their way of life. This does not mean they are immune from struggles for existence or crises at intervals. Nor does it mean that their emotional life is impoverished. But their life is very simple in its structures, rhythms, and demands. There is no growth as we would see it in developed economies. Change for the community fluctuates on a rhythmic cycle of seasons and the changing fortunes of their times. At a personal level, expectations are progressive, however. Parents give livestock to their children in the rational hope of their growing an increasing herd, which they, in turn, will distribute to their own offspring. This leads to overgrazing, such that people are used to a cycle of plenty and impoverishment. Within these expectations, the pattern of life retains its main elements and forms, quite unchanged.

Is it simplicity that creates harmony? It certainly is an element, inasmuch as one can abstract one theme from several that characterize the culture and way of life. The simplicity of the Maasai existence contributes through the fact that what befalls one individual or group generally befalls others—drought and plenty being the most important. The structure and culture also dictate a sharing of everyday life events. In visiting a chief's wife in her hut, I asked her if there is anything she

would like to know about the way of life of my people. She asked me about the construction and disposition of our houses. I explained that we often lived in large communities where we did not know our neighbors very well. She was perplexed: "How do you build your houses, then, without neighbors to help you?"

Does this conjunction of simplicity and harmony hold any parallels for business life? It is hard to find organizations that have such a simple existence, though one could identify perhaps agricultural smallholdings or mom and pop stores that live just on passing trade: businesses that seek no major market growth—just sufficient benefits to pass on to the next generation. The quality of life is indeed often happy and harmonious in such situations, though the intrusion of the market, public planning, squeezes on wealth and the like make them neither secure enough nor free from worry to emulate the Maasai. Yet these organizations, such as the Maasai, can exemplify the principle espoused by philosophers that one recipe for a contented life is to hold modest expectations.

On this principle, perhaps there is an exemplary point, for organizational life does face a future challenge of how to reverse the escalating growth expectations that market capitalism creates. The cottage industry alternative of simple, no-growth businesses is made to look attractive by the Maasai example, but is it a model in any sense for the development of the business community? Not in general, for the imperative of globalization is moving us inexorably in the opposite direction. However, increasingly at the margin, there are groups in society who seek to opt out of the rat race and migrate into this kind of harmonious equilibrium. The message here is that this can be done only to the extent that one can keep it simple. Most observable trends are in the reverse direction.

Collectivism Has to Be Culturally Reinforced

Cross-cultural scholars write much about individualism and collectivism as a key dimension of cultural difference, contrasting, for example, the preference of the developing world for group collaboration and consensus versus the Anglo-Saxon bias toward individualistic, competitive striving and the cult of the personality (Hofstede, 1998). The most primitive and enduring form of collectivism is food sharing (Ridley, 1996)—one of the fundamental processes in every kind of society. In the West, our food sharing (e.g., distribution of wealth and resources) is grossly unequal and inequitable.

The Maasai represent an opposite extreme on this continuum, intensively collectivist not only in their ethos of sharing but also in their treatment of individual differences. Contemporary behavior genetics notes that in every society, people differ on the base of heritable features of personality, ability, cognitive style, and physical appearance (Plomin, 1994). But even the most inborn of traits passes through the filter of experience. A person's genes to be tall require an environment that will nurture their potential through sufficiency of nutrition and freedom from disease or accident. It is also possible for cultural values and practices, via socialization, to overlay individual differences in character to minimize or to accentuate them. In our society, the military does the former, drama school the latter.

In the Maasai, the cult of the collective is extreme. When I asked a local chief, "What do you do when you have someone who has exceptional talent in some skill, such as musical ability?" his answer was disapproving: "We don't like it. He would not be a good murran (warrior)." Further examination revealed that the most valued abilities are those perceived to be economically useful to the collective, such as the skill to make spears, though the individuals who possess such talents are not overtly celebrated for their achievements. Likewise, whatever it takes to become a good witchdoctor—intelligence, memory, and self-belief—is discovered and employed rather than venerated or allowed to become the subject of acclamation. It was also apparent that the ability to tell stories is highly valued. Good narrators' and gossips' company may be often sought after, but without any conspicuous personal recognition. Apart from these individual differences, it seemed that other distinguishing personal qualities would be regarded as a distraction. In another locality, we asked the same question and got a different answer. Here, where the group was closer to the tourist trail and where the clan occasionally performed entertainment for cash, musical talent was valued as instrumental to the ability to purchase materials for decoration and ritual. This variation serves to underline the rule that utility to the collective is the criterion for valuing individual differentiation.

The implication is that how much individuality is displayed is a matter of collective choice. To maintain a high degree of collectivism requires a highly structured, ritualized, and normative culture. In our organizations, we achieve uniformity less by power of enculturation and more by self-selection. It is "elective affinity"—people choosing to join groups of likeminded individuals and quitting those where they feel uncomfortably different—that results in the apparent narrow bandwidth of character that segments our society horizontally. It leads to the within-group homogeneity and between-group heterogeneity of the accounting firm, the law practice, the advertising agency, and many other kinds of business (Chatman, 1991; Schneider, 1987). But within all of these sectors, individuals are striving to distinguish themselves to be valued and rewarded—a far cry from the Maasai world. Business organizations can choose to reinforce uniformity of dress and conduct-Japanese corporations built a good deal of strength through this model (Yoshimura & Anderson, 1997)—but the trends worldwide in business culture are still migrating in the opposite direction, toward the recognition of individual contribution.

A Service Ideal Can Be Cultivated at All Levels of a Social System

It was apparent, in interview after interview, that service to the collective is an overriding value. We asked every group what they would see as the exemplar of a good warrior, wife, elder, and even child. The most striking factor in responses was their uniformity. Moreover, there was a remarkable intersection with questions about what gave people greatest pleasure. A group of women spoke about the joy of being good at caring for husband, children, and animals. The good warrior is one who looks after animals. The good elder provides for his family and does not go out and get drunk. Good people, we were told, do not complain.

The Maasai scholar who we interviewed in Nairobi to check our field impressions reiterated the theme. The word respect was much used to summate the estimation of the service ideal. This is earned by "proper" and "correct" behaviors, which amount to modesty, nonviolence toward others, deference to age, and service to others.

One of the most illuminating in-depth interviews was conducted with a warrior chief—a man of extraordinary presence, around 6 ft 4 in. tall, with a lean, handsome face and body and finely braided, colored hair, possessing a deep, dark voice, leavened by a brilliant smile of large white teeth, and with alert, penetrating, yet sparkling eyes. Here was a living exemplar of the much-misused word charisma. This man had presence. His answers also revealed him to be a person of high intelligence. His acumen had earned him the responsibility for managing the financial transactions of his community. Here was someone who one felt would be trusted, followed, and revered. He probably was, but his answers betrayed no hint of leadership in the sense of exercised authority; rather, every answer to our probing just elaborated an extended concept of stewardship. His responsibility was to serve his community. Similar responses came from all our other questioning of

wives and elders about what was important to them, how they saw their roles and responsibilities, and what they regarded as deviance. They too echoed the themes of "servant leadership" (Greenleaf, 1991).

I also asked about how they dealt with mental illness and examples of people who display extremes of irrational, unpredictable, and dangerous emotions. These were reported to be quite rare but were owned as a community responsibility and source of guilt and were to be treated by the ministrations of witchdoctors. Their collectivist ethos leads the kind of behavior that in our society would be treated as criminally deviant to be treated as a shared responsibility. In our developed economies, we tend to isolate and often punish disordered personalities and treat sickness as a sign of individual weakness and mental aberrations as a form of deviance.[7] The stress literature can be seen as attempting to reverse this logic, but it fails when it only leads to organizations attempting to remove the symptoms (Quick, Nelson, & Hurrell, 1997). The deeper remedies lie in culture: Collectivism and service ideals are part of both the prevention and the cure of endemic stress. Family firms often have this ethos, but they are apt to criticize themselves for being "too soft," when actually this is just the other side to the coin of their greatest strength—their ability to embrace and integrate diversity (Nicholson & Björnberg, 2004).

Alternative Models of Leadership, Power, and Authority Operate

The charismatic chief, known colloquially and fittingly as "Cool," gave a detailed account of what being a leader meant to him. He said he had been chosen for his good behavior. Probing revealed that this connoted a mix of favorable temperament and reputation for morality. When asked about the requisite skills of leadership, he said, "Never quarrel with anyone. Don't demean anyone." He told us about when he was identified as a leader at the time of his circumcision and how he was chosen over another candidate, a murran who turned out to be docile and slow. He described the achievement that identified him early as a success in ensuring 150 cows survived during a drought, though his remarks indicate that qualities of character—steadiness, self-control, empathy, and interpersonal problem solving—were more likely to be what marked him for leadership within a culture with these values. These qualities, as it turns out, are pretty much what is currently discussed as emotional intelligence (Zeidner, Matthews, & Roberts, 2004).

I asked him to give an example of the most difficult kind of task he would have to undertake. He launched into a story of a conflict between a murran and an elder, where the former had disobeyed an injunction of the latter. What made this case difficult is that the age-set structure gives automatic authority to elders, as in many traditional cultures. This meant that early intervention had to tread a delicate line of mediation. In such a case when right is on the side of the junior party—when a murran is wronged by an elder—Cool's account showed his role to be one of fine adjustment and face saving, while giving due recognition to the fact that an offense had been given.

We asked Cool about a typical day. His account showed that much of it was spent schmoozing—walking around the manyattas talking to men and women—an essential activity to oil the wheels of the community and for the leader to retain his intelligence about the community and his ability to broker problem solving.

At the senior level, elders have a collective authority. Within this clan, there was not a single chief but also a vice chief at a different location and a third leader who was designated as a coordinator of communications, traveling the range of the tribe. The leadership role of these individuals was clearly low in the exercise of power, though high in status and authority. Whenever we raised questions about critical decisions, it was never these individuals whose authority was invoked.

Instead, it was invariably a group of elders. Their role was clearly to capture and exemplify consensual authority. Personal power did not distill in the persons of whoever was selected to take part in this collective activity because the composition would vary from time to time and from decision to decision. However, we gathered that, nonetheless, certain individuals considered especially wise or just would be called on more often than others for this duty. In this way, the leadership model matches exactly the values of the culture; individuality is acknowledged without eroding the power of the collective ideal.

Power is very much a property of the structure, which is stratified by age and gender. Women play no part, officially, in any of the decision making, though more detailed ethnographies have documented their behind-the-scenes influence and their key role in many of the social adjustments that need to be made (Hodgson, 2001). Much the same can be observed in family businesses, where women may exert an unseen influence both on decisions and, of course, through their role in schooling the next generation. My discussion with Maasai women revealed that they have strong ideas of what is correct male behavior, and one can presume that they help to enforce this through their private conversations and by the informal sanctions that may take place in intimate relationships. Yet in the literature, there is universal agreement as to their role as one of severe subjugation to male authority. As will be discussed later, the role and treatment of women in Maasai society has ethically troubling features beyond the fact of their formal powerlessness.

So here we find models of leadership at the farthest remove from those of the modern corporation, as with their cultures: a stewardship model of leadership around the exercise of emotional intelligence in interpersonal problem solving, authority by consensus decision making, and strictly stratified hierarchies of authority (Davis, Schoorman, & Donaldson, 1997). In business, leadership is the exercise of individual discretionary power, decision making is via political process of coalitions of interest, and hierarchies of authority are highly labile and are not founded on any particular fundamentals. Again, some family firms depart from the corporate model in the direction of the Maasai example, with an emphasis on settled leadership arrangements and on consensus, stewardship, and servant leadership (De Free, 1999; Greenleaf, 1991; Semler, 1993). The underlying dynamic of this are three unique aspects of family business:

1. Kinship co-ownership of a productive enterprise. This is typically what underlies the distinctive cultural strength and attachment to their products and services that mark family firms (Denison, Lief, & Ward, 2004). The Maasai display a similar emotional attachment with their animals.

2. Intergenerational transmission of assets. This is what gives family firms their renowned longevity, long-term strategic perspectives, financial prudence, and enduring, value-based distinctiveness (Lansberg, 1999). This continuity is the raison d'être of the Maasai.

3. Integration of kin and non-kin in the enterprise. The most successful family businesses are those that build clan-like structures, with family and non-family working together as a single bonded community (Gersick, Davis, Hampton, & Lansberg, 1997). That, of course, is the classic clan structure as marriage ties blend related and unrelated people to a common destiny.

Mythologies Are Central to Sustaining Strong Cultures

The mythology around which the Maasai way of life revolves is that of the warrior. We were regaled with stories about lion hunts, raids on rival tribes to steal livestock, border battles to protect their tribe against enemy incursions, and other heroic exploits. Lion hunts are an important part of the rituals of the group. They are part of the collective socialization of youth into adult ways—a source of bonding among the murran—and the means of acquiring valued accoutrements for rites and ceremonies (tail for the leader, skin for a marriage ceremony, etc.). We were told about how the group encircles a lion; one especially honored youth is given the job of rushing toward the open jaws of the lion at bay, inserting laterally a double-pointed stick and rotating it so that the lion's jaws clamping leads to its demise. Bush raids are portrayed as vital to protect the integrity of the tribe. Warriors patrol the perimeter of their range to deter their enemies. "The murran are like an army in the bush," we were told, and "enemies come frequently."

Deeper exploration and checking reveals a different reality. Lion hunts have become an extreme rarity; the last one for our host group was 15 years ago, according to one informant. The Maasai range, as specified by government regulation, is adjacent to and intersecting with wildlife conservation areas where lions are protected. Raids are also a thing of the past. The greatest threat comes from neighboring tribes letting their stock graze into another tribe's territory, as had recently occurred in our area with Samburu neighbors. The warriors do spend their time patrolling the territory, but this seems to be mainly an extended gossip network—the bush telegraph. Yet they do this kitted out for a more glorious role, adorned with their symbols of male pride and honor and carrying their useless weaponry. Autobiographical accounts from Maasai perpetuate the mythology; they are mainly heroic self-portrayals—quite at odds with the contemporary reality of Maasai life we witnessed (Lekuton, 2003; Saitoti, 1986; Spencer, 1993).

The Maasai are keen to display their mythic identity at every opportunity, especially at a time such as our arrival at their manyatta. On our first evening with them, they ritually slaughtered a goat, shared it with us, and then performed a dance. The slaughter was performed by two young murran, who first suffocated the beast, then carefully peeled back the skin at the neck, taking care not to shed a drop of blood before making an incision in the main artery of the animal's throat. Then the two murran took turns to fall to their haunches to suck the blood directly from the prostrate beast. The remainder of the blood was drained before the carcass was cooked on the open fire. Their delight in this honor was apparent. I asked one of them if it tasted good. He wrinkled his nose and shook his head but spoke with pleasure of the honor that it conferred on him.

The control of aggressive males is one of the key needs of every society, as has been observed (Coon, 1971; Harris, 1979), and the machismo and even violent aspects of the warrior cult are arguably a way this society siphons off its aggression, such that the wider culture can retain a peaceful integrity.

Their mythical sense of identity incorporates a powerful need to believe in their self-reliance. For example, I asked the Maasai in some detail about what they did about sickness. They claimed to be entirely reliant on local folk medicine and care through the ministrations of the witchdoctor. This turns out to be only partially true. Claims made that outsiders were never invited in to provide medical assistance were discounted as romantic stories by another informant.

What does this tell us of relevance to business life? For sure, we have no such reliable cultural means of containing male aggression as do the Maasai. Writers on corporate culture describe the symbolic, ritualistic, and unconscious normative themes that define the most intangible aspects of corporate identity (Goffee & Jones, 1998). Stories are a central vehicle for the transmission of values, the maintenance of norms, and the buttressing of shared identity (Martin, 2002). Culture is the taken-for-granted substratum of assumptions and beliefs in any social system. Its functional importance is that it governs what people pay attention to—what they rule in and rule out in making choices, often without conscious thought, in their everyday choices and reactions. Cultures are strong or weak. The Maasai culture is extremely strong, with its mythologies acting as a powerful binding agent. In business, writers talk about strong cultures, but they scarcely bear comparison to such an example (Deal & Kennedy, 1982). Company cultures often do have elements of what one can call heroic mythologies and legends, but there is little uniformity or consistency to them. Unlike the Maasai, if you ask two or three warriors in a firm what drives the culture, you are likely to get two or three different answers.

The leaders of corporations try to elevate their brand equity, mission statements, and strategic plans to the level of cultural norms, but the problem is that often only a small percentage of employees—those closest to the source—them seriously. The best family firms again supply the best examples, in terms of little gap between cultural self-image, mythologies, and the way of life of the community (Daily & Dollinger, 1991).

Strong Cultures Can Rapidly Decay

Our journey back to civilization was disturbing by how short we found the distance—literally—and metaphorically—between the nobility and integration of this historic culture and its extreme degradation. We called this sad journey—a one-way transition that many traditional societies have undergone (Pelto, 1973)—"the Road to Rumeruti," representing our physical journey to the border town of that name. Rumeruti somewhat resembles an African version of a Wild West frontier town—one long main street consisting of the normal provisioning stores for people going to and from the bush. The target for our reconnection with the world of commerce was, unsurprisingly, the first bar in town to consume the closest one could get to a cold beer in such a place. As we pulled up, the first and most striking phenomenon was the absence of body language signals of friendly welcome, such as those we had grown used to receiving from the people in the bush. In our new setting, travelers like us were a familiar sight, and we seemed to represent an opportunity for, at best, a somewhat cool curiosity and, at worst, petty theft. We had to abandon our beer and leave because a gang of youths was fooling around with the trailer hitched to one of our four-wheel-drive vehicles. Our two drivers, father and son,[8] advised that the situation was becoming unstable, and we had best finish our beers at a more congenial location. The youths appeared like any disaffected and low-expectation group that one finds in many transitional societies. I was reminded of the gangs hanging around the town squares of the former Eastern Germany's regional towns I saw a few years ago, oppressed by unemployment and damaged pride and now forming an aimless but menacing presence.

On the way to Rumeruti we had seen earlier signs of the same phenomenon, or what could be seen as intermediate stages to this condition. The first was a stop at the cattle ranch of a wealthy local (White) explorer. We admired his cattle and camels but were less impressed by the living conditions of his workers. These Maasai dwelt in corrugated tin lean-tos, much less commodious than the traditional Maasai dwelling, though no doubt better stocked with Western consumables. The women and children sat in the dirt around the huts in a much more listless fashion than we were used to seeing, and they eyed us with cold indifference.

Farther down the road, we stopped at a village of Maasai employed by local White farmers and service businesses and tried to conduct our usual ethnographic interviews, but we were met first with suspicious demands about why we wanted to know such things and then with demands for money. We were ready to offer our usual gifts and also cash if need be. Indeed, we did both but abandoned the interviews, sensing that we would get little reliable intelligence. Yet the few comments we did record affirmed that these people had abandoned most of their

Maasai traditions and practices. Elders were no longer revered because there was no structure to sustain such respect. Instead, they were uselessly hanging around, waiting for the next meal or conversation.

The bulk of Maasai society remains in its timeless balance. In some areas, tourism has invaded and has begun to transform their existence (especially in the much visited Maasai Mara game reserve). Here, just at the short margin where one crosses between their world and our world, one retains the impression that they have, fatally, let go with one hand—the handhold to their ancient civilization—and with the other grasped something insubstantial and un-sustaining. The only way out of the listless limbo they had entered was by the historically familiar migration to the big city—Nairobi in this case—where they would join the street people seeking advantage in scratching for a living at the margins of the human tide that flows through such a metropolis.

Does this sad story have any lessons for business organizations? It shows not so much that culture disappears but that it can get degraded quite rapidly, and those that build to greatness often do so retaining their distinctive family identity (R. C. Anderson & Reeb, 2003; O'Hara & Mandel, 2002). This is amply illustrated by the history of mergers and acquisitions, where value—often cultural value—is destroyed rather more readily than it is created (Empson, in press). Post-merger integration failure is often because of cultural residues—loyalties detached from their points of origin, for example—persisting to be a destructive force where once they were part of the organization's strength. Family businesses that sell up typically lose their identity and therefore one of the sources of their comparative advantage, quite rapidly. Yet we cannot keep cultures alive just for their aesthetic value. When the time for transition comes, as in the post-merger or post-IPO period, firms need to find ways of saying goodbye to the old and embracing the new. It is the difficulty of the latter that many organizations such as the Maasai, at their margin, face.

Ethical Challenges Are Ever Present

We take for granted that other cultures have a right to exist, especially if they are exotic and present no external threat, such as is true of many aboriginal cultures. The Maasai, with their positive social values, their pacific way of life, and their harmless environmental impacts, seem to be a prime example of a world we should leave alone and in peace. That is the policy that has been effected by the governments whose dominion cover the Maasai range: protecting them within a range of conserved land against what would otherwise be the invasion of the agrarians, as happened in former times. In earlier times of human history, the prevailing perspective on "alien" cultures has been much less relativistic and much less tolerant. Cultural imperialism was implicitly part of the economic conquest and was the norm prior to the 20th century. Priests rode in the bows of the men-o'-war that brought civilization to the "savages," with the gun and the cross as the twin instruments of conquest (Landes, 1998). Without compunction, our forebears viewed other cultures as backward, corrupt, ungodly, and in need of enlightenment. Now we shudder with guilt at the memory and try to respect the differences that survive as much as we try to honor their past.

But should we now view other cultures without criticism or without raising universal ethical questions? The Maasai present a challenging case, chiefly in one respect: the role of women. There are three aspects that are potentially troubling. One is female circumcision, or "genital mutilation," as reformers rightly term it. This was universally practiced in the area in which we were located. Not only is the practice arguably a denial of young women's rights, but also its ritual form is brutal and painful in the execution. Second is what in the West might be called licensed pedophilia. Circumcised girls quickly become wives, usually of elders, often polygynously. The warriors, during their 14-year age set, are part of a male fraternity. Given that this is at the peak of their sexual maturity and that they are the focal point of all the Maasai's glamorous self-regard in their decorative mythic identity, they clearly need a sexual outlet. On questioning them about this, the object of their amorous energy turns out to be uncircumcised, that is, prepubescent, girls. Their pre-menarche status also minimizes the risk of unwanted pregnancies among girls who will shortly be marriageable. Third is the absence of women from any formal role or status within the community, though, as I have noted, their unofficial influence may be much greater. However, the scope of this influence is limited to the domestic sphere, and the absence of women in formal decision-making position and, indeed, the absence of regard for any individual talent or needs is troubling to Western sensibilities. How can one square these practices with the values of stewardship? It is perhaps a fact of life that within societies such apparent contradictions have always prevailed. In the Maasai case, a framework of shared norms and practices acts as a protective perimeter within which humanistic values may be fully expressed, even though those same norms sanction ethically abhorrent practices and morally oppressive inter-group relations.

Ignorant bliss might summarize the situation of many of the Maasai. Of course, one has no right to rob them of this state, but one can legitimately question the ethics of denying experience and choice to people in any social system and perhaps especially when it focuses with particular force, as it does here, on one sex: women.[9] Would it constitute a return to the bad old days of cultural imperialism to assert that one should not seek to preserve such cultural arrangements? One can argue that a social system that denies women their human rights and keeps both them and many men in a state of retarded development through compulsive structures and intensive mythologies is undesirable and that the state should not seek to preserve it. The counterargument is that we have not right to pass moral judgments on one culture from the perspective of another.

What does a Darwinian perspective have to offer at this point? It does not take sides in this debate; rather, it takes both. It rejects an undiscriminating relativism because it asserts that all cultural arrangements are coevolved systems, mediating between an ancient and unchanging human nature on one hand and a changing set of environmental demands on the other. Each has costs and benefits, and therefore it says that some are less costly to human happiness and capability than others. The Maasai are, in this view, locked into a fragile equilibrium. It requires only minimal change to context and inputs to bring profound disturbance, as we have seen. The practical riposte is that change will come to the Maasai through two forces: education and money. Their blissful existence will be corroded by the power of knowledge and by the inexorable invasion of the moneyed economy. Should this change be hastened or hindered on ethical grounds? This is a question beyond the scope of this article, but it does have wider relevance.

When we look at business organizations, we tend to be a lot less shy about making ethical judgments about their standards of conduct or their treatment of their people. What is the price of the autonomy or performance of a business? One can argue, from the first principles of the new Darwinism, that some ways of working and organizing are more injurious or restrictive to the human spirit than others and that some liberate and engage human capabilities better than others. Family firms often achieve the latter, exhibiting positive qualities such as cultural inclusiveness, value-driven leadership, a high degree of identification with their own products and services, and a communitarian link with their customers, suppliers, and other stakeholders (Miller, 2004). To a degree, these are the best qualities of tribalism. We can also see the worst where firms degenerate in squabbling silos of divided interest, with detached and self-interested leadership.

Conclusion

The Maasai do inhabit a distant world in many ways, though in other ways, closer to us than we might think. Anyone who has traveled to remote locations and has had the opportunity to talk and exchange with tribal people will report how small the distance is between conversing minds. Personally, I can say that some of the Maasai with whom I met and talked were people I could relate to more easily than some people in my home community. That is a matter of social-psychological chemistry. Evolutionary psychology tells us how impressed—over-impressed—we are with what lies on the surface of physical and cultural appearance, for beneath the surface lies a genetic identity and similarity that is much greater than among members of our nearest primate cousins, the chimpanzees (Jones, 1993). It is very easy for any human to tune into and share experience with another human once you have crossed the language barrier. At the same time, within our narrow bandwidth of genetic differences we do vary in temperament, personality, intelligence, and interests in ways that mean we get along much more easily with some of our kind than we do with others. Culture, of course, is a powerful container of these differences, sometimes amplifying them, sometimes muting them. The Maasai are an extreme version of the constraint of difference.

The question with which this article opened has been answered here as follows: Cultures differ at many levels, including across types of business, not least between family and other kinds of firm. Clearly, there are major differences between the goals of businesses, whether family or non-family, and these tribes-people. That is partly a matter of complexity and differentiation, for as I have noted, the life of the Maasai is immeasurably simpler, but it shares two features especially with family firms: a mutual dependence between kinship group and the products of collective labor and a competitor relationship with other members of the wider community—in the Maasai case, other clans within the tribe, other tribes within the people, and other ethnic and tribal groups within the locality.[10] The laws of economics apply to their activities as much as they do in any business community and society (see Becker, 1991 and Sahlins, 1972, for relevant analyses). The Maasai are interested in generating surpluses and regulating consumption, not just in an idyllic life of peaceful coexistence. They strive against elements and resource insufficiencies to increase their stock, improve their welfare, and enhance the quality of their consumption. Yet like some family businesses, they will not venture into new areas of development that would erode the core of their shared experience and practice.

The Maasai case underlines the ways in which structures, norms, mythologies, and contextual conditions hold them in place and how they can be quite easily eroded or invaded by forms of change. Food sharing and the control of aggressive males are, as we have observed, critical functions in tribal communities. The Maasai solution involves powerful, inculcated norms of sharing on one hand and the mythology of the warrior on the other. In Western organizations, we do not do either of them reliably or effectively. Food sharing is unequal and often arbitrary, and ambitiously machismo males are often given dangerous license. The Enron case exemplified both of these, as do many other businesses.

The wider implication is that what we accept as normal in our businesses is a matter of choice and that if we want, say, different kinds of leadership from the dominant paradigm, then we have to do more than just train it into candidates or assume it will happen just by making judicious executive appointments. It is a matter of culture and what holds culture in place (Schein, 1985).

Notes

1. Gideon Lepalo.

2. James Ole Nairuko.

3. This Maasai tribe numbers around 30,000 in six subtribal groupings, one of which were our hosts.

4. This display is akin to the stotting (vertical leaping) of the Springbok, which similarly connotes genetic fitness.

5. Anthony Willoughby and Jo Owen of Auvian Partners.

6. We were told that around once every 2 months, visitors from outside would be seen.

7. One is reminded of Samuel Butler's novel *Erewhon* (an anagram of nowhere), written some 130 years ago as a satirical critique of socialism and Darwinism in which sickness is treated as a crime and crime as a sickness.

8. Mark and James Savage of Savage Wilderness Safaris, Nairobi, Kenya. For details, please see http://www.kilimanjaro.com/safaris/savage

9. Similar ethical questions were raised about the Taliban prior to their removal in Afghanistan.

10. The Laikipiak people have been in the headlines for their attempts to reclaim ancestral territory near the region of our field trip (Lacey, 2004).

References

Anderson, D. M. (1995). *Maasai: People of cattle*. San Francisco: Chronicle.

Anderson, R. C., & Reeb, D. M. (2003). Founding family ownership and firm performance: Evidence from the S& P 500. *Journal of Finance, 58*, 1301–1326.

Becker, G. S. (1991). *A treatise on the family* (Enlarged ed.). Boston: Harvard Business School Press.

Burt, R. (1992). *Structural holes: The social structure of competition.* Boston: Harvard Business School Press.

Chatman, J. A. (1991). Matching people and organizations: Selection and socialization in public accounting firms. *Administrative Science Quarterly, 36*, 459–484.

Coon, C. S. (1971). *The hunting peoples*. New York: Penguin.

Daily, C. M., & Dollinger, M. J. (1991). Family firms are different. *Review of Business, 13* (1), 3–5.

Davis, J. H., Schoorman, F. D., & Donaldson, L. (1997). Toward a stewardship theory of management. *Academy of Management Review, 22*, 20–47.

Deal, T. E., & Kennedy, A. A. (1982). *Corporate cultures: The rites and rituals of corporate life*. Reading, MA: Addison-Wesley.

Denison, D., Lief, C., & Ward, J. L. (2004). Culture in family-owned enterprises: Recognizing and leveraging unique strengths, *Family Business Review, 17*, 61–70.

De Pree, M. (1999). *Leading without power*. San Francisco: Jossey-Bass.

Diamond, J. (1997). *Guns, germs, and steel*. New York: Random House.

Dunbar, R. (1996). *Gossip, grooming, and evolution of language*. London: Faber & Faber.

Empson, L. (in press). *Organizational identity change: Managerial regulation and member identification in an accounting firm acquisition*. Accounting, Organizations, and Society.

Gersick, K. E., Davis, J. A., Hampton, M. M., & Lansberg, I. (1997). *Generation to generation.* Boston: Harvard Business School Press.

Goffee, R., & Jones, G. (1998). *The character of a corporation*. New York: HarperCollins.

Greenleaf, R. K. (1991). *Servant leadership: A journey into the nature of legitimate power and greatness*. New York: Paulist.

Harris, M. (1979). *Cannibals and kings*. Glasgow, UK: William Collins.

Hodgson, D. L. (2001). *Once intrepid warriors*. Bloomington: Indiana University Press.

Hofstede, G. (1998). *Culture's consequences*. Beverly Hills, CA: Sage.

Jones, S. (1993). *The language of the genes*. London: HarperCollins.

Lacey, M. (2004, September 22). Maasai, Whites and wildlife: No peaceable kingdom. *New York Times.*

Landes, D. (1998). *The wealth and poverty of nations*. New York: Norton.

Lansberg, I. (1999). *Succeeding generations*. Boston: Harvard Business School Press.

Lekuton, J. (2003). *Fighting the lion: Growing up Maasai on the African savanna.* Washington, DC: National Geographic.

Martin, J. (2002), *Organizational culture: Mapping the terrain.* Newbury Park, CA: Sage.

Miller, K. L. (2004, April 12). Europe's best companies. *Newsweek*, pp. 42–47.

Nicholson, N. (1997). Evolutionary psychology: Toward a new view of human nature and organizational society. *Human Relations, 50*, 1053–1078.

Nicholson, N. (2000). *Managing the human animal*. London: Texere.

Nicholson, N., & Björnberg, A. (2004, March). Familiness: Fatal flaw or inimitable advantage? *Families in Business, 13*, 52–54.

O'Hara, W. T., & Mandel, P. (2002, Spring). The world's oldest family companies. *Family Business*, pp. 37–49.

Pelto, P. (1973). *The snowmobile revolution: Technological and social change in the Artic*. Menlo Park, CA: Cummings.

Plomin, R. (1994). *Genetics and experience: The interplay between nature and nurture*. Thousand Oaks, CA: Sage.

Quick, J. C., Nelson, D. L., & Hurrell, J. J. (1997). *Preventive stress management in organizations*. Washington, DC: American Psychological Association.

Ridley, M. (1996). *The origins of virtue*. London: Viking.

Runciman, W. G. (1998). *The social animal*. London: HarperCollins.

Sahlins, M. D. (1972). *Stone-age economics*. Chicago: Aldine.

Saitoti, T. O. (1986). *The worlds of a Maasai warrior: An autobiography*. New York: Random House.

Schein, E. H. (1985). *Organizational culture and leadership*. San Francisco: Jossey-Bass.

Schneider, B. W. (1987). *The people make the place. Personnel psychology, 40*, 437–453.

Semler, R. (1993). *Maverick!* New York: Arrow.

Spear, T., & Waller, R. (Eds.). (1993). *Being Maasai: Ethnicity and identity in East Africa*. Oxford, UK: James Currey.

Spencer, P. (1993). *Becoming Maasai, being in time*. In T. Spear & R. Waller (Eds.), *Being Maasai: Ethnicity and identity in East Africa*. Oxford, UK: James Currey.

Tagiuri, R. L., & Davis, J. A. (1996). Bivalent attributes of the family firm. *Family Business Review, 9*, 199–208.

Tonnies, F. (1957). *Community and society* (C. P. Loomis, Trans.). East Lansing: Michigan State University Press. (Original work published 1887)

Yoshimura, N., & Anderson, P. (1997). *Inside the kaisha: Demystifying Japanese business behavior.* Boston: Harvard Business School Press.

Zeidner, M., Matthews, G., & Roberts, R. D. (2004). Emotional intelligence in the workplace: A critical review. Applied Psychology: *An International Review, 53,* 371–399.

NIGEL NICHOLSON has been a professor at London Business School since 1990, where he has held the positions of chairman of the organizational behavior department, research dean, member of the governing body, and deputy dean of the school. Before becoming a business psychologist, his first profession was journalism, and he is a frequent commentator in the media on current business issues. He is widely known for pioneering the introduction of the new science of evolutionary psychology to business through an article in *Harvard Business Review* (HBR) and also in book form: *Managing the Human Animal* (2000). His current major research interests include the psychology of family business, personality and leadership, and people skills in management. In these fields and others such as innovation, organizational change, and executive career development, he has published more than 15 books and 160 articles. One of his recent high-profile articles was published in HBR under the title "How to Motivate Your Problem People." He has just completed a major research project on risk and decision making among finance professionals, with a book forthcoming for Oxford University Press: *Traders: Risks, Decisions, and Management in Financial Markets.* He has been a guest professor at German, American, and Australian universities and has been honored in the United States with an award from the Academy of Management for his contribution to the field. He is a sought-after speaker, and at London Business School, he directs several executive programs, including the renowned High Performance People Skills and the innovative Proteus programs. At London Business School, he is currently dedicated to founding a major research and executive education initiative in the area of family business. He serves on the advisory board of the Institute for Family Business and is chairman of the evaluation panels for the JPMorgan Private Bank Family Business Honors program. He consults, coaches, and advises on all areas of his wide-ranging interests, including leader selection and development, culture change, internal communications, executive team building, and people skills for senior managers.

Too Many Bananas, Not Enough Pineapples, and No Watermelon at All
Three Object Lessons in Living with Reciprocity

DAVID COUNTS

No Watermelon at All

The woman came all the way through the village, walking between the two rows of houses facing each other between the beach and the bush, to the very last house standing on a little spit of land at the mouth of the Kaini River. She was carrying a watermelon on her head, and the house she came to was the government "rest house," maintained by the villagers for the occasional use of visiting officials. Though my wife and I were graduate students, not officials, and had asked for permission to stay in the village for the coming year, we were living in the rest house while the debate went on about where a house would be built for us. When the woman offered to sell us the watermelon for two shillings, we happily agreed, and the kids were delighted at the prospect of watermelon after yet another meal of rice and bully beef. The money changed hands and the seller left to return to her village, a couple of miles along the coast to the east.

It seemed only seconds later that the woman was back, reluctantly accompanying Kolia, the man who had already made it clear to us that he was the leader of the village. Kolia had no English, and at that time, three or four days into our first stay in Kandoka Village on the island of New Britain in Papua New Guinea, we had very little Tok Pisin. Language difficulties notwithstanding, Kolia managed to make his message clear: The woman had been outrageously wrong to sell us the watermelon for two shillings and we were to return it to her and reclaim our money immediately. When we tried to explain that we thought the price to be fair and were happy with the bargain, Kolia explained again and finally made it clear that we had missed the point. The problem wasn't that we had paid too much; it was that we had paid at all. Here he was, a leader, responsible for us while we were living in his village, and we had shamed him. How would it look if he let guests in his village *buy* food? If we wanted watermelons, or bananas, or anything else, all that was necessary was to let him know. He told us that it would be all right for us to give little gifts to people who brought food to us (and they surely would), but *no one* was to sell food to us. If anyone were to try—like this woman from Lauvore—then we should refuse. There would be plenty of watermelons without us buying them.

The woman left with her watermelon, disgruntled, and we were left with our two shillings. But we had learned the first lesson of

many about living in Kandoka. We didn't pay money for food again that whole year, and we did get lots of food brought to us. . . but we never got another watermelon. That one was the last of the season.

LESSON 1: *In a society where food is shared or gifted as part of social life, you may not buy it with money.*

Too Many Bananas

In the couple of months that followed the watermelon incident, we managed to become at least marginally competent in Tok Pisin, to negotiate the construction of a house on what we hoped was neutral ground, and to settle into the routine of our fieldwork. As our village leader had predicted, plenty of food was brought to us. Indeed, seldom did a day pass without something coming in—some sweet potatoes, a few taro, a papaya, the occasional pineapple, or some bananas—lots of bananas.

We had learned our lesson about the money, though, so we never even offered to buy the things that were brought, but instead made gifts, usually of tobacco to the adults or chewing gum to the children. Nor were we so gauche as to haggle with a giver over how much of a return gift was appropriate, though the two of us sometimes conferred as to whether what had been brought was a "two-stick" or a "three-stick" stalk, bundle, or whatever. A "stick" of tobacco was a single large leaf, soaked in rum and then twisted into a ropelike form. This, wrapped in half a sheet of newsprint (torn for use as cigarette paper), sold in the local trade stores for a shilling. Nearly all of the adults in the village smoked a great deal, and they seldom had much cash, so our stocks of twist tobacco and stacks of the Sydney *Morning Herald* (all, unfortunately, the same day's issue) were seen as a real boon to those who preferred "stick" to the locally grown product.

We had established a pattern with respect to the gifts of food. When a donor appeared at our veranda we would offer our thanks and talk with them for a few minutes (usually about our children, who seemed to hold a real fascination for the villagers and for whom most of the gifts were intended) and then we would inquire whether they could use some tobacco. It was almost never refused, though occasionally a small bottle of kerosene, a box of matches, some laundry soap, a cup of rice, or a tin of meat would be requested instead of (or even in addition to) the tobacco. Everyone, even Kolia, seemed to think this arrangement had worked out well.

Now, what must be kept in mind is that while we were following their rules—or seemed to be—we were *really still buying food.* In fact we kept a running account of what came in and what we "paid" for it. Tobacco as currency got a little complicated, but since the exchange rate was one stick to one shilling, it was not too much trouble as long as everyone was happy, and meanwhile we could account for the expenditure of "informant fees" and "household expenses." Another thing to keep in mind is that not only did we continue to think in terms of our buying the food that was brought, we thought of them as *selling it.* While it was true they never quoted us a price, they also never asked us if we needed or wanted whatever they had brought. It seemed clear to us that when an adult needed a stick of tobacco, or a child wanted some chewing gum (we had enormous quantities of small packets of Wrigley's for just such eventualities) they would find something surplus to their own needs and bring it along to our "store" and get what they wanted.

By late November 1966, just before the rainy season set in, the bananas were coming into flush, and whereas earlier we had received banana gifts by the "hand" (six or eight bananas in a cluster cut from the stalk), donors now began to bring bananas, "for the children," by the *stalk!* The Kaliai among whom we were living are not exactly specialists in banana cultivation—they only recognize about thirty varieties, while some of their neighbors have more than twice that many—but the kinds they produce differ considerably from each other in size, shape, and taste, so we were not dismayed when we had more than one stalk hanging on our veranda. The stalks ripen a bit at the time, and having some variety was nice. Still, by the time our accumulation had reached *four* complete stalks, the delights of variety had begun to pale a bit. The fruits were ripening progressively and it was clear that even if we and the kids ate nothing but bananas for the next week, some would still fall from the stalk onto the floor in a state of gross overripeness. This was the situation as, late one afternoon, a woman came bringing yet another stalk of bananas up the steps of the house.

Several factors determined our reaction to her approach: one was that there was literally no way we could possibly use the bananas. We hadn't quite reached the point of being crowded off our veranda by the stalks of fruit, but it was close. Another factor was that we were tired of playing the gift game. We had acquiesced in playing it—no one was permitted to sell us anything, and in turn we only gave things away, refusing under any circumstances to sell tobacco (or anything else) for money. But there had to be a limit. From our perspective what was at issue was that the woman wanted something and she had come to trade for it. Further, what she had brought to trade was something we neither wanted nor could use, and it should have been obvious to her. So we decided to bite the bullet.

The woman, Rogi, climbed the stairs to the veranda, took the stalk from where it was balanced on top of her head, and laid it on the floor with the words, "Here are some bananas for the children." Dorothy and I sat near her on the floor and thanked her for her thought but explained, "You know, we really have too many bananas—we can't use these; maybe you ought to give them to someone else. . . ." The woman looked mystified, then brightened and explained that she didn't want anything for them, she wasn't short of tobacco or anything. They were just a gift for the kids. Then

she just sat there, and we sat there, and the bananas sat there, and we tried again. "Look," I said, pointing up to them and counting, "we've got four stalks already hanging here on the veranda—there are too many for us to eat now. Some are rotting already. Even if we eat only bananas, we can't keep up with what's here!"

Rogi's only response was to insist that these were a gift, and that she didn't want anything for them, so we tried yet another tack: "Don't *your* children like bananas?" When she admitted that they did, and that she had none at her house, we suggested that she should take them there. Finally, still puzzled, but convinced we weren't going to keep the bananas, she replaced them on her head, went down the stairs, and made her way back through the village toward her house.

As before, it seemed only moments before Kolia was making his way up the stairs, but this time he hadn't brought the woman in tow. "What was wrong with those bananas? Were they no good?" he demanded. We explained that there was nothing wrong with the bananas at all, but that we simply couldn't use them and it seemed foolish to take them when we had so many and Rogi's own children had none. We obviously didn't make ourselves clear because Kolia then took up the same refrain that Rogi had—he insisted that we shouldn't be worried about taking the bananas, because they were a gift for the children and Rogi hadn't wanted anything for them. There was no reason, he added, to send her away with them—she would be ashamed. I'm afraid we must have seemed as if we were hard of hearing or thought he was, for our only response was to repeat our reasons. We went through it again—there they hung, one, two, three, *four* stalks of bananas, rapidly ripening and already far beyond our capacity to eat—we just weren't ready to accept any more and let them rot (and, we added to ourselves, pay for them with tobacco, to boot).

Kolia finally realized that we were neither hard of hearing nor intentionally offensive, but merely ignorant. He stared at us for a few minutes, thinking, and then asked: "Don't you frequently have visitors during the day and evening?" We nodded. Then he asked, "Don't you usually offer them cigarettes and coffee or milo?" Again, we nodded. "Did it ever occur to you to suppose," he said, "that your visitors might be hungry?" It was at this point in the conversation, as we recall, that we began to see the depth of the pit we had dug for ourselves. We nodded, hesitantly. His last words to us before he went down the stairs and stalked away were just what we were by that time afraid they might be. "When your guests are hungry, *feed them bananas!*"

LESSON 2: *Never refuse a gift, and never fail to return a gift. If you cannot use it, you can always give it away to someone else—there is no such thing as too much—there are never too many bananas.*

Not Enough Pineapples

During the fifteen years between that first visit in 1966 and our residence there in 1981 we had returned to live in Kandoka village twice during the 1970s, and though there were a great many changes in the village, and indeed for all of Papua New Guinea during that time, we continued to live according to the lessons of reciprocity learned during those first months in the field. We bought no food for money and refused no gifts, but shared our surplus. As our family grew, we continued to be accompanied by our younger children. Our place in the village came to be something like that of educated Kaliai who worked far away in New Guinea. Our friends expected us to come "home" when we had leave, but knew that our work kept us away for long periods of time. They also credited us with knowing much more about the rules of their way of life than was our due. And we sometimes shared the delusion that we understood life in the village, but even fifteen years was not long enough to relieve the need for lessons in learning to live within the rules of gift exchange.

In the last paragraph I used the word *friends* to describe the villagers intentionally, but of course they were not all our friends. Over the years some really had become friends, others were acquaintances, others remained consultants or informants to whom we turned when we needed information. Still others, unfortunately, we did not like at all. We tried never to make an issue of these distinctions, of course, and to be evenhanded and generous to all, as they were to us. Although we almost never actually refused requests that were made of us, over the long term our reciprocity in the village was balanced. More was given to those who helped us the most, while we gave assistance or donations of small items even to those who were not close or helpful.

One elderly woman in particular was a trial for us. Sara was the eldest of a group of siblings and her younger brother and sister were both generous, informative, and delightful persons. Her younger sister, Makila, was a particularly close friend and consultant, and in deference to that friendship we felt awkward in dealing with the elder sister.

Sara was neither a friend nor an informant, but she had been, since she returned to live in the village at the time of our second trip in 1971, a constant (if minor) drain on our resources. She never asked for much at a time. A bar of soap, a box of matches, a bottle of kerosene, a cup of rice, some onions, a stick or two of tobacco, or some other small item was usually all that was at issue, but whenever she came around it was always to ask for something—or to let us know that when we left, we should give her some of the furnishings from the house. Too, unlike almost everyone else in the village, when she came, she was always empty-handed. We ate no taro from her gardens, and the kids chewed none of her sugarcane. In short, she was, as far as we could tell, a really grasping, selfish old woman—and we were not the only victims of her greed.

Having long before learned the lesson of the bananas, one day we had a stalk that was ripening so fast we couldn't keep up with it, so I pulled a few for our own use (we only had one stalk at the time) and walked down through the village to Ben's house, where his five children were playing. I sat down on his steps to talk, telling him that I intended to give the fruit to his kids. They never got them. Sara saw us from across the open plaza of the village and came rushing over, shouting, "My bananas!" Then she grabbed the stalk and went off gorging herself with them. Ben and I just looked at each other.

Finally it got to the point where it seemed to us that we had to do something. Ten years of being used was long enough. So there came the afternoon when Sara showed up to get some tobacco—again.

But this time, when we gave her the two sticks she had demanded, we confronted her.

First, we noted the many times she had come to get things. We didn't mind sharing things, we explained. After all, we had plenty of tobacco and soap and rice and such, and most of it was there so that we could help our friends as they helped us, with folktales, information, or even gifts of food. The problem was that she kept coming to get things, but never came to talk, or to tell stories, or to bring some little something that the kids might like. Sara didn't argue—she agreed. "Look," we suggested, "it doesn't have to be much, and we don't mind giving you things—but you can help us. The kids like pineapples, and we don't have any—the next time you need something, bring something—like maybe a pineapple." Obviously somewhat embarrassed, she took her tobacco and left, saying that she would bring something soon. We were really pleased with ourselves. It had been a very difficult thing to do, but it was done, and we were convinced that either she would start bringing things or not come. It was as if a burden had lifted from our shoulders.

It worked. Only a couple of days passed before Sara was back, bringing her bottle to get it filled with kerosene. But this time, she came carrying the biggest, most beautiful pineapple we had seen the entire time we had been there. We had a friendly talk, filled her kerosene container, and hung the pineapple up on the veranda to ripen just a little further. A few days later we cut and ate it, and whether the satisfaction it gave came from the fruit or from its source would be hard to say, but it was delicious. That, we assumed, was the end of that irritant.

We were wrong, of course. The next afternoon, Mary, one of our best friends for years (and no relation to Sara), dropped by for a visit. As we talked, her eyes scanned the veranda. Finally she asked whether we hadn't had a pineapple there yesterday. We said we had, but that we had already eaten it. She commented that it had been a really nice-looking one, and we told her that it had been the best we had eaten in months. Then, after a pause, she asked, "Who brought it to you?" We smiled as we said, "Sara!" because Mary would appreciate our coup—she had commented many times in the past on the fact that Sara only *got* from us and never gave. She was silent for a moment, and then she said, "Well, I'm glad you enjoyed it—my father was waiting until it was fully ripe to harvest it for you, but when it went missing I thought maybe it was the one you had here. I'm glad to see you got it. I thought maybe a thief had eaten it in the bush."

LESSON 3: *Where reciprocity is the rule and gifts are the idiom, you cannot demand a gift, just as you cannot refuse a request.*

It says a great deal about the kindness and patience of the Kaliai people that they have been willing to be our hosts for all these years despite our blunders and lack of good manners. They have taught us a lot, and these three lessons are certainly not the least important things we learned.

Ties That Bind

Hopi gift culture and its first encounter with the United States

PETER M. WHITELEY

In 1852, shortly after the United States had nominally annexed Hopi country, in northern Arizona, the Hopi people arranged for a diplomatic packet to reach President Millard Fillmore at the White House. Part message and part magical gift, the packet was delivered by a delegation of five prominent men from another Pueblo tribe, the Tewas of Tesuque Pueblo in New Mexico, who wanted to gain legal protection from Anglo and Hispanic settlers who were encroaching on their lands. The delegation traveled for nearly three months, on horseback, steamboat, and train, from Santa Fe to Washington, D.C., more than 2,600 miles away. The five men spoke fluent Spanish, the dominant European language of the region at the time—which made them ideally suited to convey the gift packet and its message to the president.

At the time, no U.S. government official had visited the Hopi (and few would do so before the 1890s). Their "unique diplomatic pacquet," in the words of the nineteenth-century ethnologist Henry Rowe Schoolcraft, offered "friendship and intercommunication . . . opening, symbolically, a road from the Moqui [Hopi] country to Washington." The packet was in two parts. The first part comprised two *pahos,* or prayer-sticks, at either end of a long cotton cord, dyed for part of its length. Separating the dyed from the undyed part of the cord were six varicolored feathers, knotted into a bunch. The *pahos* "represent the Moqui [Hopi] people and the President [respectively]," Schoolcraft wrote; "the cord is the road which separates them; the [bunch of feathers] tied to the cord is the meeting point."

As well as encoding a message, the *pahos* were an offering of a kind that Hopi deities such as Taawa, the Sun god, traditionally like to receive. By giving the president *pahos* worthy of the Sun, the Hopi signaled their expectation that he would reciprocate. Just as the Sun, on receiving the appropriate offerings, would send rain clouds for sustaining life and growth, so, too, the president would send protection for Hopi lives and lands—in this instance, protection from assaults by neighboring tribes such as the Navajo.

The second part of the packet comprised a cornstalk cigarette filled with tobacco ("to be smoked by the president") and a small cornhusk package that en closed honey-soaked cornmeal. According to the Tesuque delegation, the honey-meal package was "a charm to call down rain from heaven." When the president smoked the cigarette, he would exhale clouds of smoke, which would sympathetically attract the clouds of the sky. Then, when he chewed the cornmeal and spat the wild honey on ground that needed rain, the Tesuque statement concluded, "the Moquis assure him that it [the rain] will come."

In sum, the packet was three things at once: message, offering, and gift of magical power. In conveying those elements, the Hopi sought to open diplomatic relations with the U.S.

But their intent appears to have been lost on their recipient. As so often happens when two cultures make contact, deep misunderstandings can arise: What does a gift mean? What, if anything, does the gift giver expect in return? Do the giver and the recipient both assign the same value to the gift? In twenty-five years of ethnographic fieldwork with the Hopi, it has been my goal to learn something of their history and culture. Recently I turned my attention to certain important events, such as the Millard Fillmore episode, that might shed light on how Hopi society changed as the U.S. developed. In that context Hopi gift giving and the ways it functions as a pillar of Hopi social organization have been central to my studies. One lesson of my work shines through: When nations exchange gifts, all the parties would do best to keep in mind the old adage, "It's the thought that counts."

Given the differences between Hopi and Western traditions and culture, perhaps it is not surprising that the Hopi idea of "gift" is only loosely equivalent to the Western one. In 1852 the Hopi people were still little affected by outside populations, and Hopi land use spread across much of northern Arizona and even into southern Utah. At that time, the Hopi lifestyle was traditional, based on farming, foraging, and some pastoralism. Even today, important elements of the subsistence economy persist, though wage labor and small business provide supplemental income.

The Hopi typically divide their work according to gender. Work done by men (such as farming and harvesting of crops) is perceived as a gift to the women; work done by women (such as gardening, gathering of piñion nuts, grasses, wild fruits, berries, and the like) is perceived as a gift to the men. Women also own and manage the distribution of their household's goods and crops. In fact, Hopi women control most of the material economic life, whereas Hopi men largely control the ritual and spiritual aspects.

The Hopi take part in an elaborate cycle of religious ceremonies, to which a range of specialized offices and privileges is attached. But individuals gain those distinctive social positions not through material wealth but rather through gender and kinship relations, which are ordered in a matrilineal manner. In fact, clan heads and chiefs of religious societies are typically worse off materially than the average member of the clan. Hopi leaders are supposed to be materially poor, and a wealthy individual is often criticized as *qahopi*, un-Hopi, for failing to share. Wealth and status among the Hopi is thus phrased in ritual terms: a poor person is one without ceremonial prerogatives, not one without money. So averse are the Hopi to material accumulation that in May 2004, for the second time, they voted against casino gambling, despite substantial poverty on the reservation.

Does such a primacy of value placed on ceremonial roles explain the evanescent nature of the gift given to President Fillmore? In what world of meaning did the packet represent great value? Indeed, what's in a gift?

Anthropologists have been making hay of that last question ever since 1925, when the French anthropologist Marcel Mauss published his groundbreaking *Essai sur le Don* (translated into English as "The Gift"). Mauss convincingly argued that in small-scale societies (10,000 or fewer persons) gifts are "total social facts." What he meant is that, in gift- or barter-based social systems, divisions of social life into discrete domains—such as economy, politics, law, or religion—are meaningless; each sphere interpenetrates and overlaps the others.

As in strict barter, an exchange in Hopi culture that begins by making a gift to someone does not involve money, but it does require reciprocity. Thus goods, services, or knowledge "given" to an individual or a group are answered with something of equivalent value. "Gifts" develop an interconnectedness between Hopi individuals in a way that outright purchases cannot. Furthermore, the Hopi offer girls in a much broader range of circumstances than people in Western cultures do, and the value of those gifts extends to the religious realm, tying individuals and groups to each other and to the realm of the spirits.

Probably the key to understanding a gift-based system such as that of the Hopi is to recognize that such systems are built on kinship. "Kinship"—the godzilla that has driven multitudes of college students screaming from anthropology 101—is, in this regard at least, straightforward. It means simply that the great majority of human social activity is framed in terms of reciprocal family ties. Where all personal relationships are cast within the "kinship idiom" there are no members of the society who are not kin to me, nor I to them.

Kinship terms encode behavioral expectations as well as familial role. As anthropologists never tire of saying, such terms are primarily social, not biological: obviously if I call fifteen women "mother," as the average Hopi can do, I do not assume that each woman physically gave birth to me. But my "mothers" all have rights and duties in relation to me. And, reciprocally, I have duties and rights with respect to them: in fact, their duties are my rights, and my duties are their rights in the relationship. That is what reciprocity is all about. You give me food, I plant your cornfield, to give a crude example. But, in a kinship society, such a basic structure of mutual expectations forms the foundation for an entire apparatus of courtesy and manners, deference and respect, familiarity or distance. Those expectations are concretely expressed by gifts—spontaneous and planned, routine and special, trivial and grand. Gifts are thus communications in a language of social belonging.

So averse are the Hopi to material accumulation that in May 2004 they voted against casino gambling.

So-called gift economies entail a certain kind of sociality, or sense of what it means to belong to a community. In such an economy, one gives a gift to mark social relations built on kinship and altruism, but without the expectation of direct repayment. According to some arguments, gifts are also given to foster a sense of community, as well as sustainable interrelations with the local environment. In fact, in some respects the giver still "owns" some part of the gift, and it is the intangible connection between the two parties, mediated by the gift, that forms the basis of interpersonal relationships.

In contrast, in exchange economies, commodities dominate social interchange. Competitive markets, governed by the profit motive, connect buyer and seller, and social relations are characterized by individualism. A gift, once given, belongs entirely to the recipient; only when the item given has sentimental value does it keep the bond between giver and recipient alive.

That is not to say the Hopi did not engage in the more impersonal, "Western" forms of material exchange. In the Hopi language, as in English, several words describe how an item is transferred from one person to another: *maqa* ("to give"); *hùuya* ("to barter or trade"); and *tu'i* ("to buy"). Those words all antedate the arrival of Europeans—and anthropological classifications. Barter and purchase, as well as gifts, have all long been present in Hopi life. Furthermore, gift exchange in the West can also function as it does among the Hopi, as part of kinship obligations or ordinary social life.

What is distinctive about Hopi custom is the fact that the gift economy is responsible for the great majority of exchanges. Furthermore, there is no such thing as a free gift. The strong interpersonal bonds created by a gift make giving almost de rigueur at ceremonial events. Gifts, particularly gifts of food or utensils, are transmitted during ceremonies of personal milestones (at a birth or a marriage), as well as at public gatherings.

For example, at the annual so-called basket dances, girls and women distribute a variety of objects they have collected for the occasion. The dances illustrate the Hopi lack of acquisitiveness. The women form a semicircle and dance and sing; after each song two girls fling gifts into the crowd of men assembled outside the circle. Among the gifts are valuable baskets and buckskins, though inexpensive utensils and manufactured items are also popular. Each man zealously grabs for the flying objects, and if two men happen to catch the same item, both wrestle with the object, often until it has been totally destroyed.

Although gift giving has been a pillar of Hopi society, trade has also flourished in Hopi towns since prehistory, with a network that extended from the Great Plains to the Pacific Coast, and from the Great Basin, centered on present-day Nevada and Utah, to the Valley of Mexico. Manufactured goods, raw materials, and gems drove the trade, supplemented by exotic items such as parrots. The Hopis were producers as well, manufacturing large quantities of cotton cloth and ceramics for the trade. To this day, interhousehold trade and barter, especially for items of traditional manufacture for ceremonial use (such as basketry, bows, cloth, moccasins, pottery, and rattles), remain vigorous.

For hundreds of years, at least, the Hopi traded with the Rio Grande Pueblos to acquire turquoise, *heishi* (shell necklaces), and buckskins; one long string of *heishi,* for instance, was worth two Hopi woven cotton mantas. Similarly, songs, dances, and other ritual elements were often exchanged for an agreed-upon equivalent.

The high value the Hopi placed on the items they acquired by trade correlate, in many respects, with the value Europeans placed on them. Silver, for instance, had high value among both Westerners and Native Americans as money and as jewelry. *Siiva,* the Hopi word both for "money" and for "silver jewelry" was borrowed directly from the English word "silver" Paper money itself was often treated the way traditional resources were: older Hopi men bundled it and stored it in trunks, stacked by denomination.

It was not until the 1890s, however, that silver jewelry began to be produced by the Hopi. A man named Sikyatala learned silversmithing from a Zuni man, and his craftsmanship quickly made silver jewelry into treasured adornments. Those among the Hopi who cared for it too much, though, were criticized for vanity; one nickname, Siisiva ("[wearing] a lot of silver"), characterized a fop.

Some jewels, such as turquoise, traditionally had a sacred value, beyond adornment. Even today, flakes of turquoise are occasionally offered to the spirits in religious ceremonies. Turquoise and shell necklaces appear in many ritual settings, frequently adorning the costumes of *katsinas* (ceremonial figures) and performers in the social dances.

How much the Hopi value turquoise becomes apparent toward the close of a ritual enactment known as the Clown Ceremony. The "clowns"—more than mere entertainers—represent unbridled human impulses. Warrior *katsinas* arrive to punish the clowns for licentious behavior and teach them good Hopi behavior: modest and quiet in conduct, careful and decorous in speech, abstemious and sharing about food, and unselfish about other things. The clowns fail miserably (and hilariously) at their lessons. Eventually the warrior chief presents an ultimatum: stop flaunting chaos or die. The clown chief then offers him a turquoise necklace as a "mortgage" on the clowns' lives. The warrior chief accepts, the downs receive a lesser punishment, and community life goes on—not with perfection, but with a human mixture of the virtuous and the flawed.

I n Hopi tradition, the first clan among the Hopi, and the one that supplied the *kikmongwi,* or village chief, was Bear. When other clans arrived, their leaders approached the *kikmongw*i to request entry into the village. He asked what they had to contribute, such as a beneficial ceremony. So challenged, each clan performed its ceremony, and if successful, say, in producing rain, its members were invited to live in the village, assigned an area for housing, and granted agricultural lands to work in the valley below. In return, the clan agreed to perform its ceremony, as part of a cycle of ceremonies throughout the year, and to intermarry with the other clans of the community, a practice called exogamous marriage. In that way, the Snake clan brought the Snake Dance, the Badger clan introduced principal katsina ceremonies, and the Fire clan brought the Warriors' society to the Hopi village. The villages thus came to be made up of mutually interdependent clans.

One of the essential principles expressed here, and the very cornerstone of Hopi society and sociality, is the exchange of mutually beneficial gifts—ceremonies for land, people in exogamous marriage—and the relationships reconfigured by those exchanges. And the same model is extended to the supernatural world: the gods must be propitiated with offerings of ritual gifts, and thus reminded of their dependence upon and obligations to mortal people.

The items sent to President Fillmore conform to the archetypal Hopi offering. Seeking to incorporate the president into the Hopi world, the appropriate strategy was to give him valuable presents that sought something in return, and to make sure he understood what that meant. Addressing him with prayer-sticks the way they might address the Sun father, the delegation sought to engage him within the gifting and kinship idiom. The instructions delivered with the packet—even across a succession of translations—spoke clearly of the Hopi intent. As with the turquoise mortgage of the *katsina* clowns, the idea of reciprocity is central. If the president wants more of, say, rain-magic, he must give back: he must receive the gift and its political proposal, and provide something in return.

A las, the magico-religious sensibility of the Hopi worldview and the offer of serial reciprocity clashed with Manifest Destiny and the assimilationist ideology of Fillmore's presidency. Historical records make it clear that he did not smoke the cigarette, nor chew nor spit the honey-meal, and, so far as we know, he sent no formal reply. None of the objects has survived.

What the five men of the Tesuque delegation received no doubt perplexed them as much as the packet they delivered perplexed the president: Each man was given a Millard Fillmore peace medal, a Western-style business suit, and a daguerreotype portrait (all now lost, as well). They also got a tour of standard destinations in Washington, including the Patent Office and the Smithsonian Institution, where they were introduced to the "wonders of electricity," according to a contemporary newspaper account in the *Daily National Intelligencer.* In their meeting with Fillmore they heard the president say he "hoped the Great Spirit would bless and sustain them till they again returned to the bosom of their families."

Certainly Fillmore expressed the goodwill of the U.S. toward the Pueblos in general and to the Tesuque party in particular—who, in all probability, conveyed that sentiment to the Hopi. But the dissonance between gift and exchange economies helps explain why the Hopis did not achieve their goals. (The U.S. did not protect the Hopi from intrusions by the Navajo or by anyone else.)

The Hopi sought to embrace the president in their own sphere of sociality and mutuality—to extend kinship to him. But in a social system like the president's, where gifts are not total social facts, the political belongs in a separate domain from the religious or the economic, and kinship is secondary. The gift of a jeweled sword, for instance, might have impressed Fillmore more, but for the Hopi, its strictly symbolic value—as an item for display, but with no political, religious, or social value—would not have ensured a return, a social connection built on mutual exchange. More, by Hopi standards, presenting such a gift might have seemed inhospitable and materialistic, indeed, undiplomatic and even selfish. Thus does understanding fail between nations.

From *Natural History,* November 2004, pp. 26–31. Copyright © 2004 by Natural History Magazine. Reprinted by permission.

UNIT 4
Other Families, Other Ways

Unit Selections

Key Points to Consider

- If the incest taboo has to do with biology, then why is it culturally variable?

- Why do you think "fraternal polyandry" is socially acceptable in Tibet but not in our society?

- How have dietary changes affected birth rates and women's health?

- Under what circumstances did Western marriages become "love-based?"

- What are the pros and cons of arranged marriages versus freedom of choice?

- Does the stability of Japanese marriages necessarily imply compatibility and contentment?

Student Web Site
www.mhcls.com/online

Internet Reference
Further information regarding this Web site may be found in this book's preface or online.

Kinship and Social Organization
http://www.umanitoba.ca/anthropology

Since most people in small-scale societies of the past spent their whole lives within a local area, it is understandable that their primary interactions—economic, religious, and otherwise—were with their relatives. It also makes sense that through marriage customs, they strengthened those kinship relationships that clearly defined their mutual rights and obligations. Indeed, the resulting family structure may be surprisingly flexible and adaptive, as witnessed in the essays "When Brothers Share a Wife" by Melvyn Goldstein, and "Arranging a Marriage in India" by Serena Nanda.

For these reasons, anthropologists have looked upon family and kinship as the key mechanisms for transmitting culture from one generation to the next. Social changes may have been slow to take place throughout the world, but as social horizons have widened, family relationships and community alliances are increasingly based upon new principles. Even as birth rates have increased, kinship networks have diminished in size and strength. As people have increasingly become involved with others as coworkers in a market economy, our associations depend more and more upon factors such as personal aptitudes, educational backgrounds, and job opportunities. Is it any wonder that people "fall in love," as if marriage has always been a matter of individual decision-making, even though it hardly ever was historically? (See "What's Love Got to Do with It?)

Yet the family is still there. Except for some rather unusual exceptions, the family is smaller, but still functions in its age-old nurturing and protective role, even under conditions where there is little affection (see "Who Needs Love! In Japan, Many Couples Don't" by Nicholas Kristof) or under conditions of extreme poverty and a high infant mortality rate (see "Death Without Weeping" by Nancy Scheper-Hughes). Beyond the immediate family, the situation is in a state of flux. Certain ethnic groups, especially those in poverty, still have a need for the broader network and in some ways seem to be reformulating those ties.

We do not know where the changes described in this section will lead us and which ones will ultimately prevail. One thing is certain: anthropologists will be there to document the trends, for the discipline of anthropology has had to change as well. One important feature of the essays in this section is the growing interest of anthropologists in the study of complex societies where old theoretical perspectives are increasingly inadequate.

Current trends, however, do not necessarily mean the eclipse of the kinship unit. The large family network is still the best guarantee of individual survival and well-being in an urban setting.

When Brothers Share a Wife

Among Tibetans, the good life relegates many women to spinsterhood

MELVYN C. GOLDSTEIN

Eager to reach home, Dorje drives his yaks hard over the 17,000-foot mountain pass, stopping only once to rest. He and his two older brothers, Pema and Sonam, are jointly marrying a woman from the next village in a few weeks, and he has to help with the preparations.

Dorje, Pema, and Sonam are Tibetans living in Limi, a 200-square-mile area in the northwest corner of Nepal, across the border from Tibet. The form of marriage they are about to enter—fraternal polyandry in anthropological parlance—is one of the world's rarest forms of marriage but is not uncommon in Tibetan society, where it has been practiced from time immemorial. For many Tibetan social strata, it traditionally represented the ideal form of marriage and family.

The mechanics of fraternal polyandry are simple. Two, three, four, or more brothers jointly take a wife, who leaves her home to come and live with them. Traditionally, marriage was arranged by parents, with children, particularly females, having little or no say. This is changing somewhat nowadays, but it is still unusual for children to marry without their parents' consent. Marriage ceremonies vary by income and region and range from all the brothers sitting together as grooms to only the eldest one formally doing so. The age of the brothers plays an important role in determining this: very young brothers almost never participate in actual marriage ceremonies, although they typically join the marriage when they reach their midteens.

The eldest brother is normally dominant in terms of authority, that is, in managing the household, but all the brothers share the work and participate as sexual partners. Tibetan males and females do not find the sexual aspect of sharing a spouse the least bit unusual, repulsive, or scandalous, and the norm is for the wife to treat all the brothers the same.

Offspring are treated similarly. There is no attempt to link children biologically to particular brothers, and a brother shows no favoritism toward his child even if he knows he is the real father because, for example, his other brothers were away at the time the wife became pregnant. The children, in turn, consider all of the brothers as their fathers and treat them equally, even if they also know who is their real father. In some regions children use the term "father" for the eldest brother and "father's brother" for the others, while in other areas they call all the

brothers by one term, modifying this by the use of "elder" and "younger."

Unlike our own society, where monogamy is the only form of marriage permitted, Tibetan society allows a variety of marriage types, including monogamy, fraternal polyandry, and polygyny. Fraternal polyandry and monogamy are the most common forms of marriage, while polygyny typically occurs in cases where the first wife is barren. The widespread practice of fraternal polyandry, therefore, is not the outcome of a law requiring brothers to marry jointly. There is choice, and in fact, divorce traditionally was relatively simple in Tibetan society. If a brother in a polyandrous marriage became dissatisfied and wanted to separate, he simply left the main house and set up his own household. In such cases, all the children stayed in the main household with the remaining brother(s), even if the departing brother was known to be the real father of one or more of the children.

The Tibetans' own explanation for choosing fraternal polyandry is materialistic. For example, when I asked Dorje why he decided to marry with his two brothers rather than take his own wife, he thought for a moment, then said it prevented the division of his family's farm (and animals) and thus facilitated all of them achieving a higher standard of living. And when I later asked Dorje's bride whether it wasn't difficult for her to cope with three brothers as husbands, she laughed and echoed the rationale of avoiding fragmentation of the family and land, adding that she expected to be better off economically, since she would have three husbands working for her and her children.

Exotic as it may seem to Westerners, Tibetan fraternal polyandry is thus in many ways analogous to the way primogeniture functioned in nineteenth-century England. Primogeniture dictated that the eldest son inherited the family estate, while younger sons had to leave home and seek their own employment—for example, in the military or the clergy. Primogeniture maintained family estates intact over generations by permitting only one heir per generation. Fraternal polyandry also accomplishes this but does so by keeping all the brothers together with just one wife so that there is only one *set* of heirs per generation.

While Tibetans believe that in this way fraternal polyandry reduces the risk of family fission, monogamous marriages among brothers need not necessarily precipitate the division of the family estate: brothers could continue to live together, and the family land could continue to be worked jointly. When I asked Tibetans about this, however, they invariably responded that such joint families are unstable because each wife is primarily oriented to her own children and interested in their success and well-being over that of the children of the other wives. For example, if the youngest brother's wife had three sons while the eldest brother's wife had only one daughter, the wife of the youngest brother might begin to demand more resources for her children since, as males, they represent the future of the family. Thus, the children from different wives in the same generation are competing sets of heirs, and this makes such families inherently unstable. Tibetans perceive that conflict will spread from the wives to their husbands and consider this likely to cause family fission. Consequently, it is almost never done.

Although Tibetans see an economic advantage to fraternal polyandry, they do not value the sharing of a wife as an end in itself. On the contrary, they articulate a number of problems inherent in the practice. For example, because authority is customarily exercised by the eldest brother, his younger male siblings have to subordinate themselves with little hope of changing their status within the family. When these younger brothers are aggressive and individualistic, tensions and difficulties often occur despite there being only one set of heirs.

In addition, tension and conflict may arise in polyandrous families because of sexual favoritism. The bride normally sleeps with the eldest brother, and the two have the responsibility to see to it that the other males have opportunities for sexual access. Since the Tibetan subsistence economy requires males to travel a lot, the temporary absence of one or more brothers facilitates this, but there are also other rotation practices. The cultural ideal unambiguously calls for the wife to show equal affection and sexuality to each of the brothers (and vice versa), but deviations from this ideal occur, especially when there is a sizable difference in age between the partners in the marriage.

Dorje's family represents just such a potential situation. He is fifteen years old and his two older brothers are twenty-five and twenty-two years old. The new bride is twenty-three years old, eight years Dorje's senior. Sometimes such a bride finds the youngest husband immature and adolescent and does not treat him with equal affection; alternatively, she may find his youth attractive and lavish special attention on him. Apart from that consideration, when a younger male like Dorje grows up, he may consider his wife "ancient" and prefer the company of a woman his own age or younger. Consequently, although men and women do not find the idea of sharing a bride or bridegroom repulsive, individual likes and dislikes can cause familial discord.

Two reasons have commonly been offered for the perpetuation of fraternal polyandry in Tibet: that Tibetans practice female infanticide and therefore have to marry polyandrously, owing to a shortage of females; and that Tibet, lying at extremely high altitudes, is so barren and bleak that Tibetans would starve without resort to this mechanism. A Jesuit who lived in Tibet during the eighteenth century articulated this second view: "One reason for this most odious custom is the sterility of the soil, and the small amount of land that can be cultivated owing to the lack of water.

The crops may suffice if the brothers all live together, but if they form separate families they would be reduced to beggary."

Both explanations are wrong, however. Not only has there never been institutionalized female infanticide in Tibet, but Tibetan society gives females considerable rights, including inheriting the family estate in the absence of brothers. In such cases, the woman takes a bridegroom who comes to live in her family and adopts her family's name and identity. Moreover, there is no demographic evidence of a shortage of females. In Limi, for example, there were (in 1974) sixty females and fifty-three males in the fifteen- to thirty-five-year age category, and many adult females were unmarried.

The second reason is also incorrect. The climate in Tibet is extremely harsh, and ecological factors do play a major role perpetuating polyandry, but polyandry is not a means of preventing starvation. It is characteristic, not of the poorest segments of the society, but rather of the peasant landowning families.

In the old society, the landless poor could not realistically aspire to prosperity, but they did not fear starvation. There was a persistent labor shortage throughout Tibet, and very poor families with little or no land and few animals could subsist through agricultural labor, tenant farming, craft occupations such as carpentry, or by working as servants. Although the per person family income could increase somewhat if brothers married polyandrously and pooled their wages, in the absence of inheritable land, the advantage of fraternal polyandry was not generally sufficient to prevent them from setting up their own households. A more skilled or energetic younger brother could do as well or better alone, since he would completely control his income and would not have to share it with his siblings. Consequently, while there was and is some polyandry among the poor, it is much less frequent and more prone to result in divorce and family fission.

An alternative reason for the persistence of fraternal polyandry is that it reduces population growth (and thereby reduces the pressure on resources) by relegating some females to lifetime spinsterhood. Fraternal polyandrous marriages in Limi (in 1974) averaged 2.35 men per woman, and not surprisingly, 31 percent of the females of child-bearing age (twenty to forty-nine) were unmarried. These spinsters either continued to live at home, set up their own households, or worked as servants for other families. They could also become Buddhist nuns. Being unmarried is not synonymous with exclusion from the reproductive pool. Discreet extramarital relationships are tolerated, and actually half of the adult unmarried women in Limi had one or more children. They raised these children as single mothers, working for wages or weaving cloth and blankets for sale. As a group, however, the unmarried woman had far fewer offspring than the married women, averaging only 0.7 children per woman, compared with 3.3 for married women, whether polyandrous, monogamous, or polygynous. While polyandry helps regulate population, this function of polyandry is not consciously perceived by Tibetans and is not the reason they consistently choose it.

If neither a shortage of females nor the fear of starvation perpetuates fraternal polyandry, what motivates brothers, particularly younger brothers, to opt for this system of marriage? From the perspective of the younger brother in a landholding family, the main incentive is the attainment or maintenance of the good life. With polyandry, he can expect a more secure and higher standard of living, with access not only to this family's land and animals but also to its inherited collection of clothes, jewelry, rugs, saddles, and horses. In addition, he will experience less work pressure and much greater security because all responsibility does not fall on one "father." For Tibetan brothers, the question is whether to trade off the greater personal freedom inherent in monogamy for the real or potential economic security, affluence, and social prestige associated with life in a larger, labor-rich polyandrous family.

A brother thinking of separating from his polyandrous marriage and taking his own wife would face various disadvantages. Although in the majority of Tibetan regions all brothers theoretically have rights to their family's estate, in reality Tibetans are reluctant to divide their land into small fragments. Generally, a younger brother who insists on leaving the family will receive only a small plot of land, if that. Because of its power and wealth, the rest of the family usually can block any attempt of the younger brother to increase his share of land through litigation. Moreover, a younger brother may not even get a house and cannot expect to receive much above the minimum in terms of movable possessions, such as furniture, pots, and pans. Thus, a brother contemplating going it on his own must plan on achieving economic security and the good life not through inheritance but through his own work.

The obvious solution for younger brothers—creating new fields from virgin land—is generally not a feasible option. Most Tibetan populations live at high altitudes (above 12,000 feet), where arable land is extremely scarce. For example, in Dorje's village, agriculture ranges only from about 12,900 feet, the lowest point in the area, to 13,300 feet. Above that altitude, early frost and snow destroy the staple barley crop. Furthermore, because of the low rainfall caused by the Himalayan rain shadow, many areas in Tibet and northern Nepal that are within the appropriate altitude range for agriculture have no reliable sources of irrigation. In the end, although there is plenty of unused land in such areas, most of it is either too high or too arid.

Even where unused land capable of being farmed exists, clearing the land and building the substantial terraces necessary for irrigation constitute a great undertaking. Each plot has to be completely dug out to a depth of two to two and half feet so that the large rocks and boulders can be removed. At best, a man might be able to bring a few new fields under cultivation in the first years after separating from his brothers, but he could not expect to acquire substantial amounts of arable land this way.

In addition, because of the limited farmland, the Tibetan subsistence economy characteristically includes a strong emphasis on animal husbandry. Tibetan farmers regularly maintain cattle, yaks, goats, and sheep, grazing them in the areas too high for agriculture. These herds produce wool, milk, cheese, butter, meat, and skins. To obtain these resources, however, shepherds must accompany the animals on a daily basis. When first setting up a monogamous household, a younger brother like Dorje would find it difficult to both farm and manage animals.

In traditional Tibetan society, there was an even more critical factor that operated to perpetuate fraternal polyandry—a form of hereditary servitude somewhat analogous to serfdom in Europe. Peasants were tied to large estates held by aristocrats, monasteries, and the Lhasa government. They were allowed the use of some farmland to produce their own subsistence but were required to provide taxes in kind and corvée (free labor) to their lords. The corvée was a substantial hardship, since a peasant household was in many cases required to furnish the lord with one laborer daily for most of the year and more on specific occasions such as the harvest. This enforced labor, along with the lack of new land and ecological pressure to pursue both agriculture and animal husbandry, made polyandrous families particularly beneficial. The polyandrous family allowed an internal division of adult labor, maximizing economic advantage. For example, while the wife worked the family fields, one brother could perform the lord's corvée, another could look after the animals, and a third could engage in trade.

Although social scientists often discount other people's explanations of why they do things, in the case of Tibetan fraternal polyandry, such explanations are very close to the truth. The custom, however, is very sensitive to changes in its political and economic milieu and, not surprisingly, is in decline in most Tibetan areas. Made less important by the elimination of the traditional serf-based economy, it is disparaged by the dominant non-Tibetan leaders of India, China, and Nepal. New opportunities for economic and social mobility in these countries, such as the tourist trade and government employment, are also eroding the rationale for polyandry, and so it may vanish within the next generation.

MELVYN C. GOLDSTEIN, now a professor of anthropology at Case Western Reserve University in Cleveland, has been interested in the Tibetan practice of fraternal polyandry (several brothers marrying one wife) since he was a graduate student in the 1960s.

From *Natural History,* March 1987, pp. 39–48. Copyright © 1987 by Natural History Magazine. Reprinted by permission.

Death Without Weeping

Has poverty ravaged mother love in the shantytowns of Brazil?

NANCY SCHEPER-HUGHES

I have seen death without weeping,
The destiny of the Northeast is death,
Cattle they kill,
To the people they do something worse
  —*Anonymous Brazilian singer (1965)*

"Why do the church bells ring so often?" I asked Nailza de Arruda soon after I moved into a corner of her tiny mud-walled hut near the top of the shantytown called the Alto do Cruzeiro (Crucifix Hill). I was then a Peace Corps volunteer and community development/ health worker. It was the dry and blazing hot summer of 1965, the months following the military coup in Brazil, and save for the rusty, clanging bells of N. S. das Dores Church, an eerie quiet had settled over the market town that I call Bom Jesus da Mata. Beneath the quiet, however, there was chaos and panic. "It's nothing," replied Nailza, "just another little angel gone to heaven."

Nailza had sent more than her share of little angels to heaven, and sometimes at night I could hear her engaged in a muffled but passionate discourse with one of them, two-year-old Joana. Joana's photograph, taken as she lay propped up in her tiny cardboard coffin, her eyes open, hung on a wall next to one of Nailza and Ze Antonio taken on the day they eloped.

Nailza could barely remember the other infants and babies who came and went in close succession. Most had died unnamed and were hastily baptized in their coffins. Few lived more than a month or two. Only Joana, properly baptized in church at the close of her first year and placed under the protection of a powerful saint, Joan of Arc, had been expected to live. And Nailza had dangerously allowed herself to love the little girl.

In addressing the dead child, Nailza's voice would range from tearful imploring to angry recrimination: "Why did you leave me? Was your patron saint so greedy that she could not allow me one child on this earth?" Ze Antonio advised me to ignore Nailza's odd behavior, which he understood as a kind of madness that, like the birth and death of children, came and went. Indeed, the premature birth of a stillborn son some months later "cured" Nailza of her "inappropriate" grief, and the day came when she removed Joana's photo and carefully packed it away.

More than fifteen years elapsed before I returned to the Alto do Cruzeiro, and it was anthropology that provided the vehicle of my return. Since 1982 I have returned several times in order to pursue a problem that first attracted my attention in the 1960s. My involvement with the people of the Alto do Cruzeiro now spans a quarter of a century and three generations of parenting in a community where mothers and daughters are often simultaneously pregnant.

The Alto do Cruzeiro is one of three shantytowns surrounding the large market town of Bom Jesus in the sugar plantation zone of Pernambuco in Northeast Brazil, one of the many zones of neglect that have emerged in the shadow of the now tarnished economic miracle of Brazil. For the women and children of the Alto do Cruzeiro the only miracle is that some of them have managed to stay alive at all.

The Northeast is a region of vast proportions (approximately twice the size of Texas) and of equally vast social and developmental problems. The nine states that make up the region are the poorest in the country and are representative of the Third World within a dynamic and rapidly industrializing nation. Despite waves of migrations from the interior to the teeming shantytowns of coastal cities, the majority still live in rural areas on farms and ranches, sugar plantations and mills.

Life expectancy in the Northeast is only forty years, largely because of the appallingly high rate of infant and child mortality. Approximately one million children in Brazil under the age of five die each year. The children of the Northeast, especially those born in shantytowns on the periphery of urban life, are at a very high risk of death. In these areas, children are born without the traditional protection of breast-feeding, subsistence gardens, stable marriages, and multiple adult caretakers that exists in the interior. In the hillside shantytowns that spring up around cities or, in this case, interior market towns, marriages are brittle, single parenting is the norm, and women are frequently forced into the shadow economy of domestic work in the homes of the rich or into unprotected and oftentimes "scab" wage labor on the surrounding sugar plantations, where they clear land for planting and weed for a pittance, sometimes less than a dollar a day. The women of the Alto may not bring their babies with them into the homes of the wealthy, where the often-sick infants are considered sources of contamination, and they cannot carry the little ones to the riverbanks where they wash clothes because the river is heavily infested with schistosomes and other deadly parasites. Nor can they carry their young children to the plantations, which are often several miles away. At wages of a dollar a day, the women of the Alto cannot hire baby sitters. Older children who are not in school will sometimes serve as somewhat indifferent caretakers. But any child not in school is also expected to find wage work. In most cases, babies are simply left at home alone, the door securely fastened. And so many also die alone and unattended.

Bom Jesus da Mata, centrally located in the plantation zone of Pernambuco, is within commuting distance of several sugar plantations and mills. Consequently, Bom Jesus has been a magnet for rural workers forced off their small subsistence plots by large landowners wanting to use every available piece of land for sugar cultivation. Initially, the rural migrants to Bom Jesus were squatters who were given tacit approval by the mayor to put up temporary straw huts on each of the three hills overlooking the town. The Alto do Cruzeiro is the oldest, the largest, and the poorest of the shantytowns. Over the past three decades many of the original migrants have become permanent residents, and the primitive and temporary straw huts have been replaced by small homes (usually of two rooms) made of wattle and daub, sometimes covered with plaster. The more affluent residents use bricks and tiles. In most Alto homes, dangerous kerosene lamps have been replaced by light bulbs. The once tattered rural garb, often fashioned from used sugar sacking, has likewise been replaced by store-brought clothes, often castoffs from a wealthy *patrão* (boss). The trappings are modern, but the hunger, sickness, and death that they conceal are traditional, deeply rooted in a history of feudalism, exploitation, and institutionalized dependency.

My research agenda never wavered. The questions I addressed first crystalized during a veritable "die-off" of Alto babies during a severe drought in 1965. The food and water shortages and the political and economic chaos occasioned by the military coup were reflected in the handwritten entries of births and deaths in the dusty, yellowed pages of the ledger books kept at the public registry office in Bom Jesus. More than 350 babies died in the Alto during 1965 alone—this from a shantytown population of little more than 5,000. But that wasn't what surprised me. There were reasons enough for the deaths in the miserable conditions of shantytown life. What puzzled me was the seeming indifference of Alto women to the death of their infants, and their willingness to attribute to their own tiny offspring an aversion to life that made their death seem wholly natural, indeed all but anticipated.

Although I found that it was possible, and hardly difficult, to rescue infants and toddlers from death by diarrhea and dehydration with a simple sugar, salt, and water solution (even bottled Coca-Cola worked fine), it was more difficult to enlist a mother herself in the rescue of a child she perceived as ill-fated for life or better off dead, or to convince her to take back into her threatened and besieged home a baby she had already come to think of as an angel rather than as a son or daughter.

I learned that the high expectancy of death, and the ability to face child death with stoicism and equanimity, produced patterns of nurturing that differentiated between those infants thought of as thrivers and survivors and those thought of as born already "wanting to die." The survivors were nurtured, while stigmatized, doomed infants were left to die, as mothers say, *a mingua,* "of neglect." Mothers stepped back and allowed nature to take its course. This pattern, which I call mortal selective neglect, is called passive infanticide by anthropologist Marvin Harris. The Alto situation, although culturally specific in the form that it takes, is not unique to Third World shantytown communities and may have its correlates in our own impoverished urban communities in some cases of "failure to thrive" infants.

I use as an example the story of Zezinho, the thirteen-month-old toddler of one of my neighbors, Lourdes. I became involved with Zezinho when I was called in to help Lourdes in the delivery of another child, this one a fair and robust little tyke with a lusty cry. I noted that while Lourdes showed great interest in the newborn, she totally ignored Zezinho who, wasted and severely malnourished, was curled up in a fetal position on a piece of urine- and feces-soaked cardboard placed under his mother's hammock. Eyes open and vacant, mouth slack, the little boy seemed doomed.

When I carried Zezinho up to the community day-care center at the top of the hill, the Alto women who took turns caring for one another's children (in order to free themselves for part-time work in the cane fields or washing clothes) laughed at my efforts to save Ze, agreeing with Lourdes that here was a baby without a ghost of a chance. Leave him alone, they cautioned. It makes no sense to fight with death. But I did do battle with Ze, and after several weeks of force-feeding (malnourished babies lose their interest in food), Ze began to succumb to my ministrations. He acquired some flesh across his taut chest bones, learned to sit up, and even tried to smile. When he seemed well enough, I returned him to Lourdes in her miserable scrap-material lean-to, but not without guilt about what I had done. I wondered whether returning Ze was at all fair to Lourdes and to his little brother. But I was busy and washed my hands of the matter. And Lourdes did seem more interested in Ze now that he was looking more human.

When I returned in 1982, there was Lourdes among the women who formed my sample of Alto mothers—still struggling to put together some semblance of life for a now grown Ze and her five other surviving children. Much was made of my reunion with Ze in 1982, and everyone enjoyed retelling the story of Ze's rescue and of how his mother had given him up for dead. Ze would laugh the loudest when told how I had had to force-feed him like a fiesta turkey. There was no hint of guilt on the part of Lourdes and no resentment on the part of Ze. In fact, when questioned in private as to who was the best friend he ever had in life, Ze took a long drag on his cigarette and answered without a trace of irony, "Why my mother, of course." "But of course," I replied.

Part of learning how to mother in the Alto do Cruzeiro is learning when to let go of a child who shows that it "wants" to die or that it has no "knack" or no "taste" for life. Another part is learning when it is safe to let oneself love a child. Frequent child death remains a powerful shaper of maternal thinking and practice. In the absence of firm expectation that a child will survive, mother love as we conceptualize it (whether in popular terms or in the psychobiological notion of maternal bonding) is attenuated and delayed with consequences for infant survival. In an environment already precarious to young life, the emotional detachment of mothers toward some of their babies contributes even further to the spiral of high mortality—high fertility in a kind of macabre lock-step dance of death.

The average woman of the Alto experiences 9.5 pregnancies, 3.5 child deaths, and 1.5 stillbirths. Seventy percent of all child deaths in the Alto occur in the first six months of life, and 82 percent by the end of the first year. Of all deaths in the community each year, about 45 percent are of children under the age of five.

Women of the Alto distinguish between child deaths understood as natural (caused by diarrhea and communicable diseases) and those resulting from sorcery, the evil eye, or other magical or supernatural afflictions. They also recognize a large category of infant deaths seen as fated and inevitable. These hopeless cases are classified by mothers under the folk terminology "child sickness" or "child attack." Women say that there are at least fourteen different types of hopeless child sickness, but most can be subsumed under two categories—chronic and acute. The chronic cases refer to infants who are born small and wasted. They are deathly pale, mothers say, as well as weak and passive. They demonstrate no vital force, no liveliness. They do not suck vigorously; they hardly cry. Such babies can be this way at birth or they can be born sound but soon show no resistance, no "fight" against the common crises of infancy: diarrhea, respiratory infections, tropical fevers.

The acute cases are those doomed infants who die suddenly and violently. They are taken by stealth overnight, often following convulsions that bring on head banging, shaking, grimacing, and shrieking. Women say it is horrible to look at such a baby. If the infant begins to foam at the mouth or gnash its teeth or go rigid with its eyes turned back inside its head, there is absolutely no hope. The infant is "put aside"—left alone—often on the floor in a back room, and allowed to die. These symptoms (which accompany high fevers, dehydration, third-stage malnutrition, and encephalitis) are equated by Alto women with madness, epilepsy, and worst of all, rabies, which is greatly feared and highly stigmatized.

Most of the infants presented to me as suffering from chronic child sickness were tiny, wasted famine victims, while those labeled as victims of acute child attack seemed to be infants suffering from the deliriums of high fever or the convulsions that can accompany electrolyte imbalance in dehydrated babies.

Local midwives and traditional healers, praying women, as they are called, advise Alto women on when to allow a baby to die. One midwife explained: "If I can see that a baby was born unfortuitously, I tell the mother that she need not wash the infant or give it a cleansing tea. I tell her just to dust the infant with baby powder and wait for it to die." Allowing nature to take its course is not seen as sinful by these often very devout Catholic women. Rather, it is understood as cooperating with God's plan.

Often I have been asked how consciously women of the Alto behave in this regard. I would have to say that consciousness is always shifting between allowed and disallowed levels of awareness. For example, I was awakened early one morning in 1987 by two neighborhood children who had been sent to fetch me to a hastily organized wake for a two-month-old infant whose mother I had unsuccessfully urged to breast-feed. The infant was being sustained on sugar water, which the mother referred to as *soro* (serum), using a medical term for the infant's starvation regime in light of his chronic diarrhea. I had cautioned the mother that an infant could not live on *soro* forever.

The two girls urged me to console the young mother by telling her that it was "too bad" that her infant was so weak that Jesus had to take him. They were coaching me in proper Alto etiquette. I agreed, of course, but asked, "And what do *you* think?" Xoxa, the eleven-year-old, looked down at her dusty flip-flops and blurted out, "Oh, Dona Nanci, that baby never got enough to eat, but you must never say that!" And so the death of hungry babies remains one of the best kept secrets of life in Bom Jesus da Mata.

Most victims are waked quickly and with a minimum of ceremony. No tears are shed, and the neighborhood children form a tiny procession, carrying the baby to the town graveyard where it will join a multitude of others. Although a few fresh flowers may be scattered over the tiny grave, no stone or wooden cross will mark the place, and the same spot will be reused within a few months' time. The mother will never visit the grave, which soon becomes an anonymous one.

What, then, can be said of these women? What emotions, what sentiments motivate them? How are they able to do what, in fact, must be done? What does mother love mean in this inhospitable context? Are grief, mourning, and melancholia present, although deeply repressed? If so, where shall we look for them? And if not, how are we to understand the moral visions and moral sensibilities that guide their actions?

I have been criticized more than once for presenting an unflattering portrait of poor Brazilian women, women who are, after all, themselves the victims of severe social and institutional neglect. I have described these women as allowing some of their children to die, as if this were an unnatural and inhuman act rather than, as I would assert, the way any one of us might act, reasonably and rationally, under similarly desperate conditions. Perhaps I have not emphasized enough the real pathogens in this environment of high risk: poverty, deprivation, sexism, chronic hunger, and economic exploitation. If mother love is, as many psychologists and some feminists believe, a seemingly natural and universal maternal script, what does it mean to women for whom scarcity, loss, sickness, and deprivation have made that love frantic and robbed them of their grief, seeming to turn their hearts to stone?

Throughout much of human history—as in a great deal of the impoverished Third World today—women have had to give birth and to nurture children under ecological conditions and social arrangements hostile to child survival, as well as to their own well-being. Under circumstances of high childhood mortality, patterns of selective neglect and passive infanticide may be seen as active survival strategies.

They also seem to be fairly common practices historically and across cultures. In societies characterized by high childhood mortality and by a correspondingly high (replacement) fertility, cultural practices of infant and child care tend to be organized primarily around survival goals. But what this means is a pragmatic recognition that not all of one's children can be expected to live. The nervousness about child survival in areas of northeast Brazil, northern India, or Bangladesh, where a 30 percent or 40 percent mortality rate in the first years of life is common, can lead to forms of delayed attachment and a casual or benign neglect that serves to weed out the worst bets so as to enhance the life chances of healthier siblings, including those yet to be born. Practices similar to those that I am describing have been recorded for parts of Africa, India, and Central America.

Life in the Alto do Cruzeiro resembles nothing so much as a battlefield or an emergency room in an overcrowded inner-city public hospital. Consequently, mortality is guided by a kind of "life-boat ethics," the morality of triage. The seemingly studied indifference toward the suffering of some of their infants, conveyed in such sayings as "little critters have no feelings," is understandable in light of these women's obligation to carry on with their reproductive and nurturing lives.

In their slowness to anthropomorphize and personalize their infants, everything is mobilized so as to prevent maternal over-attachment and, therefore, grief at death. The bereaved mother is told not to cry, that her tears will dampen the wings of her little angel so that she cannot fly up to her heavenly home. Grief at the death of an angel is not only inappropriate, it is a symptom of madness and of a profound lack of faith.

Infant death becomes routine in an environment in which death is anticipated and bets are hedged. While the routinization of death in the context of shantytown life is not hard to understand, and quite possible to empathize with, its routinization in the formal institutions of public life in Bom Jesus is not as easy to accept uncritically. Here the social production of indifference takes on a different, even a malevolent, cast.

In a society where triplicates of every form are required for the most banal events (registering a car, for example), the registration of infant and child death is informal, incomplete, and rapid. It requires no documentation, takes less than five minutes, and demands no witnesses other than office clerks. No questions are asked concerning the circumstances of the death, and the cause of death is left blank, unquestioned and unexamined. A neighbor, grandmother, older sibling, or common-law husband may register the death. Since most infants die at home, there is no question of a medical record.

From the registry office, the parent proceeds to the town hall, where the mayor will give him or her a voucher for a free baby coffin. The full-time municipal coffinmaker cannot tell you exactly how many baby coffins are dispatched each week. It varies, he says, with the seasons. There are more needed during the drought months and during the big festivals of Carnaval and Christmas and São Joao's Day because people are too busy, he supposes, to take their babies to the clinic. Record keeping is sloppy.

Similarly, there is a failure on the part of city-employed doctors working at two free clinics to recognize the malnutrition of babies who are weighed, measured, and immunized without comment and as if they were not, in fact, anemic, stunted, fussy, and irritated starvation babies. At best the mothers are told to pick up free vitamins or a health "tonic" at the municipal chambers. At worst, clinic personnel will give tranquilizers and sleeping pills to quiet the hungry cries of "sick-to-death" Alto babies.

The church, too, contributes to the routinization of, and indifference toward, child death. Traditionally, the local Catholic church taught patience and resignation to domestic tragedies that were said to reveal the imponderable workings of God's will. If an infant died suddenly, it was because a particular saint had claimed the child. The infant would be an angel in the service of his or her heavenly patron. It would be wrong, a sign of a lack of faith, to weep for a child with such good fortune. The infant funeral was, in the past, an event celebrated with joy. Today, however, under the new regime of "liberation theology," the bells of N. S. das Dores parish church no longer peal for the death of Alto babies, and no priest accompanies the procession of angels to the cemetery where their bodies are disposed of casually and without ceremony. Children bury children in Bom Jesus da Mata. In this most Catholic of communities, the coffin is handed to the disabled and irritable municipal gravedigger, who often chides the children for one reason or another. It may be that the coffin is larger than expected and the gravedigger can find no appropriate space. The children do not wait for the gravedigger to complete his task. No prayers are recited and no sign of the cross made as the tiny coffin goes into its shallow grave.

When I asked the local priest, Padre Marcos, about the lack of church ceremony surrounding infant and childhood death today in Bom Jesus, he replied; "In the old days, child death was richly celebrated. But those were the baroque customs of a conservative church that wallowed in death and misery. The new church is a church of hope and joy. We no longer celebrate the death of child angels. We try to tell mothers that Jesus doesn't want all the dead babies they send him." Similarly, the new church has changed its baptismal customs, now often refusing to baptize dying babies brought to the back door of a church or rectory. The mothers are scolded by the church attendants and told to go home and take care of their sick babies. Baptism, they are told, is for the living; it is not to be confused with the sacrament of extreme unction, which is the anointing of the dying. And so it appears to the women of the Alto that even the church has turned away from them, denying the traditional comfort of folk Catholicism.

The contemporary Catholic church is caught in the clutches of a double bind. The new theology of liberation imagines a kingdom of God on earth based on justice and equality, a world without hunger, sickness, or childhood mortality. At the same time, the church has not changed its official position on sexuality and reproduction, including its sanctions against birth control, abortion, and sterilization. The padre of Bom Jesus da Mata recognizes this contradiction intuitively, although he shies away from discussions on the topic, saying that he prefers to leave questions of family planning to the discretion and the "good consciences" of his impoverished parishioners. But this, of course, sidesteps the extent to which those good consciences have been shaped by traditional church teachings in Bom Jesus, especially by his recent predecessors. Hence, we can begin to see that the seeming indifference of Alto mothers toward the death of some of their infants is but a pale reflection of the official indifference of church and state to the plight of poor women and children.

Nonetheless, the women of Bom Jesus are survivors. One woman, Biu, told me her life history, returning again and again to the themes of child death, her first husband's suicide, abandonment by her father and later by her second husband, and all the other losses and disappointments she had suffered in her long forty-five years. She concluded with great force, reflecting on the days of Carnaval '88 that were fast approaching:

> No, Dona Nanci, I won't cry, and I won't waste my life thinking about it from morning to night. . . . Can I argue with God for the state that I'm in? No! And so I'll dance and I'll jump and I'll play Carnaval! And yes, I'll laugh and people will wonder at a *pobre* like me who can have such a good time.

And no one did blame Biu for dancing in the streets during the four days of Carnaval—not even on Ash Wednesday, the day following Carnaval '88 when we all assembled hurriedly to assist in the burial of Mercea, Biu's beloved *casula,* her last-born daughter who had died at home of pneumonia during the festivities. The rest of the family barely had time to change out of their costumes. Severino, the child's uncle and godfather, sprinkled holy water over the little angel while he prayed: "Mercea, I don't know whether you were called, taken, or thrown out of this world. But look down at us from your heavenly home with tenderness, with pity, and with mercy." So be it.

NANCY SCHEPER-HUGHES is a professor in the Department of Anthropology at the University of California, Berkeley. She has written *Death Without Weeping: Violence of Everyday Life in Brazil* (1992).

What's Love Got to Do with It

A Brief History of Marriage

STEPHANIE COONTZ

It's remarkable to realize that no one under the age of 30 is old enough to actually remember the fairy-tale wedding of Lady Diana Spencer to Prince Charles back in 1981. Yet almost everyone knows about the disillusion and drama that set in a few years later, when it became clear that they weren't going to live "happily ever after." As soon as Diana had the two sons the monarchy needed to serve as "an heir and a spare," Charles returned to his longtime lover, and Diana, bitterly angry, went on to take a series of lovers of her own. As Diana famously complained to a television interviewer, she hadn't known at the time of her wedding that there'd be three persons involved in her marriage. Many individuals still identify so much with the disappointed princess that they've reacted with fury to the announcement that Prince Charles will finally marry the woman with whom he's had a 35-year relationship.

But having only three people involved in a marriage would have seemed downright lonely to most people of the past, and for thousands of years it would have seemed strange for anyone to have entered a marriage with such high expectations for personal happiness as Diana and the millions of her admirers had.

George Bernard Shaw once described marriage as an institution that brings two people together under the influence of the most violent, delusive, and transient of passions, and requires them to swear they'll remain in that abnormal, exhausting condition until death do them part. His comment pokes fun at the unrealistic expectations attached to the cultural ideal that marriage should be based on true love. But for thousands of years, people would not have gotten the joke, because almost no one believed that people should marry for love. When individuals did advocate such a bizarre belief, it was no laughing matter, but a serious threat to social order.

In ancient India, falling in love before marriage was considered a disruptive, antisocial act. In some Chinese dialects, a term for *love* didn't traditionally apply to feelings between husband and wife: it was used to describe an illicit, socially disapproved relationship. Both the ancient Greeks and medieval Europeans thought lovesickness was a type of insanity, and that it was almost indecent to love a spouse too ardently. The Greek philosopher Plato did hold love in high regard, because he felt that it led men to behave honorably; however, he was referring not to the love of women, "such as the meaner men feel," but to the love of a man for another man, which was the Greek ideal for the purest form of love.

Once the Greeks became Christians, they got far less tolerant of same-sex relationships. But for the first thousand years of Christianity, the church didn't like heterosexual love much better than it liked homosexual love. "It's better to marry than to burn," said Paul, but it's better still to remain single and celibate. Right up until the 16th century, the Christian church taught that married love was only one step above unmarried fornication: The Virgin Mary was the most admired woman; the widow the next. The wife occupied the lowest rung of respectable womanhood.

The hierarchy of good things was different for the aristocracy, but for them, too, the pleasures of marriage were way down on the totem pole. The courtly love poems and songs that have so influenced our own sense of what romance is all about were originally based on the notion that adultery was the purest form of love. In 12th-century France, the author of the first treatise on courtly love wrote that marriage is no excuse for not loving. By this he meant that marriage was no excuse for not loving someone *outside* the marriage!

In most cultures of the past, it was inconceivable that young people would choose their spouse on the basis of an unpredictable feeling like love. Marriage wasn't about the happiness of two individuals—it was a political and economic arrangement between two families. For the propertied classes, marriage was a way of consolidating wealth, merging resources, forging political alliances, and even concluding peace treaties.

Marriage was also an economic and political transaction in the lower classes. Farms or businesses could rarely be run by a single person, so prospective partners' skills, resources, tools, and useful in-laws were more important than their attractiveness. For a farmer or artisan, getting married was like picking your most crucial employee, and it was a foolish man indeed who would choose her for her looks, or fire her because he didn't love her anymore.

Certainly, people fell in love in the ancient and medieval world—sometimes even with their own spouse. But marriage was far too vital an economic and political institution to be entered into solely on the basis of something as irrational as love, and too important to be left to the whims of two young people. For thousands of years, the theme song for most courtships and weddings could have been "what's love got to do with it?"

Married love began to get a better reputation with the Protestant Reformation in the 16th century. Protestants argued that the clergy should be allowed, even encouraged, to marry, and that Roman Catholics were wrong to call marriage a necessary evil or a second-best existence to celibacy. Rather, said Luther, marriage was "a glorious estate."

But Protestants were just as suspicious of ardent love between husband and wife as were Roman Catholics, and they were even more hostile toward young people's right to freely choose their own mate. Protestants insisted that a marriage wasn't valid unless the parents agreed to it, even if the couple had gone through a ceremony and later had children together. Luther argued that parents didn't have the right to force a child into a loveless match, but they were totally justified in forbidding a match, no matter how much the couple loved each other, or in annulling a match for which they hadn't given permission. Both Catholic and Protestant theologians criticized women who used endearing nicknames for their husbands, because such familiarity undermined the lines of authority that ought to govern marriage.

It wasn't until the 18th century that a decisive change began to occur in popular attitudes toward love and marriage, spurred by two seismic social revolutions. First, the spread of wage labor made young people less dependent on their parents to get a start in life. A man didn't have to delay marriage until he inherited land or took over a business from his father. A woman could earn her own dowry. This made it harder for parents to control their children's courting.

Second, the freedoms afforded by the market economy had their parallel in new philosophical ideas. During the 18th-century Enlightenment and the age of revolution, influential thinkers across Europe began to champion individual rights and insist that the pursuit of happiness was a legitimate goal. They advocated marrying for love, rather than for wealth or status.

By the end of the 1700s, personal choice of partners had replaced arranged marriage as a social ideal, and individuals were encouraged to make that choice on the basis of love. For the first time in 5,000 years, marriage came to be seen as a private relationship between two individuals, rather than one link in a larger system of political and economic alliances. The measure of a successful marriage was no longer how big a financial settlement was involved, how many useful in-laws were acquired, or how many children were produced, but how well a family met the emotional needs of its individual members.

But these new ideas, conservatives immediately complained, posed a crisis of social order. If marriage was suddenly to be about love and lifelong intimacy, they worried, what would hold a marriage together if love and intimacy disappeared? And how could household order be maintained if marriages were based on love, rather than power?

Traditionalists had good cause to fret. The 1780s and 1790s saw a crisis over these questions, especially in regions influenced by the radical ideas of the American and French revolutions. In America, New Jersey gave women the vote, and several states enacted measures that made it easier for young people to choose their own partners. Most states began to liberalize divorce laws.

The French revolutionaries went further. They redefined marriage as a freely chosen civil contract, made divorce more accessible than it would be again until 1975, and decriminalized homosexual acts, on the grounds that such penalties violated the principle that the state should respect people's private choices. They mandated that families couldn't favor boys over girls in inheritance. Traditionalists thought the world was coming to an end.

At the end of the 18th century, however, the most radical innovations were rolled back. In France, Napoleon repealed the no-fault divorce laws and struck down equal inheritance for women. In America, New Jersey revoked the right of women to vote, and most states adopted restrictions on women's political activity. At the same time, women lost access to many occupations that had formerly been open to them.

But the ideas fostered by these revolutions had made it impossible to fall back on the old saying that women had to obey their husbands as subjects had to obey the king. So people cast about for a new understanding of the relationship between men and women and the nature of marriage—one that didn't unleash the "chaos" of equality, but didn't insist too much on women's subordination or raise uncomfortable parallels between the right to rebel against political tyrants and women's right to rebel against domestic ones.

The result was a compromise between egalitarian and patriarchal views of marriage. There was a new outrage against forcing women into loveless marriages, reflected in the art and literature of the day. But women, in or out of marriage, weren't extended the same rights as men. Instead, women were said to possess such a unique moral worth and such a delicate constitution that they shouldn't be exposed to the risks that men had to take by participating in business or politics. The exclusion of women from politics, in this new theory, wasn't an assertion of male privilege, but a mark of deference to women's talents and needs.

And those needs began to be defined in totally new ways. In the Middle Ages, popular culture had painted women as the lusty sex, more prone to passion and sexual excess than men. Suddenly this was turned on its head. It became accepted wisdom in the 19th century that the "normal" woman lacked any sexual drives at all—another reason to protect her from too much freedom.

By the early 19th century, idealization of love, marriage, home, hearth, and female purity was the bedrock of popular culture. Poems were written about the "angel in the house" and the sanctity of home, completely overturning an older popular culture that focused on community rather than family celebrations.

When Queen Victoria walked down the aisle wearing white instead of the multicolored costumes of the past, a new "tradition" was instantly invented, and people began to lose the memory of a time when female purity, loving marriage, and domesticity weren't the most cherished subjects of popular culture. One author summed up the new view by saying that if you had just four letters with which to express all the affection and morality and meaning in life, you would simply spell out H-O-M-E.

In the late 18th century, conservatives had warned that unions based on love and the desire for personal happiness were inherently unstable. If love was the most important reason to marry, how could society condemn people who stayed single rather than enter a loveless marriage? If love disappeared from a marriage, why shouldn't the couple be allowed to go their separate ways? If men and women were true soul mates, why should they not be equal partners in society?

In the 19th century, the doctrine that men and women had innately different natures and occupied separate spheres of life seemed to sidestep these problems by allowing people to romanticize love and marriage without unleashing the radical demands that had rocked society in the 1790s. The doctrine of separate spheres held back the inherent individualism of the "pursuit of happiness" by making men and women dependent upon each other, insisting that each party was incomplete without marriage. It justified women's confinement to the home without having to rely on patriarchal assertions about men's right to rule. Men were protecting women, it was said, not dominating them, by reserving political and economic roles for themselves, and women in return would rescue men from material corruption because of their own pure, sexless natures. For a while, the doctrine of female purity seemed to resolve the problem of how to justify women's exclusion from political, economic, and sexual rights without returning to the naked patriarchal controls of the past.

But there were two serious problems with the compromise between the radical implications of love and the traditional constraints of marriage. First of all, the idealized home was out of reach for most of the population, and in fact, middle-class women's domesticity and seclusion depended on the denial of domesticity to the working-class women, men, and children who took over the chores that had formerly taken up the bulk of middle-class wives' time. In the southern United States, slave holders had no respect for the "sanctity" of marriage, motherhood, or protected childhood when it came to their slaves, and even after emancipation, most African Americans had neither the time nor the resources for wives to be full-time homemakers and children to stay home to be nurtured by their mothers.

In the North, women and children who couldn't survive on their husbands' or fathers' wages worked as domestic servants in other people's homes and provided cheap factory labor. Without their work, middle-class homemakers would have had scant time to minister to the emotional needs of their husbands and children. In mid-19th-century cities, providing enough water to maintain what advice writers called "a fairly clean" home required a servant to lug the equivalent of 100 bottles of water from the public pipe every day.

Even for those who could afford to practice the new ideals of domesticity and gender segregation, there was a problem. The doctrine of difference said that men and women were complementary figures who could be completed only by marriage, but it also drove a wedge between the sexes by emphasizing their differences. Women began to see men as a threat to their pure nature and their more refined friendships. In letters and diaries, women often referred to men as "the grosser sex." For their part, men found it easier to worship an angel in the abstract than to constantly curb their manners and restrain their own enjoyments to put up with the conventions of ladylike behavior on a daily basis.

If the doctrine of difference inhibited emotional intimacy between men and women, the cult of female purity made physical intimacy even more problematic, creating a huge distinction in men's minds between good sex and "good" women. Many men couldn't think about a woman they respected in sexual terms; they often went to prostitutes for sexual relief, and frequently passed venereal diseases on to their wives. For many women, marital sex was a source of anxiety, guilt, or disgust, yet Victorian women suffered from an epidemic of ailments that were almost certainly associated with sexual frustration. They flocked to hydrotherapy centers, where strong volleys of water sometimes relieved their symptoms. Physicians regularly massaged women's pelvic areas to alleviate "hysteria." In fact, the mechanical vibrator was invented at the end of the 19th century to relieve physicians of this time-consuming chore!

No wonder there was a revolt against Victorian prudery and the doctrine of separate spheres. The sexual revolution of the early 20th century wasn't a revolt against marriage—it was an attempt to make marriage more satisfying and to make married love more central to people's identity. And it succeeded dramatically. In the early 20th century, the age of marriage fell, the proportion of men and women who remained single all their lives fell, and the same-sex bonds and intense extended-family ties that had once coexisted with marital ties were devalued, or even labeled deviant. This was when marriage became the happy ending for every story, and when expectations of emotional and sexual satisfaction in marriage led people to elevate marriage above all other personal and family ties. Marriage became a much more important goal, especially for women, and more people reported themselves happy in marriage, than in the past. But the more that people expected to find love and sexual satisfaction in marriage, the more discontented they became when a marriage proved unsatisfying. Divorce rates tripled during the early 1900s. By the end of the 1920s, hundreds of books and articles worried about *The Bankruptcy of Marriage; The Revolt of Women;* and *The Marriage Crisis* and asked, "Is Marriage on the Skids?"

The crisis was put on the back burner during the 1930s and 1940s by the Great Depression and World War II, and in the 1950s, it was almost completely forgotten, as the love-based, male-breadwinner family swept aside all other family forms and values. The reaction against the hardship and turmoil of the '30s and '40s combined with postwar prosperity and unprecedented government subsidies for male-breadwinner families during the 1950s to create what many people see as the Golden Age of Marriage.

By the 1960s, marriage had become nearly universal in North America and Western Europe, with 95 percent of all persons marrying. And as people married at a younger age, life spans lengthened, and divorce rates fell or held steady, individuals were spending much more of their lives in marriage than ever before or since. By 1959, almost half of all American women were married by age 19, and 70 percent were married by age 24. There were also more full-time housewives in society than ever before or since.

Never before had so many people shared the experience of courting their own mates, getting married when they wanted to, and setting up their own households. And never before had married couples been so independent of community groups and extended family ties. The postwar period was characterized by the overwhelming dominance of the nuclear family, male-breadwinner model of marriage. Any departure from this model—whether late marriage, non-marriage, divorce, single motherhood, or even delayed childbearing—was considered deviant.

A 1957 survey in the United States reported that four out of five people believed that anyone who preferred to remain single was "sick," "neurotic," or "immoral." Even larger majorities agreed that, once married, the husband should be the breadwinner and the wife should stay home. As late as 1961, one survey of young women aged 16 to 21 found that almost all expected to be married by age 22, most wanted to have four children, and they expected to quit work permanently when their first child was born.

But under the surface of that placidity, disillusion and discontent were mounting, for both sexes. Hugh Hefner founded *Playboy* magazine in 1953 as a voice of revolt against male family responsibilities. He urged men to "enjoy the pleasures the female has to offer without becoming emotionally involved"—or, worse yet, financially responsible: *Playboy's* first issue, in April 1953, featured the article "Miss Gold-Digger of 1953," assailing women who expected husbands to support them.

Housewives had their own discontents. In poll after poll, women who married in the 1950s said that they didn't want their daughters to have the same life that they'd had. Instead, they wanted their daughters to marry later in life and get more education. The limits that these wives and mothers had experienced in their marriages had led them to encourage behaviors in their children that, in combination with the new economic and political trends of the 1960s and 1970s, overturned prior gender roles and marriage patterns. As African Americans, young people, and women challenged the restrictions they'd faced in social life and the economy brought more women into the workforce on new terms, all the old contradictions of the love-based, male-breadwinner marriage reemerged, and this time they exploded.

It took more than 150 years to establish the love-based, male-breadwinner marriage as the dominant model in North America and Western Europe. It took less than 25 years to dismantle it. In barely two decades, marriage lost its role as "the master event," which governed young people's sexual initiation, their assumption of adult roles and work patterns, and their transition into parenthood. People began marrying later. Divorce rates soared. Premarital sex became the norm. Acceptance of gay and lesbian relations increased. The division of labor between husband as breadwinner and wife as homemaker, which sociologists in the 1950s had believed was vital for industrial society, fell apart. And many of the mores that once governed why people marry, what predicts marital satisfaction, who divorces, and how cohabitation affects future marital behavior began to change in fundamental and unexpected ways.

Today researchers chase a moving target as they study the new dynamics and relationships of married life. And all of us struggle to understand and come to terms with these changes in our own families. It doesn't help when the mass media and political pundits assure us that if we just tried harder, we could recapture a Golden Age of "traditional" marriage. Such illusions merely burden us with unrealistic nostalgia for what love and marriage "used to be," feeding our guilt and our fears about family change, instead of showing us the grounds for hope: the fact that many people are now discovering how to sustain commitments and make deeper connections both inside and outside marriage. Our challenge today is to reject romanticized views of the past, which make us feel guilty for not living in a sit-com marriage, and to find ways to help all people—whatever kind of family they live in, whether they're currently married or not—build healthier relationships and meet their obligations to dependents.

STEPHANIE COONTZ, MA, author of *The Way We Never Were,* teaches history and family studies at The Evergreen State College in Olympia, Washington, and serves as director of research and public education at the Council on Contemporary Families. This article is adapted from her latest book, *Marriage, A History: From Obedience to Intimacy, or How Love Conquered Marriage,* published by Viking Press. Contact coontzs@msn.com.

Arranging a Marriage in India

SERENA NANDA

Sister and doctor brother-in-law invite correspondence from North Indian professionals only, for a beautiful, talented, sophisticated, intelligent sister, 5'3", slim, M.A. in textile design, father a senior civil officer. Would prefer immigrant doctors, between 26–29 years. Reply with full details and returnable photo. A well-settled uncle invites matrimonial correspondence from slim, fair, educated South Indian girl, for his nephew, 25 years, smart, M.B.A., green card holder, 5'6". Full particulars with returnable photo appreciated.

Matrimonial Advertisements,
India Abroad

In India, almost all marriages are arranged. Even among the educated middle classes in modern, urban India, marriage is as much a concern of the families as it is of the individuals. So customary is the practice of arranged marriage that there is a special name for a marriage which is not arranged: It is called a "love match."

On my first field trip to India, I met many young men and women whose parents were in the process of "getting them married." In many cases, the bride and groom would not meet each other before the marriage. At most they might meet for a brief conversation, and this meeting would take place only after their parents had decided that the match was suitable. Parents do not compel their children to marry a person who either marriage partner finds objectionable. But only after one match is refused will another be sought.

Young men and women do not date and have very little social life involving members of the opposite sex.

As a young American woman in India for the first time, I found this custom of arranged marriage oppressive. How could any intelligent young person agree to such a marriage without great reluctance? It was contrary to everything I believed about the importance of romantic love as the only basis of a happy marriage. It also clashed with my strongly held notions that the choice of such an intimate and permanent relationship could be made only by the individuals involved. Had anyone tried to arrange my marriage, I would have been defiant and rebellious!

At the first opportunity, I began, with more curiosity than tact, to question the young people I met on how they felt about this practice. Sita, one of my young informants, was a college graduate with a degree in political science. She had been waiting for over a year while her parents were arranging a match for her. I found it difficult to accept the docile manner in which this well-educated young woman awaited the outcome of a process that would result in her spending the rest of her life with a man she hardly knew, a virtual stranger, picked out by her parents.

"How can you go along with this?" I asked her, in frustration and distress. "Don't you care who you marry?"

"Of course I care," she answered." This is why I must let my parents choose a boy for me. My marriage is too important to be arranged by such an inexperienced person as myself. In such matters, it is better to have my parents' guidance."

I had learned that young men and women in India do not date and have very little social life involving members of the opposite sex. Although I could not disagree with Sita's reasoning, I continued to pursue the subject.

"But how can you marry the first man you have ever met? Not only have you missed the fun of meeting a lot of different people, but you have not given yourself the chance to know who is the right man for you."

"Meeting with a lot of different people doesn't sound like any fun at all," Sita answered. "One hears that in America the girls are spending all their time worrying about whether they will meet a man and get married. Here we have the chance to enjoy our life and let our parents do this work and worrying for us."

She had me there. The high anxiety of the competition to "be popular" with the opposite sex certainly was the most prominent feature of life as an American teenager in the late fifties. The endless worrying about the rules that governed our behavior and about our popularity ratings sapped both our self-esteem and our enjoyment of adolescence. I reflected that absence of this competition in India most certainly may have contributed to the self-confidence and natural charm of so many of the young women I met.

And yet, the idea of marrying a perfect stranger, whom one did not know and did not "love," so offended my American ideas of individualism and romanticism, that I persisted with my objections.

"I still can't imagine it," I said. "How can you agree to marry a man you hardly know?"

"But of course he will be known. My parents would never arrange a marriage for me without knowing all about the boy's family background. Naturally we will not rely only on what the family tells us. We will check the particulars out ourselves. No one will want their daughter to marry into a family that is not good. All these things we will know beforehand."

Impatiently, I responded, "Sita, I don't mean know the family, I mean, know the man. How can you marry someone you don't know personally and don't love? How can you think of spending your life with someone you may not even like?"

"If he is a good man, why should I not like him?" she said. "With you people, you know the boy so well before you marry, where will be the fun to get married? There will be no mystery and no romance. Here we have the whole of our married life to get to know and love our husband. "This way is better, is it not?"

Her response made further sense, and I began to have second thoughts on the matter. Indeed, during months of meeting many intelligent young Indian people, both male and female, who had the same ideas as Sita, I saw arranged marriages in a different light. I also saw the importance of the family in Indian life and realized that a couple who took their marriage into their own hands was taking a big risk, particularly if their families were irreconcilably opposed to the match. In a country where every important resource in life—a job, a house, a social circle—is gained through family connections, it seemed foolhardy to cut oneself off from a supportive social network and depend solely on one person for happiness and success.

Six years later I returned to India to again do fieldwork, this time among the middle class in Bombay, a modern, sophisticated city. From the experience of my earlier visit, I decided to include a study of arranged marriages in my project. By this time I had met many Indian couples whose marriages had been arranged and who seemed very happy. Particularly in contrast to the fate of many of my married friends in the United States who were already in the process of divorce, the positive aspects of arranged marriages appeared to me to outweigh the negatives. In fact, I thought I might even participate in arranging a marriage myself. I had been fairly successful in the United States in "fixing up" many of my friends, and I was confident that my matchmaking skills could be easily applied to this new situation, once I learned the basic rules. "After all," I thought, "how complicated can it be? People want pretty much the same things in a marriage whether it is in India or America."

An opportunity presented itself almost immediately. A friend from my previous Indian trip was in the process of arranging for the marriage of her eldest son. In India there is a perceived shortage of "good boys," and since my friend's family was eminently respectable and the boy himself personable, well educated, and nice looking, I was sure that by the end of my year's fieldwork, we would have found a match.

The basic rule seems to be that a family's reputation is most important. It is understood that matches would be arranged only within the same caste and general social class, although some crossing of subcastes is permissible if the class positions of the bride's and groom's families are similar. Although dowry is now prohibited by law in India, extensive gift exchanges took place with every marriage. Even when the boy's family do not "make demands," every girl's family nevertheless feels the obligation to give the traditional gifts, to the girl, to the boy, and to the boy's family. Particularly when the couple would be living in the joint

family—that is, with the boy's parents and his married brothers and their families, as well as with unmarried siblings—which is still very common even among the urban, upper-middle class in India, the girls' parents are anxious to establish smooth relations between their family and that of the boy. Offering the proper gifts, even when not called "dowry," is often an important factor in influencing the relationship between the bride's and groom's families and perhaps, also, the treatment of the bride in her new home.

In a society where divorce is still a scandal and where, in fact, the divorce rate is exceedingly low, an arranged marriage is the beginning of a lifetime relationship not just between the bride and groom but between their families as well.

In a society where divorce is still a scandal and where, in fact, the divorce rate is exceedingly low, an arranged marriage is the beginning of a lifetime relationship not just between the bride and groom but between their families as well. Thus, while a girl's looks are important, her character is even more so, for she is being judged as a prospective daughter-in-law as much as a prospective bride. Where she would be living in a joint family, as was the case with my friend, the girls's ability to get along harmoniously in a family is perhaps the single most important quality in assessing her suitability.

My friend is a highly esteemed wife, mother, and daughter-in-law. She is religious, soft-spoken, modest, and deferential. She rarely gossips and never quarrels, two qualities highly desirable in a woman. A family that has the reputation for gossip and conflict among its womenfolk will not find it easy to get good wives for their sons. Parents will not want to send their daughter to a house in which there is conflict.

My friend's family were originally from North India. They had lived in Bombay, where her husband owned a business, for forty years. The family had delayed in seeking a match for their eldest son because he had been an Air Force pilot for several years, stationed in such remote places that it had seemed fruitless to try to find a girl who would be willing to accompany him. In their social class, a military career, despite its economic security, has little prestige and is considered a drawback in finding a suitable bride. Many families would not allow their daughters to marry a man in an occupation so potentially dangerous and which requires so much moving around.

The son had recently left the military and joined his father's business. Since he was a college graduate, modern, and well traveled, from such a good family, and, I thought, quite handsome, it seemed to me that he, or rather his family, was in a position to pick and choose. I said as much to my friend.

While she agreed that there were many advantages on their side, she also said, "We must keep in mind that my son is both short and dark; these are drawbacks in finding the right match." While the boy's height had not escaped my notice, "dark" seemed to me inaccurate; I would have called him "wheat" colored perhaps, and in any case, I did not realize that color would be a consideration. I discovered, however, that while a boy's skin color is a less important consideration than a girl's, it is still a factor.

An important source of contacts in trying to arrange her son's marriage was my friend's social club in Bombay. Many of the women had daughters of the right age, and some had already expressed an interest in my friend's son. I was most enthusiastic about the possibilities of one particular family who had five daughters, all of whom were pretty, demure, and well educated. Their mother had told my friend, "You can have your pick for your son, whichever one of my daughters appeals to you most."

I saw a match in sight. "Surely," I said to my friend, "we will find one there. Let's go visit and make our choice." But my friend held back; she did not seem to share my enthusiasm, for reasons I could not then fathom.

When I kept pressing for an explanation of her reluctance, she admitted, "See, Serena, here is the problem. The family has so many daughters, how will they be able to provide nicely for any of them? We are not making any demands, but still, with so many daughters to marry off, one wonders whether she will even be able to make a proper wedding. Since this is our eldest son, it's best if we marry him to a girl who is the only daughter, then the wedding will truly be a gala affair." I argued that surely the quality of the girls themselves made up for any deficiency in the elaborateness of the wedding. My friend admitted this point but still seemed reluctant to proceed.

"Is there something else," I asked her, "some factor I have missed?" "Well," she finally said, "there is one other thing. They have one daughter already married and living in Bombay. The mother is always complaining to me that the girl's in-laws don't let her visit her own family often enough. So it makes me wonder, will she be that kind of mother who always wants her daughter at her own home? This will prevent the girl from adjusting to our house. It is not a good thing." And so, this family of five daughters was dropped as a possibility.

Somewhat disappointed, I nevertheless respected my friend's reasoning and geared up for the next prospect. This was also the daughter of a woman in my friend's social club. There was clear interest in this family and I could see why. The family's reputation was excellent; in fact, they came from a subcaste slightly higher than my friend's own. The girl, who was an only daughter, was pretty and well educated and had a brother studying in the United States. Yet, after expressing an interest to me in this family, all talk of them suddenly died down and the search began elsewhere.

"What happened to that girl as a prospect?" I asked one day. "You never mention her any more. She is so pretty and so educated, what did you find wrong?"

"She is too educated. We've decided against it. My husband's father saw the girl on the bus the other day and thought her forward. A girl who 'roams about' the city by herself is not the girl for our family." My disappointment this time was even greater, as I thought the son would have liked the girl very much. But then I thought, my friend is right, a girl who is going to live in a joint family cannot be too independent or she will make life miserable for everyone. I also learned that if the family of the girl has even a slightly higher social status than the family of the boy, the bride may think herself too good for them, and this

too will cause problems. Later my friend admitted to me that this had been an important factor in her decision not to pursue the match.

The next candidate was the daughter of a client of my friend's husband. When the client learned that the family was looking for a match for their son, he said, "Look no further, we have a daughter." This man then invited my friends to dinner to see the girl. He had already seen their son at the office and decided that "he liked the boy." We all went together for tea, rather than dinner—it was less of a commitment—and while we were there, the girl's mother showed us around the house. The girl was studying for her exams and was briefly introduced to us.

After we left, I was anxious to hear my friend's opinion. While her husband liked the family very much and was impressed with his client's business accomplishments and reputation, the wife didn't like the girl's looks. "She is short, no doubt, which is an important plus point, but she is also fat and wears glasses." My friend obviously thought she could do better for her son and asked her husband to make his excuses to his client by saying that they had decided to postpone the boy's marriage indefinitely.

"If a mistake is made we have not only ruined the life of our son or daughter, but we have spoiled the reputation of our family as well."

By this time almost six months had passed and I was becoming impatient. What I had thought would be an easy matter to arrange was turning out to be quite complicated. I began to believe that between my friend's desire for a girl who was modest enough to fit into her joint family, yet attractive and educated enough to be an acceptable partner for her son, she would not find anyone suitable. My friend laughed at my impatience: "Don't be so much in a hurry," she said. "You Americans want everything done so quickly. You get married quickly and then just as quickly get divorced. Here we take marriage more seriously. We must take all the factors into account. It is not enough for us to learn by our mistakes. This is too serious a business. If a mistake is made we have not only ruined the life of our son or daughter, but we have spoiled the reputation of our family as well. And that will make it much harder for their brothers and sisters to get married. So we must be very careful."

What she said was true and I promised myself to be more patient, though it was not easy. I had really hoped and expected that the match would be made before my year in India was up. But it was not to be. When I left India my friend seemed no further along in finding a suitable match for her son than when I had arrived.

Two years later, I returned to India and still my friend had not found a girl for her son. By this time, he was close to thirty, and I think she was a little worried. Since she knew I had friends all over India, and I was going to be there for a year, she asked me to "help her in this work" and keep an eye out for someone suitable. I was flattered that my judgment was respected, but knowing now how complicated the process was, I had lost my earlier confidence as a matchmaker. Nevertheless, I promised that I would try.

Appendix
Further Reflections on Arranged Marriage . . .

This essay was written from the point of view of a family seeking a daughter-in-law. Arranged marriage looks somewhat different from the point of view of the bride and her family. Arranged marriage continues to be preferred, even among the more educated, Westernized sections of the Indian population. Many young women from these families still go along, more or less willingly, with the practice, and also with the specific choices of their families. Young women do get excited about the prospects of their marriage, but there is also ambivalence and increasing uncertainty, as the bride contemplates leaving the comfort and familiarity of her own home, where as a "temporary guest" she had often been indulged, to live among strangers. Even in the best situation she will now come under the close scrutiny of her husband's family. How she dresses, how she behaves, how she gets along with others, where she goes, how she spends her time, her domestic abilities—all of this and much more—will be observed and commented on by a whole new set of relations. Her interaction with her family of birth will be monitored and curtailed considerably. Not only will she leave their home, but with increasing geographic mobility, she may also live very far from them, perhaps even on another continent. Too much expression of her fondness for her own family, or her desire to visit them, may be interpreted as an inability to adjust to her new family, and may become a source of conflict. In an arranged marriage the burden of adjustment is clearly heavier for a woman than for a man. And that is in the best of situations.

In less happy circumstances, the bride may be a target of resentment and hostility from her husband's family, particularly her mother-in-law or her husband's unmarried sisters, for whom she is now a source of competition for the affection, loyalty, and economic resources of their son or brother. If she is psychologically, or even physically abused, her options are limited, as returning to her parents' home, or divorce, are still very stigmatized. For most Indians, marriage and motherhood are still considered the only suitable roles for a woman, even for those who have careers, and few women can comfortably contemplate remaining unmarried. Most families still consider "marrying off" their daughters as a compelling religious duty and social necessity. This increases a bride's sense of obligation to make the marriage a success, at whatever cost to her own personal happiness.

The vulnerability of a new bride may also be intensified by the issue of dowry, which although illegal, has become a more pressing issue in the consumer conscious society of contemporary urban India. In many cases, where a groom's family is not satisfied with the amount of dowry a bride brings to her marriage, the young bride will be constantly harassed to get her parents to give more. In extreme cases, the bride may even be murdered, and the murder disguised as an accident or suicide. This also offers the husband's family an opportunity to arrange another match for him, thus bringing in another dowry. This phenomena, called dowry death, calls attention not just to the "evils of dowry" but also to larger issues of the powerlessness of women as well.

—Serena Nanda
March 1998

It was almost at the end of my year's stay in India that I met a family with a marriageable daughter whom I felt might be a good possibility for my friend's son. The girl's father was related to a good friend of mine and by coincidence came from the same village as my friend's husband. This new family had a successful business in a medium-sized city in central India and were from the same subcaste as my friend. The daughter was pretty and chic; in fact, she had studied fashion design in college. Her parents would not allow her to go off by herself to any of the major cities in India where she could make a career, but they had compromised with her wish to work by allowing her to run a small dress-making boutique from their home. In spite of her desire to have a career, the daughter was both modest and home-loving and had had a traditional, sheltered upbringing. She had only one other sister, already married, and a brother who was in his father's business.

I mentioned the possibility of a match with my friend's son. The girl's parents were most interested. Although their daughter was not eager to marry just yet, the idea of living in Bombay—a sophisticated, extremely fashion-conscious city where she could continue her education in clothing design—was a great inducement. I gave the girl's father my friend's address and suggested that when they went to Bombay on some business or whatever, they look up the boy's family.

Returning to Bombay on my way to New York, I told my friend of this newly discovered possibility. She seemed to feel there was potential but, in spite of my urging, would not make any moves herself. She rather preferred to wait for the girl's family to call upon them. I hoped something would come of this introduction, though by now I had learned to rein in my optimism.

A year later I received a letter from my friend. The family had indeed come to visit Bombay, and their daughter and my friend's daughter, who were near in age, had become very good friends. During that year, the two girls had frequently visited each other. I thought things looked promising.

Last week I received an invitation to a wedding: My friend's son and the girl were getting married. Since I had found the match, my presence was particularly requested at the wedding. I was thrilled. Success at last! As I prepared to leave for India, I began thinking, "Now, my friend's younger son, who do I know who has a nice girl for him . . .?"

Edited by Philip R. DeVita.

From *Stumbling Toward Truth: Anthropologists at Work,* Waveland Press, 2000, pp. 196–204. Copyright © 1992 by Serena Nanda. Reprinted by permission of the author.

Who Needs Love!
In Japan, Many Couples Don't

Nicholas D. Kristof

Omiya, Japan—Yuri Uemura sat on the straw tatami mat of her living room and chatted cheerfully about her 40-year marriage to a man whom, she mused, she never particularly liked.

"There was never any love between me and my husband," she said blithely, recalling how he used to beat her. "But, well, we survived."

A 72-year-old midwife, her face as weathered as an old baseball and etched with a thousand seams, Mrs. Uemura said that her husband had never told her that he liked her, never complimented her on a meal, never told her "thank you," never held her hand, never given her a present, never shown her affection in any way. He never calls her by her name, but summons her with the equivalent of a grunt or a "Hey, you."

"Even with animals, the males cooperate to bring the females some food," Mrs. Uemura said sadly, noting the contrast to her own marriage. "When I see that, it brings tears to my eyes."

In short, the Uemuras have a marriage that is as durable as it is unhappy, one couple's tribute to the Japanese sanctity of family.

The divorce rate in Japan is at a record high but still less than half that of the United States, and Japan arguably has one of the strongest family structures in the industrialized world. As the United States and Europe fret about the disintegration of the traditional family, most Japanese families remain as solid as the small red table on which Mrs. Uemura rested her tea.

It does not seem that Japanese families survive because husbands and wives love each other more than American couples, but rather because they perhaps love each other less.

A study published last year by the Population Council, an international nonprofit group based in New York, suggested that the traditional two-parent household is on the wane not only in America but throughout most of the world. There was one prominent exception: Japan.

In Japan, for example, only 1.1 percent of births are to unwed mothers—virtually unchanged from 25 years ago. In the United States, the figure is 30.1 percent and rising rapidly.

Yet if one comes to a little Japanese town like Omiya to learn the secrets of the Japanese family, the people are not as happy as the statistics.

"I haven't lived for myself," Mrs. Uemura said, with a touch of melancholy, "but for my kids, and for my family, and for society."

Mrs. Uemura's marriage does not seem exceptional in Japan, whether in the big cities or here in Omiya. The people of Omiya, a community of 5,700 nestled in the rain-drenched hills of the Kii Peninsula in Mie Prefecture, nearly 200 miles southwest of Tokyo, have spoken periodically to a reporter about various aspects of their daily lives. On this visit they talked about their families.

Survival Secrets
Often, the Couples Expect Little

Osamums Torida furrowed his brow and looked perplexed when he was asked if he loved his wife of 33 years.

"Yeah, so-so, I guess," said Mr. Torida, a cattle farmer. "She's like air or water. You couldn't live without it, but most of the time, you're not conscious of its existence."

The secret to the survival of the marriage, Mr. Torida acknowledged, was not mutual passion.

"Sure, we had fights about our work," he explained as he stood beside his barn. "But we were preoccupied by work and our debts, so we had no time to fool around."

That is a common theme in Omiya. It does not seem that Japanese families survive because husbands and wives love each other more than American couples, but rather because they perhaps love each other less.

"I think love marriages are more fragile than arranged marriages," said Tomika Kusukawa, 49, who married her high-school sweetheart and now runs a car repair shop with him. "In love marriages, when something happens or if the couple falls out of love, they split up."

If there is a secret to the strength of the Japanese family it consists of three ingredients: low expectations, patience, and shame.

GETTING ALONG

Matchmaker, Matchmaker

How countries compare on an index of compatibility of spouses, based on answers to questions about politics, sex, social issues, religion and ethics, from a survey by the Dentsu Research Institute and Leisure Development Center in Japan. A score of 500 would indicate perfect compatibility.

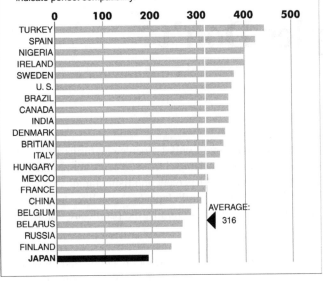

New York Times

The advantage of marriages based on low expectations is that they have built in shock absorbers. If the couple discover that they have nothing in common, that they do not even like each other, then that is not so much a reason for divorce as it is par for the course.

Even the discovery that one's spouse is having an affair is often not as traumatic in a Japanese marriage as it is in the West. A little sexual infidelity on the part of a man (though not on the part of his wife) was traditionally tolerated, so long as he did not become so besotted as to pay his mistress more than he could afford.

Tsuzuya Fukuyama, who runs a convenience store and will mark her 50th wedding anniversary this year, toasted her hands on an electric heater in the front of the store and declared that a woman would be wrong to get angry if her husband had an affair.

The durability of the Japanese family is particularly wondrous because couples are, by international standards, exceptionally incompatible.

"It's never just one side that's at fault," Mrs. Fukuyama said sternly. "Maybe the husband had an affair because his wife wasn't so hot herself. So she should look at her own faults."

Mrs. Fukuyama's daughter came to her a few years ago, suspecting that her husband was having an affair and asking what to do.

"I told her, 'Once you left this house, you can only come back if you divorce; if you're not prepared to get a divorce, then

you'd better be patient,'" Mrs. Fukuyama recalled. "And so she was patient. And then she got pregnant and had a kid, and now they're close again."

The word that Mrs. Fukuyama used for patience is "gaman," a term that comes up whenever marriage is discussed in Japan. It means toughing it out, enduring hardship, and many Japanese regard gaman with pride as a national trait.

Many people complain that younger folks divorce because they do not have enough gaman, and the frequency with which the term is used suggests a rather bleak understanding of marriage.

"I didn't know my husband very well when we married, and afterward we used to get into bitter fights," said Yoshiko Hirowaki, 56, a store owner. "But then we had children, and I got very busy with the kids and with this shop. Time passed."

Now Mrs. Hirowaki has been married 34 years, and she complains about young people who do not stick to their vows.

"In the old days, wives had more gaman," she said. "Now kids just don't have enough gaman."

The durability of the Japanese family is particularly wondrous because couples are, by international standards, exceptionally incompatible.

One survey asked married men and their wives in 37 countries how they felt about politics, sex, religion, ethics and social issues. Japanese couples ranked dead last in compatibility of views, by a huge margin. Indeed, another survey found that if they were doing it over again, only about one-third of Japanese would marry the same person.

A national survey found that 30 percent of fathers spend less than 15 minutes a day on weekends talking with or playing with their children.

Incompatibility might not matter so much, however, because Japanese husbands and wives spend very little time talking to each other.

"I kind of feel there's nothing new to say to her," said Masayuki Ogita, an egg farmer, explaining his reticence.

In a small town like Omiya, couples usually have dinner together, but in Japanese cities there are many "7-11 husbands," so called because they leave at 7 A.M. and return after 11 P.M.

Masahiko Kondo now lives in Omiya, working in the chamber of commerce, but he used to be a salesman in several big cities. He would leave work each morning at 7, and about four nights a week would go out for after-work drinking or mah-jongg sessions with buddies.

"I only saw my baby on Saturdays or Sundays," said Mr. Kondo, a lanky good-natured man of 37. "But in fact, I really enjoyed that life. It didn't bother me that I never spent time with my kid on weekdays."

Mr. Kondo's wife, Keiko, had her own life, spent with her child and the wives of other workaholic husbands.

"We had birthday parties, but they were with the kids and the mothers," she remembers. "No fathers ever came."

A national survey found that 30 percent of fathers spend less than 15 minutes a day on weekdays talking with or playing with their children. Among eighth graders, 51 percent reported that they never spoke with their fathers on weekdays.

Traditionally, many companies were reluctant to promote employees who had divorced or who had major problems at home.

As a result, the figures in Japan for single-parent households can be deceptive. The father is often more a theoretical presence than a homework-helping reality.

Still, younger people sometimes want to see the spouses in daylight, and a result is a gradual change in focus of lives from work to family. Two decades ago, nearly half of young people said in surveys that they wanted their fathers to put priority on work rather than family. Now only one-quarter say that.

Social Pressures
Shame Is Keeping Bonds in Place

For those who find themselves desperately unhappy, one source of pressure to keep plugging is shame.

"If you divorce, you lose face in society," said Tatsumi Kinoshita, a tea farmer. "People say, 'His wife escaped.' So folks remain married because they hate to be gossiped about."

Shame is a powerful social sanction in Japan, and it is not just a matter of gossip. Traditionally, many companies were reluctant to promote employees who had divorced or who had major problems at home.

"If you divorce, it weakens your position at work," said Akihiko Kanda, 27, who works in a local government office. "Your bosses won't give you such good ratings, and it'll always be a negative factor."

The idea, Mr. Kanda noted, is that if an employee cannot manage his own life properly, he should not be entrusted with important corporate matters.

Financial sanctions are also a major disincentive for divorce. The mother gets the children in three-quarters of divorces, but most mothers in Japan do not have careers and have few financial resources. Fathers pay child support in only 15 percent of all divorces with children, partly because women often hesitate to go to court to demand payments and partly because men often fail to pay even when the court orders it.

"The main reason for lack of divorce is that women can't support themselves," said Mizuko Kanda, a 51-year-old housewife. "My friends complain about their husbands and say that they'd divorce if they could, but they can't afford to."

The result of these social and economic pressures is clear.

Even in Japan, there are about 24 divorces for every 100 marriages, but that compares with 32 in France, and 42 in England, and 55 in the United States.

The Outlook
Change Creeps in, Imperiling Family

But society is changing in Japan, and it is an open question whether these changes will undermine the traditional family as they have elsewhere around the globe.

The nuclear family has already largely replaced the extended family in Japan, and shame is eroding as a sanction. Haruko Okumura, for example, runs a kindergarten and speaks openly about her divorce.

"My Mom was uneasy about it, but I never had an inferiority complex about being divorced," said Mrs. Okumura, as dozens of children played in the next room. "And people accepted me easily."

Mrs. Okumura sees evidence of the changes in family patterns every day: fathers are playing more of a role in the kindergarten. At Christmas parties and sports contests, fathers have started to show up along with mothers. And Mrs. Okumura believes that divorce is on the upswing.

"If there's a weakening of the economic and social pressures to stay married," she said, "surely divorce rates will soar."

Already divorce rates are rising, approximately doubling over the last 25 years. But couples are very reluctant to divorce when they have children, and so single-parent households account for exactly the same proportion today as in 1965.

Shinsuke Kawaguchi, a young tea farmer, is one of the men for whom life is changing. Americans are not likely to be impressed by Mr. Kawaguchi's open-mindedness, but he is.

"I take good care of my wife," he said. "I may not say 'I love you,' but I do hold her hand. And I might say, after she makes dinner, 'This tastes good.'"

"Of course," Mr. Kawaguchi quickly added, "I wouldn't say that unless I'd just done something really bad."

Even Mrs. Uemura, the elderly woman whose husband used to beat her, said that her husband was treating her better.

"The other day, he tried to pour me a cup of tea," Mrs. Uemura recalled excitedly. "It was a big change. I told all my friends."

UNIT 5

Gender and Status

Unit Selections

Key Points to Consider

- What is a "berdache" and how does it highlight the ways in which different societies accommodate atypical individuals?

- Why do many cultures the world over treat menstruating women as taboo?

- How and why do perceptions of feminine beauty vary from culture to culture?

Student Web Site

www.mhcls.com/online

Internet References

Further information regarding these Web sites may be found in this book's preface or online.

Arranged Marriages
  http://women3rdworld.miningco.com/cs/arrangedmarriage/
Bonobo Sex and Society
  http://songweaver.com/info/bonobos.html
FGM Research
  http://www.amnesty.org/ailib/intcam/femgen/fgm1.htm
OMIM Home Page-Online Mendelian Inheritance in Man
  http://www3.ncbi.nlm.nih.gov/omim/
Reflections on Sinai Bedouin Women
  http://www.sherryart.com/women/bedouin.html

The McGraw-Hill Companies, Inc/Kim David, photographer

The feminist movement in the United States has had a significant impact upon the development of anthropology. Feminists have rightly charged that anthropologists have tended to gloss over the lives of women in studies of society and culture. In part this is because, until recent times, most anthropologists have been men. The result has been an undue emphasis upon male activities as well as male perspectives in descriptions of particular societies.

These charges, however, have proven to be a firm corrective. In the last few years, anthropologists have begun to study women and, more particularly, the sexual division of labor and its relation to biology as well as to social and political status. In addition, these changes in emphasis have been accompanied by an increase in the number of women in the field. (See "A Woman's Curse?" by Meredith Small.)

Feminist anthropologists have begun to attack critically many of the established anthropological beliefs. They have shown, for example, that field studies of nonhuman primates, which were often used to demonstrate the evolutionary basis of male dominance, distorted the actual evolutionary record by focusing primarily on baboons. (Male baboons are especially dominant and aggressive.) Other, less-quoted primate studies show how dominance and aggression are highly situational phenomena, sensitive to ecological variation. Feminist anthropologists have also shown that the subsistence contribution of women has likewise been ignored by anthropologists. A classic case is that of the !Kung, a hunting and gathering people in southern Africa, where women provide the bulk of the foodstuffs, including most of the available protein, and who, not coincidentally, enjoy a more egalitarian relationship than usual with men.

Thus, since political control is a matter of cultural variation, male authority is not biologically predetermined. In fact, there are many cultures in which some men may play a more feminine or, at least, asexual role, as described in "The Berdache Tradition" and, as we see in and "Where Fat Is a Mark of Beauty," gender relationships are deeply embedded in social experience.

The Berdache Tradition

WALTER L. WILLIAMS

Because it is such a powerful force in the world today, the Western Judeo-Christian tradition is often accepted as the arbiter of "natural" behavior of humans. If Europeans and their descendant nations of North America accept something as normal, then anything different is seen as abnormal. Such a view ignores the great diversity of human existence.

This is the case of the study of gender. How many genders are there? To a modern Anglo-American, nothing might seem more definite than the answer that there are two: men and women. But not all societies around the world agree with Western culture's view that all humans are either women or men. The commonly accepted notion of "the opposite sex," based on anatomy, is itself an artifact of our society's rigid sex roles.

Among many cultures, there have existed different alternatives to "man" or "woman." An alternative role in many American Indian societies is referred to by anthropologists as *berdache*. . . . The role varied from one Native American culture to another, which is a reflection of the vast diversity of aboriginal New World societies. Small bands of hunter-gatherers existed in some areas, with advanced civilizations of farming peoples in other areas. With hundreds of different languages, economies, religions, and social patterns existing in North America alone, every generalization about a cultural tradition must acknowledge many exceptions.

This diversity is true for the berdache tradition as well, and must be kept in mind. My statements should be read as being specific to a particular culture, with generalizations being treated as loose patterns that might not apply to peoples even in nearby areas.

Briefly, a berdache can be defined as a morphological male who does not fill a society's standard man's role, who has a non-masculine character. This type of person is often stereotyped as effeminate, but a more accurate characterization is androgyny. Such a person has a clearly recognized and accepted social status, often based on a secure place in the tribal mythology. Berdaches have special ceremonial roles in many Native American religions, and important economic roles in their families. They will do at least some women's work, and mix together much of the behavior, dress, and social roles of women and men. Berdaches gain social prestige by their spiritual, intellectual, or craftwork/artistic contributions, and by their reputation for hard work and generosity. They serve a mediating function between women and men, precisely because their character is seen as distinct from either sex. They are not seen as men, yet they are not seen as women either. They occupy an alternative gender role that is a mixture of diverse elements.

In their erotic behavior berdaches also generally (but not always) take a nonmasculine role, either being asexual or becoming the passive partner in sex with men. In some cultures the berdache might become a wife to a man. This male-male sexual behavior became the focus of an attack on berdaches as "sodomites" by the Europeans who, early on, came into contact with them. From the first Spanish conquistadors to the Western frontiersmen and the Christian missionaries and government officials, Western culture has had a considerable impact on the berdache tradition. In the last two decades, the most recent impact on the tradition is the adaptation of a modern Western gay identity.

To Western eyes berdachism is a complex and puzzling phenomenon, mixing and redefining the very concepts of what is considered male and female. In a culture with only two recognized genders, such individuals are gender nonconformist, abnormal, deviant. But to American Indians, the institution of another gender role means that berdaches are not deviant—indeed, they do conform to the requirements of a custom in which their culture tells them they fit. Berdachism is a way for society to recognize and assimilate some atypical individuals without imposing a change on them or stigmatizing them as deviant. This cultural institution confirms their legitimacy for what they are.

Societies often bestow power upon that which does not neatly fit into the usual. Since no cultural system can explain everything, a common way that many cultures deal with these inconsistencies is to imbue them with negative power, as taboo, pollution, witchcraft, or sin. That which is not understood is seen as a threat. But an alternative method of dealing with such things, or people, is to take them out of the realm of threat and to sanctify them.[1] The berdaches' role as mediator is thus not just between women and men, but also between the physical and the spiritual. American Indian cultures have taken what Western culture calls negative, and made it a positive; they have successfully utilized the different skills and insights of a class of people that Western culture has stigmatized and whose spiritual powers have been wasted.

Many Native Americans also understood that gender roles have to do with more than just biological sex. The standard

Western view that one's sex is always a certainty, and that one's gender identity and sex role always conform to one's morphological sex is a view that dies hard. Western thought is typified by such dichotomies of groups perceived to be mutually exclusive: male and female, black and white, right and wrong, good and evil. Clearly, the world is not so simple; such clear divisions are not always realistic. Most American Indian worldviews generally are much more accepting of the ambiguities of life. Acceptance of gender variation in the berdache tradition is typical of many native cultures' approach to life in general.

Overall, these are generalizations based on those Native American societies that had an accepted role for berdaches. Not all cultures recognized such a respected status. Berdachism in aboriginal North America was most established among tribes in four areas: first, the Prairie and western Great Lakes, the northern and central Great Plains, and the lower Mississippi Valley; second, Florida and the Caribbean; third, the Southwest, the Great Basin, and California; and fourth, scattered areas of the Northwest, western Canada, and Alaska. For some reason it is not noticeable in eastern North America, with the exception of its southern rim. . . .

American Indian Religions

Native American religions offered an explanation for human diversity by their creation stories. In some tribal religions, the Great Spiritual Being is conceived as neither male nor female but as a combination of both. Among the Kamia of the Southwest, for example, the bearer of plant seeds and the introducer of Kamia culture was a man-woman spirit named Warharmi.[2] A key episode of the Zuni creation story involves a battle between the kachina spirits of the agricultural Zunis and the enemy hunter spirits. Every four years an elaborate ceremony commemorates this myth. In the story a kachina spirit called *ko'lhamana* was captured by the enemy spirits and transformed in the process. This transformed spirit became a mediator between the two sides, using his peacemaking skills to merge the differing lifestyles of hunters and farmers. In the ceremony, a dramatic reenactment of the myth, the part of the transformed *ko'lhamana* spirit, is performed by a berdache.[3] The Zuni word for berdache is *lhamana*, denoting its closeness to the spiritual mediator who brought hunting and farming together.[4] The moral of this story is that the berdache was created by the deities for a special purpose, and that this creation led to the improvement of society. The continual reenactment of this story provides a justification for the Zuni berdache in each generation.

In contrast to this, the lack of spiritual justification in a creation myth could denote a lack of tolerance for gender variation. The Pimas, unlike most of their Southwestern neighbors, did not respect a berdache status. *Wi-kovat,* their derogatory word, means "like a girl," but it does not signify a recognized social role. Pima mythology reflects this lack of acceptance, in a folk tale that explains male androgyny as due to Papago witchcraft. Knowing that the Papagos respected berdaches, the Pimas blamed such an occurrence on an alien influence.[5] While the Pimas' condemnatory attitude is unusual, it does point out the importance of spiritual explanations for the acceptance of gender variance in a culture.

Other Native American creation stories stand in sharp contrast to the Pima explanation. A good example is the account of the Navajos, which presents women and men as equals. The Navajo origin tale is told as a story of five worlds. The first people were First Man and First Woman, who were created equally and at the same time. The first two worlds that they lived in were bleak and unhappy, so they escaped to the third world. In the third world lived two twins, Turquoise Boy and White Shell Girl, who were the first berdaches. In the Navajo language the world for berdache is *nadle*, which means "changing one" or "one who is transformed." It is applied to hermaphrodites—those who are born with the genitals of both male and female—and also to "those who pretend to be *nadle*," who take on a social role that is distinct from either men or women.[6]

In the third world, First Man and First Woman began farming, with the help of the changing twins. One of the twins noticed some clay and, holding it in the palm of his/her hand, shaped it into the first pottery bowl. Then he/she formed a plate, a water dipper, and a pipe. The second twin observed some reeds and began to weave them, making the first basket. Together they shaped axes and grinding stones from rocks, and hoes from bone. All these new inventions made the people very happy.[7]

The message of this story is that humans are dependent for many good things on the inventiveness of *nadle*. Such individuals were present from the earliest eras of human existence, and their presence was never questioned. They were part of the natural order of the universe, with a special contribution to make.

Later on in the Navajo creation story, White Shell Girl entered the moon and became the Moon Bearer. Turquoise Boy, however, remained with the people. When First Man realized that Turquoise Boy could do all manner of women's work as well as women, all the men left the women and crossed a big river. The men hunted and planted crops. Turquoise Boy ground the corn, cooked the food, and weaved cloth for the men. Four years passed with the women and men separated, and the men were happy with the *nadle*. Later, however the women wanted to learn how to grind corn from the *nadle,* and both the men and women had decided that it was not good to continue living separately. So the women crossed the river and the people were reunited.[8]

They continued living happily in the third world, until one day a great flood began. The people ran to the highest mountaintop, but the water kept rising and they all feared they would be drowned. But just in time, the ever-inventive Turquoise Boy found a large reed. They climbed upward inside the tall hollow reed, and came out at the top into the fourth world. From there, White Shell Girl brought another reed, and the climbed again to the fifth world, which is the present world of the Navajos.[9]

These stories suggest that the very survival of humanity is dependent on the inventiveness of berdaches. With such a mythological belief system, it is no wonder that the Navajos held *nadle* in high regard. The concept of the *nadle* is well formulated in the creation story. As children were educated by these stories, and all Navajos believed in them, the high status accorded to gender variation was passed down from generation to generation. Such stories also provided instruction for *nadle* themselves to live by. A spiritual explanation guaranteed a special place for a person who was considered different but not deviant.

For American Indians, the important explanations of the world are spiritual ones. In their view, there is a deeper reality than the here-and-now. The real essence or wisdom occurs when one finally gives up trying to explain events in terms of "logic" and "reality." Many confusing aspects of existence can better be explained by actions of a multiplicity of spirits. Instead of a concept of a single god, there is an awareness of "that which we do not understand." In Lakota religion, for example, the term *Wakan Tanka* is often translated as "god." But a more proper translation, according to the medicine people who taught me, is "The Great Mystery."[10]

While rationality can explain much, there are limits to human capabilities of understanding. The English language is structured to account for cause and effect. For example, English speakers say, "It is raining," with the implication that there is a cause "it" that leads to rain. Many Indian languages, on the other hand, merely note what is most accurately translated as "raining" as an observable fact. Such an approach brings a freedom to stop worrying about causes of things, and merely to relax and accept that our human insights can go only so far. By not taking ourselves too seriously, or overinflating human importance, we can get beyond the logical world.

The emphasis of American Indian religions, then, is on the spiritual nature of all things. To understand the physical world, one must appreciate the underlying spiritual essence. Then one can begin to see that the physical is only a faint shadow, a partial reflection, of a supernatural and extrarational world. By the Indian view, everything that exists is spiritual. Every object—plants, rocks, water, air, the moon, animals, humans, the earth itself—has a spirit. The spirit of one thing (including a human) is not superior to the spirit of any other. Such a view promotes a sophisticated ecological awareness of the place that humans have in the larger environment. The function of religion is not to try to condemn or to change what exists, but to accept the realities of the world and to appreciate their contributions to life. Everything that exists has a purpose.[11]

One of the basic tenets of American Indian religion is the notion that everything in the universe is related. Nevertheless, things that exist are often seen as having a counterpart: sky and earth, plant and animal, water and fire. In all of these polarities, there exist mediators. The role of the mediator is to hold the polarities together, to keep the world from disintegrating. Polarities exist within human society also. The most important category within Indian society is gender. The notions of Woman and Man underlie much of social interaction and are comparable to the other major polarities. Women, with their nurtural qualities, are associated with the earth, while men are associated with the sky. Women gatherers and farmers deal with plants (of the earth), while men hunters deal with animals.

The mediator between the polarities of woman and man, in the American Indian religious explanation, is a being that combines the elements of both genders. This might be a combination in a physical sense, as in the case of hermaphrodites. Many Native American religions accept this phenomenon in the same way that they accept other variations from the norm. But more important is their acceptance of the idea that gender can be combined in ways other than physical hermaphroditism. The physical aspects of a thing or a person, after all, are not nearly as important as its spirit. American Indians use the concept of a person's *spirit* in the way that other Americans use the concept of a person's *character.* Consequently, physical hermaphroditism is not necessary for the idea of gender mixing. A person's character, their spiritual essence, is the crucial thing.

The Berdache's Spirit

Individuals who are physically normal might have the spirit of the other sex, might range somewhere between the two sexes, or might have a spirit that is distinct from either women or men. Whatever category they fall into, they are seen as being different from men. They are accepted spiritually as "Not Man." Whichever option is chosen, Indian religions offer spiritual explanations. Among the Arapahos of the Plains, berdaches are called *haxu'xan* and are seen to be that way as a result of a supernatural gift from birds or animals. Arapaho mythology recounts the story of Nih'a'ca, the first *haxu'xan.* He pretended to be a woman and married the mountain lion, a symbol for masculinity. The myth, as recorded by ethnographer Alfred Kroeber about 1900, recounted that "These people had the natural desire to become women, and as they grew up gradually became women. They gave up the desires of men. They were married to men. They had miraculous power and could do supernatural things. For instance, it was one of them that first made an intoxicant from rainwater."[12] Besides the theme of inventiveness, similar to the Navajo creation story, the berdache role is seen as a product of a "natural desire." Berdaches "gradually became women," which underscores the notion of woman as a social category rather than as a fixed biological entity. Physical biological sex is less important in gender classification than a person's desire—one's spirit.

They myths contain no prescriptions for trying to change berdaches who are acting out their desires of the heart. Like many other cultures' myths, the Zuni origin myths simply sanction the idea that gender can be transformed independently of biological sex.[13] Indeed, myths warn of dire consequences when interference with such a transformation is attempted. Prince Alexander Maximilian of the German state of Wied, traveling in the northern Plains in the 1830s, heard a myth about a warrior who once tried to force a berdache to avoid women's clothing. The berdache resisted, and the warrior shot him with an arrow. Immediately the berdache disappeared, and the warrior saw only a pile of stones with his arrow in them. Since then, the story concluded, no intelligent person would try to coerce a berdache.[14] Making the point even more directly, a Mandan myth told of an Indian who tried to force *mihdake* (berdaches) to give up their distinctive dress and status, which led the spirits to punish many people with death. After that, no Mandans interfered with berdaches.[15]

With this kind of attitude, reinforced by myth and history, the aboriginal view accepts human diversity. The creation story of the Mohave of the Colorado River Valley speaks of a time when people were not sexually differentiated. From this perspective, it is easy to accept that certain individuals might combine elements of masculinity and femininity.[16] A respected Mohave elder, speaking in the 1930s, stated this viewpoint simply: "From the very beginning of the world it was meant that there should be [berdaches], just as it was instituted that there should be shamans. They were intended for that purpose."[17]

This elder also explained that a child's tendencies to become a berdache are apparent early, by about age nine to twelve, before the child reaches puberty: "That is the time when young persons become initiated into the functions of their sex. . . . None but young people will become berdaches as a rule."[18] Many tribes have a public ceremony that acknowledges the acceptance of berdache status. A Mohave shaman related the ceremony for his tribe: "When the child was about ten years old his relatives would begin discussing his strange ways. Some of them disliked it, but the more intelligent began envisaging an initiation ceremony." The relatives prepare for the ceremony without letting the boy know if it. It is meant to take him by surprise, to be both an initiation and a test of his true inclinations. People from various settlements are invited to attend. The family wants the community to see it and become accustomed to accepting the boy as an *alyha.*

On the day of the ceremony, the shaman explained, the boy is led into a circle: "If the boy showed a willingness to remain standing in the circle, exposed to the public eye, it was almost certain that he would go through with the ceremony. The singer, hidden behind the crowd, began singing the songs. As soon as the sound reached the boy he began to dance as women do." If the boy is unwilling to assume *alyha* status, he would refuse to dance. But if his character—his spirit—is *alyha,* "the song goes right to his heart and he will dance with much intensity. He cannot help it. After the fourth song he is proclaimed." After the ceremony, the boy is carefully bathed and receives a woman's skirt. He is then led back to the dance ground, dressed as an *alyha,* and announces his new feminine name to the crowd. After that he would resent being called by his old male name.[19]

Among the Yuman tribes of the Southwest, the transformation is marked by a social gathering, in which the berdache prepares a meal for the friends of the family.[20] Ethnographer Ruth Underhill, doing fieldwork among the Papago Indians in the early 1930s, wrote that berdaches were common among the Papago Indians, and were usually publicly acknowledged in childhood. She recounted that a boy's parents would test him if they noticed that he preferred female pursuits. The regular pattern, mentioned by many of Underhill's Papago informants, was to build a small brush enclosure. Inside the enclosure they placed a man's bow and arrows, and also a woman's basket. At the appointed time the boy was brought to the enclosure as the adults watched from outside. The boy was told to go inside the circle of brush. Once he was inside, the adults "set fire to the enclosure. They watched what he took with him as he ran out and if it was the basketry materials, they reconciled themselves to his being a berdache."[21]

What is important to recognize in all of these practices is that the assumption of a berdache role was not forced on the boy by others. While adults might have their suspicions, it was only when the child made the proper move that he was considered a berdache. By doing woman's dancing, preparing a meal, or taking the woman's basket he was making an important symbolic gesture. Indian children were not stupid, and they knew the implications of these ceremonies beforehand. A boy in the enclosure could have left without taking anything, or could have taken both the man's and the woman's tools. With the community standing by watching, he was well aware that his choice would mark his assumption of berdache status. Rather than being seen as an involuntary test of his reflexes, this ceremony may be interpreted as a definite statement by the child to take on the berdache role.

Indians do not see the assumption of berdache status, however, as a free will choice on the part of the boy. People felt that the boy was acting out his basic character. The Lakota shaman Lame Deer explained:

> They were not like other men, but the Great Spirit made them *winktes* and we accepted them as such. . . . We think that if a woman has two little ones growing inside her, if she is going to have twins, sometimes instead of giving birth to two babies they have formed up in her womb into just one, into a half-man/half-woman kind of being. . . . To us a man is what nature, or his dreams, make him. We accept him for what he wants to be. That's up to him.[22]

While most of the sources indicate that once a person becomes a berdache it is a lifelong status, directions from the spirits determine everything. In at least one documented case, concerning a nineteenth-century Klamath berdache named Lele'ks, he later had a supernatural experience that led him to leave the berdache role. At that time Lele'ks began dressing and acting like a man, then married women, and eventually became one of the most famous Klamath chiefs.[23] What is important is that both in assuming berdache status and in leaving it, supernatural dictate is the determining factor.

Dreams and Visions

Many tribes see the berdache role as signifying an individual's proclivities as a dreamer and a visionary. . . .

Among the northern Plains and related Great Lakes tribes, the idea of supernatural dictate through dreaming—the vision quest—had its highest development. The goal of the vision quest is to try to get beyond the rational world by sensory deprivation and fasting. By depriving one's body of nourishment, the brain could escape from logical thought and connect with the higher reality of the supernatural. The person doing the quest simply sits and waits for a vision. But a vision might not come easily; the person might have to wait for days.

The best way that I can describe the process is to refer to my own vision quest, which I experienced when I was living on a Lakota reservation in 1982. After a long series of prayers and blessings, the shaman who had prepared me for the ceremony took me out to an isolated area where a sweat lodge had been set up for my quest. As I walked to the spot, I worried that I might not be able to stand it. Would I be overcome by hunger? Could I tolerate the thirst? What would I do if I had to go to the toilet? The shaman told me not to worry, that a whole group of holy people would be praying and singing for me while I was on my quest.

He had me remove my clothes, symbolizing my disconnection from the material would, and crawl into the sweat lodge. Before he left me I asked him, "What do I think about?" He said, "Do not think. Just pray for spiritual guidance." After a prayer he closed the flap tightly and I was left in total darkness. I still do not understand what happened to me during my vision quest, but during the day and a half that I was out there, I never once felt hungry or thirsty or the need to go to the toilet. What happened was an intensely personal experience that I cannot and do not wish to explain, a process of being that cannot be described in rational terms.

When the shaman came to get me at the end of my time, I actually resented having to end it. He did not need to ask if my vision quest were successful. He knew that it was even before seeing me, he explained, because he saw an eagle circling over me while I underwent the quest. He helped interpret the signs I had seen, then after more prayers and singing he led me back to the others. I felt relieved, cleansed, joyful, and serene. I had been through an experience that will be a part of my memories always.

If a vision quest could have such an effect on a person not even raised in Indian society, imagine its impact on a boy who from his earliest years had been waiting for the day when he could seek his vision. Gaining his spiritual power from his first vision, it would tell him what role to take in adult life. The vision might instruct him that he is going to be a great hunter, a craftsman, a warrior, or a shaman. Or it might tell him that he will be a berdache. Among the Lakotas, or Sioux, there are several symbols for various types of visions. A person becomes *wakan* (a sacred person) if she or he dreams of a bear, a wolf, thunder, a buffalo, a white buffalo calf, or Double Woman. Each dream results in a different gift, whether it is the power to cure illness or wounds, a promise of good hunting, or the exalted role of a *heyoka* (doing things backward).

A white buffalo calf is believed to be a berdache. If a person has a dream of the sacred Double Woman, this means that she or he will have the power to seduce men. Males who have a vision of Double Woman are presented with female tools. Taking such tools means that the male will become a berdache. The Lakota word *winkte* is composed of *win,* "woman," and *kte,* "would become."[24] A contemporary Lakota berdache explains, "To become a *winkte,* you have a medicine man put you up on the hill, to search for your vision. "You can become a *winkte* if you truly are by nature. You see a vision of the White Buffalo Calf Pipe. Sometimes it varies. A vision is like a scene in a movie."[25] Another way to become a *winkte* is to have a vision given by a *winkte* from the past.[26] . . .

By interpreting the result of the vision as being the work of a spirit, the vision quest frees the person from feeling responsible for his transformation. The person might even claim that the change was done against his will and without his control. Such a claim does not suggest a negative attitude about berdache status, because it is common for people to claim reluctance to fulfill their spiritual duty no matter what vision appears to them. Becoming any kind of sacred person involves taking on various social responsibilities and burdens.[27] . . .

A story was told among the Lakotas in the 1880s of a boy who tried to resist following his vision from Double Woman. But according to Lakota informants "few men succeed in this effort after having taken the strap in the dream." Having rebelled against the instructions given him by the Moon Being, he committed suicide.[28] The moral of that story is that one should not resist spiritual guidance, because it will lead only to grief. In another case, an Omaha young man told of being addressed by a spirit as "daughter," whereupon he discovered that he was unconsciously using feminine styles of speech. He tried to use male speech patterns, but could not. As a result of this vision, when he returned to his people he resolved himself to dress as a woman.[29] Such stories function to justify personal peculiarities as due to a fate over which the individual has no control.

Despite the usual pattern in Indian societies of using ridicule to enforce conformity, receiving instructions from a vision inhibits others from trying to change the berdache. Ritual explanation provides a way out. It also excuses the community from worrying about the cause of that person's difference, or the feeling that it is society's duty to try to change him.[30] Native American religions, above all else, encourage a basic respect for nature. If nature makes a person different, many Indians conclude, a mere human should not undertake to counter this spiritual dictate. Someone who is "unusual" can be accommodated without being stigmatized as "abnormal." Berdachism is thus not alien or threatening; it is a reflection of spirituality.

Notes

1. Mary Douglas, *Purity and Danger* (Baltimore: Penguin, 1966), p. 52. I am grateful to Theda Perdue for convincing me that Douglas's ideas apply to berdachism. For an application of Douglas's thesis to berdaches, see James Thayer, "The Berdache of the Northern Plains: A Socioreligious Perspective," *Journal of Anthropological Research 36* (1980): 292–93.

2. E. W. Gifford, "The Kamia of Imperial Valley," *Bureau of American Ethnology Bulletin 97* (1931): 12.

3. By using present tense verbs in this text, I am not implying that such activities are necessarily continuing today. I sometimes use the present tense in the "ethnographic present," unless I use the past tense when I am referring to something that has not continued. Past tense implies that all such practices have disappeared. In the absence of fieldwork to prove such disappearance, I am not prepared to make that assumption, on the historic changes in the berdache tradition.

4. Elsie Clews Parsons, "The Zuni La' Mana," *American Anthropologist 18* (1916): 521; Matilda Coxe Stevenson, "Zuni Indians," *Bureau of American Ethnology Annual Report 23* (1903): 37; Franklin Cushing, "Zuni Creation Myths," *Bureau of American Ethnology Annual Report 13* (1894): 401–3. Will Roscoe clarified this origin story for me.

5. W. W. Hill, "Note on the Pima Berdache," *American Anthropologist 40* (1938): 339.

6. Aileen O'Bryan, "The Dine': Origin Myths of the Navaho Indians," *Bureau of American Ethnology Bulletin 163* (1956): 5; W. W. Hill, "The Status of the Hermaphrodite and Transvestite in Navaho Culture,"*American Anthropologist 37* (1935): 273.

7. Martha S. Link, *The Pollen Path: A Collection of Navajo Myths* (Stanford: Stanford University Press, 1956).

8. O'Bryan, "Dine'," pp. 5, 7, 9–10.

9. Ibid.

10. Lakota informants, July 1982. See also William Powers, *Oglala Religion* (Lincoln: University of Nebraska Press, 1977).

11. For this admittedly generalized overview of American Indian religious values, I am indebted to traditionalist informants of many tribes, but especially those of the Lakotas. For a discussion of native religions see Dennis Tedlock, *Finding the Center* (New York: Dial Press, 1972); Ruth Underhill, *Red Man's Religion* (Chicago: University of Chicago Press, 1965); and Elsi Clews Parsons, *Pueblo Indian Religion* (Chicago: University of Chicago Press, 1939).

12. Alfred Kroeber, "The Arapaho," *Bulletin of the American Museum of Natural History 18* (1902–7): 19.

13. Parsons, "Zuni La' Mana," p. 525.

14. Alexander Maximilian, *Travels in the interior of North America, 1832–1834,* vol. 22 of *Early Western Travels,* ed. Reuben Gold Thwaites, 32 vols. (Cleveland: A. H. Clark, 1906), pp. 283–84, 354. Maximilian was quoted in German in the early homosexual rights book by Ferdinand Karsch-Haack, *Das Gleichgeschlechtliche Leben der Naturvölker* (The same-sex life of nature peoples) (Munich: Verlag von Ernst Reinhardt, 1911; reprinted New York: Arno Press, 1975), pp. 314, 564.

15. Oscar Koch, *Der Indianishe Eros* (Berlin: Verlag Continent, 1925), p. 61.

16. George Devereux, "Institutionalized Homosexuality of the Mohave Indians," *Human Biology 9* (1937): 509.

17. Ibid., p. 501

18. Ibid.

19. Ibid., pp. 508–9.

20. C. Daryll Forde, "Ethnography of the Yuma Indians," *University of California Publications in American Archaeology and Ethnology 28* (1931): 157.

21. Ruth Underhill, *Social Organization of the Papago Indians* (New York: Columbia University Press, 1938), p. 186. This story is also mentioned in Ruth Underhill, ed., *The Autobiography of a Papago Woman* (Menasha, Wisc.: American Anthropological Association, 1936), p. 39.

22. John Fire and Richard Erdoes, *Lame Deer, Seeker of Visions* (New York: Simon and Schuster, 1972), pp. 117, 149.

23. Theodore Stern, *The Klamath Tribe: A People and Their Reservation* (Seattle: University of Washington Press, 1965), pp. 20, 24; Theodore Stern, "Some Sources of Variability in Klamath Mythology,"*Journal of American Folklore 69* (1956): 242ff; Leshe Spier, *Klamath Ethnography* (Berkeley: University of California Press, 1930), p. 52.

24. Clark Wissler, "Societies and Ceremonial Associations in the Oglala Division of the Teton Dakota," *Anthoropological Papers of the american Museum of Natural History 11,* pt. 1 (1916): 92; Powers, *Oglala Religion,* pp. 57–59.

25. Ronnie Loud Hawk, Lakota informant 4, July 1982.

26. Terry Calling Eagle, Lakota informant 5, July 1982.

27. James S. Thayer, "The Berdache of the Northern Plains: A Socioreligious Perspective," *Journal of Anthropological Research 36* (1980): 289.

28. Fletcher, "Elk Mystery," p. 281.

29. Alice Fletcher and Francis La Flesche, "The Omaha Tribe," *Bureau of American Ethnology Annual Report 27* (1905–6): 132.

30. Harriet Whitehead offers a valuable discussion of this element of the vision quest in "The Bow and the Burden Strap: A New Look at Institutionalized Homosexuality in Native North America," in *Sexual Meanings,* ed. Sherry Ortner and Harriet Whitehead (Cambridge: Cambridge University Press, 1981), pp. 99–102. See also Erikson, "Childhood," p. 329.

A Woman's Curse?

Why do cultures the world over treat menstruating women as taboo? An anthropologist offers a new answer— and a challenge to Western ideas about contraception

MEREDITH F. SMALL

The passage from girlhood to womanhood is marked by a flow of blood from the uterus. Without elaborate ceremony, often without discussion, girls know that when they begin to menstruate, their world is changed forever. For the next thirty years or so, they will spend much energy having babies, or trying not to, reminded at each menstruation that either way, the biology of reproduction has a major impact on their lives.

Anthropologists have underscored the universal importance of menstruation by documenting how the event is interwoven into the ideology as well as the daily activities of cultures around the world. The customs attached to menstruation take peculiarly negative forms: the so-called menstrual taboos. Those taboos may prohibit a woman from having sex with her husband or from cooking for him. They may bar her from visiting sacred places or taking part in sacred activities. They may forbid her to touch certain items used by men, such as hunting gear or weapons, or to eat certain foods or to wash at certain times. They may also require that a woman paint her face red or wear a red hip cord, or that she segregate herself in a special hut while she is menstruating. In short, the taboos set menstruating women apart from the rest of their society, marking them as impure and polluting.

Anthropologists have studied menstrual taboos for decades, focusing on the negative symbolism of the rituals as a cultural phenomenon. Perhaps, suggested one investigator, taking a Freudian perspective, such taboos reflect the anxiety that men feel about castration, an anxiety that would be prompted by women's genital bleeding. Others have suggested that the taboos serve to prevent menstrual odor from interfering with hunting, or that they protect men from microorganisms that might otherwise be transferred during sexual intercourse with a menstruating woman. Until recently, few investigators had considered the possibility that the taboos—and the very fact of menstruation—might instead exist because they conferred an evolutionary advantage.

In the mid-1980s the anthropologist Beverly I. Strassmann of the University of Michigan in Ann Arbor began to study the ways men and women have evolved to accomplish (and regulate) reproduction. Unlike traditional anthropologists, who focus on how culture affects human behavior, Strassmann was convinced that the important role played by biology was being neglected. Menstruation, she suspected, would be a key for observing and understanding the interplay of biology and culture in human reproductive behavior.

To address the issue, Strassmann decided to seek a culture in which making babies was an ongoing part of adult life. For that she had to get away from industrialized countries, with their bias toward contraception and low birthrates. In a "natural-fertility population," she reasoned, she could more clearly see the connection between the physiology of women and the strategies men and women use to exploit that physiology for their own reproductive ends.

Strassmann ended up in a remote corner of West Africa, living in close quarters with the Dogon, a traditional society whose indigenous religion of ancestor worship requires that menstruating women spend their nights at a small hut. For more than two years Strassmann kept track of the women staying at the hut, and she confirmed the menstruations by testing urine samples for the appropriate hormonal changes. In so doing, she amassed the first long-term data describing how a traditional society appropriates a physiological event—menstruation—and refracts that event through a prism of behaviors and beliefs.

What she found explicitly challenges the conclusions of earlier investigators about the cultural function of menstrual taboos. For the Dogon men, she discovered, enforcing visits to the menstrual hut serves to channel parental resources into the upbringing of their own children. But more, Strassmann, who also had training as a reproductive physiologist, proposed a new theory of why menstruation itself evolved as it did—and again, the answer is essentially a story of conserving resources. Finally, her observations pose provocative questions about women's health in industrialized societies, raising serious doubts about the tactics favored by Western medicine for developing contraceptive technology.

Menstruation is the visible stage of the ovarian cycle, orchestrated primarily by hormones secreted by the ovaries: progesterone and a family of hormones called estrogens. At the beginning of each cycle (by convention, the first day of a woman's period) the levels of the estrogens begin to rise. After about five days, as their concentrations increase, they cause the blood- and nutrient-rich inner lining of the uterus, called the endometrium, to thicken and acquire a densely branching network of blood vessels. At about the middle of the cycle, ovulation takes place, and an egg makes its way from one of the two ovaries down one of the paired fallopian tubes to the uterus. The follicle from which the egg was released in the ovary now begins to secrete progesterone as well as estrogens, and the progesterone causes the endometrium to swell and become even richer with blood vessels—in short, fully ready for a pregnancy, should conception take place and the fertilized egg become implanted.

If conception does take place, the levels of estrogens and progesterone continue to rise throughout the pregnancy. That keeps the endometrium thick enough to support the quickening life inside the uterus. When the baby is born and the new mother begins nursing, the estrogens and progesterone fall to their initial levels, and lactation hormones keep them suppressed. The uterus thus lies quiescent until frequent lactation ends, which triggers the return to ovulation.

If conception does not take place after ovulation, all the ovarian hormones also drop to their initial levels, and menstruation—the shedding of part of the uterine lining—begins. The lining is divided into three layers: a basal layer that is constantly maintained, and two superficial layers, which shed and regrow with each menstrual cycle. All mammals undergo cyclical changes in the state of the endometrium. In most mammals the sloughed-off layers are resorbed into the body if fertilization does not take place. But in some higher primates, including humans, some of the shed endometrium is not resorbed. The shed lining, along with some blood, flows from the body through the vaginal opening, a process that in humans typically lasts from three to five days.

Of course, physiological facts alone do not explain why so many human groups have infused a bodily function with symbolic meaning. And so in 1986 Strassmann found herself driving through the Sahel region of West Africa at the peak of the hot season, heading for a sandstone cliff called the Bandiagara Escarpment, in Mali. There, permanent Dogon villages of mud or stone houses dotted the rocky plateau. The menstrual huts were obvious: round, low-roofed buildings set apart from the rectangular dwellings of the rest of the village.

The Dogon are a society of millet and onion farmers who endorse polygyny, and they maintain their traditional culture despite the occasional visits of outsiders. In a few Dogon villages, in fact, tourists are fairly common, and ethnographers had frequently studied the Dogon language, religion and social structure before Strassmann's arrival. But her visit was the first time someone from the outside wanted to delve into an intimate issue in such detail.

It took Strassmann a series of hikes among villages, and long talks with male elders under the thatched-roof shelters where they typically gather, to find the appropriate sites for her research. She gained permission for her study in fourteen villages, eventually choosing two. That exceptional welcome, she thinks, emphasized the universality of her interests. "I'm working on all the things that really matter to [the Dogon]—fertility, economics—so they never questioned my motives or wondered why I would be interested in these things," she says. "It seemed obvious to them." She set up shop for the next two and a half years in a stone house in the village, with no running water or electricity. Eating the daily fare of the Dogon, millet porridge, she and a research assistant began to integrate themselves into village life, learning the language, getting to know people and tracking visits to the menstrual huts.

Following the movements of menstruating women was surprisingly easy. The menstrual huts are situated outside the walled compounds of the village, but in full view of the men's thatched-roof shelters. As the men relax under their shelters, they can readily see who leaves the huts in the morning and returns to them in the evening. And as nonmenstruating women pass the huts on their way to and from the fields or to other compounds, they too can see who is spending the night there. Strassmann found that when she left her house in the evening to take data, any of the villagers could accurately predict whom she would find in the menstrual huts.

The huts themselves are cramped, dark buildings—hardly places where a woman might go to escape the drudgery of work or to avoid an argument with her husband or a co-wife. The huts sometimes become so crowded that some occupants are forced outside—making the women even more conspicuous. Although babies and toddlers can go with their mothers to the huts, the women consigned there are not allowed to spend time with the rest of their families. They must cook with special pots, not their usual household possessions. Yet they are still expected to do their usual jobs, such as working in the fields.

Why, Strassmann wondered, would anyone put up with such conditions?

The answer, for the Dogon, is that a menstruating woman is a threat to the sanctity of religious altars, where men pray and make sacrifices for the protection of their fields, their families and their village. If menstruating women come near the altars, which are situated both indoors and outdoors, the Dogon believe that their aura of pollution will ruin the altars and bring calamities upon the village. The belief is so ingrained that the women themselves have internalized it, feeling its burden of responsibility and potential guilt. Thus violations of the taboo are rare, because a menstruating woman who breaks the rules knows that she is personally responsible if calamities occur.

Nevertheless, Strassmann still thought a more functional explanation for menstrual taboos might also exist, one closely related to reproduction. As she was well aware, even before her studies among the Dogon, people around the world have a fairly sophisticated view of how reproduction works. In general, people everywhere know full well that menstruation signals the absence of a pregnancy and the possibility of another one. More precisely, Strassmann could frame her hypothesis by reasoning as follows: Across cultures, men and women recognize that a lack of menstrual cycling in a woman implies she is either pregnant, lactating or menopausal. Moreover, at least among natural-fertility cultures that do not practice birth control, continual cycles during peak reproductive years imply to people in those cultures that a woman is sterile. Thus, even though people might not be able to pinpoint ovulation, they can easily identify whether a woman will soon be ready to conceive on the basis of whether she is menstruating. And that leads straight to Strassmann's insightful hypothesis about the role of menstrual taboos: information about menstruation can be a means of tracking paternity.

"There are two important pieces of information for assessing paternity," Strassmann notes: timing of intercourse and timing of menstruation. "By forcing women to signal menstruation, men are trying to gain equal access to one part of that critical information." Such information, she explains, is crucial to Dogon men, because they invest so many resources in their own offspring. Descent is marked through the male line; land and the food that comes from the land is passed down from fathers to sons. Information about paternity is thus crucial to a man's entire lineage. And because each man has as many as four wives, he cannot possibly track them all. So forcing women to signal their menstrual periods, or lack thereof, helps men avoid cuckoldry.

To test her hypothesis, Strassmann tracked residence in the menstrual huts for 736 consecutive days, collecting data on 477 complete cycles. She noted who was at each hut and how long each woman stayed. She also collected urine from ninety-three women over a ten-week period, to check the correlation between residence in the menstrual hut and the fact of menstruation.

The combination of ethnographic records and urinalyses showed that the Dogon women mostly play by the rules. In 86 percent of the hormonally detected menstruations, women went to the hut. Moreover, none of the tested women went to the hut when they were not menstruating. In the remaining 14 percent of the tested menstruations, women stayed home from the hut, in violation of the taboo, but some were near menopause and so not at high risk for pregnancy. More important, none of the women who violated the taboo did it twice in a row. Even they were largely willing to comply.

Thus, Strassmann concluded, the huts do indeed convey a fairly reliable signal, to men and to everyone else, about the status of a woman's fertility. When she leaves the hut, she is considered ready to conceive. When she stops going to the hut, she is evidently pregnant or menopausal. And women of prime reproductive age who visit the hut on a regular basis are clearly infertile.

It also became clear to Strassmann that the Dogon do indeed use that information to make paternity decisions. In several cases a man was forced to marry a pregnant woman, simply because everyone knew that the man had been the woman's first sexual partner after her last visit to the menstrual hut. Strassmann followed one case in which a child was being brought up by a man because he was the mother's first sexual partner after a hut visit, even though the woman soon married a different man. (The woman already knew she was pregnant by the first man at the time of her marriage, and she did not visit the menstrual hut before she married. Thus the truth was obvious to everyone, and the real father took the child.)

In general, women are cooperative players in the game because without a man, a woman has no way to support herself or her children. But women follow the taboo reluctantly. They complain about going to the hut. And if their husbands convert from the traditional religion of the Dogon to a religion that does not impose menstrual taboos, such as Islam or Christianity, the women quickly cease visiting the hut. Not that such a religious conversion quells a man's interest in his wife's fidelity: far from it. But the rules change. Perhaps the sanctions of the new religion against infidelity help keep women faithful, so the men can relax their guard. Or perhaps the men are willing to trade the reproductive advantages of the menstrual taboo for the economic benefits gained by converting to the new religion. Whatever the case, Strassmann found an almost perfect correlation between a husband's religion and his wives' attendance at the hut. In sum, the taboo is established by men, backed by supernatural forces, and internalized and accepted by women until the men release them from the belief.

But beyond the cultural machinations of men and women that Strassmann expected to find, her data show something even more fundamental—and surprising—about female biology. On average, she calculates, a woman in a natural-fertility population such as the Dogon has only about 110 menstrual periods in her lifetime. The rest of the time she will be prepubescent, pregnant, lactating or menopausal. Women in industrialized cultures, by contrast, have more than three times as many cycles: 350 to 400, on average, in a lifetime. They reach menarche (their first menstruation) earlier—at age twelve and a half, compared with the onset age of sixteen in natural-fertility cultures. They have fewer babies, and they lactate hardly at all. All those factors lead women in the industrialized world to a lifetime of nearly continuous menstrual cycling.

The big contrast in cycling profiles during the reproductive years can be traced specifically to lactation. Women in more traditional societies spend most of their reproductive years in lactation amenorrhea, the state in which the hormonal changes required for nursing suppress ovulation and inhibit menstruation. And it is not just that the Dogon bear more children (eight to nine on average); they also nurse each child on demand rather than in scheduled bouts, all through the night as well as the day, and intensely enough that ovulation simply stops for about twenty months per child. Women in industrialized societies typically do not breast-feed as intensely (or at all), and rarely breast-feed each child for as long as the Dogon women do. (The average for American women is four months.)

The Dogon experience with menstruation may be far more typical of the human condition over most of evolutionary history than is the standard menstrual experience in industrialized nations. If so, Strassmann's findings alter some of the most closely held beliefs about female biology. Contrary to what the Western medical establishment might think, it is not particularly "normal" to menstruate each month. The female body, according to Strassmann, is biologically designed to spend much more time in lactation amenorrhea than in menstrual cycling. That in itself suggests that oral contraceptives, which alter hormone levels to suppress ovulation and produce a bleeding, could be forcing a continual state of cycling for which the body is ill-prepared. Women might be better protected against reproductive cancers if their contraceptives mimicked lactation amenorrhea and depressed the female reproductive hormones, rather than forcing the continual ebb and flow of menstrual cycles.

Strassmann's data also call into question a recently popularized idea about menstruation: that regular menstrual cycles might be immunologically beneficial for women. In 1993 the controversial writer Margie Profet, whose ideas about evolutionary and reproductive biology have received vast media attention, proposed in *The Quarterly Review of Biology* that menstruation could have such an adaptive value. She noted that viruses and bacteria regularly enter the female body on the backs of sperm, and she hypothesized that the best way to get them out is to flush them out. Here, then, was a positive, adaptive role for something unpleasant, an evolutionary reason for suffering cramps each month. Menstruation, according to Profet, had evolved to rid the body of pathogens. The "anti-pathogen" theory was an exciting hypothesis, and it helped win Profet a MacArthur Foundation award. But Strassmann's work soon showed that Profet's ideas could not be supported because of one simple fact: under less-industrialized conditions, women menstruate relatively rarely.

Instead, Strassmann notes, if there is an adaptive value to menstruation, it is ultimately a strategy to conserve the body's resources. She estimates that maintaining the endometrial lining during the second half of the ovarian cycle takes substantial metabolic energy. Once the endometrium is built up and ready to receive a fertilized egg, the tissue requires a sevenfold metabolic increase to remain rich in blood and ready to support a pregnancy. Hence, if no pregnancy is forthcoming, it makes a lot of sense for the body to let part of the endometrium slough off and then regenerate itself, instead of maintaining that rather costly but unneeded tissue. Such energy conservation is common among vertebrates: male rhesus monkeys have shrunken testes during their nonbreeding season, Burmese pythons shrink their guts when they are not digesting, and hibernating animals put their metabolisms on hold.

Strassmann also suggests that periodically ridding oneself of the endometrium could make a difference to a woman's long-term survival. Because female reproductive hormones affect the brain and other tissues, the metabolism of the entire body is involved during cycling. Strassmann estimates that by keeping hormonal low through half the cycle, a woman can save about six days' worth of energy for every four nonconceptive cycles. Such caloric conservation might have proved useful to early hominids who lived by hunting and gathering, and even today it might be helpful for women living in less affluent circumstances than the ones common in the industrialized West.

But perhaps the most provocative implications of Strassmann's work have to do with women's health. In 1994 a group of physicians and anthropologists published a paper, also in *The Quarterly Review of Biology,* suggesting that the reproductive histories and lifestyles of women in industrialized cultures are at odds with women's naturally evolved biology, and that the differences lead to greater risks of reproductive cancers. For example, the investigators estimated that women in affluent cultures may have a hundredfold greater risk of breast cancer than do women who subsist by hunting and gathering. The increased risk is probably caused not only by low levels of exercise and a high-fat diet, but also by a relatively high number of menstrual cycles over a lifetime. Repeated exposure to the hormones of the ovarian cycle—because of early menarche, late menopause, lack of pregnancy and little or no breast-feeding—is implicated in other reproductive cancers as well.

Those of us in industrialized cultures have been running an experiment on ourselves. The body evolved over millions of years to move across the landscape looking for food, to live in small kin-based groups, to make babies at intervals of four years or so and to invest heavily in each child by nursing intensely for years. How many women now follow those traditional patterns? We move little, we rely on others to get our food, and we rarely reproduce or lactate. Those culturally initiated shifts in lifestyles may pose biological risks.

Our task is not to overcome that biology, but to work with it. Now that we have a better idea of how the female body was designed, it may be time to rework our lifestyles and change some of our expectations. It may be time to borrow from our distant past or from our contemporaries in distant cultures, and treat our bodies more as nature intended.

MEREDITH F. SMALL is a professor of anthropology at Cornell University in Ithaca, New York. Her latest book, *Our Babies, Ourselves: How Biology And Culture Shape The Way We Parent,* was published in May 1998 [see Laurence A. Marschall's review in Books in Brief, November/December 1998].

This article is reprinted from *The Sciences,* January/February 1999, pp. 24–29. Copyright © 1999 by New York Academy of Sciences. www.nyas.org. Reprinted by permission. For subscription, email: publicationse@nyas.org.

Where Fat Is a Mark of Beauty

In a rite of passage, some Nigerian girls spend months gaining weight and learning customs in a special room. "To be called a 'slim princess' is an abuse," says a defender of the practice.

Ann M. Simmons

Akpabuyo, Nigeria—Margaret Bassey Ene currently has one mission in life: gaining weight.

The Nigerian teenager has spent every day since early June in a "fattening room" specially set aside in her father's mud-and-thatch house. Most of her waking hours are spent eating bowl after bowl of rice, yams, plantains, beans and *gari,* a porridge-like mixture of dried cassava and water.

After three more months of starchy diet and forced inactivity, Margaret will be ready to reenter society bearing the traditional mark of female beauty among her Efik people: fat.

In contrast to many Western cultures where thin is in, many culture-conscious people in the Efik and other communities in Nigeria's southeastern Cross River state hail a woman's rotundity as a sign of good health, prosperity and allure.

The fattening room is at the center of a centuries-old rite of passage from maidenhood to womanhood. The months spent in pursuit of poundage are supplemented by daily visits from elderly matrons who impart tips on how to be a successful wife and mother. Nowadays, though, girls who are not yet marriage-bound do a tour in the rooms purely as a coming-of-age ceremony. And sometimes, nursing mothers return to the rooms to put on more weight.

"The fattening room is like a kind of school where the girl is taught about motherhood," said Sylvester Odey, director of the Cultural Center Board in Calabar, capital of Cross River state. "Your daily routine is to sleep, eat and grow fat."

Like many traditional African customs, the fattening room is facing relentless pressure from Western influences. Health campaigns linking excess fat to heart disease and other illnesses are changing the eating habits of many Nigerians, and urban dwellers are opting out of the time-consuming process.

Effiong Okon Etim, an Efik village chief in the district of Akpabuyo, said some families cannot afford to constantly feed a daughter for more than a few months. That compares with a stay of up to two years, as was common earlier this century, he said.

But the practice continues partly because "people might laugh at you because you didn't have money to allow your child to pass through the rite of passage," Etim said. What's more, many believe an unfattened girl will be sickly or unable to bear children.

Etim, 65, put his two daughters in a fattening room together when they were 12 and 15 years old, but some girls undergo the process as early as age 7, after undergoing the controversial practice of genital excision.

Bigger Is Better, According to Custom

As for how fat is fat enough, there is no set standard. But the unwritten rule is the bigger the better, said Mkoyo Edet, Etim's sister.

"Beauty is in the weight," said Edet, a woman in her 50s who spent three months in a fattening room when she was 7. "To be called a 'slim princess' is an abuse. The girl is fed constantly whether she likes it or not."

In Margaret's family, there was never any question that she would enter the fattening room.

"We inherited it from our forefathers; it is one of the heritages we must continue," said Edet Essien Okon, 25, Margaret's stepfather and a language and linguistics graduate of the University of Calabar. "It's a good thing to do; it's an initiation rite."

His wife, Nkoyo Effiong, 27, agreed: "As a woman, I feel it is proper for me to put my daughter in there, so she can be educated."

Effiong, a mother of five, spent four months in a fattening room at the age of 10.

Margaret, an attractive girl with a cheerful smile and hair plaited in fluffy bumps, needs only six months in the fattening room because she was already naturally plump, her stepfather said.

During the process, she is treated as a goddess, but the days are monotonous. To amuse herself, Margaret has only an instrument made out of a soda bottle with a hole in it, which she taps on her hand to play traditional tunes.

Still, the 16-year-old says she is enjoying the highly ritualized fattening practice.

"I'm very happy about this," she said, her belly already distended over the waist of her loincloth. "I enjoy the food, except for *gari.*"

Day in, day out, Margaret must sit cross-legged on a special stool inside the secluded fattening room. When it is time to eat, she sits on the floor on a large, dried plantain leaf, which also serves as her bed. She washes down the mounds of food with huge pots of water and takes traditional medicine made from leaves and herbs to ensure proper digestion.

As part of the rite, Margaret's face is decorated with a white, claylike chalk.

"You have to prepare the child so that if a man sees her, she will be attractive," Chief Etim said.

Tufts of palm leaf fiber, braided and dyed red, are hung around Margaret's neck and tied like bangles around her wrists and ankles. They are adjusted as she grows.

Typically, Margaret would receive body massages using the white chalk powder mixed with heavy red palm oil. But the teen said her parents believe the skin-softening, blood-stimulating massages might cause her to expand further than necessary.

Margaret is barred from doing her usual chores or any other strenuous physical activities. And she is forbidden to receive visitors, save for the half a dozen matrons who school Margaret in the etiquette of the Efik clan.

They teach her such basics as how to sit, walk and talk in front of her husband. And they impart wisdom about cleaning, sewing, child care and cooking—Efik women are known throughout Nigeria for their chicken pepper soup, pounded yams and other culinary creations.

"They advise me to keep calm and quiet, to eat the *gari,* and not to have many boyfriends so that I avoid unwanted pregnancy," Margaret said of her matron teachers. "They say that unless you have passed through this, you will not be a full-grown woman."

What little exercise Margaret gets comes in dance lessons. The matrons teach her the traditional *ekombi,* which she will be expected to perform before an audience on the day she emerges from seclusion—usually on the girl's wedding day, Etim said.

But Okon said his aim is to prepare his stepdaughter for the future, not to marry her off immediately. Efik girls receive more education than girls in most parts of Nigeria, and Okon hopes Margaret will return to school and embark on a career as a seamstress before getting married.

Weddings Also Steeped in Tradition

Once she does wed, Margaret will probably honor southeastern Nigeria's rich marriage tradition. It begins with a letter from the family of the groom to the family of the bride, explaining that "our son has seen a flower, a jewel, or something beautiful in your family, that we are interested in," said Josephine Effah-Chukwuma, program officer for women and children at the Constitutional Rights Project, a law-oriented nongovernmental organization based in the Nigerian commercial capital of Lagos.

If the girl and her family consent, a meeting is arranged. The groom and his relatives arrive with alcoholic beverages, soft drinks and native brews, and the bride's parents provide the food. The would-be bride's name is never uttered, and the couple are not allowed to speak, but if all goes well, a date is set for handing over the dowry. On that occasion, the bride's parents receive about $30 as a token of appreciation for their care of the young woman. "If you make the groom pay too much, it is like selling your daughter," Effah-Chukwuma said. Then, more drinks are served, and the engagement is official.

On the day of the wedding, the bride sits on a specially built wooden throne, covered by an extravagantly decorated canopy. Maidens surround her as relatives bestow gifts such as pots, pans, brooms, plates, glasses, table covers—everything she will need to start her new home. During the festivities, the bride changes clothes three times.

The high point is the performance of the *ekombi,* in which the bride twists and twirls, shielded by maidens and resisting the advances of her husband. It is his task to break through the ring and claim his bride.

Traditionalists are glad that some wedding customs are thriving despite the onslaught of modernity.

Traditional weddings are much more prevalent in southeastern Nigeria than so-called white weddings, introduced by colonialists and conducted in a church or registry office.

"In order to be considered married, you have to be married in the traditional way," said Maureen Okon, a woman of the Qua ethnic group who wed seven years ago but skipped the fattening room because she did not want to sacrifice the time. "Tradition identifies a people. It is important to keep up a culture. There is quite a bit of beauty in Efik and Qua marriages."

UNIT 6
Religion, Belief, and Ritual

Unit Selections

Key Points to Consider

- How can modern medicine be combined with traditional healing to take advantage of the best aspects of both? In what respects do perceptions of disease affect treatment and recovery?

- Why should scarce research funds be used to assess indigenous peoples knowledge and approaches to health?

- How do beliefs about the supernatural contribute to a sense of personal security, individual responsibility, and social harmony?

- How does the experience of autism differ between the United States and India?

- How has voodoo become such an important form of social control in rural Haiti?

- In what ways are magic rituals practical and rational?

- How do rituals and taboos get established in the first place?

- How important are ritual and taboo in our modern industrial society?

Student Web Site
www.mhcls.com/online

Internet References
Further information regarding these Web sites may be found in this book's preface or online.

Anthropology Resources Page
   http://www.usd.edu/anth/
Yahoo: Society and Culture: Death
   http://dir.yahoo.com/Society_and_Culture/Death_and_Dying/

M. Freeman/PhotoLink/Getty Images

The anthropological interest in religion, belief, and ritual is not concerned with the scientific validity of such phenomena, but rather with the way in which people relate various concepts of the supernatural to their everyday lives. From this practical perspective, some anthropologists have found that traditional spiritual healing is just as helpful in the treatment of illness as is modern medicine (see "Ancient Teachings, Modern Lessons"); that voodoo is a form of social control (as in "The Secrets of Haiti's Living Dead"); and that the ritual and spiritual preparation for playing the game of baseball can be just as important as spring training (see "Baseball Magic").

Every society is composed of feeling, thinking, and acting human beings who at one time or another are either conforming to or altering the social order into which they were born. As described in "The Adaptive Value of Religious Ritual," "religion is an ideological framework that gives special legitimacy and validity to human experience within any given socio-cultural system." In this way, monogamy as a marriage form, or monarchy as a political form, ceases to be simply one of many alternative ways in which a society can be organized, but becomes, for the believer, the only legitimate way. Religion considers certain human values and activities as sacred and inviolable. It is this mythic function that helps to explain the strong ideological attachments that some people have, regardless of the scientific merits of their points of view.

While under some conditions religion may in fact be "the opiate of the masses," under other conditions such a belief system may be a rallying point for social and economic protest. A con-

temporary example of the former might be the "Moonies" (members of the Unification Church founded by Sun Myung Moon), while a good example of the latter is the role of the black church in the American civil rights movement, along with the prominence of such religious figures as Martin Luther King Jr. and Jesse Jackson. A word of caution must be set forth concerning attempts to understand belief systems of other cultures. At times the prevailing attitude seems to be, "What I believe in is religion, and what you believe in is superstition." While anthropologists generally do not subscribe to this view, some tend to explain behavior that seems, on the surface, to be incomprehensible and impractical as some form of religious ritual. The articles in this unit should serve as a strong warning concerning the pitfalls of that approach.

"Eyes of the Ngangas" and "Remapping the World of Autism" show how important a person's traditional belief systems, combined with community involvement, can be to the physical and psychological well-being of the individual. This perspective is so important that the treatment of illness is hindered without it. Thus, beliefs about the supernatural may be subtle, informal, and yet absolutely necessary for social harmony and stability.

Mystical beliefs and ritual are not absent from the modern world. "Body Ritual Among the Nacirema" reveals that our daily routines have mystic overtones and "Baseball Magic" examines the need for ritual and taboo in the "great American pastime."

In summary, the writings in this unit show religion, belief, and ritual in relationship to practical human affairs.

Eyes of the *Ngangas:* Ethnomedicine and Power in Central African Republic

People of the Third World have a variety of therapies available for combating diseases, but because of cost, availability, and cultural bias, most rely on ethnomedical traditional treatment rather than "biomedical" or Western therapies. Dr. Lehmann's field research focuses on the importance of *ngangas* (traditional healers) as a source of primary health care for both the Aka Pygmy hunters and their horticultural neighbors, the Ngando of Central African Republic. Tracing the basis and locus of the *ngangas*' mystical diagnostic and healing powers, he shows that they are particularly effective with treatments for mental illness and, to an unknown extent, with herbal treatment of physical illnesses as well. The powers of the Aka *ngangas,* however, are also used to reduce the tensions between themselves and their patrons and to punish those Ngando who have caused the hunters harm. Lehmann points out the necessity of recognizing and treating the social as well as the biological aspects of illness and appeals to health care planners to establish counterpart systems that mobilize popular and biomedical specialists to improve primary health care in the Third World.

ARTHUR C. LEHMANN

*E*thnomedicine (also referred to as folk, traditional, or popular medicine) is the term used to describe the primary health care system of indigenous people whose medical expertise lies outside "biomedicine" the "modem" medicine of Western societies. Biomedicine does exist in the Third World, but it is unavailable to the masses of inhabitants for a number of reasons. Conversely, although popular medicine has largely been supplanted by biomedicine in the Western World, it still exists and is revived from time to time by waves of dissatisfaction with modem medicine and with the high cost of health care, by the health food movement, and by a variety of other reasons. The point is, all countries have pluralistic systems of health care, but for many members of society the combat against the diseases that have plagued mankind is restricted to the arena of popular medicine.

This is particularly true in the developing nations, such as those of the sub-Saharan regions of Africa, where over 80 percent of the population live in rural areas with a dearth of modem medical help (Bichmann 1979; Green 1980). Between 1984 and the present, I have made six field trips to one such rural area (the most recent in 1994), to study the primary health care practices of Aka Pygmy hunter-gatherers and their horticultural neighbors, the Ngando of Central African Republic (C.A.R.).

The Aka and the Ngando

Several groups of the Pygmies live in a broad strip of forested territory stretching east and west across the center of Equatorial Africa. The two largest societies are the Mbuti of the Inturi Forest of Zaire and the Aka, who live in the Southern Rainforest that extends from the Lobaye River in Central African Republic into the People's Republic of the Congo and into Cameroun (Cavalli-Sforza 1971). Like the Mbuti, the Aka are long-time residents of their region. It is on the edge of the Southern Rainforest in and near the village of Bagandu that the Aka Pygmies and the Ngando come into most frequent contact. The proximity, particularly during the dry season from December to April, allows for comparisons of health care systems that would be difficult otherwise, for the Aka move deep into the forest and are relatively inaccessible for a good portion of the year.

Since Turnbull described the symbiotic relationship between Mbuti Pygmies and villagers in Zaire (1965), questions remain as to why Pygmy hunters continue their association with their sedentary neighbors. Bahuchet's work shows that the relationship between the Aka and the Ngando of C.A.R. is one of voluntary mutual dependence in which both groups benefit; indeed, the Aka consider the villagers responsible for their well-being (1985: 549). Aka provide the Ngando with labor, meat, and forest materials while the Ngando pay the Aka with plantation foods, clothes, salt, cigarettes, axes and knives, alcohol, and infrequently, money.

This mutual dependence extends to the health care practices of both societies. Ngando patrons take seriously ill Aka to the dispensary for treatment; Aka consider this service a form of payment that may be withheld by the villagers as a type of punishment. On the other hand, Aka *ngangas* (traditional healers) are called upon to diagnose and treat Ngando illnesses. The powers believed to be held by the *ngangas* are impressive, and few, particularly rural residents, question these powers or the roles they play in everyday life in Central African Republic.

Eyes of the *Ngangas*

The people believe that the *ngangas* intervene on their behalf with the supernatural world to combat malevolent forces and also use herbal expertise to protect them from the myriad of tropical diseases. Elisabeth Motte (1980) has recorded an extensive list of medicines extracted by the *ngangas* from the environment to counter both natural and supernatural illnesses; 80 percent are derived from plants and the remaining 20 percent from animals and minerals.

Both Aka and Ngando *ngangas* acquire their power to diagnose and cure through an extensive apprenticeship ordinarily served under the direction of their fathers, who are practicing healers themselves. This system of inheritance is based on primogeniture, although other than first sons may be chosen to become *ngangas*. Although Ngando *ngangas* may be either male or female, the vast majority are males; all Aka *ngangas* are males. In the absence of the father or if a younger son has the calling to become a healer, he may study under an *nganga* outside the immediate family.

During my six trips to the field, *ngangas* permitted me to question them on their training and initiation into the craft; it became apparent that important consistencies existed. First, almost all male *ngangas* are first sons. Second, fathers expect first sons to become *ngangas*; as they said, "It is natural." Third, the apprenticeship continues from boyhood until the son is himself a *nganga*, at which time he trains his own son. Fourth, every *nganga* expresses firm belief in the powers of his teacher to cure and, it follows, in his own as well. As is the case with healers around the world, despite the trickery sometimes deemed necessary to convince clients of the effectiveness of the cure, the *ngangas* are convinced that their healing techniques will work unless interrupted by stronger powers. Fifth, every *nganga* interviewed maintained strongly that other *ngangas* who were either envious or have a destructive spirit can destroy or weaken the power of a healer, causing him to fail. Sixth, and last, the origin and locus of the *ngangas'* power is believed to be in their eyes.

Over and over I was told that during the final stages of initiation, the master *nganga* had vaccinated the initiate's eyes and placed "medicine" in the wound, thus giving the new *nganga* power to divine and effectively treat illnesses. At first I interpreted the term *vaccination* to mean simply the placement of "medicine" in the eyes, but I was wrong. Using a double-edged razor blade and sometimes a needle, the master *nganga* may cut his apprentice's lower eyelids, the exterior corners of the eyes, or below the eyes (although making marks below the eyes is now considered "antique" I was told); he concludes the ceremony by placing magical medicine in the cuts. At this moment, the student is no longer an apprentice; he has achieved the status of an *nganga* and the ability to diagnose illnesses with the newly acquired power of his eyes.

Not until my last field trip in 1994 did I witness a master *nganga* actually cut the whites of his apprentice's eyes. At the end of an hour-long interview with an *nganga*, which focused on my eliciting his concept of disease etiology in treatment of illness, I casually posed the question I had asked other *ngangas* many times before: "Do you vaccinate your apprentice's eyes?" The *nganga* beckoned his apprentice seated nearby, and, to my amazement, the apprentice immediately placed his head on the master's lap. I quickly retrieved my camcorder which I had just put away! The master removed a razor blade from a match box, spread the student's eyelids apart, deftly made five cuts on the whites of each eye, and squeezed the juice of a leaf (the "medicine") into the wounds. This astounding procedure performed on perhaps the most sensitive of all human parts took less than a total of three minutes and did not appear to cause the apprentice any degree of pain, albeit his eyes were red and his tears profuse.

During the career of an *nganga*, his eyes will be vaccinated many times, thus, it is believed, rejuvenating the power of the eyes to correctly diagnose illness and ensure proper therapy. It is clear that the multiple powers of *ngangas* to cure and to protect members of their band from both physical and mental illnesses as well as from a variety of types of supernatural attacks reside in their eyes.

It follows that the actual divinatory act involves a variety of techniques, particular to each *nganga*, that allows him to use his powers to "see" the cause or the illness and determine its treatment. Some bum a dear, rocklike amber resin called *paka* found deep in the rain forest, staring into the flames to learn the mystery of illness and the appropriate therapy. Some stare into the rays of the sun during diagnosis or gaze into small mirrors to unlock the secret powers of the ancestors in curing. Others concentrate on plates filled with water or large, brilliant chunks of glass. The most common but certainly the most incongruous method of acquiring a vision by both Aka and Ngando *ngangas* today is staring into a light bulb. These are simply stuck into the ground in front of the *nganga* or, as is the case among many village healers, the light bulb is floated in a glass of water during consultation. The appearance of a light bulb surfacing from an Aka *nganga's* healing paraphernalia in the middle of a rain forest is, to say the least, unique. Western methods of divining—of knowing the unknown—were not, and to some degree are not now, significantly different from the techniques of the *ngangas*. Our ways of "seeing," involving gazing at and "reading" tea leaves, crystal balls, cards, palms, and stars, are still considered appropriate techniques by many.

Therapy Choices and Therapy Managers

A wide variety of therapies coexist in contemporary Africa, and the situation in the village of Bagandu is no exception. The major sources of treatment are Aka *ngangas*, Ngando *ngangas*, kinship therapy (family councils called to resolve illness-causing conflicts between kin), home remedies, Islamic healers (marabouts), and the local nurse at the government dispensary, who is called "doctor" by villagers and hunters alike. In addition, faith healers, herbalists, and local specialists (referred to as "fetishers") all attempt, in varying degrees, to treat mental or physical illness in Bagundu. Intennittently Westerners, such as missionaries, personnel from the U.S. Agency for International

Development, and anthropologists, also treat physical ailments. Bagandu is a large village of approximately 3,400 inhabitants, however; most communities are much smaller and have little access to modem treatment. And, as Cavalli-Sforza has noted,

> If the chances of receiving Western medical help for Africans living in remote villages are very limited, those of Pygmies are practically nonexistent. They are even further removed from hospitals. African health agents usually do not treat Pygmies. Medical help comes exceptionally and almost always from rare visiting foreigners. (Cavalli-Sforza 1986: 421)

Residents of Bagandu are fortunate in having both a government dispensary and a pharmacy run by the Catholic church, but prescriptions are extremely costly relative to income, and ready cash is scarce. A more pressing problem is the availability of drugs. Frequently the "doctor" has only enough to treat the simplest ailments such as headaches and small cuts; he must refer thirty to forty patients daily to the Catholic pharmacy, which has more drugs than the dispensary but still is often unable to fill prescriptions for the most frequently prescribed drugs such as penicillin, medicine to counteract parasites, and antibiotic salves. Although the doctor does the best he can under these conditions, patients must often resort only to popular medical treatment—in spite of the fact that family members, the therapy managers, have assessed the illness as one best treated by biomedicine. In spite, too, of the regular unavailability of medicine, the doctor's diagnosis and advice is still sought out—"although many people will consent to go to the dispensary only after having exhausted the resources of traditional medicine" (Motte 1980: 311).

Popular, ethnomedical treatment is administered by kin, ngangas (among both the Aka and Ngando villagers), other specialists noted for treatment of specific maladies, and Islamic marabouts, who are recent immigrants from Chad. According to both Aka and Ngando informants, the heaviest burden for health care falls to these ethnomedical systems. Ngando commonly utilize home, kin remedies for minor illnesses, but almost 100 percent indicated that for more serious illnesses they consulted either the doctor or ngangas (Aka, Ngando, or both); to a lesser extent they visited specialists. The choice of treatment, made by the family therapy managers, rests not only on the cause and severity of the illness, but also on the availability of therapists expert in the disease or problem, their: cost, and their proximity to the patient. Rarely do the residents of Bagandu seek the aid of the marabouts, for example, in part because of the relatively high cost of consultation. Clearly, both popular and biomedical explanations for illness play important roles in the maintenance of health among Bagandu villagers, although popular medicine is the most important therapy resource available. Popular medicine is especially vital for the Aka hunters, whose relative isolation and inferior status (in the eyes of the Ngando) have resulted in less opportunity for biomedical treatment. Yet even they seek out modem medicine for illnesses.

Whatever the system of treatment chosen, it is important to understand that "the management of illness and therapy by a set of close kin is a central aspect of the medical scene in central Africa. . . . The therapy managing group . . . exercises a brokerage function between the sufferer and the specialist" (Janzen 1978: 4). It is the kingroup that determines which therapy is to be used.

Explanations of Illness

The choice of therapy in Bagandu is determined by etiology and severity, as in the West. Unlike Western medicine, however, African ethnomedicine is not restricted to an etiology of only natural causation. Both the Aka and the Ngando spend a great deal of time, energy, and money (or other forms of payments) treating illnesses perceived as being the result of social and cultural imbalances, often described in supernatural terms. Aka and Ngando nosology has accommodated biomedicine without difficulty, but traditional etiology has not become less important to the members of these societies. Frequent supernatural explanations of illness by Aka and Ngando informants inevitably led me to the investigation of witchcraft, curses, spells, or the intervention of ancestors and nameless spirits, all of which were viewed as being responsible for poor health and misfortune. The Aka maintain, for example, that the fourth leading cause of death in Bagandu is witchcraft (diarrhea is the principal cause; measles, second, and convulsions, third [Hewlett 1986: 56]). During my research, it became apparent that a dual model of disease explanation exists among the Aka and Ngando: first, a naturalistic model that fits its Western biomedical counterpart well, and second, a supernaturalistic explanation.

Interviews with village and Pygmy ngangas indicated that their medical systems are not significantly different. Indeed, both groups agree that their respective categories of illness etiology are identical. Further, the categories are not mutually exclusive: an illness may be viewed as being natural, but it may be exacerbated by supernatural forces such as witchcraft and spells. Likewise, this phenomenon can be reversed: an illness episode may be caused by supernatural agents but progress into a form that is treatable through biomedical techniques. For example, my relatively educated and ambitious young field assistant, a villager, was cut on the lower leg by a piece of stone while working on a new addition to his house. The wound, eventually becoming infected, caused swelling throughout the leg and groin. As was the case in some of his children's illnesses, the explanation for the wound was witchcraft. It was clear to him that the witch was a neighbor who envied his possessions and his employment by a foreigner. Although the original cut was caused by a supernatural agent, the resulting infection fitted the biomedical model. Treatment by a single injection of penicillin quickly brought the infection under control, although my assistant believed that had the witch been stronger the medicine would not have worked. Here is a case in which, "in addition to the patient's physical signs and social relationships," the passage of time is also crucial to "the unfolding of therapeutic action" (Feierman 1985: 77). As the character of an illness changes with time as the illness runs its course, the therapy manager's decisions may change, because the perceived etiology can shift as a result of a variety of signs, such as a slow-healing wound or open conflict in the patient's social group (Janzen 1978: 9)

Studies on disease etiologies among select African societies (Bibeau 1979; Janzen 1978; Warren 1974) reported that most illnesses had natural causes, and this finding holds for the Ngando villagers as well. At first glance, these data would seem to reduce the importance of *nganga*s and of popular medicine generally, but it is necessary to recognize that *nganga*s treat both natural and supernatural illnesses utilizing both medical and mystical techniques. The question posed by Feierman, "Is popular medicine effective?" (1985: 5), is vital to the evaluation of *nganga*s as healers. Surely some traditional medicines used by these cures must in many cases work, and work regularly enough to earn the sustained support of the general public.

Illnesses of God and Illnesses of Man

Both the Ngando and Aka explanations for natural illnesses lack clarity. Some *nganga*s refer to them as "illnesses of God"; others simply identify them as "natural"; and still others frequently use both classifications, regularly assigning each label to specific ailments. Hewlett maintains that the Aka sometimes labelled unknown maladies as illnesses of God (1986: personal communication). On the other hand, the Bakongo of neighboring Zaire defined illnesses of God as those "generally, mild conditions which respond readily to therapy when no particular disturbance exists in the immediate social relationships of the sufferer. . . . The notion of 'god' does not imply divine intervention or retribution but simply that the cause is an affliction in the order of things unrelated to human intentions" (Janzen 1978: 9).

Both Janzen's and Hewlett's data are accurate, but my field data show as well as that the explanations of natural illnesses among the Ngando and Aka not only refer to normal mild diseases and sometimes unknown ones but also to specific illnesses named by the *nganga*s and the residents of Bagandu. The confusion surrounding these mixed explanations of disease causation is an important topic for future ethnosemantic or other techniques of emic inquiry by ethnographers.

Residents of Bagandu and both Aka and Ngando *nganga*s categorized sickness caused by witchcraft, magic, curses, spells, and spirits as "illnesses of man." This is the second major disease category. Witchcraft, for example, while not the main cause of death, is the most frequently named cause of illness in Bagandu. Informants in Bagandu cite the frequency of witchcraft accusations as proof of their viewpoint. Antisocial or troublesome neighbors are frequently accused of being witches and are jailed if the charge is proven. Maladies of all sorts, such as sterility among females, are also commonly attributed to the innate and malevolent power of witches. These types of explanations are not unusual in rural Africa. What is surprising are reports of new illnesses in the village caused by witches.

All Ngando informants claimed, furthermore, that the problem of witchcraft has not diminished over time; on the contrary, it has increased. The thinking is logical: because witchcraft is believed to be inherited, any increase in population is seen also as an inevitable increase in the number of witches in the village. Population figures in the region of the Southern Rainforest have increased somewhat in the past few decades despite epidemics such as measles; accordingly, the incidence of maladies attributed to witches has increased. One informant from Bagandu strongly insisted that witches are not only more numerous but also much more powerful today than before. Offiong (1983) reported a marked increase of witchcraft in Nigeria and adjacent states in West Africa, caused not by inflation of population but by the social strain precipitated by the frustration accompanying lack of achievement after the departure of colonial powers.

Insanity is not a major problem among the Ngando. When it does occur, it is believed to be caused by witchcraft, clan or social problems, evil spirits, and breaking taboos. Faith healers, marabouts, and *nganga*s are seen as effective in the treatment of mental illness due to witchcraft or other causes. The role of faith healers is particularly important in the lives of members of the Prophetical Christian Church in Bagandu. They have strong faith in the healing sessions and maintain that the therapy successfully treats the victims of spirits' attacks. Informants also claim the therapy lasts a long time.

The curse is a common method of venting anger in Bagandu, used by both male and female witches. Informants stated that women use curses more than men and that the subjects of their attacks are often males. The curses of witches are counted as being extremely dangerous in the intended victim. One villager accused the elderly of using the curse as a weapon most frequently. Spell-casting is also common in the area, and males often use spells as a method of seduction.

Most, if not all, residents of Bagandu use charms, portable "fetishes," and various types of magical objects placed in and around their houses for protection. Some of these objects are counter-magical: they simultaneously protect the intended victim and turn the danger away from the victim to the attackers. Counter-magic is not always immediate; results may take years to appear. Charms, fetishes, and other forms of protection are purchased from *nganga*s, marabouts, and other specialists such as herbalists. For example, the Aka and Ngando alike believe that wearing a mole's tooth on a bracelet is the most powerful protection from attacks by witches.

To a lesser extent, spirits are also believed to cause illness. It is problematic whether or not this source of illness deserves a separate category of disease causation. Bahuchet thinks not; rather, he holds that spirit-caused illnesses should be labeled illnesses of God (1986: personal communication). It is interesting to note that in addition to charms and other items put to use in Bagandu, residents supplicate ancestors for aid in times of difficulty. If the ancestors do not respond, and if the victim of the misfortune practices Christianity, he or she will seek the aid of God. Non-Christians and Christians alike commonly ask diviners the cause of their problem, after which they seek the aid of the proper specialist. Revenge for real or imagined attacks on oneself or on loved ones is common. One method is to point a claw of a mole at the wrongdoer. Ngando informants maintain the victim dies soon after. Simple possession of a claw, if discovered, means jail for the owner.

My initial survey of Aka and Ngando *nganga*s in 1984 brought out other origins of illness. Two *nganga*s in Bagandu specifically cited the devil, rather than unnamed evil spirits, as a cause for disease. The higher exposure of villagers to Christianity may account for this attribution: seven denominations are currently represented in the churches of Bagandu. Urban *ngangas* questioned in Bangui, the capital, stressed the use of poison as a cause of illness and death. Although poisonings do not figure prominently as a cause of death among the Aka and Ngando, it is common belief that *ngangas* and others do use poison.

Finally, while not a cause for illness, informants maintained that envious *ngangas* have the power to retard or halt the progress of a cure administered by another. All *ngangas* interviewed in 1984 and 1985 confirmed not only that they have the power to interrupt the healing process of a patient but also that they frequently invoke it. Interestingly, *ngangas* share this awesome power with witches, who are also believed by members of both societies to be able to spoil the "medicine" of healers. This kind of perception of the *ngangas*' power accounts, in part, for their dual character: primarily beneficial to the public, they can also be dangerous.

While the numerical differences in the frequency of physiologically and psychologically rooted illnesses in Bagandu are unknown, Ngando respondents in a small sample were able to list a number of supernaturally caused illnesses that are treatable by *ngangas,* but only a few naturally caused ones. Among the naturalistic illnesses were illnesses of the spleen; *laltungba,* deformation of the back; and *Kongo,* "illness of the rainbow." According to Hewlett (1986: 53), *Kongo* causes paralysis of the legs (and sometimes of the arms) and death after the victim steps on a dangerous mushroom growing on a damp spot in the forest where a rainbow-colored snake has rested. Had the Ngando sample been more exhaustive, it is probable that the list of natural diseases would have been greater, although perhaps not as high as the twenty natural illnesses the *ngangas* said they could treat successfully. That impressive list includes malaria, hernia, diarrhea, stomach illness, pregnancy problems, dysentery, influenza, abscesses, general fatigue, traumas (snake bite, miscellaneous wounds, and poisoning), and general and specific bodily pain (spleen, liver, ribs, head, and uterus).

Powers of the *Ngangas*

The powers of the *ngangas* are not limited to controlling and defeating supernatural or natural diseases alone. In the village of Bagandu and in the adjacent Southern Rainforest where the Ngando and Aka hunters come into frequent contact, tensions exist due to the patron-client relationship, which by its very economic nature is negative. These tensions are magnified by ethnic animosity. Without the Akas' mystical power, their economic and social inferiority would result in an even more difficult relationship with the Ngando. Here the powers of the Pygmy *ngangas* play an important part in leveling, to bearable limits, the overshadowing dominance of the Ngando, and it is here that the *ngangas* demonstrate their leadership outside the realm of health care. Each Aka has some form of supernatural protection provided by the *nganga* of his camp to use while in the village. Still, the need exists for the extraordinary powers of the *nganga* himself for those moments of high tension when Aka are confronted by what they consider the most menacing segments of the village population: the police, the mayor, and adolescent males, all of whom, as perceived by the Aka, are dangerous to their personal safety while in the village.

In the summer of 1986, I began to study the attitudes of village patrons toward their Aka clients and, conversely, the attitudes of the so-called wayward servants (Turnbull's term for the Mbuti Pygmy of Zaire, 1965) toward the villagers. Participant observation and selective interviews of patrons, on the one hand, and of hunters, on the other, disclosed other important tangents of power of the Aka in general and of their *ngangas* in particular. First, the Aka often have visible sources of power such as scarification, cords worn on the wrist and neck, and bracelets strung with powerful charms for protection against village witches. These protective devices are provided the Aka by their *ngangas.* Second, and more powerful still, are the hidden powers of the Aka in general, bolstered by the specific powers of the *ngangas.* Although the villagers believe the hunters' power is strongest in the forest, and therefore weaker in the village setting, Aka power commands the respect of the farmers. Third, the villagers acknowledge the Aka expertise in the art of producing a variety of deadly poisons, such as *sepi,* which may be used to punish farmers capable of the most serious crimes against the Pygmies. The obvious functions of these means of protection and retribution, taken from the standpoint of the Aka, are positive. Clearly these powers reduce the tension of the Aka while in the village, but they also control behavior of villagers toward the hunters to some undefinable degree.

Villagers interpret the variety of punishments which the Aka are capable of meting out to wrongdoers as originating in their control of mystical or magical. powers. Interestingly, even poisonings are viewed in this way by villagers because of the difficulty of proving that poison rather than mystical power caused illness or death. Although the use of poison is rare, it is used and the threat remains. Georges Guille-Escuret, a French ethnohistorian working in Bagandu in 1985, reported to me that prior to my arrival in the field that year three members of the same household had died on the same day. The head of the family had been accused of repeated thefts of game from the traps and from the camp of an Aka hunter. When confronted with the evidence—a shirt the villager had left at the scene of the thefts—the family rejected the demands of the hunter for compensation for the stolen meat. Soon thereafter, the thief, his wife, and his mother died on the same day. Villagers, who knew of the accusations of theft, interpreted the deaths as the result of poisoning or the mystical powers of the hunter.

Stories of Aka revenge are not uncommon, nor are the Akas' accusations of wrongdoing leveled against the villagers. To the Ngando farmers, the powers of the Aka *ngangas* include the ability to cause death through the use of fetishes, to cause illness to the culprit's eyes, and to direct lightning to strike the perpetrator. These and other impressive powers to punish are seen as real threats to villagers—but the power of the *ngangas* to cure is even more impressive.

Attempts in my research to delineate the strengths and weaknesses of the *ngangas* and other health care specialists discovered a number of qualities/characteristics widely held to be associated with each. First, each specialist is known for specific medical abilities; that is, Aka and Ngando *ngangas* recognize the therapeutic expertise of others in a variety of cures. A *nganga* from Bangui maintained that Aka *ngangas* were generally superior to the village healers in curing. This view is shared by a number of villagers interviewed, who maintained that the power of Aka *ngangas* is greater than that of their own specialists.

The Aka strongly agree with this view, and in a sense the Aka are more propertied in the realm of curing than are the villagers. There is no question that the Aka are better hunters. Despite the Ngandos' greater political and economic power in the area and the social superiority inherent in their patron status, the Ngando need the Aka. All these elements help balance the relationship between the two societies, although the supernatural and curative powers of Aka *ngangas* have not previously been considered to be ingredients in the so-called symbiotic relationship between Pygmy hunters and their horticultural neighbors.

Second, *ngangas* noted for their ability to cure particular illnesses are often called upon for treatment by other *ngangas* who have contracted the disease. Third, with one exception, all the *ngangas* interviewed agree that European drugs, particularly those contained in hypodermic syringes and in pills, are effective in the treatment of natural diseases. One dissenting informant from the capital disdained biomedicine altogether because, as he said, "White men don't believe in us." Fourth, of the fourteen Aka and Ngando *ngangas* interviewed in 1985, only five felt that it was possible for a *nganga* to work successfully with the local doctor (male nurse) who directed the dispensary in Bagandu. All five of these *ngangas* said that if such cooperation did come about, their special contribution would be the treatment of patients having illnesses of man, including mental illness resulting from witchcraft, from magical and spiritual attacks, and from breaking taboos. None of the *ngangas* interviewed had been summoned to work in concert with the doctor. Fifth, as a group of the *ngangas* held that biomedical practitioners are unable to successfully treat mental illnesses and other illnesses resulting from attacks of supernatural agents. In this the general population of the village agree. This is a vitally important reason for the sustained confidence in popular therapy in the region—a confidence that is further strengthened by the belief that the *ngangas* can treat natural illnesses as well. Sixth, the village doctor recognized that the *ngangas* and marabouts do have more success in the treatment of mental illnesses than he does. Although the doctor confided that he has called in a village *nganga* for consultation in a case of witchcraft, he also disclosed that upon frequent occasions he had to remedy the treatment administered by popular specialists for natural diseases. It is important to recognize that unlike biomedical specialists in the capital, the local doctor does appreciate the talents of traditional therapists who successfully practice ethnopsychiatry.

All respondents to this survey recognized the value of biomedicine in the community, and little variation in the types of cures the doctor could effect was brought out. No doubts were raised regarding the necessity of both biomedicine and popular therapy to the proper maintenance of public health. The spheres of influence and expertise of both types of practitioners, while generally agreed upon by participants of the Ngando survey, did show some variation, but these were no more serious than our own estimates of the abilities of our physicians in the West.

In short, all informants utilized both systems of therapy when necessary and if possible.

The continuation of supernatural explanations of illness by both the Ngando and the Aka results in part from tradition, in combination with their lack of knowledge of scientific disease etiology, and in part because of the hidden positive functions of such explanations. Accusations of witchcraft and the use of curses and malevolent magic function to express the anxiety, frustrations, and social disruptions in these societies. These are traditional explanations of disease, with more than a single focus, for they focus on both the physical illness and its sociological cause. "Witchcraft (and by extension other supernatural explanations for illness and disaster) provides an indispensable component in many philosophies of misfortune. It is the friend rather than the foe of mortality" (Lewis 1986: 16). Beyond this rationale, reliance upon practitioners of popular medicine assures the patient that medicine is available for treatment in the absence of Western drugs.

The Role of Ethnomedicine

Among the Aka and Ngando and elsewhere, systems of popular medicine have sustained African societies for centuries. The evolution of popular medicine has guaranteed its good fit to the cultures that have produced it; even as disruptive an element of the system as witchcraft can claim manifest and latent functions that contribute to social control and the promotion of proper behavior.

Unlike Western drug therapies, no quantifiable measure exists for the effectiveness of popular medicine. Good evidence from World Health Organization studies can be brought forth, however, to illustrate the relatively high percentage of success of psychotherapeutic treatment through ethnomedicine in the Third World compared to that achieved in the West. The results of my research in Bagandu also demonstrate the strong preference of villagers for popular medicine in cases involving mental illness and supernaturally caused mental problems. At the same time, the doctor is the preferred source of therapy for the many types of natural disease, while *ngangas* and other specialists still have the confidence of the public in treating other maladies; referred to as illnesses of man and some illnesses of God. Whatever the perceived etiology by kingroup therapy managers, both popular and biomedical therapists treat natural illnesses. It is in this realm of treatment that it is most important to ask, "What parts of popular medicine work?" rather than, "Does popular medicine work?" Because evidence has shown that psychotherapy is more successful in the hands of traditional curers, it is therefore most important to question the effectiveness of popular therapy in handling natural illnesses. Currently, the effectiveness of traditional drugs used for natural diseases is unknown; however, the continued support of popular therapists by both rural and urban Africans indicates a strength in the system. The effectiveness of the *ngangas* may be both psychological and pharmaceutical, and if the ecological niche does provide drugs that do cure natural illnesses, it is vital that these be determined and manufactured commercially in their countries of origin. If we can assume that some traditional drugs are effective, governments must utilize the expertise of healers in identifying these.

It is unrealistic to attempt to train popular therapists in all aspects of biomedicine, just as it is unrealistic to train biomedical specialists in the supernatural treatments applied by popular practitioners. However, neither type of therapist, nor the public, will benefit from the expertise of the other if they remain apart. The task is to make both more effective by incorporating the best of each into a counterpart system that focuses on a basic training of healers in biomedicine. This combination must certainly be a more logical and economic choice than attempting to supply biomedical specialists to every community in Central African Republic, a task too formidable for any country north or south of the Sahara. The significance of this proposal is magnified by the massive numbers for whom biomedicine is unavailable, those who must rely only upon ethnomedicine.

Even if available to all, biomedicine alone is not the final answer to disease control in the Third World. Hepburn succinctly presents strong arguments against total reliance upon the biomedical approach:

> Biomedicine is widely believed to be effective in the cure of sickness. A corollary of this is the belief that if adequate facilities could be provided in the Third World and "native" irrationalities and cultural obstacles could be overcome, the health problems of the people would largely be eliminated. However, this belief is not true, because the effectiveness of biomedicine is limited in three ways. First, many conditions within the accepted defining properties of biomedicine (i.e., physical diseases) cannot be treated effectively. Second, by concentrating on the purely physical, biomedicine simply cannot treat the social aspects of sickness (i.e., illness). Third, cures can only be achieved under favorable environmental and political conditions: if these are not present, biomedicine will be ineffective (1988: 68).

The problems facing societies in Africa are not new. These same issues faced Westerners in the past, and our partial solutions, under unbelievably better conditions, took immense time and effort to achieve. If primary health care in the non-Western world is to improve, the evolutionary process must be quickened by the utilization of existing popular medical systems as a counterpart of biomedicine, by the expansion of biomedical systems, and by the cooperation of international funding agencies with African policymakers, who themselves must erase their antagonism toward ethnomedicine.

Ancient Teachings, Modern Lessons

DAVID A. TAYLOR

In recent years, researchers have looked for areas where indigenous knowledge, also called local or traditional knowledge, can meet modern science for better environmental health. A 1999 conference titled "Science for the 21st Century—A New Commitment" that was cosponsored by the United Nations Educational, Scientific and Cultural Organization (UNESCO) produced a declaration recognizing that "traditional and local knowledge systems, as dynamic expressions of perceiving and understanding the world, can make and historically have made a valuable contribution to science and technology."

The declaration suggested that as a fund of cultural heritage and empirical information, indigenous knowledge should be preserved and researched. The conference called on the International Council for Science—a Paris-based nongovernmental organization composed of 98 multidisciplinary national scientific research councils and 26 international single-discipline scientific unions—to study how traditional knowledge might best relate with science. (One tool for doing this is ethnography, the study and systematic recording of human cultures.) More recently, researchers shared results at the Seventh International Congress of Ethnobiology, held at the University of Georgia in Athens in October 2000.

These efforts have sparked warnings from those who view them merely as gestures of political correctness—gestures that, while validating minority cultures, threaten to compromise the rigor of the scientific method. Perhaps more importantly, critics say that unmerited trust in tradition can endanger human health. A month before the UNESCO conference, the 17 May 1999 issue of *Forensic Science International* published an analysis of forensic data from Johannesburg, South Africa, where traditional remedies containing toxic substances were cited as causes for over 200 deaths in a five-year period. And a 14 October 1999 *Nature* editorial responding to the UNESCO conference declaration acknowledged that traditional knowledge deserves more respect from modern science than it has received, but noted that "such acceptance also requires due caution and a rigorous assessment of more and less deserving forms of traditional knowledge." The editorial further warned that integrating different forms of knowledge would not be easy.

For one thing, indigenous knowledge rarely comes in the form of scientific data. Often it involves complex narratives. Yet as viewers of detective dramas know, even a tangential discussion can sometimes yield important clues. In her 1997 book *The Spirit Catches You and You Fall Down* about the health care received by a young Hmong girl in California with epilepsy, Anne Fadiman wrote, "The Hmong have a phrase, *hais cuaj txub kaum txub,* which means 'to speak of all kinds of things.' It is often used at the beginning of an oral narrative as a way of reminding the listeners that the world is full of things that may not seem to be connected but actually are; that no event occurs in isolation; that you can miss a lot by sticking to the point; and that the storyteller is likely to be rather long-winded."

Fadiman proceeds to show how the girl's immigrant family and cultural origins in Southeast Asia—and her American doctors' approach to them—seriously influenced the treatment she received. The girl's family interpreted her doctors' behavior as uncaring and regarded the medical treatment with suspicion; thus, they decided to forgo the recommended treatment. It is a story of contrasting ways of understanding health, and it's a situation that is likely to occur more and more often as populations spread across the globe.

Drug Discovery: The Greatest Interest?

Perhaps the greatest interest in indigenous knowledge comes from its potential for discovering new drugs and new uses for indigenous medicines. The ethnobotanical approach to drug discovery has experienced a resurgence in recent decades [see *EHP* 105:1186–1191 (1997)] and has yielded many new medicines, including several that the National Cancer Institute considers promising for the treatment of AIDS, cancer, and other serious illnesses.

Joshua Rosenthal, a program officer for the NIH International Cooperative Biodiversity Groups (ICBG), notes that traditionally used compounds have yielded new antimalarial drugs (for example, artemisinin is derived from the herb *Artemisia annua,* also known as sweet Annie or qing hao and long used in Chinese medicine to combat fevers), painkillers (a potent alkaloid from the skin of the frog *Epipedobates tricolor*—used to make poison darts for immobilizing small animals—is being tested at Abbot Laboratories), and antidiarrheal medicines (such as Normal Stool Formula from Shaman Pharmaceuticals, which uses the sap of the Amazonian rain forest tree *Croton lechleri*). In addition to the drugs themselves, says Rosenthal, indigenous knowledge can help to identify mechanisms of action for therapeutic agents. "In starting from the knowledge that something works when tested in broad-based functional assays," he says, "we have the opportunity to discover new molecular targets that we might not have identified using approaches that begin with our current understanding of a disease."

The ICBG program, begun in 1992, aims to integrate drug discovery, biodiversity conservation, and sustainable economic benefits for populations where new drugs are found. Starting from the broad outline of the United Nations Convention on Biological Diversity—a 1992 global agreement that recognized the need for drug discovery to provide fair returns to the places where drugs orginate and support in the form of financial, political, and other incentives for communities to conserve the natural sources of new medicines—the ICBG developed regional research groups in Latin America, Africa, and Southeast Asia.

The program is a partnership in which traditional knowledge can guide the search for new medicines and support decisions for research follow-up. In turn, modern medicine channels research findings back to traditional healers and communities. Under the program, scientists propose studies and approach traditional healers for insights on how they use plants, which may lead to broader medical application of natural compounds. The pairing of scientists and traditional healers varies depending on the program and the study proposed.

Achieving a feasible, equitable solution hasn't been easy. The convention provided an important framework and recognition of the relationships between drug discovery, ecosystems, and traditional knowledge. However, its implementation has often mired in national politics, according to Rosenthal. Constructing agreements among international companies, universities, national governments, and local communities that return benefits to source communities without obstructing the research process is very difficult. "Very few countries have been able to do it yet," he notes. In one instance, well-intentioned researchers encountered a politically charged atmosphere in Chiapas, Mexico, where minority indigenous groups, stung by previous injustices and a lack of respect for their customs, moved to block sharing of their traditional knowledge with Western medicine.

Efforts to compare the effectiveness of scientific and traditional systems have had limited success. In Suriname, one study aimed to compare the rate of drug discovery of an ethnobotanically led process with that of a conventional approach of random biologic assays. It found a slightly higher success rate for the traditional approach, but the study encountered two main difficulties. First, the biologic assays skewed the basis for comparison toward the modern drug discovery model because those assays screen mainly for illnesses faced by temperate-zone populations, and not for health problems such as malaria or tuberculosis that are far more common in the tropics where the plants grow. Second, the fast turnover in the types of bioassays used by pharmaceutical companies—sometimes a complete change in a matter of months—meant that there was no consistent bioassay benchmark for compounds studied even a year apart. "It's difficult to get a comparison of all the samples hitting the same screens," Rosenthal says.

What the ICBG has found are promising areas of interchange between traditional systems and modern medicine, not only in the drug discovery process but also in creating channels for information exchange between very different knowledge systems. In Central and West Africa, researchers have worked with traditional healers' unions, providing opportunities for the healers to learn about Western medical research and exploring the potential of traditional medicine for treating HIV/AIDS and malaria. A network of medical professionals from both systems has emerged, with leadership from Maurice Iwu, a Nigerian-born ethnopharmacologist. Iwu is working on a treatment for infection with the Ebola virus using a traditional West African chewstick (a tooth cleaning instrument) made from the *Garcinia kola* tree.

Shaman Pharmaceuticals, a small company based in South San Francisco, California, notes its debt to indigenous knowledge from the start. "[Indigenous] knowledge greatly reduces the number of plants that we screen intensively and increases our potential for success," observes Steven King, the company's senior vice president for ethnobotany and conservation. Shaman takes pains to create new paths for sharing the benefits of the discovery process and provides direct reciprocal payments to the communities it works with. But because money alone isn't always the best way to share profits with a remote community with no bank, Shaman also uses other means including public health projects that provide potable water. Such projects are managed by the company's nonprofit foundation, The Healing Forest Conservancy.

"Historically, ethnobotany and forest conservation projects have not been conducted with public health and medical projects," King and coauthors noted in the 1996 book *Valuing Local Knowledge: Indigenous People and Intellectual Property Rights*. But when modern industries such as mining, oil extraction, and logging damage ecosystems where promising plants are found, there can be grave environmental health effects, including contamination of streams and drinking water with toxic runoff from mines.

Public health projects can address these impacts, for example by providing clean water and preventive medicine. The Healing Forest Conservancy has provided clean water for Quechua villages in Ecuador and Dayak villages in Indonesia. According to King, such projects, when integrated thoughtfully, can complement indigenous medical systems. For example, projects can involve local people in project planning and implementation, and can address health priorities that they identify.

Still, the narrowly focused discovery process used by most pharmaceutical companies is poorly suited for gauging other values of indigenous knowledge. For a more systematic look, Rosenthal points to a new NIH grants program through the National Center for Complementary and Alternative Medicine, called Traditional, Indigenous Systems of Medicine. Begun in 2000, the program is intended to fund examinations of systems of traditional knowledge such as the Indian system of Ayurveda, American Indian medicine, traditional Chinese medicine, and Latin American folk medicine with the goal of increasing the quality of clinical research evaluating the efficacy of such traditional, indigenous systems of medicine. Such studies must, according to the program's announcement, study the system in the cultural context of its origin and as adopted and adapted in other cultures.

Nutrition and Ecosystem Knowledge from the Past

While the path from ethnomedicine to new drugs is fairly direct, other sciences are also using ethnographic methods to assess indigenous knowledge for health benefits. Nutrition and agriculture may also benefit by exploring farmers' crop-breeding choices and local nutritional strategies. At the ethnobiology conference in Georgia, plant breeder Mary Eubanks, president of Sun Dance Genetics in Durham, North Carolina, and adjunct professor of plant genetics at Duke University, proposed that archaeobotanical investigations into the cultivation history of maize can yield safer, more robust varieties free of the potential health risks of genetically engineered varieties.

Traditional cultivation practices use naturally occurring genetic variation and a wider genetic base, making the varieties they yield less vulnerable to diseases and pests. By contrast, a genetically engineered crop has a narrower genetic base and therefore less variability to defend the crop from devastation by pests and disease that could cause food shortages and thus nutritional deficiencies. In the March 2000 issue of *Latin American Antiquity*, Eubanks and her coauthor observed that "the evolution of maize is intricately interwoven with culture history and environmental change." They emphasized that "the more we know about important crop plants, their relationships to their wild relatives . . . and how and under what conditions humans exploited and altered them . . . the greater our chances will be for identifying beneficial genes from wild plants"—and possibly recovering beneficial traits lost over time.

Elsewhere, anthropologists have found lessons for modern agriculture in traditional landscape management systems. In Indonesia, Bali's volcanic slopes and deep ravines make it difficult to irrigate rice fields. Traditionally the Balinese have diverted water through tunnels—some longer than a kilometer—to networks of canals and aqueducts. These networks are coordinated by rituals at community "water temples" across the island. Besides formalizing who takes care of each stretch of canal, the rituals bring together the people who maintain the system. While at a temple for a ritual, canal managers might discuss the sequence of opening locks, fields to be inundated, water volume, and other group decisions to be made. The hierarchy of water temples starts upstream at the volcanic Lake Batur and extends down to the smallest group of water users, about the size of a neighborhood.

With the introduction of modern farming practices in the 1970s and 1980s, however, agricultural scientists advised farmers to plant modern rice varieties, which can produce higher yields but which also require more fertilizers and pesticides. They also advised farmers to plant their fields independently, without waiting for communal workdays or synchronizing with others who use the canals.

In the mid-1980s Steven Lansing, an ecological anthropologist doing field research in Bali, heard farmers complain of rising pest damage to rice crops. Pest outbreaks were hurting rice yields despite the introduction of the modern varieties and cropping patterns. By 1987 rodent infestations were more serious than they had ever been before. Continued crop losses were threatening the area's nutritional status and introducing other risks of disease from the rats that infested the crop fields.

To assess the effects of various influences on the situation, Lansing and a computer expert developed a computer model of two river systems in southern Bali based on hydrology, rice growth, pest dynamics, and social/behavioral factors, including the community water temple rituals. Using the model, Lansing found that the water temple network managed water resources more effectively and kept pest damage low. By clustering planting and harvesting of nearby fields, the network created a sort of artificial ecosystem that kept pest populations in check. The computer model showed that the rice system reached a stable level of high productivity after several seasons of such management. Under the fragmented, random planting schedule of the introduced method, pest problems increased both in the model and in the rice fields. These results helped convince officials that the communal water temple network had important benefits.

Stuart Plattner, a program director at the National Science Foundation, which supported the work, observed that Lansing's research started from a traditional ethnographic perspective and followed connections that emerged between religion and irrigation, undeterred by officials who insisted that the two were unrelated. "Things that we think are separate are not at all separate," Plattner wrote in a 6 April 1997 article in the *Earth Times*. "Steve Lansing has been tremendously successful in making that point." Balinese scientists have since presented the experience of combining new and traditional agricultural technologies at international workshops.

Studies in which indigenous knowledge and modern science meaningfully complement each other remain few, but other promising examples come from Canada's far north. Researchers there have documented environmental health from both indigenous and scientific perspectives. Studies funded by the West Kitikmeot/Slave Study Society, a nonprofit partnership of government, industry, aboriginal, and environmental organizations, have monitored the effects of mining and other development on the environment and people in the area between the Great Slave Lake in the Northwest Territories and Bathurst Inlet to the north in Nunavut. In that area, indigenous peoples such as the Dogrib, Dene, and Inuit predominate. Outside influences have heavily impacted the health and social conditions of these groups and have prompted many of them to look within their traditional systems for solutions.

One pair of studies in the late 1990s examined caribou migration patterns using satellite collars placed on each herd's leader in one and traditional oral narrative accounts from Dogrib elders in the other. Dogrib elders advised wildlife scientist Anne Gunn in developing the satellite-collar study, and information from the Dogrib traditional knowledge study of caribou was placed in a geographic information system database for further analysis.

Caribou provided a natural starting point for collaboration: elders and scientists shared concerns over declining caribou population and habitat, and indigenous groups in the region have long relied on caribou for nutrition, cultural health, and identity. The groups' diet and materials for clothing and shelter comes from caribou (some use the animal's skins for tipis, for example). Perhaps more importantly, the groups interpret the health of their society through their relationship with the caribou and take pride in their ability to hunt and track. In that way, caribou give them a sense of belonging and order. (When placed in new surroundings without bearings on where to find caribou, for example, some groups lose a sense of purpose; alcoholism rates are often higher among these groups.)

The two studies correlated closely on migration patterns and showed that traditional Dogrib methods for diverting caribou from mine sites—where they risk exposure to toxic residues—were effective. Other studies have tracked the health effects of mining with community observations about contaminated plant, wildlife, and water resources and adverse symptoms experienced by mine workers. A *State of Knowledge* report posted on the society's Web site at http://www.wkss.nt.ca/ synthesizes these studies.

The West Kitikmeot/Slave Society even studied how Dogrib place-names convey information about biologic features of the people's natural surroundings. A 1998 report by the Dogrib Renewable Resources Committee titled *Habitat of Dogrib Traditional Territory: Place Names as Indicators of Bio-Geographical Knowledge* documents indigenous knowledge of the area as a baseline for tracking changes in ecosystems. In documenting over 2,100 sites, the study found that Dogrib place names such as "gooseberry lake" and "red-throated loons on big fish lake" signaled facets of habitat and local biodiversity that have since been incorporated in habitat maps based on satellite images.

Where Language, Health, and the Environment Overlap

For Luisa Maffi, an anthropological linguist, the place-name study confirms that language is a vital key to indigenous peoples' community health. "The obvious fact is that much of knowledge, if not all, is encoded in language," says Maffi, who is also president of Terralingua, a nonprofit research group that conducts studies on ecosystems and cultural diversity in order to support maintenance of that diversity. Their studies involve ethnographic interviews and local participation in ecosystem inventories.

Maffi says that the number of languages in an area can be a good indicator of cultural range, which in turn is linked to the store of knowledge of a given ecosystem and its biological diversity. "If you look at a map of the world's biodiversity hot spots and overlay on that a map of linguistic diversity, you see a striking overlap," she says. That suggests a correlation between the number of discrete cultures in an area and biological diversity.

Terralingua has explored that correlation globally in a project with the World Wide Fund For Nature International that mapped biocultural diversity as a step toward sustaining ecosystems. On a smaller scale, the group's Sierra Tarahumara Diversity Project aims to understand those interrelationships in a part of northern Mexico where mining and logging have degraded the environment and undermined local cultures by discouraging the use of native language on the job and presenting Western consumer goods that may entice young workers away from Tarahumara customs. Indigenous societies in the Sierra Tarahumara depend on both subsistence agriculture and a wide

array of local plant and animal species for their survival. Project researchers have met with Tarahumara communities to assess priorities, document the linkages among biologic, cultural, and linguistic resources, assess local impacts of commercial activities (including tourism), and suggest various alternatives. The project aims to advance basic scientific research as well as conservation planning.

Besides expressing how people understand their environment, Maffi finds that people's words express how they perceive symptoms of illness. When a minority language is marginalized, that can affect the quality of health care the speakers receive. In the Chiapas region of Mexico, Maffi found that the Tzeltal Maya had a sophisticated range of terms for describing symptoms in their language (distinguishing a wheezing cough from a hacking cough, for example). Yet when a field medic would visit the village and ask the townspeople about their illnesses in Spanish, she said, "People would be completely unable to talk about it, to convey the subtleties that they could in their own language." That chasm, she says, together with the medic's impatience with local customs, seriously affected the quality of health care they received.

Community Health

A community's environmental health therefore depends not just on integrating local knowledge with scientific understanding, but on recognizing the differences in power and access enjoyed by different cultures. Many indigenous cultures exist at the margins of mainstream society, tend to be poor, and often lack political clout in managing natural resources or influencing the allocation of funds for their public health care, education, and other needs. In a November 1999 speech, Gro Harlem Brundtland, director-general of the World Health Organization, said, "Indigenous peoples continue to be subject to systematic denial of their fundamental human rights—to cultural identity, to land, to liberty, to health, and to life itself."

This disparity supports society's mandate for cultural competence among health professionals today, according to Richard Levinson, associate executive director of programs and policy at the American Public Health Association (APHA), a nonprofit professional organization. "Cultural competence means that health professionals need to understand the cultural characteristics of the groups from which their patients come," says Levinson. Physicians treating the Hmong family of Anne Fadiman's book, for example, needed a basic familiarity with the Hmong community's approach to health and illness in order to understand how to treat them. Levinson says that in the United States that concept has extended beyond immigrant groups to include long-naturalized populations such as Latino and African-American communities, which may trust their local experience more than outside health professionals.

Dwight Conquergood, an associate professor of performance studies at Northwestern University in Evanston, Illinois, who in 1985 was a young ethnographer at a refugee camp in Thailand, demonstrated this principle at a community level by engaging Hmong values and customs in a campaign to eradicate rabies. Efforts by the camp's medical staff to get pets inoculated produced no results. Fadiman's book relates that Conquergood organized a "rabies parade," with Hmong participants and characters from Hmong folktales explaining the etiology of rabies. The day after the procession, wrote Fadiman, "The vaccination stations were so besieged by dogs—dogs carried in their owners' arms, dogs dragged on rope leashes, dogs rolled in on two-wheeled pushcarts—that the health workers could hardly inoculate them fast enough."

Anthropology has also supplied methods for applying community-based knowledge to environmental health research. Elizabeth Guillette, an anthropologist with the Center for Bio-environmental Research at Tulane and Xavier Universities in New Orleans, Louisiana, has applied those methods to gain valuable information related to long-term pesticide exposure. In some cases, ethnographic interviews helped to guide the direction of research. For example, mothers in a Mexican pesticide exposure study begun in 1995 repeatedly noted that their children engaged in less play than the parents recalled from their own childhoods. That led Guillette to investigate the children's abilities through directed activities. She found that pesticide-exposed children indeed did have less endurance and coordination than lesser-exposed children [see *EHP* 106:347–353 (1998); *EHP* 108 (suppl 3):389–393 (2000)].

Again, channeling study findings back to the community is an important but often neglected part of the research process. "It does not have to take a lot of time," Guillette says, and it can yield further benefits. She presented her results on pesticide exposure to the study groups in the Mexican cohort and has since noticed a decline in home use of pesticides.

Community-based initiatives to monitor environmental health foster collaboration between Western science and indigenous knowledge. In Canada, the Dogrib and neighboring Dene have launched ambitious efforts that include technical training, counsel by elders in documenting local knowledge, and developing indicators of nutritional status, economic development, and mining conditions. Residents have helped to identify hazardous waste sites for cleanup and mapped their locations for others to view on the Nunavut Planning Commission's Web site, located online at http://npc.nunavut. ca/. Similar efforts are under way among the Mohawk Nation in Akwesasne, New York [see *EHP* 106(suppl 3):833–840 (1998)].

Considering the Merits of Two Systems

Still, questions remain: Why should efforts by small groups, many with problems rarely found in industrialized societies, concern the broader medical community? These would not seem to be promising sources of health wisdom as indigenous communities tend to have shorter life expectancies than the mainstream population and are more likely to suffer from problems such as emerging infectious diseases that are less common in the rest of the population. And why should scarce research funds be used to assess nonscientific approaches to health?

Levinson responds that indigenous peoples are not just marginal groups with remote illnesses. A continuing rise in travel and immigration brings new people—along with their beliefs about the medical conditions they face—to industrialized countries. According to the American Medical Student Association, a national student-run organization, generalist physicians can soon expect more than 40% of their patients to be from minority cultures. The association offers training material on cross-cultural competency in a downloadable document titled *Module on Cross-Cultural Issues in Health,* located online at http://www.amsa.org/programs/ccimain.cfm.

"[The United States has] always been a nation of immigrants," says Levinson, inextricably tying it to the health concerns of groups around the world; health concerns that appear distant now will eventually be ours, he maintains. "In terms of health, we really have one world," he says, adding that an international flow of emerging infectious diseases means that insular attitudes about these illnesses must change.

As for why to consider indigenous knowledge, Levinson reiterates the importance of health professionals understanding where their patients come from so they will be alert not only to possible dangers but also to possible benefits as well. Many traditional customs, such as practicing yoga and taking herbal remedies, have a healthy effect. "The problem," says Levinson, "is when the practices are harmful, for example native drugs that contain toxic substances or rituals that may prevent appropriate diagnosis or treatment. Either way, good treatment requires awareness of these factors."

Experiences from ethnomedicine, ecosystem management, and community health all suggest that health professionals in the twenty-first century may gain new tools by innovatively combining the best of science with the best of the old ways. These lessons are not lost on the medical professionals in California who dealt with Lia Lee, the Hmong girl with epilepsy. In a response to a review of Fadiman's book in the March–April 1998 issue of *Pediatric Nursing,* June L. Harney Boffman, who worked in the Merced County Medical Center during the period covered by the book, urged that nurses, doctors, and social workers recognize the power of belief. "Knowing is in the context of one's world," Boffman wrote. "This should never be overlooked in the future."

From *Environmental Health Perspectives,* vol. 109, no. 5, 2001. Published by National Institute of Environmental Health Sciences. www.ehponline.org

The Adaptive Value of Religious Ritual

Rituals promote group cohesion by requiring members to engage in behavior that is too costly to fake

RICHARD SOSIS

I was 15 years old the first time I went to Jerusalem's Old City and visited the 2,000-year-old remains of the Second Temple, known as the Western Wall. It may have foreshadowed my future life as an anthropologist, but on my first glimpse of the ancient stones I was more taken by the people standing at the foot of the structure than by the wall itself. Women stood in the open sun, facing the Wall in solemn worship, wearing long-sleeved shirts, head coverings and heavy skirts that scraped the ground. Men in their thick beards, long black coats and fur hats also seemed oblivious to the summer heat as they swayed fervently and sang praises to God. I turned to a friend, "Why would anyone in their right mind dress for a New England winter only to spend the afternoon praying in the desert heat?" At the time I thought there was no rational explanation and decided that my fellow religious brethren might well be mad.

Of course, "strange" behavior is not unique to ultraorthodox Jews. Many religious acts appear peculiar to the outsider. Pious adherents the world over physically differentiate themselves from others: Moonies shave their heads, Jain monks of India wear contraptions on their heads and feet to avoid killing insects, and clergy almost everywhere dress in outfits that distinguish them from the rest of society. Many peoples also engage in some form of surgical alteration. Australian aborigines perform a ritual operation on adolescent boys in which a bone or a stone is inserted into the penis through an incision in the urethra. Jews and Muslims submit their sons to circumcision, and in some Muslim societies daughters are also subject to circumcision or other forms of genital mutilation. Groups as diverse as the Nuer of Sudan and the Iatmul of New Guinea force their adolescents to undergo ritual scarification. Initiation ceremonies, otherwise known as rites of passage, are often brutal. Among Native Americans, Apache boys were forced to bathe in icy water, Luiseno initiates were required to lie motionless while being bitten by hordes of ants, and Tukuna girls had their hair plucked out.

How can we begin to understand such behavior? If human beings are rational creatures, then why do we spend so much time, energy and resources on acts that can be so painful or, at the very least, uncomfortable? Archaeologists tell us that our

species has engaged in ritual behavior for at least 100,000 years, and every known culture practices some form of religion. It even survives covertly in those cultures where governments have attempted to eliminate spiritual practices. And, despite the unparalleled triumph of scientific rationalism in the 20th century, religion continued to flourish. In the United States a steady 40 percent of the population attended church regularly throughout the century. A belief in God (about 96 percent), the afterlife (about 72 percent), heaven (about 72 percent) and hell (about 58 percent) remained substantial and remarkably constant. Why do religious beliefs, practices and institutions continue to be an essential component of human social life?

Such questions have intrigued me for years. Initially my training in anthropology did not provide an answer. Indeed, my studies only increased my bewilderment. I received my training in a subfield known as human behavioral ecology, which studies the adaptive design of behavior with attention to its ecological setting. Behavioral ecologists assume that natural selection has shaped the human nervous system to respond successfully to varying ecological circumstances. All organisms must balance trade-offs: Time spent doing one thing prevents them from pursuing other activities that can enhance their survival or reproductive success. Animals that maximize the rate at which they acquire resources, such as food and mates, can maximize the number of descendants, which is exactly what the game of natural selection is all about.

Behavioral ecologists assume that natural selection has designed our decision-making mechanisms to optimize the rate at which human beings accrue resources under diverse ecological conditions—a basic prediction of *optimal foraging theory*. Optimality models offer predictions of the "perfectly adapted" behavioral response, given a set of environmental constraints. Of course, a perfect fit with the environment is almost never achieved because organisms rarely have perfect information and because environments are always changing. Nevertheless, this assumption has provided a powerful framework to analyze a variety of decisions, and most research (largely conducted among foraging populations) has shown that our species broadly conforms to these expectations.

If our species is designed to optimize the rate at which we extract energy from the environment, why would we engage in religious behavior that seems so counterproductive? Indeed, some religious practices, such as ritual sacrifices, are a conspicuous display of wasted resources. Anthropologists can explain why foragers regularly share their food with others in the group, but why would anyone share their food with a dead ancestor by burning it to ashes on an altar? A common response to this question is that people believe in the efficacy of the rituals and the tenets of the faith that give meaning to the ceremonies. But this response merely begs the question. We must really ask why natural selection has favored a psychology that believes in the supernatural and engages in the costly manifestations of those beliefs.

Ritual Sacrifice

Behavioral ecologists have only recently begun to consider the curiosities of religious activities, so at first I had to search other disciplines to understand these practices. The scholarly literature suggested that I wasn't the only one who believed that intense religious behavior was a sign of madness. Some of the greatest minds of the past two centuries, such as Marx and Freud, supported my thesis. And the early anthropological theorists also held that spiritual beliefs were indicative of a primitive and simple mind. In the 19th century, Edward B. Tylor, often noted as one of the founding fathers of anthropology, maintained that religion arose out of a misunderstanding among "primitives" that dreams are real. He argued that dreams about deceased ancestors might have led the primitives to believe that spirits can survive death.

Eventually the discipline of anthropology matured, and its practitioners moved beyond the equation that "primitive equals irrational." Instead, they began to seek functional explanations of religion. Most prominent among these early 20th-century theorists was the Polish-born anthropologist Bronislaw Malinowski. He argued that religion arose out of "the real tragedies of human life, out of the conflict between human plans and realities." Although religion may serve to allay our fears of death, and provide comfort from our incessant search for answers, Malinowski's thesis did not seem to explain the origin of rituals. Standing in the midday desert sun in several layers of black clothing seems more like a recipe for increasing anxiety than treating it. The classical anthropologists didn't have the right answers to my questions. I needed to look elsewhere.

Fortunately, a new generation of anthropologists has begun to provide some explanations. It turns out that the strangeness of religious practices and their inherent costs are actually the critical features that contribute to the success of religion as a universal cultural strategy and why natural selection has favored such behavior in the human lineage. To understand this unexpected benefit we need to recognize the adaptive problem that ritual behavior solves. William Irons, a behavioral ecologist at Northwestern University, has suggested that the universal dilemma is the promotion of cooperation within a community. Irons argues that the primary adaptive benefit of religion is its ability to facilitate cooperation within a group—while hunting, sharing food, defending against attacks and waging war—all critical activities in our evolutionary history. But, as Irons points out, although everyone is better off if everybody cooperates, this ideal is often very difficult to coordinate and achieve. The problem is that an individual is even better off if everyone else does the cooperating, while he or she remains at home enjoying an afternoon siesta. Cooperation requires social mechanisms that prevent individuals from free riding on the efforts of others. Irons argues that religion is such a mechanism.

The key is that religious rituals are a form of communication, which anthropologists have long maintained. They borrowed this insight from ethologists who observed that many species engage in patterned behavior, which they referred to as "ritual." Ethologists recognized that ritualistic behaviors served as a form of communication between members of the same species, and often between members of different species. For example, the males of many avian species engage in courtship rituals—such as bowing, head wagging, wing waving and hopping (among many other gestures)—to signal their amorous intents before a prospective mate. And, of course, the vibration of a rattlesnake's tail is a powerful threat display to other species that enter its personal space.

Irons's insight is that religious activities signal commitment to other members of the group. By engaging in the ritual, the member effectively says, "I identify with the group and I believe in what the group stands for." Through its ability to signal commitment, religious behavior can overcome the problem of free riders and promote cooperation within the group. It does so because trust lies at the heart of the problem: A member must assure everyone that he or she will participate in acquiring food or in defending the group. Of course, hunters and warriors may make promises—"you have my word, I'll show up tomorrow"—but unless the trust is already established such statements are not believable.

It turns out that there is a robust way to secure trust. Israeli biologist Amotz Zahavi observes that it is often in the best interest of an animal to send a dishonest signal—perhaps to fake its size, speed, strength, health or beauty. The only signal that can be believed is one that is too costly to fake, which he referred to as a "handicap." Zahavi argues that natural selection has favored the evolution of handicaps. For example, when a springbok antelope spots a predator it often *stots*—it jumps up and down. This extraordinary behavior puzzled biologists for years: Why would an antelope waste precious energy that could be used to escape the predator? And why would the animal make itself more visible to something that wants to eat it? The reason is that the springbok is displaying its quality to the predator—its ability to escape, effectively saying, "Don't bother chasing me. Look how strong my legs are, you won't be able to catch me." The only reason a predator believes the springbok is because the signal is too costly to fake. An antelope that is not quick enough to escape cannot imitate the signal because it is not strong enough to repeatedly jump to a certain height. Thus, a display can provide honest information if the signals are so costly to perform that lower quality organisms cannot benefit by imitating the signal.

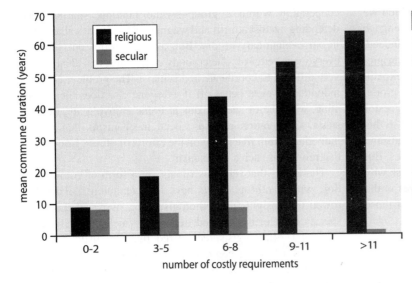

behaviors that are constrained

consumption of:
coffee, alcohol, tobacco, meat, other foods or
beverages

use and ownership of:
photographs, jewelry, certain technology, other
material items

activities:
monogamous marriage, gambling, communication
with the outside, living as a nuclear family,
maintaining rights to biological children

behaviors that are required

trial period for membership, surrender of material
belongings, learn a body of knowledge, endure
public sessions of criticism, certain clothing styles,
certain hairstyles, fasting

In much the same way, religious behavior is also a costly signal. By donning several layers of clothing and standing out in the midday sun, ultraorthodox Jewish men are signaling to others: "Hey! Look, I'm a *haredi* Jew. If you are also a member of this group you can trust me because why else would I be dressed like this? No one would do this *unless* they believed in the teachings of ultraorthodox Judaism and were fully committed to its ideals and goals." The quality that these men are signaling is their level of commitment to a specific religious group.

Adherence to a set of religious beliefs entails a host of ritual obligations and expected behaviors. Although there may be physical or psychological benefits associated with some ritual practices, the significant time, energy and financial costs involved serve as effective deterrents for anyone who does not believe in the teachings of a particular religion. There is no incentive for nonbelievers to join or remain in a religious group, because the costs of maintaining membership—such as praying three times a day, eating only kosher food, donating a certain part of your income to charity and so on—are simply too high.

Those who engage in the suite of ritual requirements imposed by a religious group can be trusted to believe sincerely in the doctrines of their respective religious communities. As a result of increased levels of trust and commitment among group members, religious groups minimize costly monitoring mechanisms that are otherwise necessary to overcome free-rider problems that typically plague communal pursuits. Hence, the adaptive benefit of ritual behavior is its ability to promote and maintain cooperation, a challenge that our ancestors presumably faced throughout our evolutionary history.

Benefits of Membership

One prediction of the "costly signaling theory of ritual" is that groups that impose the greatest demands on their members will elicit the highest levels of devotion and commitment. Only committed members will be willing to dress and behave in ways that differ from the rest of society. Groups that maintain more-committed members can also offer more because it's easier for them to attain their collective goals than groups whose members

are less committed. This may explain a paradox in the religious marketplace: Churches that require the most of their adherents are experiencing rapid rates of growth. For example, the Church of Jesus Christ of Latter-day Saints (Mormons), Seventh-day Adventists and Jehovah's Witnesses, who respectively abstain from caffeine, meat and blood transfusions (among other things), have been growing at exceptional rates. In contrast, liberal Protestant denominations such as the Episcopalians, Methodists and Presbyterians have been steadily losing members.

Economist Lawrence Iannaccone, of George Mason University, has also noted that the most demanding groups also have the greatest number of committed members. He found that the more distinct a religious group was—how much the group's lifestyle differed from mainstream America—the higher its attendance rates at services. Sociologists Roger Finke and Rodney Stark, of Penn State and the University of Washington, respectively, have argued that when the Second Vatican Council in 1962 repealed many of the Catholic Church's prohibitions and reduced the level of strictness in the church, it initiated a decline in church attendance among American Catholics and reduced the enrollments in seminaries. Indeed, in the late 1950s almost 75 percent of American Catholics were attending Mass weekly, but since the Vatican's actions there has been a steady decline to the current rate of about 45 percent.

The costly signaling theory of ritual also predicts that greater commitment will translate into greater cooperation within groups. My colleague Eric Bressler, a graduate student at McMaster University, and I addressed this question by looking at data from the records of 19th-century communes. All communes face an inherent problem of promoting and sustaining cooperation because individuals can free ride on the efforts of others. Because cooperation is key to a commune's survival, we employed commune longevity as a measure of cooperation. Compared to their secular counterparts, the religious communes did indeed demand more of their members, including such behavior as celibacy, the surrender of all material possessions and vegetarianism. Communes that demanded more of their members survived longer, overcoming the fundamental challenges of cooperation. By placing greater demands on their

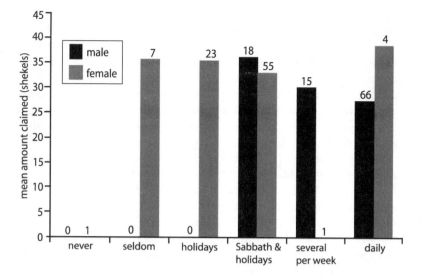

members, they were presumably able to elicit greater belief in and commitment toward the community's common ideology and goals.

I also wanted to evaluate the costly signaling theory of ritual within modern communal societies. The kibbutzim I had visited in Israel as a teenager provided an ideal opportunity to examine these hypotheses. For most of their 100-year history, these communal societies have lived by the dictum, "From each according to his abilities, to each according to his needs." The majority of the more than 270 kibbutzim are secular (and often ideologically antireligious); fewer than 20 are religiously oriented. Because of a massive economic failure—a collective debt of more than $4 billion—the kibbutzim are now moving in the direction of increased privatization and reduced communality. When news of the extraordinary debt surfaced in the late 1980s, it went largely unnoticed that the religious kibbutzim were financially stable. In the words of the Religious Kibbutz Movement Federation, "the economic position of the religious kibbutzim is sound, and they remain uninvolved in the economic crisis."

The success of the religious kibbutzim is especially remarkable given that many of their rituals inhibit economic productivity. For example, Jewish law does not permit Jews to milk cows on the Sabbath. Although rabbinic rulings now permit milking by kibbutz members to prevent the cows from suffering, in the early years none of this milk was used commercially. There are also significant constraints imposed by Jewish law on agricultural productivity. Fruits are not allowed to be eaten for the first few years of the tree's life, agricultural fields must lie fallow every seven years, and the corners of fields can never be harvested—they must be left for society's poor. Although these constraints appear detrimental to productivity, the costly signaling theory of ritual suggests that they may actually be the key to the economic success of the religious kibbutzim.

I decided to study this issue with economist Bradley Ruffle of Israel's Ben Gurion University. We developed a game to determine whether there were differences in how the members of secular and religious kibbutzim cooperated with each other. The game involves two members from the same kibbutz who remain anonymous to each other. Each member is told there are 100 shekels in an envelope to which both members have access. Each participant decides how many shekels to withdraw and keep. If the sum of both requests exceeds 100 shekels, both members receive no money and the game is over. However, if the requests are less than or equal to 100 shekels, the money remaining in the envelope is increased by 50 percent and divided evenly among the participants. Each member also keeps the original amount he or she requested. The game is an example of a common-pool resource dilemma in which publicly accessible goods are no longer available once they are consumed. Since the goods are available to more than one person, the maintenance of the resources requires individual self-restraint; in other words, cooperation.

After we controlled for a number of variables, including the age and size of the kibbutz and the amount of privatization, we found not only that religious kibbutzniks were more cooperative with each other than secular kibbutzniks, but that male religious kibbutz members were also significantly more cooperative than female members. Among secular kibbutzniks we found no sex differences at all. This result is understandable if we appreciate the types of rituals and demands imposed on religious Jews. Although there are a variety of requirements that are imposed equally on males and females, such as keeping kosher and refraining from work on the Sabbath, male rituals are largely performed in public, whereas female rituals are generally pursued privately. Indeed, none of the three major requirements imposed exclusively on women—attending a ritual bath, separating a portion of dough when baking bread and lighting Shabbat and holiday candles—are publicly performed. They are not rituals that signal commitment to a wider group; instead they appear to signal commitment to the family. Men, however, engage in highly visible rituals, most notably public prayer, which they are expected to perform three times a day. Among male religious kibbutz members, synagogue attendance is positively correlated with cooperative behavior. There is no similar correlation among females. This is not surprising given that women are not required to attend services, and so their presence does not signal commitment to the group. Here the costly signaling theory of ritual provides a unique explanation of these findings. We expect that further work will provide even more insight into the ability of ritual to promote trust, commitment and cooperation.

We know that many other species engage in ritual behaviors that appear to enhance trust and cooperation. For example, anthropologists John Watanabe of Dartmouth University and Barbara Smuts at the University of Michigan have shown that greetings between male olive baboons serve to signal trust and commitment between former rivals. So why are human rituals often cloaked in mystery and the supernatural? Cognitive anthropologists Scott Atran of the University of Michigan and Pascal Boyer at Washington University in St. Louis have pointed out that the counterintuitive nature of supernatural concepts are more easily remembered than mundane ideas, which facilitates their cultural transmission. Belief in supernatural agents such as gods, spirits and ghosts also appears to be critical to religion's ability to promote long-term cooperation. In our study of 19th-century communes, Eric Bressler and I found that the strong positive relationship between the number of costly requirements imposed on members and commune longevity only held for religious communes, not secular ones. We were surprised by this result because secular groups such as militaries and fraternities appear to successfully employ costly rituals to maintain cooperation. Cultural ecologist Roy Rappaport explained, however, that although religious and secular rituals can both promote cooperation, religious rituals ironically generate greater belief and commitment because they sanctify unfalsifiable statements that are beyond the possibility of examination. Since statements containing supernatural elements, such as "Jesus is the son of God," cannot be proved or disproved, believers verify them "emotionally." In contrast to religious propositions, the kibbutz's guiding dictum, taken from Karl Marx, is not beyond question; it can be evaluated by living according to its directives by distributing labor and resources appropriately. Indeed, as the economic situation on the kibbutzim has worsened, this fundamental proposition of kibbutz life has been challenged and is now disregarded by many who are pushing their communities to accept differential pay scales. The ability of religious rituals to evoke emotional experiences that can be associated with enduring supernatural concepts and symbols differentiates them from both animal and secular rituals and lies at the heart of their efficiency in promoting and maintaining long-term group cooperation and commitment.

Evolutionary research on religious behavior is in its infancy, and many questions remain to be addressed. The costly signaling theory of ritual appears to provide some answers, and, of course, it has given me a better understanding of the questions I asked as a teenager. The real value of the costly signaling theory of ritual will be determined by its ability to explain religious phenomena across societies. Most of us, including ultraorthodox Jews, are not living in communes. Nevertheless, contemporary religious congregations that demand much of their members are able to achieve a close-knit social community—an impressive accomplishment in today's individualistic world.

Religion has probably always served to enhance the union of its practitioners; unfortunately, there is also a dark side to this unity. If the intragroup solidarity that religion promotes is one of its significant adaptive benefits, then from its beginning religion has probably always played a role in intergroup conflicts. In other words, one of the benefits for individuals of intragroup solidarity is the ability of unified groups to defend and compete against other groups. This seems to be as true today as it ever was, and is nowhere more apparent than the region I visited as a 15-year-old boy—which is where I am as I write these words. As I conduct my fieldwork in the center of this war zone, I hope that by appreciating the depth of the religious need in the human psyche, and by understanding this powerful adaptation, we can learn how to promote cooperation rather than conflict.

Bibliography

Atran, S. 2002. *In Gods We Trust*. New York: Oxford University Press.

Iannaccone, L. 1992. Sacrifice and stigma: Reducing free-riding in cults, communes, and other collectives. *Journal of Political Economy* 100:271–291.

Iannaccone, L. 1994. Why strict churches are strong. *American Journal of Sociology* 99:1180–1211.

Irons, W. 2001. Religion as a hard-to-fake sign of commitment. In *Evolution and the Capacity for Commitment*, ed. R. Nesse, pp. 292–309. New York: Russell Sage Foundation.

Rappaport, R. 1999. *Ritual and Religion in the Making of Humanity*. Cambridge: Cambridge University Press.

Sosis, R. 2003. Why aren't we all Hutterites? Costly signaling theory and religious behavior. *Human Nature* 14:91–127.

Sosis, R., and C. Alcorta. 2003. Signaling, solidarity, and the sacred: The evolution of religious behavior. *Evolutionary Anthropology* 12:264–274.

Sosis, R., and E. Bressler. 2003. Cooperation and commune longevity: A test of the costly signaling theory of religion. *Cross-Cultural Research* 37:211–239.

Sosis, R., and B. Ruffle. 2003. Religious ritual and cooperation: Testing for a relationship on Israeli religious and secular kibbutzim. *Current Anthropology* 44:713–722.

Zahavi, A., and A. Zahavi. 1997. *The Handicap Principle*. New York: Oxford University Press.

RICHARD SOSIS is an assistant professor of anthropology at the University of Connecticut. His research interests include the evolution of cooperation, utopian societies and the behavioral ecology of religion. Address: Department of Anthropology, U-2176, University of Connecticut, Storrs, CT 06269–2176. Internet: richard.sosis@uconn.edu

Remapping the World of Autism

Roy Richard Grinker

As an anthropologist, I have learned that the best way to learn about the rules of any society is to see them broken. That is why sickness, when it prevents people from living up to the rules of social behavior, can teach us so much about culture. When everything goes smoothly and expectations are met, the rules fade into the background of social life and become almost invisible. We learn more when things go wrong, as I found out when I started a research project to study autism across cultures. I wanted to know if autism existed in other cultures, and if so, what people did about it. I traveled to Korea, South Africa, and India, and communicated by telephone and email to mothers and fathers in more than a dozen other countries.

What I discovered in all of these places was that brave and dedicated parents, like the Indian mothers described in this article, wage a constant battle to balance the rules of their society with their own personal beliefs about their children. In every country, it is a mother's eyes that are the first to truly see her child and accept her child's difference. But simply to see a child with autism is not the same thing as helping him or integrating him into a social world. Those doors have to be worked open.

As we will see, a group mothers in India can teach us a great deal about the obstacles to mental health care in India and the rules of Hindu society. These mothers all raised boys with autism, a disorder that always emerges before the age of three, in boys four times more often than in girls, with a constellation of symptoms, sometimes severe and sometimes moderate, that includes impairments in language and social interaction, and restricted interests and activities. Although the symptoms of autism are the same everywhere, the meaning of those symptoms varies from culture to culture. For these mothers, raising a child with autism in India became an act of resistance against the expectations of their culture. Their stories also help us understand the difference between the concepts of "disease" and "illness." In the view of anthropologist Arthur Kleinman, a disease occurs when something is wrong with our bodily organs or systems, whereas illness is the experience of negative or unwanted changes in our bodies or our ability to function in society. Autism is both a disease and an illness, and it cannot be otherwise.

The experiences of autism—as an illness, not as a disease—even by mothers from the same country can be vastly different. These experiences are shaped by the kind of community each woman lives in, her ancestry, the gender roles that are valued in her culture and how they are played out in her home, her culture's tolerance for diversity and difference, and even her own personality and personal will to care for her child in the face of harsh criticism from the people closest to her. Anthropology can play an important role in understanding how culture affects and will continue to affect the way we view autism, and therefore also, the way we raise our children.

In India, most of the children who would be given the diagnosis of autism if they were in the United States are instead called either mentally retarded (MR) or mad (in Hindi, *paagol*). With either diagnosis, the family must face an extraordinary amount of social stigma. Tamara Daley, an American psychologist who has studied autism in India, believes that many doctors in India actually do know something about autism but are reluctant to give the diagnosis, either because they think there is nothing that can be done to help anyway or because they assume the families they see, many of which are illiterate or poorly educated, will be unable to understand what autism means. Until 1999 the Indian government did not even recognize autism as a disorder.

Consider the case of a teenage boy I met in New Delhi named Rohit. Before he was two, Rohit's parents knew something was wrong. He didn't speak much, showed no interest in social interaction, had rigid, patterned behaviors, and an odd gait. Rohit's parents tried religious healers but when there was no improvement in his behavior, they moved on to medical doctors who diagnosed him with mental retardation.

By the age of 5, Rohit was interested mostly in memorizing license plate numbers and showed great skill in identifying vehicle makes and models. By the age of 8, his speech though still delayed was articulate and fluent, but he had no friends. He still kissed and hugged his mother in public, which is inappropriate in India, and used obscene words when talking to neighbors. Pediatricians said that Rohit needed a more lively social environment. No elementary school would take him, so his parents paid $60 a month to place him in a good private school for a diverse array of children with special needs, many of whom were blind, deaf, mentally retarded, or had cerebral palsy. Rohit was enrolled under the diagnosis "mental retardation."

Six years later, when Rohit was 14, and just as socially impaired as ever, a British-trained psychiatrist in Delhi came to the school to give a lecture to parents about developmental disorders, including autism, and urged the school to administer an autism rating scale to its students. The idea was to screen potential cases for further diagnostic assessment. Rohit's parents resisted. They had already seen dozens of doctors over the years and each time they were told that Rohit was mentally retarded. They'd already gotten comfortable with the diagnosis.

After the lecture, still knowing little about autism, they told the school director, "Rohit cannot have autism because he looks fine physically." Ten months later, the school prevailed over the parents' objections. Rohit was tested and then diagnosed with autism. Further examination showed no evidence of mental retardation. In fact, his IQ is above average. The psychiatrist promptly prescribed a small dose of an anti-depressant that helps reduce anxiety and, in people with autism, facilitates assertiveness. Within three months the family reported that Rohit's social relatedness had improved noticeably. It had taken them fifteen years to get proper treatment for Rohit.

There is emerging in India a disjunction between doctors, who often rely on outdated medical literature, and parents, who are increasingly well informed. The parents' source is the internet, a central character in nearly every autism story I've ever heard, anywhere. Many Indian parents have set up Google alerts to send themselves daily notices of every news article published on autism in any newspaper in the world. Through such information, autism is slowly but surely becoming less exotic in India and so also less shameful.

One day, as I talked to a group of three Bengali mothers waiting to pick up their children from the only school for autistic children in New Delhi (pop. 14 million), called Open Door, I noticed a remarkable similarity to some of the positive conversations I had heard in the United States. In the U.S. parents often talk about whether Albert Einstein or Isaac Newton were high functioning autistic people. Newton, for example, spoke little, had few friends, and was extremely awkward socially. In India, such comparisons involve religious figures. One of the Bengali women commented to me, "You know, our god, Siva, was like an autistic person. He couldn't relate to others, he walked around naked." The other women lit up and joined in. "He had no friends!" "Yes, he was totally disconnected from the world." "He was abnormal." Of course, they are right, and this is why Siva's parents-in-law to-be were so outraged that their daughter might marry him.

"I heard that Ramakrishna was autistic too," one woman said, but she could not say why. She was referring to the Bengali saint, Sri Ramakrishna Paramahansa, who was illiterate and bizarre, but revered in India. As a child, he wore girl's clothing and acted like a girl, sometimes pretending that he was a widow or an abandoned wife, and he worshipped the Lord Krishna through *madhurya bhava,* a woman's deeply spiritual desire for her lover. He was thought to be *paagol* (mad) but also divinely inspired.

There is a long tradition of unusual saints and other holy men and women in India who had special powers but who were incapable of having appropriate social relationships. In this context, it is not that surprising to hear mothers describe their children with autism as untainted by the evils of civilization and with terms like "pure" and "close to God." In fact, an important stage of the ideal Hindu life course is the eventual separation from the social world, the renunciation of society, with the greatest value given to the forest dweller who abrogates all social ties and family obligations.

Despite the extraordinary cultural variation of India—where there are close to four hundred different languages in a country roughly one third the size of the United States—Hindu child rearing practices are remarkably consistent. Among all Hindu communities, the mother and child are nearly inseparable for the first two years of life, with mothers holding their children at the hip even when working around the house. Up until the age of two or two and a half, children are kings, sleeping with their mothers, the breast always accessible enough so they never have to cry for long. Weaning usually occurs between the ages of 2 and 3 but in many cases, where there is no younger sibling, a child may breast-feed until the age of 5 or 6.

In general, Hindu boys are tied to their mothers until about the age of 5, when mothers no longer indulge them and they enter the world of the father and his extended family. Some Indian psychoanalysts have suggested that the tie between the child and the mother, especially between the son and mother, is so close that it is almost pathological. A boy is so important to a mother's status in her family and society at large that her emotional attachment to him—or reverence—may be excessive from a western perspective. The father is typically disengaged during early childhood. While the child is enmeshed with his mother, however, the father and the extended family are always nearby. Gently the mother weans the child not only from the breast but from the dependence on her and pushes him or her into the bosom of the extended family: the father and, figuratively speaking, dozens of mothers.

The mother essentially renounces the son around the time he enters primary school. Mothers tease their children by suggesting that they will give them away, discouraging attention-getting behaviors, encouraging self-restraint, and, if they do indulge the child, rejecting them afterwards. For example, a mother might say, "you had your milk, now get out of the house." Other relatives push him to voluntarily abandon his mother. They guide him to either the extended family, joint family, or both, rather than to independence, and promote a familial rather than an individual identity. This structure is changing rapidly, especially in urban India and in the Indian diaspora, where men and women are entering competitive marketplaces that place a high value on individualism. Still, just as Americans idealize the nuclear family at a time when nearly half of all American children live in single parent households, the ideals of the conventional Hindu family persist. For the mothers of children with autism, however, the disorder disrupts any hope of having their children merge with either an extended or joint family.

Throughout the world, autism is commonly considered a disorder that is about being socially disconnected, and this is true in India as well. Still, in India, autism takes a culturally specific form where the child is largely disconnected from his or her extended family and the maternal bonds remain unbroken. Mothers of children with autism don't feel comfortable asking their in-laws to take a greater role in raising them. Such a mother will not trust her child to anyone. The mother of a mute and mentally retarded autistic child knows her child is incapable of leaving her to spend more time with the extended family, even if the extended family is willing. She will not even try a simple gesture of separation, such as asking a child to get permission from his or her grandparents to eat candy or play a game. Common acts that Hindu mothers use to foster separation, such as teasing the child, have no impact when a child cannot comprehend the meaning (for example, handing the child to a distant relative and saying, "You take him! I don't want him anymore! I've cared for him enough!").

Shubrha and her husband Rajiv lived with their son Gautam in a joint family enclave until Rajiv was relocated to Delhi. "It was a relief in many ways to be away from my in-laws," Shubrha told me. They never blamed me for causing his mental problems and behaviors, but they did blame me for not doing the right things to help him. They said I was too overprotective, that I kept him home too much, that he didn't have an exciting environment to help him learn how to talk or be social. After a while the constant criticism gets to you and you think to yourself, 'okay, if you know how to do it, *you* do it, you are *supposed* to do it anyway if you are his grandmother,' but then nothing ever happens. But that was okay for me because I knew I could take care of him better than anyone."

When Gautham was almost 11, he started to go to a school for children with mental retardation not far from his home in Delhi. Though he had been toilet trained a year earlier, he now started to soil his pants on the way home from school, sometimes putting his hands into his pants and playing with his feces. Once home, he refused to let anyone wash him, so Shubrha had to have someone physically restrain him while she cleaned him up. After a few weeks, Shubrha decided that the only way to extinguish that behavior was to let him sit and stink in his own feces. "It was horrible," she said. "The house smelled so bad, Gautham had rashes on his thighs and buttocks. I had to keep scented candles and incense burning most of the time, but I held out because I knew the only way to stop the behavior was to show no reaction to it. My husband kept saying, 'how much longer can you take it?' I think it took the better part of a year but it worked."

Within a few years, Rajiv and Shubrha divorced. Shubrha now felt free to raise Gautam by herself, often in ways that others might find shocking. When Gautham was about 15 years old, he began to show an interest in sex. He became increasingly irritable and violent and sometimes scratched and hit himself. "No one gives you advice about handling these sexual matters," Shubrha said, "especially in India where people have so many hang-ups about sex." At a conference about special education in Delhi, Shubrha met a young American graduate student and asked for his thoughts. Gautam, he believed, needed some kind of course in sex education, but since Gautam was nonverbal, he needed to be educated with visual aids like photographs and videos. Such images are illegal in India, but Shubrha knew she had to break the law. With the graduate student's help, Gautam learned how to manage his urges and his mood improved dramatically.

From the perspective of most parents, what Shubrha did might seem bizarre, but I found it made perfect sense, and that it was a deeply compassionate act. Parents of autistic children everywhere improvise, they do what works, and they know their children learn *concretely,* through what is real, visible and tangible rather than through abstract discussions, like lectures about the birds and the bees. There is no denying that Shubrha clearly improved Gautham's emotional health and taught him what is arguably an important life skill. And that is something she can be proud of.

Amla, another Bengali mother living near Delhi, considers that she has become a "Bohemian." By this she means that she is ill-suited to the society in which she lives, and that she dislikes convention, including materialism and her conservative parents-in-law. "My husband Anil became a Bohemian too, which made him an unsuitable husband, or at least a poor provider. A couple of times he came home without a paycheck and a receipt showing he'd donated the whole thing to a shelter or a hospital." When their autistic and only son, Sunil, was twelve, her husband died suddenly of a heart attack. Normally, the eldest son arranges the cremation and lights the fire by putting a flame to the deceased's lips to symbolize the spirit leaving the body.

"It was chaos in the house," she recalls, "people coming into the house, and the body was there—the typical Hindu thing—and Sunil was going crazy. He was unable to comprehend what was going on, why his father was lying dead in our house, and the crying visitors were too much. He stuck his fingers in his ears and screamed and screamed. I was devastated enough, but I couldn't do this to him." So Amla did what few Hindu women are prepared to do. She took Anil to an electric crematorium and lit the cremation fire herself.

These days one can find urban Hindu women arranging funerals and even cremating their husbands—all Hindus cremate, unlike Muslims who bury—but it is still a clear violation of Hindu laws, and in a conservative family it is unforgivable. Traditionally, women are not allowed to step foot in the burning grounds, and this is true among all Hindus, regardless of linguistic or ethnic group. Her side of the family was appalled, and her husband's family vowed never to see her again.

Mamta's village sits at the foothills of the Himalayas, near the old British hill stations in northern India. She comes to Action for Autism wearing jeans, teeshirt and sandals one day and then a traditional Indian sari the next. She tells me that when her first child, Ohjyu, was eighteen months old, he didn't seem to behave like the other children did. "I took him to a baby show. They have judges, and mothers exhibit the babies. The babies all did little tasks and won prizes. But my baby wouldn't do anything. I had no idea what was wrong and I didn't even know the word autism."

On the way home from the baby show, she remembered having seen an article about developmental delays in an old issue of the Indian magazine, *Outlook,* and dug it out of the trash. The article listed the symptoms of autism, some of which Ohjyu had, like poor eye contact, speech delay, and an inability to respond to his name.

"That killed me. It was so painful and I didn't share it with anyone, not even my husband. I knew he would be unwilling to believe that something was wrong. I didn't tell my own parents."

Eventually, however, Mamta convinced her husband to take Ohjyu to a pediatrician. The doctor said that Ohjyu's speech was delayed because they lived in an isolated home in the mountains. He recommended taking him into a more stimulating environment, which she and her husband arranged by moving to the city of Gwalior. Although she contemplated terminating her second pregnancy for fear of having another disabled child, her husband refused to even consider it. In Gwalior, little changed for the better with Ohjyu; in fact, he looked worse. So they moved back to Nainital.

Unable to watch the progressive deterioration of her son and against the advice of her husband, and the outrage of her parents-in-law, she devised a plan. She was going to learn how to interact with him and help him learn, even if it meant abandoning her husband and parents-in-law in their mountain village for months, an action many of her friends and neighbors thought was outrageous. Mamta could only imagine the insults hurled behind her back. She took the wide-eyed Ohjyu, along with his infant sister, on the 7 hour train ride to New Delhi. There, a child psychologist diagnosed Ohjyu, then four years old, with autism. Armed with this diagnosis she decided that she was going to reach Ohjyu.

"I belong to a people called the Kumaon, and we don't have many medical experts. I knew something was wrong, but, convincing my people? I cried nights. I was irritable,

depressed. My husband avoided me and spent more time working. But now it's out. I spend most of my time with my mother-in-law, and we don't fight much. I respect her power. But I did disobey her. She didn't want me to go to Delhi or see the psychologist. Now when I see these other mothers here in Delhi, I say, 'you have to do what you have to do.'"

Mamta's mother-in-law resisted attempts to understand Ohjyu's developmental problems because she believed it was her husband's family's responsibility. So, on their behalf and leaving Mamta at home, she traveled into the hills to see holy men and tantrics, some of whom said that Ohjyu was possessed by a demon. She eventually reached a conclusion and told Mamta: her husband's family had failed to please the god of the subcaste.

It is hard to exaggerate the importance of boys in Hindu families. Sons carry on the family line and carry out the rituals that are crucial to success in this and subsequent worlds. So in Mamta's community when a girl is born, goats must be sacrificed to please the unhappy village god; only then will they make it possible for boys to be born and be born healthy. When Ohjyu was born, it had been thirteen years since Mamta's parents-in-law had made the last sacrifice. "They wanted to do the sacrifice earlier," Mamta says, "but something kept happening to prevent it. They'd get ready to kill the goats, and then someone would be born. But you can't do the sacrifice at that time without causing big problems. Then someone would die and you can't do the sacrifice then either." So Mamta's parents-inlaw now promised to sacrifice fourteen goats, at a cost of about 1,500 rupees (about $35, U.S.) per goat, to the *devi,* or god, a form of Lord Shiva named Khandenagh. The god is represented by a small pile of stones in a temple in the mountains, where it is tended by priests who perform a small worship ceremony for the devi twice a day.

So when I asked Mamta if her parents-in-law blamed *her* for Ohjyu's condition, she seemed perplexed. "They blame themselves for not making the sacrifices. But they do blame me for learning about autism, for leaving them, and for listening to the autism center instead of the priests."

Shubrha, Amla, Mamta and the other women I met in India were not going to let stigma, or tradition, or even law get in the way of helping their children. The disturbances they had to deal with were collective because they felt the pressures of Hindu custom. But even if there were no social stigma, they would still be left with personal and emotional turmoil. That is because diseases, however much we see them as biological or material in nature, are total life-changing experiences for parents, families, and communities. The writer, Susan Sontag, once argued that we'd all be better off if diseases were seen only as biological events. She protested the punitive uses of diseases as metaphors—the way tuberculosis was once the figure of death, or the way people talk about the evils of society as cancers. She argued that if we could rid ourselves of any non-material discussion of illness, there would be less stigma and more social support for the ill, not only those suffering from the most stigmatizing diseases such as AIDS and leprosy, but also for people with more invisible afflictions such as mental illnesses. But if we see a cancer, for example, simply as a tumor, we might easily ignore the complexity of human experience. If we see autism as just a brain disorder, we might miss the little victories that people experience each day as they cope with this illness, not only in the United States, but in New Delhi, and the hills of northern India.

ROY RICHARD GRINKER is Professor of Anthropology at The George Washington University and the father of a teenager with autism. He is the author of *Unstrange Minds: Remapping the World of Autism* (Basic Books, 2007; http://www.unstrange.com)

The Secrets of Haiti's Living Dead

A Harvard botanist investigates mystic potions, voodoo rites, and the making of zombies.

GINO DEL GUERCIO

Five years ago, a man walked into l'Estère, a village in central Haiti, approached a peasant woman named Angelina Narcisse, and identified himself as her brother Clairvius. If he had not introduced himself using a boyhood nickname and mentioned facts only intimate family members knew, she would not have believed him. Because, eighteen years earlier, Angelina had stood in a small cemetery north of her village and watched as her brother Clairvius was buried.

The man told Angelina he remembered that night well. He knew when he was lowered into his grave, because he was fully conscious, although he could not speak or move. As the earth was thrown over his coffin, he felt as if he were floating over the grave. The scar on his right cheek, he said, was caused by a nail driven through his casket.

The night he was buried, he told Angelina, a voodoo priest raised him from the grave. He was beaten with a sisal whip and carried off to a sugar plantation in northern Haiti where, with other zombies, he was forced to work as a slave. Only with the death of the zombie master were they able to escape, and Narcisse eventually returned home.

Legend has it that zombies are the living dead, raised from their graves and animated by malevolent voodoo sorcerers, usually for some evil purpose. Most Haitians believe in zombies, and Narcisse's claim is not unique. At about the time he reappeared, in 1980, two women turned up in other villages saying they were zombies. In the same year, in northern Haiti, the local peasants claimed to have found a group of zombies wandering aimlessly in the fields.

But Narcisse's case was different in one crucial respect; it was documented. His death had been recorded by doctors at the American-directed Schweitzer Hospital in Deschapelles. On April 30, 1962, hospital records show, Narcisse walked into the hospital's emergency room spitting up blood. He was feverish and full of aches. His doctors could not diagnose his illness, and his symptoms grew steadily worse. Three days after he entered the hospital, according to the records, he died. The attending physicians, an American among them, signed his death certificate. His body was placed in cold storage for twenty hours, and then he was buried. He said he remembered hearing his doctors pronounce him dead while his sister wept at his bedside.

At the Centre de Psychiatrie et Neurologie in Port-au-Prince, Dr. Lamarque Douyon, a Haitian-born, Canadian-trained psychiatrist, has been systematically investigating all reports of zombies since 1961. Though convinced zombies were real, he had been unable to find a scientific explanation for the phenomenon. He did not believe zombies were people raised from the dead, but that did not make them any less interesting. He speculated that victims were only made to *look* dead, probably by means of a drug that dramatically slowed metabolism. The victim was buried, dug up within a few hours, and somehow reawakened.

The Narcisse case provided Douyon with evidence strong enough to warrant a request for assistance from colleagues in New York. Douyon wanted to find an ethnobotanist, a traditional-medicines expert, who could track down the zombie potion he was sure existed. Aware of the medical potential of a drug that could dramatically lower metabolism, a group organized by the late Dr. Nathan Kline—a New York psychiatrist and pioneer in the field of psychopharmacology—raised the funds necessary to send someone to investigate.

The search for that someone led to the Harvard Botanical Museum, one of the world's foremost institutes of ethnobiology. Its director, Richard Evans Schultes, Jeffrey professor of biology, had spent thirteen years in the tropics studying native medicines. Some of his best-known work is the investigation of curare, the substance used by the nomadic people of the Amazon to poison their darts. Refined into a powerful muscle relaxant called D-tubocurarine, it is now an essential component of the anesthesia used during almost all surgery.

Schultes would have been a natural for the Haitian investigation, but he was too busy. He recommended another Harvard ethnobotanist for the assignment, Wade Davis, a 28-year-old Canadian pursuing a doctorate in biology.

Davis grew up in the tall pine forests of British Columbia and entered Harvard in 1971, influenced by a *Life* magazine story on the student strike of 1969. Before Harvard, the only Americans he had known were draft dodgers, who seemed very exotic. "I used to fight forest fires with them," Davis says. "Like everybody else, I thought America was where it was at. And I wanted to go to Harvard because of that Life article. When I got there, I realized it wasn't quite what I had in mind."

Davis took a course from Schultes, and when he decided to go to South America to study plants, he approached his professor for guidance. "He was an extraordinary figure," Davis remembers. "He was a man who had done it all. He had lived alone for years in the Amazon." Schultes sent Davis to the rain forest with two letters of introduction and two pieces of advice: wear a pith helmet and try ayahuasca, a powerful hallucinogenic vine. During that expedition and others, Davis proved himself an "outstanding field man," says his mentor. Now, in early 1982, Schultes called him into his office and asked if he had plans for spring break.

"I always took to Schultes's assignments like a plant takes to water," says Davis, tall and blond, with inquisitive blue eyes. "Whatever Schultes told me to do, I did. His letters of introduction opened up a whole world." This time the world was Haiti.

Davis knew nothing about the Caribbean island—and nothing about African traditions, which serve as Haiti's cultural basis. He certainly did not believe in zombies. "I thought it was a lark," he says now.

Davis landed in Haiti a week after his conversation with Schultes, armed with a hypothesis about how the zombie drug—if it existed—might be made. Setting out to explore, he discovered a country materially impoverished, but rich in culture and mystery. He was impressed by the cohesion of Haitian society; he found none of the crime, social disorder, and rampant drug and alcohol abuse so common in many of the other Caribbean islands. The cultural wealth and cohesion, he believes, spring from the country's turbulent history.

During the French occupation of the late eighteenth century, 370,000 African-born slaves were imported to Haiti between 1780 and 1790. In 1791, the black population launched one of the few successful slave revolts in history, forming secret societies and overcoming first the French plantation owners and then a detachment of troops from Napoleon's army, sent to quell the revolt. For the next hundred years Haiti was the only independent black republic in the Caribbean, populated by people who did not forget their African heritage. "You can almost argue that Haiti is more African than Africa," Davis says. "When the west coast of Africa was being disrupted by colonialism and the slave trade, Haiti was essentially left alone. The amalgam of beliefs in Haiti is unique, but it's very, very African."

Davis discovered that the vast majority of Haitian peasants practice voodoo, a sophisticated religion with African roots. Says Davis, "It was immediately obvious that the stereotypes of voodoo weren't true. Going around the countryside, I found clues to a whole complex social world." Vodounists believe they communicate directly with, indeed are often possessed by, the many spirits who populate the everyday world. Vodoun society is a system of education, law, and medicine; it embodies a code of ethics that regulates social behavior. In rural areas, secret vodoun societies, much like those found on the west coast of Africa, are as much or more in control of everyday life as the Haitian government.

Although most outsiders dismissed the zombie phenomenon as folklore, some early investigators, convinced of its reality, tried to find a scientific explanation. The few who sought a zombie drug failed. Nathan Kline, who helped finance Davis's

expedition, had searched unsuccessfully, as had Lamarque Douyon, the Haitian psychiatrist. Zora Neale Hurston, an American black woman, may have come closest. An anthropological pioneer, she went to Haiti in the Thirties, studied vodoun society, and wrote a book on the subject, *Tell My Horse,* first published in 1938. She knew about the secret societies and was convinced zombies were real, but if a power existed, she too failed to obtain it.

Davis obtained a sample in a few weeks.

He arrived in Haiti with the names of several contacts. A BBC reporter familiar with the Narcisse case had suggested he talk with Marcel Pierre. Pierre owned the Eagle Bar, a bordello in the city of Saint Marc. He was also a voodoo sorcerer and had supplied the BBC with a physiologically active powder of unknown ingredients. Davis found him willing to negotiate. He told Pierre he was a representative of "powerful but anonymous interests in New York," willing to pay generously for the priest's services, provided no questions were asked. Pierre agreed to be helpful for what Davis will only say was a "sizable sum." Davis spent a day watching Pierre gather the ingredients—including human bones—and grind them together with mortar and pestle. However, from his knowledge of poison, Davis knew immediately that nothing in the formula could produce the powerful effects of zombification.

Three weeks later, Davis went back to the Eagle Bar, where he found Pierre sitting with three associates. Davis challenged him. He called him a charlatan. Enraged, the priest gave him a second vial, claiming that this was the real poison. Davis pretended to pour the powder into his palm and rub it into his skin. "You're a dead man," Pierre told him, and he might have been, because this powder proved to be genuine. But, as the substance had not actually touched him, Davis was able to maintain his bravado, and Pierre was impressed. He agreed to make the poison and show Davis how it was done.

The powder, which Davis keeps in a small vial, looks like dry black dirt. It contains parts of toads, sea worms, lizards, tarantulas, and human bones. (To obtain the last ingredient, he and Pierre unearthed a child's grave on a nocturnal trip to the cemetery.) The poison is rubbed into the victim's skin. Within hours he begins to feel nauseated and has difficulty breathing. A pins-and-needles sensation afflicts his arms and legs, then progresses to the whole body. The subject becomes paralyzed; his lips turn blue for lack of oxygen. Quickly—sometimes within six hours—his metabolism is lowered to a level almost indistinguishable from death.

As Davis discovered, making the poison is an inexact science. Ingredients varied in the five samples he eventually acquired, although the active agents were always the same. And the poison came with no guarantee. Davis speculates that sometimes instead of merely paralyzing the victim, the compound kills him. Sometimes the victim suffocates in the coffin before he can be resurrected. But clearly the potion works well enough often enough to make zombies more than a figment of Haitian imagination.

Analysis of the powder produced another surprise. "When I went down to Haiti originally," says Davis, "my hypothesis was that the formula would contain *concombre zombi,* the 'zombie's

Richard Schultes

His students continue his tradition of pursuing botanical research in the likeliest of unlikely places.

Richard Evans Schultes, Jeffrey professor of biology emeritus, has two homes, and they could not be more different. The first is Cambridge, where he served as director of the Harvard Botanical Museum from 1970 until last year, when he became director emeritus. During his tenure he interested generations of students in the exotic botany of the Amazon rain forest. His impact on the field through his own research is worldwide. The scholarly ethnobotanist with steel-rimmed glasses, bald head, and white lab coat is as much a part of the Botanical Museum as the thousands of plant specimens and botanical texts on the museum shelves.

In his austere office is a picture of a crew-cut, younger man stripped to the waist, his arms decorated with tribal paint. This is Schultes's other persona. Starting in 1941, he spent thirteen years in the rain forests of South America, living with the Indians and studying the plants they use for medicinal and spiritual purposes.

Schultes is concerned that many of the people he has studied are giving up traditional ways. "The people of so-called primitive societies are becoming civilized and losing all their forefathers' knowledge of plant lore," he says. "We'll be losing the tremendous amounts of knowledge they've gained over thousands of years. We've interested in the practical aspects with the hope that new medicines and other things can be developed for our own civilization."

Schultes's exploits are legendary in the biology department. Once, while gathering South American plant specimens hundreds of miles from civilization, he contracted beri-beri. For forty days he fought creeping paralysis and overwhelming fatigue as he paddled back to a doctor. "It was an extraordinary feat of endurance," says disciple Wade Davis. "He is really one of the last nineteenth-century naturalists."

Hallucinogenic plants are one of Schultes's primary interests. As a Harvard undergraduate in the Thirties, he lived with Oklahoma's Kiowa Indians to observe their use of plants. He participated in their peyote ceremonies and wrote his thesis on the hallucinogenic cactus. He has also studied other hallucinogens, such as morning glory seeds, sacred mushrooms, and ayahuasca, a South American vision vine. Schultes's work has led to the development of anesthetics made from curare and alternative sources of natural rubber.

Schultes's main concern these days is the scientific potential of plants in the rapidly disappearing Amazon jungle. "If chemists are going to get material on 80,000 species and then analyze them, they'll never finish the job before the jungle is gone," he says. "The short cut is to find out what the [native] people have learned about the plant properties during many years of living in the very rich flora."

—G.D.G.

---

cucumber,' which is a *Datura* plant. I thought somehow *Datura* was used in putting people down." *Datura* is a powerful psychoactive plant, found in West Africa as well as other tropical areas and used there in ritual as well as criminal activities. Davis had found *Datura* growing in Haiti. Its popular name suggested the plant was used in creating zombies.

But, says Davis, "there were a lot of problems with the *Datura* hypothesis. Partly it was a question of how the drug was administered. *Datura* would create a stupor in huge doses, but it just wouldn't produce the kind of immobility that was key. These people had to appear dead, and there aren't many drugs that will do that."

One of the ingredients Pierre included in the second formula was a dried fish, a species of puffer or blowfish, common to most parts of the world. It gets its name from its ability to fill itself with water and swell to several times its normal size when threatened by predators. Many of these fish contain a powerful poison known as tetrodotoxin. One of the most powerful nonprotein poisons known to man, tetrodotoxin turned up in every sample of zombie powder that Davis acquired.

Numerous well-documented accounts of puffer fish poisoning exist, but the most famous accounts come from the Orient, where *fugu* fish, a species of puffer, is considered a delicacy. In Japan, special chefs are licensed to prepare *fugu*. The chef removes enough poison to make the fish nonlethal, yet enough remains to create exhilarating physiological effects—tingles up and down the spine, mild prickling of the tongue and lips,

euphoria. Several dozen Japanese die each year, having bitten off more than they should have.

"When I got hold of the formula and saw it was the *fugu* fish, that suddenly threw open the whole Japanese literature," says Davis. Case histories of *fugu* poisoning read like accounts of zombification. Victims remain conscious but unable to speak or move. A man who had "died" after eating *fugu* recovered seven days later in the morgue. Several summers ago, another Japanese poisoned by *fugu* revived after he was nailed into his coffin. "Almost all of Narcisse's symptoms correlated. Even strange things such as the fact that he said he was conscious and could hear himself pronounced dead. Stuff that I thought had to be magic, that seemed crazy. But, in fact, that is what people who get *fugu*-fish poisoning experience."

Davis was certain he had solved the mystery. But far from being the end of his investigation, identifying the poison was, in fact, its starting point. "The drug alone didn't make zombies," he explains. "Japanese victims of puffer-fish poisoning don't become zombies, they become poison victims. All the drug could do was set someone up for a whole series of psychological pressures that would be rooted in the culture. I wanted to know why zombification was going on," he says.

He sought a cultural answer, an explanation rooted in the structure and beliefs of Haitian society. Was zombification simply a random criminal activity? He thought not. He had discovered that Clairvius Narcisse and "Ti Femme," a second victim he interviewed, were village pariahs. Ti Femme was regarded as a thief. Narcisse had abandoned his children and deprived his brother of land that was rightfully his. Equally suggestive, Narcisse claimed that his aggrieved brother had sold him to a *bokor*, a voodoo priest who dealt in black magic; he made cryptic reference to having been tried and found guilty by the "masters of the land."

Gathering poisons from various parts of the country, Davis had come into direct contact with the vodoun secret societies. Returning to the anthropological literature on Haiti and pursuing his contacts with informants, Davis came to understand the social matrix within which zombies were created.

Davis's investigations uncovered the importance of the secret societies. These groups trace their origins to the bands of escaped slaves that organized the revolt against the French in the late eighteenth century. Open to both men and women, the societies control specific territories of the country. Their meetings take place at night, and in many rural parts of Haiti the drums and wild celebrations that characterize the gatherings can be heard for miles.

Davis believes the secret societies are responsible for policing their communities, and the threat of zombification is one way they maintain order. Says Davis, "Zombification has a material basis, but it also has a societal logic." To the uninitiated, the practice may appear a random criminal activity, but in rural vodoun society, it is exactly the opposite—a sanction imposed by recognized authorities, a form of capital punishment. For rural Haitians, zombification is an even more severe punishment than death, because it deprives the subject of his most valued possessions: his free will and independence.

The vodounists believe that when a person dies, his spirit splits into several different parts. If a priest is powerful enough, the spiritual aspect that controls a person's character and individuality, known as *ti bon ange*, the "good little angel," can be captured and the corporeal aspect, deprived of its will, held as a slave.

From studying the medical literature on tetrodotoxin poisoning, Davis discovered that if a victim survives the first few hours of the poisoning, he is likely to recover fully from the ordeal. The subject simply revives spontaneously. But zombies remain without will, in a trance-like state, a condition vodounists attribute to the power of the priest. Davis thinks it possible that the psychological trauma of zombification may be augmented by *Datura* or some other drug; he thinks zombies may be fed a *Datura* paste that accentuates their disorientation. Still, he puts the material basis of zombification in perspective: "Tetrodotoxin and *Datura* are only templates on which cultural forces and beliefs may be amplified a thousand times."

Davis has not been able to discover how prevalent zombification is in Haiti. "How many zombies there are is not the question," he says. He compares it to capital punishment in the United States: "It doesn't really matter how many people are electrocuted, as long as it's a possibility." As a sanction in Haiti, the fear is not of zombies, it's of becoming one.

Davis attributes his success in solving the zombie mystery to his approach. He went to Haiti with an open mind and immersed himself in the culture. "My intuition unhindered by biases served me well," he says. "I didn't make any judgments." He combined this attitude with what he had learned earlier from his experiences in the Amazon. "Schultes's lesson is to go and live with the Indians as an Indian." Davis was able to participate in the vodoun society to a surprising degree, eventually even penetrating one of the Bizango societies and dancing in their nocturnal rituals. His appreciation of Haitian culture is apparent. "Everybody asks me how did a white person get this information? To ask the question means you don't understand Haitians—they don't judge you by the color of your skin."

As a result of the exotic nature of his discoveries, Davis has gained a certain notoriety. He plans to complete his dissertation soon, but he has already finished writing a popular account of his adventures. To be published in January by Simon and Schuster, it is called *The Serpent and the Rainbow,* after the serpent that vodounists believe created the earth and the rainbow spirit it married. Film rights have already been optioned; in October Davis went back to Haiti with a screenwriter. But Davis takes the notoriety in stride. "All this attention is funny," he says. "For years, not just me, but all Schultes's students have had extraordinary adventures in the line of work. The adventure is not the end point, it's just along the way of getting the data. At the Botanical Museum, Schultes created a world unto itself. We didn't think we were doing anything above the ordinary. I still don't think we do. And you know," he adds, "the Haiti episode does not begin to compare to what others have accomplished—particularly Schultes himself."

GINO DEL GUERCIO is a national science writer for United Press International.

Body Ritual Among the Nacirema

Horace Miner

The anthropologist has become so familiar with the diversity of ways in which different peoples behave in similar situations that he is not apt to be surprised by even the most exotic customs. In fact, if all of the logically possible combinations of behavior have not been found somewhere in the world, he is apt to suspect that they must be present in some yet undescribed tribe. This point has, in fact, been expressed with respect to clan organization by Murdock (1949: 71). In this light, the magical beliefs and practices of the Nacirema present such unusual aspects that it seems desirable to describe them as an example of the extremes to which human behavior can go.

Professor Linton first brought the ritual of the Nacirema to the attention of anthropologists twenty years ago (1936: 326), but the culture of this people is still very poorly understood. They are a North American group living in the territory between the Canadian Cree, the Yaqui and Tarahumare of Mexico, and the Carib and Arawak of the Antilles. Little is known of their origin, though tradition states that they came from the east. According to Nacirema mythology, their nation was originated by a culture hero, Notgnishaw, who is otherwise known for two great feats of strength—the throwing of a piece of wampum across the river Pa-To-Mac and the chopping down of a cherry tree in which the Spirit of Truth resided.

Nacirema culture is characterized by a highly developed market economy which has evolved in a rich natural habitat. While much of the people's time is devoted to economic pursuits, a large part of the fruits of these labors and a considerable portion of the day are spent in ritual activity. The focus of this activity is the human body, the appearance and health of which loom as a dominant concern in the ethos of the people. While such a concern is certainly not unusual, its ceremonial aspects and associated philosophy are unique.

The fundamental belief underlying the whole system appears to be that the human body is ugly and that its natural tendency is to debility and disease. Incarcerated in such a body, man's only hope is to avert these characteristics through the use of the powerful influences of ritual and ceremony. Every household has one or more shrines devoted to this purpose. The more powerful individuals in the society have several shrines in their houses and, in fact, the opulence of a house is often referred to in terms of the number of such ritual centers it possesses. Most houses are of wattle and daub construction, but the shrine rooms of the more wealthy are walled with stone. Poorer families imitate the rich by applying pottery plaques to their shrine walls.

While each family has at least one such shrine, the rituals associated with it are not family ceremonies but are private and secret. The rites are normally only discussed with children, and then only during the period when they are being initiated into these mysteries. I was able, however, to establish sufficient rapport with the natives to examine these shrines and to have the rituals described to me.

The focal point of the shrine is a box or chest which is built into the wall. In this chest are kept the many charms and magical potions without which no native believes he could live. These preparations are secured from a variety of specialized practitioners. The most powerful of these are the medicine men, whose assistance must be rewarded with substantial gifts. However, the medicine men do not provide the curative potions for their clients, but decide what the ingredients should be and then write them down in an ancient and secret language. This writing is understood only by the medicine men and by the herbalists who, for another gift, provide the required charm.

The charm is not disposed of after it has served its purpose, but is placed in the charm-box of the household shrine. As these magical materials are specific for certain ills, and the real or imagined maladies of the people are many, the charm-box is usually full to overflowing. The magical packets are so numerous that people forget what their purposes were and fear to use them again. While the natives are very vague on this point, we can only assume that the idea in retaining all the old magical materials is that their presence in the charm-box, before which the body rituals are conducted, will in some way protect the worshipper.

Beneath the charm-box is a small font. Each day every member of the family, in succession, enters the shrine room, bows his head before the charm-box, mingles different sorts of holy water in the font, and proceeds with a brief rite of ablution. The holy waters are secured from the Water Temple of the community, where the priests conduct elaborate ceremonies to make the liquid ritually pure.

In the hierarchy of magical practitioners, and below the medicine men in prestige, are specialists whose designation is best translated "holy-mouth-men." The Nacirema have an almost pathological horror and fascination with the mouth, the condition of which is believed to have a supernatural influence on all social relationships. Were it not for the rituals of the mouth, they believe that their teeth would fall out, their gums bleed, their jaws shrink, their friends desert them, and their lovers reject them. (They also believe that a strong relationship exists between oral and moral characteristics. For example, there is a ritual ablution of the mouth for children which is supposed to improve their moral fiber.)

The daily body ritual performed by everyone includes a mouth-rite. Despite the fact that these people are so punctilious about care of the mouth, this rite involves a practice which strikes the uninitiated stranger as revolting. It was reported to me that the ritual consists of inserting a small bundle of hog hairs into the mouth, along with certain magical powders, and then moving the bundle in a highly formalized series of gestures.

In addition to the private mouth-rite, the people seek out a holy-mouth-man once or twice a year. These practitioners have an impressive set of paraphernalia, consisting of a variety of augers, awls, probes, and prods. The use of these objects in the exorcism of the evils of the mouth involves almost unbelievable ritual torture of the client. The holy-mouth-man opens the client's mouth and, using the above mentioned tools, enlarges any holes which decay may have created in the teeth. Magical materials are put into these holes. If there are no naturally occurring holes in the teeth, large sections of one or more teeth are gouged out so that the supernatural substance can be applied. In the client's view, the purpose of these ministrations is to arrest decay and to draw friends. The extremely sacred and traditional character of the rite is evident in the fact that the natives return to the holy-mouth-men year after year, despite the fact that their teeth continue to decay.

It is to be hoped that, when a thorough study of the Nacirema is made, there will be a careful inquiry into the personality structure of these people. One has but to watch the gleam in the eye of a holy-mouth-man, as he jabs an awl into an exposed nerve, to suspect that a certain amount of sadism is involved. If this can be established, a very interesting pattern emerges, for most of the population shows definite masochistic tendencies. It was to these that Professor Linton referred in discussing a distinctive part of the daily body ritual which is performed only by men. This part of the rite involves scraping and lacerating the surface of the face with a sharp instrument. Special women's rites are performed only four times during each lunar month, but what they lack in frequency is made up in barbarity. As part of this ceremony, women bake their heads in small ovens for about an hour. The theoretically interesting point is that what seems to be a preponderantly masochistic people have developed sadistic specialists.

The medicine men have an imposing temple, or *latipso*, in every community of any size. The more elaborate ceremonies required to treat very sick patients can only be performed at this temple. These ceremonies involve not only the thaumaturge but a permanent group of vestal maidens who move sedately about the temple chambers in distinctive costume and headdress.

The *latipso* ceremonies are so harsh that it is phenomenal that a fair proportion of the really sick natives who enter the temple ever recover. Small children whose indoctrination is still incomplete have been known to resist attempts to take them to the temple because "that is where you go to die." Despite this fact, sick adults are not only willing but eager to undergo the protracted ritual purification, if they can afford to do so. No matter how ill the supplicant or how grave the emergency, the guardians of many temples will not admit a client if he cannot give a rich gift to the custodian. Even after one has gained admission and survived the ceremonies, the guardians will not permit the neophyte to leave until he makes still another gift.

The supplicant entering the temple is first stripped of all his or her clothes. In every-day life the Nacirema avoids exposure of his body and its natural functions. Bathing and excretory acts are performed only in the secrecy of the household shrine, where they are ritualized as part of the body-rites. Psychological shock results from the fact that body secrecy is suddenly lost upon entry into the *latipso*. A man, whose own wife has never seen him in an excretory act, suddenly finds himself naked and assisted by a vestal maiden while he performs his natural functions into a sacred vessel. This sort of ceremonial treatment is necessitated by the fact that the excreta are used by a diviner to ascertain the course and nature of the client's sickness. Female clients, on the other hand, find their naked bodies are subjected to the scrutiny, manipulation, and prodding of the medicine men.

Few supplicants in the temple are well enough to do anything but lie on their hard beds. The daily ceremonies, like the rites of the holy-mouth-men, involve discomfort and torture. With ritual precision, the vestals awaken their miserable charges each dawn and roll them about on their beds of pain while performing ablutions, in the formal movements of which the maidens are highly trained. At other times they insert magic wands in the supplicant's mouth or force him to eat substances which are supposed to be healing. From time to time the medicine men come to their clients and jab magically treated needles into their flesh. The fact that these temple ceremonies may not cure, and may even kill the neophyte, in no way decreases the people's faith in the medicine men.

There remains one other kind of practitioner, known as a "listener." This witch-doctor has the power to exorcise the devils that lodge in the heads of people who have been bewitched. The Nacirema believe that parents bewitch their own children. Mothers are particularly suspected of putting a curse on children while teaching them the secret body rituals. The counter-magic of the witch-doctor is unusual in its lack of ritual. The patient simply tells the "listener" all his troubles and fears, beginning with the earliest difficulties he can remember. The memory displayed by the Nacirema in these exorcism sessions is truly remarkable. It is not uncommon for the patient to bemoan the rejection he felt upon being weaned as a babe, and a few individuals even see their troubles going back to the traumatic effects of their own birth.

In conclusion, mention must be made of certain practices which have their base in native esthetics but which depend upon the pervasive aversion to the natural body and its functions. There are ritual fasts to make fat people thin and ceremonial feasts to make thin people fat. Still other rites are used to make women's breasts large if they are small, and smaller if they are large. General dissatisfaction with breast shape is symbolized in the fact that the ideal form is virtually outside the range of human variation. A few women afflicted with almost inhuman hypermammary development are so idolized that they make a handsome living by simply going from village to village and permitting the natives to stare at them for a fee.

Reference has already been made to the fact that excretory functions are ritualized, routinized, and relegated to secrecy. Natural reproductive functions are similarly distorted. Intercourse is taboo as a topic and scheduled as an act. Efforts are made to avoid pregnancy by the use of magical materials or by limiting intercourse to certain phases of the moon. Conception is actually very infrequent. When pregnant, women dress so as to hide their condition. Parturition takes place in secret, without friends or relatives to assist, and the majority of women do not nurse their infants.

Our review of the ritual life of the Nacirema has certainly shown them to be a magic-ridden people. It is hard to understand how they have managed to exist so long under the burdens which they have imposed upon themselves. But even such exotic customs as these take on real meaning when they are viewed with the insight provided by Malinowski when he wrote (1948:70):

> Looking from far and above, from our high places of safety in the developed civilization, it is easy to see all the crudity and irrelevance of magic. But without its power and guidance early man could not have mastered his practical difficulties as he has done, nor could man have advanced to the higher stages of civilization.

References

Linton, Ralph. 1936. *The Study of Man.* New York, D. Appleton-Century Co.

Malinowski, Bronislaw. 1948. *Magic, Science, and Religion.* Glencoe, The Free Press.

Murdock, George P. 1949. *Social Structure.* New York, The Macmillan Co.

From *American Anthropologist*, by Horace Miner, June 1956, pp. 503–507.

Baseball Magic

GEORGE GMELCH

On each pitching day for the first three months of a winning season, Dennis Grossini, a pitcher on a Detroit Tiger farm team, arose from bed at exactly 10:00 A.M. At 1:00 P.M. he went to the nearest restaurant for two glasses of iced tea and a tuna sandwich. Although the afternoon was free, he changed into the sweatshirt and supporter he wore during his last winning game, and, one hour before the game, he chewed a wad of Beech-Nut chewing tobacco. After each pitch during the game he touched the letters on his uniform and straightened his cap after each ball. Before the start of each inning he replaced the pitcher's resin bag next to the spot where it was the inning before. And after every inning in which he gave up a run, he washed his hands.

When asked which part of the ritual was most important, he said, "You can't really tell what's most important so it all becomes important. I'd be afraid to change anything. As long as I'm winning, I do everything the same."

Trobriand Islanders, according to anthropologist Bronislaw Malinowski, felt the same way about their fishing magic. Among the Trobrianders, fishing took two forms: in the *inner lagoon* where fish were plentiful and there was little danger, and on the *open sea* where fishing was dangerous and yields varied widely. Malinowski found that magic was not used in lagoon fishing, where men could rely solely on their knowledge and skill. But when fishing on the open sea, Trobrianders used a great deal of magical ritual to ensure safety and increase their catch.

Baseball, America's national pastime, is an arena in which players behave remarkably like Malinowski's Trobriand fishermen. To professional ballplayers, baseball is more than just a game. It is an occupation. Since their livelihoods depend on how well they perform, many use magic to try to control the chance that is built into baseball. There are three essential activities of the game—pitching, hitting, and fielding. In the first two, chance can play a surprisingly important role. The pitcher is the player least able to control the outcome of his own efforts. He may feel great and have good stuff warming up in the bullpen and then get into the game and not have it. He may make a bad pitch and see the batter miss it for a strike out or see it hit hard but right into the hands of a fielder for an out. His best pitch may be blooped for a base hit. He may limit the opposing team to just a few hits yet lose the game, or he may give up a dozen hits but still win. And the good and bad luck don't

always average out over the course of a season. Some pitchers end the season with poor won-loss records but good earned run averages, and vice versa. For instance, this past season Andy Benes gave up over one run per game more than his teammate Omar Daal but had a better won-loss record. Benes went 14–13, while Daal was only 8–12. Both pitched for the same team—the Arizona Diamondbacks—which meant they had the same fielders behind them. Regardless of how well a pitcher performs, on every outing he depends not only on his own skill, but also upon the proficiency of his teammates, the ineptitude of the opposition, and luck.

Hitting, which many observers call the single most difficult task in the world of sports, is also full of risk and uncertainty. Unless it's a home run, no matter how well the batter hits the ball, fate determines whether it will go into a waiting glove, whistle past a fielder's diving stab, or find a gap in the outfield. The uncertainty is compounded by the low success rate of hitting: the average hitter gets only one hit in every four trips to the plate, while the very best hitters average only one hit every three trips. Fielding, as we will return to later, is the one part of baseball where chance does not play much of a role.

How does the risk and uncertainty in pitching and hitting affect players? How do they try to exercise control over the outcomes of their performance? These are questions that I first became interested in many years ago as both a ballplayer and an anthropology student. I'd devoted much of my youth to baseball, and played professionally as first baseman in the Detroit Tigers organization in the 1960s. It was shortly after the end of one baseball season that I took an anthropology course called "Magic, Religion, and Witchcraft." As I listened to my professor describe the magical rituals of the Trobriand Islanders, it occurred to me that what these so-called "primitive" people did wasn't all that different from what my teammates and I did for luck and confidence at the ball park.

Routines and Rituals

The most common way players attempt to reduce chance and their feelings of uncertainty is to develop and follow a daily routine, a course of action which is regularly followed. Talking about the routines ballplayers follow, Pirates coach Rich Donnelly said:

They're like trained animals. They come out here [ballpark] and everything has to be the same, they don't like anything that knocks them off their routine. Just look at the dugout and you'll see every guy sitting in the same spot every night. It's amazing, everybody in the same spot. And don't you dare take someone's seat. If a guy comes up from the minors and sits here, they'll say, 'Hey, Jim sits here, find another seat.' You watch the pitcher warm up and he'll do the same thing every time. And when you go on the road it's the same way. You've got a routine and you adhere to it and you don't want anybody knocking you off it.

Routines are comforting, they bring order into a world in which players have little control. And sometimes practical elements in routines produce tangible benefits, such as helping the player concentrate. But what players often do goes beyond mere routine. Their actions become what anthropologists define as *ritual*—prescribed behaviors in which there is no empirical connection between the means (e.g., tapping home plate three times) and the desired end (e.g., getting a base hit). Because there is no real connection between the two, rituals are not rational, and sometimes they are actually irrational. Similar to rituals are the nonrational beliefs that form the basis of taboos and fetishes, which players also use to reduce chance and bring luck to their side. But first let's look more closely at rituals.

Most rituals are personal, that is, they're performed by individuals rather than by a team or group. Most are done in an unemotional manner, in much the same way players apply pine tar to their bats to improve the grip or dab eye black on their upper cheeks to reduce the sun's glare. Baseball rituals are infinitely varied. A ballplayer may ritualize any activity—eating, dressing, driving to the ballpark—that he considers important or somehow linked to good performance. For example, Yankee pitcher Denny Neagle goes to a movie on days he is scheduled to start. Pitcher Jason Bere listens to the same song on his Walkman on the days he is to pitch. Jim Ohms puts another penny in the pouch of his supporter after each win. Clanging against the hard plastic genital cup, the pennies made a noise as he ran the bases toward the end of a winning season. Glenn Davis would chew the same gum every day during hitting streaks, saving it under his cap. Infielder Julio Gotay always played with a cheese sandwich in his back pocket (he had a big appetite, so there might also have been a measure of practicality here). Wade Boggs ate chicken before every game during his career, and that was just one of dozens of elements in his pre and post game routine, which also included leaving his house for the ballpark at precisely the same time each day (1:47 for a 7:05 game). Former Oriole pitcher Dennis Martinez would drink a small cup of water after each inning and then place it under the bench upside down, in a line. His teammates could always tell what inning it was by counting the cups.

Many hitters go through a series of preparatory rituals before stepping into the batter's box. These include tugging on their caps, touching their uniform letters or medallions, crossing themselves, tapping or bouncing the bat on the plate, or swinging the weighted warm-up bat a prescribed number of times. Consider Red Sox Nomar Garciaparra. After each pitch he steps out of the batters box, kicks the dirt with each toe, adjusts his right batting glove, adjusts his left batting glove, and touches his helmet before getting back into the box. Mike Hargrove, former Cleveland Indian first baseman, had so many time consuming elements in his batting ritual that he was known as "the human rain delay." Both players believe their batting rituals helped them regain their concentration after each pitch. But others wonder if they have become prisoners of their own superstitions. Also, players who have too many or particularly bizarre rituals risk being labeled as "flakes," and not just by teammates but by fans and media as well. For example, pitcher Turk Wendell's eccentric rituals, which included wearing a necklace of teeth from animals he had killed, made him a cover story in the *New York Times Sunday Magazine.*

Some players, especially Latin Americans, draw upon rituals from their Roman Catholic religion. Some make the sign of the cross or bless themselves before every at bat, and a few like the Rangers' Pudge Rodriguez do so before every pitch. Others, like the Detroit Tiger Juan Gonzalez, also visibly wear religious medallions around their necks, while some tuck them discretely inside their undershirts.

One ritual associated with hitting is tagging a base when leaving and returning to the dugout between innings. Some players don't "feel right" unless they tag a specific base on each trip between the dugout and the field. One of my teammates added some complexity to his ritual by tagging third base on his way to the dugout only after the third, sixth, and ninth innings. Asked if he ever purposely failed to step on the bag, he replied, "Never! I wouldn't dare. It would destroy my confidence to hit." Baseball fans observe a lot of this ritual behavior, such as fielders tagging bases, pitchers tugging on their caps or touching the resin bag after each bad pitch, or smoothing the dirt on the mound before each new batter or inning, never realizing the importance of these actions to the player. The one ritual many fans do recognize, largely because it's a favorite of TV cameramen, is the "rally cap"—players in the dugout folding their caps and wearing them bill up in hopes of sparking a rally.

Most rituals grow out of exceptionally good performances. When a player does well, he seldom attributes his success to skill alone. He knows that his skills were essentially the same the night before. He asks himself, "What was different about today which explains my three hits?" He decides to repeat what he did today in an attempt to bring more good luck. And so he attributes his success, in part, to an object, a food he ate, not having shaved, a new shirt he bought that day, or just about any behavior out of the ordinary. By repeating that behavior, he seeks to gain control over his performance. Outfielder John White explained how one of his rituals started:

I was jogging out to centerfield after the national anthem when I picked up a scrap of paper. I got some good hits that night and I guess I decided that the paper had something to do with it. The next night I picked up a gum wrapper and had another good night at the plate . . . I've been picking up paper every night since.

Outfielder Ron Wright of the Calgary Cannons shaves his arms once a week and plans to continue doing so until he has a bad year. It all began two years before when after an injury he shaved his arm so it could be taped, and proceeded to hit three homers over the next few games. Now he not only has one of the smoothest swings in the minor leagues, but two of the smoothest forearms. Wade Boggs' routine of eating chicken before every game began when he was a rookie in 1982. He noticed a correlation between multiple hit games and poultry plates (his wife has over 40 chicken recipes). One of Montreal Expos farmhand Mike Saccocio's rituals also concerned food, "I got three hits one night after eating at Long John Silver's. After that when we'd pull into town, my first question would be, "Do you have a Long John Silver's?" Unlike Boggs, Saccocio abandoned his ritual and looked for a new one when he stopped hitting well.

When in a slump, most players make a deliberate effort to change their rituals and routines in an attempt to shake off their bad luck. One player tried taking different routes to the ballpark; several players reported trying different combinations of tagging and not tagging particular bases in an attempt to find a successful combination. I had one manager who would rattle the bat bin when the team was not hitting well, as if the bats were in a stupor and could be aroused by a good shaking. Similarly, I have seen hitters rub their hands along the handles of the bats protruding from the bin in hopes of picking up some power or luck from bats that are getting hits for their owners. Some players switch from wearing their contact lenses to glasses. Brett Mandel described his Pioneer League team, the Ogden Raptors, trying to break a losing streak by using a new formation for their pre-game stretching.[1]

Taboo

Taboos are the opposite of rituals. The word taboo comes from a Polynesian term meaning prohibition. Breaking a taboo, players believe, leads to undesirable consequences or bad luck. Most players observe at least a few taboos, such as never stepping on the white foul lines. A few, like the Mets Turk Wendell and Red Sox Nomar Garciaparra, leap over the entire basepath. One teammate of mine would never watch a movie on a game day, despite the fact that we played nearly every day from April to September. Another teammate refused to read anything before a game because he believed it weakened his batting eye.

Many taboos take place off the field, out of public view. On the day a pitcher is scheduled to start, he is likely to avoid activities he believes will sap his strength and detract from his effectiveness. Some pitchers avoid eating certain foods, others will not shave on the day of a game, refusing to shave again as long as they are winning. Early in the 1989 season Oakland's Dave Stewart had six consecutive victories and a beard by the time he lost.

Taboos usually grow out of exceptionally poor performances, which players, in search of a reason, attribute to a particular behavior. During my first season of pro ball I ate pancakes before a game in which I struck out three times. A few weeks later I had another terrible game, again after eating pancakes.

The result was a pancake taboo: I never again ate pancakes during the season. Pitcher Jason Bere has a taboo that makes more sense in dietary terms: after eating a meatball sandwich and not pitching well, he swore off them for the rest of the season.

While most taboos are idiosyncratic, there are a few that all ball players hold and that do not develop out of individual experience or misfortune. These form part of the culture of baseball, and are sometimes learned as early as Little League. Mentioning a no-hitter while one is in progress is a well-known example. It is believed that if a pitcher hears the words "no-hitter," the spell accounting for this hard to achieve feat will be broken and the no-hitter lost. This taboo is also observed by many sports broadcasters, who use various linguistic subterfuges to inform their listeners that the pitcher has not given up a hit, never saying "no-hitter."

Fetishes

Fetishes or charms are material objects believed to embody "supernatural" power that can aid or protect the owner. Good luck charms are standard equipment for some ballplayers. These include a wide assortment of objects from coins, chains, and crucifixes to a favorite baseball hat. The fetishized object may be a new possession or something a player found that happens to coincide with the start of a streak and which he holds responsible for his good fortune. While playing in the Pacific Coast League, Alan Foster forgot his baseball shoes on a road trip and borrowed a pair from a teammate. That night he pitched a no-hitter, which he attributed to the shoes. Afterwards he bought them from his teammate and they became a fetish. Expo farmhand Mark LaRosa's rock has a different origin and use:

> I found it on the field in Elmira after I had gotten bombed. It's unusual, perfectly round, and it caught my attention. I keep it to remind me of how important it is to concentrate. When I am going well I look at the rock and remember to keep my focus, the rock reminds me of what can happen when I lose my concentration.

For one season Marge Schott, former owner of the Cincinnati Reds, insisted that her field manager rub her St. Bernard "Schotzie" for good luck before each game. When the Reds were on the road, Schott would sometimes send a bag of the dog's hair to the field manager's hotel room.

During World War II, American soldiers used fetishes in much the same way. Social psychologist Samuel Stouffer and his colleagues found that in the face of great danger and uncertainty, soldiers developed magical practices, particularly the use of protective amulets and good luck charms (crosses, Bibles, rabbits' feet, medals), and jealously guarded articles of clothing they associated with past experiences of escape from danger.[2] Stouffer also found that prebattle preparations were carried out in fixed ritual-like order, similar to ballplayers preparing for a game.

Uniform numbers have special significance for some players who request their lucky number. Since the choice is usually limited, they try to at least get a uniform that contains their lucky number, such as 14, 24, 34, or 44 for the player whose lucky number is four. When Ricky Henderson came to the Blue Jays in 1993 he paid outfielder Turner Ward $25,000 for the right to wear number 24. Oddly enough, there is no consensus about the effect of wearing number 13. Some players will not wear it, others will, and a few request it. Number preferences emerge in different ways. A young player may request the number of a former star, hoping that—through what anthropologists call *imitative* magic—it will bring him the same success. Or he may request a number he associates with good luck. While with the Oakland A's Vida Blue changed his uniform number from 35 to 14, the number he wore as a high-school quarterback. When 14 did not produce better pitching performance, he switched back to 35. Former San Diego Padre first baseman Jack Clark changed his number from 25 to 00, hoping to break out of a slump. That day he got four hits in a double header, but also hurt his back. Then, three days later, he was hit in the cheekbone by a ball thrown in batting practice.

Colorado Rockies Larry Walker's fixation with the number three has become well known to baseball fans. Besides wearing 33, he takes three practice swings before stepping into the box, he showers from the third nozzle, sets his alarm for three minutes past the hour and he was wed on November 3 at 3:33 P.M. Fans in ballparks all across America rise from their seats for the seventh inning stretch before the home club comes to bat because the number seven is lucky, although the origin of this tradition has been lost.

Clothing, both the choice and the order in which they are put on, combine elements of both ritual and fetish. Some players put on their uniform in a ritualized order. Expos farmhand Jim Austin always puts on his left sleeve, left pants leg, and left shoe before the right. Most players, however, single out one or two lucky articles or quirks of dress for ritual elaboration. After hitting two home runs in a game, for example, ex-Giant infielder Jim Davenport discovered that he had missed a buttonhole while dressing for the game. For the remainder of his career he left the same button undone. For outfielder Brian Hunter the focus is shoes, "I have a pair of high tops and a pair of low tops. Whichever shoes don't get a hit that game, I switch to the other pair." At the time of our interview, he was struggling at the plate and switching shoes almost every day. For Birmingham Baron pitcher Bo Kennedy the arrangement of the different pairs of baseball shoes in his locker is critical:

I tell the clubies [clubhouse boys] when you hang stuff in my locker don't touch my shoes. If you bump them move them back. I want the Pony's in front, the turfs to the right, and I want them nice and neat with each pair touching each other. . . . Everyone on the team knows not to mess with my shoes when I pitch.

During streaks—hitting or winning—players may wear the same clothes day after day. Once I changed sweatshirts midway through the game for seven consecutive nights to keep a hitting streak going. Clothing rituals, however, can become impractical. Catcher Matt Allen was wearing a long sleeve turtle neck shirt on a cool evening in the New York-Penn League when he had a three-hit game. "I kept wearing the shirt and had a good week," he explained. "Then the weather got hot as hell, 85 degrees and muggy, but I would not take that shirt off. I wore it for another ten days—catching—and people thought I was crazy." Also taking a ritual to the extreme, Leo Durocher, managing the Brooklyn Dodgers to a pennant in 1941, is said to have spent three and a half weeks in the same gray slacks, blue coat, and knitted blue tie. During a 16-game winning streak, the 1954 New York Giants wore the same clothes in each game and refused to let them be cleaned for fear that their good fortune might be washed away with the dirt. Losing often produces the opposite effect. Several Oakland A's players, for example, went out and bought new street clothes in an attempt to break a fourteen-game losing streak.

Baseball's superstitions, like most everything else, change over time. Many of the rituals and beliefs of early baseball are no longer observed. In the 1920s and 1930s sportswriters reported that a player who tripped en route to the field would often retrace his steps and carefully walk over the stumbling block for "insurance." A century ago players spent time on and off the field intently looking for items that would bring them luck. To find a hairpin on the street, for example, assured a batter of hitting safely in that day's game. Today few women wear hairpins—a good reason the belief has died out. To catch sight of a white horse or a wagon-load of barrels were also good omens. In 1904 the manager of the New York Giants, John McGraw, hired a driver with a team of white horses to drive past the Polo Grounds around the time his players were arriving at the ballpark. He knew that if his players saw white horses, they'd have more confidence and that could only help them during the game. Belief in the power of white horses survived in a few backwaters until the 1960s. A gray haired manager of a team I played for in Drummondville, Quebec, would drive around the countryside before important games and during the playoffs looking for a white horse. When he was successful, he would announce it to everyone in the clubhouse.

One belief that appears to have died out recently is a taboo about crossed bats. Some of my Latino teammates in the 1960s took it seriously. I can still recall one Dominican player becoming agitated when another player tossed a bat from the batting cage and it landed on top of his bat. He believed that the top bat might steal hits from the lower one. In his view, bats contained a finite number of hits, a sort of baseball "image of limited good." It was once commonly believed that when the hits in a bat were used up no amount of good hitting would produce any more. Hall of Famer Honus Wagner believed each bat contained only 100 hits. Regardless of the quality of the bat, he would discard it after its 100th hit. This belief would have little relevance today, in the era of light bats with thin handles—so thin that the typical modern bat is lucky to survive a dozen hits without being broken. Other superstitions about bats do survive, however. Position players on the Class A Asheville Tourists, for example, would not let pitchers touch or swing their bats, not even to warm up. Poor-hitting players, as most pitchers are, were said to pollute or weaken the bats.

Uncertainty and Magic

The best evidence that players turn to rituals, taboos, and fetishes to control chance and uncertainty is found in their uneven application. They are associated mainly with pitching and hitting—the activities with the highest degree of chance—and not fielding. I met only one player who had any ritual in connection with fielding, and he was an error prone shortstop. Unlike hitting and pitching, a fielder has almost complete control over the outcome of his performance. Once a ball has been hit in his direction, no one can intervene and ruin his chances of catching it for an out (except in the unlikely event of two fielders colliding). Compared with the pitcher or the hitter, the fielder has little to worry about. He knows that, in better than 9.7 times out of 10, he will execute his task flawlessly. With odds like that there is little need for ritual.

Clearly, the rituals of American ballplayers are not unlike that of the Trobriand Islanders studied by Malinowski many years ago.[3] In professional baseball, fielding is the equivalent of the inner lagoon while hitting and pitching are like the open sea.

While Malinowski helps us understand how ballplayers respond to chance and uncertainty, behavioral psychologist B. F. Skinner sheds light on why personal rituals get established in the first place.[4] With a few grains of seed Skinner could get pigeons to do anything he wanted. He merely waited for the desired behavior (e.g., pecking) and then rewarded it with some food. Skinner then decided to see what would happen if pigeons were rewarded with food pellets regularly, every fifteen seconds, regardless of what they did. He found that the birds associate the arrival of the food with a particular action, such as tucking their head under a wing or walking in clockwise circles. About ten seconds after the arrival of the last pellet, a bird would begin doing whatever it associated with getting the food and keep doing it until the next pellet arrived. In short, the pigeons behaved as if their actions made the food appear. They learned to associate particular behaviors with the reward of being given seed.

Ballplayers also associate a reward—successful performance—with prior behavior. If a player touches his crucifix and then gets a hit, he may decide the gesture was responsible for his good fortune and touch his crucifix the next time he comes to the plate. If he gets another hit, the chances are good that he will touch his crucifix each time he bats. Unlike pigeons, however, most ballplayers are quicker to change their rituals once they no longer seem to work. Skinner found that once a pigeon associated one of its actions with the arrival of food or water, only sporadic rewards were necessary to keep the ritual going. One pigeon, believing that hopping from side to side brought pellets into its feeding cup, hopped ten thousand times without a pellet before finally giving up. But, then, didn't Wade Boggs eat chicken before every game, through slumps and good times, for seventeen years?

Obviously the rituals and superstitions of baseball do not make a pitch travel faster or a batted ball find the gaps between the fielders, nor do the Trobriand rituals calm the seas or bring fish. What both do, however, is give their practitioners a sense of control, with that added confidence, at no cost. And we all know how important that is. If you really believe eating chicken or hopping over the foul lines will make you a better hitter, it probably will.

Bibliography

Malinowski, B. *Magic, Science and Religion and Other Essays* (Glencoe, Ill., 1948).

Mandel, Brett. *Minor Players, Major Dreams.* Lincoln, Nebraska: University of Nebraska Press, 1997.

Skinner, B.F. *Behavior of Organisms: An Experimental Analysis* (D. Appleton-Century Co., 1938).

Skinner, B.F. *Science and Human Behavior* (New York: Macmillan, 1953).

Stouffer, Samuel. *The American Soldier.* New York: J. Wiley, 1965.

Torrez, Danielle Gagnon. *High Inside: Memoirs of a Baseball Wife.* New York: G.P. Putnam's Sons, 1983.

Notes

1. Mandel, *Minor Players, Major Dreams,* 156.
2. Stouffer, *The American Soldier.*
3. Malinowski, B. *Magic, Science and Religion and Other Essays.*
4. Skinner, B.F. *Behavior of Organisms: An Experimental Analysis.*

Department of Anthropology, Union College; e-mail gmelchg@union.edu

Revised version of "Superstition and Ritual in American Baseball," from *Elysian Fields Quarterly,* Vol. 11, No. 3, 1992, pp. 25–36. Copyright © 2000 George Gmelch. Reprinted by permission of George Gmelch.

UNIT 7

Sociocultural Change: The Impact of the West

Unit Selections

Key Points to Consider

- What is a subsistence system? What have been the effects of colonialism on formerly subsistence-oriented socioeconomic systems?

- How do cash crops inevitably lead to class distinctions and poverty?

- What ethical obligations do you think industrial societies have toward respecting the human rights and cultural diversity of traditional communities?

- If the Aztecs did not think of the Spanish Conquistadores as Gods, what did they really think of them?

- Are the disparities of wealth and power in the world fair?

- What should your nation's policy be towards genocidal practices in other countries?

- How has indigenous exploitation persisted in Africa even with political independence?

- Should the biodiversity of game parks in Ethiopia be under corporate management or indigenous control?

- Can Minority Languages Be Saved?

Student Web Site

www.mhcls.com/online

Internet References

Further information regarding these Web sites may be found in this book's preface or online.

Human Rights and Humanitarian Assistance
http://www.etown.edu/vl/humrts.html

The Indigenous Rights Movement in the Pacific
http://www.inmotionmagazine.com/pacific.html

RomNews Network—Online
http://www.romnews.com/community/index.php

WWW Virtual Library: Indigenous Studies
http://www.cwis.org/wwwvl/indig-vl.html

Courtesy of Robert Buss

The origins of academic anthropology lie in the colonial and imperial ventures of the past five hundred years. During this period, many people of the world were brought into a relationship with Europe and the United States that was usually exploitative and often socially and culturally disruptive. For over a century, anthropologists have witnessed this process and the transformations that have taken place in those social and cultural systems brought under the umbrella of a world economic order. Early anthropological studies—even those widely regarded as pure research—directly or indirectly served colonial interests. Many anthropologists certainly believed that they were extending the benefits of Western technology and society while preserving the cultural rights of those people whom they studied. But representatives of poor nations challenge this view, and are far less generous in describing the past role of the anthropologist. Most contemporary anthropologists, however, have a deep moral commitment to defending the legal, political, and economic rights of the people with whom they work.

When anthropologists discuss social change, they usually mean change brought about in pre-industrial societies through long-standing interaction with the nation-states of the industrialized world. In early anthropology, contact between the West and the remainder of the world was characterized by the terms "acculturation" and "culture contact." These terms were used to describe the diffusion of cultural traits between the developed and the less-developed countries. Often this was analyzed as a one-way process in which cultures of the less developed world were seen, for better or worse, as receptacles for Western cultural traits. Nowadays, many anthropologists believe that the diffusion of cultural traits across social, political, and economic boundaries was emphasized at the expense of the real issues of dominance, subordinance, and dependence that characterized the colonial experience. Just as important, many anthropologists recognize that the present-day forms of cultural, economic, and political interaction between the developed and the so-called underdeveloped world are best characterized as neo-colonial.

Most of the authors represented in this unit take the perspective that anthropology should be critical as well as descriptive. They raise questions about cultural contact and subsequent economic and social disruption.

In keeping with the notion that the negative impact of the West on traditional cultures began with colonial domination, this unit opens with "Why Can't People Feed Themselves?" and includes "The Arrow of Disease." Continuing with "The Price of Progress," we see that "progress" for the West has often meant poverty, hunger, disease, and death for traditional peoples.

Even the widely disseminated narrative account of the Conquest of Mexico, says Camilla Townsend ("Burying the White Gods: New Perspectives on the Conquest of Mexico), was nothing more than a dehumanizing fabrication—a convenient explanation that ignored the facts.

Of course, traditional peoples are not the only losers in the process of cultural destruction. In "The Battle for Cattle" and "Rangers by Birth," we learn that the more we deprive the traditional stewards (the indigenous peoples) of their land, the greater the loss in overall biodiversity. And if we don't acknowledge native peoples' intellectual property rights to therapeutic plant materials (See "Digging Into the Roots of Research Ethics."), we may lose that as well. All of humanity stands to suffer as a vast store of human knowledge—embodied in tribal subsistence practices, language, medicine, and folklore—is obliterated, in a manner not unlike the burning of the library of Alexandria 1,600 years ago. We can only hope that it is not too late to save what is left.

Why Can't People Feed Themselves?

FRANCES MOORE LAPPÉ AND JOSEPH COLLINS

Question: You have said that the hunger problem is not the result of overpopulation. But you have not yet answered the most basic and simple question of all: Why can't people feed themselves? As Senator Daniel P. Moynihan put it bluntly, when addressing himself to the Third World, "Food growing is the first thing you do when you come down out of the trees. The question is, how come the United States can grow food and you can't?"

Our Response: In the very first speech I, Frances, ever gave after writing *Diet for a Small Planet,* I tried to take my audience along the path that I had taken in attempting to understand why so many are hungry in this world. Here is the gist of that talk that was, in truth, a turning point in my life:

When I started I saw a world divided into two parts: a *minority* of nations that had "taken off" through their agricultural and industrial revolutions to reach a level of unparalleled material abundance and a *majority* that remained behind in a primitive, traditional, undeveloped state. This lagging behind of the majority of the world's peoples must be due, I thought, to some internal deficiency or even to several of them. It seemed obvious that the underdeveloped countries must be deficient in natural resources—particularly good land and climate—and in cultural development, including modern attitudes conducive to work and progress.

But when looking for the historical roots of the predicament, I learned that my picture of these two separate worlds was quite false. My two separate worlds were really just different sides of the same coin. One side was on top largely because the other side was on the bottom. Could this be true? How were these separate worlds related?

Colonialism appeared to me to be the link. Colonialism destroyed the cultural patterns of production and exchange by which traditional societies in "underdeveloped" countries previously had met the needs of the people. Many precolonial social structures, while dominated by exploitative elites, had evolved a system of mutual obligations among the classes that helped to ensure at least a minimal diet for all. A friend of mine once said: "Precolonial village existence in subsistence agriculture was a limited life indeed, but it's certainly not Calcutta." The misery of starvation in the streets of Calcutta can only be understood as the end-point of a long historical process—one that has destroyed a traditional social system.

"Underdeveloped," instead of being an adjective that evokes the picture of a static society, became for me a verb (to "underdevelop") meaning the *process* by which the minority of the world has transformed—indeed often robbed and degraded—the majority.

That was in 1972. I clearly recall my thoughts on my return home. I had stated publicly for the first time a world view that had taken me years of study to grasp. The sense of relief was tremendous. For me the breakthrough lay in realizing that today's "hunger crisis" could not be described in static, descriptive terms. Hunger and underdevelopment must always be thought of as a *process*.

To answer the question "why hunger?" it is counterproductive to simply *describe* the conditions in an underdeveloped country today. For these conditions, whether they be the degree of malnutrition, the levels of agricultural production, or even the country's ecological endowment, are not static factors—they are not "givens." They are rather the *results* of an ongoing historical process. As we dug ever deeper into that historical process for the preparation of this book, we began to discover the existence of scarcity-creating mechanisms that we had only vaguely intuited before.

We have gotten great satisfaction from probing into the past since we recognized it is the only way to approach a solution to hunger today. We have come to see that it is the *force* creating the condition, not the condition itself, that must be the target of change. Otherwise we might change the condition today, only to find tomorrow that it has been recreated—with a vengeance.

Asking the question "Why can't people feed themselves?" carries a sense of bewilderment that there are so many people in the world not able to feed themselves adequately. What astonished us, however, is that there are not *more* people in the world who are hungry—considering the weight of the centuries of effort by the few to undermine the capacity of the majority to feed themselves. No, we are not crying "conspiracy!" If these forces were entirely conspiratorial, they would be easier to detect and many more people would by now have risen up to resist. We are talking about something more subtle and insidious; a heritage of a colonial order in which people with the advantage of considerable power sought their own self-interest, often arrogantly believing they were acting in the interest of the people whose lives they were destroying.

The Colonial Mind

The colonizer viewed agriculture in the subjugated lands as primitive and backward. Yet such a view contrasts sharply with documents from the colonial period now coming to light. For example, A. J. Voelker, a British agricultural scientist assigned to India during the 1890s wrote:

> Nowhere would one find better instances of keeping land scrupulously clean from weeds, of ingenuity in device of water-raising appliances, of knowledge of soils and their capabilities, as well as of the exact time to sow and reap, as one would find in Indian agriculture. It is wonderful too, how much is known of rotation, the system of "mixed crops" and of fallowing. . . . I, at least, have never seen a more perfect picture of cultivation."[1]

None the less, viewing the agriculture of the vanquished as primitive and backward reinforced the colonizer's rationale for destroying it. To the colonizers of Africa, Asia, and Latin America, agriculture became merely a means to extract wealth—much as gold from a mine—on behalf of the colonizing power. Agriculture was no longer seen as a source of food for the local population, nor even as their livelihood. Indeed the English economist John Stuart Mill reasoned that colonies should not be thought of as civilizations or countries at all but as "agricultural establishments" whose sole purpose was to supply the "larger community to which they belong." The colonized society's agriculture was only a subdivision of the agricultural system of the metropolitan country. As Mill acknowledged, "Our West India colonies, for example, cannot be regarded as countries. . . . The West Indies are the place where England *finds it convenient* to carry on the production of sugar, coffee and a few other tropical commodities."[2]

Prior to European intervention, Africans practiced a diversified agriculture that included the introduction of new food plants of Asian or American origin. But colonial rule simplified this diversified production to single cash crops—often to the exclusion of staple foods—and in the process sowed the seeds of famine.[3] Rice farming once had been common in Gambia. But with colonial rule so much of the best land was taken over by peanuts (grown for the European market) that rice had to be imported to counter the mounting prospect of famine. Northern Ghana, once famous for its yams and other foodstuffs, was forced to concentrate solely on cocoa. Most of the Gold Coast thus became dependent on cocoa. Liberia was turned into a virtual plantation subsidiary of Firestone Tire and Rubber. Food production in Dahomey and southeast Nigeria was all but abandoned in favor of palm oil; Tanganyika (now Tanzania) was forced to focus on sisal and Uganda on cotton.

The same happened in Indochina. About the time of the American Civil War the French decided that the Mekong Delta in Vietnam would be ideal for producing rice for export. Through a production system based on enriching the large landowners,

Vietnam became the world's third largest exporter of rice by the 1930s; yet many landless Vietnamese went hungry.[4]

Rather than helping the peasants, colonialism's public works programs only reinforced export crop production. British irrigation works built in nineteenth-century India did help increase production, but the expansion was for spring export crops at the expense of millets and legumes grown in the fall as the basic local food crops.

Because people living on the land do not easily go against their natural and adaptive drive to grow food for themselves, colonial powers had to force the production of cash crops. The first strategy was to use physical or economic force to get the local population to grow cash crops instead of food on their own plots and then turn them over to the colonizer for export. The second strategy was the direct takeover of the land by large-scale plantations growing crops for export.

Forced Peasant Production

As Walter Rodney recounts in *How Europe Underdeveloped Africa,* cash crops were often grown literally under threat of guns and whips.[5] One visitor to the Sahel commented in 1928: "Cotton is an artificial crop and one the value of which is not entirely clear to the natives . . . " He wryly noted the "enforced enthusiasm with which the natives . . . have thrown themselves into . . . planting cotton."[6] The forced cultivation of cotton was a major grievance leading to the Maji Maji wars in Tanzania (then Tanganyika) and behind the nationalist revolt in Angola as late as 1960.[7]

Although raw force was used, taxation was the preferred colonial technique to force Africans to grow cash crops. The colonial administrations simply levied taxes on cattle, land, houses, and even the people themselves. Since the tax had to be paid in the coin of the realm, the peasants had either to grow crops to sell or to work on the plantations or in the mines of the Europeans.[8] Taxation was both an effective tool to "stimulate" cash cropping and a source of revenue that the colonial bureaucracy needed to enforce the system. To expand their production of export crops to pay the mounting taxes, peasant producers were forced to neglect the farming of food crops. In 1830, the Dutch administration in Java made the peasants an offer they could not refuse; if they would grow government-owned export crops on one fifth of their land, the Dutch would remit their land taxes.[9] If they refused and thus could not pay the taxes, they lost their land.

Marketing boards emerged in Africa in the 1930s as another technique for getting the profit from cash crop production by native producers into the hands of the colonial government and international firms. Purchases by the marketing boards were well below the world market price. Peanuts bought by the boards from peasant cultivators in West Africa were sold in Britain for more than *seven times* what the peasants received.[10]

The marketing board concept was born with the "cocoa hold-up" in the Gold Coast in 1937. Small cocoa farmers refused to sell to the large cocoa concerns like United Africa Company (a subsidiary of the Anglo-Dutch firm, Unilever—which we know as Lever Brothers) and Cadbury until they got a higher price. When the British government stepped in and agreed to buy the cocoa directly in place of the big business concerns, the smallholders must have thought they had scored at least a minor victory. But had they really? The following year the British formally set up the West African Cocoa Control Board. Theoretically, its purpose was to pay the peasants a reasonable price for their crops. In practice, however, the board, as sole purchaser, was able to hold down the prices paid the peasants for their crops when the world prices were rising. Rodney sums up the real "victory":

> None of the benefits went to Africans, but rather to the British government itself and to the private companies. . . . Big companies like the United African Company and John Holt were given . . . quotas to fulfill on behalf of the boards. As agents of the government, they were no longer exposed to direct attack, and their profits were secure.[11]

These marketing boards, set up for most export crops, were actually controlled by the companies. The chairman of the Cocoa Board was none other than John Cadbury of Cadbury Brothers (ever had a Cadbury chocolate bar?) who was part of a buying pool exploiting West African cocoa farmers.

The marketing boards funneled part of the profits from the exploitation of peasant producers indirectly into the royal treasury. While the Cocoa Board sold to the British Food Ministry at low prices, the ministry upped the price for British manufacturers, thus netting a profit as high as 11 million pounds in some years.[12]

These marketing boards of Africa were only the institutionalized rendition of what is the essence of colonialism—the extraction of wealth. While profits continued to accrue to foreign interests and local elites, prices received by those actually growing the commodities remained low.

Plantations

A second approach was direct takeover of the land either by the colonizing government or by private foreign interests. Previously self-provisioning farmers were forced to cultivate the plantation fields through either enslavement or economic coercion.

After the conquest of the Kandyan Kingdom (in present day Sri Lanka), in 1815, the British designated all the vast central part of the island as crown land. When it was determined that coffee, a profitable export crop, could be grown there, the Kandyan lands were sold off to British investors and planters at a mere five shillings per acre, the government even defraying the cost of surveying and road building.[13]

Java is also a prime example of a colonial government seizing territory and then putting it into private foreign hands. In 1870, the Dutch declared all uncultivated land—called waste land—property of the state for lease to Dutch plantation enterprises. In addition, the Agrarian Land Law of 1870 authorized foreign companies to lease village-owned land. The peasants, in chronic need of ready cash for taxes and foreign consumer goods, were only too willing to lease their land to the foreign companies for very modest sums and under terms dictated by

the firms. Where land was still held communally, the village headman was tempted by high cash commissions offered by plantation companies. He would lease the village land even more cheaply than would the individual peasant or, as was frequently the case, sell out the entire village to the company.[14]

The introduction of the plantation meant the divorce of agriculture from nourishment, as the notion of food value was lost to the overriding claim of "market value" in international trade. Crops such as sugar, tobacco, and coffee were selected, not on the basis of how well they feed people, but for their high price value relative to their weight and bulk so that profit margins could be maintained even after the costs of shipping to Europe.

Suppressing Peasant Farming

The stagnation and impoverishment of the peasant food-producing sector was not the mere by-product of benign neglect, that is, the unintended consequence of an overemphasis on export production. Plantations—just like modern "agro-industrial complexes"—needed an abundant and readily available supply of low-wage agricultural workers. Colonial administrations thus devised a variety of tactics, all to undercut self-provisioning agriculture and thus make rural populations dependent on plantation wages. Government services and even the most minimal infrastructure (access to water, roads, seeds, credit, pest and disease control information, and so on) were systematically denied. Plantations usurped most of the good land, either making much of the rural population landless or pushing them onto marginal soils. (Yet the plantations have often held much of their land idle simply to prevent the peasants from using it—even to this day. Del Monte owns 57,000 acres of Guatemala but plants only 9000. The rest lies idle except for a few thousand head of grazing cattle.)[15]

In some cases a colonial administration would go even further to guarantee itself a labor supply. In at least twelve countries in the eastern and southern parts of Africa the exploitation of mineral wealth (gold, diamonds, and copper) and the establishment of cash-crop plantations demanded a continuous supply of low-cost labor. To assure this labor supply, colonial administrations simply expropriated the land of the African communities by violence and drove the people into small reserves.[16] With neither adequate land for their traditional slash-and-burn methods nor access to the means—tools, water, and fertilizer—to make continuous farming of such limited areas viable, the indigenous population could scarcely meet subsistence needs, much less produce surplus to sell in order to cover the colonial taxes. Hundreds of thousands of Africans were forced to become the cheap labor source so "needed" by the colonial plantations. Only by laboring on plantations and in the mines could they hope to pay the colonial taxes.

The tax scheme to produce reserves of cheap plantation and mining labor was particularly effective when the Great Depression hit and the bottom dropped out of cash crop economies. In 1929 the cotton market collapsed, leaving peasant cotton producers, such as those in Upper Volta, unable to pay their colonial taxes. More and more young people, in some years as many as

80,000, were thus forced to migrate to the Gold Coast to compete with each other for low-wage jobs on cocoa plantations.[17]

The forced migration of Africa's most able-bodied workers—stripping village food farming of needed hands—was a recurring feature of colonialism. As late as 1973 the Portuguese "exported" 400,000 Mozambican peasants to work in South Africa in exchange for gold deposited in the Lisbon treasury.

The many techniques of colonialism to undercut self-provisioning agriculture in order to ensure a cheap labor supply are no better illustrated than by the story of how, in the mid-nineteenth century, sugar plantation owners in British Guiana coped with the double blow of the emancipation of slaves and the crash in the world sugar market. The story is graphically recounted by Alan Adamson in *Sugar without Slaves.*[18]

Would the ex-slaves be allowed to take over the plantation land and grow the food they needed? The planters, many ruined by the sugar slump, were determined they would not. The planter-dominated government devised several schemes for thwarting food self-sufficiency. The price of crown land was kept artificially high, and the purchase of land in parcels smaller than 100 acres was outlawed—two measures guaranteeing that newly organized ex-slave cooperatives could not hope to gain access to much land. The government also prohibited cultivation on as much as 400,000 acres—on the grounds of "uncertain property titles." Moreover, although many planters held part of their land out of sugar production due to the depressed world price, they would not allow any alternative production on them. They feared that once the ex-slaves started growing food it would be difficult to return them to sugar production when world market prices began to recover. In addition, the government taxed peasant production, then turned around and used the funds to subsidize the immigration of laborers from India and Malaysia to replace the freed slaves, thereby making sugar production again profitable for the planters. Finally, the government neglected the infrastructure for subsistence agriculture and denied credit for small farmers.

Perhaps the most insidious tactic to "lure" the peasant away from food production—and the one with profound historical consequences—was a policy of keeping the price of imported food low through the removal of tariffs and subsidies. The policy was double-edged: first, peasants were told they need not grow food because they could always buy it cheaply with their plantation wages; second, cheap food imports destroyed the market for domestic food and thereby impoverished local food producers.

Adamson relates how both the Governor of British Guiana and the Secretary for the Colonies Earl Grey favored low duties on imports in order to erode local food production and thereby release labor for the plantations. In 1851 the governor rushed through a reduction of the duty on cereals in order to "divert" labor to the sugar estates. As Adamson comments, "Without realizing it, he [the governor] had put his finger on the most mordant feature of monoculture: . . . its convulsive need to destroy any other sector of the economy which might compete for 'its' labor."[19]

Many colonial governments succeeded in establishing dependence on imported foodstuffs. In 1647 an observer in the West Indies wrote to Governor Winthrop of Massachusetts: "Men are so intent upon planting sugar that they had rather buy food at very dear rates than produce it by labour, so infinite is the profitt of sugar workes. . . ."[20] By 1770, the West Indies were importing most of the continental colonies' exports of dried fish, grain, beans, and vegetables. A dependence on imported food made the West Indian colonies vulnerable to any disruption in supply. This dependence on imported food stuffs spelled disaster when the thirteen continental colonies gained independence and food exports from the continent to the West Indies were interrupted. With no diversified food system to fall back on, 15,000 plantation workers died of famine between 1780 and 1787 in Jamaica alone.[21] The dependence of the West Indies on imported food persists to this day.

Suppressing Peasant Competition

We have talked about the techniques by which indigenous populations were forced to cultivate cash crops. In some countries with large plantations, however, colonial governments found it necessary to *prevent* peasants from independently growing cash crops not out of concern for their welfare, but so that they would not compete with colonial interests growing the same crop. For peasant farmers, given a modicum of opportunity, proved themselves capable of outproducing the large plantations not only in terms of output per unit of land but, more important, in terms of capital cost per unit produced.

In the Dutch East Indies (Indonesia and Dutch New Guinea) colonial policy in the middle of the nineteenth century forbade the sugar refineries to buy sugar cane from indigenous growers and imposed a discriminatory tax on rubber produced by native smallholders.[22] A recent unpublished United Nations study of agricultural development in Africa concluded that large-scale agricultural operations owned and controlled by foreign commercial interests (such as the rubber plantations of Liberia, the sisal estates of Tanganyika [Tanzania], and the coffee estates of Angola) only survived the competition of peasant producers because "the authorities actively supported them by suppressing indigenous rural development."[23]

The suppression of indigenous agricultural development served the interests of the colonizing powers in two ways. Not only did it prevent direct competition from more efficient native producers of the same crops, but it also guaranteed a labor force to work on the foreign-owned estates. Planters and foreign investors were not unaware that peasants who could survive economically by their own production would be under less pressure to sell their labor cheaply to the large estates.

The answer to the question, then, "Why can't people feed themselves?" must begin with an understanding of how colonialism actively prevented people from doing just that.

Colonialism

- forced peasants to replace food crops with cash crops that were then expropriated at very low rates;
- took over the best agricultural land for export crop plantations and then forced the most able-bodied

workers to leave the village fields to work as slaves or for very low wages on plantations;

- encouraged a dependence on imported food;
- blocked native peasant cash crop production from competing with cash crops produced by settlers or foreign firms.

These are concrete examples of the development of under-development that we should have perceived as such even as we read our history schoolbooks. Why didn't we? Somehow our schoolbooks always seemed to make the flow of history appear to have its own logic—as if it could not have been any other way. I, Frances, recall, in particular, a grade-school, social studies pamphlet on the idyllic life of Pedro, a nine-year-old boy on a coffee plantation in South America. The drawings of lush vegetation and "exotic" huts made his life seem romantic indeed. Wasn't it natural and proper that South America should have plantations to supply my mother and father with coffee? Isn't that the way it was *meant* to be?

Notes

1. Radha Sinha, *Food and Poverty* (New York: Holmes and Meier, 1976), p. 26.

2. John Stuart Mill, *Political Economy,* Book 3, Chapter 25 (emphasis added).

3. Peter Feldman and David Lawrence, "Social and Economic Implications of the Large-Scale Introduction of New Varieties of Foodgrains," Africa Report, preliminary draft (Geneva: UNRISD, 1975), pp. 107–108.

4. Edgar Owens, *The Right Side of History,* unpublished manuscript, 1976.

5. Walter Rodney, *How Europe Underdeveloped Africa* (London: Bogle-L'Ouverture Publications, 1972), pp. 171–172.

6. Ferdinand Ossendowski, *Slaves of the Sun* (New York: Dutton, 1928), p. 276.

7. Rodney, *How Europe Underdeveloped Africa,* pp. 171–172.

8. Ibid., p. 181.

9. Clifford Geertz, *Agricultural Involution* (Berkeley and Los Angeles: University of California Press, 1963), pp. 52–53.

10. Rodney, *How Europe Underdeveloped Africa,* p. 185.

11. Ibid., p. 184.

12. Ibid., p. 186.

13. George L. Beckford, *Persistent Poverty: Underdevelopment in Plantation Economies of the Third World* (New York: Oxford University Press, 1972), p. 99.

14. Ibid., p. 99, quoting from Erich Jacoby, *Agrarian Unrest in Southeast Asia* (New York: Asia Publishing House, 1961), p. 66.

15. Pat Flynn and Roger Burbach, North American Congress on Latin America, Berkely, California, recent investigation.

16. Feldman and Lawrence, "Social and Economic Implications," p. 103.

17. Special Sahelian Office Report, Food and Agriculture Organization, March 28, 1974, pp. 88–89.

18. Alan Adamson, *Sugar Without Slaves: The Political Economy of British Guiana, 1838–1904* (New Haven and London: Yale University Press, 1972).

19. Ibid., p. 41.

20. Eric Williams, *Capitalism and Slavery* (New York: Putnam, 1966), p. 110.

21. Ibid., p. 121.

22. Gunnar Myrdal, *Asian Drama,* vol. 1 (New York: Pantheon, 1966), pp. 448–449.

23. Feldman and Lawrence, "Social and Economic Implications," p. 189.

FRANCES MOORE LAPPÉ and **DR. JOSEPH COLLINS** are founders and directors of the Institute for Food and Development Policy, located in San Francisco and New York.

The Arrow of Disease

When Columbus and his successors invaded the Americas, the most potent weapon they carried was their germs. But why didn't deadly disease flow in the other direction, from the New World to the Old?

JARED DIAMOND

The three people talking in the hospital room were already stressed out from having to cope with a mysterious illness, and it didn't help at all that they were having trouble communicating. One of them was the patient, a small, timid man, sick with pneumonia caused by an unidentified microbe and with only a limited command of the English language. The second, acting as translator, was his wife, worried about her husband's condition and frightened by the hospital environment. The third person in the trio was an inexperienced young doctor, trying to figure out what might have brought on the strange illness. Under the stress, the doctor was forgetting everything he had been taught about patient confidentiality. He committed the awful blunder of requesting the woman to ask her husband whether he'd had any sexual experiences that might have caused the infection.

As the young doctor watched, the husband turned red, pulled himself together so that he seemed even smaller, tried to disappear under his bed sheets, and stammered in a barely audible voice. His wife suddenly screamed in rage and drew herself up to tower over him. Before the doctor could stop her, she grabbed a heavy metal bottle, slammed it onto her husband's head, and stormed out of the room. It took a while for the doctor to elicit, through the man's broken English, what he had said to so enrage his wife. The answer slowly emerged: he had admitted to repeated intercourse with sheep on a recent visit to the family farm; perhaps that was how he had contracted the mysterious microbe.

This episode, related to me by a physician friend involved in the case, sounds so bizarrely one of a kind as to be of no possible broader significance. But in fact it illustrates a subject of great importance: human diseases of animal origins. Very few of us may love sheep in the carnal sense. But most of us platonically love our pet animals, like our dogs and cats; and as a society, we certainly appear to have an inordinate fondness for sheep and other livestock, to judge from the vast numbers of them that we keep.

Some of us—most often our children—pick up infectious diseases from our pets. Usually these illnesses remain no more than a nuisance, but a few have evolved into far more. The major killers of humanity throughout our recent history—smallpox, flu, tuberculosis, malaria, plague, measles, and cholera—are all infectious diseases that arose from diseases of animals. Until World War II more victims of war died of microbes than of gunshot or sword wounds. All those military histories glorifying Alexander the Great and Napoleon ignore the ego-deflating truth: the winners of past wars were not necessarily those armies with the best generals and weapons, but those bearing the worst germs with which to smite their enemies.

The grimmest example of the role of germs in history is much on our minds this month, as we recall the European conquest of the Americas that began with Columbus's voyage of 1492. Numerous as the Indian victims of the murderous Spanish conquistadores were, they were dwarfed in number by the victims of murderous Spanish microbes. These formidable conquerors killed an estimated 95 percent of the New World's pre-Columbian Indian population.

Why was the exchange of nasty germs between the Americas and Europe so unequal? Why didn't the reverse happen instead, with Indian diseases decimating the Spanish invaders, spreading back across the Atlantic, and causing a 95 percent decline in *Europe's* human population?

Similar questions arise regarding the decimation of many other native peoples by European germs, and regarding the decimation of would-be European conquistadores in the tropics of Africa and Asia.

Naturally, we're disposed to think about diseases from our own point of view: What can we do to save ourselves and to kill the microbes? Let's stamp out the scoundrels, and never mind what *their* motives are!

In life, though, one has to understand the enemy to beat him. So for a moment, let's consider disease from the microbes' point of view. Let's look beyond our anger at their making us sick in bizarre ways, like giving us genital sores or diarrhea, and ask why it is that they do such things. After all, microbes are as much a product of natural selection as we are, and so their actions must have come about because they confer some evolutionary benefit.

Basically, of course, evolution selects those individuals that are most effective at producing babies and at helping those babies find suitable places to live. Microbes are marvels at this latter requirement. They have evolved diverse ways of spreading from one person to another, and from animals to people. Many of our symptoms of disease actually represent ways in which some clever bug modifies our bodies or our behavior such that we become enlisted to spread bugs.

The most effortless way a bug can spread is by just waiting to be transmitted passively to the next victim. That's the strategy practiced by microbes that wait for one host to be eaten by the next—salmonella bacteria, for example, which we contract by eating already-infected eggs or meat; or the worm responsible for trichinosis, which waits for us to kill a pig and eat it without properly cooking it.

As a slight modification of this strategy; some microbes don't wait for the old host to die but instead hitchhike in the saliva of an insect that bites the old host and then flies to a new one. The free ride may be provided by mosquitoes, fleas, lice, or tsetse flies, which spread malaria, plague, typhus, and sleeping sickness, respectively. The dirtiest of all passive-carriage tricks is perpetrated by microbes that pass from a woman to her fetus—microbes such as the ones responsible for syphilis, rubella (German measles), and AIDS. By their cunning these microbes can already be infecting an infant before the moment of its birth.

Other bugs take matters into their own hands, figuratively speaking. They actively modify the anatomy or habits of their host to accelerate their transmission. From our perspective, the open genital sores caused by venereal diseases such as syphilis are a vile indignity. From the microbes' point of view, however, they're just a useful device to enlist a host's help in inoculating the body cavity of another host with microbes. The skin lesions caused by smallpox similarly spread microbes by direct or indirect body contact (occasionally very indirect, as when U.S. and Australian whites bent on wiping out "belligerent" native peoples sent them gifts of blankets previously used by smallpox patients).

More vigorous yet is the strategy practiced by the influenza, common cold, and pertussis (whooping cough) microbes, which induce the victim to cough or sneeze, thereby broadcasting the bugs toward prospective new hosts. Similarly the cholera bacterium induces a massive diarrhea that spreads bacteria into the water supplies of potential new victims. For modification of a host's behavior, though, nothing matches the rabies virus, which not only gets into the saliva of an infected dog but drives the dog into a frenzy of biting and thereby infects many new victims.

Thus, from our viewpoint, genital sores, diarrhea, and coughing are "symptoms" of disease. From a bug's viewpoint, they're clever evolutionary strategies to broadcast the bug. That's why it's in the bug's interests to make us "sick." But what does it

gain by killing us? That seems self-defeating, since a microbe that kills its host kills itself.

Though you may well think it's of little consolation, our death is really just an unintended by-product of host symptoms that promote the efficient transmission of microbes. Yes, an untreated cholera patient may eventually die from producing diarrheal fluid at a rate of several gallons a day. While the patient lasts, though, the cholera bacterium profits from being massively disseminated into the water supplies of its next victims. As long as each victim thereby infects, on average, more than one new victim, the bacteria will spread, even though the first host happens to die.

So much for the dispassionate examination of the bug's interests. Now let's get back to considering our own selfish interests: to stay alive and healthy, best done by killing the damned bugs. One common response to infection is to develop a fever. Again, we consider fever a "symptom" of disease, as if it developed inevitably without serving any function. But regulation of body temperature is under our genetic control, and a fever doesn't just happen by accident. Because some microbes are more sensitive to heat than our own bodies are, by raising our body temperature we in effect try to bake the bugs to death before we get baked ourselves.

We and our pathogens are now locked in an escalating evolutionary contest, with the death of one contestant the price of defeat, and with natural selection playing the role of umpire.

Another common response is to mobilize our immune system. White blood cells and other cells actively seek out and kill foreign microbes. The specific antibodies we gradually build up against a particular microbe make us less likely to get reinfected once we are cured. As we all know there are some illnesses, such as flu and the common cold, to which our resistance is only temporary; we can eventually contract the illness again. Against other illnesses, though—including measles, mumps, rubella, pertussis, and the now-defeated menace of smallpox—antibodies stimulated by one infection confer lifelong immunity. That's the principle behind vaccination—to stimulate our antibody production without our having to go through the actual experience of the disease.

Alas, some clever bugs don't just cave in to our immune defenses. Some have learned to trick us by changing their antigens, those molecular pieces of the microbe that our antibodies recognize. The constant evolution or recycling of new strains of flu, with differing antigens, explains why the flu you got two years ago didn't protect you against the different strain that arrived this year. Sleeping sickness is an even more slippery customer in its ability to change its antigens rapidly.

Among the slipperiest of all is the virus that causes AIDS, which evolves new antigens even as it sits within an individual patient, until it eventually overwhelms the immune system.

Our slowest defensive response is through natural selection, which changes the relative frequency with which a gene appears from generation to generation. For almost any disease some people prove to be genetically more resistant than others. In an epidemic, those people with genes for resistance to that particular microbe are more likely to survive than are people lacking such genes. As a result, over the course of history human populations repeatedly exposed to a particular pathogen tend to be made up of individuals with genes that resist the appropriate microbe just because unfortunate individuals without those genes were less likely to survive to pass their genes on to their children.

Fat consolation, you may be thinking. This evolutionary response is not one that does the genetically susceptible dying individual any good. It does mean, though, that a human population as a whole becomes better protected.

In short, many bugs have had to evolve tricks to let them spread among potential victims. We've evolved counter-tricks, to which the bugs have responded by evolving counter-counter-tricks. We and our pathogens are now locked in an escalating evolutionary contest, with the death of one contestant the price of defeat, and with natural selection playing the role of umpire.

T he form that this deadly contest takes varies with the pathogens: for some it is like a guerrilla war, while for others it is a blitzkrieg. With certain diseases, like malaria or hookworm, there's a more or less steady trickle of new cases in an affected area, and they will appear in any month of any year. Epidemic diseases, though, are different: they produce no cases for a long time, then a whole wave of cases, then no more cases again for a while.

Among such epidemic diseases, influenza is the most familiar to Americans, this year having been a particularly bad one for us (but a great year for the influenza virus). Cholera epidemics come at longer intervals, the 1991 Peruvian epidemic being the first one to reach the New World during the twentieth century. Frightening as today's influenza and cholera epidemics are, through, they pale beside the far more terrifying epidemics of the past, before the rise of modern medicine. The greatest single epidemic in human history was the influenza wave that killed 21 million people at the end of the First World War. The black death, or bubonic plague, killed one-quarter of Europe's population between 1346 and 1352, with death tolls up to 70 percent in some cities.

The infectious diseases that visit us as epidemics share several characteristics. First, they spread quickly and efficiently from an infected person to nearby healthy people, with the result that the whole population gets exposed within a short time. Second, they're "acute" illnesses: within a short time, you either die or recover completely. Third, the fortunate ones of us who do recover develop antibodies that leave us immune against a recurrence of the disease for a long time, possibly our entire lives. Finally, these diseases tend to be restricted to humans; the bugs causing them tend not to live in the soil or in other animals. All four of these characteristics apply to what Americans think of as the once more-familiar acute epidemic diseases of childhood, including measles, rubella, mumps, pertussis, and smallpox.

It is easy to understand why the combination of those four characteristics tends to make a disease run in epidemics. The rapid spread of microbes and the rapid course of symptoms mean that everybody in a local human population is soon infected, and thereafter either dead or else recovered and immune. No one is left alive who could still be infected. But since the microbe can't survive except in the bodies of living people, the disease dies out until a new crop of babies reaches the susceptible age—and until an infectious person arrives from the outside to start a new epidemic.

A classic illustration of the process is given by the history of measles on the isolated Faeroe Islands in the North Atlantic. A severe epidemic of the disease reached the Faeroes in 1781, then died out, leaving the islands measles-free until an infected carpenter arrived on a ship from Denmark in 1846. Within three months almost the whole Faeroes population—7,782 people—had gotten measles and then either died or recovered, leaving the measles virus to disappear once again until the next epidemic. Studies show that measles is likely to die out in any human population numbering less than half a million people. Only in larger populations can measles shift from one local area to another, thereby persisting until enough babies have been born in the originally infected area to permit the disease's return.

Rubella in Australia provides a similar example, on a much larger scale. As of 1917 Australia's population was still only 5 million, with most people living in scattered rural areas. The sea voyage to Britain took two months, and land transport within Australia itself was slow. In effect, Australia didn't even consist of a population of 5 million, but of hundreds of much smaller populations. As a result, rubella hit Australia only as occasional epidemics, when an infected person happened to arrive from overseas and stayed in a densely populated area. By 1938, though, the city of Sydney alone had a population of over one million, and people moved frequently and quickly by air between London, Sydney, and other Australian cities. Around then, rubella for the first time was able to establish itself permanently in Australia.

What's true for rubella in Australia is true for most familiar acute infectious diseases throughout the world. To sustain themselves, they need a human population that is sufficiently numerous and densely packed that a new crop of susceptible children is available for infection by the time the disease would otherwise be waning. Hence the measles and other such diseases are also known as "crowd diseases."

C rowd diseases could not sustain themselves in small bands of hunter-gatherers and slash-and-burn farmers. As tragic recent experience with Amazonian Indians and Pacific Islanders confirms, almost an entire tribelet may be wiped out by an epidemic brought by an outside visitor, because no one in the tribelet has any antibodies against the microbe. In addition, measles and some other "childhood" diseases are more likely to kill infected adults than children, and all adults in the tribelet are susceptible. Having killed most of the tribelet, the epidemic then disappears. The small population size explains why tribelets can't sustain epidemics introduced from the outside; at the same time it explains why they could never evolve epidemic diseases of their own to give back to the visitors.

That's not to say that small human populations are free from all infectious diseases. Some of their infections are caused by microbes capable of maintaining themselves in animals or in soil, so the disease remains constantly available to infect people. For example, the yellow fever virus is carried by African wild monkeys and is constantly available to infect rural human populations of Africa. It was also available to be carried to New World monkeys and people by the transAtlantic slave trade.

Other infections of small human populations are chronic diseases, such as leprosy and yaws, that may take a very long time to kill a victim. The victim thus remains alive as a reservoir of microbes to infect other members of the tribelet. Finally, small human populations are susceptible to nonfatal infections against which we don't develop immunity, with the result that the same person can become reinfected after recovering. That's the case with hookworm and many other parasites.

All these types of diseases, characteristic of small, isolated populations, must be the oldest diseases of humanity. They were the ones that we could evolve and sustain through the early millions of years of our evolutionary history, when the total human population was tiny and fragmented. They are also shared with, or are similar to the diseases of, our closest wild relatives, the African great apes. In contrast, the evolution of our crowd diseases could only have occurred with the buildup of large, dense human populations, first made possible by the rise of agriculture about 10,000 years ago, then by the rise of cities several thousand years ago. Indeed, the first attested dates for many familiar infectious diseases are surprisingly recent: around 1600 B.C. for smallpox (as deduced from pockmarks on an Egyptian mummy), 400 B.C. for mumps, 1840 for polio, and 1959 for AIDS.

Agriculture sustains much higher human population densities than does hunting and gathering—on average, 10 to 100 times higher. In addition, hunter-gatherers frequently shift camp, leaving behind their piles of feces with their accumulated microbes and worm larvae. But farmers are sedentary and live amid their own sewage, providing microbes with a quick path from one person's body into another person's drinking water. Farmers also become surrounded by disease-transmitting rodents attracted by stored food.

The explosive increase in world travel by Americans, and in immigration to the United States, is turning us into another melting pot—this time of microbes that we'd dismissed as causing disease in far-off countries.

Some human populations make it even easier for their own bacteria and worms to infect new victims, by intentionally gathering their feces and urine and spreading it as fertilizer on the fields where people work. Irrigation agriculture and fish farming provide ideal living conditions for the snails carrying schistosomes, and for other flukes that burrow through our skin as we wade through the feces-laden water.

If the rise of farming was a boon for our microbes, the rise of cities was a veritable bonanza, as still more densely packed human populations festered under even worse sanitation conditions. (Not until the beginning of the twentieth century did urban populations finally become self-sustaining; until then, constant immigration of healthy peasants from the countryside was necessary to make good the constant deaths of city dwellers from crowd diseases.) Another bonanza was the development of world trade routes, which by late Roman times effectively joined the populations of Europe, Asia, and North Africa into one giant breeding ground for microbes. That's when smallpox finally reached Rome as the "plague of Antonius," which killed millions of Roman citizens between A.D. 165 and 180.

Similarly, bubonic plague first appeared in Europe as the plague of Justinian (A.D. 542–543). But plague didn't begin to hit Europe with full force, as the black death epidemics, until 1346, when new overland trading with China provided rapid transit for flea-infested furs from plague-ridden areas of Central Asia. Today our jet planes have made even the longest intercontinental flights briefer than the duration of any human infectious disease. That's how an Aerolíneas Argentinas airplane, stopping in Lima, Peru, earlier this year, managed to deliver dozens of cholera-infected people the same day to my city of Los Angeles, over 3,000 miles away. The explosive increase in world travel by Americans, and in immigration to the United States, is turning us into another melting pot—this time of microbes that we previously dismissed as just causing exotic diseases in far-off countries.

When the human population became sufficiently large and concentrated, we reached the stage in our history when we could at last sustain crowd diseases confined to our species. But that presents a paradox: such diseases could never have existed before. Instead they had to evolve as new diseases. Where did those new diseases come from?

Evidence emerges from studies of the disease-causing microbes themselves. In many cases molecular biologists have identified the microbe's closest relative. Those relatives also prove to be agents of infectious crowd diseases—but ones confined to various species of domestic animals and pets! Among animals too, epidemic diseases require dense populations, and they're mainly confined to social animals that provide the necessary large populations. Hence when we domesticated social animals such as cows and pigs, they were already afflicted by epidemic diseases just waiting to be transferred to us.

For example, the measles virus is most closely related to the virus causing rinderpest, a nasty epidemic disease of cattle and many wild cud-chewing mammals. Rinderpest doesn't affect humans. Measles, in turn, doesn't affect cattle. The close similarity of the measles and rinderpest viruses suggests that the rinderpest virus transferred from cattle to humans, then became the measles virus by changing its properties to adapt to us. That transfer isn't surprising, considering how closely many peasant farmers live and sleep next to cows and their accompanying feces, urine, breath, sores, and blood. Our intimacy with cattle has been going on for 8,000 years since we domesticated them—ample time for the rinderpest virus to discover us nearby. Other familiar infectious diseases can similarly be traced back to diseases of our animal friends.

Given our proximity to the animals we love, we must constantly be getting bombarded by animal microbes. Those invaders get winnowed by natural selection, and only a few succeed in establishing themselves as human diseases. A quick survey of current diseases lets us trace four stages in the evolution of a specialized human disease from an animal precursor.

In the first stage, we pick up animal-borne microbes that are still at an early stage in their evolution into specialized human pathogens. They don't get transmitted directly from one person to another, and even their transfer from animals to us remains uncommon. There are dozens of diseases like this that we get directly from pets and domestic animals. They include cat scratch fever from cats, leptospirosis from dogs, psittacosis from chickens and parrots, and brucellosis from cattle. We're similarly susceptible to picking up diseases from wild animals, such as the tularemia that hunters occasionally get from skinning wild rabbits.

In the second stage, a former animal pathogen evolves to the point where it does get transmitted directly between people and causes epidemics. However, the epidemic dies out for several reasons—being cured by modern medicine, stopping when everybody has been infected and died, or stopping when everybody has been infected and become immune. For example, a previously unknown disease termed *o'nyong-nyong* fever appeared in East Africa in 1959 and infected several million Africans. It probably arose from a virus of monkeys and was transmitted to humans by mosquitoes. The fact that patients recovered quickly and became immune to further attack helped cause the new disease to die out quickly.

The annals of medicine are full of diseases that sound like no known disease today but that once caused terrifying epidemics before disappearing as mysteriously as they had come. Who alive today remembers the "English sweating sickness" that swept and terrified Europe between 1485 and 1578, or the "Picardy sweats" of eighteenth- and nineteenth-century France?

A third stage in the evolution of our major diseases is represented by former animal pathogens that establish themselves in humans and that do not die out; until they do, the question of whether they will become major killers of humanity remains up for grabs. The future is still very uncertain for Lassa fever, first observed in 1969 in Nigeria and caused by a virus probably derived from rodents. Better established is Lyme disease, caused by a spirochete that we get from the bite of a tick. Although the first known human cases in the United States appeared only as recently as 1962, Lyme disease is already reaching epidemic proportions in the Northeast, on the West Coast, and in the upper Midwest. The future of AIDS, derived from monkey viruses, is even more secure, from the virus's perspective.

The final stage of this evolution is represented by the major, long-established epidemic diseases confined to humans. These diseases must have been the evolutionary survivors of far more pathogens that tried to make the jump to us from animals—and mostly failed.

Diseases represent evolution in progress, as microbes adapt by natural selection to new hosts. Compared with cows' bodies, though, our bodies offer different immune defenses and different chemistry. In that new environment, a microbe must evolve new ways to live and propagate itself.

The best-studied example of microbes evolving these new ways involves myxomatosis, which hit Australian rabbits in 1950. The myxoma virus, native to a wild species of Brazilian rabbit, was known to cause a lethal epidemic in European domestic rabbits, which are a different species. The virus was intentionally introduced to Australia in the hopes of ridding the continent of its plague of European rabbits, foolishly introduced in the nineteenth century. In the first year, myxoma produced a gratifying (to Australian farmers) 99.8 percent mortality in infected rabbits. Fortunately for the rabbits and unfortunately for the farmers, the death rate then dropped in the second year to 90 percent and eventually to 25 percent, frustrating hopes of eradicating rabbits completely from Australia. The problem was that the myxoma virus evolved to serve its own interest, which differed from the farmers' interests and those of the rabbits. The virus changed to kill fewer rabbits and to permit lethally infected ones to live longer before dying. The result was bad for Australian farmers but good for the virus: a less lethal myxoma virus spreads baby viruses to more rabbits than did the original, highly virulent myxoma.

For a similar example in humans, consider the surprising evolution of syphilis. Today we associate syphilis with genital sores and a very slowly developing disease, leading to the death of untreated victims only after many years. However, when syphilis was first definitely recorded in Europe in 1495, its pustules often covered the body from the head to the knees, caused flesh to fall off people's faces, and led to death within a few months. By 1546 syphilis had evolved into the disease with the symptoms known to us today. Apparently, just as with myxomatosis, those syphilis spirochetes evolved to keep their victims alive longer in order to transmit their spirochete offspring into more victims.

H ow, then, does all this explain the outcome of 1492—that Europeans conquered and depopulated the New World, instead of Native Americans conquering and depopulating Europe?

In the century or two following Columbus's arrival in the New World, the Indian population declined by about 95 percent. The main killers were European germs, to which the Indians had never been exposed.

Part of the answer, of course, goes back to the invaders' technological advantages. European guns and steel swords were more effective weapons than Native American stone axes and wooden clubs. Only Europeans had ships capable of crossing the ocean and horses that could provide a decisive advantage in battle. But that's not the whole answer. Far more Native Americans died in bed than on the battlefield—the victims of germs, not of guns and swords. Those germs undermined Indian resistance by killing most Indians and their leaders and by demoralizing the survivors.

The role of disease in the Spanish conquests of the Aztec and Inca empires is especially well documented. In 1519 Cortés landed on the coast of Mexico with 600 Spaniards to conquer the fiercely militaristic Aztec Empire, which at the time had a population of many millions. That Cortés reached the Aztec capital of Tenochtitlán, escaped with the loss of "only" two-thirds of his force, and managed to fight his way back to the coast demonstrates both Spanish military advantages and the initial naïveté of the Aztecs. But when Cortés's next onslaught came, in 1521, the Aztecs were no longer naïve; they fought street by street with the utmost tenacity.

What gave the Spaniards a decisive advantage this time was smallpox, which reached Mexico in 1520 with the arrival of one infected slave from Spanish Cuba. The resulting epidemic proceeded to kill nearly half the Aztecs. The survivors were demoralized by the mysterious illness that killed Indians and spared Spaniards, as if advertising the Spaniards' invincibility. By 1618 Mexico's initial population of 20 million had plummeted to about 1.6 million.

Pizarro had similarly grim luck when he landed on the coast of Peru in 1531 with about 200 men to conquer the Inca Empire. Fortunately for Pizarro, and unfortunately for the Incas, smallpox had arrived overland around 1524, killing much of the Inca population, including both Emperor Huayna Capac and his son and designated successor, Ninan Cuyoche. Because of the vacant throne, two other sons of Huayna Capac, Atahuallpa and Huáscar, became embroiled in a civil war that Pizarro exploited to conquer the divided Incas.

When we in the United States think of the most populous New World societies existing in 1492, only the Aztecs and Incas come to mind. We forget that North America also supported populous Indian societies in the Mississippi Valley. Sadly, these societies too would disappear. But in this case conquistadores contributed nothing directly to the societies' destruction; the conquistadores' germs, spreading in advance, did everything. When De Soto marched through the Southeast in 1540, he came across Indian towns abandoned two years previously because nearly all the inhabitants had died in epidemics. However, he was still able to see some of the densely populated towns lining the lower Mississippi. By a century and a half later, though, when French settlers returned to the lower Mississippi, almost all those towns had vanished. Their relics are the great mound sites of the Mississippi Valley. Only recently have we come to realize that the mound-building societies were still largely intact when Columbus arrived, and that they collapsed between 1492 and the systematic European exploration of the Mississippi.

When I was a child in school, we were taught that North America had originally been occupied by about one million Indians. That low number helped justify the white conquest of what could then be viewed as an almost empty continent. However, archeological excavations and descriptions left by the first European explorers on our coasts now suggest an initial number of around 20 million. In the century or two following Columbus's arrival in the New World, the Indian population is estimated to have declined by about 95 percent.

The main killers were European germs, to which the Indians had never been exposed and against which they therefore had neither immunologic nor genetic resistance. Smallpox, measles, influenza, and typhus competed for top rank among the killers. As if those were not enough, pertussis, plague, tuberculosis, diphtheria, mumps, malaria, and yellow fever came close behind. In countless cases Europeans were actually there to witness the decimation that occurred when the germs arrived. For example, in 1837 the Mandan Indian tribe, with one of the most elaborate cultures in the Great Plains, contracted smallpox thanks to a steamboat traveling up the Missouri River from St. Louis. The population of one Mandan village crashed from 2,000 to less than 40 within a few weeks.

The one-sided exchange of lethal germs between the Old and New worlds is among the most striking and consequence-laden facts of recent history. Whereas over a dozen major infectious diseases of Old World origins became established in the New World, not a single major killer reached Europe from the Americas. The sole possible exception is syphilis, whose area of origin still remains controversial.

That one-sidedness is more striking with the knowledge that large, dense human populations are a prerequisite for the evolution of crowd diseases. If recent reappraisals of the pre-Columbian New World population are correct, that population was not far below the contemporaneous population of Eurasia. Some New World cities, like Tenochtitlán, were among the world's most populous cities at the time. Yet Tenochtitlán didn't have awful germs waiting in store for the Spaniards. Why not?

One possible factor is the rise of dense human populations began somewhat later in the New World than in the Old. Another is that the three most populous American centers—the Andes, Mexico, and the Mississippi Valley—were never connected by regular fast trade into one gigantic breeding ground for microbes, in the way that Europe, North Africa, India, and China became connected in late Roman times.

The main reason becomes clear, however, if we ask a simple question: From what microbes could any crowd diseases of the Americas have evolved? We've seen that Eurasian crowd diseases evolved from diseases of domesticated herd animals. Significantly, there were many such animals in Eurasia. But there were only five animals that became domesticated in the Americas: the turkey in Mexico and parts of North America, the guinea pig and llama/alpaca (probably derived from the same original wild species) in the Andes, and Muscovy duck in tropical South America, and the dog throughout the Americas.

That extreme paucity of New World domestic animals reflects the paucity of wild starting material. About 80 percent of the big wild mammals of the Americas became extinct at the end of the last ice age, around 11,000 years ago, at approximately the same time that the first well-attested wave of Indian hunters spread over the Americas. Among the species that disappeared were ones that would have yielded useful domesticates, such as American horses and camels. Debate still rages as to whether those extinctions were due to climate changes or to the impact of Indian hunters on prey that had never seen humans. Whatever the reason, the extinctions removed most of the basis for Native American animal domestication—and for crowd diseases.

The few domesticates that remained were not likely sources of such diseases. Muscovy ducks and turkeys don't live in enormous flocks, and they're not naturally endearing species (like young lambs) with which we have much physical contact. Guinea pigs may have contributed a trypanosome infection like Chagas' disease or leishmaniasis to our catalog of woes, but that's uncertain.

Initially the most surprising absence is of any human disease derived from llamas (or alpacas), which are tempting to consider as the Andean equivalent of Eurasian livestock. However, llamas had three strikes against them as a source of human pathogens: their wild relatives don't occur in big herds as do wild sheep, goats, and pigs; their total numbers were never remotely as large as the Eurasian populations of domestic livestock, since llamas never spread beyond the Andes; and llamas aren't as cuddly as piglets and lambs and aren't kept in such close association with people. (You may not think of piglets as cuddly, but human mothers in the New Guinea highlands often nurse them, and they frequently live right in the huts of peasant farmers.)

The importance of animal-derived diseases for human history extends far beyond the Americas. Eurasian germs played a key role in decimating native peoples in many other parts of the world as well, including the Pacific islands, Australia, and southern Africa. Racist Europeans used to attribute those conquests to their supposedly better brains. But no evidence for such better brains has been forthcoming. Instead, the conquests were made possible by Europeans nastier germs, and by the technological advances and denser populations that Europeans ultimately acquired by means of their domesticated plants and animals.

So on this 500th anniversary of Columbus's discovery, let's try to regain our sense of perspective about his hotly debated achievements. There's no doubt that Columbus was a great visionary, seaman, and leader. There's also no doubt that he and his successors often behaved as bestial murderers. But those facts alone don't fully explain why it took so few European immigrants to initially conquer and ultimately supplant so much of the native population of the Americas. Without the germs Europeans brought with them—germs that were derived from their animals—such conquests might have been impossible.

JARED DIAMOND is a contributing editor of *Discover,* a professor of physiology at the UCLA School of Medicine, a recipient of a MacArthur genius award, and a research associate in ornithology at the American Museum of Natural History. Expanded versions of many of his *Discover* articles appear in his book *The Third Chimpanzee: The Evolution and Future of the Human Animal,* which won Britain's 1992 COPUS prize for best science book. Not least among his many accomplishments was his rediscovery in 1981 of the long-lost bowerbird of New Guinea. Diamond wrote about pseudo-hermaphrodites for *Discover's* special June issue on the science of sex.

Burying the White Gods: New Perspectives on the Conquest of Mexico

Camilla Townsend

In 1552, Francisco López de Gómara, who had been chaplain and secretary to Hernando Cortés while he lived out his old age in Spain, published an account of the conquest of Mexico. López de Gómara himself had never been to the New World, but he could envision it nonetheless. "Many [Indians] came to gape at the strange men, now so famous, and at their attire, arms and horses, and they said, 'These men are gods!'"[1] The chaplain was one of the first to claim in print that the Mexicans had believed the conquistadors to be divine. Among the welter of statements made in the Old World about inhabitants of the New, this one found particular resonance. It was repeated with enthusiasm, and soon a specific version gained credence: the Mexicans had apparently believed in a god named Quetzalcoatl, who long ago had disappeared in the east, promising to return from that direction on a certain date. In an extraordinary coincidence, Cortés appeared off the coast in that very year and was mistaken for Quetzalcoatl by the devout Indians. Today, most educated persons in the United States, Europe, and Latin America are fully versed in this account, as readers of this piece can undoubtedly affirm. In fact, however, there is little evidence that the indigenous people ever seriously believed the newcomers were gods, and there is no meaningful evidence that any story about Quetzalcoatl's returning from the east ever existed before the conquest. A number of scholars of early Mexico are aware of this, but few others are. The cherished narrative is alive and well, and in urgent need of critical attention.[2]

In order to dismantle a construct with such a long history, it will be necessary first to explain the origins and durability of the myth and then to offer an alternate explanation of what happened in the period of conquest and what the indigenous were actually thinking. In proposing an alternative, I will make three primary assertions: first, that we must put technology in all its forms—beyond mere weaponry—front and center in our story of conquest; second, that we can safely do this because new evidence from scientists offers us explanations for divergent technological levels that have nothing to do with differences in intelligence; and third, that the Mexicans themselves immediately became aware of the technology gap and responded to it with intelligence and savvy rather than wide-eyed talk of gods. They knew before we did, it seems, that technology was the crux.

In the last twenty years, scholars have made room for alternative narratives in many arenas, demonstrating that power imbalances explain the way we tell our stories. Yet despite our consciousness of narrative as political intervention, the story of the white gods in the conquest of Mexico has remained largely untouched. It is essentially a pornographic vision of events, albeit in a political rather than asexual sense. What most males say they find so enticing about pornography is not violent imagery—which after all takes center stage relatively rarely—but rather the idea that the female is *not* concerned about any potential for violence or indeed any problematic social inequalities or personal disagreements but instead enthusiastically and unquestioningly adores—even worships—the male. Certainly, such a narrative may be understood to be pleasurable in the context of the strife-ridden relationships of the real world. Likewise, it perhaps comes as no surprise that the relatively powerful conquistadors and their cultural heirs should prefer to dwell on the Indians' adulation for them, rather than on their pain, rage, or attempted military defense. It is, however, surprising that this element has not been more transparent to recent scholars.

Perhaps this relatively dehumanizing narrative has survived among us—in an era when few such have—because we have lacked a satisfactory alternative explanation for the conquest. Without such a misunderstanding, how could a handful of Spaniards permanently defeat the great Aztec state?[3] It is a potentially frightening question—at least to those who do not want the answer to be that one group was more intelligent or more deserving than another. The notion that the Indians were too devout for their own good, and hence the victims of a calendric coincidence of tragic consequences, is highly appealing. We can argue that it was no one's fault if the Indians thought the Spanish were gods and responded to them as such. The belief was part and parcel of their cosmology and does not by any means indicate that they were lacking in intelligence or that their culture was "less developed." Thus even those participating in colonial semiosis with a sympathetic ear, who study Indian narratives alongside colonists' fantasies, often avoid or deny the Europeans' superior ability to conquer *in a technical sense,* making statements that simply are not believable. One has suggested that, "but for the cases of some spectacularly successful conquistadors," the indigenous might have killed off all approaching colonizers as successfully as the South Sea Islanders did away with Captain Cook, another that, if the last Aztec king, Cuauhtemoc, had met with better fortune, the Aztecs might have "embarked upon their own version of the Meiji era in Japan."[4]

The obvious explanation for conquest, many would argue, is technology. The Spanish had a technological advantage large enough to ensure their victory, especially if we acknowledge that their technology included not only blunderbusses and powder but also printing presses, steel blades and armor, crossbows, horses and riding equipment, ships, navigation tools—and indirectly, as a result of the latter three, an array of diseases.[5] But even here we are in dangerous waters, as some would thereby infer a difference in intelligence. Felipe Fernández-Armesto writes: "I hope to contribute to the explosion of what I call the *conquistador-myth*: the notion that Spaniards displaced incumbent elites in the early modern New World because they were in some sense better, or better-equipped, technically, morally or intellectually."[6] But why need we conflate the latter three? One group can be better equipped technically without being better equipped morally or intellectually. A people's technology is *not* necessarily a function of their intelligence. Even a superficial observer of the Aztecs must notice their accurate calendar, their extraordinary goldwork and poetry, their pictoglyph books: such an observer calls them intellectually deficient at his or her peril.

Science can now offer historians clear explanations for the greater advancement of technology among certain peoples without presupposing unequal intelligence. Biologist Jared Diamond presents this new knowledge coherently and powerfully in *Guns, Germs, and Steel: The Fates of Human Societies,* which has not received the attention it deserves from historians.[7] He sets out to provide a non-racist explanation for "Why the Inca Emperor Atahuallpa Did Not Capture King Charles I of Spain." After marshalling well-known evidence that turning from a hunter-gatherer lifestyle to sedentary farming leads to increasing population and the proliferation of technological advances—including guns, steel, and (indirectly) germs—he says that we must then ask ourselves why farming developed earlier and/or spread more rapidly in certain parts of the world. The answer lies in the constellation of suitable—that is, protein-rich—wild plants available in a particular environment at a particular time—which scientists can now reconstruct. It is a highly risky endeavor to turn from hunting and gathering to farming. It makes no sense to do so, except on a part-time basis, for sugar cane, bananas, or squash, for instance; it makes a great deal of sense to do it for the wheat and peas of the Fertile Crescent (and certain other species that spread easily on the wide and relatively ecologically constant east-west axis of Eurasia). In the case of the Americas, one rushes to ask, "What about corn?" Indeed, it turns out that after the millennia of part-time cultivation that it took to turn the nearly useless wild *teosinte* with its tiny bunches of seeds into something approaching today's ears of corn, Mesoamericans became very serious full-time agriculturalists. But by then, they had lost valuable time—or so we say if they were in a race with Eurasia. In 1519, it would turn out that, unbeknownst to either side, they *had* been in something akin to a race. Establishing that the Mexicans had not had protein-rich crops available to them for as long as their conquerors, and thus had not been sedentary as long, allows us to understand the technical disparities that existed without resorting to comparisons of intelligence or human worth.

Diamond's work relieves us of an old burden. We may proceed more freely with our business as historians.

Our first task must be to ask ourselves whence came the myths associated with the conquest. The simple truth is that, by the 1550s, some Indians were themselves saying that they (or rather, their parents) had presumed the white men to be gods. Their words became widely available to an international audience in 1962, when Miguel León-Portilla published *The Broken Spears: The Aztec Account of the Conquest of Mexico,* translated from his 1959 *Visión de los vencidos.* The work was perfectly timed to meet with the political sympathies of a generation growing suspicious of the conquistadors' version of events. The volume was printed in at least eleven other languages and has remained a common reference for a variety of scholars. It is an invaluable book, communicating the fear, pain, and anger experienced by the Mexica when their great city of Tenochtitlan crumbled.[8] Yet, ironically, the same text that lets sixteenth-century Nahuas speak "within hearing distance of the rest of the world"[9] also traps them in stereotype, quoting certain statements made at least a generation after the conquest as if they were transparent realities. "When Motecuhzoma heard that [the Spanish] were inquiring about his person, and when he learned that the 'gods' wished to see him face to face, his heart shrank within him and he was filled with anguish. He wanted to run away and hide."[10]

Numerous scholars have analyzed these words while ignoring their context. The best-known such work is Tzvetan Todorov's *Conquest of America: The Question of the Other.* Although quick to say there is no "natural inferiority" (indeed, he aptly points out that it is the Indians who rapidly learn the language of the Spanish, not the other way around), he insists that it is the Spaniards' greater adeptness in manipulating signs that gives them victory. While the Spanish believe in man-man communication ("What are we to do?"), the Indians only envision man-world communication ("How are we to know?"). Thus the Indians have a "paralyzing belief that the Spaniards are gods" and are "inadequate in a situation requiring improvisation."[11] Popular historians have been equally quick to accept this idea of indigenous reality, often with the best intentions. Hugh Thomas's recent monumental 800-page volume is a case in point. Thomas uses apocryphal accounts as if they had been tape-recorded conversations in his portrayal of the inner workings of Moctezuma's[12] court. "The Emperor considered flight. He thought of hiding . . . He decided on . . . a cave on the side of Chapultepec." Thomas does this, I believe, not out of naïveté but out of a genuine desire to incorporate the Indian perspective. He does not want to describe the intricate politics of the Spanish while leaving the Indian side vague, rendering it less real to his readers.[13]

With such friends, though, perhaps the indigenous and their cultural heirs do not need enemies. A different approach is definitely needed, or the white gods will continue to inhabit our narratives. In beginning anew, let us first ask what sources we have available. We in fact have only one set of documents that were undoubtedly written at the time of conquest by someone who was certainly there—the letters of Cortés. The *Cartas* are masterful constructions, loaded with political agendas, but we are at least certain of their origin, and Cortés never wrote that he was taken for a god. Andrés de Tapia, a Spanish noble who was a captain under Cortés, wrote an account predating López de Gómara's, and, in the 1560s, two aging conquistadors wrote their memoirs: Francisco de Aguilar, who by then had renounced worldly wealth and was living in a Dominican monastery, dictated a short narration, and Bernal Díaz del Castillo, then a landholder in Guatemala, wrote a long and spicy manuscript that has come to be beloved by many.[14]

Besides the testimony of these few conquistadors, we have the writings of priests who were on the scene early, and who were bent on making a careful study of indigenous beliefs, the better to convert the natives. In 1524, twelve Franciscan "Apostles" arrived in Mexico City and were warmly greeted by Cortés. One of them, Fray Toribio de Benavente (known to posterity by his Nahuatl name, "Motolinía" or "Poor One"), wrote extensively.[15] The efforts of the Franciscans led to the founding in 1536 of a formal school for Indian noblemen in Tlatelolco in Mexico City and culminated during the 1550s in the work of Bernardo de Sahagún, who spent years orchestrating a grand project in which students did extensive interviews with surviving notables of the *ancien régime*. The most complete extant version is the Florentine Codex.[16] The Dominican Fray Diego Durán, though not born until the 1530s, is also particularly valuable to us because he moved with his family from Seville to Mexico "before he lost his 'milk teeth,'" was raised by Nahuatl-speaking servants, and became fluent in the language.[17]

The last group of sources were produced by the indigenous themselves, but here is the heart of the problem: we have none that date from the years of conquest or even from the 1520s or 1530s. There are sixteen surviving pre-conquest codices (none from Mexico City itself, where the conquerors' book burning was most intense), and then, dating from the 1540s, statements written in Nahuatl using the Roman alphabet, which was then rapidly becoming accessible to educated indigenous through the school of Tlatelolco.[18] The most famous such document about the conquest is the lengthy Book Twelve of the Florentine Codex. Although it was organized by Sahagún, and the Spanish glosses were written by him, the Nahuatl is the work of his Indian aides.[19] At the end of the century, a few indigenous men wrote histories. Don Fernando de Alva Ixtlilxochitl, a descendant of the last king of Texcoco, near Tenochtitlan, was prolific.[20] Though removed in time, he is worth reading, having access to secretly preserved codices; he railed against Spaniards who had confused matters by making false assertions that were taken as truth.[21]

These, then, are the rather limited documents we have to work with. James Lockhart has used circumstantial evidence to argue that we must be mistaken in our notion that the Mexicans responded to the Spanish in the early years with fatalism and awe. Even though we have no indigenous records produced at contact, we have a corpus of materials from the 1550s, including not only explicit commentary on events but also the data preserved in litigation and church records:

What we find . . . is a picture dominated in so many aspects by patently untouched pre-conquest patterns that it does not take much imagination to reconstruct a great deal of the situation during the missing years. It would be a most unlikely scenario for a people to have spent twenty-five undocumented years in wide-mouthed amazement inspired by some incredible intruders, and then, the moment we can see them in the documents, to have relapsed into going about their business, seeking the advantage of their local entities, interpreting everything about the newcomers as some familiar aspect of their own culture.[22]

It is in this context that we must approach the later understanding that the Aztecs were convinced that their own omens had for years been predicting the coming of the cataclysm, and that Cortés was recognized as Quetzalcoatl and the Europeans as gods. The most important source for all of these legends is Book Twelve of the Florentine Codex. Lockhart notes that it reads very much as if it were two separate documents: the first part, covering the period from the sighting of the European sails to the Spaniards' violent attack on warrior-dancers participating in a religious festival, reads like an apocryphal fable (complete with comets as portents), while the second part, covering the period from the Aztec warriors' uprising against the Spaniards after the festival to their ultimate defeat over a year later, reads like a military archivist's record of events.[23] Indeed, this phenomenon makes sense: the old men being interviewed in the 1550s would likely have participated as young warriors in the battles against the Spanish, or at least have been well aware of what was transpiring. On the other hand, they would most certainly *not* have been privy to the debates within Moctezuma's inner circle when the Spaniards' arrival first became known: the king's closest advisers were killed in the conquest, and at any rate would have been older men even in 1520.

Still, the fact that the informants for the Florentine were not acquainted with the inner workings of Moctezuma's court only proves that they were unlikely to have the first part of the story straight; it tells us nothing about why they chose to say what they did. It seems likely that they retroactively sought to find particular auguries associated with the conquest. The Florentine's omens do not appear to have been commonly accepted, as they do not appear in other Nahuatl sources.[24] Interestingly, Fernández-Armesto notes that the listed omens fall almost exactly in line with certain Greek and Latin texts that are known to have been available to Sahagún's students.[25]

Why would Sahagún's assistants have been so eager to come up with a compelling narrative about omens? We must bear in mind that they were the sons and grandsons of Tenochtitlan's most elite citizens—descendants of priests and nobles. It was their own class, even their own family members, who might have been thought to be at fault if it were true that they had had no idea that the Spaniards existed prior to their arrival. Durán later recorded some of the accusations against seers as they had been reported to him:

Motecuhzoma, furious, cried, "It is your position, then, to be deceivers, tricksters, to pretend to be men of science and forecast that which will take place in the future, deceiving everyone by saying that you know what will happen in the world, that you see what is within the hills, in the center of the earth, underneath the waters, in the caves and in the earth's clefts, in the springs and water holes. You call yourselves 'children of the night' but everything is a lie, it is all pretense."[26]

Here Moctezuma himself is the speaker; whether any particular individual ever gave vent to such rage at the time is unknowable. What is clear is that the person speaking years later still felt deceived. It begins to seem not merely unsurprising, but indeed necessary, that Sahagún's elite youths should insist that their forebears *had* read the signs and had known what was to happen. In their version, the Truth was paralyzing and left their forebears vulnerable, perhaps even more so than they might have been.[27]

The idea that Cortés was understood to be the god Quetzalcoatl returning from the east is also presented as fact in Book Twelve. Moctezuma sends gifts for different gods, to see which are most welcome to the newcomers, and then decides it is Quetzalcoatl who has come. There are numerous obvious problems with the story. First, Quetzalcoatl was not a particularly prominent god in the pantheon worshiped in Mexico's great city. The one city in the empire where Quetzalcoatl was prominent, Cholula, was the only one to mount a concerted attack against Cortés as he made his way to the Aztec capital. Many aspects of the usual post-conquest description of Quetzalcoatl—that he was a peace-loving god who abhorred human sacrifice, for example—are obviously European mythological constructs, thus rendering the whole story somewhat suspect. Furthermore, in the Codex itself, when the earlier explorer Juan de Grijalva lands on the coast in 1518, *he* is taken to be Quetzalcoatl. So much for the explanation that Cortés happened to land in the right year, causing all the pieces to fall into place in the indigenous imagination.

Susan Gillespie has made a careful study of every sixteenth-century text (pre- and post-conquest) where Quetzalcoatl appears, and has proven that the story as we know it did not exist until Sahagún edited the Florentine Codex in the 1560s. Quetzalcoatl certainly was a deity in the Nahua tradition. If we take as our only sources the pre-conquest codices, archaeological remains of temples, and recitations of pre-conquest religious ceremonies recorded elsewhere, we are left with certain definite elements. Quetzalcoatl was, as his name indicates, a feathered serpent, a flying reptile (much like a dragon), who was a boundary maker (and transgressor) between earth and sky. Like most gods, he could take various forms and was envisioned differently in various villages and epochs: he could be the wind, for example. His name became a priestly title, an honorific for those liminal humans whose role it was to connect those on earth to those beyond. In myth, he was associated with the city of the Toltecs, an ancient state-building people who had preceded the Aztecs in the Central Valley of Mexico. As the invading Mexica often claimed legitimacy by insisting that they were the heirs of the Toltecs, the symbol of Quetzalcoatl often appeared as an iconographic legitimator of a kingly line. In the Aztec ritual calendar, different deities were associated with each cyclically repeating date: Quetzalcoatl was tied to the year Ce Acatl (One Reed), which is correlated to the year 1519 (among others) in the Western calendar.[28]

There is no evidence of any ancient myths recounting the departure or return of such a god, but, in the early years after conquest, discrete elements of the story that has become so familiar to us do appear separately in various documents, with the main character being mortal rather than divine. The wandering hero is called Huemac or Topiltzin ("Our Lord" as in "Our Nobleman"); he is not given the name "Quetzalcoatl" until the 1540s, and then not in Nahuatl language texts. He is sometimes said to have ruled Tollan; the city is sometimes said to have fallen in connection with his exile; the prophecy of his return is occasionally made.[29] Motolinía rendered the story relevant to Cortés: Quetzalcoatl (in his version, a mortal apotheosized into a god, in good European tradition) was sent away to build up other lands, but people in Mexico awaited his return, and when they saw the sails of Cortés they said, "Their god was coming, and because of the white sails, they said he was bringing by sea his own temples." Then, remembering that all the Spaniards were supposed to have been gods, Motolinía quickly added, "When they disembarked, they said that it was not their god, but rather many gods."[30]

The elements did not all appear in the same narration until Sahagún's Codex drew them together in the 1560s—although references to the more traditional god Quetzalcoatl and a separate mortal hero named Huemac are also peppered throughout the Codex. By that time, Spanish priests had been interacting with the locals for years, and new European elements had been incorporated almost seamlessly: as they were wont to do elsewhere, the priests had theorized that a Christian saint had previously visited the New World, and such a man makes his appearance in these stories as the hero Quetzalcoatl, now a peace-loving man who is driven into exile because of the people's belief in the devil (the god Huitzilopochtli), and who foretells his own return.[31] In about 1570, the author of the "Anales de Cuauhtitlan" became the first Nahua to put all these elements together. To the generation of the 1570s, it seemed logical that their forebears had believed thus, for it provided a needed explanation why they had made such an ineffective defense.[32]

Even if it is untrue that anyone in 1519 thought Cortés was Quetzalcoatl, there remains the question of whether or not Cortés and his men were in general perceived to be gods. Cortés did not claim that he was accorded godly status. It is, however, apparently true that the Nahuas frequently referred to the Spanish as *teotl* or *teutl* (plural *teteo'* or *teteu'*), which the Spanish rendered in their own texts as *teul* (plural *teules*); they translated this word as "god." Sahagún's students in the 1550s clearly believed their parents had used *teotl* as a form of address in their dealings with the Spanish, and this was a matter less open to reinterpretation than some others.[33] Several conquistadors insisted on it. Perhaps the best question is not whether the Indians used the word *teotl* in their groping efforts to categorize the Spaniards before they had any political relation to them but rather why they did so, what it meant to them.

To turn an obvious point into a less obvious one, the indigenous had to call the Spaniards something, and it was not at all clear what that something should be. It is noteworthy that in Durán's history the issue first surfaces in the initial communication efforts of the Indian translator Malinche. "She responded, 'The leader of these men says he has come to greet your master Motecuhzoma, that his only intention is to go to the city of Mexico." But in the next interchange: "The Indian woman answered in the following way: 'These gods say that they kiss your hands and that they will eat."[34] In the Nahua universe as it had existed up until this point, a person was always labeled as being from a particular village or city-state, or, more specifically, as one who filled a given social role (a tribute collector, prince, servant). These new people fit nowhere; undoubtedly, they had a village or city-state somewhere, but it was not in the known world, and their relationship to it was not clear. Later, they were called "Caxtilteca" (people of Castile), but that came after closer acquaintance. There was no word for

"Indian," of course, and the indigenous struggled in certain situations. How to describe the woman translator, for example, who came with the newcomers but was not one of them? She became "a woman, one of us people here."[35] If there were no "Indians," there were no "Spanish" in opposition to them. So what to call the new arrivals? One of them might be a *tecuhtli,* a dynastic lord ruling over his own people, but he was not so in relation to "us people here." The Nahuatl word for king was *tlatoani,* meaning "he who speaks." Tellingly, in Nahuatl texts where the Spaniards have previously been referred to as *teotl,* first Cortés and then the viceroy become *tlatoani* after the Europeans vanquish the Indians and are in a position of authority over them.[36]

In the Florentine Codex, the moment of political surrender is described by the warriors: "There goes the lord Cuauhtemoc going to give himself to the gods" (*teteu'*). Yet, in the preceding pages, the enemy has been described as execrable rather than divine: in fact, when the Spaniards are temporarily expelled, the warriors perform ceremonies "in gratitude to their gods (*teotl*) for having freed them from their enemies." Tellingly, in the negotiations *after* the surrender, when the Spaniards are demanding full restitution of all the gold and jewels they were ever given, they are termed "our lords" as in "our earthly overlords" (*totecuiovan,* from *tecuhtli*), but in a moment of rage, a leading priest whose tone indicates he does not yet feel he owes allegiance cries out, "Let the god (*teotl*), the Captain [Cortés] pay heed!" He then refuses to pay, until the defeated Cuauhtemoc calms him and uses the word *tecuhtli* again.[37]

Sixteenth-century dictionaries say that *teotl* meant simply *dios,* but they, we must remember, were written years later, after semantic shifts had occurred in the process of Indians and priests working together.[38] Bernal Díaz first says that *teotl* meant "god" (*dios*) or "demon" (*demonio*). We might assume he meant "demon" only in the sense that the Christians called the entire Nahua pantheon "devils," but an anecdote that he relates indicates otherwise. The Spaniards seem to have been given to understand—quite accurately—that the word could mean "devil" in the sense of a capricious immortal over whom mortals had no control, or a ceremonial human impersonator of such a character. After the Spanish had gleaned the word's meaning, they thought to reinforce the notion as follows:

> [Cortés said], "I think we'll send Heredia against them." Heredia was an old Basque musketeer with a very ugly face covered with scars, a huge beard, and one blind eye. He was also lame in one leg . . . So old Heredia shouldered his musket and went off with [the Indians] firing shots in the air as he went through the forest, so that the Indians should both hear and see him. And the *caciques* sent the news to the other towns that they were bringing along a *Teule* to kill the Mexicans [Aztecs] who were at Cingapacinga. I tell this story here merely as a joke and to show Cortés' guile.[39]

This story is barely comprehensible unless one accepts that the Spanish had been told the word *teotl* encompassed notions of "powerful one" and "deity impersonator." For the impression one is left with here is not that the locals thought the Spaniards were glorious and divine beings but rather that they envisioned them as bizarre sorcerers who owed allegiance to no one and whose powers could potentially be turned against the Aztec overlords and tax collectors. It is even conceivable that the indigenous were

referring to "deity impersonators" as potential sacrifice victims for the Aztecs; certainly, *teotl* is used in that sense in descriptions of religious ceremonies elsewhere in the Florentine.

That the word had some ambiguity embedded within it is made clear in several texts. Durán's history—written in Spanish by a Spaniard who spoke Nahuatl and had Nahuatl sources—provides revealing examples. While the Spaniards are wending their way toward the city of Mexico, Moctezuma decides to send out medicine men to combat them. If the newcomers were really understood to be "gods" according to the term's definition in Spanish, then such an action makes no sense—since sorcerers fought human enemies, not gods. Durán's narrator deals with this inconsistency by having a close adviser to the king mention tactfully that such a step will probably be useless. Not long after, Moctezuma prepares to "receive the gods" in his city but then makes the following speech within the same paragraph: "Woe to us! . . . In what way have we offended the gods? What has happened? Who are these men who have arrived? Whence have they come?"[40] Given the varied implications of the term *teotl,* it is not surprising that the Spaniards chose to understand it simply as "god" and to forget about the Heredia incident. Bernal Díaz himself, after his initial avowal, never mentions the second definition again. In other cases, it is clear that the Spanish chose translations of ambiguous passages most in keeping with the notion that they were perceived as divine.[41]

Motolinía was the only Spaniard present in the early 1520s who explicitly addressed this issue. He asserted that, in the first villages the Spaniards entered, the locals thought that the horse-and-man figures were single beings, like classical centaurs, one imagines. Within days, they learned of their error, saw that "the man was a man and the horse a beast," and so had to seek new words. They used *mazatl* (deer) to refer to the horses, and they used the Spanish corruption of their own initial label (*teotl*), or *teul,* to refer to the people, as the Spanish were now introducing themselves as such. They knew no other word for the newcomers until after the victory, when they were instructed to call them *cristianos.* Some Spaniards complained about that shift, Motolinía says scornfully, preferring to be called *Teules.*[42]

I n the debates about what really happened at the time of conquest, two facts stand out. Acknowledging them both simultaneously is perhaps counterintuitive, as they appear to be in opposition to each other; they are not. First, it was much more difficult than is commonly imagined for the Spanish to vanquish the Aztecs; the Europeans were in desperate straits on more than one occasion. Second, it was inevitable that Cortés and his men—or some other soon-to-follow expedition—would conquer the Aztecs. They had the technological advantage. The outcome was no coincidence. The Spanish conquest of the Mexicans against large numerical odds was replicated in innumerable other confrontations in the Americas—between Francisco Pizarro and the Incas, Hernando de Soto and the Alabama Indians, the English settlers and the Algonkians, etc.—and much later between Europeans and Africans. Yet the victory was never facile, for those less well equipped in a technological sense still did all they could to defend their own interests.

Cortés rapidly learned from his translators what he needed to know—that the Aztec army was the most powerful in the land, that the king offered city-states the alternative of joining the empire peacefully and paying an annual tribute or of fighting and facing brutal defeat, that the Spaniards' most effective strategy would be to turn people against the hated overlords. In July 1519, he scuttled his ships so his men would not be tempted to turn back, and struck inland to seek the Aztec capital of Tenochtitlan. First, however, he sent one ship to Spain with the news of his coastal explorations, the information he had received thus far about the Mexican empire, and his hopes of claiming that state on behalf of Carlos V. He did this partly because he was a traitor in a legal sense, having launched his expedition from Cuba without the governor's permission, and so needed to make a case in his own defense. Equally important, he knew he would need reinforcements and supplies. In order not to lose contact with the wider world, he left a number of men in the newly founded town of Vera Cruz who would be there to meet reinforcements (or enemies) when they arrived. That the Veracruzanos not starve or be killed, Cortés took several coastal Indian chiefs hostage.[43]

The story has been told many times of how Cortés and his men made their way to Tenochtitlan—fighting when necessary, turning the Indians against each other through clever ruses, detecting plots and putting them down, and finally coming face-to-face with the great Moctezuma on the causeway leading to the island city. There, according to Cortés, Moctezuma welcomed him, and shortly after agreed to become a vassal of the Spanish king. One week later, following an ancient European tactic of war, Cortés claimed to have seized Moctezuma's person and placed him under house arrest, so that he could rule through him, and Moctezuma agreed to remain in custody even when Cortés later offered to release him upon a promise of good behavior. Cortés ruled the empire successfully for over five months and then learned that an army from the Caribbean under Captain Narváez had landed at Vera Cruz in pursuit of him. Leaving a contingent in the city, Cortés made for the coast, and there he brought the hundreds of newcomers over to his side. Yet the temporary division in the Spanish ranks had become visible to the indigenous, and they rebelled, ejecting the Spaniards from their city in the famed Noche Triste.

Even though posterity has tended to accept it, the story is in fact more than a little difficult to believe. The idea that the Aztecs peacefully surrendered their kingdom fits well with the notion that the Mexica responded to the Europeans as gods. If we do not proceed on that assumption, however, the story flies in the face of common sense. The Spanish numbered only about five hundred, the city folk a quarter of a million. The Spanish had only one translator to tell them what was occurring; Moctezuma's people could watch every move that every Spaniard made. Simply to eat every day, the Spaniards were desperately dependent on those they dreamed of ruling. How vulnerable they were in this regard becomes painfully clear in the Codex Aubin, in which a resident of Tenochtitlan recalled that, when the people later stopped feeding the invaders, the horses began to eat the straw mats that lined the floors. Although it is certainly true that the Spanish maintained a "seize the king" policy both before and after Tenochtitlan, early in their dealings with the impressive Aztecs, the newly arrived Spanish were unlikely to have been arrogantly sure of their course. They certainly did not have the power to arrest the emperor without bringing on a state of chaos, as events proved.[44]

John Elliott and others have explained the content of Cortés's letter to the king, which subsequently formed the basis for the story as we have come to know it.[45] Besides justifying the actions he had taken without receiving royal permission, Cortés was using language to leap another legalistic hurdle: Carlos V could only annex territories that came to him voluntarily or through a just war. It was thus very important that Moctezuma swear fealty to the Spanish monarch early in the letter, *before* his people rebelled, when they technically became traitors. Placing Moctezuma under arrest without his protesting the Spaniards' right to do so was a crucial symbolic step.

Francis Brooks has argued that there is strong evidence against Cortés having immediately arrested Moctezuma. First, although he was supposedly in full control of the kingdom from November to May, Cortés made no effort to inform anyone else in the world of his successes, even though he had men perfectly capable of building ships, as they later proved. Second, Cortés's own story contradicts itself often, describing Moctezuma as a prisoner one moment and in control the next.[46] Cortés himself describes what he was doing during those months—continuing to become acquainted with Moctezuma and the city, consulting the mapmakers, sending representatives to visit surrounding towns, collecting gifts of gold, and waiting for his ship to return with an answer from Spain.[47] It is perfectly possible to believe that he was doing all these things as an honored visitor but not as the leader of a handful of coup-staging interlopers.

It is, however, equally certain that Moctezuma was put in irons before the end of the drama. There is real evidence that it occurred in April of 1520, coinciding with the sudden appearance of his rival Captain Narváez. At that point, Cortés had nothing left to lose. On the one hand, a Spanish army larger than his own had arrived on the coast with the intention of arresting him; on the other hand, the Aztecs were aware of this turn of events and planned to use it to their advantage. Only with a gun to Moctezuma's head could Cortés assure the newly arrived Spaniards that he was in control of the kingdom and gain their allegiance, as well as stave off an indigenous uprising. Numerous sworn witnesses in later court cases claimed that Spanish soldiers guarded Moctezuma around the clock in this period. Durán mentions eighty days of confinement, which would indeed place the arrest in April.[48] Cortés claimed that Moctezuma begged to be of service to the Spanish king in defending the land against these evil new arrivals, but that scenario is so preposterous as to be laughable, except when considered in the legalistic light discussed above. Indeed, no other Spaniard writing about these events described them thus: the others universally described Moctezuma's obvious hostility (or duplicity).[49] One is left thinking that Cortés did protest too much; it is quite likely that, rather than swearing eternal friendship, he chose this moment to have Moctezuma clapped in irons. Yet precisely because his situation was so precarious, it was particularly important that he portray his control of the region as long-term.[50]

The accounts of the other conquistadors are replete with inconsistencies concerning their purported power. "While I stayed . . . I did not see a living creature killed or sacrificed," wrote Cortés. "The great Moctezuma continued to show his accustomed good will towards us, but never ceased his daily sacrifices of human beings. Cortés tried to dissuade him but met with no success," wrote Bernal Díaz.[51] In the midst of describing Moctezuma's palaces, Francisco de Aguilar seemed almost visibly to recall that he was supposed to be describing a prisoner: "They brought him . . . fish of all kinds, besides . . . fruits from the seacoast . . . The plates and cups of his dinner service were very clean. He was not served on gold or silver because he was in captivity, but it is likely that he had a great table service of gold and silver."[52] Aguilar went on to say (as per Cortés) that the arrest had taken place because the Spanish had learned that Moctezuma had plotted against them and had ordered one of the men left in Vera Cruz to be killed. Aguilar and Andrés de Tapia and a third man had been sent to the coast to ascertain the truth of the matter. But de Tapia's own account says Indians were sent on that errand.[53] His description of the five-month period of supposed Spanish control seems odd: "In this manner we stayed on, the marques keeping us so close to our quarters that no one stepped a musket-shot away without permission."[54]

The friars who wrote about the events also undermined the notion of an immediate arrest,[55] and, although later indigenous sources accept it, the earliest known indigenous record does not. The Annals of Tlatelolco was probably written in the mid-1540s, possibly based on a story that had been memorized in the late 1520s. Here, Moctezuma is detained sometime after Cortés finds he must leave for the seashore and before the Spanish initiate a massacre at a religious festival, leading directly to their own expulsion. Until that point, the city's only relationship with the newcomers had been to provide them with food, water, and firewood, as they would have done for any honored guests.[56]

Just as we must refrain from imagining that the Spanish arrived with the power to arrest Moctezuma immediately, we must also avoid the equally wrong-headed assumption that they were able to defeat the Aztecs militarily with a few well-aimed shots. When Cortés struck inland from Vera Cruz, he had only fifteen horses with him. Later, when the Aztecs rebelled and ejected the Spanish from the city, between four and six hundred men were killed as they fled along the causeways leading out of the city, along with at least a thousand Tlaxcalan allies. Narrow passages rendered the Europeans vulnerable to attack: on at least two different occasions, over forty Spaniards were ambushed and killed while traveling through gorges.

Yet, in the end, it was no accident that the Europeans won. I have recounted the difficulties the Spanish faced, the impossibility of their having taken over immediately, in order to be more credible in saying that Europeans were bound to destroy the Mexicans eventually. Although it can be argued that diseases weakened both the Mexica and the Spaniards' Indian allies, and thus were not determinant, there remained a huge divide between the military capabilities of the two sides. Outside the city, on open ground, the Spanish were nearly invincible. After regrouping in the wake of their expulsion from the city, Cortés launched a campaign against Tenochtitlan. Several weeks and numerous battles later, one Spaniard died of his wounds, and Cortés mourned "the first of my company to be killed . . . on this campaign."[57] What nearby village chief could say the same? The Spanish had learned how to use what they had to enable groups of two hundred men to withstand masses of enemies. Both their harquebus and crossbow firings were able to slice through the Indians' cotton armor, and, because of their weapons' range, they could attack lethally when

the Indians were still distant; furthermore, mounted Europeans carrying long metal lances could forge a path through the throngs. The Indians could fire their arrows at six times the rate of a Spanish blunderbuss, but to no avail, because metal armor rendered the Europeans nearly impervious.[58]

The horses were of utmost importance. Three horses could turn a dire situation into a rout. They could even solve the problem of food supplies: clusters of armed horsemen could take a village or market by surprise and return with what the Spanish needed. The Europeans' own engineering experience was also crucial. As soon as they arrived in Tenochtitlan, Cortés put his master shipbuilder to work on four brigantines in case they should be needed to escape across the lake. They later came in handy in the final battles in the canals of the city: "The key to the war lay with them . . . As the wind was good, we bore down through the middle of them, and although they fled as fast as they were able, we sank a huge number of canoes and killed or drowned many of the enemy, which was the most remarkable sight in the world."[59]

It is true as many have maintained that the Spanish would have been crushed by greater numbers in the long run or starved to death had they not worked with Indian allies ("special forces" style). A few hundred Spaniards became an unbeatable force only when combined with thousands of indigenous pouring in behind them. Cortés himself and several other chroniclers willingly attest to this. "When the inhabitants of the city saw . . . the great multitude of our allies—although without us, they would have had no fear of them—they fled, and our allies pursued them."[60] What we must understand, though, is that the technological advantage was what, in the last analysis, made it possible for the Spanish to retain their indigenous allies. The indigenous learned quickly that they did not have the requisite technology: they saw that their civilian populations could not survive the onslaughts of the Spaniards even in the short term, and they recognized the undeniable long-range importance of the Europeans' maritime connections to distant lands.

Much ink has been spilt over the question of why the Tlaxcalans, for example, traditional enemies of the Mexica, briefly battled the Spaniards, then sided with them as their unwavering and most significant allies. The Tlaxcalans had little love for the Mexica and could not afford the luxury of acquiring another powerful enemy in the persons of the Spanish. Cortés, however, tells us what the clincher was. "I burnt more than ten villages, in one of which there were more than three thousand houses, where the inhabitants fought with us, although there was no one [no warriors] there to help them." He kept 'round the clock guard of their camp with their long-range weapons to make sure the Tlaxcalans did not retaliate in kind, "which would have been so disastrous." When they sued for peace, Cortés explained, "They would rather be Your Highness's vassals than see their houses destroyed and their women and children killed."[61] Likewise, when Cortés and the other survivors of the Noche Triste made it back to Tlaxcala, they made it their business within days to attack villages that were not friendly to them. Most sued for peace. "They see how those who do so are well received and favored by me," wrote Cortés, "whereas those who do not are destroyed daily."[62] Meanwhile, Moctezuma offered one year's tax relief to those who refrained from going over to the Spanish, but that was a distant carrot compared to the immediate threat constituted by mounted lancers riding through town. When a set of villages received emissaries from Tenochtitlan, the Spanish torched the towns. "On the following day three chieftains from those towns came begging my forgiveness for what had happened and asking me to destroy nothing more, for they promised that they would never again receive anyone from Tenochtitlan."[63]

More important than any weapons or horses the Spanish had with them, however, were Spanish ships, which had the potential to bring endless reinforcements. One of Cortés's first acts after fleeing from Tenochtitlan had been to send two expeditions loaded with treasure, which they were to use to purchase horses and weapons. Before they could return, in mid-1520, seven ships loaded with men and supplies appeared off the coast, for word had spread since Cortés had dispatched his initial messages in 1519.[64] Three more fully stocked vessels would arrive in early 1521. Even though we have since tended to overlook it, Europeans of the time understood how crucial this factor was. When Aguilar narrated his memory of the post–Noche Triste period, he said first that other ships had arrived and then that the Indian towns had chosen to "offer themselves peaceably."[65] Cortés recalled, "One of my lads, who knew that nothing in the world would give me such pleasure as to learn of the arrival of this [new] ship and the aid it brought, set out by night [to bring me word], although the road was dangerous."[66] Indeed, Cortés was so well aware of the importance of his connection to the rest of the world that he made it his first order of business to build and staff forts along the road from Tenochtitlan to the sea, before proceeding with a campaign against Tenochtitlan.

At last he was ready: "When, on the twenty-eight of April . . . I called all my men out on parade and reckoned eighty-six horsemen, 118 crossbowmen and harquebusiers, some 700 foot soldiers with swords and bucklers, three large iron guns, fifteen small bronze field guns and ten hundredweight of powder, . . . [t]hey knew well . . . that God had helped us more than we had hoped, and ships had come with horses, men and arms."[67] After only a few days of battle, it was clear to many of the towns surrounding Tenochtitlan how well supplied the Spanish now were. "The natives of Xochimilco . . . and certain of the Otomí, . . . came to offer themselves as Your Majesty's vassals, begging me to forgive them for having delayed so long." After a major defeat suffered by the Spanish, in which forty were captured and sacrificed, many of the Spaniards' allies withdrew again. It is commonly accepted that they returned only when the Nahua priests' predictions of a great victory to occur within the ensuing eight days did not come true. Cortés, though, outlines events as follows: first messengers arrived from Vera Cruz telling of the arrival of yet another ship and bringing powder and crossbows to prove it, and then, in the next sentence, "all the lands round about" demonstrated their good sense and came over to the Spaniards' side.[68] Perhaps, after all, the Indians' decisions were less spiritually than practically motivated.

We must now expand our list of relevant technological implements to include printing presses. The comparatively quick and widespread communication channels available to the Spanish gave them a geopolitical perspective throughout the events that the Aztecs, for all their intelligence, even brilliance, simply lacked. At the end of sixteenth century, Matteo Ricci, a Jesuit missionary to China, would make a comment about books that the Aztecs would have appreciated, although they themselves envisioned texts in other ways: "The whole point of writing things down . . . is that your voice carries for thousands of miles."[69] Matteo Ricci read the Spanish, Portuguese, and Italian explorers, who themselves read Ibn Battutah and Marco Polo. As Todorov put it, "Did not Columbus himself set sail because he had read Marco Polo's narrative?"[70] In 1504, Amerigo Vespucci published his suggestion that what Columbus had found was not the tip of the Orient but a New World, and, by 1511, Peter Martyr's Latin compendium of reported observations on the New World was available to educated Europeans everywhere—within five years, it would even make its way into the best-read fiction of the day.[71] In 1509, the Spanish crown promulgated a law that no royal official was to do anything to impede the sending of any information about the Indies back to Spain.[72]

Albrecht Dürer is known for having spoken with awe of Aztec art that had been shipped back by Cortés and that he saw in an exhibit in the town hall in Brussels: "All the days of my life I have seen nothing that rejoiced my heart so much as these things, for I have seen among them wonderful works of art, and I marveled at the subtle intellects of men in foreign parts."[73] What is less well known is that Dürer saw these objects in July of 1520. Over a year before the conquest was complete, the Europeans were already putting on exhibits of their findings and spreading the word throughout their continent. Yet, on the other side of the sea, the Aztecs did not even know what to call the newcomers in their midst. The inequality of their positions is stunning, the subtle intellect of the Aztec artists notwithstanding.

What, then, were the indigenous thinking? Available evidence indicates that the Aztecs responded to their situation with clear-sighted analysis of the technological differential, rather than by prostrating themselves before the "white gods."[74] As difficult as it is, let us first consider what we know of Moctezuma's thoughts. The version of the king's response that later became popular was the vision of Moctezuma sighing and lapsing into paralyzing depression, but the evidence that we have about the steps taken by Moctezuma indicates that he actually behaved like the experienced twenty-year sovereign he was. All sources agree that, after the first sighting of a Spanish ship in 1517, he had the sea watched from various vantage points. When Cortés and his men landed near today's Vera Cruz and began conversing with the locals, Moctezuma sent court painters to record the numbers of men, "deer," and boats.[75] Even though the Spaniards saw these paintings as quaint, we must keep in mind that Moctezuma moved within a world in which accurate counts concerning distant territories were kept as pictoglyphic records as a matter of course.[76] As the Spanish began their ascent toward Tenochtitlan, Moctezuma organized a veritable war room. "A report of everything that was happening was given and relayed to Moctezuma. Some of the messengers would be arriving as others were leaving . . . There was no time when they weren't listening, when reports weren't being given."[77] Cortés also reported that Moctezuma's messengers were present in every town they visited, watching every step they took. Bernal Díaz said by the time the Spaniards got to the capital, the sermon they had given frequently along the way had been repeated so often to Moctezuma that he asked them not to give it again, as the arguments were by now familiar to him.[78] Despite his intelligence and his organizational apparatus, however, Moctezuma still had the problem that his frame of reference was not as wide as that of the Spaniards: Durán's informant said that he called for priests and sages from different parts of the kingdom to consult their libraries and traditions and tell him who these strangers were, but they could find nothing. Only one man said anything useful, describing the power of the Spaniards and mentioning that the first explorers were merely there to scout a route, that others would return.[79]

The words of Moctezuma's that we have come from Cortés, who claimed to quote a long speech of greeting in which Moctezuma turned over his kingdom to the Spaniard.[80] The elaborate statement may well have been loosely based on something that Moctezuma actually said—minus the immediate surrender of his entire kingdom—as it employs the classic courtly Nahuatl style, makes no reference to Cortés being Quetzalcoatl or any other god, and mentions facts that would otherwise have been unknown to the Spanish at this early date—that the Aztecs themselves were migrants to the region and had a long history of banished kings—which Moctezuma found sufficient to explain the arrival of the newcomers. Later, Cortés actually has Moctezuma insist to his Spanish audience that he himself is *not* a god, and does not possess untold wealth: "I know that [my enemies] have told you the walls of my houses are made of gold, and that the floor mats in my rooms . . . are likewise of gold, and that I was, and claimed to be, a god; . . . The houses as you see are of stone and lime and clay . . . Then he raised his clothes and showed me his body, saying, 'See that I am of flesh and blood like you and all other men.'" This may have been invented by Cortés.[81] But a Nahuatl speaker would have been very likely to use "floor mats" and "flesh and blood" as important metaphors; their poets did so frequently. Indeed, one is hard-pressed to think of a convincing political reason for Cortés to throw in this particular paragraph. On the other hand, Moctezuma had every reason to make the statement—to minimize the extent of his wealth and in order to work his way around in courtly and indirect speech in true Nahuatl style to his impolite punch line: he wanted it known that he did not believe the Spaniards to be gods. One is even more inclined to read the statement this way in that it is apparently how the Spanish read it then, judging from the style in which both López de Gómara and Bernal Díaz recounted the incident. Bernal Díaz embellished: "You must take the [stories] as a joke, as I take the story of your thunders and lightnings."[82]

If we cannot be certain of what Moctezuma said, we can at least analyze his actions as a text of sorts: indeed, his decision to allow the Spaniards and many hundreds of their Tlaxcalan allies to enter his city has been analyzed for many years as if it were a declaration of sentiment. In lieu of the traditional interpretation that he was a coward or a fool, scholars have proffered various motivations—caution, a desire for secrecy, a need to wait for the dry season.[83] There is a central explanation for Moctezuma's decision, however. Besides attempting to turn the potential conquerors back by offering them annual tribute, the emperor apparently did try to have the Spanish killed at least twice while they were still distant; somebody certainly gave the order to attack them. Yet, when the Spaniards were nearing the city, "Moctezuma did not give orders for anyone to meet them in battle."[84] He could not: he knew now that the Spaniards won battles in the open field. Even if

he had had time to arm every warrior in his kingdom and then surround and destroy the Spanish with the sheer force of numbers, he would have been politically destroyed. The casualties would have been immense, beyond anything ever seen, and the people of the Central Valley accepted the arrogance of their Mexica neighbors in exchange for peace and the privilege of living close to power. If the Aztecs could not deliver a quick victory on the outskirts of their own capital, they were doomed; so if his army could not win quickly and easily here—and Moctezuma knew they could not—then they could not fight. At the time, Cortés and his followers did not understand the political situation well enough to grasp this fact; centuries later, posterity tends to lose sight of the realities of that world. Not so those who wrote a few decades later. Said López de Gómara: "It seemed unfitting and dishonorable for him to make war upon Cortés and fight a mere handful of strangers who said they were ambassadors. Another reason was that he did not wish to stir up trouble for himself (and this was the truest reason), for it was clear that he would immediately have to face an uprising among the Otomí, the Tlaxcalans, and many others." Said Bernal Díaz: "Moctezuma's captains and *papas* also advised him that if he tried to prevent our entry *we would fight him in his subject towns.*"[85]

It is reasonable to assume that, while Cortés and his men were in the city gathering information about the kingdom, Moctezuma was also attempting to gather information about them. It may have been his hope that they would eventually leave of their own accord. Almost all accounts except the letter by Cortés indicate that it was Moctezuma's messengers who first told of the arrival of Captain Narváez: it was the Mexican king who told the Spanish the news, not the other way around. Whether Moctezuma was initially behind it or not, his people did raise a rebellion against the Spanish as soon as Cortés returned from the coast. Moctezuma himself became known for the speeches he made from the rooftops in which he asked the warriors to lay down their arms. "Let the Mexica hear: we are not their match, may they be dissuaded [from further fighting]."[86] By then, he was in irons, and so has been seen as a coward doing his best to save his life. But it is possible that he, the warrior king who had led so many successful campaigns, preached peace in relation to the Spanish out of true conviction that his people would be destroyed if they pursued violence. In interpreting his actions, we would do well to remember that if so, *he was right.* Moctezuma, with his knowledge of the capabilities of both sides, was one of the few Mexica in a position to be able to see the *longue durée.*[87]

Inga Clendinnen has studied the reactions of the Mexica warriors to the Spanish. She finds evidence that, despite the great respect the Aztecs had for the horses, they held the Spanish men themselves in outright contempt. When the Spanish returned to retake the city, there is no evidence that the warriors operated according to sacred signs or astrology; instead, they put immediate practicality before all else. Contrary to popular opinion, they did not fight to take prisoners for sacrifice rather than to kill: they did not even want the Spanish for sacrifice, and, when they had a chance to destroy them, did so with a blow to the back of the head, as they did with criminals. In general, the only use the warriors made of sacrifice in this campaign was as a tool to instill terror in the hearts of the Spanish who were close enough to see what they were doing.[88]

We have significant evidence about the military men's attitude toward technology. The Aztecs cleverly used their own inventions against their enemies whenever they could. When the Spanish approached the city in what was to be the final campaign, the Indians secretly opened a dike in an effort to trap the opposing forces on an island that was connected to land by only one causeway.[89] More often, though, the indigenous were in the position of needing to decode Spanish tactics and technology as quickly as possible, rather than showing off their own. Through keen observation, they were able to make remarkable headway. First, there was the question of seizing some of the Spaniards' powerful weapons and learning to use them. They quickly put captured lances to use but recognized that the Spaniards' other weapons were more powerful: "The crossbowman aimed the bolt well, he pointed it right at the person he was going to shoot, and when it went off, it went whining, hissing and humming. And the arrows missed nothing, they all hit someone, went all the way through someone. The guns were pointed and aimed right at people . . . It came upon people unawares, giving no warning when it killed them. However many were fired at died, when some dangerous part was hit: the forehead, the nape of the neck, the heart, the chest, the stomach, or the abdomen."[90] These weapons, however, were more difficult to use: at one point, some captured crossbowmen were apparently either forced to shoot at their countrymen or to give lessons to Aztec soldiers; in either case, the arrows went astray. And the guns of course would not work without powder, even if the Aztecs could have learned to make bullets. When they captured a cannon, they recognized they had neither the expertise nor the ammunition to make it useful to themselves. The best they could do was make it impossible for the Spanish ever to regain it: they wisely sank it in the lake.[91] The second pressing concern was to thwart Spanish technology even if they could not harness it themselves. The natives made extra long spears and managed to take an occasional horseman by surprise, killing the beast and pulling down the rider. Canoe men learned to zigzag so rapidly that guns could not be trained on them, and, once, they were able to lure two Spanish boats into shallow water and capture them.[92] Yet what they could do in this regard was limited.

As frustrated as they were by their technological shortcomings in comparison to the Spanish, at no point do the warriors seem to have responded as if they were awestruck. In one case, the Spanish decided to build a catapult to turn against the city. Cortés wanted to believe that the Indian observers were petrified: "Even if it were to have had no other effect, which indeed it had not, the terror it caused was so great that we thought the enemy might surrender. But neither of our hopes was fulfilled, for the carpenters failed to operate their machine."[93] Little did he know that, in Indian memory, the incident would border on the humorous:

And then those Spaniards installed a catapult on top of an altar platform with which to hurl stones at the people . . . Then they wound it up, then the arm of the catapult rose up. But the stone did not land on the people, but fell [almost straight down] behind the marketplace at Xomolco. Because of that the Spaniards there argued among themselves. They looked as if they were jabbing their fingers in one another's faces, chattering a great deal. And [meanwhile] the catapult kept returning back and forth, going one way and then the other.[94]

Indeed, this relatively straightforward view of Spanish accomplishments is pervasive in Nahua accounts of the war. European technology is mentioned frequently—not as something mystifying in the hands of gods but as the clear and concrete explanation for indigenous military losses. As early as the Annals of Tlatelolco, writers mentioned at the key point in their narration that "the war leaders were dying from the guns and iron bolts." As late as the end of the century, Ixtlilxochitl mentions that a local king decides to heed his sister and not try to stop Cortés: she warned of "a young man with a light in one hand that would exceed that of the sun, and in the other an *espada,* which was the weapon that this newly arrived nation used."[95] The Florentine Codex, in the middle of the century, is full of the "We are not their match" concept to which Moctezuma gives full voice before he dies; indeed, it is the messengers' comment upon their first return from seeing the newcomers.

Reading Book Twelve from start to finish, including the first part, which contains the obviously revisionist account of the facts, as well as the more faithful second section, one is left with two predominant images—which surely speak to the most profound impressions the Indians received and passed on to their children. Both images are direct reflections of the technological discrepancy between the peoples involved, of which the narrators are clearly very much aware. First, page by page, the mounted Spaniards in their clanking armor with their metallic weapons move ever closer to the great city. That the Spanish had passed through the Iron Age was certainly not lost on the Mexica. The word *tepoztli* (metal, or iron) appears more than any other. The initial report Moctezuma is given is presented in three sections. First come the Spaniards' weapons. "Their war gear was all iron. They clothed their bodies in iron, they put iron on their heads, their swords were iron, their bows were iron, and their shields and lances were iron." Next, the horses are described, and last the vicious dogs who accompany their masters. Later, when the Indians attempt to fight, they lose dramatically. "Not just a few but a huge number of them were destroyed." After killing yet more Indians in Cholula, the Spanish set out again: "Their iron lances and halberds seem to sparkle, and their iron swords were curved like a stream of water. Their cuirasses and iron helmets seemed to make a clattering sound." When they file into Tenochtitlan, their metal weapons and armor are described in even greater detail, filling whole pages.[96]

Secondly, throughout the narrative, although the Indians do not know who the newcomers were, the newcomers know enough about the world to search for Moctezuma; they will not rest until they find him. First, Cortés uses his knowledge to flatter. "I want to see and behold [your city], for word has gone out in Spain that you are very strong, great warriors." The Spaniards ask many questions. "When Moctezuma heard this, that many and persistent inquiries were being made about him, that the gods wanted to see his face, he was greatly anguished." Later: "When they saw [an Aztec general] they said, 'Is this one then Moctezuma?'" On the causeway, Cortés greets the king: "Is it not you? Is it not you then? Moctezuma?" and Moctezuma at last answers, "Yes, it is me."[97] This element makes the indigenous feel at least as vulnerable as do the metal weapons: the Spaniards have somehow used their knowledge to make their way to the heart of Aztec power, but the Aztecs could not begin to envision a similar expedition to the seat of Carlos V. They now knew about the ships, but only a few—probably Moctezuma, for example—had seen the compasses and printed books in the possession of the Spaniards. Ordinary people could only begin to piece together an explanation. What is remarkable is that they knew this is what needed to be explained.

This is a case in which the ending is only the beginning. In the first few years after the conquest was complete, the Aztecs exhibited few signs of believing that gods walked in their midst. Motolinía tells us that, for the first five years, no one paid any attention to the priests who were attempting to reach out to the people. In 1526, the Franciscans held a marriage ceremony for a prince, but when they tried to convince others to follow his example, the Indians said dismissively that Spanish men themselves had more than one woman. When the fathers opened a school and Cortés ordered the indigenous nobles to send their sons, the families sent servants as substitutes. They had no intention of turning their children over to such men and were confident that the newcomers were too stupid or ill informed to know the difference.[98] What would they have said if they could have known that posterity would insist they believed the Spaniards to be divine?

Notes

I would like to thank the friends and colleagues who read, critiqued, and improved earlier versions of this work: Antonio Barrera, James Lockhart, Frederick Luciani, John Graham Nolan, David Robinson, Andrew Rotter, Kira Stevens, Gary Urton, and Anja Utgennant, as well as Michael Grossberg, Allyn Roberts, and the anonymous *AHR* reviewers.

1. Lesley Byrd Simpson, trans. and ed., *Cortés: The Life of the Conqueror by His Secretary* (Berkeley, Calif., 1965), excerpted from Francisco López de Gómara, *Historia de la conquista de México* (Zaragoza, 1552), 137. (Although all research was conducted in the Spanish originals, in the interest of communication I have here cited published English translations wherever there exists an edition that is generally considered definitive. Where there is none, I have provided translations myself.)

2. Several scholars have recently alluded to the unlikelihood of the commonly accepted scenario, among them Susan D. Gillespie, *The Aztec Kings: The Construction of Rulership in Mexica History* (Tucson, Ariz., 1989); James Lockhart, ed. and trans., *We People Here: Nahuatl Accounts of the Conquest of Mexico* (Berkeley, Calif., 1993); and Ross Hassig, *Time, History and Belief in Aztec and Colonial Mexico* (Austin, Tex., 2001). None have made it the focus of any work. This stands in contrast to South Pacific history, at least as written by anthropologists. Gananath Obeyesekere set out to challenge the "fact" that Captain Cook was received as the god Lono in Hawai'i in 1779 in *The Apotheosis of Captain Cook: European Mythmaking in the Pacific* (Princeton, N.J., 1992), thereby earning for himself several awards but also the anger of Marshall Sahlins in *How "Natives" Think: About Captain Cook, for Example* (Chicago, 1995). Prominent Mexicanists who have accepted the legends include David Carrasco, *Quetzalcoatl and the Irony of Empire: Myths and Prophecies in the Aztec Tradition* (Chicago, 1982); Jacques Lafaye, *Quetzalcóatl and Guadalupe: The Formation*

of Mexican National Consciousness, 1531–1813, Benjamin Keen, trans. (Chicago, 1976); Miguel León-Portilla, ed., *The Broken Spears,* Lysander Kemp, trans. (Boston, 1962); and H. B. Nicholson, *Topiltzin Quetzalcoatl: The Once and Future Lord of the Toltecs* (Boulder, Colo., 2001). Similar ideas about the Indians having accepted the newly arrived whites as gods developed elsewhere in the New World as well, but space limitations prevent treatment of that subject here. For musings on the situation in the Andean world, see Olivia Harris, " 'The Coming of the White People': Reflections on the Mythologisation of History in Latin America," *Bulletin of Latin American Research* 14, no. 1 (1995): 9–24.

3. On the word "Aztec": this was a term introduced generations later by outsiders to talk about a political conglomeration. The ethnic group who held power called themselves the Mexica (pronounced me-SHEE-ka). They, and most of the people they governed, were Nahuas, or speakers of the Nahuatl language. For ease of communication, I will most often use the more generally known term. On the nature of the Aztec state: it is now understood by experts that the "empire" in fact consisted of profoundly divided ethnic groups residing in separate city-states, thus rendering it particularly vulnerable to the invading Europeans, as will be discussed. However, in conversations with colleagues from other fields, I have learned that it is essential to state unequivocally that the Aztecs did represent an advanced state—with a capital city larger than any in Europe, a regularized taxation system in which accounts of collections and expenditures were kept, and a profoundly imperialist tendency toward expansionism. For a discussion of the great differences between, for example, the Aztecs and the more nomadic groups familiar to most U.S. historians, see John E. Kicza, *Resilient Cultures: America's Native Peoples Confront European Colonization, 1500–1800* (Upper Saddle River, N.J., 2003).

4. Felipe Fernández-Armesto, "Aztec Auguries and Memories of the Conquest of Mexico," *Renaissance Studies* 6 (1992): 303; Hugh Thomas, *Conquest: Montezuma, Cortés and the Fall of Old Mexico* (London, 1993), 601.

5. Scholars have argued that the Europeans' advanced agricultural lifestyle, alongside animals and their use of ships, contributed to the spread of disease and hence the development of antibodies that the American indigenous did not have. The point may be moot in the case of the defeat of the Aztecs, for, although their soldiers were brought low by smallpox, the same was true of the Spaniards' allies, on whom they relied for their victory. See Ross Hassig, *Mexico and the Spanish Conquest* (London, 1994), 101–02.

6. Fernández-Armesto, "Aztec Auguries," 288.

7. Jared Diamond, *Guns, Germs, and Steel: The Fates of Human Societies* (New York, 1997). Gale Stokes included this Pulitzer Prize-winning book in a review essay, "The Fates of Human Societies: A Review of Recent Macrohistories," *AHR* 106 (April 2001): 508–25. He begins, "Not many historians would subtitle their book, 'The Fates of Human Societies,' " and goes on to say that it is biologist Jared Diamond who has had the nerve. Although Stokes's overall argument is that macrohistory when done well (and he implicitly includes Diamond's work in this category) certainly has its uses, Diamond's theme of "Eurasia-meets-the-rest-of-the-world [and wins]" is lost in the rest of the essay, which focuses instead on the equally interesting question of why Europe, as opposed to China,

became the leader of the modern world. Almost nothing has been written about the book in Latin Americanist journals. To my knowledge, only one recent textbook on colonial America opens with an explicit consideration of Diamond's argument: Stanley N. Katz, John M. Murrin, and Douglas Greenberg, eds., *Colonial America: Essays in Politics and Social Development,* 5th edn. (New York, 2001).

8. León-Portilla has done important work beyond the ivory tower as well, bringing Nahuatl-speaking indigenous poets to work at Mexico's most prestigious universities and supporting *indigenista* movements in other ways. His political significance must not be underestimated.

9. Jorge Klor de Alva, "Foreword," to León-Portilla, *Broken Spears,* xi.

10. León-Portilla, *Broken Spears,* 35. Most of the book conveys similar images, coming from texts written in the 1550s and later. As of 2000, a new textbook became available that translates Nahuatl primary sources into English (*Victors and Vanquished: Spanish and Nahua Views of the Conquest of Mexico,* published by Bedford/St. Martin's). The book's editor, Stuart B. Schwartz, is well acquainted with the work of his colleague James Lockhart on early Mexico, and includes mention of some controversy over the existence of the Quetzalcoatl myth—but unfortunately only after recounting the story as if it were true. Books that promise to be helpful in teaching include Matthew Restall, *Seven Myths of the Spanish Conquest* (New York, 2003); Stephanie Wood, *Transcending Conquest: Nahua Views of Spanish Colonial Mexico* (Norman, Okla., forthcoming); and another by James Lockhart (see note 18 below).

11. Tzvetan Todorov, *The Conquest of America: The Question of the Other* (New York, 1984), 63, 69, 75, 87. See Inga Clendinnen's analysis of this text in "Cortés, Signs, and the Conquest of Mexico," in Anthony Grafton and Ann Blair, eds., *The Transmission of Culture in Early Modern Europe* (Philadelphia, 1990). See also Clendinnen, "Fierce and Unnatural Cruelty: Cortés and the Conquest of Mexico," *Representations* 33 (1991): 65–100.

12. On the spelling of the Mexican emperor's name: the English and Germans later used "Montezuma," but none of the players on the scene did. The correct spelling of the name in Nahuatl is debatable and, in any case, somewhat alienating to non-Nahuatl speakers. I am using the most common Spanish form ("Moctezuma") except where quoting someone who uses a different version.

13. Thomas, *Conquest,* 180. There are many such examples in the book. Nor is this argument limited only to Thomas. Viewers of Michael Wood's recent BBC series "Conquistadors" (2000) will not have failed to detect his interest in and sympathy for the Indians. Yet he, too, subscribes to the white gods theory and quotes the *Broken Spears* text verbatim—and without raising hackles. His reviewer in *The Chronicle Review* mentions that he might well be more critical of the "Black Legend" concerning Spain but argues that "his treatment of the natives is politically faultless" (Diana de Armas Wilson, "Killing for God and for Gold," May 4, 2001). There is a beautiful new trade book that likewise takes the old stories for granted: Neil Baldwin, *Legends of the Plumed Serpent: Biography of a Mexican God* (New York, 1998).

14. The most useful edition of Cortés is *Letters from Mexico,* J. H. Elliott, intro., and Anthony Pagden, trans. and ed. (New Haven, Conn., 1986). Bernal Díaz is valuable despite the fact that he takes the structure of his book, almost section by section, from López de Gómara, alternating between plagiarizing his words and arguing vociferously and explicitly with them. A few have even argued that he fantasized his own participation in the conquest, given that he situates himself at the heart of all the action and that his name fails to appear on one list of participants housed in the Archive of the Indies in Spain. But all the chroniclers plagiarized; all exaggerated their own role; and no extant list of men or equipment is complete. There is evidence that he was there (in 1540, both Cortés and the viceroy wrote to the emperor on his behalf), and the text includes many details that only a participant would have thought of or gotten right. The most careful positioning of Bernal Díaz in relation to his contemporaries has been accomplished by Rolena Adorno, "Discourses on Colonialism: Bernal Díaz, Las Casas, and the Twentieth Century Reader," *Modern Language Notes* 103 (1988): 239–58; and "The Discursive Encounter of Spain and America: The Authority of Eyewitness Testimony in the Writing of History," *William and Mary Quarterly* 49 (1992): 210–28. The edition of Bernal Díaz used here is *The Conquest of New Spain,* J. M. Cohen, ed. (London, 1963), trans. from *Historia verdadera de la conquista de la nueva España por Bernal Díaz del Castillo,* Joaquín Ramírez Cabañas, ed. (Mexico City, 1955). The chronicles of Andrés de Tapia and Francisco de Aguilar are found in Patricia de Fuentes, ed., *The Conquistadors: First-Person Accounts of the Conquest of Mexico* (Norman, Okla., 1993). Another supposedly firsthand account is now known as the chronicle of the "Anonymous Conquistador." It appears to have been written by someone who never actually saw Mexico City. Bernardino Vásquez de Tapia also left a brief military summary. Another conquistador named Ruy González later wrote a letter to the king, but, as the latter two do not help significantly with the issue under discussion, I will leave them aside. See Arthur P. Stabler and John E. Kicza, "Ruy González's 1553 Letter to Emperor Charles V: An Annotated Translation," *The Americas* 42 (1986).

15. He had some direct sources: in the earliest days, Motolinía worked with Malinche, the Indian woman translator who had worked with Cortés; later, he came to know well the young Indian nobles who studied Latin and other subjects with the fathers, even though communication was at first minimal. He noted with humor, "The first one who taught singing . . . was an old friar who barely knew a single word of the Indians' language, . . . and he spoke as quickly as if he were speaking to students in Spain. Those of us who heard him could not help laughing . . . It was a marvelous thing that even though at first they understood nothing . . . in a short time they understood and learned the songs." Fray Toribio de Benavente Motolinía, *Historia de los indios de la Nueva España* (Madrid, 1988), 271.

16. The original is housed in the Laurenziana Medicean Library, Florence. A facsimile edition is *Códice florentino* (Florence, 1979). An English edition is Arthur J. O. Anderson and Charles Dibble, eds., *The Florentine Codex: General History of the Things of New Spain* (Salt Lake City, 1950–82). Sahagún's earliest version of the text is published as *The Primeros*

Memoriales, Thelma Sullivan, H. B. Nicholson, Arthur J. O. Anderson, Charles Dibble, Eloise Quiñones, and Wayne Ruwet, eds. (Norman, Okla., 1997). On the Franciscan agenda in general, see John Leddy Phelan, *The Millennial Kingdom of the Franciscans in the New World,* 2d edn. rev. (Berkeley, Calif., 1970).

17. He interviewed extensively, often asking about codices he knew villagers still had, once venting his frustration at "Indian wordiness in telling fables—when anyone is willing to listen to them they go on forever," but generally providing a sympathetic ear and recording certain perspectives that are obviously indigenous. Of course, we must approach his work cautiously: he did, for example, insert statements clearly made by contemporaries into the mouths of historical figures. He has Moctezuma make this bitter speech before the Spaniards arrive: "They will reign and I shall be the last king of this land. Even though some of our descendants and relatives may remain, even though they may be made governors and given states, they will not be true lords and kings but subordinates, like tax collectors or gatherers of the tribute that my ancestors and I have won. Our descendants' only task will be to comply with the commands and orders of the strangers." Diego Durán, *The History of the Indies of New Spain,* Doris Heyden, ed. (Norman, Okla., 1994), 511–12.

18. James Lockhart in *We People Here* has gathered together the only six of these statements that describe the conquest and were written before 1560, after which date it is unlikely that people who had clear memories of the events still lived. This is an invaluable collection because it includes careful transcriptions of both the Nahuatl text and the Spanish summaries, and yet it is accessible to everyone because it includes translations of each. A "student-friendly" edition is in preparation at Stanford University Press.

19. On the methods of interviewing and the names and positions of those Indians who did the interviewing, see Lockhart, *We People Here;* and Alfredo López Austin, "The Research Method of Fray Bernardino de Sahagún," in Munro S. Edmonson, ed., *Sixteenth-Century Mexico: The Work of Sahagún* (Albuquerque, N. Mex., 1974).

20. There were a number of indigenous (or mestizo, but Indian-identified) writers in this period, including a grandson of Moctezuma named Don Fernando de Alvarado Tezozomac, Diego Muñoz Camargo from Tlaxcala, and Don Domingo de San Antón Muñón Chimalpahin from Chalco. None left work as extensive or as useful in the case of this particular project as Ixtlilxochitl, and so in the interest of space, I am leaving them aside. Chimalpahin, however, deserves special mention because he wrote for a Nahua audience. In his accounts, the Spaniards appear not as gods but as a set of foreign invaders. The year summaries for 1519–1522 resemble other year summaries. "The year Three House, 1521: At this time Quauhtemoctzin [Cuauhtemoc] was installed as ruler of Tenochtitlan in Izcalli in the ancient month count, and in February in the Christian month count, when the Spaniards still occupied Tlaxcala. He was a son of Ahuitzotzin." Arthur J. O. Anderson and Susan Schroeder, eds., *Codex Chimalpahin* (Norman, Okla., 1997), 167. See also Susan Schroeder, "Looking Back at the Conquest: Nahua Perceptions of Early Encounters from the Annals of Chimalpahin," in Eloise Quiñones Keber, ed., *Chipping Away on Earth* (Lancaster, Calif., 1994), 377–97.

21. For example: "No me he querido aprovechar de las historias que hartan de esta material, por la diversidad y confusión que

tienen entre sí los autores que hartan de ellas, por las falsas relaciones y contrarias interpretaciones que se les dieron." Fernando de Alva Ixtlilxochitl, "Sumaria Relación de la Historia General de Esta Nueva España desde el origen del mundo hasta la Era de Ahora," in *Obras históricas,* Edmundo O'Gorman, ed., vol. 1 (Mexico City, 1975), 525. There is no question that Ixtlilxochitl is a problematic source if one is looking for a "pure" Indian voice: he sometimes relied, for example, on the "Codex Xolotl" (Charles Dibble, ed., *Códice Xolotl* [Mexico City, 1951]), which is clearly a post-conquest creation, and he was personally and politically embedded in elite Creole culture. For a discussion of the latter issue, see Jorge Cañizares-Esguerra, *How to Write the History of the New World: Historiographies, Epistemologies, and Identities in the Eighteenth-Century Atlantic World* (Stanford, Calif., 2001), esp. 221–25. I read him, however, as having a distinctly indigenous perspective in subtle ways. For example, he inserts "por lengua de Marina" (through the words of Malinche) frequently when summarizing communications made with the Spanish—even, in one case, when a local king was asking Cortés and his men to accept some local girls as sleeping partners. "Historia de la nación chichimeca," in *Obras históricas,* O'Gorman, ed., vol. 2 (Mexico City, 1977), 214.

22. Lockhart, *We People Here,* 5.

23. Lockhart, *We People Here,* 18. It is worth noting that other sources purportedly based on interviews with those involved reflect this same bipartite treatment—a history that reads like a recitation of myths suddenly becomes a detailed and realistic description of battle scenes. See Ixtlilxochitl, "Compendio Histórico del Reino de Texcoco," in *Obras históricas,* vol. 1. Ross Hassig also concludes after working extensively with the second part of Book Twelve, "The Aztecs did not lose their faith, they lost a war." *Mexico and the Spanish Conquest,* 149.

24. The one exception was the Tlaxcalan Diego Muñoz Camargo. Writing in 1580, he claimed that people in his city were also preoccupied with the foretellings of the white gods, but as proof he offered the same set of omens that took the Aztec capital as their point of reference, "an unimaginable attribute of a source resting on authentic Tlaxcalan tradition" (Lockhart, *We People Here,* 17). The repetition of details shows that Muñoz Camargo clearly copied straight from the Florentine.

25. Fernández-Armesto, "Aztec Auguries."

26. Durán, *History of the Indies of New Spain,* 493. This is a motif in Durán's text.

27. In other versions, less famous to us today, the seers and sorcerers similarly speak the Truth, but to no effect because Moctezuma has grown proud and will not listen. See Stephen Colston, " 'No Longer Will There Be a Mexico': Omens, Prophecies, and the Conquest of the Aztec Empire," *American Indian Quarterly* 9 (1985): 244. Ixtlilxochitl relies on this tradition in "Compendio Histórico del Reino de Texcoco," in *Obras históricas,* 1: 450–51. Additionally, Sahagún's young men were mostly from Tlatelolco, once a neighboring city-state, not Tenochtitlan proper, and although they were in many ways identified with the Aztecs, their ancestors had in fact been conquered; thus, as Kevin Terraciano has pointed out to me in a personal communication, they may have found it satisfying to represent the heart of the Aztec state as crumbling in panic.

28. Gillespie, *Aztec Kings,* esp. 197–98. For a detailed study of the feathered serpent motif throughout Mesoamerica, see Enrique Florescano, *The Myth of Quetzalcoatl* (Baltimore, 1999).

29. Following is a drastic oversimplification of the transformation of the narrative: I refer the reader to Gillespie's *Aztec Kings* for further details (185–95). In the 1530s, in the first three Spanish texts recounting Aztec history, supposedly as told to the writers by locals, two would-be kings fight, and one ends up leading his followers away (also a common trope in the pre-Hispanic codices); in one version, probably recorded by a well-known friar and linguist, Andres de Olmos, the important hero is named Ce Acatl (One Reed), which is as close as we come to the name "Quetzalcoatl." In the early 1540s, however, while the mortal hero is still "Huemac" in the Nahuatl text "Historia Tolteca Chichimeca" from the Puebla area, he is in Spanish texts explicitly named Quetzalcoatl, apparently in honor of the god in several cases, or as a man who was deified after his death (a common element of European mythology) in Motolinía's and Andrés de Tapia's works.

30. Motolinía, *Historia de los Indios,* 107–08.

31. For a full treatment of the church's intellectual wrestling with the Indian question, see Lafaye, *Quetzalcoatl and Guadalupe.* The most popular version among clerics held it that Quetzalcoatl had in fact been the apostle St. Thomas. It was not only the New World's Christian missionaries who looked for evidence that God had sent previous emissaries to the lands they hoped to convert. By the late sixteenth century, the Jesuits in China also believed they had found proof of an earlier presence. (Personal communication from David Robinson.)

32. At the end of the century, various authors continued to "mix and match" the contrasting elements. In the case of Ixtlilxochitl, his personal trajectory regarding the legend closely paralleled that of his century. As a very young man, while he is still according to his own testimony struggling simply to decipher certain codices or stories and summarize them, he describes the rise and fall of the hero Topiltzin, making no mention whatsoever of Quetzalcoatl or of anyone fleeing by sea or promising to return. There is a fragmentary document attached to a later work, apparently intended to be a commentary on an accompanying picture, now lost, in which he suddenly says that Topiltzin at last went east and died there and was burned to ashes along with all his treasure, but that he promised to return in the year One Reed, which was when the Spanish came. In a later work, Ixtlilxochitl introduces a section on the pre-Toltec period, which he had never mentioned before, and here he presents a sinless virgin hero "whom they called Quetzalcoatl, or by another name, Huemac" who had come from the east and would come again. The character does not appear anywhere else in the volume; the narrative continues in a more traditional vein. In the magnum opus he wrote before his death, Ixtlilxochitl begins with a full chapter on Quetzalcoatl, who by now is a fully delineated character, indeed, the first great historian of the Americas (implicitly a precursor to Ixtlilxochitl himself), who leaves records of his own great works for posterity to find, and who passes away by sea, promising that when he returned his children would become "the lords and possessors of the earth." Thus Ixtlilxochitl left Aztec history intact yet framed it between the by-now expected departure of the early saint and the arrival of the Spanish. Ixtlilxochitl, "Sumaria Relación de las cosas de la Nueva España" [c. 1600] (273, 387), and "Compendio Histórico del Reino de Texcoco" [c. 1608] (529), in *Obras históricas,* vol. 1; Ixtlilxochitl, "Historia de la Nación Chichimeca," in *Obras históricas,* 2: 7–9. Durán inserts the story even more awkwardly into his manuscript.

33. Lockhart, *We People Here,* 20.

34. Durán, *History of the Indies,* 499–500.

35. This phrase was used in writing a few more times in the sixteenth century, and Lockhart has taken it as the very apt title of his book.

36. "Annals of Tlatelolco" and "Historia Tolteca-Chichimeca," both in Lockhart, *We People Here,* 271, 287.

37. "Book Twelve of the Florentine Codex," in Lockhart, *We People Here,* 244, 179, 252, respectively. The priest's resistance to using the term that binds him as a vassal is particularly noteworthy in that the Spanish tortured those Mexica leaders who did not participate in helping them locate missing gold and jewels.

38. Louise Burkhart has studied the Franciscans' early efforts to "translate" religion. Theirs was no easy task, as the Nahuas did not see the universe as a struggle between good and evil but rather between order and chaos. There was, for example, no word for "sin," and so the word for "damage" was made to suffice. By the 1530s, the word chosen for "devil" or "demon" was *tlacatecolotl,* or human-owl, a shape-changing sorcerer of legends, so that *teotl* could mean "God" in the Christian sense. In 1519, however, the Spanish were on their own in trying to understand and translate Nahuatl concepts. They seem to have come remarkably close in their initial comprehension of what they were being called. "A single divine principle—*teotl*—was responsible for the nature of the cosmos, negative aspects of it as well as positive ones . . . *Teotl* could manifest itself in ritual objects, images, and human deity-impersonators—forms not necessarily consistent with the Western conception of deity." Burkhart, *The Slippery Earth: Nahua-Christian Moral Dialogue in Sixteenth-Century Mexico* (Tucson, Ariz., 1989), 36–42.

39. Bernal Díaz, *Conquest of New Spain,* 112, 117.

40. Durán, *History of the Indies,* 513, 524–25.

41. In the Florentine Codex, for example, Sahagún's students wrote that when Moctezuma was in hopes of establishing a tributary relationship with the Spanish by giving them annual gifts, he ordered his men, "Xicmotlatlauhtilican in totecuio in teotl." This translates best as "Address our political lord, the *teul,* in a courtly manner," but it was given in the Spanish gloss done by Sahagún as "Worship the god in my name." Lockhart, *We People Here,* 68–69.

42. Motolinía, *Historia de los Indios,* 193–94. A similar corruption that became a permanent name, with no meaning attached, is "Malinche." After receiving her as a slave, the Spaniards christened her "Marina." As she was the all-important translator, the Indians added the honorific "-tzin" and called her "Malintzin." (They did not have the sound for "r" in their language.) The Spanish heard "Malinchi" or "Malinche," and that became her name, familiar to both groups, with few people knowing how it had come about.

43. Cortés, "Second Letter," in Elliott and Pagden, *Letters from Mexico,* 51. It is important to note that, in the earliest dealings with the Nahuas, it was the lord of Cempoala who took the initiative and made overtures to Cortés, not the other way around.

44. James Lockhart and Stuart Schwartz have noted in *Early Latin America* (Cambridge, 1983) both that a standard mode of operation was developed early on in the period of conquest and that the Aztecs more than any other group gave the Spaniards

pause. I would argue that by the time Pizarro faced Atahualpa in Peru, he had reason to have greater confidence than Cortés could immediately have had that he could use the techniques even when facing a great empire.

45. J. H. Elliott, "Introduction," to Cortés, *Letters from Mexico;* Clendinnen, "Cortés, Signs, and the Conquest of Mexico." See also Eulalia Guzmán, *Relaciones de Hernán Cortés a Carlos V sobre la invasión de Anahuac* (Mexico City, 1958).

46. Francis Brooks, "Motecuzoma Xocoyotl, Hernán Cortés and Bernal Díaz del Castillo: The Construction of an Arrest," *Hispanic American Historical Review* 75 (1995): 164–65. López de Gómara did see the awkwardness of the communication issue, and wrote, "Now that Cortés saw himself rich and powerful, he formed three plans: One was to send to Santo Domingo and the other islands news of the country and his good fortune." He then implied that Cortés had never quite had the time to see to it before Captain Narváez and his men appeared. López de Gómara, *Cortés: The Life of the Conqueror,* 187.

47. Cortés, "Second Letter," in Elliott and Pagden, *Letters from Mexico,* 113.

48. Brooks, "Motecuzoma," 181; Durán, *History of the Indies,* 531.

49. This even includes López de Gómara, usually faithful to the Cortesian narrative, in *Cortés: The Life of the Conqueror,* 188–89.

50. The fact that no Spaniard ever publicly accused Cortés of lying about his ability to arrest the Mexican king within a week of his arrival is not as significant as it first appears. Even those many conquistadors who later came to hate him (and even testify against him on other matters, financial and personal) would have understood, consciously and unconsciously, the importance of maintaining a united voice regarding the Spanish legal right to govern the indigenous population. Juan Cano, married to Moctezuma's daughter Isabel, did later claim in a lawsuit over his wife's inheritance that it was untrue that the Mexica lords had gathered before the conquest to swear loyalty to the Spanish and cede their property, or that, if they had gathered together, they could not possibly have understood the purport of the proceedings. Significantly, he reversed himself in his next document and attempted to use other legal precedents to protect his wife's property: someone had apparently made it quite clear to him how quickly he would lose the judges' sympathy if he touched on the issue of the Spanish right to rule in the first place. For the latter, see "Relaciones de la Nueva España" (Madrid, 1990), 153, cited in Thomas, *Conquest,* 325.

51. Cortés, "Second Letter," in Elliott and Pagden, *Letters from Mexico,* 107; Bernal Díaz, *Conquest of New Spain,* 276.

52. "The Chronicle of Fray Francisco de Aguilar," in Fuentes, *Conquistadors,* 148.

53. "The Chronicle of Andrés de Tapia," in Fuentes, *Conquistadors,* 39.

54. "Chronicle of Andrés de Tapia," in Fuentes, *Conquistadors,* 44.

55. Motolinía skipped from Moctezuma's welcoming speech on the causeway to the arrival of Narváez, without addressing who ruled in the interim (*Historia de los Indios,* 55). Durán writes in his own inimitable style: "According to traditions and to paintings kept by certain [indigenous] elders, it is said that Motecuhzoma left the sanctuary with his feet in chains [the day he welcomed the Spaniards]. And I saw this in a painting

that belonged to an ancient chieftain from the province of Tezcoco. Motecuhzoma was depicted in irons, wrapped in a mantle and carried on the shoulders of his dignitaries. This seems difficult to believe, since I have never met a Spaniard who will concede this point to me. But as all of them deny other things that have always been obvious, and remain silent about them in their histories, writings and narrations, I am sure they would also deny and omit this, one of the worst and most atrocious acts committed by them. A conqueror, who is now a friar, told me that though the imprisonment of Motecuhzoma might be true, it was done with the idea of protecting the lives of the Spanish captain and his men" (*History of the Indies,* 530–31). Durán, anxious to demonstrate the ways in which the Indians were victimized, is willing to move the day of arrest forward to the day of arrival—even more impossible to believe. But his source is a native picture that would, if in the standard format, only have been meant to portray a significant episode, not necessarily to give it a date. It was apparently that same native source that told Durán Moctezuma had been imprisoned eighty days. Interestingly, the "conqueror who is now a friar" was probably Aguilar, who said in his statement for public consumption that Moctezuma had been arrested as a traitor to the Spanish king, not in a desperate power ploy intended to protect their own lives.

56. "Annals of Tlaltelolco," in Lockhart, *We People Here,* 257. There has been controversy surrounding the age of this manuscript, as it bears the date "1528" in the scribe's handwriting, but this would not have been possible, as Nahuatl speakers had not yet learned to write their language in the Latin alphabet. Lockhart convincingly dates it to the 1540s in *We People Here,* 39–42. This document's potentially very early date makes it essential that we consult it in the general matter under discussion in this article. Even though it makes no reference whatsoever to Cortés being taken for Quetzalcoatl, it does use the word *teotl* or "god" to designate the Spaniards, as we would expect, given the analysis of Book Twelve. What the speakers may have meant by this has been addressed by Anja Utgennant, University of Cologne, "Gods, Christians and Enemies: The Representation of the Conquerors in a Nahuatl Account," paper presented at "El Cambio Cultural en el México del siglo XVI," University of Vienna, June 6–13, 2002.

57. Cortés, "Third Letter," in Elliott and Pagden, *Letters from Mexico,* 176.

58. Hassig, *Mexico and the Spanish Conquest,* 52, 65–68. Hassig notes that a few did fall to slingstones, and others died when minor wounds became infected.

59. Cortés, "Third Letter," in Elliott and Pagden, *Letters from Mexico,* 212.

60. Cortés, "Second Letter" (131) and "Third Letter" (218), in Elliott and Pagden, *Letters from Mexico.* There are numerous additional examples.

61. Cortés, "Second Letter," in Elliott and Pagden, *Letters from Mexico,* 60, 62, 66. In case Cortés had some unfathomable reason for making this story up, confirmation is easily found in the words of a Tlaxcalan warrior as recounted to Durán: "If you wish to have my opinion I shall give it to you: have pity upon your children, brothers, the old men and women and orphans who are to die, all of them innocent, perishing only because we [noblemen] wish to make a defense." *History of the Indies,* 522. Some of the other conquistadors clearly felt squeamish

about this, or wanted to defend themselves from the likes of Las Casas, for later accounts include strange stories of villages they could have plundered at this point but did not. (See Aguilar, Tapia, and Bernal Díaz.) Durán notes the inconsistency and says the Indians definitely remembered events the way Cortés did.

62. Cortés, "Second Letter," in Elliott and Pagden, *Letters from Mexico,* 156, 158.

63. Cortés, "The Third Letter," in Elliott and Pagden, *Letters from Mexico,* 181. The Florentine Codex, like Durán, confirms these stories, only telling them with a tragic rather than triumphant tone.

64. Two were sent to the aid of Narváez; four constituted an independently got-up exploratory venture from Jamaica, and one was sent by Cortés's father in Spain.

65. Aguilar, in Fuentes, *Conquistadors,* 157; Bernal Díaz, in *Conquest of New Spain,* 309, also comments on the affection and joy with which new arrivals were greeted.

66. Cortés, "Third Letter," in Elliott and Pagden, *Letters from Mexico,* 182. See also 147–48, 164–65, 191–92.

67. Cortés, "Third Letter," in Elliott and Pagden, *Letters from Mexico,* 207.

68. Cortés, "Third Letter," in Elliott and Pagden, *Letters from Mexico,* 221, 247.

69. Jonathan D. Spence, *The Memory Palace of Matteo Ricci* (New York, 1984), 22.

70. Todorov, *Conquest of America,* 13. Indeed, Columbus annotated his copy of Marco Polo's book.

71. One of the speakers created by Sir Thomas More in *Utopia* was supposed to have sailed with Vespucci: his utopia was thus a New World island. More drew explicitly from Vespucci's 1504 work as well as from Martyr's 1511 volume, seamlessly stirring in elements of ancient European tales of fantasy. It was a popular book: *Utopia* was published in Latin in 1516, 1517, 1518, and 1519, in German in 1524, and in English in 1551. Interestingly, the 1517 edition contained a map of "Utopia" drawn by Ambrosius Holbein (younger brother to Hans Holbein); it bears striking resemblances to a stylized map of Tenochtitlan that appeared in Nuremberg in 1524 in a Latin translation of Cortés's Second and Third Letters (supposedly based on a sketch sent back by Cortés).

72. Lewis Hanke, *The Spanish Struggle for Justice in the Conquest of America* (Philadelphia, 1949), 9. Jared Diamond in his previously cited chapter "Collision at Cajamarca: Why the Inca Emperor Atahualpa Did Not Capture King Charles I of Spain," in *Guns, Germs, and Steel,* shows in an interesting way that Spanish guns alone could not have accomplished Pizarro's purpose for him but that the total constellation of Spanish technology was of paramount importance.

73. Dürer's diary, quoted in Benjamin Keen, *The Aztec Image in Western Thought* (New Brunswick, N.J., 1971), 69.

74. We must sift our usual expectations. The Spanish, for example, imagined that the Nahuas were overawed by their first sight of European ships, and we have tended to repeat this. In fact, they seem to have recognized them for what they were—boats that were larger and more impressive than their own. Durán asserts that the native messenger found them "wondrous and terrifying" but then elaborates that the messenger "described how, while he had been walking next to the seashore, he had seen a round

[water]hill [the same word used for "village" or "settlement"] or [water]house [same word used for "boat"] moving from one side to another until it had anchored next to some rocks on the beach." Durán, *History of the Indies,* 495. Durán's text gives the Spanish for "hill" and "house," contributing to the myth that the Indians perceived the boats as floating mountains or great houses, like temples. However, any Nahuatl speaker cannot help but wonder what his Nahuatl source originally said, as the word for "village" or "settlement" in Nahuatl is "water-hill," and the word for "boat" is "water-house." Thus it is quite likely that the speaker meant to say, "He saw some sort of settlement, a boat, moving from side to side," and his Spanish hearer or reader mistakenly removed the prefix meaning "water" from the two words, thinking it referred to the fact that the messenger had seen these things in the water. This view is supported by another messenger's comment a few pages later (505): "Before showing him the paintings he narrated that some men would come to this land in a great wooden hill. This wooden hill would be so big that it would lodge many men, serving them as a home. Within it they would eat and sleep." In the Florentine Codex, after the famous hyperbole, Moctezuma's emissaries reached the Spanish ship by canoe and reported matter-of-factly: "They [the newcomers] hitched the prow of the [Indians'] boat with an iron staff and hauled them in. Then they put down a ladder" (Lockhart, *We People Here,* 70).

75. Several conquistadors, Durán's source, and the Florentine Codex all refer to this event.

76. Cortés, "Second Letter," in Elliott and Pagden, *Letters from Mexico,* 94. Walter Mignolo, *The Darker Side of the Renaissance: Literacy, Territoriality and Colonization* (Ann Arbor, Mich., 1995), studies Spanish resistance to seeing the kinds of information conveyed in Aztec records and maps; see esp. 296–313. On the topic in general, start with Elizabeth Hill Boone, "Aztec Pictorial Histories: Records without Words," in Boone and Mignolo, eds., *Writing without Words: Alternative Literacies in Mesoamerica and the Andes* (Durham, N. C., 1994).

77. Florentine Codex, in Lockhart, *We People Here,* 94.

78. Bernal Díaz, *Conquest of New Spain,* 222.

79. Durán, *History of the Indies,* 503–06.

80. Some form of the speech Cortés attributes to Moctezuma appears in most of the later Spanish accounts, and a variation in the Florentine Codex. For several centuries, it was assumed that these sources were quoting the king verbatim; more recently, it has been assumed that the king said nothing of the kind. The truth probably lies in between. For examples of courtly Nahuatl speech, see Frances Karttunen and James Lockhart, eds., *The Art of Nahuatl Speech: The Bancroft Dialogues* (Los Angeles, 1987).

81. J. H. Elliott, "The Mental World of Hernán Cortés," *Transactions of the Royal Historical Society,* 5th ser., 17 (1967): 41–58.

82. López de Gómara, *Cortés: The Life of the Conqueror,* 140–42; Bernal Díaz, *Conquest of New Spain,* 223–24.

83. See esp. Clendinnen, "Cortés, Signs, and the Conquest of Mexico," 97–98; and Hassig, *Mexico and the Spanish Conquest,* 77.

84. Florentine Codex, in Lockhart, *We People Here,* 106.

85. López de Gómara, *Cortés: The Life of the Conqueror,* 134; Bernal Díaz, *Conquest of New Spain,* 205 (emphasis added).

86. Florentine Codex, in Lockhart, *We People Here,* 138. Almost all the sources mention such speeches on his part.

87. It is possible to get a sense of what the commoners thought about the Spanish during all this time. Nahua sources refer not only to the foreigners' insatiable demand for gold but also to the overwhelming quantities of food and water that they consumed—and that the city folk were asked by Moctezuma to provide. Not only food, added Sahagún's students, but also hundreds of bowls, pitchers, and pans. One presumes that there may also have been the usual tensions over women, but only a single particularly egregious incident regarding lewd glances at sacred women made its way into the oral tradition that was passed on to Sahagún. "[Before the ceremonies] the women who had fasted for a year ground up the amaranth . . . in the temple courtyard. The Spaniards came out well adorned in battle equipment . . . arrayed as warriors. They passed among the grinding women, circling around them, looking at each one, looking upon their faces. And when they were through looking at them, they went into the great palace." Far from regarding the Spanish as gods, the city dwellers apparently saw them as dish thieves and profaners of the sacred. Florentine Codex, in Lockhart, *We People Here,* 122, 128.

88. Clendinnen, "Cortés, Signs, and the Conquest of Mexico," esp. 107–14. She notes that there may have been one exception—a single incident in which the Indians seem to have come close to killing Cortés and apparently chose not to, perhaps hoping to take him alive so as to sacrifice his still-beating heart to the gods. Hassig, *Time, History and Belief,* echoes her incredulity that Aztec political and military leaders were making practical decisions based on religious tradition rather than realpolitik.

89. Cortés, "Third Letter," in Elliott and Pagden, *Letters from Mexico,* 175.

90. Florentine Codex, in Lockhart, *We People Here,* 146.

91. Clendinnen, "Cortés, Signs, and the Conquest of Mexico,"107; and Hassig, *Mexico and the Spanish Conquest,* 121, both working with the texts of Cortés, Bernal Díaz, Durán, and the Florentine Codex. It is possible that Indians were learning to make some of the Spanish goods, since Cortés mentions having nails, pitch, oars, and sails made locally, but he probably meant that Spaniards were manufacturing them. "Second Letter," in Elliott and Pagden, *Letters from Mexico,* 157.

92. The Spanish describe such memorable events as atrocities, but they are recounted with pride in the Florentine Codex; Lockhart, *We People Here,* 188, 192, 210, 232. For a thorough discussion, see Hassig, *Mexico and the Spanish Conquest,* 129–33.

93. Cortés, "Third Letter," in Elliott and Pagden, *Letters from Mexico,* 257.

94. Florentine Codex, in Lockhart, *We People Here,* 230. Lockhart also comments on this incident in the same volume (7).

95. Ixtlilxochitl, "Historia de la Nación Chichimeca," in *Obras históricas,* 2: 244.

96. Florentine Codex, in Lockhart, *We People Here,* 80, 90, 96, 110.

97. Florentine Codex, in Lockhart, *We People Here,* 74, 86, 98, 116.

98. Motolinía, *Historia de los Indios,* 147–48, 173, 276. If we believe that the 1540s write-up of the initial conversations between the Franciscan Apostles and the Aztec priests represents a close approximation of what was said, then we have a 1524 indigenous statement to the effect that not only are the Spaniards not divine but they do not even have the right to determine how the indigenous shall worship. The speech begins with exaggerated courtesy, "Our lords, leading personages of much esteem, you are very welcome to our lands and towns. We ourselves, being inferior and base, are unworthy of looking upon the faces of such valiant personages." In true courtly Nahuatl style, the speaker builds gradually to his point: "All of us together feel that it is enough to have lost, enough that the power and royal jurisdiction have been taken from us. As for our gods, we will die before giving up serving and worshiping them. This is our determination; do what you will . . . We have no more to say, lords." "Chapter 7: In Which the Reply of the Principal Holy Men to the Twelve Is Found," *Coloquios y doctrina cristiana,* in Kenneth Mills and William B. Taylor, eds., *Colonial Spanish America: A Documentary History* (Wilmington, Del., 1998), 21–22. Jorge Klor de Alva has worked extensively with the *coloquios* on the question of their veracity. See, for example, "The Aztec-Spanish Dialogues of 1524," *Alcheringia/Ethnopoetics* 4 (1980): 52–193. While acknowledging that we have only a text based on notes made at the time, he asserts the probability that the notes reflect a genuine resistance to the Spanish priests, as other evidence suggests. The notion that the Aztecs simply accepted what the Christians had to say in a "spiritual conquest" has been abandoned by scholars. To begin, see Burkhart, *Slippery Earth;* and most recently, Viviana Díaz Balsera, "A Judeo-Christian Tlaloc or a Nahua Yahweh? Domination, Hybridity and Continuity in the Nahua Evangelization Theater," *Colonial Latin American Review* 10 (2001): 209–28.

CAMILLA TOWNSEND is an associate professor of history at Colgate University. She is a comparativist, whose book *Tales of Two Cities: Race and Economic Culture in Early Republican North and South America* (Austin, Tex., 2000) explores contrasting colonial legacies in the Chesapeake and the Andean region. Recently, she has concluded that New Spain is crucial to comparative colonial studies and has made the study of Nahuatl her focus. Her book *Malintzin: The Woman Who Went with Cortés* is forthcoming from the University of New Mexico Press, and a study of "The Chalcan Woman's Song" in the *Canares Mexicanos* is in process.

From *The American Historical Review,* Vol. 108, no. 3, June 2003, pp. 659–687. Copyright © 2003 by American Historical Association. Reprinted by permission.

The Price of Progress

John Bodley

In aiming at progress . . . you must let no one suffer by too drastic a measure, nor pay too high a price in upheaval and devastation, for your innovation.

Maunier, 1949: 725

Until recently, government planners have always considered economic development and progress beneficial goals that all societies should want to strive toward. The social advantage of progress—as defined in terms of increased incomes, higher standards of living, greater security, and better health—are thought to be positive, *universal* goods, to be obtained at any price. Although one may argue that tribal peoples must sacrifice their traditional cultures to obtain these benefits, government planners generally feel that this is a small price to pay for such obvious advantages.

In earlier chapters [in *Victims of Progress,* 3rd ed.], evidence was presented to demonstrate that autonomous tribal peoples have not *chosen* progress to enjoy its advantages, but that governments have *pushed* progress upon them to obtain tribal resources, not primarily to share with the tribal peoples the benefits of progress. It has also been shown that the price of forcing progress on unwilling recipients has involved the deaths of millions of tribal people, as well as their loss of land, political sovereignty, and the right to follow their own life style. This chapter does not attempt to further summarize that aspect of the cost of progress, but instead analyzes the specific effects of the participation of tribal peoples in the world-market economy. In direct opposition to the usual interpretation, it is argued here that the benefits of progress are often both illusory and detrimental to tribal peoples when they have not been allowed to control their own resources and define their relationship to the market economy.

Progress and the Quality of Life

One of the primary difficulties in assessing the benefits of progress and economic development for any culture is that of establishing a meaningful measure of both benefit and detriment. It is widely recognized that *standard of living,* which is the most frequently used measure of progress, is an intrinsically ethnocentric concept relying heavily upon indicators that lack universal cultural relevance. Such factors as GNP, per capita income, capital formation, employment rates, literacy, formal education, consumption of manufactured goods, number of doctors and hospital beds per thousand persons, and the amount of money spent on government welfare and health programs may be irrelevant measures of actual *quality* of life for autonomous or even semiautonomous tribal cultures. In its 1954 report, the Trust Territory government indicated that since the Micronesian population was still largely satisfying its own needs within a cashless subsistence economy, "Money income is not a significant measure of living standards, production, or well-being in this area" (TTR, 1953: 44). Unfortunately, within a short time the government began to rely on an enumeration of certain imported consumer goods as indicators of a higher standard of living in the islands, even though many tradition-oriented islanders felt that these new goods symbolized a lowering of the quality of life.

A more useful measure of the benefits of progress might be based on a formula for evaluating cultures devised by Goldschmidt (1952: 135). According to these less ethnocentric criteria, the important question to ask is: Does progress or economic development increase or decrease a given culture's ability to satisfy the physical and psychological needs of its population, or its stability? This question is a far more direct measure of quality of life than are the standard economic correlates of development, and it is universally relevant. Specific indication of this *standard* of living could be found for any society in the nutritional status and general physical and mental health of its population, the incidence of crime and delinquency, the demographic structure, family stability, and the society's relationship to its natural resource base. A society with high rates of malnutrition and crime, and one degrading its natural environment to the extent of threatening its continued existence, might be described as at a lower standard of living than is another society where these problems did not exist.

Careful examination of the data, which compare, on these specific points, the former condition of self-sufficient tribal peoples with their condition following their incorporation into the world-market economy, leads to the conclusion that their standard of living is *lowered,* not raised, by economic progress—and often to a dramatic degree. This is perhaps the most outstanding and inescapable fact to emerge from the years of research that anthropologists have devoted to the study of culture change and modernization. Despite the best intentions of those who have promoted change and improvement, all too often the results have been poverty, longer working hours, and much greater physical exertion, poor health, social disorder, discontent, discrimination, overpopulation, and environmental deterioration—combined with the destruction of the traditional culture.

Diseases of Development

Perhaps it would be useful for public health specialists to start talking about a new category of diseases. . . . Such diseases could be called the "diseases of development" and would consist of those pathological conditions which are based on the usually unanticipated consequences of the implementation of developmental schemes.

Hughes & Hunter, 1972: 93

Economic development increases the disease rate of affected peoples in at least three ways. First, to the extent that development is successful, it makes developed populations suddenly become vulnerable to all of the diseases suffered almost exclusively by "advanced" peoples. Among these are diabetes, obesity, hypertension, and a variety of circulatory problems. Second, development disturbs traditional environmental balances and may dramatically increase certain bacterial and parasite diseases. Finally, when development goals prove unattainable, an assortment of poverty diseases may appear in association with the crowded conditions of urban slums and the general breakdown in traditional socioeconomic systems.

Outstanding examples of the first situation can be seen in the Pacific, where some of the most successfully developed native peoples are found. In Micronesia, where development has progressed more rapidly than perhaps anywhere else, between 1958 and 1972 the population doubled, but the number of patients treated for heart disease in the local hospitals nearly tripled, mental disorder increased eightfold, and by 1972 hypertension and nutritional deficiencies began to make significant appearances for the first time (TTR, 1959, 1973, statistical tables).

Although some critics argue that the Micronesian figures simply represent better health monitoring due to economic progress, rigorously controlled data from Polynesia show a similar trend. The progressive acquisition of modern degenerative diseases was documented by an eight-member team of New Zealand medical specialists, anthropologists, and nutritionists, whose research was funded by the Medical Research Council of New Zealand and the World Health Organization. These researchers investigated the health status of a genetically related population at various points along a continuum of increasing cash income, modernizing diet, and urbanization. The extremes on this acculturation continuum were represented by the relatively traditional Pukapukans of the Cook Islands and the essentially Europeanized New Zealand Maori, while the busily developing Rarotongans, also of the Cook Islands, occupied the intermediate position. In 1971, after eight years of work, the team's preliminary findings were summarized by Dr. Ian Prior, cardiologist and leader of the research, as follows:

We are beginning to observe that the more an islander takes on the ways of the West, the more prone he is to succumb to our degenerative diseases. In fact, it does not seem too much to say our evidence now shows that the farther the Pacific natives move from the quiet, carefree life of their ancestors, the closer they come to gout, diabetes, atherosclerosis, obesity, and hypertension.

Prior, 1971: 2

In Pukapuka, where progress was limited by the island's small size and its isolated location some 480 kilometers from the nearest port, the annual per capita income was only about thirty-six dollars and the economy remained essentially at a subsistence level. Resources were limited and the area was visited by trading ships only three or four times a year; thus, there was little opportunity for intensive economic development. Predictably, the population of Pukapuka was characterized by relatively low levels of imported sugar and salt intake, and a presumably related low level of heart disease, high blood pressure, and diabetes. In Rarotonga, where economic success was introducing town life, imported food, and motorcycles, sugar and salt intakes nearly tripled, high blood pressure increased approximately ninefold, diabetes two- to threefold, and heart disease doubled for men and more than quadrupled for women, while the number of grossly obese women increased more than tenfold. Among the New Zealand Maori, sugar intake was nearly eight times that of the Pukapukans, gout in men was nearly double its rate on Pukapuka, and diabetes in men was more than fivefold higher, while heart disease in women had increased more than sixfold. The Maori were, in fact, dying of "European" diseases at a greater rate than was the average New Zealand European.

Government development policies designed to bring about changes in local hydrology, vegetation, and settlement patterns and to increase population mobility, and even programs aimed at reducing certain diseases, have frequently led to dramatic increases in disease rates because of the unforeseen effects of disturbing the preexisting order. Hughes and Hunter (1972) published an excellent survey of cases in which development led directly to increased disease rates in Africa. They concluded that hasty development intervention in relatively balanced local cultures and environments resulted in "a drastic deterioration in the social and economic conditions of life."

Traditional populations in general have presumably learned to live with the endemic pathogens of their environments, and in some cases they have evolved genetic adaptations to specific diseases, such as the sickle-cell trait, which provided an immunity to malaria. Unfortunately, however, outside intervention has entirely changed this picture. In the late 1960s, sleeping sickness suddenly increased in many areas of Africa and even spread to areas where it did not formerly occur, due to the building of new roads and migratory labor, both of which caused increased population movement. Large-scale relocation schemes, such as the Zande Scheme, had disastrous results when natives were moved from their traditional disease-free refuges into infected areas. Dams and irrigation developments inadvertently created ideal conditions for the rapid proliferation of snails carrying schistosomiasis (a liver fluke disease), and major epidemics suddenly occurred in areas where this disease had never before been a problem. DDT spraying programs have been temporarily successful in controlling malaria, but there is often a rebound effect that increases the problem when spraying is discontinued, and the malarial mosquitoes are continually evolving resistant strains.

Urbanization is one of the prime measures of development, but it is a mixed blessing for most former tribal peoples. Urban health standards are abysmally poor and generally worse than in rural areas for the detribalized individuals who have crowded into the towns and cities throughout Africa, Asia, and Latin America seeking wage employment out of new economic necessity. Infectious diseases related to crowding and poor sanitation are rampant in urban centers, while greatly increased stress and poor nutrition aggravate a variety of other health problems. Malnutrition and other diet-related conditions are, in fact, one of the characteristic hazards of progress faced by tribal peoples and are discussed in the following sections.

The Hazards of Dietary Change

The traditional diets of tribal peoples are admirably adapted to their nutritional needs and available food resources. Even though these diets may seem bizarre, absurd, and unpalatable to outsiders, they are unlikely to be improved by drastic modifications. Given the delicate balances and complexities involved in any subsistence system, change always involves risks, but for tribal people the effects of dietary change have been catastrophic.

Under normal conditions, food habits are remarkably resistant to change, and indeed people are unlikely to abandon their traditional diets voluntarily in favor of dependence on difficult-to-obtain exotic imports. In some cases it is true that imported foods may be identified with powerful outsiders and are therefore sought as symbols of greater prestige. This may lead to such absurdities as Amazonian Indians choosing to consume imported canned tunafish when abundant high-quality fish is available in their own rivers. Another example of this situation occurs in tribes where mothers prefer to feed their infants expensive nutritionally inadequate canned milk from unsanitary, but *high status,* baby bottles. The high status of these items is often promoted by clever traders and clever advertising campaigns.

Aside from these apparently voluntary changes, it appears that more often dietary changes are forced upon unwilling tribal peoples by circumstances beyond their control. In some areas, new food crops have been introduced by government decree, or as a consequence of forced relocation or other policies designed to end hunting, pastoralism, or shifting cultivation. Food habits have also been modified by massive disruption of the natural environment by outsiders—as when sheepherders transformed the Australian Aborigines' foraging territory or when European invaders destroyed the bison herds that were the primary element in the Plains Indians' subsistence patterns. Perhaps the most frequent cause of diet change occurs when formerly self-sufficient peoples find that wage labor, cash cropping, and other economic development activities that feed tribal resources into the world-market economy must inevitably divert time and energy away from the production of subsistence foods. Many developing peoples suddenly discover that, like it or not, they are unable to secure traditional foods and must spend their newly acquired cash on costly, and often nutritionally inferior, manufactured foods.

Overall, the available data seem to indicate that the dietary changes that are linked to involvement in the world-market economy have tended to *lower* rather than raise the nutritional levels of the affected tribal peoples. Specifically, the vitamin, mineral, and protein components of their diets are often drastically reduced and replaced by enormous increases in starch and carbohydrates, often in the form of white flour and refined sugar.

Any deterioration in the quality of a given population's diet is almost certain to be reflected in an increase in deficiency diseases and a general decline in health status. Indeed, as tribal peoples have shifted to a diet based on imported manufactured or processed foods, there has been a dramatic rise in malnutrition, a massive increase in dental problems, and a variety of other nutritional-related disorders. Nutritional physiology is so complex that even well-meaning dietary changes have had tragic consequences. In many areas of Southeast Asia, government-sponsored protein supplementation programs supplying milk to protein-deficient populations caused unexpected health problems and increased mortality. Officials failed to anticipate that in cultures where adults do not normally drink milk, the enzymes needed to digest it are no longer produced and milk *intolerance* results (Davis & Bolin, 1972). In Brazil, a similar milk distribution program caused an epidemic of permanent blindness by aggravating a preexisting vitamin A deficiency (Bunce, 1972).

Teeth and Progress

There is nothing new in the observation that savages, or peoples living under primitive conditions, have, in general, excellent teeth. . . . Nor is it news that most civilized populations possess wretched teeth which begin to decay almost before they have erupted completely, and that dental caries is likely to be accompanied by periodontal disease with further reaching complications.

Hooton, 1945: xviii

Anthropologists have long recognized that undisturbed tribal peoples are often in excellent physical condition. And it has often been noted specifically that dental caries and the other dental abnormalities that plague industrialized societies are absent or rare among tribal peoples who have retained their traditional diets. The fact that tribal food habits may contribute to the development of sound teeth, whereas modernized diets may do just the opposite, was illustrated as long ago as 1894 in an article in the *Journal of the Royal Anthropological Institute* that described the results of a comparison between the teeth of ten Sioux Indians were examined when they came to London as members of Buffalo Bill's Wild West Show and were found to be completely free of caries and in possession of all their teeth, even though half of the group were over thirty-nine years of age. Londoners' teeth were conspicuous for both their caries and their steady reduction in number with advancing age. The difference was attributed primarily to the wear and polishing caused by the traditional Indian diet of coarse food and the fact that they chewed their food longer, encouraged by the absence of tableware.

One of the most remarkable studies of the dental conditions of tribal peoples and the impact of dietary change was conducted in the 1930s by Weston Price (1945), an American dentist who was interested in determining what caused normal, healthy teeth. Between 1931 and 1936, Price systematically explored tribal areas throughout the world to locate and examine the most isolated peoples who were still living on traditional foods. His fieldwork covered Alaska, the Canadian Yukon, Hudson Bay, Vancouver Island, Florida, the Andes, the Amazon, Samoa, Tahiti, New Zealand, Australia, New Caledonia, Fiji, the Torres Strait, East Africa, and the Nile. The study demonstrated both the superior quality of aboriginal dentition and the devastation that occurs as modern diets are adopted. In nearly every area where traditional foods were still being eaten, Price found perfect teeth with normal dental arches and virtually no decay, whereas caries and abnormalities increased steadily as new diets were adopted. In many cases the change was sudden and striking. Among Eskimo groups subsisting entirely on traditional food he found caries totally absent, whereas in groups eating a considerable quantity of store-bought food approximately 20 percent of their teeth were decayed. This figure rose to more than 30 percent with Eskimo groups subsisting almost exclusively on purchased or government-supplied food, and reached an incredible 48 percent among the Vancouver Island Indians. Unfortunately for many of these people, modern dental treatment did not accompany the new food, and their suffering was appalling. The loss of teeth was, of course, bad enough in itself, and it certainly undermined the population's resistance to many new diseases, including tuberculosis. But new foods were also accompanied by crowded, misplaced teeth, gum diseases, distortion of the face, and pinching of the nasal cavity. Abnormalities in the dental arch appeared in the new generation following the change in diet, while caries appeared almost immediately even in adults.

Price reported that in many areas the affected peoples were conscious of their own physical deterioration. At a mission school in Africa, the principal asked him to explain to the native schoolchildren why they were not physically as strong as children who had had no contact with schools. On an island in the Torres Strait the natives knew exactly what was causing their problems and resisted—almost to the point of bloodshed—government efforts to establish a store that would make imported food available. The government prevailed, however, and Price was able to establish a relationship between the length of time the government store had been established and the increasing incidence of caries among a population that showed an almost 100 percent immunity to them before the store had been opened.

In New Zealand, the Maori, who in their aboriginal state are often considered to have been among the healthiest, most perfectly developed of people, were found to have "advanced" the furthest. According to Price:

Their modernization was demonstrated not only by the high incidence of dental caries but also by the fact that

90 percent of the adults and 100 percent of the children had abnormalities of the dental arches.

Price, 1945: 206

Malnutrition

Malnutrition, particularly in the form of protein deficiency, has become a critical problem for tribal peoples who must adopt new economic patterns. Population pressures, cash cropping, and government programs all have tended to encourage the replacement of traditional crops and other food sources that were rich in protein with substitutes, high in calories but low in protein. In Africa, for example, protein-rich staples such as millet and sorghum are being replaced systematically by high-yielding manioc and plantains, which have insignificant amounts of protein. The problem is increased for cash croppers and wage laborers whose earnings are too low and unpredictable to allow purchase of adequate amounts of protein. In some rural areas, agricultural laborers have been forced systematically to deprive nonproductive members (principally children) of their households of their minimal nutritional requirements to satisfy the need of the productive members. This process has been documented in northeastern Brazil following the introduction of large-scale sisal plantations (Gross & Underwood, 1971). In urban centers the difficulties of obtaining nutritionally adequate diets are even more serious for tribal immigrants, because costs are higher and poor quality foods are more tempting.

One of the most tragic, and largely overlooked, aspects of chronic malnutrition is that it can lead to abnormally undersized brain development and apparently irreversible brain damage; it has been associated with various forms of mental impairment or retardation. Malnutrition has been linked clinically with mental retardation in both Africa and Latin America (see, for example, Mönckeberg, 1968), and this appears to be a worldwide phenomenon with serious implications (Montagu, 1972).

Optimistic supporters of progress will surely say that all of these new health problems are being overstressed and that the introduction of hospitals, clinics, and the other modern health institutions will overcome or at least compensate for all of these difficulties. However, it appears that uncontrolled population growth and economic impoverishment probably will keep most of these benefits out of reach for many tribal peoples, and the intervention of modern medicine has at least partly contributed to the problem in the first place.

The generalization that civilization frequently has a broad negative impact on tribal health has found broad empirical support (see especially Kroeger & Barbira-Freedman [1982] on Amazonia; Reinhard [1976] on the Arctic; and Wirsing [1985] globally), but these conclusions have not gone unchallenged. Some critics argue that tribal health was often poor before modernization, and they point specifically to tribals' low life expectancy and high infant mortality rates. Demographic statistics on tribal populations are often problematic because precise data are scarce, but they do show a less favorable profile than that enjoyed by many industrial societies. However, it should be remembered that our present life expectancy is a recent phenomenon that has been very costly in terms of medical research and technological advances. Furthermore, the benefits of our health system are not enjoyed equally by all members of our society. High infant mortality could be viewed as a relatively inexpensive and egalitarian tribal public health program that offered the reasonable expectation of a healthy and productive life for those surviving to age fifteen.

Some critics also suggest that certain tribal populations, such as the New Guinea highlanders, were "stunted" by nutritional deficiencies created by tribal culture and are "improved" by "acculturation" and cash cropping (Dennett & Connell, 1988). Although this argument does suggest that the health question requires careful evaluation, it does not invalidate the empirical generalizations already established. Nutritional deficiencies undoubtedly occurred in densely populated zones in the central New Guinea highlands. However, the specific case cited above may not be widely representative of other tribal groups even in New Guinea, and it does not address the facts of outside intrusion or the inequities inherent in the contemporary development process.

Ecocide

"How is it," asked a herdsman . . . "how is it that these hills can no longer give pasture to my cattle? In my father's day they were green and cattle thrived there; today there is no grass and my cattle starve." As one looked one saw that what had once been a green hill had become a raw red rock.

Jones, 1934

Progress not only brings new threats to the health of tribal peoples, but it also imposes new strains on the ecosystems upon which they must depend for their ultimate survival. The introduction of new technology, increased consumption, lowered mortality, and the eradication of all traditional controls have combined to replace what for most tribal peoples was a relatively stable balance between population and natural resources, with a new system that is imbalanced. Economic development is forcing *ecocide* on peoples who were once careful stewards of their resources. There is already a trend toward widespread environmental deterioration in tribal areas, involving resource depletion, erosion, plant and animal extinction, and a disturbing series of other previously unforeseen changes.

After the initial depopulation suffered by most tribal peoples during their engulfment by frontiers of national expansion, most tribal populations began to experience rapid growth. Authorities generally attribute this growth to the introduction of modern medicine and new health measures and the termination of intertribal warfare, which lowered morality rates, as well as to new technology, which increased food production. Certainly all of these factors played a part, but merely lowering mortality rates would not have produced the rapid population growth that most tribal areas have experienced if traditional birth-spacing mechanisms had not been eliminated at the same time. Regardless of which factors were most important, it is clear that all of the natural and cultural checks on population growth have suddenly been pushed aside by culture change, while tribal lands have been steadily reduced and consumption levels have risen. In many tribal areas, environmental deterioration due to overuse of resources has set in, and in other areas such deterioration is imminent as resources continue to dwindle relative to the expanding population and increased use. Of course, population expansion by tribal peoples may have positive political consequences, because where tribals can retain or regain their status as local majorities they may be in a more favorable position to defend their resources against intruders.

Swidden systems and pastoralism, both highly successful economic systems under traditional conditions, have proved particularly vulnerable to increased population pressures and outside efforts to raise productivity beyond its natural limits. Research in Amazonia demonstrates that population pressures and related resource depletion can be created indirectly by official policies that restrict swidden peoples to smaller territories. Resource depletion itself can then become a powerful means of forcing tribal people into participating in the world-market economy—thus leading to further resource depletion. For example, Bodley and Benson (1979) showed how the Shipibo Indians in Peru were forced to further deplete their forest resources by cash cropping in the forest area to replace the resources that had been destroyed earlier by the intensive cash cropping necessitated by the narrow confines of their reserve. In this case, certain species of palm trees that had provided critical housing materials were destroyed by forest clearing and had to be replaced by costly purchased materials. Research by Gross (1979) and other showed similar processes at work among four tribal groups in central Brazil and demonstrated that the degree of market involvement increases directly with increases in resource depletion.

The settling of nomadic herders and the removal of prior controls on herd size have often led to serious overgrazing and erosion problems where these had not previously occurred. There are indications that the desertification problem in the Sahel region of Africa was aggravated by programs designed to settle nomads. The first sign of imbalance in a swidden system appears when the planting cycles are shortened to the point that garden plots are reused before sufficient forest regrowth can occur. If reclearing and planting continue in the same area, the natural patterns of forest succession may be disturbed irreversibly and the soil can be impaired permanently. An extensive tract of tropical rainforest in the lower Amazon of Brazil was reduced to a semiarid desert in just fifty years through such a process (Ackermann, 1964). The soils in the Azande area are also now seriously threatened with laterization and other problems as a result of the government-promoted cotton development scheme (McNeil, 1972).

The dangers of overdevelopment and the vulnerability of local resource systems have long been recognized by both anthropologists and tribal peoples themselves. But the pressures for change have been overwhelming. In 1948 the Maya villagers of Chan Kom complained to Redfield (1962) about the shortening of their swidden cycles, which they correctly attributed to increasing population pressures. Redfield told them, however, that they had no choice but to go "forward with technology" (Redfield, 1962: 178). In Assam, swidden cycles were shortened from an average of twelve years to only two or three within just twenty years, and anthropologists warned that the limits of swiddening would soon be reached (Burling, 1963: 311–312). In the Pacific, anthropologists warned of population pressures on limited resources as early as the 1930s (Keesing, 1941: 64–65). These warnings seemed fully justified, considering the fact that the crowded Tikopians were prompted by population pressures on their tiny island to suggest that infanticide be legalized. The warnings have been dramatically reinforced since then by the doubling of Micronesia's population in just the fourteen years between 1958 and 1972, from 70,600 to 114,645, while consumption levels have soared. By 1985 Micronesia's population had reached 162,321.

The environmental hazards of economic development and rapid population growth have become generally recognized only since worldwide concerns over environmental issues began in the early 1970s. Unfortunately, there is as yet little indication that the leaders of the new developing nations are sufficiently concerned with environmental limitations. On the contrary, governments are forcing tribal peoples into a self-reinforcing spiral of population growth and intensified resource exploitation, which may be stopped only by environmental disaster or the total impoverishment of the tribals.

The reality of ecocide certainly focuses attention on the fundamental contrasts between tribal and industrial systems in their use of natural resources, who controls them, and how they are managed. Tribal peoples are victimized because they control resources that outsiders demand. The resources exist because tribals managed them conservatively. However, as with the issue of the health consequences of detribalization, some anthropologists minimize the adaptive achievements of tribal groups and seem unwilling to concede that ecocide might be a consequence of cultural change. Critics attack an exaggerated "noble savage" image of tribals living in perfect harmony with nature and having no visible impact on their surroundings. They then show that tribals do in fact modify the environment, and they conclude that there is no significant difference between how tribals and industrial societies treat their environments. For example, Charles Wagley declared that Brazilian Indians such as the Tapirape

are not "natural men." They have human vices just as we do.... They do not live "in tune" with nature any more than I do; in fact, they can often be as destructive of their environment, within their limitations, as some civilized men. The Tapirape are not innocent or childlike in any way.

Wagley, 1977: 302

Anthropologist Terry Rambo demonstrated that the Semang of the Malaysian rain forests have a measurable impact on their environment. In his monograph *Primitive Polluters,* Rambo (1985) reported that the Semang live in smoke-filled houses. They sneeze and spread germs, breathe, and thus emit carbon dioxide. They clear small gardens, contributing "particulate matter" to the air and disturbing the local climate because cleared areas proved measurably warmer and drier than the shady forest. Rambo concluded that his research "demonstrates the essential functional similarity of the environmental interactions of primitive and civilized societies" (1985: 78) in contrast to a "noble sav-

age" view (Bodley, 1983) which, according to Rambo (1985: 2), mistakenly "claims that traditional peoples almost always live in essential harmony with their environment."

This is surely a false issue. To stress, as I do, that tribals tend to manage their resources for sustained yield within relatively self-sufficient subsistence economies is not to make them either innocent children or natural men. Nor is it to deny that tribals "disrupt" their environment and may never be in absolute "balance" with nature.

The ecocide issue is perhaps most dramatically illustrated by two sets of satellite photos taken over the Brazilian rain forests of Rôndonia (Allard & McIntyre, 1988: 780–781). Photos taken in 1973, when Rôndonia was still a tribal domain, show virtually unbroken rain forest. The 1987 satellite photos, taken after just fifteen years of highway construction and "development" by outsiders, show more than 20 percent of the forest destroyed. The surviving Indians were being concentrated by FUNAI (Brazil's national Indian foundation) into what would soon become mere islands of forest in a ravaged landscape. It is irrelevant to quibble about whether tribals are noble, child-like, or innocent, or about the precise meaning of balance with nature, carrying capacity, or adaptation, to recognize that for the past 200 years rapid environmental deterioration on an unprecedented global scale has followed the wresting of control of vast areas of the world from tribal groups by resource-hungry industrial societies.

Deprivation and Discrimination

Contact with European culture has given them a knowledge of great wealth, opportunity and privilege, but only very limited avenues by which to acquire these things.

Crocombe, 1968

Unwittingly, tribal peoples have had the burden of perpetual relative deprivation thrust upon them by acceptance—either by themselves or by the governments administering them—of the standards of socioeconomic progress set for them by industrial civilizations. By comparison with the material wealth of industrial societies, tribal societies become, by definition, impoverished. They are then forced to transform their cultures and work to achieve what many economists now acknowledge to be unattainable goals. Even though in many cases the modest GNP goals set by development planners for the developing nations during the "development decade" of the 1960s were often met, the results were hardly noticeable for most of the tribal people involved. Population growth, environmental limitations, inequitable distribution of wealth, and the continued rapid growth of the industrialized nations have all meant that both the absolute and the relative gap between the rich and poor in the world is steadily widening. The prospect that tribal peoples will actually be able to attain the levels of resource consumption to which they are being encouraged to aspire is remote indeed except for those few groups who have retained effective control over strategic mineral resources.

Tribal peoples feel deprivation not only when the economic goals they have been encouraged to seek fail to materialize, but also when they discover that they are powerless, second-class citizens who are discriminated against and exploited by the dominant society. At the same time, they are denied the satisfactions of their traditional cultures, because these have been sacrificed in the process of modernization. Under the impact of major economic change family life is disrupted, traditional social controls are often lost, and many indicators of social anomie such as alcoholism, crime, delinquency, suicide, emotional disorders, and despair may increase. The inevitable frustration resulting from this continual deprivation finds expression in the cargo cults, revitalization movements, and a variety of other political and religious movements that have been widespread among tribal peoples following their disruption by industrial civilization.

Bibliography

Ackermann, F. L. 1964. *Geologia e Fisiografia da Região Bragantina, Estado do Pará.* Manaus, Brazil: Conselho Nacional de Pesquisas, Instituto Nacional de Pesquisas da Amazonia.

Allard, William Albert, and Loren McIntyre. 1988. Rondônia's settlers invade Brazil's imperiled rain forest. *National Geographic* 174(6):772–799.

Bodley, John H. 1970. *Campa Socio-Economic Adaptation.* Ann Arbor: University Microfilms.

———. 1983. *Der Weg der Zerstörung: Stammesvölker und die industrielle Zivilization.* Munich: Trickster-Verlag. (Translation of *Victims of Progress.*)

Bodley, John H., and Foley C. Benson. 1979. Cultural ecology of Amazonian palms. *Reports of Investigations,* no. 56. Pullman: Laboratory of Anthropology, Washington State University.

Bunce, George E. 1972. Aggravation of vitamin A deficiency following distribution of non-fortified skim milk: An example of nutrient interaction. In *The Careless Technology: Ecology and International Development,* ed. M. T. Farvar and John P. Milton, pp. 53–60. Garden City, N.Y.: Natural History Press.

Burling, Robbins. 1963. *Rengsanggri: Family and Kinship in a Garo Village.* Philadelphia: University of Pennsylvania Press.

Davis, A. E., and T. D. Bolin. 1972. Lactose intolerance in Southeast Asia. In *The Careless Technology: Ecology and International Development,* ed. M. T. Farvar and John P. Milton, pp. 61–68. Garden City, N.Y.: Natural History Press.

Dennett, Glenn, and John Connell. 1988. Acculturation and health in the highlands of Papua New Guinea. *Current Anthropology* 29(2):273–299.

Goldschmidt, Walter R. 1972. The interrelations between cultural factors and the acquisition of new technical skills. In *The Progress of Underdeveloped Areas,* ed. Bert F. Hoselitz, pp. 135–151. Chicago: University of Chicago Press.

Gross, Daniel R., et al. 1979. Ecology and acculturation among native peoples of Central Brazil. *Science* 206(4422): 1043–1050.

Hughes, Charles C., and John M. Hunter. 1972. The role of technological development in promoting disease in Africa. In *The Careless Technology: Ecology and International Development,* ed. M. T. Farvar and John P. Milton, pp. 69–101. Garden City, N.Y.: Natural History Press.

Keesing, Felix M. 1941. *The South Seas in the Modern World.* Institute of Pacific Relations International Research Series. New York: John Day.

Kroeger, Axel, and François Barbira-Freedman. 1982. *Culture Change and Health: The Case of South American Rainforest Indians.* Frankfurt am Main: Verlag Peter Lang. (Reprinted in Bodley, 1988a:221–236.)

McNeil, Mary. 1972. Lateritic soils in distinct tropical environments: Southern Sudan and Brazil. In *The Careless Technology: Ecology an International Development,* ed. M. T. Farvar and John P. Milton, pp. 591–608. Garden City, N.Y.: Natural History Press.

Mönckeberg, F. 1968. Mental retardation from malnutrition. *Journal of the American Medical Association* 206:30–31.

Montagu, Ashley. 1972. Sociogenic brain damage. *American Anthropologist* 74(5):1045–1061.

Rambo, A. Terry. 1985. *Primitive Polluters: Semang Impact on the Malaysian Tropical Rain Forest Ecosystem.* Anthropological Papers no. 76, Museum of Anthropology, University of Michigan.

Redfield, Robert. 1953. *The Primitive World and Its Transformations.* Ithaca, N.Y.: Cornell University Press.

———. 1962. *A Village That Chose Progress: Chan Kom Revisited.* Chicago: University of Chicago Press, Phoenix Books.

Smith, Wilberforce. 1894. The teeth of ten Sioux Indians. *Journal of the Royal Anthropological Institute* 24:109–116.

TTR: *See under* United States.

United States, Department of the Interior, Office of Territories. 1953. *Report on the Administration of the Trust Territory of the Pacific Islands* (by the United States to the United Nations) for the Period July 1, 1951, to June 30, 1952.

———. 1954. *Annual Report, High Commissioner of the Trust Territory of the Pacific Islands to the Secretary of the Interior* (for 1953).

United States, Department of State. 1955. *Seventh Annual Report to the United Nations on the Administration of the Trust Territory of the Pacific Islands* (July 1, 1953, to June 30, 1954).

———. 1959. *Eleventh Annual Report to the United Nations on the Administration of the Trust Territory of the Pacific Islands* (July 1, 1957, to June 30, 1958).

———. 1964. *Sixteenth Annual Report to the United Nations on the Administration of the Trust Territory of the Pacific Islands* (July 1, 1962 to June 30, 1963).

———. 1973. *Twenty-Fifth Annual Report to the United Nations on the Administration of the Trust Territory of the Pacific Islands* (July 1, 1971, to June 30, 1972).

The Battle for Cattle

LISA MATTHEWS

"Yantai!" shouted Jane Kamuasi from the inside of the candle-lit kitchen.

Playing outside with her brothers by the light of a small headlamp and the countless stars, Yantai heard Jane tell her to get some vegetables for the evening meal. Moments later, the wooden door to Jane's modified mud-and-cow-dung home pushed open. Yantai's delicate frame and bright eyes appeared through the darkness; she was carrying a handful of plum tomatoes and a shallot.

Yantai had gone across the yard to the Kamuasi's more modern metal sheeting house to fetch the vegetables. There, my companion, Mike, and two other men were watching the African Cup of Nations soccer tournament—Togo vs. Congo—on a small black-and-white television powered by roof-top solar panels. Jane and I finished cooking the *sukuma wiki* (finely chopped kale with garlic and tomatoes) on a metal charcoal burner, and cut the corn-flour *ugali*. Then we stepped outside into the dark night to bring the supper to the men watching television.

We placed the food containers onto the coffee tables, and I said hello to Jane's visitors: Francis Sakuda, executive director of the Simba Maasai Outreach Organization (SIMOO), and John Partishou, a friend, huddled in a red plaid *shuka,* or blanket. Before searching in the hutch for the bowls and spoons, Jane lowered her head for Francis to touch the top—a sign of greeting and respect offered to members of the same clan and elders.

After everyone had served themselves, the TV suddenly flickered into black and white fuzz. Kindalele, Jane's eldest son and TV fix-it wizard, got up to adjust the battery to no avail. It died moments later. We would have to wait to see a newspaper before learning the score. The candle lantern cast shadows about the room, and for a moment, silence enveloped the plywood-walled room.

But the family was used to the vagaries of their improvised system, and easily switched to conversation. Soon we were deep in a discussion about U.S. government policy at home and abroad. "We saw pictures on TV from the hurricane in New Orleans," Francis said. "What a terrible tragedy for all those people." Then, reflecting on the ongoing drought that has crippled East Africa, he observed, "They have too much water, and we don't have enough."

They were all surprised that the U.S. government did not do more to address the suffering caused by the hurricane. I said that the U.S. government faced a great deal of fury and criticism from African American leaders who felt the slowed response was based on their racial identity. "The Kenyan government response regarding this drought has been poor, too," remarked Francis, leaving unspoken the stronger parallel: The government response has been poor because of the Maasai's cultural identity. In Kenya, pastoralists are viewed as backwards, and their lands viewed as fallow, despite the fact that pastoralists, who represent 25 percent of the population, produce 80 percent of the country's meat and an estimated 40 percent of Kenya's gross domestic product. And because they are seen in this light, they receive far less help than they need. Despite mobilizing some food and water resources, the Kenyan government has not been successful in preventing deaths or providing enough for its people facing starvation, disrupted living conditions, and a crumbling economy.

Maasai culture is intimately tied to livestock. Cattle are not only used for milk, blood, and meat, but also are an integral part of the spiritual and cultural Maasai way of life. One Maasai elder explained to me that if you do not have a cow, you have no respect, no voice in the Maasai community. The Maasai have a belief that all of the cattle in the entire world belong to them, and the gift of a cow is the most sincere gesture of sympathy. After the World Trade Center attacks on September 11, the small village of Enoosaen gave 14 head of cattle to the United States embassy—double one of the Maasai's lucky numbers, seven. In their traditional council-of-elders justice system, a person would be fined 149 cattle for committing a murder, an unfathomable punishment.

In a culture like this, a man watching his cattle die of starvation during a drought is not just watching his food source or his income drop; he is watching his value as a man vanish. That idea was brought home to me when I expressed some irritation at seeing the men sitting around watching TV while the women did all the cooking. John Partishou said, "Because the cattle are not here, you are not able to see what the men really do."

The cattle were not there because too many had died in the drought, and Jane's husband, Daniel, had moved them close to Nairobi, a day's drive from the Kamuasi's village of Ilnarooj. The village is one of six in the Olishaibor community, on the fringe of the Great Rift Valley in the shadow of the Ngong Hills. As we sat talking in the Kamuasi's *boma* (homestead), Daniel was in Nairobi, having walked two hours to the nearest city to catch a bus. He was checking on his remaining cows, goats, and sheep. In the course of the nine-month drought Daniel had lost 10 cattle and 6 sheep, out of an already small herd at home. Jane said that watching the cows perish brought a terrible sadness to their family—it's like the loss of a family member, she said.

"The drought is really affecting us—we depend on our live-stock, but now because the livestock have gone [to Nairobi] we can't depend on them for milk," said Joyce Tunta, another member of the Oloshoiboi community.

As hard as the drought has been for the Maasai in Oloshoiboi, though, it is far worse for those in the forest highlands of central Kenya. There, Maasai have uprooted their families to live in temporary camps around Mount Kenya, hoping to find viable pasture in the higher, wetter country. That hope has not panned out.

John Tingoi, the Program Coordinator for a local community-based organization, OSILIGI (meaning "hope" in Maa) took Mike and me to visit the Mount Kenya camps, about four hours north of Nairobi. Turning off the paved road, we bounced along the dirt and grassy ruts for a while, then stopped just before we reached the camps. My stomach lurched from the stench of rotting flesh. From the truck, I could spot the sinew, muscles, and bones of at least eight carcasses decaying in the heat of the sun. For fear I would be sick, I could not get out of the truck; but John and the others were eager to show Mike the carcasses burgeoning with maggots. They wanted us to understand up-close the impact of the drought and the effects of their relocation to the forest. Mike later commented that he could taste the rot on his tongue.

About 300 Maasai and other pastoralists from Samburu and Laikipia districts were living within this region of the forest. Fifty or so homes were set up just on the outskirts of a grassy clearing. Many had walked for days, some for weeks, in search of pasture. One man from Samburu had lost 150 head of cattle from starvation on the way to the forest, where the grass is short and dry, but abundant. They had no where else to turn.

John pulled up to the temporary home—a makeshift tent of tarp and blankets enclosed by a fence of thorn bushes—where he and his family had been living for two months. Unlike typical Maasai home sites separated by a good 15 or 20 minute walk, the temporary camps formed a small Maasai city.

The ground sank as I stepped out of the truck and tiny dried goat droppings fell into my sandals. We were inundated with swarms of flies.

John introduced me to his young girls, who were playing in the goat pen we were standing in. John's youngest girl came up to me to say, "Supa," and bowed her head for us to greet her. She tried in vain to shoo the death flies from the corners of her mouth and eyes. We walked through the pen and to the fence enclosing their temporary camp. John's wife was cooking tea on the fire. When she got up to say hello to us, flies buzzed around the area, clouding their tent. John said that above all else, keeping warm was the most difficult part of living here, especially at night when the temperature drops to about 40 degrees Fahrenheit. He said that many people in the temporary camps have been sick, and he was concerned about his young girls.

On the day I visited, the government was implementing a one-time livestock-purchasing program to help provide some income for the struggling herdsmen. I talked to a group of Maasai through the translation of John Tingoi's. Many believed that the government support is helpful, but it is not enough.

Nkidayu Kereti Sururu and Lenguar Meretuni Leruso said that moving to Mt. Kenya is a mixed blessing—there is plenty of pasture, but the change in climate at the higher elevation has stressed the animals, which are dying of pneumonia and other diseases. The cold nights also make the cows more susceptible to East Coast Fever, a fatal disease carried by ticks, and even healthy cows are not interested in drinking the frigid river water.

Moving to Mt. Kenya is also risky, Leruso said, because the Maasai don't have proper access to a market to sell their livestock. He explained that agriculturalist tribes in Kenya take advantage of the drought-plagued Maasai, buying the meat for much less than what it is worth. Typically, a cow is worth approximately 18,000 Kenyan shillings, but now they are only selling for 10,000 Ksh, or less. On top of that, he said, prices for basic goods have increased in the area. "Many of the herders are starving," Lenguar said.

The group collectively complained that the government was not purchasing the weak cows, as they had promised, and were instead buying their best cows, the ones that were more likely to survive the drought. John Elipa, from the Kenyan Agricultural Development Corporation, said that the cows bought from these pastoralists would be taken to ranches, fattened, and resold, to create a revolving fund for drought relief. He emphasized that the program helps in the short term as well, because the Maasai who sell a few cows can afford to buy food for their families.

John said that he is eager for the rains so he can return to his permanent home in Doldol, a small, mostly Maasai community. The only road to Doldol, approximately 60 kilometers north of Nanuki, is bordered by an electric fence. In 2000, the last year of severe drought, more than 11,000 cows died on this road on their way to Mt. Kenya. John said many were enticed by the grass on the other side of the fence and electrocuted.

As we drove down this road, John pointed out a great clearing in the distance, where the grand graduation ceremony for the young *moran* (warriors) used to take place. This was Maasai land, roughly 1 million acres that once served as the cushion for droughts like this one, but it was coerced from the Maasai to make way for white settlement in British East Africa at the turn of the 20th century.

This land, part of what is known today as the White Highlands, has been the root of contention between the Maasai and the Kenyan government since independence in 1963. "The Maasai experienced the biggest colonial land rip-off in all of Africa," said William Ole Ntimama, Maasai Minister of Parliament for Narok North.

With the stroke of a pen on June 15, 1895, Maasai land became part of British East Africa. Using force, intimidation, and coercion, colonial officials succeeded in signing two agreements with Maasai representatives, the first in 1904 and the second in 1911. The 1904 agreement removed the Maasai from the most fertile lands in all of Kenya, paving the way for white farmers and agribusinesses. The lands ranged from the great swamp around what is now Nairobi, to the plains around Mount Kenya, to the volcanic rich lands around Lake Naivasha and Nakruru. Today, the volcanic soil and cool rains surrounding the lakes are used for floriculture and coffee and tea plantations. The Maasai's former lands are home to an array of national parks, including Hell's Gate and Mount Kenya.

In exchange for their best grazing resources in the Central Rift Valley, the Maasai secured two permanent reserves, one north of the railway line in Laikipia and the second south in what are today Kajiado and Narok districts. Similar to American Indians, the Maasai were hoodwinked into giving up their best lands in exchange for a reservation—convinced that it would ensure the right to the reservation for eternity. But as in the United States, white settlement in the Rift Valley increased, and pressure for Maasai land in Laikipia grew. More coercion, back-door deals, and schemes by both British officials and Maasai leaders led to the second treaty of 1911, which forced the Maasai at gun-point to exchange 4,500 square miles in the northern reserve for 6,500 in the more arid Southern Rift Valley. In mirror to the Trail of Tears experienced by American Indian groups in the early 1800s, hundreds of Maasai perished from exposure during this grueling trek across the Mau escarpment. Livestock died by the thousands. Some Maasai in Laikipia refused to move and hid amongst other groups in the neighboring Mokogodo forest, passing as Il-Dorobos, or people without cattle. James Legei, who also works with OSILIGI, said, "Only recently [within the past 20 years] have Maasai in the south realized that Maasai are still living in Laikipia."

The Mau Mau rebellion, a largely Kikuyu movement, successfully fought for sovereignty in 1963. From the very infancy of independence, the Kikuyu majority established a firm grasp on Kenyan political power. Kikuyu agricultural-based ideologies fit into the policies of land use the British had established, and Kikuyu leaders quickly replicated the colonial systems they fought to drive from Kenya.

A delegation of 10 Maasai traveled to the Lancaster House Conference in London in 1963 to participate in negotiating the terms of decolonization and to advocate for the return of the Northern Highlands to Maasai communities. The delegation issued a written plea: "It is as a direct result of having been induced to leave the best-watered and most fertile areas that the Maasai have endured the most recent disastrous famine, following drought and flood ... Being confined to marginal areas of rainfall, whenever the rains fail, [Maasai] are the first to suffer."

The fledgling Kenyan government had the opportunity to redistribute Maasai lands after independence, but instead bowed to British pressure to keep the highlands for the elite. As a result, the former Northern Reserve lands today are owned by no more than 40 descendents of the white colonialists and are bordered by electric fences. They are home to several five-star tourist lodges and seasonal multi-million dollar celebrity ranches. The land is full of grass, trees, and an abundance of wildlife. John Tingoi commented that if the Maasai tried to graze their cattle on their former lands, they would be shot.

Colonial settlement and land appropriation eroded the southern reserve as well. Since 1911 the British Magadi Soda Company has extracted thousands of tons of soda ash from Lake Magadi in the center of the reserve. Revenues from the ash, used to make glass and detergent, have not supported community development or education. The Masai Mara, probably one of the world's most famous game parks, was etched out of the southern reserve in 1974. Ben Ole Tongoyo from Touch of Love Integrated Development Program comes from Maji Moto, a community adjacent to the park. He says that a percentage of the park revenue goes to the community, but that there is no accountability from an independent party. "Most of the money pads the pockets of the local officials and never reaches the grassroots."

Population influx into the already arid southern Maasai lands has resulted in long-term impacts on the land and the environment. "Weather patterns are changing," said Francis Sakuda. He said that Oloshoiboi once flourished with a great diversity of wild animals. Now, only a few herds of giraffe and an occasional leopard grace their lands.

Governments in Africa don't want to explore the indigenous question because the few elites who have power are benefiting from indigenous exploitation, John Tingoi said. Officials claim that "all Africans are indigenous" because governments are complicit in dispossessing indigenous peoples from their lands and resources. Tingoi said that when other Kenyan tribes, like the Kikuyu, arrived in the Rift Valley they found Maasai, who been living there for hundreds of years.

Maasai red *shukas* and colorful beadwork grace the covers of tourism books of East Africa and postcards throughout Kenya. This image of the fierce and proud warrior is appropriated, bought, stolen, and sold by the majority of mainstream Kenyans, tourism companies, and conservationists without any real benefit to Maasai communities themselves. The government purports to embrace their culture, but the Kenyan government does not support or respect their pastoral way of life. The Maasai are continually pushed to the margins of Kenyan society without adequate access to healthcare, sanitation, and water resources, education, information, or transportation services. It is a direct result of their continued colonialization by the rest of Kenyan society that the Maasai claim indigeniety.

From Jane Kamuasi's house in the Ngong Hills, it's a 45-minute hike across the rocky terrain and down a steep slope to the closest spring. On a typical week, Jane fetches water twice or three times for her family. On our way down, we met numerous groups of women coming and going from the spring. Some were lucky enough to have donkeys; others, wearing no more than flimsy tennis shoes with no laces, were carrying seven or eight gallons of water in a jug with a head-strap. Some of the women had walked for three hours to get to the water source.

The spring amounted to no more than a trickle of water into a puddle of mud. Donkeys and goats were drinking from the same source, separated by a small mud dam. To ensure our health, Jane made sure that we would not drink this water, but most people don't have that luxury. Two weeks later, she said that the puddle had dried up. The women were then forced to walk even further.

Traditionally, the Maasai would move with their families and cattle to the areas that receive more rainfall; colonialism and the market economy have changed this nomadic way of life. But they are still steadfast in keeping their traditions and language. "The Maasai have been so successful keeping their traditions alive," said Samuel Mushokia Muchiri, a Kikuyu. "That's what makes them indigenous—they have not conformed to the ways of the West like so many of the other tribes in Kenya," he said.

The government knows that the Maasai are indigenous—they just don't want to recognize it in policy, said Tingoi. Ruth Emanikor, a Turkana woman who works with the Indigenous Information Network based in Nairobi, said that Kenyan government officials are afraid to decentralize resources because with empowerment comes agitation for additional rights. But, she said, it is clear they need to implement a law recognizing indigenous peoples. And that is what the Maasai are pushing for. Instead of waiting for the government to enact policies supporting their children's' education, infrastructure development, and civic education, communities are taking matters into their own hands.

The constitutional referendum process in November 2005 proved to be the perfect opportunity for Maasai to mobilize action, create a political base, and begin to push for their rights.

"For the first time, Maasai communities voted as a block [to defeat the draft constitution]," said Mary Simat, the chairwoman of Maasai Women's Empowerment and Education Development. The draft constitution would have posed a serious threat to Maasai and other pastoralists' land rights because the government would be able to claim lands that were "idle."

The constitutional referendum process also motivated various Maasai organizations to formulate a strategy for reclaiming their lands in the Northern Reserve. They formed the Maa Civil Society Forum with the express purpose of opening a dialogue to redress historical wrongs committed against the Maasai during the colonial period and perpetuated after independence. "All of the Kenyan governments have been hostile to the Maasai," said Ben Ole Koisaba, the chairman of the forum. The Maasai have been powerless for too long, and there are no safety nets for this drought in Maasai land, he said.

Back at her *boma*, Jane Kamuasi said she is proud to have voted in the recent constitutional referendum. Francis Sakuda said, "Jane is a role model to other women in Oloshoiboi. She has shown other women who have families that they too can become educated and work to improve their community."

LISA MATTHEWS is the Program Officer for Cultural Survival.

Rangers by Birth

Mursi, Suri, Nyangatom, Dizi and Me'en have managed the biodiversity in Ethiopia's Omo area for centuries. Is it Wise to push them aside in the name of conservation?

WILL HURD

The midday heat brings the men together under a small shade tree on the edge of a plateau overlooking the Omo River in Ethiopia. Long fighting sticks and cow skins for sitting have been stored in the branches, among dried grass that has been stuffed there to increase the shade. The tree is just outside the cluster of small grass huts that is Benna Orr (Stones Village). The men look out over a large island in the river where the tall Mursi sorghum grows. The island and surrounding banks are dotted with makeshift grain huts, where the women thresh grain or talk and eat, hiding from the brunt of the sun.

Hogo (Beans) is here under the tree, as are Uligidangdor (Greybull), Char Koro Ramai (Long Leopard Tail), Nebi Jare (Buffalo Legs), Ari Holi (White Ox) and many of the other men of Stones Village. They are making rope from the sword-like extensions of *kashwi* (*Sansevieria,* or bowstring hemp), which is found only near the river. As the Mursis' ever-present, emphatic speech and raucous laughter ring out, Hogo grips the sharp stick with his toes, scraping off the outer fibers to get the long, weavable strands. His finished rope will be taken back to the cattle camps on the plains for leads on calves and bulls.

From atop the plateau, I can see the place where we ford the Omo River to Greybull's garden. The water is fast here, and the crocodiles can't navigate well in the current. Crocodiles are ever-present around the village, basking on the river's shores or floating with their eyes just above water. Although the swift current at the ford makes for a somewhat safer crossing, it is still treacherous. The water is up over our waists, and I can only avoid being swept away by holding onto Greybull, a massive man whose hands and feet are at least one-and-a-half times larger than mine. One time, a friend of Greybull's got drunk while weeding his garden, and we joked that if he tried to cross the river home he would end up in Bongos, a village three days downriver.

Many times I have tried to define the Mursi by their most dominant quality, but it is difficult to choose just one. Are they herdsman foremost, or botanists, orators, or rangers? The Mursi excel at all of these occupations. Like the Suri and Nyangatom—the other cattle herders in the area—the Mursi are so thoroughly entwined with cattle that it has been said they think in terms of cattle. All words for colors are described as colors of cattle coats. When shown a color they don't have a name for, they say, "There is no such beast." It

is dizzying to listen to them rattling off plant names while walking through the bush. I never learned a measurable fraction of the plants most Mursi know, plants for building huts, carving milk containers, for veterinary and human medicine; plants to eat or to tie around the arms as rattles during initiation. They even have a water-clarifier, a root called *kamogi,* (*Maerua subcordata*). It is shaved and spun on a stick in brown, murky water, causing the dirt particles to drop to the bottom, leaving clear water. It is used when the rains come. The rain drags more dirt into the Omo, which the Mursi say makes them sick.

The Mursi also know animals. As trackers they know where animals are, what they eat, and how they behave. It is astonishing to watch them come across a riot of tracks and quickly decipher how many *marchan* (lesser kudu) crossed the path. Their localized, empirical knowledge of animals of the area—animals amongst which they and their ancestors have lived for thousands of years—greatly surpasses the knowledge of the highlanders who are employed as park rangers in Omo National Park, which surrounds the Mursi. At one point the warden of the national park asked if I had ever seen *gusheny* (blue monkeys) and wondered where they could be found. The Mursi had already shown me the monkeys—just one of the animals they know intimately. Unfortunately, the Mursi and other nearby indigenous groups are seen as a liability for the park rather than an asset. As a result, the Mursi live under the constant threat of relocation that would destroy their culture.

Omo National Park was established in 1966 on the territories of five tribes: the Suri, Dizi, Mursi, Me'en and Nyangatom. Virtually the entire park is the home of these five tribes or used by them for cultivation, cattle raising, bee-keeping, food gathering, and occasional hunting. The Suri, who have the largest territory, are closely related to the Mursi, their languages being mutually intelligible. The Mursi became Mursi 150 years ago, when they branched off from the larger Suri group by crossing to the east bank of the Omo River. The Mursi say they and the Suri "are one people." The Suri and the Mursi still primarily follow an animist religion, and the Mursi practice a form of divination by reading cow entrails.

The Nyangatom cultivate sorghum and graze cattle in the southern regions of the park and are culturally and linguistically different from the rest of the groups. The Nyangatom men often have facial tattoos of raised bumps, and the women wear hundreds of beaded necklaces, which collectively resemble a small inner tube. The Dizi and Me'en are highland agriculturalists who live in the northern regions of the park.

The total combined population of all these tribes is around 140,000, but the number of people who use the land inside the park is difficult to estimate, especially as Mursi, Suri, and Nyangatom are seminomadic. They change residences several times throughout the year. Fifty thousand would be a reasonable approximation for the number of park inhabitants.

Although the creation of Omo Park forced the Mursi and other tribal people out of certain areas, the park mostly existed on paper, infringing little on the lives of the local people. This all stands to change, as the park now has a new manager, the African Parks Foundation of the Netherlands.

African Parks Foundation is the brainchild of billionaire Paul van Vlissingen, whose family business is based on liquid petroleum gas distribution and a global retail business. The foundation is partially funded by Rob Walton, the chairman of Wal-Mart, who is also on the board of African Parks Foundation of America. In November 2005 the foundation signed a contract to lease the park for 25 years, a change of management that could have a huge impact on the five local groups, restricting their access to vital resources and even physically displacing them.

Government park officials have been collecting signatures from local people, on documents they cannot read, by which they give their "consent" to the park boundaries. These documents will then be used to gazette, or legally establish, the park's boundaries, a process that will make the local people illegal squatters on their own land. There was no meaningful consultation with local residents about where the boundaries should be drawn, and those who signed these documents (of which they were not given copies) either did so unwillingly or did not appreciate the full implications of what they were doing.

This development comes on the heels of forced resettlement from the other park in Ethiopia that African Parks Foundation has taken over, Nech Sar National Park, near Arba Minch. In 2004, the government moved 3,800 Kore who traditionally cultivated within the park. They claim to have allocated land outside of the Park to 1,800 of the Kore. The whereabouts of the remaining 2,000 Kore people is still unknown. No compensation was paid for lost property or crops. Approximately 5,500 Guji-Oromo, a seminomadic pastoral people who traditionally reside within the park, have been harassed and a number chased from the park. According to a report by the Guji themselves, which neither the government nor APF have denied, 463 of their houses were burned down by Ethiopian park officials and police in November 2004—ten months after APF signed a contract in which the government stipulated that all residents of the park would be removed. Despite this, the Guji-Oromo remain, pushed to two small corners of the park. This does not bode well for the Mursi under the tree or the other tribal peoples of the Omo Park area.

There is no extra space for a park to be created in the Omo area. The resources are fully used by indigenous peoples' different strategies for deriving a living throughout the year. In the case of the Mursi, they plant along the riverbank in the renewed silt after the rainy season and inland during the rains. They also graze cattle on the surrounding plains. If large sections of land are taken, they could not survive without becoming permanently dependant on food aid.

African Parks Foundation has been asked many times to add a "no evictions" clause to its contracts with the government. They have been asked to make the contract available to tribal people so they can seek independent legal advice. They have also been asked to sign written agreements with the local groups, safeguarding their rights to secure livelihoods and co-manage the park. On all these counts the foundation has refused. And the Ethiopian government, no doubt anticipating large tourist revenues, has abdicated it's responsibility to help the Mursi.

But will the park plan succeed if local groups are marginalized? In the end, would this be good for biodiverstiy? Mark Dowie writes in his recent article in *Orion* magazine, "Many conservationists are beginning to realize that most of the areas they have sought to protect are rich in biodiversity precisely because the people who were living there had come to understand the value and mechanisms of biological diversity. Some will even admit that wrecking the lives of 10 million or more poor, powerless people has been an enormous mistake—not only a moral . . . and economic mistake, but an ecological one as well."

The fact that Omo National Park can be mistaken for a wilderness by Westerners is a tribute to the benign environmental impact of the livelihood strategies of local people. This is a landscape created in part by millennia of human use; there is evidence of similar agricultural practices in the area dating back 5,000 years. Pastoralists open grasslands by burning the dense brush, promoting the growth of new grass, which is good for both cattle and wildlife. The Mursi know that they live well with the biodiversity: "In the Elma valley," said one Mursi *bari* (elder), "We have zebras, hartebeest and buffalo. In your land you have destroyed all your animals, so, after you have come here to see things, we can go together to your land so that I can see what kind of animals you have."

The local groups in the area do not derive much of their economy from hunting—1 or 2 percent at the most and usually when they are hungry. The guns they have are 30-year-old AK-47s, with barrels that have widened from use, making an already-inaccurate gun more inaccurate. Hunting is close range, and in the case of one of the most often-hunted animals, cape buffalo, extremely dangerous. What would be of more interest to the Mursi is having real decision-making power in the use of their land and getting a fair share of the tourism revenue from the park. What is certain is that having hungry, angry, displaced people at the outer edges of the park is a recipe for park failure. A large proportion of the park budget would be needed for policing activities.

A better approach would be for African Parks Foundation to truly partner with the local groups, not just hire some as game guards. The collective knowledge of people who have lived among the animals in this area for thousands of years should be seen as an asset for the park. One has to ask if African Parks Foundation, with a corporate manager at the helm, is really in a better position to manage the biodiversity than the local people. If the Suri, Dizi, Mursi, Me'en and Nyangatom are given real decision-making power in Omo National Park, it could be the most exciting conservation project in Africa.

WILL HURD lived with the Mursi for four months. He founded Native Solutions to Conservation Refugees in response to a Mursi request to help them stay on their land. For more information on the Mursi, Suri, Dizi, Me'en and Nyangatom and their possible displacement visit http://conservationrefugees.org/.

Digging Into the Roots of Research Ethics

How a Canadian ethnobotanist became a champion of research that advances the lot of indigenous peoples

LILA GUTERMAN

A recent spate of scandals in science suggests that researchers often risk violating ethical standards to advance their personal or professional standing.

Kelly P. Bannister, an ethnobotanist at the University of Victoria here, has risked quite a bit in precisely the opposite direction. As a graduate student in the late 1990s, she twice bucked norms of science to deter commercialization of her research and to share the results of her work with indigenous peoples in Canada.

While studying how an indigenous group in British Columbia uses plants for food and medicine, she withheld extracts of the plants from her graduate supervisor, who wanted to sell them to a pharmaceutical company. Then, when she finished her dissertation, she had it sealed for five years. She didn't want companies to profit from her published work, perhaps at the expense—or at least at the displeasure—of the Indian groups that had collaborated with her.

The decisions cost her time, stress, and the coin of the academic realm—publications. Ms. Bannister also lost her graduate supervisor after the dispute over her plant samples.

Her choices could have withered her research career. But surprisingly, perhaps *because* she continues to rank her own interests lower than those of the aboriginal peoples she works with, her career is flourishing.

Ms. Bannister, 41, an adjunct professor of environmental studies, directs a research-and-policy center dedicated to environmental projects at Victoria. She is in demand for publishing on the ethics of research involving aboriginal peoples, and she sits on several university, national, and international committees working to reform research policies.

Her studies focus on making academic research, writ large, more equitable to the indigenous groups it often studies. She concentrates on intellectual property—the stories, songs, and traditions of aboriginal peoples, which have in the past often been exploited or published without the agreement of those who shared them with the researchers.

"As academics," says George P. Nicholas, a professor of archaeology at British Columbia's Simon Fraser University, who has collaborated with Ms. Bannister, "we can look at the problems and identify their causes and say, Here are some solutions. It's another thing entirely to make a commitment . . . to talk to the communities as well as to deal with academic institutions, professional societies, and international policy-making organizations."

Ms. Bannister, he says, "perhaps more than anyone else I know, has been willing to make that kind of commitment."

Dressed Down

Kelly Bannister grew up in the small city of Nanaimo, on the east coast of Vancouver Island. This instigator of progressive change is the daughter of conservative parents, her father a self-made businessman. A former college runner, she still bears the leanness and energy of an athlete and wears shorts and trail shoes to work. She and her husband, Ronald, and their 3-year-old daughter, Katia, live on tiny, forested Thetis Island, a 20-minute ferry ride across the Strait of Georgia from Vancouver Island.

Ms. Bannister did not set out to focus on research ethics. She earned bachelor's and master's degrees in microbiology at the University of Victoria. After several years teaching there, she embarked on an almost accidental transition from molecular biology to ethnobotany.

She happened to meet Nancy J. Turner, a professor and ethnobotany researcher at Victoria. "I said, 'ethno-what?'" Ms. Bannister remembers. But she was intrigued by what she learned, and signed up to be a research assistant in Ms. Turner's group in the summer of 1995, doing laboratory tests of samples from plants used by the Secwepemc people, in the southern interior of British Columbia.

That fall she began studying for her Ph.D. in the botany department of the University of British Columbia, under a supervisor named G.H. Neil Towers, a prominent plant chemist. She continued doing research on Ms. Turner's project studying traditional uses of plants among the Secwepemc and working in Mr. Towers's laboratory to analyze the specimens.

Early on she discovered that her research would have to involve more than fieldwork, lab work, and publishing. During one of her first meetings with the tribal elders, she presented her research proposal. As Ms. Bannister recalls, one elder stood up and challenged her, saying, "They've taken our land. They've taken our culture. And now they're going to take the only things we have left, our medicines."

Ms. Bannister was deeply shaken by that challenge, even though the elder noted that she had not meant to include Ms. Bannister in her indictment.

"I came away thinking, 'I can't do this, I can't do this,'" Ms. Bannister remembers.

Prospecting or Piracy?

The Secwepemc elder's attitude is not unusual, says Doris M. Cook, a senior policy adviser at the Canadian Institutes of Health Research. Many aboriginal people around the world have become skeptical of research after scientists working with them have broken promises or neglected to inform them of the results of the studies.

Ms. Cook, who is Mohawk, recalls researchers in her community studying how industrial pollution had affected people's health. The local people did not hear of the results for 17 years. What's more, a published report—which Ms. Cook found 20 years after the original study—listed the names of all of the participants, violating the original requirement of anonymity.

"In the past," she says, "the benefits of research have accrued to the researchers and their institutions, in the forms of higher education, Ph.D.'s, postdocs, articles, and career advancement. Aboriginal people have not really benefited from it."

Ethnobotany has proven particularly controversial. The field aims to understand how people use plants, but it is also intimately tied to bioprospecting (sometimes called "biopiracy"), which involves attempts to develop pharmaceuticals from plants used by local people. Critics say drug companies benefit by appropriating, or even stealing, indigenous knowledge, some of which is obtained via academic research.

Ronald E. Ignace, who was chief of one of the Secwepemc bands for 20 years, says his people were "burned" when researchers claimed copyright to publications resulting from the elders' sharing of the band's stories.

As a result, the Secwepemc set conditions for researchers who want to study their knowledge or practices: the copyright to any publications had to go to an educational nonprofit group that Mr. Ignace had started; researchers could use what they learned only for educational purposes; and researchers' field notes would belong to the Secwepemc museum.

Despite her dressing-down by the tribal elder, Ms. Bannister decided that she could do the research in accordance with the group's conditions. But she soon learned that her own philosophy differed from that of her supervisor, who felt that the

university laboratory should earn money for supplies by selling the plant extracts to a drug company. (Mr. Towers died in 2004.)

Despite being just a third-year graduate student, Ms. Bannister took a stand. She insisted that she could not go along with his plan without the approval of representatives of the Secwepemc people. Mr. Towers refused to meet with them. A few weeks later, Ms. Bannister received a letter from Mr. Towers resigning as her supervisor.

To keep her Ph.D. program going, Iain E.P. Taylor, now a professor emeritus who was then the head of the botany department at the University of British Columbia, agreed to become her supervisor jointly with Ms. Turner, who had an adjunct position at Victoria. "When the rug was being pulled out from under me, he gave me another rug to stand on," Ms. Bannister says of Mr. Taylor.

"Neil Towers was a great subscriber to the commons," says Mr. Taylor. "Kelly was certainly one of his most talented students. He and she banged heads over this agreement."

Mr. Towers later rejoined Ms. Bannister's dissertation committee, although not as her supervisor, and was at her dissertation defense.

Sharing the Fruits

Ms. Bannister's dissertation, which she completed in 2000, turned out to be "good, sound, solid stuff," says Mr. Taylor, who is one of the few people to have seen her raw data. (They remain unpublished today.) Making the laboratory results all the more interesting, he says, was the cultural context that she provided along with her data.

For instance, she described the way the Secwepemc cook a plant called balsamroot for use as food, and the different way they prepare it for use as a medicine.

She received permission from the University of British Columbia to place her dissertation in "restricted access"—a step normally taken by students wishing to apply for patent protection—for five years, so that she could work with the Secwepemc people to publish her work (and that of others doing ethnobotanical research with the band) in a book format that would be useful to them.

Ms. Bannister refused to seek publication of her data in a scientific journal. "Publication is the first and easiest source for biotechnology and pharmaceutical and other corporate entities to just come in and scoop up the information for free, and without any connection to the original knowledge holders," she says. "I didn't want to contribute to it."

Adds Mr. Nicholas, who served on her dissertation committee: "That's an extremely brave stance—some would say foolish stance—for a new Ph.D."

"It's a principle," she says. "Me, tiny little me, standing up for my principles."

It wouldn't be the last time. When the five-year period ended, in June 2005, the publishing efforts were not complete and she received a yearlong extension, followed by a three-month extension this June. Ms. Bannister is putting together draft chapters for academic and tribal review. The University of Victoria will publish the book as part of its Western Geographic series. The press will share the copyright and potential royalties with the Secwepemc people. The book will contain an explicit statement, the wording to be worked out with tribal representatives, that the Secwepemc retain rights to their cultural innovations and expect to be contacted for any future use of the information.

"What I'm trying to counter," she says, "is the severing between the community source of knowledge and expertise, and the end publication, in which the academic authors usually are the ones who are credited for the information." Typically, she says, "those at the last stages of the invention or the discovery or the knowledge creation are the ones who get the most reward." She chooses to share the attribution instead.

Sidney N. Jules, who is Secwepemc, says he is sure that Ms. Bannister's work will be useful for the band. "A lot of the people that she did research with have passed on," he says. "If she didn't do the research when she did, we would have lost a lot of knowledge." Her slow and collaborative approach to publishing, he says, "certainly showed that she was aware of the cultural aspects and understood the importance of not just exploiting the information."

New Agreements

In the years since receiving her Ph.D., Ms. Bannister has continued doing ethnobotanical research—but only outside academe. She works as a consultant with indigenous groups when they request it and does not publish academic articles on that work.

Her work at the University of Victoria has concentrated on the intellectual-property and ethical issues of research collaborations between academic researchers and indigenous peoples.

In one project, she worked with local and indigenous groups around Clayoquot Sound, on the west coast of Vancouver Island, to develop standards for conducting research there. The 30-page document called on scientists to involve local people in the research through employment or volunteer work, to work out in advance any restrictions on the data, and to decide who would own, or profit from, commercial rights to the material.

An appendix provides a draft letter of consent for use when the research involves any of five Indian bands in the area, together known as the Central Region Nuu-chah-nulth First Nations. The research participants and the scientists sign it, acknowledging that the participants own and control the information they provide, and that they "will have an opportunity to deny publication or public distribution of any of the information [they] provide."

Those requirements are controversial, says Rodney Dobell, a professor emeritus of public policy at Victoria, who was principal investigator and a collaborator with Ms. Bannister on a three-year grant from the Social Sciences and Humanities Research Council of Canada for work around Clayoquot Sound. "This is

where you start to run into problems with researchers, who feel they are in control of the interpretation of the evidence they've gathered," he says. "This is still a somewhat unsettled area."

The standards took two years to develop, until August 2003. Such work is important to creating trusting relationships in research, says Michael F. Brown, a professor of anthropology at Williams College and author of the 2003 book *Who Owns Native Culture?* (Harvard University Press). "That's why the work of Kelly Bannister and some of her colleagues is so remarkable, because they've put in the time to work out collaborative contracts," he says. "But the front-end commitment is huge."

The process, Ms. Bannister acknowledges, "took a lot longer than we thought it would." But the slowness can be typical of working out agreements with politically and culturally diverse peoples, she says. And academe often fails to acknowledge that. "The timelines we have to adhere to stem from funders and from reward and promotion criteria," she says. "Those systemic pressures can set us up to fail or to be inadequate in developing standards" for research.

R. Michael M'Gonigle, a professor of environmental law and policy at Victoria and an author of the new book *Planet U: Sustaining the World, Reinventing the University*, (New Society Publishers), concurs: "What's needed is a shift in the university reward system to value the needs of the community, to value [researchers] giving on-the-ground results."

Mr. Brown agrees with much of what Ms. Bannister stands for. "There should be legitimate and durable protections for indigenous peoples in certain areas," he declares. But he does not think that aboriginal people should own information, other than forms that can be copyrighted, related to their cultures. When it comes to academic publications, such ownership, he says, "assumes that the anthropologist or biologist just absorbs information, doesn't process it, doesn't analyze it, doesn't contribute anything to it."

Were he presented with the condition that an Indian group had to own the copyright on anything he published, he says, he would decline to do research with that group. "If I write it," he says, "it's mine."

Ignorance, Not Malice

Ms. Bannister says she has never felt deprived of credit for her work with indigenous groups. Sharing copyright is just one possible answer. Sometimes the solution is simply quoting the person who gave the information. "What I have a problem with is distancing the knowledge from the original source," she says. "Particularly for academics, whose whole enterprise rests on due credit."

She and others see reason for optimism. Aboriginal groups are increasingly standing up for themselves, professional groups are developing codes of ethics, and grant-making bodies in Canada and elsewhere are exploring new ethical requirements for researchers working with indigenous peoples. International agreements, like the Convention on Biological Diversity, accepted by 150 governments in 1992, encourage signatories to recognize the importance of the knowledge of indigenous peoples and to collaborate and share benefits with them. The World Intellectual Property Organization has been working since 1998 on a program to protect traditional knowledge, and is discussing draft provisions.

Ms. Bannister is working with the University of Victoria, the Canadian government, and internationally in an attempt to change the ethical rules and support systems for researchers working with aboriginal groups and other local peoples. She is also collaborating with Mr. Nicholas of Victoria on a major new international project to study intellectual-property problems, and potential solutions, in archaeology.

Much of her work, she says, boils down to raising awareness: "A lot of the source of the problems that arise is ignorance. I actually don't think that people have malicious intent to harm and deceive."

Ms. Bannister's work in pushing for change is important, says Marianne Ignace, an associate professor of anthropology and First Nations studies at Simon Fraser University, and the wife of Ronald Ignace, the former chief of a Secwepemc band. "The natural-science community badly needs people like Kelly to alert them to those kinds of issues," she says.

Ms. Bannister's own experience in graduate school woke her up to the perspective of aboriginal people who are under the researchers' microscopes—and to the conflicting demands on the researchers themselves.

"My learning curve was as valuable as anything else I've experienced in terms of understanding the pulls by my academic obligations in one direction and the expectations and needs of the community in another direction," she says. "I can't continue to be here at the university if I'm not going to work on the systemic problem."

Can Minority Languages Be Saved?

Globalization vs. Culture

The increasing mobility of people, goods, and information has driven a powerful trend toward cultural uniformity and the extinction of local languages. But languages that have young people, business, and government on their side are alive and thriving.

Eric Garland

Globalized economics and media are changing the face of culture around the globe, reducing the number of languages that humans speak. As the world economy becomes more integrated, a common tongue has become more important than ever to promote commerce, and that puts speakers of regional dialects and minority languages at a distinct disadvantage. In addition, telecommunications has pressured languages to become more standardized, further squeezing local variations of language.

Over the past 500 years, as nation-states developed and became more centralized, regional dialects and minority languages have been dominated by the centrist dialects of the ruling parties. Cornish has given way to English, Breton to French, Bavarian to High German, and Fu-jian-wa to Cantonese. Linguists concur that minority languages all over the world are giving way to more dominant languages, such as English, Mandarin, and Spanish, among others. The realities of commerce and the seductive power of world pop culture are placing pressure on speakers of minority languages to learn majority languages or suffer the consequences: greater difficulty doing business, less access to information, etc.

These pressures are inducing a rapid die-off of languages around the world. Languages have been disappearing steadily, with 3,000 of the world's languages predicted to disappear in the next 100 years. According to the United Nations Environment Program, there are 5,000 to 7,000 spoken languages in the world, with 4,000 to 5,000 of these classed as indigenous, used by native tribes. More than 2,500 are in danger of immediate extinction, and many more are losing their link with the natural world, becoming museum pieces rather than living languages.

Futurists have noted this loss with no little despair, for significant, culturally specific information may disappear along with a language. For instance, knowledge about unique medicines and treatments used by aboriginal groups could be lost forever if the language used to transmit that information is banned by a majority culture.

The common wisdom is that globalization is the wave of the future, and in many respects this is undeniable. However, swept up in this conventional wisdom is the notion that languages and cultures will simply cease to exist, and people will instead choose "global" cultures and languages that will transcend boundaries.

This is not the only potential scenario. It is possible for globalization and new technology to safeguard cultural identity while simultaneously allowing free exchanges of ideas and goods. For centuries, dialects and languages have been unifying to facilitate national identity, scientific research, and commerce. Without question, there will be a need for common languages, as standardization allows growth in software and in people. But global prosperity and new technologies may also allow smaller cultures to preserve their niches. It is clear from several modern examples that a dying or dead language can turn around and become vibrant again, depending on people's determination and the government policies that are put in place.

Reversing Language Loss

The idea of saving languages is very modern. When linguistics scholar Joshua A. Fishman first wrote of "reversing language shift" in his book of that title (1990), one reviewer actually laughed at the notion. The conventional wisdom among linguists, historians, and sociologists was that, if your culture and language were on the way out, their doom was assured in a globalized world. After all, the prevailing trends are toward globalization and a unified world. Tiny dialects—such as Breton, the Celtic language spoken in Brittany, a province on the northwestern coast of France—are not a benefit in the global economy, since they are difficult to learn, poorly adapted to modern life, and unintelligible to almost everyone beyond a small region.

Learning or relearning a native language is often a political statement, an act of self-definition, one that brings solidarity with our neighbors. It is political power, cultural reverence, and perhaps a

feeling of control in a world where political and cultural borders are collapsing all around us. Minority languages may also have a place alongside majority forms of communication. The International Committee for the Defense of the Breton Language suggests that early bilingualism can help prepare young people to master several languages, which will be an advantage—if not a necessity—for the future in Europe.

Changing world geopolitics is already reforming the pressures on languages. The fall of the Soviet Union actually spurred a trend toward reversing language loss. In many of the former Soviet republics, older Turkic languages have been revived, now that the Russian influence is gone. Turkey is spending $1.5 billion to encourage the resurgence of Turkish throughout the region. Language is power, economic and otherwise, and the Turks are capitalizing on the possibility of extending their reach, causing a reverse of language shift in the region.

It is becoming clear that, when people have a strong cultural reason to reverse language shift, they can effectively resist the onslaught of majority languages. Moreover, the mass-media technologies that allowed the one-way dialogue of majority languages to drive out minority languages and dialects are now helping those silenced languages to make a comeback. Speakers of these smaller languages can use interactive technologies such as Web sites, e-mail, and message boards to talk back to the world by creating and distributing media in their own language to a global diaspora.

Québec: Case Study in Reversing Language Shift

Some minority languages are resurging despite the pressures of globalization. An excellent example of this phenomenon is Québec, which has shown that smaller languages, given sufficient economic power and policy planning, can resist even the strongest linguistic force on the planet: English.

Québec is a Canadian province of about 7 million inhabitants, where more than 95% are native French speakers. Since France signed the Treaty of Paris in 1763 and ceded command of New France to the English, North America's French-speaking inhabitants have been surrounded by English-speakers, who held almost all official and economic power over Québec. Though most Québec inhabitants lived and died speaking French, British government officials and factory bosses generally required the use of English.

As the twentieth century stretched on, even young Québecois began to turn toward bilingualism in English and away from French education. After hundreds of years of survival, Canadian French appeared headed toward extinction. This created great tension among the people of Québec, culminating in the 1960s with the *Revolution Tranquille,* during which native francophone Québecois demanded the use of French as the only official language of the province.

Today, Québecois strongly defend their language and have passed laws to make it the medium of commerce and governance. Québec passed the *Loi 101,* requiring the public use of French in all cases and relegating English to a secondary status. French is now the dominant language of commerce and government in Québec; English is also available on an incidental basis in federal matters, but French must always be offered. On the commercial side, even the extremely technical language of technology is translated into French for use in the province, such as for textbooks and training manuals.

In the media, all billboards and public signs must appear in French; English words, if used, must be accompanied by a French translation. Also, the technology that supported the English language in Canada is now used to maintain the regular use of French. The Canadian government now pays for the support of fully bilingual national media, both the English-language Canadian Broadcasting Company and its French equivalent, Radio-Canada. Both stations require a certain percentage of their offering to be original Canadian content. The government has decreed that the airwaves will be filled with Canadian French (not even European French) programming. From the news to game shows, Canadian French is clearly the language of the province's popular culture.

Another policy that effectively supports the reversal of language shift in Québec is the encouragement of immigrants to speak the local language. West Africans, Haitians, Dominicans, Poles, and Greeks are all encouraged to speak French when arriving in places such as Montréal and Québec City; many immigrants remain bilingual in their native tongue and French, even though the powerful influence of English can be felt all around from the rest of Canada and the United States.

Québec is an example of a place where a language heading toward extinction has assured its own survival by education, political will, and commercial expedience. The technologies that initially placed pressure on the people to learn English, such as mass media (TV, radio, public signage, and print), has been appropriated to support the local language now and in the future. It is an example of the technologies of globalization being used to support the minority culture.

Dead Languages Reborn: The Case of Hebrew

Hebrew demonstrates how a language can be brought back from the dead to form the basis of a national identity. Israel united first as a state and then deliberately as a linguistically unified culture.

At the end of the nineteenth century, there were 10 million Yiddish-speaking Jews around the world, but none were habitual or primary speakers of Hebrew. Eliezer Ben-Yehuda, called the father of Modern Hebrew, is responsible for the adaptation of ancient Hebrew dialects into the Modern Hebrew language currently associated with the state of Israel.

The transition to a modern language still has some bumps. Words have needed to be invented by language councils even to describe the activities of daily life. In the first years of Israel, the state published posters asking speakers of German, Yiddish, and Russian to learn Hebrew from their children, who were being taught the new form. Once there was a second generation, where children saw their parents, policemen, and librarians speaking Hebrew, a national language was born.

Modern Hebrew is an established language in no threat of extinction because it adheres to the three most important factors in maintaining a language for the future: It is the language of education for the young, of commerce, and of official government activity. It is important to note that the forces of globalization and dominant languages like English and French do not appear to be a threat to this young language. A local TV and film industry provides Hebrew-based entertainment and a common popular culture for young people. Similarly, the rapid development of technologies and Internet sites for Hebrew has promoted the spread of the language all over the world. Modern life is not a threat to this recently revived language.

The resurgence of Hebrew in Israel offers a role model for speakers of languages such as Welsh, Irish Gaelic, Catalan, and Basque. Representatives from Catalonia and the Basque country have been sent to Israel to study the effect that Hebrew has had in solidifying the idea of Israel as a nation-state.

Minority Languages in Europe

A number of minority languages in western Europe still exist despite overwhelming pressure from the majority, centrist languages of the nations in which they co-exist. English, French, and Castilian Spanish are clearly the dominant languages, even in the geographical areas where the minority ethnicities exist. But the future of the local languages depends not so much on the strength of the national languages as on the relationship of the local language to education, government, and commerce.

Here is an overview of some of the trends in Europe's less-widely spoken languages.

Catalan: Seeking Freedom in Castilian Spain

Catalan is an example of a language that has resisted the pressures of homogenization. Catalan is the national language of the tiny nation of Andorra and the "co-official" language of the Catalonia region of eastern Spain, the Balearic Islands, and regions of Sardinia and France. Sharing roots with both French and Spanish, Catalan is far from a small minority tongue, with 7.5 million speakers.

During the Franco regime (1939–1975), the use of Catalan was banned, along with all other regional languages of Spain, such as Basque and Galician. With the death of Franco in 1975, the ban was lifted, and new Catalan newspapers and television channels were launched. Catalan is now Catalonia's official language for all government, commerce, education, and culture. The new strength of the language may lead to the formation of a semiautonomous Catalonian state within federal Spain.

Irish Gaelic: Reviving Ireland's Native Tongue

Despite suffering centuries of repression under English landlords who would repeatedly outlaw the native language, Irish Gaelic is increasing in strength and relevance. According to the 2004 census, 1.6 million people, or 45% of Ireland's total population, were competent speakers of Irish Gaelic, or *gaeilge,* up from 1.4 million speakers in 1996. It has been the official language of the free state of Ireland since 1922, but English remains the most commonly spoken language in Ireland.

Education is increasing the total number of Irish speakers throughout the country, especially among younger Irish citizens. There is also a burgeoning media culture entirely in the Irish language. The television network TG4 provides news, current affairs, sports, and even a soap opera, *Ros na Run,* entirely in Irish Gaelic. The majority of Irish Web sites are still in English, and those written in Gaelic either pertain to cultural matters such as music or the language itself or are of official government publications.

The government appears to be the greatest driver of the Irish language, if not popular culture. A growing number of legal precedents support Ireland's right to require the use of its indigenous language. For example, in 1989, European courts accepted the right of the Irish government to require Dutch art teacher Anita Groener to learn Irish Gaelic as a prerequisite to her employment.

Still, the use of Irish language in government has been perfunctory until recently. The ability to function in the Irish language is legally required for all government bureaucrats, but fluency was not required, and Irish was rarely used. Meanwhile, English was a daily necessity. But with the Official Languages Act of 2003, the use of Irish in the government has increased, enabling any Irish citizen to obtain government services entirely in Gaelic.

Still, the future success of Irish remains uncertain. The impact of increased education and of the Official Languages Act is likely to give some buoyancy to the language, but its establishment as a monoglot language of commerce remains unlikely.

Welsh: Language Becomes an Important Argument for Political Autonomy

The Celtic language of Welsh, or *cymraeg,* has been overshadowed by its dominant neighbor, English. The Welsh people do not share the Scots' streak of independence, so their language has mostly existed only as a provincial tongue—one associated with farmers and not landed gentry. Over the past two centuries, the language has been eroded to the point that the Welsh monoglot population is less than 1% of the nation, having declined as a result of two world wars, television, and the increasing choice of Wales as a retirement community for many Englishmen.

Yet, the Welsh people and their language have prevailed, even in the face of the economic and technological trends of globalization. The use of the Welsh language is a cultural and political statement for many in Wales, but especially in the agrarian north. In Wales, as in Scotland, the regional nationalist party has won representation in Parliament. In Wales, more than 20% of the population speaks Welsh fluently.

Today, Welsh is offered regularly as a second language in schools and is increasingly the language of primary instruction once again. The percentage of Welsh children up to age 14 who are able to speak Welsh increased from 15% in 1971 to 25% in 1991. Welsh language media are limited but growing. A separate Welsh TV channel, S4C, began broadcasting in 1982 and now features news, cultural programming, and children's shows. Today, in the government sector, several high-level public jobs require bilingualism, but in the commercial realm, English remains the unchallenged *lingua franca.*

The Welsh language may be on the upswing compared to the trends of the latter part of the twentieth century, but still there may not be a future for a nation of monoglot Welshmen. A strong majority (80%) of Welshmen do not see Welsh as the key to nationhood. For now, the Welsh language as a primary driver of nationalism is in question, even though the Welsh language is in resurgence.

Consistent policies expanding the use of Welsh ensure its survival, and it is less in danger of disappearing than it was a century ago. However, its use as the monoglot language of commerce or government seems unlikely in the future.

Scots Gaelic: A Museum Piece of a Language

Indigenous Scots Gaelic (*ghaíhlig*), stands in sharp relief to the experiences of native Welsh and Irish Gaelic. Scotland has virtually no Gaelic-only speakers. No public services are available in the language, and making it the national language is not even an issue.

This indifference to an indigenous national language is perhaps due to the unique history of the Scottish culture vis-à-vis its English neighbors. After conquering the Scots in 1746, the English victors outlawed the Scots language and culture, along with the wearing of the tartan. Over time, the prohibition of Scottish culture was changed to assimilation. The British military began adopting some traditions, such as music (bagpipe and drums), as well as the wearing of the tartan for the Black Watch. English royalty established new homes in Scotland, and the notion of the Highlander became romanticized: In effect, Scottish culture became the property of the British, as much a distinct political statement as local languages are in Ireland and Wales.

Today, there are 60,000 speakers of Scots Gaelic, but they are on average considerably older than speakers of many resurging languages. Many Scots regard the Scottish language as a relic of the past. There is no mandatory education in Scots Gaelic, and French is more popular as a second language in high schools.

Scottish-language media is limited compared with Irish Gaelic and Welsh. There are newspapers in the Highlands that feature sections in Scots Gaelic, but no major dailies in the language. Radio may feature the local language for music, but news broadcasts are in English. Scottish youth are not using the Internet to perpetuate the local language. The technological forces of globalization overwhelmingly demand the English language.

The national linguistic identity of Scotland seems more likely to focus on the use of proper English in public settings and a secondary strong regional accent for use among countrymen. A full resurgence of the local language appears unlikely.

Breton: Overcoming French Suppression and Increasing the Use of the Native Tongue

Western France is considered one of the seven Celtic nations, home of the Breton people who speak a Celtic language called *brezhoneg*. The Breton language suffered centuries of repression at the hands of the central French government, but Brittany retains a strong cultural and historical identity. Today, 200,000 to 300,000 people still speak Breton, down from the 1.2 million who spoke it at the start of the twentieth century. Now, however, it is gaining greater popularity and public acceptance, mostly through educational and cultural means. Though government services and commerce are conducted almost exclusively in French, Breton language instruction in schools supports its preservation.

Breton may attain an equal cultural status in Brittany, so long as young people are still allowed to form identities through the Breton language, but it is unlikely to enjoy the success of supremacy achieved by Canadian French and Catalan, since there is little commercial or governmental support for Breton.

Minority Languages for the Future

Globalized commerce and media are not necessarily the death knell for local languages, because certain trends support their preservation. Whereas one-way mass media technologies such as TV, radio, and print served to support majority languages, today's computer technology is turning the tables. It is considerably less expensive now to produce video and audio in any language, and communications technologies allow you to transmit these media to a diaspora anywhere in the world.

In the future, with lower prices for powerful computers and dramatic advances in broadband Internet (such as IPv6 architecture that will soon turn any Internet connection into a broadcast device), majority languages may no longer possess an advantage in distributing information to the public. In the future, anybody anywhere on Earth could conceivably receive the evening news in Welsh or Irish Gaelic. Also, the availability of cheap, powerful multimedia will allow teachers to translate educational materials into a local language more easily. These educational technologies will be essential to the survival and prosperity of languages in the future. Only education of the youth assures the continuity of a language.

The availability of government services in a chosen language is the only path to its legitimacy in a political sense, but even more critical is for a minority language to be used in commerce.

The pressures of globalization on minority languages are undeniable, and many will likely disappear. However, extinction is not a certainty. The trend toward the homogeneity of global culture has stimulated many people to search for their native roots and hold tighter to their cultural identity.

We are living in interesting times, linguistically, as powerful national languages encounter fierce resistance in their drive to dislodge local languages. New technologies are offering people greater freedom to choose their own cultural identity, and many are choosing minority local languages. The linguistic giants will not be the only choice in the future.

ERIC GARLAND is the principal of Competitive Futures Inc., a futures consultancy, www.competitivefutures.com. His last article for *The Futurist*, "Scenarios in Practice: Futuring in the Pharmaceutical Industry," appeared in January–February 2006.

What Native Peoples Deserve

Roger Sandall

The Roosevelt Indian Reservation in the Amazon rain forest is not a happy place. Last year, the Cinta Larga Indians slaughtered 29 miners there, and in October the Brazilian who was trying to mediate the conflict was murdered at a cash machine. Neither of these events represented anything new. The reserve, located 2,100 miles northwest of Rio de Janeiro, and named for Theodore Roosevelt when he visited Brazil in 1913, is also where a notorious massacre of Cinta Larga by rubber tappers took place in 1963; only one child in the village survived.

The immediate cause of the recent violence is not rubber but diamonds. The Roosevelt Indian Reservation may be sitting on one of the world's largest deposits, and no one wants to leave it in the ground—neither the Indians, nor the itinerant diggers (*garimpeiros*), nor the government. But, under present Brazilian law, no one is free to begin digging, either. And this brings us to the deeper cause of murder and mayhem in the region.

Under Brazil's constitution, the country's Indians are not full citizens. Instead, they are legal minors, with the status of a protected species. This has one singular benefit for the Indians: the twelve Cinta Larga responsible for last year's killing of 29 wildcat prospectors may enjoy immunity from prosecution and never face jail. But there is also a downside. As wards of the state, the Indians are denied the right to mine their own land.

As for outsiders, they must apply for permits to dig, and face endless bureaucratic delays that more often than not lead nowhere. The outcome is predictable: frustrated in their own wishes, and hard-pressed by the impatient diggers, Indians make private deals, which then go sour—and the shooting starts.

At issue here is not just the law; the law is itself the product of an idea, or a set of ideas, concerning certain underlying questions. What should be done about endangered enclave societies in the midst of a modern nation? Can they, or their land, or their minerals be cut off and preserved, frozen in time, pristine and inviolate, forever? Should they be?

The massacre of the Cinta Larga in 1963 gave rise to a Brazilian state inquiry that became known as the Figueiredo Report (after the official in charge of the investigation). The inquiry was meant to find out about the shockingly grave deficiencies and abuses that were then being tolerated by the Indian Protection Service, including the use of individual Indians as slaves. Once it was completed, the old agency was closed down, and a new one created to replace it.

There the matter might have rested had not the London *Sunday Times* caught a whiff of scandal. The paper dispatched the travel writer Norman Lewis to Brazil; though he did not meet any Indians, he found all he needed in the Figueiredo Report. "By the descriptions of all who had seen them," Lewis reported, "there were no more inoffensive and charming human beings on the planet than the forest Indians of Brazil."

Having established a scene of primal innocence, Lewis proceeded to tell of the atrocities against the Cinta Larga, warning that they were being pushed to the brink of extinction and that there might not be a single Indian left by 1980. He concluded: "What a tragedy, what a reproach it will be for the human race if this is allowed to happen!" Reprinted all over the globe, his sensational article had profound and lasting effects.

The first of these effects was to enshrine a form of extreme protectionism, not only as a temporary means to an end—the human and cultural survival of the indigenous peoples of Brazil—but as an end in itself. Soon, all those working for Indian interests were of a single opinion: the only way to protect these tribal peoples was to create inviolable sanctuaries where they would "live their own lives preserving their own culture on their own land."

The second effect was to galvanize a number of English explorers, writers, and anthropologists into setting up a permanent international lobby. The name of this flourishing body is Survival, self-described as "the world's leading organization supporting tribal peoples." Two men who have been associated with it from the outset are John Hemming and Robin Hanbury-Tenison.

Hemming, who served for two decades as the director of the Royal Geographical Society, has written a number of books about South America, among them an indispensable three-volume history of the impact of civilization on Brazil's indigenous peoples—*Red Gold, Amazon Frontier,* and *Die If You Must,* the last of which appeared in 2003.* Hanbury-Tenison, Hemming's long-time friend, was also a founder of Survival and is today its president. Less well-known but also important is

---

*Macmillan, 887 pp., $28.50 (paper)

the documentary filmmaker Adrian Cowell, who has spoken up on behalf of the Amazonian Indians for nearly 50 years.

According to a recent article by Hemming in the British monthly *Prospect,* the campaign to ensure the survival of the Amazonian peoples appears to have succeeded. This is also the gist of the final chapter of *Die If You Must,* where he wrote:

> The Indians will survive physically. Their populations have grown steadily since a nadir of near-extinction in the mid-20th century. Having fallen to little more than 100,000 in the 1950's, they have more than tripled to some 350,000 and are generally rising fast.

The health of the Indians is basically good, Hemming reported in *Die If You Must.* The killers of yesteryear—measles, TB, pneumonia, cholera, and smallpox—are rare. Their land is also secure: "a remarkable 11 percent of the land-mass of Brazil is now reserved for Indians. The 587 indigenous areas total almost 260 million acres—an area greater than France, Germany, and Benelux combined." Environmentalist ideals and indigenous interests have been reconciled: "From the air, [one reservation] now stands out as an immense rectangle of verdant vegetation framed by the dismal brown of arid ranch-lands."

It was in the 1950's and 60's that Hemming, Hanbury-Tenison, and Cowell, three young men from Oxford and Cambridge, launched themselves on the world. They were talented and energetic, they had good connections, and above all they shared a boyish taste for adventure. At Eton they probably read about Lawrence of Arabia; at Oxford, where Hemming and Hanbury-Tenison roomed together, they already knew that "exploring" was what they wanted to do most. They regarded the rain forests of Brazil as a natural field for their endeavors, and in no time they were paddling up the Amazon in canoes.

Adrian Cowell was a Cambridge man, and his precocity as an explorer makes an impressive tale in itself. As a student in 1954 he joined a university Trans-Africa Expedition. The following year he was in Asia. Then, as he relates in *The Heart of the Forest* (1961), "the Oxford and Cambridge Expedition to South America . . . brought me to the Amazon forest." Thereafter he joined the Brazilian Centro Expedition, an enterprise associated with the creation of the new national capital of Brasilia. Its purpose was "to canoe down the Xingu River and burn an airstrip at the exact geographical center of Brazil."

It was all tremendous fun and very romantic—a word that occurs spontaneously in the books of Hanbury-Tenison, who has written voluminously about his explorations and today runs a booking agency for exotic locations. Here, from his website, is a typical passage about an early adventure in Afghanistan:

> A sound like distant thunder made me look up at the rich blue cloudless sky before I turned to see twenty wild horsemen in turbans and flowing robes bearing down on me. They carried long-barreled rifles and had daggers in their belts. Beside their spirited horses loped large, hairy hounds. With their Genghis Khan moustaches and fine, aquiline noses they were almost caricatures of the bandits we had been warned about. I should have been frightened,

but all I could think was that if I had to go I could not have found a more romantic end.

This tells us quite a bit about the attitude of all three men toward indigenous peoples. In light of that attitude, Hanbury-Tenison must have been taken aback when, in 1971, he called on the anthropologist Margaret Mead at the Museum of Natural History in New York to tell her about Survival International (as Survival was then called), and she gave him a piece of her mind. Mead at the age of seventy was a very different person from the idealistic young woman who had visited Samoa in 1926. By 1971, she was fiercely *un*romantic, and the spectacle of yet another young Oxford "explorer" embarking on yet another expedition up the Amazon must have set her teeth on edge. With sturdy good sense she tried to talk him out of his fantasies.

In his 1973 book, *A Question of Survival,* Hanbury-Tenison describes this "small, beady-eyed dumpling of a lady who sailed into the attack as I came through the door":

> The main point that annoyed [Mead] was the concept, unstated by me, that primitive peoples were any better off as they were. She said she was "maddened by antibiotic-ridden idealists who wouldn't stand three weeks in the jungle" . . . and the whole "noble savage" concept almost made her foam at the mouth. "All primitive peoples," she said, "lead miserable, unhappy, cruel lives, most of which are spent trying to kill each other." The reason they lived in the unpleasant places they did, like the middle of the Brazilian jungle, was that nobody else would.

There was much talk in those days about the pharmaceutical benefits of rain forests, and Hanbury-Tenison and his friends were sure that the Amazon was about to make a huge contribution to the world's health. (This was a little before the discovery of the supposed wonders of jojoba oil.) But Mead was having none of it:

> She said that to protect [the Indians] on the grounds that they could be useful to us or contribute anything was nonsense. "No primitive person has *ever* contributed *anything,* or ever will," she said. She had no time for suggestions of medical knowledge or the value of jungle lore.

The only grounds on which Mead relented were broadly humanitarian. For one thing, the Indians' "art, culture, dancing, music, etc. was pleasant and attractive and their grandchildren might thank us for trying to preserve or at best record it now that we have the proper technical means [i.e., tape and film] for doing so." For another thing, "it was bad for the world to let these people die, and the effort to prevent their extermination was good for mankind even if it failed."

> For the rest, however, Mead vehemently denied that the Indians had any special reasons for being protected, as she denied any advantage of one race over another. She also claimed emphatically that they all wanted one thing only, and that was to have as many material possessions and comforts as possible. Those still running away in the jungle were the ones who had encountered the most unpleasant savagery from Europeans, and even though

they might be having no contact now, if they could possibly get hold of any aluminum pots they would use them.

Although faithfully recorded by Hanbury-Tenison, Mead's argument was as lost on him in 1971 as it is lost today on legions of like-minded people who teach or mouth the slogans of multiculturalism. What Mead herself failed to grasp was that, naive though he may have sounded, Hanbury-Tenison and his friends had been radicalized, and they were never going to accept her bleak view of the tribal world. It was not that they had been reading Marx; instead, they had been reading Norman Lewis's digest of the worst parts of the Figueiredo Report, including Figueiredo's judgment that "the Indians [had] suffered tortures similar to those of Treblinka and Dachau."

Torture, indeed, was too tame a word for what had taken place. In 1963, there had been massacres of the Cinta Larga tribe in Rondonia. One gunman's taped testimony describes how an employee of a rubber company named Chico Luis

gave the chief a burst with his tommy gun to make sure, and after that he let the rest of them have it. . . . [A]ll the other guys had to do was finish off anyone still showing signs of life. . . . [T]here was a young Indian girl they didn't shoot, with a kid of about five in one hand, yelling his head off. . . . Chico shot the kid through the head with his .45 and then grabbed hold of the woman—who by the way was very pretty. "Be reasonable," I said, "why do you have to kill her?" In my view it was a waste. "What's wrong with giving her to the boys? They haven't set eyes on a woman for six weeks. Or we could give her as a present to [their boss] de Brito."

But Chico would not listen:

He tied the Indian girl up and hung her head downward from a tree, legs apart, and chopped her in half right down the middle with his machete. Almost with a single chop I'd say. The village was like a slaughterhouse. He calmed down after he'd cut the woman up, and told us to burn down all the huts and throw the bodies into the river.

This is unbearable: but it is not essentially different from what had happened to many Indians in Latin America after 1492. The lawless frontier was for centuries a refuge for loners, criminals, and violent psychopaths who had nothing to lose and could act with impunity. Those who went searching for El Dorado in the 1540's behaved like packs of marauding wolves, seizing food from the same Indian villagers whom they then enslaved as porters, and who were tortured or killed when they failed to cooperate. As one learns from Hemming's three-volume work, this sort of thing has had a very long history indeed.

Colonial nations fashion their heroes from the timber at hand, much of which is twisted and full of knots. Australia, for example, invites its citizens to admire an unappealing Irish bandit named Ned Kelly. But the Kellys smell sweet alongside Brazil's much romanticized *bandeirantes.* What are often referred to as

expeditions of "pathfinders" from São Paulo into the interior in the first half of the 17th century were mostly slave raids aimed at catching, chaining, and marching back to the coast as many Indians as a group of well-armed and ruthless men could seize.

To be sure, there was sometimes a genuinely exploratory aspect to such forays. In *Red Gold,* Hemming offers a balanced account of this phase of Brazilian expansion inland, and fairly describes the ordeals of the *bandeirantes* themselves. Since slave-raiding was a central feature of traditional Indian culture, too, the journeys engaged whites, Indians, and those of mixed ancestry (*mamelucos*) in a common enterprise:

The Indians contributed their forest skills and geographical knowledge. They soon grasped the purpose of the mission and became expert enslavers of other natives. Although brutalized and worked hard by the captains of the *bandeiras,* the Indians probably enjoyed service on them. It was quite normal for Tupi warriors to make long marches through the forests to attack enemy tribes.

In the course of his own periodic visits to Brazil, Adrian Cowell appears to have come rather closer to the realities of Amazonian Indian life than either Hanbury-Tenison or Hemming. As a result, although aware of the horrors long endured by Indians at the hands of slavers, settlers, and frontier psychopaths, he was also more prepared to face up to the grimmer aspects of the native cultures themselves, and of the horrors Indians had long inflicted on each other.

In *The Heart of the Forest* (1961), Cowell writes in idyllic prose of the partnership he formed with an Indian hunter, carrying his friend's gun and studying his craft, teaching himself to decoy wildfowl by imitating their calls. But he also reports how, in 1958 on the Xingu River, there were continual killings of itinerant Brazilian rubber tappers (*seringueiros*) by Indians, and of Indians by *seringueiros.* A Juruna Indian told him how

first we lived lower down the Xingu and worked for the *seringueiros,* but they killed many [Indians] with rifles. So we came up here past the great rapids and lived till the *seringueiros* say they are friends and gave us rifles. So we went downriver again and worked for the *seringueiros* till they killed more Juruna. Then we killed many *seringueiros* and came back here and killed Trumai and Kamayura Indians. Then the Txukahamae tribe came and killed almost all of us so that we are only twelve now.

That is the way things were and always had been. And this, too, was a seemingly ineradicable aspect of the culture that Cowell thought worthy of being saved. Back in 1967, he had joined the brothers Claudio and Orlando Villas-Boas in an attempt to contact and "pacify" the elusive Kreen-Akrore. But violence in the camp was making it hard to manage a community where different tribal groups had been brought together for their own safety. The captions on a page of photographs in Cowell's 1973 book, *The Tribe that Hides from Man,* read like the list of casualties on some exotic war memorial: "*Above:* Javaritu, a Trumai killed by Tapiokap. *Above:* Pionim, a Kayabi, killed Tapiokap to avenge his brother-in-law." And so on.

Much has been written about the endeavor of the Villas-Boas brothers to establish the Xingu Indian refuge and entice the tribal remnants of the Kayabi or Txikao or Suya to join it. A passage from *The Tribe that Hides from Man* offers a glimpse into the thought processes of Claudio, a "Marxist philosopher" in the Latin American manner:

> Look around this camp and you will see Indians are more loving than we are. But the expression of their love is confined to the limits of this society. They cut a hole in the wilderness to contain their family, but outside this camp is the jungle where they kill meat for food, bamboo for arrows, leaves for their beds. Killing is the essence of forest existence, and if you stopped it, the forest and the Indian would die. Within the Indian mind there is a complete division between the duties within the group and the absence of duty in the land of killing outside.

At one time, Claudio suggested that Indians should feel free to kill white *seringueiros* or any other uninvited marauders who came into the Xingu Park. While warning them of the inevitable costs of this practice as a permanent way of life, he understood that, according to the tribal code, revenge killing was natural, habitual, and inevitable. Nor was this the only aspect of Amazonian Indian culture that was hard to reconcile with modern life. Strict rules of seclusion were found among all the upper-Xingu tribes. Women were subjected to draconian punishments for violations of taboo. In a British television documentary from the 1970's, a young Mehinacu woman was asked what would happen if she were to glimpse, even accidentally, the sacred flutes played by the men. She would be gang-raped, she replied, smiling sadly as if in recognition that in the genteel world of her white interviewer, such sexual punishments—culturally authorized, approved, indeed mandatory—were unthinkable.

Hemming's account of Amazonian life is hard on the efforts of Christian missionaries, and especially hard on Jesuits ("fanatical missionaries intent on replacing native society and beliefs with their own Christian model"). One line of grudging appreciation will be followed by the word "but" and ten lines of disparagement. As his impressive study proceeds from volume to volume, he is consistently severe, his language becomes more tendentious, and an austere secularism dictates his judgment of religious matters. In his recent article in *Prospect,* he seems to approve wholeheartedly only of the politically radical priests who began to appear in the 1960's—"trained anthropologists who did not try to undermine indigenous beliefs and ceased to be aggressive proselytizers." Before that point, his view of Catholic missionary activity is mainly negative.

But what exactly were the religious authorities to do when they first arrived from Portugal and had to deal, for example, with the Tupinamba? Did they not have a clear obligation both to undermine and to prohibit certain indigenous beliefs? In modern times, we have seen the rise of whole political cultures

gripped by pathology, with hideous consequences; so, too, sick ethnic cultures evolved historically in the tribal world. Few quite so sick as the Tupinamba have been recorded before or since.

They loved human flesh. Prestige and power centered on the ritual slaughtering of prisoners. In an account prepared by Alfred Métraux for the Smithsonian's *Handbook of South American Indians* (1948), we read that the killing and eating of these prisoners (who were fattened for the purpose) "were joyful events which provided these Indians with the opportunity for merrymaking, aesthetic displays, and other emotional outlets." Métraux then describes what took place at a cannibal feast after the victim's skull was shattered:

> Old women rushed to drink the warm blood, and children were invited to dip their hands in it. Mothers would smear their nipples with blood so that even babies could have a taste of it. The body, cut into quarters, was roasted on a barbecue, and the old women, who were the most eager for human flesh, licked the grease running along the sticks. Some portions, reputed to be delicacies or sacred, such as the fingers or the grease around the liver or heart, were allotted to distinguished guests.

That Portuguese settlers in the 16th century did not cope very well with this aspect of the Indian tribal world is probably true. That the missionaries who came after them did not handle the situation as they might have done is also likely. But if they had been around at the time, would John Hemming, or Robin Hanbury-Tenison, or Adrian Cowell, or the entire staff of Survival have done much better? Would any of us?

"All primitive peoples," Margaret Mead had said to her young Oxford visitor, "lead miserable, unhappy, cruel lives, most of which are spent trying to kill each other." She was overdoing it, but she had a point—a point largely lost sight of in today's systematic sentimentalizing of the Stone Age.

Of course, as we have seen, Mead also acknowledged that certain aspects of Indian culture—"their art, culture, dancing, music, etc."—deserved to survive, for the enjoyment of the people themselves and for the admiration of humanity as a whole. That, indeed, is more or less what has happened today in the Xingu Park and places like it elsewhere. On display in such places is a pacified, deranged, and somewhat feminized version of Amazonian culture, of the kind that middle-class travelers from the West like to see: a theatrical world where dressing-up in feathered regalia, ritual ceremonies, and communal dancing never stop.

Hemming, who welcomes the prospect of self-determination, claims that "modern indigenous policy seeks to empower tribes to manage their own affairs." Yet both self-determination and empowerment imply literacy and modern education; and here the picture is less clear. Officially, the children are learning to read and write, and in the last chapter of *Die If You Must*—a chapter with the title "Present and Future" Hemming makes three rather perfunctory references to schooling. But at the same time, he strongly implies that in his vision of the future it does not matter whether the children learn to read and write or not, because others will be there to do things for them.

Who are these others? According to Hemming, the external political affairs of the Indians on the Xingu reserve are "supported by a remarkable contingent of 33 non-government organizations, a fireless band of missionaries, anthropologists, well-wishers, journalists, doctors, and lawyers, both in Brazil and abroad." As for their internal welfare, that is served by a "resident tribe of whites, composed of social scientists, doctors, teachers, nurses, biologists, and agronomists from all parts of Brazil." With friends like these, who needs self-determination?

What Hemming is describing is the fruit of the inviolable-sanctuary approach to cultural survival. This rests on what might be called fortress theory, and has two cardinal principles: that "culture" and "people" and "land" should be seen as indivisible, and that they can be kept this way forever in a suitably constructed territorial redoubt. Whatever is happening in the world around them, ethnic cultures should, insofar as possible, be preserved unchanged. With the help of an army of administrative personnel, custodially responsible for seeing to it that they go on wanting only the same things they have always wanted, their heritage will be kept alive. Social change—at least as it affects these picturesque tribal peoples—is bad, and should be stopped.

Among the Xingu Park Indians, it is in fact safe to say that the older generation remains strongly attached to its remote lands, and intends to go on living there, hunting animals and gathering fruits. But what do younger Indians want to do with their lives? If there is one thing we have learned from modern history, it is that individuals often outgrow their ethnic cultures,

find life in a fortress claustrophobic, and choose to move on. In contrast to museum exhibits, real human beings have a way of developing ideas and ambitions and desires—including for aluminum pots—beyond the ken of conservators. Fortress theory, multicultural "essentialism," and the enduring cult of the noble savage are the enemies of those ambitions and human desires.

In the final paragraph of *Die If You Must,* Hemming wonders uneasily whether the pessimists might have the last laugh after all—whether the Amazon's "beautiful, ancient, and intricate cultures will be maintained only artificially as curiosities for tourists, researchers, or politically correct enthusiasts." That is quite possible. But it is hardly the only undesirable possibility. Preserving ancient cultural patterns is laudable, but it is not enough. No society in history has ever stood still, and however beautiful, and ancient, and intricate traditional cultures may be, it is wrong to lock people up inside them and throw away the key. Uprooting the dishonest and patronizing Western cult of the noble savage will be the work of generations; but as far as today's Amazonian Indians are concerned, the main priority must surely be to ensure that those among them who do not want to play the obliging role of historical curiosities, endlessly dressing up for visitors whose expectations they feel bound to fulfill, are able to find something else to do in the modern world—on the reservation or off it. In that quest we can only wish them well.

ROGER SANDALL taught anthropology for many years at the University of Sydney in Australia and is the author most recently of *The Culture Cult.* His essay, "Can Sudan Be Saved?," appeared in the December 2004 COMMENTARY.

Test Your Knowledge Form

We encourage you to photocopy and use this page as a tool to assess how the articles in *Annual Editions* expand on the information in your textbook. By reflecting on the articles you will gain enhanced text information. You can also access this useful form on a product's book support Web site at *http://www.mhcls.com/online/*.

NAME:

DATE:

TITLE AND NUMBER OF ARTICLE:

BRIEFLY STATE THE MAIN IDEA OF THIS ARTICLE:

LIST THREE IMPORTANT FACTS THAT THE AUTHOR USES TO SUPPORT THE MAIN IDEA:

WHAT INFORMATION OR IDEAS DISCUSSED IN THIS ARTICLE ARE ALSO DISCUSSED IN YOUR TEXTBOOK OR OTHER READINGS THAT YOU HAVE DONE? LIST THE TEXTBOOK CHAPTERS AND PAGE NUMBERS:

LIST ANY EXAMPLES OF BIAS OR FAULTY REASONING THAT YOU FOUND IN THE ARTICLE:

LIST ANY NEW TERMS/CONCEPTS THAT WERE DISCUSSED IN THE ARTICLE, AND WRITE A SHORT DEFINITION:

We Want Your Advice

ANNUAL EDITIONS revisions depend on two major opinion sources: one is our Advisory Board, listed in the front of this volume, which works with us in scanning the thousands of articles published in the public press each year; the other is you—the person actually using the book. Please help us and the users of the next edition by completing the prepaid article rating form on this page and returning it to us. Thank you for your help!

ANNUAL EDITIONS: Anthropology 08/09

ARTICLE RATING FORM

Here is an opportunity for you to have direct input into the next revision of this volume.
We would like you to rate each of the articles listed below, using the following scale:

1. **Excellent: should definitely be retained**
2. **Above average: should probably be retained**
3. **Below average: should probably be deleted**
4. **Poor: should definitely be deleted**

Your ratings will play a vital part in the next revision.
Please mail this prepaid form to us as soon as possible.
Thanks for your help!

RATING	ARTICLE	RATING	ARTICLE
	1. Before: The Sixties		21. The Berdache Tradition
	2. Eating Christmas in the Kalahari		22. A Woman's Curse?
	3. Tricking and Tripping		23. Where Fat Is a Mark of Beauty
	4. Anthropology and Counterinsurgency: The Strange Story of Their Curious Relationship		24. Eyes of the Ngangas: Ethnomedicine and Power in Central Africa
	5. One Hundred Percent American		25. Ancient Teachings, Modern Lessons
	6. Who's Speech Is Better?		26. The Adaptive Value of Religious Ritual
	7. Do You Speak American?		27. Remapping the World of Autism
	8. Fighting for Our Lives		28. The Secrets of Haiti's Living Dead
	9. "I Can't Even Open My Mouth"		29. Body Ritual Among the Nacirema
	10. Shakespeare in the Bush		30. Baseball Magic
	11. Understanding Eskimo Science		31. Why Can't People Feed Themselves?
	12. The Inuit Paradox		32. The Arrow of Disease
	13. Meeting the Maasai: Messages for Management		33. Burying the White Gods: New Perspectives on the Conquest of Mexico
	14. Too Many Bananas, Not Enough Pineapples, and No Watermelon at All		34. The Price of Progress
	15. Ties That Bind		35. The Battle for Cattle
	16. When Brothers Share a Wife		36. Rangers by Birth
	17. Death Without Weeping		37. Digging Into the Roots of Research Ethics
	18. What's Love Got to Do with It		38. Can Minority Languages Be Saved?
	19. Arranging a Marriage in India		39. What Native Peoples Deserve
	20. Who Needs Love! In Japan, Many Couples Don't		

BUSINESS REPLY MAIL
FIRST CLASS MAIL PERMIT NO. 551 DUBUQUE IA

POSTAGE WILL BE PAID BY ADDRESSEE

McGraw-Hill Contemporary Learning Series
501 BELL STREET
DUBUQUE, IA 52001

NO POSTAGE
NECESSARY
IF MAILED
IN THE
UNITED STATES

ABOUT YOU

Name

Date

Are you a teacher? ☐ A student? ☐
Your school's name

Department

Address

City

State

Zip

School telephone #

YOUR COMMENTS ARE IMPORTANT TO US!

Please fill in the following information:
For which course did you use this book?

Did you use a text with this ANNUAL EDITION? ☐ yes ☐ no
What was the title of the text?

What are your general reactions to the Annual Editions concept?

Have you read any pertinent articles recently that you think should be included in the next edition? Explain.

Are there any articles that you feel should be replaced in the next edition? Why?

Are there any World Wide Web sites that you feel should be included in the next edition? Please annotate.

May we contact you for editorial input? ☐ yes ☐ no
May we quote your comments? ☐ yes ☐ no